Classical Sociological Theory

BLACKWELL READERS IN SOCIOLOGY

Each volume in this authoritative series aims to provide students and scholars with comprehensive collections of classic and contemporary readings for all the major sub-fields of sociology. They are designed to complement single-authored works, or to be used as stand-alone textbooks for courses. The selected readings sample the most important works that students should read and are framed by informed editorial introductions. The series aims to reflect the state of the discipline by providing collections not only on standard topics but also on cutting-edge subjects in sociology to provide future directions in teaching and research.

Forthcoming
Social Movements edited by Jeff Goodwin and James Jasper

Classical Sociological Theory

Edited by

Craig Calhoun, Joseph Gerteis, James Moody,
Steven Pfaff, Kathryn Schmidt, and Indermohan Virk

BLACKWELL
Publishers

Copyright © Blackwell Publishers Ltd 2002; editorial matter and organization copyright © Craig Calhoun, Joseph Gerteis, James Moody, Steven Pfaff, Kathryn Schmidt, and Indermohan Virk 2002

First published 2002

2 4 6 8 10 9 7 5 3 1

Blackwell Publishers Inc.
350 Main Street
Malden, Massachusetts 02148
USA

Blackwell Publishers Ltd
108 Cowley Road
Oxford OX4 1JF
UK

Library of Congress Cataloging-in-Publication Data has been applied for
ISBN 0–631–21347–3 (hardback); 0–631–21348–1 (paperback)

British Library Cataloguing in Publication Data
A CIP catalogue record for this book is available from the British Library.

Typeset in Sabon, 10 on 12pt
by Set Systems, Saffron Walden, Essex
Printed in Great Britain by TJ International, Padstow, Cornwall

This book is printed on acid-free paper.

Contents

Contributors

Craig Calhoun is Professor of Sociology and History at New York University and since 1999 has been President of the Social Science Research Council. He was previously editor of *Sociological Theory*. His books include *Neither Gods Nor the Emperors: Students and the Struggle for Democracy in China* (1995), *Critical Social Theory: Culture, History, and the Challenge of Difference* (1995), and *Nationalism* (1997). He is also editor-in-chief of the *Oxford Dictionary of the Social Sciences*.

Joseph Gerteis is Assistant Professor of Sociology at the University of Minnesota, Twin Cities. His work explores the influence of categorical identities on social action in politics and social movements. His recent work examines southern labor movements of the late nineteenth century.

James Moody is Assistant Professor of Sociology at Ohio State University. He studies informal social organization through social networks, including the distribution of sexually transmitted diseases, adolescent friendship structure, and relations through the Internet.

Steven Pfaff is Assistant Professor of Sociology at the University of Washington. His scholarly interests include sociological theory, comparative and historical sociology and research on collective action and social movements. His current research focuses on popular protest in the East German revolution of 1989–90.

Kathryn Schmidt is Lecturer in Sociology at the University of Northern Iowa. Her research explores how gender and sexuality structure organizational processes and workplace relations.

Indermohan Virk is a Ph.D. candidate in the Department of Sociology at the University of North Carolina at Chapel Hill and a Visiting Lecturer at Indiana University. Her current research addresses the transformation of public space and its impact on the public sphere in the late twentieth-century United States.

Acknowledgments

The authors and publishers gratefully acknowledge the following for permission to reproduce copyright material:

1   Karl Marx, "Contribution to the Critique of Hegel's Philosophy of Law." From Karl Marx and Frederick Engels, *Collected Works, Volume 3*. Richard Dixon et al., translators. Copyright © 1975 by International Publishers, pp. 175–81, 184–7;

2   Karl Marx, "Economic and Philosophic Manuscripts of 1844." From Karl Marx and Frederick Engels, *Collected Works, Volume 3*. Richard Dixon et al., translators. Copyright © 1975 by International Publishers, pp. 270–82;

3   Karl Marx, "Commodities." From Karl Marx and Frederick Engels, *Collected Works, Volume 35*. Richard Dixon et al., translators. Copyright © 1975 by International Publishers, pp. 45–56, 81–94;

4   Karl Marx, "The General Formula for Capital." From Karl Marx and Frederick Engels, *Collected Works, Volume 35*. Richard Dixon et al., translators. Copyright © 1975 by International Publishers, pp. 157–66;

5   Karl Marx, "Division of Labour and Manufacture." From Karl Marx and Frederick Engels, *Collected Works, Volume 35*. Richard Dixon et al., translators. Copyright © 1975 by International Publishers, pp. 341–4, 364–6;

6   Karl Marx, "The So-Called Primitive Accumulation." From Karl Marx and Frederick Engels, *Collected Works, Volume 35*. Richard Dixon et al., translators. Copyright © 1975 by International Publishers, pp. 704–7, 748–51;

7   Karl Marx, "Classes." From Karl Marx and Frederick Engels, *Collected Works, Volume 37*. Richard Dixon et al., translators. Copyright © 1975 by International Publishers, pp. 870–1;

8   Karl Marx and Frederick Engels, "Manifesto of the Communist Party." From Karl Marx and Frederick Engels, *Collected Works, Volume 6*. Richard Dixon et al., translators. Copyright © 1975 by International Publishers, pp. 481–2, 485 506;

9   Karl Marx, "The Eighteenth Brumaire of Louis Bonaparte." From Karl Marx and Frederick Engels, *Collected Works, Volume 11*. Richard Dixon et al., translators. Copyright © 1975 by International Publishers, pp. 103–12, 194–7;

10 Emile Durkheim, "The Rules of Sociological Method." Reprinted and edited with the permission of the Free Press, a division of Simon & Schuster, Inc. From Emile Durkheim, *The Rules of Sociological Method*. Translated by W. D. Halls. Edited by Steven Lukes. Copyright © 1982 by Steven Lukes.

Translation, copyright © 1982 by Macmillan Publishers, Ltd., pp. 35–8, 50–9, 119–25, 127–32, 143–5;

11   Emile Durkheim, "The Division of Labor in Society." Reprinted and edited with the permission of The Free Press, a division of Simon & Schuster, Inc. From Emile Durkheim, *The Division of Labor in Society*. Introduction by Lewis A. Coser. Translated by W. D. Halls. Copyright © 1984 by Lewis A. Coser. Translation, copyright © 1984 by Higher & Further Education Division, Macmillan Publishers Ltd., p. 1–2, 24–9, 38–41, 60–3, 68–71, 83–5, 200–5, 301–6;

12   Emile Durkheim, "The Elementary Forms of the Religious Life." Reprinted and edited with the permission of The Free Press, a division of Simon & Schuster, Inc. From Emile Durkheim, *Elementary Forms of the Religious Life*. Translated by W. D. Swain. Copyright © 1965 by the Free Press, pp. 15–19, 21–2, 28–33, 467–75;

13   Max Weber, " 'Objectivity' in Social Science." Reprinted and edited with the permission of the Free Press, a division of Simon & Schuster, Inc. From Max Weber, *The Methodology of the Social Sciences*. Translated and edited by Edward A. Shils and Henry A. Finch. Copyright © 1949 by the Free Press, renewed 1977 by Edward A. Shils, pp. 89–99, 110–12;

14   Max Weber, "Basic Sociological Terms." Reprinted and edited with the permission of The Free Press, a division of Simon & Schuster, Inc. From Max Weber, *The Theory of Social and Economic Organization*. Translated by A. M. Henderson and Talcott Parsons. Edited by Talcott Parsons. Copyright © 1947, renewed 1975 by Talcott Parsons, pp. 88–103, 107–17;

15   Max Weber, "The Protestant Ethic and the Spirit of Capitalism." From Max Weber, *The Protestant Ethic and the Spirit of Capitalism*. Translated by Talcott Parsons. Copyright © 1930, Charles Scribner's Sons, pp. 35–40, 47–65, 74–8, 170–83;

16   Max Weber, "The Distribution of Power Within the Political Community: Class, Status, Party." Used by permission of Oxford University Press, Inc. From *From Max Weber: Essays in Sociology*. Edited by H. H. Gerth and C. Wright Mills. Translated by H. H. Gerth and C. Wright Mills. Copyright © 1946, 1958 by H. H. Gerth and C. Wright Mills, pp. 180–95;

17   Max Weber, "The Types of Legitimate Domination." Reprinted and edited with the permission of The Free Press, a Division of Simon & Schuster, Inc. From *The Theory of Social and Economic Organization* by Max Weber. Translated by A. M. Henderson and Talcott Parsons. Edited by Talcott Parsons. Copyright © 1947, renewed 1975 by Talcott Parsons, pp. 324–5, 328–30, 333–4, 341–3, 358–64, 367, 369–70;

18   Max Weber, "Bureaucracy." From *From Max Weber: Essays in Sociology* by Max Weber. Edited by H. H. Gerth and C. Wright Mills. Translated by H. H. Gerth and C. Wright Mills. Copyright © 1946, 1958 by H. H. Gerth and C.

Wright Mills. Used by permission of Oxford University Press, Inc., pp. 135–44, 149–58, 163–4, 173–8;

19 George Herbert Mead, "The Self." From *Mind, Self and Society: From the Standpoint of a Social Behaviorist*, by George H. Mead. Edited and with an introduction by Charles W. Morris. Copyright © 1934 by the University of Chicago, renewed 1962 by Charles W. Morris. University of Chicago Press, 1934, pp. 135–44, 149–58, 163–4, 173–8;

20 Georg Simmel, "The Stranger." From *Georg Simmel: On Individuality and Social Forms*, by Georg Simmel. Edited and with an introduction by Donald N. Levine. Copyright © 1971 by the University of Chicago. University of Chicago Press, 1971, pp. 143–9;

21 "Group Expansion and the Development of Individuality." From *Georg Simmel: On Individuality and Social Forms*, by Georg Simmel. Edited and with an introduction by Donald N. Levine. Copyright © 1971 by the University of Chicago. University of Chicago Press, 1971, pp. 252–66, 268–74, 290–2;

22 Sigmund Freud, "Civilization and its Discontents." From *Civilization and its Discontents* by Sigmund Freud. Translated by James Strachey. Copyright © 1961 by James Strachey, renewed 1989 by Alix Strachey. Used by permission of W. W. Norton & Company, Inc.;

23 W. E. B. Du Bois, "The Souls of Black Folk." From *The Souls of Black Folk* by W. E. B. Du Bois. First published 1903. Bantam Books, 1989, pp. 1–9;

24 Karl Mannheim, "Ideology and Utopia." *From Ideology and Utopia: An Introduction to the Sociology of Knowledge*, by Karl Mannheim. Translated by Louis Worth and Edward Shils. Used by permission of Routledge Publishers, pp. 55–9, 94–6, 192–200, 203–4;

25 Max Horkheimer, "Traditional and Critical Theory." From *Critical Theory: Selected Essays*, by Max Horkheimer. Translated by Matthew J. O'Connell et al. English Translation copyright © 1972 by Herder and Herder, Inc. Used by permission of the Continuum Publishing Group, pp. 188–243;

26 Theodor Adorno, "Cultural Criticism and Society." From *Prisms*, by Theodor Adorno. Translated by Samuel Weber and Shierry Weber. Copyright © 1967 by Theodor W. Adorno. Published by MIT Press, 1981, pp. 19–34;

27 Herbert Marcuse. "One-Dimensional Man." From *One-Dimensional Man: Studies in the Ideology of Advanced Industrial Society"* by Herbert Marcuse. Copyright © 1964 by Herbert Marcuse. Reprinted by permission of Beacon Press, Boston, pp. 1, 3–5, 7–8, 71–80, 82–3;

28 Talcott Parsons, "The Structure of Social Action." Reprinted and edited with the permission of The Free Press, a division of Simon & Schuster, Inc. From *The Structure of Social Action* by Talcott Parsons. Copyright © 1949 by The

Free Press, renewed 1977 by Talcott Parsons, pp. 43–5, 51–2, 56, 58–69, 719–26;

29 Talcott Parsons, "The Position of Sociological Theory." From "The Position of Sociology Theory," by Talcott Parsons. *American Sociological Review* 13, 2. Copyright © 1948 by The American Sociological Association, pp. 156–63;

30 Talcott Parsons, "An Outline of the Social System." Reprinted and edited with permission of The Free Press, a division of Simon & Schuster, Inc. From *Theories of Society* by Talcott Parsons, Edward A. Shils, Kaspar D. Naegle, Jesse R. Pitts. Copyright © 1961 by the Free Press, pp. 36–43, 44–7, 70–2;

31 Robert K. Merton, "On Sociological Theories of the Middle Range." Reprinted and edited with the permission of The Free Press, a division of Simon & Schuster, Inc. From *Social Theory and Social Structure* by Robert K. Merton. Copyright © 1949, 1957 by The Free Press, renewed 1977, 1985 by Robert K. Merton, pp. 39–53;

32 Robert K. Marton, "Manifest and Latent Functions." Reprinted and edited with the permission of The Free Press, a division of Simon & Schuster, Inc. From *Social Theory and Social Structure* by Robert K. Merton. Copyright © 1949, 1957 by The Free Press, renewed 1977, 1985 by Robert K. Merton, pp. 114–15, 117–22, 124–6;

33 Robert K. Merton, "The Bearing of Empirical Research on Sociological Theory." Reprinted and edited with the permission of The Free Press, a division of Simon & Schuster, Inc. From *Social Theory and Social Structure* by Robert K. Merton. Copyright © 1949, 1957 by The Free Press, renewed 1977, 1985 by Robert K. Merton, pp. 156–63, 165–71.

The publishers apologize for any errors or omissions in the above list and would be grateful to be notified of any corrections that should be incorporated in the next edition or reprint of this book.

Introduction

Sociology is the development of systematic knowledge about social life, the way it is organized, how it changes, its creation in social action, and its disruption and renewal in social conflict. Sociological theory is both a guide to sociological inquiry and an attempt to bring order to its results.

Sociological theory is not simply a collection of answers to questions about what society is like. It offers many answers, but it also offers help in posing better questions and developing inquiries that can answer them. Like all of science, thus, it is a process. It is always under development, responding to changes in our social lives and to improvements in our sociological knowledge. In this sense, the playwright and poet LeRoi Jones once compared writing and hunting. "Hunting is not those heads on the wall," he said.[1] He meant that hunting is an adventure; it is a project. Hunting is something one can do better or worse, but one can never know precisely what one will find. The same is true of writing, and of the pursuit of knowledge. Theory is our most developed way of organizing the knowledge we have, but that knowledge is never complete. Of necessity, therefore, theory is also a guide to new research and a way of organizing debates over what our partial knowledge tells us.

The adventure of sociological theory is relatively new – perhaps 200 years old at most.[2] But it is closely connected to a long history of social thought, extending back to the ancient world. Greek philosophers, Roman lawyers, and Jewish and Christian religious scholars all contributed significantly to the "prehistory" of sociological theory. They not only thought about society, they thought in systematic ways about what made it possible, how it could be made better, and what caused social order sometimes to collapse. Nonetheless, sociological theory did not develop until the modern era – mainly the eighteenth and nineteenth centuries. The change that mattered most was the rise of science.

From Social Thought to Social Science

Science transformed the ways in which people understood the conditions of their own lives and relationships as well as the ways they understood astronomy or gravity.[3] At the most general level, and aside from any of its specific discoveries or theories, the scientific revolution brought an emphasis on new learning. That is, researchers set out to gather as much knowledge as possible and especially as much empirical knowledge as possible, and to organize it as systematically as possible. Earlier systems for classifying knowledge were often abandoned, particularly where they were based on surface appearance rather than deeper underlying and causally significant relations. In a thousand different fields from astronomy to the study of moths, from the breeding of farm animals to the growth of human population, the internal structure of human bodies to the way our sensory organs work, early scientists tried to see as objectively as possible, and to search as widely as possible for things to see. In most of these fields some knowledge already existed. Modern science not only added to it, but subjected it to questioning and tests.

Partly as an inevitable consequence of this, science challenged the authority of traditions and venerable institutions including churches and governments. This was direct in some cases – famously that of Galileo – where scientific research produced results that contradicted old doctrines and the teachings of current religious authorities. But even more general and pervasive was the notion that the best knowledge was that based on logic and evidence, because this meant reasoning for oneself and looking at the world for oneself and thus potentially reasoning and looking anew. When early scientists stressed the importance of logic and rational thought on the one hand and empirical evidence on the other, they specifically meant to challenge the notion that we should simply believe what we are taught. They meant that even the most respected authorities and the most venerated traditions could sometimes be wrong. The starting points of science are to think for oneself, in the most rigorous way possible, and to trust the evidence of one's senses, especially when it is rooted in experiment or careful observation and demonstration and not casual everyday experience. This isn't the whole of science, however, not least because reason and evidence can come into conflict with each other. Science also involves, on the one hand, efforts to distinguish what is "objective" in facts from the language in which we state them or the specific (and often more or less artificial) circumstances under which we collect data (sometimes supplementing our senses with technology). And it is on the other hand efforts to discern logical order in enormously complex and always incomplete collections of facts.

This is something different from simply offering a summary of established facts. In the first place, facts always require interpretation, and making interpretation systematic is one of the main tasks of theory. In addition, knowledge advances by the process the philosopher of science Karl Popper called "conjecture and refutation."[4] That is, a scientist puts forward propositions about how the world works; these are initially conjectures, products of imagination as well as knowledge. They become the basis for hypotheses, and research and analysis confirm or reject them. Thus, seeing patterns and connections in social life depends on imagination; theorists must try to see how things fit together. But refutation drives the development of knowledge forward as much as imagination. Refutation of an important hypothesis stimulates a rethinking of the whole pattern of knowledge that is organized by a theory.

Empirical research also depends on theory to specify the objects of its analysis: how do we know what constitutes a community, for example, or a religion? Appealing to common sense doesn't solve the problem. Common sense is generally formed on the basis of a particular religion or a particular experience of community – and this is a source of bias if one is seeking knowledge of religion or community in general, in all social contexts. Even more basically, concepts are like lenses that enable us to see phenomena. Take the concept "self-fulfilling prophecy," developed by the American sociologist Robert Merton in the mid-twentieth century.[5] This calls our attention to a common aspect of human actions that may take place in many different contexts and which we wouldn't otherwise relate to each other. Aided by the concept, we can easily see the commonality among teachers' predictions of students' future success or failure in school, the labeling of criminals (who then find it hard to get legitimate jobs), and the comments of famous securities analysts on TV about what stocks are likely to go up or down. In none of the cases is the outcome of the predictions independent of the predictions themselves.

Theories also contain propositions, statements about how the world works. As communities grow larger, one prominent sociological proposition holds, they will become more internally differentiated. Any factual proposition like this can be tested by turning it into a hypothesis – a prediction – and by specifying facts that would count as refuting it. In this case, research seems so far mostly to confirm the growth/differentiation correlation (though there are exceptions and qualifications). Another proposed correlation is that as science and rationalization advance in modern societies, religion will decline; this secularization hypothesis is more controversial. In some societies the decline is evident, in others less so. But even where most people still say they are religious, both the content of religious teaching and the place of religion in people's lives have often changed. This suggests one reason why theories grow complicated. It is impossible to get a serious grasp on the relationship between science and religion without considering that each refers to many different things, and that many other features of social reality shape the relations between them. Politics, for example, may change the relationship between science and religion, leading some to back one against the other, defining legal boundaries between the two, or joining specific versions of each in a sense of national identity. Theories provide frameworks for relating different research results to each other and developing explanations: community relationships organize less of social life as markets expand; professionals perform services once the province of family, friends, and neighbors; and governments and corporations grow stronger and more formally organized. These changes also, of course, give a new context to religion. One of the most important things theory does is offer a systematic account of the overall workings of social life within which one can place specific topics. It is important to be systematic – to rely on theory rather than just vague assumptions – partly because this enables one to correct assumptions when new research challenges them.

Theory is concerned with the development of concepts with which to grasp social life, with identifying patterns in social relations and social action, with producing explanations for both specific features of life in society and changes in overall forms of society. It is thus an indispensable part of sociology, crucial to its standing as a science. At the same time, sociological thory is more than a tool for sociologists. It is also a crucial basis for reflection on social life, informing moral deliberations and public decisions. This is true first because sociological theory – along with the rest of social science – enables us to understand specific events, institutions, and social trends. It is a different thing, for example, to experience living in a city and to have a theoretical understanding of why cities have grown to enormous size. Secondly, sociological theory helps us to see the connections among different events, institutions and trends. It helps us answer questions like how changes in gender roles and relations affect families, schools, workplaces, and politics. It helps us to see general patterns in social life – differences and similarities among countries, for example, or among historical periods. Thirdly, sociological theory helps us relate personal life to society. This is important at all scales from interpersonal relations like love or friendship to large-scale patterns in economy, government, or culture. Sociological theory helps us to see to what extent we can choose the conditions we live under, and also to what extent our choices are shaped by our backgrounds and other social factors. It helps us literally to judge what is possible and what is not, and what are the likely consequences of different courses of action.

Sociological theory does not tell us what parties to vote for, what religion to profess – if any – or what moral values are right. But it does enable us to make systematic and informed judgments about what policies will promote the values we hold dear and which will be likely to undermine them. Among its main contributions is assistance in being systematic in assessing social phenomena and proposals for social change. It also helps us to be systematic in working out our own ideas, to see when there are tensions between different values we hold. In many cases, sociological theory does not settle arguments, but helps us to see more deeply what is at stake in them. Take the idea that people are basically rational actors who make decisions on the basis of self-interest. Sociological theory includes explorations of how much of social life can be explained in these terms – and it includes some phenomena, like marriage decisions, that people usually insist have nothing to do with such strategic analysis. At the same time, sociological theory also explores the ways in which culture shapes ideas of what is rational, what is of interest, and even what the self is like. It explores how being embedded in networks of social relations or in institutions such as a church or a business corporation may shape what kinds of actions we choose. And it considers whether in addition to strategic interests people are moved by emotions such as anger and love or sentiments such as sympathy for others.

Thinking about social relationships is basic to having them. Creating a family involves not just biological reproduction but the development of social roles and the identification of one family as distinct from others. All human societies that we know of differentiate their members on the basis of gender, age, and kinship or descent. These distinctions help to organize social life; they are also charged with moral significance. Thinking about social life, in short, is part of how we create it.

Like a family, an army, a city, a religion, a kingdom, or a nation must be imagined and made the object of thought in order to exist as such. This does not mean that it will be well or systematically understood (and indeed, many social factors influence us without our ever being aware of them). The thought that helps a city to exist may name it, but not grasp why its population grows. It will probably include some understanding of its governance, of who belongs in it by right and who is tolerated as an outsider, and of the place of markets or temples within it. All of these and likely many other features of the city will be the objects of reflection by its members – and perhaps by others, such as invaders who would conquer it. Thought about society is a basic part of human culture, in short, whether in mythic or scientific or purely practical forms.

Social thought developed in the context of religion as people explored the ultimate meaning of their life together and the moral norms that guided it. It developed in law as people sought to resolve practical problems of organizing social life. Eventually political inquiry came to explore what kind of society a particular form of government produced – or conversely, what sort of government a given form of society could support. Ideas about what would constitute a good society developed out of each of these traditions, and have been a part of philosophy since its earliest phases. Alongside this large question people posed more specific ones about family, friendship, and ways to organize armies or religious communities. Should there be more hierarchy or more equality? Must men and women be kept sharply distinct or should they be allowed similar roles? Is freedom compatible with unity? Some of these general reflections on social life were remarkably insightful and still repay study. But they did not add up to sociological theory.

To do so, they had to meet two basic criteria. First, they had to offer empirical claims that could be the basis of either tests (and thereby confirmation, correction, or improvement) or comparisons among theories (and thereby judgment as to which more accurately grasped social reality). In this sense, the idea of theory is embedded in the notion of science and the specifically scientific use of empirical observations. Second, theories were not *sociological* theories unless they focused on social life as a specific and distinct object of study. In the simplest sense, sociological theories needed to be about society, in its own right, and not simply as an adjunct of religion, law, or politics. Of course, just what society was or is could be debated. Early sociological theorists tended to assume that it meant more or less the same thing as nation – so one spoke of French society or English society. But it also meant local communities, voluntary organizations, interpersonal relationships, and public communication. It included culture and social action as well as social structure. Society only began to command the attention of theorists during the seventeenth and eighteenth centuries.

The Idea of Society and the Roots of Sociological Theory

The concept of society – social action and relationships and organizations – came to the fore not simply as an intellectual development but in response to enormous changes in social life itself. Among the many changes, four stand out as especially significant for the development of sociological theory:

The rise of individualism

Individualism may seem the opposite of a concern for society, but it did not mean the absence of society so much as a different way of organizing and thinking about it.[6] Conceived as the product of individual thought and action, or judged on the criterion of how well it meets individuals' needs, society looks different from when it is approached as ordered according to divine law or dictated by kings.

Individualism's most important early appearance was in religion. Especially in the Protestant Reformation, the notion became widespread that people should read the Bible for themselves (not leave that to priests), pray in terms they made up for themselves (not simply by official prayers handed down by the church), and develop a personal relationship with God. These ideas had an influence on the rise of science, which was itself rooted in modern individualism and also helped to undermine traditional authorities.

Individualism had a similar impact in social life and on thinking about society, introducing a shift from inherited (or ascribed) to chosen (or achieved) relationships. Individualism led people to think for themselves about social relationships and social organizations, not simply accept those which had been passed down from earlier ages. This was reflected in changing commitments to family and community. Increasingly, these social relationships were approached as objects of personal choice. Migration away from rural communities reflected individual's pursuit of economic gain, and an urban economy open to strangers from the countryside or even other countries encouraged individual decisions to relocate. Perhaps even more dramatically, marriages were increasingly understood as personal relationships, ideally founded on love between individuals, rather than mainly alliances between broader kin groups.

The idea that individual relationships ought to be products of choice suggested also that social relationships in general could be chosen. In the seventeenth and eighteenth centuries, theorists borrowed the idea of a contract from economic life (and from the biblical notion of a covenant between God and His chosen people) to describe social life generally.[7] Thomas Hobbes, John Locke, and Jean-Jacques Rousseau were among the most important early "social contract" theorists. They sought to describe how society could come into being on the basis of a contract among individuals, and they sought to use reasoning about what sorts of social arrangements free people would agree to as a way to analyze whether actually existing social organization was just. Early social contract theory focused mostly on political questions, but it contributed to the rise of sociological theory by approaching the question of what political arrangements were legitimate through examination of how social relations might come into being. Locke and Rousseau especially distinguished society from government and gave it priority.

Emphasizing individual responsibility in religion and in the choice of relationships was also linked to a positive value on everyday, ordinary personal life. Christianity had tended previously to exalt the spiritual and otherworldly. During the early modern period, Christian thinkers placed new emphasis on how religion could guide personal life; marriage, family, and work all gained positive value, thus, because affairs of this world were not seen merely as preparation for the hereafter. This suggested also that individuals should apply themselves to building a better society here on earth, not simply waiting for salvation after death. As the poet William Blake put it, "I will not cease from mental fight, Nor shall my sword sleep in my hand, Till we have built Jerusalem, In England's green and pleasant land."[8]

The rise of modern states

There had long been kings and other sorts of rulers, of course. What changed with modernity was the capacity of states to regulate and shape different aspects of social life.[9] States built roads, raised citizen armies, operated schools and prisons, and collected taxes to pay for all these and other activities. At one level, thus, states helped to organize societies. At another level, though, states were distinct from society. This was made evident in a distinctive modern phenomenon – revolution.[10]

Revolution involved "the people" rising up to change the political institutions under which they lived, and often to try to reorganize society more generally. Blake suggested something of the underlying idea when he said that Englishmen should build a New Jerusalem. Among other things the English, American, and French Revolutions all signaled a change in how people thought about the legitimacy of government. It was not enough to know that a king was the oldest son of his father or that he claimed divine right to rule. People demanded evidence that government ruled in the best interests of the people. But who were the people? Revolutionary thought signaled also the growing prominence of a new idea, the nation, understood as the group of people and the cultural identity that endured as governments came and went. The idea of nation deeply influenced the idea of society, suggesting that it should be understood as a bounded, internally organized population at the level of a country.[11] This concept proved extremely influential, although in fact social organization was always both more local and more international than a nation-state centered concept of society suggested.

The distinction of state from society was affirmed in the concept of "civil society" – that is, society that was a free product of relations among private persons.[12] Contract was a model for those relations, but not the only one. Friendship, religious community, and the self-governance of medieval guilds and cities also offered models. During the eighteenth and early nineteenth centuries, several theorists responded to a growing importance for civil society. They laid part of the foundation for sociological theory in emphasizing how much of human life was organized at a level between the interior privacy of intimate family life (or indeed, the inner personality of the individual) and the exterior direction of the state. Society was the crucial middle ground in which relationships could not be explained entirely by either psychology or by politics. And, as the Scot Adam Ferguson wrote, society had its own history, distinct from that of politics.[13]

The development of large-scale markets, capitalism and modern industry

One crucial thing that people did in "civil society" was to pursue material interests and well-being. The pace of economic change in the late eighteenth and early nineteenth centuries was so rapid and its impact so great that contemporaries borrowed the previously political idea of revolution to describe it: the industrial revolution.[14]

The industrial revolution was actually felt first in agriculture; rapidly rising farm productivity meant that large nonagricultural populations could be supported by relatively few farmers. This shaped both the decline of rural villages and the rise of cities. Both phenomena called attention to the idea of society, as people questioned whether the economic changes were good for social relations. One enduring sociological theme reflects this: the distinction of community from association or civil society, in which the former reflects the image of small scale, tight-knit, and directly interpersonal relations in villages or small towns while the latter reflects the image of impersonal, looser relationships in the city, and the loss of direct ties to indirect ones through markets, media, and formal organizations.[15]

The transformation of productivity by division of labor, factories, and technology was a crucial feature of the late eighteenth and early nineteenth centuries in Britain and took place slightly later in other European countries, America, and eventually much of the world. It not only had sociological effects (e.g., on community) but was itself a sociological as well as an economic phenomenon. It contributed to the rise of the idea of society most crucially through two notions: the division of labor and the market. Adam Smith was influential in establishing the importance of both, and thus counts as a founder of sociology as well as economics.[16]

In his famous book, *The Wealth of Nations*, Smith described the division of labor as a social process, and one basic to growing productivity.[17] Instead of combining a number of skills in the person of one craftsman, this involved training workers to be specialists in each. Instead of a pin maker, thus, there was someone who straightened wire, someone who sharpened its point, someone who made a head, and someone who attached it. In addition, crucially, there was also an entrepreneur or manager who organized and supervised the process. As individuals, each of these people might be less skilled than the former pin maker (and all but the manager would be paid less), but together they could produce more and cheaper pins. This made for economic efficiency. It also demonstrated, however, how different people with different jobs were in fact dependent on each other in a larger social organization – something true of society on a large scale as well as each workplace. For pin making, the necessary social organization was produced by entrepreneurs and managers. For society at large, one might think the government had the same role and in fact many people thought and still think just this. But Smith argued that govenment was not the only way to achieve social organization on a large scale. At least equally important (and often more efficient) was the market.

Insofar as people operated as buyers and sellers (of their labor and managerial ingenuity as well as of physical goods), the market operated through the law of supply and demand to condition each to behave efficiently. Much more could be produced on the basis of a social division of labor mediated by the market than by individuals or families aiming at self-subsistence. Smith suggested that individual people were led to create social value, as if by an "invisible hand." In other words, the market was self-organizing. Smith emphasized this point not only to show its economic importance but also to illustrate how relationships among ordinary people, rather than decisions of the king or laws enforced by the state, could provide for social order.

European exploration of the rest of the world and the trade, war, and colonization that followed in its wake

Economic expansion was among the most important forces driving European exploration of the rest of the globe. This also had roots in religion, however, as missionaries sought to convert nonbelievers to Christianity. It was shaped by state-building as European kings and later republics sought to expand their power through empires. It was even a product of science, as explorers sought to prove the world round and to discover new biological species even while also serving economic and political employers. Exploration – and exploitation – were also both connected to early social science. Theorists provided accounts of the inferiority of non-European peoples. They provided justifications for colonial rule. But they also learned enormously, most importantly about culture, about differences in forms of social organization, and about the complex manner in which different ways of life are held together.

The eighteenth-century French social theorist, the Baron of Montesquieu, thus helped to pave the way for sociology. He asked why different countries had different legal and political systems, and sought the answer in cultural differences that he called "the spirit" behind laws.[18] Montesquieu, like most of his contemporaries, combined prejudice with fact, speculating for example, that warm climates made some people naturally lazy and thus in need of more despotic rule. But he was also part of a broad current of European thought that first recognized that social conditions were not natural nor immutable partly through seeing how many different sorts of social institutions there were in the rest of the world. Instead of conceptualizing this through the notion of social contract, Montesquieu emphasized the way that culture knits together a whole package of knowledge, beliefs, practices, and values.

Although Europeans often tried to impose their culture – and political, economic, and religious practices – on the people they colonized elsewhere in the world, they also tried to understand them. This become a powerful inducement to the development of sociological theory and social science generally. Some developed evolutionary theories to try to explain differences in social organization as the product of growth or progress. Indeed, some of these theorists came before and influenced Darwin's biological theory of evolution. Others later joined the two, like Herbert Spencer, who was simultaneously a sociologist and a biologist and the coiner of the term "survival of the fittest." Eventually many social scientists became critics of colonialism, and sought to point out that difference did not always mean either superiority or inferiority.

European expansion into the rest of the world had material effects that were also important influences on the rise of social theory. Wealth extracted from other lands and long-distance trade contributed to the growth of capitalism; the need to administer far-flung colonies contributed to the development of more scientific approaches to government and formal organizations. The idea of America figured prominently. In the beginning, wrote John Locke, all the world was America.[19] He meant that the entire world was organized in the minimalist fashion he thought typical of the aboriginal Native Americans. Both the confrontation with small-scale, non-state-centered societies elsewhere and the development of transnational empires helped counterbalance the tendency to equate society with nation-state. For later theorists, the significance of America (as of other settler societies such as Australia) was to dramatize the experiment of creating new social forms completely by choice, with little inheritance behind them. In the 1830s, for example, the Frenchman Alexis de Toqueville visited the United States to learn about Europe's future. This lay, he thought with democracy, which he understood as a society based on free individualistic choice and relatively social equality. His account, *Democracy in America*, became a classic of sociological theory, taking up the question (following Montesquieu) of what social and culture conditions made stable democratic government possible – and what might make it collapse into anarchy or tyranny.[20]

Sociological theory was born, in short, in reflection on both momentous changes in Europe and the pattern of similarities and differences discerned among human societies around the world. Science offered a new method for developing knowledge; both social change and the confrontation with social difference made ordinary people, business leaders, and government officials all seek new knowledge about society. The changes and the confrontations with difference were often disruptive, but by their very disruptions called attention to the issue of how society worked.

The Twentieth Century: Synthesis and Critique

The First World War marked a watershed in sociological theory. Marxist internationalism, for example, confronted the power of nationalism. The optimism of nineteenth-century evolutionism and faith in progress was deeply challenged. Several of the great founders of modern sociology – like Weber and Durkheim – lived through the war and struggled after it with a growing concern for the fate of modern society.

At the same time, the world war itself signaled – albeit ironically – a new level of interconnections among the different European countries and between affairs in Europe and elsewhere. In Russia, for example, the First World War was a precipitating factor in the communist revolution of 1917. This introduced a new kind of East–West split, no longer between Occident and Orient but between capitalist and communist countries. Much of the rest of twentieth century history was shaped by it. The First World War also marked the emergence of the United States as a global military power, entering the war late but decisively. And the nature of the war itself revealed that power depended on the ability to mobilize industry, transport systems, and a wide variety of citizens. Success in war, in other words, depended on social organization and not only that of the military itself.

Perhaps it is not surprising that after the war the United States also began to emerge more prominently as a force in sociological theory. Indeed, an American, Talcott Parsons, sought to pick up the projects of the great classical sociological theorists of Europe and synthesize them into a new social theory. At the heart of his conception was the effort to reconcile social action and social structure, the ways in which people could make choices about their lives and the ways in which all of social life depended on underlying patterns that were beyond individual choice. In some ways, Parsons' sociological theory mirrored a basic issue in the developing self-understanding of the Western, non-communist societies. Capitalism and democracy both presented the importance of individuals and their choices as basic to modern life. "Free enterprise," consumer choice, and open elections were central to the idea of the "free world," as opposed to communism. Parsons embraced that idea, but at the same time recognized how incomplete it was. If choice – by both managers and consumers – was basic to capitalism, so was the idea of the market as a self-regulating system. If open elections were basic to democracy, so was the concentration of power in the state bureaucracy (rather, for example, than independent feudal lords).

These concerns were not unique to Talcott Parsons. Many social theorists took on the challenge of trying effectively to relate action to structure. For some, like Karl Mannheim, the question was to what extent ideas reflected the social positions of those who espoused them. Mannheim asked whether intellectuals in some sense might occupy a special social position that enabled them to be more objective. For others, like George Herbert Mead, the question was how the individual might come into being as a result of social processes, through communication with others and through a recognition of how he or she fitted into the large patterns of social interaction. We only gain full individuality, Mead suggested, when we can see ourselves at least in part as others see us – and for this we need social learning. At the same time, in the words of another great American sociologist, Charles Horton Cooley, "self and society are twinborn."[21] Imagining individuals as existing before and separate from society misunderstands both. But, society cannot make individuals in any shape; human nature is recalcitrant, limiting the options and pressing in specific directions. Sigmund Freud made this point as strongly as anyone in the early twentieth century.[22] Not only did nature matter, though, human beings were internally complex creatures, driven by conflicting tendencies, wants, and needs. Emotions mattered alongside reason and often in conflict with it.

Talcott Parsons, in his synthesis, approached personality, culture, and society as quasi-autonomous systems, three different levels of analysis of human life. Many of his critics charged that he smoothed out the conflicts and contradictions in each, and thus presented more harmony and consensus than was accurate. Perhaps this was most visible in the contrast between his presentation of the economy as working "functionally" to supply the needs of everyone and of all different parts of society and Marx's account of class conflict and the inherent contradictions and recurrent crises of capitalism. Likewise, in terms of personality, though Parsons drew on Freud, he emphasized the ideal of full and successful integration of the personality more than the inevitability of internal conflicts. Though he drew on Weber, he emphasized the capacity of culture to integrate human societies and guide evolution more than he did the cultural contradictions of modern life, the ways in which rationalization undermined creative individual spirit or consumerism granted people choice but reduced its meaning. Weber, after all, had talked gloomily of an "iron cage" in which capitalism and bureaucracy started out creating individual opportunity and effective social organization and ultimately trapped people in a social system without spirit.

The Second World War and the Great Depression that preceded it seemed to many to point out the merit in Weber's pessimism. Max Horkheimer, Theodor Adorno, and colleagues initially based at Frankfurt's Institute for Social Research combined influences from Weber, Marx, and Freud (among other sources) to produce a "critical theory." This aimed at understanding the ways in which rationalization could turn against reason and the limits to both capitalist development and bureaucratic states. The critical theorists were particularly influential in analyzing the rise of fascism, an ideology which combined heavy emphases on science and technology with an effort to restore "nature" and "spirit" to modern life. Adorno organized a research team to study the social factors – like a repressive work environment – that contributed to an "authoritarian personality" which made people will to join movements like fascism. Critical theory examined the rationalization of modern life that produced not only Parsons' functional social system, but a reduction of human choices to consumer options and a loss of capacity to advance liberty by transforming institutions. Part of the problem was that people found it hard to grasp that they had the capacity to remake the social world – not as individuals, but as members of social movements, creators of culture, and citizens in democratic society.

Sociological theory was often divided between those who stressed the successes of social integration and those who emphasized its limits and failures, and the importance of conflict to how society really worked. Parsons and other twentieth-century theorists drew on Durkheim and many nineteenth-century theorists to produce a new sociological theory that shared an emphasis on how the whole of society could be greater than the sum of its parts, and how the needs of each part for the others encouraged "functional integration." This theory has proved powerful in accounting for many of the ways that society does indeed coalesce despite diversity and differentiation. Like economic theories of the market as an "invisible hand," this sociological functionalism suggests that freely formed relationships can be self-regulating. But the functionalists didn't say very much about the extent to which power and violence determined how the system got started, who was wealthy, who was protected, and who was vulnerable. Their critics did a much better job with pointing out the "visible hand" of corporate power, military power, and other ways in which some social actors could control others or prosper at their expense. The critics also stressed the ways that history was not simple progress but a story of conflicts and crises. Where funtionalists tended to approach conflict as the breakdown of social relations, others drew on Georg Simmel who had pointed out that conflict was itself socially organized, a form of social relations.

These criticisms would become increasingly powerful in the last third of the twentieth century and remain basic to the debates that define contemporary sociological theory. We will turn to many of them in Part II of this anthology. Functionalism and closely related theories dominated sociological discussions until the 1960s. Increasing controversy over them was linked to other controversies that came to the fore in the 1960s, over poverty, race, war, and new kinds of international domination and exploitation. There has been no group of theories that has ever attained comparable hegemony over the field as a whole – and the field has suffered some disunity as a result, as well as being opened to new creativity. The functionalist synthesis were not the last word in sociological theory, but they remain enormously influential. To stress only functional integration and not power may be one-sided, but such integration is nonetheless of vital importance.

Conclusion

It is not easy to say when sociological theory started. As we have seen, ideas from the ancient world and especially from the seventeeth and eighteenth centuries contributed importantly. But it was only in the nineteenth century that sociological theory gained autonomy from other theories which privileged politics or economics or indeed, law or religion. August Comte coined the name sociology in 1838–9. He and his contemporary de Tocqueville were more clearly sociologists than their forebears Montesquieu and Rousseau (though both of the earlier writers did develop sociological theories). Likewise, Karl Marx built on the work of Adam Smith as well as on theorists of civil society like G. W. F. Hegel. But Marx's work is more specifically sociological, concerned with capitalism not only as an economic system but as a social formation, a kind of society with specific forms of power relations, cities, culture, and social movements. The creation of sociological theory did not end with the mid-nineteenth-century theorists like Comte, Tocqueville, and Marx who pioneered the mixture of scientific observation and rational analysis that would remain central. Indeed, it was a generation of successors who came of age in the 1890s who exerted the most enduring influence on the institutionalization of sociological theory within universities.[23] Emile Durkheim and Max Weber are the most important of these. And of course, the development of sociological theory continued in the twentieth century and continues now in the twenty-first. Many of the themes are rooted in the social changes of the early modern era. The division of labor that Adam Smith analyzed was a basic starting point for Emile Durkheim's theory of social solidarity. Both remain key influences on contemporary theorists. The question of division of labor is being rethought in the contexts of global organization of production and new technologies that dramatically shift the relationships between knowledge and industrial production.

Similarly, the work of Max Weber has been described as a dialogue with the ghost of Karl Marx. Weber saw much truth in Marx's analysis of capitalism, but also thought it one-sided, and insisted on the importance of religion and culture in ways contrary to Marx. Both are influential today among the theorists who ask how the globalization of economic activity will affect – or be affected by – cultures and religions around the world. The story of the development of sociological theory, in short, is one in which progress in the creation of new theory does not necessarily make older theory obsolete. On the contrary, some of the great classical sociological theories remain both influential and relevant today. They represent brilliant intellectual achievements and we learn much by thinking with the scholars who created them. They also offer signposts in intellectual argument, helping us to identify where later thinkers stand on basic questions by how they identify with or challenge earlier thinkers. Sometimes, too, social change makes us see new lessons in old theories. Marx's work is perhaps the extreme case here, partly because its later use has been so heavily shaped by politics.

Because Marx's theory was an influence on communism – indeed, taken as a sort of sacred text for communism – many assumed that the post-1989 collapse of communism made Marx's work irrelevant and for a time it lost prestige. As attention turned to globalization, however, and as globalization pitted different social interests against each other in a variety of conflicts, new readers found much of interest in Marx's theory. As early as 1848, for example, he and his collaborator Friedrich Engels discerned tendencies that seemed new to others a hundred and fifty years later. "exploitation of the world market gives a cosmopolitan character to production and consumption in every country . . . All old-established national industries have been destroyed or are daily being destroyed . . . In place of the old local and national seclusion and self-sufficiency, we have intercourse in every direction, universal inter-dependence of nations."[24]

This was prescient, but it was not the last word. As we noted at the beginning of this introductory essay, there is no last word. Theory is not the correct answer to all our questions. It offers many answers, but all of them provisional, all of them subject to revision and improvement on the basis of new evidence. Science is about asking questions. Some of these are new questions, some are old ones that have puzzled theorists as long as theory has existed. What is the relationship between individual and society? Between creative action and seemingly stable structures of relations? How do growth in economies or populations or knowledge itself change society? What, with Tocqueville, are the social and cultural conditions for democracy? What, with Durkheim, are the social and cultural conditions for solidarity and moral order? Can religion guide social life in the future as much as it did some times in the past? Are strong local communities necessarily undermined by global economic competition?

Sociological theorists have made great strides in answering these and other pressing questions, and also great strides in figuring out why they are hard to answer conclusively. Theories like the ones excerpted in the rest of this book are indispensable tools for grappling with basic questions in social life. That life is always part structure – to be analyzed as objectively as possible, and part action, to be understood in terms of reasons and possibilities. Theory, in other words, guides not just our search for right answers, but our search for right actions. Our actions will change the world for better or worse, and we will still need theory to understand it.

Notes

1   In *The Fiction of LeRoi Jones/Amiri Baraka* (Chicago: Chicago Review Press; orig. 1964). Jones later changed his name to Amiri Baraka.

2   There is no altogether satisfactory history of sociological theory. Several textbooks that cover much of its development are listed in the bibliography. For a serious account of the key modern theorists, see Lewis Coser, *Masters of Sociological Thought* (New York: Harcourt Brace Jovanovich, 1977); for a somewhat lighter review, see Randall Collins and Makowsky, *Discovery of Society* (New York: McGraw-Hill, rev. ed., 1997). For more depth on specific theorists, see George Ritzer, ed., *The Blackwell Companion to the Major Social Theorists* (Cambridge, MA: Blackwell, 2000). For a more historical account, see Tom Bottomore and Robert Nisbet, eds., *A History of Sociological Analysis* (New York: Basic Books, 1978).

3   There are many histories of modern science; a readable and authoritative one is Brian Silver, *The Ascent of Science* (Oxford: Oxford University Press, 1997); to situate the rise of science in Western intellectual history more generally, see Jacob Bronowski and Bruce Mazlish, *The Western Intellectual Tradition, from Leonardo to Hegel* (New York: Harper Collins 1986).

4   Karl R. Popper, *Conjectures and Refutations: The Growth of Scientific Knowledge* (London: Routledge, 1992).

5   Robert K. Merton *Social Theory and Social Structure* (Glencoe, IL: Free Press, 1957).

6   On the early history of individualism as a sociological concept, see Steven Lukes, *Individualism* (Oxford: Blackwell, 1973).

7   See David Zaret, *The Heavenly Contract* (Chicago: University of Chicago Press, 1985) and C. B. MacPherson, *The Political Theory of Possessive Individualism* (Cambridge: Cambridge University Press, 1976).

8   William Blake, "The New Jerusalem," in *The Complete Poetry and Prose of William Blake* (New York: Anchor, 1982).

9   For sociological accounts of the rise of the modern state, see Anthony Giddens, *The Nation-State and Violence* (Berkeley: University of California Press, 1984); Michael

Mann, *The Sources of Social Power*, vols. 1 and 2 (Cambridge: Cambridge University Press, 1983, 1993); Gianfranco Poggi, *The State: Its Nature, Development, and Progress* (Stanford: Stanford University Press, 1991).

10   On the specific place of revolutions within the early modern era, see Jack Goldstone, *Revolution and Rebellion in the Early Modern World* (Berkeley: University of California Press, 1991).

11   See Craig Calhoun, *Nationalism* (Minneapolis: University of Minnesota Press, 1997) and "Nationalism, Political Community, and the Representation of Society: Or, Why Feeling at Home Is Not a Substitute for Public Space," *European Journal of Social Theory*, Vol. 2 (1999), No. 2, pp. 217–31.

12   See Jean Cohen and Andrew Arato, *The Political Theory of Civil Society* (Cambridge, MA: MIT Press, 1992); also John Keane, *Civil Society* (Stanford: Stanford University Press, 1999); Adam Seligman, *Civil Society* (New York: Free Press, 1992); Craig Calhoun, "Public Sphere/Civil Society: History of the Concepts" *International Encyclopedia of Social and Behavioral Sciences* (Amsterdam: Elsevier, 2001).

13   *An Essay on the History of Civil Society* (Cambridge: Cambridge University Press, 1996; orig. 1767).

14   The term "industrial revolution" was first used by French writers in the early nineteenth century and rapidly appropriated into English thought; Raymond Williams, *Culture and Society, 1780–1950* (Harmondsworth: Penguin, 1958).

15   The classic sociological account of this contrast is Ferdinand Toennies, *Community and Association/Gemeinschaft und Gesellschaft* (New Brunswick, NJ: Transaction Publishers, 1988; orig. 1887). Toennies' term "gesellschaft" should arguably be translated as "civil society."

16   See David A. Reissman, *Adam Smith's Sociological Economics* (London: Croom Helm, 1976).

17   Adam Smith, *An Inquiry into the Nature and Causes of the Wealth of Nations* (Chicago: University of Chicago Press, 1977; orig. 1776).

18   Charles Louis de Secondat, Baron de Montesquieu, *The Spirit of Laws* (Berkeley: University of California Press, 1978; orig. 1748).

19   John Locke, *Second Treatise on Government* (Englewood Cliffs, NJ: Prentice-Hall, 1952; orig. 1690).

20   Alexis de Tocqueville, *Democracy in America* (New York: Harper, 2000; orig. 1840, 1844).

21   C. H. Cooley, *Social Organization* (New York: Scribners, 1902).

22   See, notably, *Civilization and its Discontents* (New York: Norton 1961; orig. 1930).

23   See H. Stuart Hughes, *Consciousness and Society: The Reorientation of European Social Thought, 1890–1930* (New York: Knopf, 1961) and Talcott Parsons, *The Structure of Social Action* (Glencoe: Free Press, 1967; orig. 1937).

24   Karl Marx and Friedrich Engels, *Manifesto of the Communist Party*, pp. 477–519 in *Collected Works* (New York: International Publishers, 1975), p. 488.

Part I

The Sociological Theory of Karl Marx and Friedrich Engels

Introduction to Part I

Although he is conventionally regarded as one of the "founding fathers" of modern sociology, Karl Marx (1818–83) was not a professional academic. Nor was he directly a part of the nascent field of sociology in his day. Instead Marx was trained as a philosopher and saw himself as an economist and social critic. His enduring legacy in sociology results from the way that his work brought a theoretical focus to empirical social analysis. Marx provided a theory to understand the connection between the concrete economic relationships among people and the broad patterns of social order that emerge from them in specific eras – an argument now known as "historical materialism." In developing historical materialism as a theoretical system, Marx and his collaborator Friedrich Engels laid the foundation of what was to become a Marxist school of sociological thought and analysis. Marx continues to fascinate not only because of his brilliance as a philosopher and social scientist, but because he represents the epitome of the scholar-activist, the social critic who is, to paraphrase Marx's own words in the *Theses on Feuerbach*, not content with criticizing the world but who is also trying to change it.

Marx's Life and Intellectual Outlook

Karl Marx was born in Trier, a commercial city in western Germany near the border of France, in 1818. He was the son of a prosperous merchant family and attended University (first in Bonn, and then in Berlin) in order to study law. Marx soon shifted his interest to philosophy, eventually earning a doctorate at Jena. Abandoning the idea of a university career, Marx became a political journalist and a member of a radical philosophical circle known as the "Young Hegelians." In 1842, he met Friedrich Engels, who would be his friend, collaborator, and benefactor throughout his life. Owing to press censorship and political repression in the Prussian dominions, Marx, now married, moved to Paris. There he met many of the most important literary and political figures of his day. His continuing political journalism led to his being charged with high treason by the Prussian government in 1844. In 1845, under pressure from Prussia, the French government banished Marx from Paris as well and he moved to Brussels, then briefly to Cologne. Marx finally settled in London in 1849.

Throughout his career Marx was strenuously engaged both in the development of a philosophical system based on the principle of negative critique of existing social conditions and as political activist, journalist, and agitator. Early in his career, Marx rejected the idea that liberal reform – that is, gradual political emancipation and the right to political participation in a democratic state – would be enough to redress the social crisis and gross inequalities of the capitalist system. For Marx, the mistake of liberal political theory was that it assumed that a particular class – the bourgeoisie – would claim political and social rights, and then extend them to the rest of society. According to Marx, this was a mistake, because it missed the real material foundation of such rights in the power that adheres to the ownership of property. Thus, bourgeois democracy depends on the possession of rights that actually reside only in wealth. In Western countries at least, the abolition of slavery meant that workers were formally free under law, but according to Marx, this was an empty reality so long as real power flowed from economic possession. While Marx advocated the extension of suffrage and other democratic rights, he never considered these the goals of political struggle, only a means by which a revolutionary transformation of society might be achieved.

Alongside Engels, Marx became involved in an organization known as the Communist League, which advocated radical socialism as an answer to the social and political crises created by the industrial revolution in Europe. In February 1848, Marx and Engels published the *Manifesto of the Communist Party*, a call to arms for a great working-class social revolution and one of the most important political and social tracts ever written. Alongside its polemics, the *Manifesto* sketched out a philosophy of world history as the struggle between contending social classes. This class struggle could only be resolved through putting an end to the alienation between people created by the institution of private property. As if on cue, revolutionary insurrections grew out of economic crisis and social unrest in France in February and in Germany in March 1848. Marx and Engels returned to Germany and took an active part in the revolution, editing a radical Cologne newspaper and involving themselves in political struggles.

Marx's move to England followed the collapse of the revolution and the triumph of reactionary forces in Germany and France. Marx began to devote his energy to the full-time study of economics, spending long hours in the public reading room of the British Museum. Marx supported himself through the contributions of wealthy friends like Engels, and through work as a journalistic contributor to many publications, including the *New York Daily Tribune*. Many of Marx's journalistic works on such subjects as the collapse of the second French republic, the consequences of British imperialism in India, and on slavery and the Civil War in the United States are recognized as masterpieces of social analysis. In 1864, Marx helped to found the first international socialist movement, the International Working Men's Association in London. In 1867, Marx published the first volume of his masterpiece, *Capital*, which he intended as a radical critique of the science of economics and of the material basis of bourgeois society. In the following years, Marx labored on a second and third volume (which remained uncompleted) and remained an active force in steering the political affairs of the international socialist movement. In 1883, Marx died and was buried in London. Engels then adopted the role as the leading intellectual in the socialist movement until his own death in 1895.

Marx's Philosophy and Social Thought

Marx's philosophical system was influenced, first and foremost, by the work of the prominent philosopher Georg Wilhelm Friedrich Hegel and his followers. However,

Marx's thought also had a more practical and empirically engaged dimension than did Hegel's. This can be seen in Marx's ongoing dialogue and critique of the early science of economics, which provided the core themes of his sociological thought. Marx objected to the overly abstract and ideal conception of the world represented by Hegel's philosophy. For Marx, Hegel's discussion of "spirit" as the force driving the history of the world was an abstract mystification of the actual force in world history: an active humanity making and unmaking the material world. Marx also rejected Hegel's claims about the role of the state. Rather than civil society growing out of the state, Marx argued that the state sprang from society. Marx's confrontation with Hegel's thought is reflected in the "Contribution to the Critique of Hegel's Philosophy of Law" (excerpted below).

Marx's material analysis has radical implications for how we understand knowledge. For Marx, humanity's objective economic activity is the base upon which the ideas and institutions were balanced. As a result, ideas cannot be understood in isolation, but rather only in direct relation to the social context within which they were born. In the *German Ideology* Marx noted, "The production of ideas, of conceptions, of consciousness, is directly interwoven with material activity and material intercourse of men and appear at this stage as the direct efflux of their material behavior." In other words, it is not ideas that determine the material world, but rather the other way around. Marx called this "turning Hegel over on his head."

Nevertheless, Marx adopted much from the method, if not the content, of Hegel's philosophy, particularly Hegel's dialectical mode of logic. Simply put, "dialectic" refers to a process of change in human society where the contradictions contained in a given idea or era produce a change that can be seen as its negation. Where Hegel focused on the dialectical relation of ideas, Marx's dialectic was based on social relations of the material world, analyzing the way that opposing forces produce contradiction and conflict. So, for example, increasing exploitation of workers by the capitalists may have the consequence of causing workers to become more militant. In the face of this militancy, the capitalists may become more exploitative and repressive in order to crush their resistance. This may inadvertently help the workers to realize that only a complete revolution against existing conditions can be their salvation. Marx argued that social analysts must be aware of the reciprocal economic relationships among social actors and the broader social structure that results from them.

Marx used social criticism as his standard form of social analysis. Marx defined criticism as the "radical negation of social reality." Instead of accepting existing social relations on face value, Marx subjected them to analysis. In rejecting Hegel's idealization of the state, for example, Marx provides a searing critique of calls for state-led development as an alternative to market forces and proclaims the proletariat the social force destined to negate the existing order and replace it with another. For Marx and his followers, the purpose of social critique was to measure society's claims about itself against the reality of its operations. This focus is apparent in Engels' early classic, *The Condition of the Working Class in England in 1844*, an attempt based on an empirical survey of existing conditions in order to critique the idealized claims of the proponents of capitalist development. Hegel had remarked, "Periods of bliss are history's blank pages." As is dazzlingly presented in Marx's celebrated essay *The Eighteenth Brumaire of Louis Bonaparte* excerpted below, in his own analysis of historical events, Marx's attention was focused on periods of conflict. Marx understood processes of social change in terms of the clash of opposing interests and the material forces that determine them.

Like Hegel, Marx saw human history as one of estrangement and conflict. And Marx broke with the economists by arguing for what we might see today as a *sociology* of economic relations. Marx tried to reveal in his posthumously published *Economic and Philosophical Manuscripts of 1844* (excerpted below) that the cause of this was not alienation from an abstract "spirit," but a deeply human process, involving social estrangement and material dispossession. Marx argued that the foundation of society was humankind's joint involvement in free, productive and creative work. However, for Marx the history of civilization revealed the progressive coercion of human labor and the dispossession of the product of labor from its producers. Driven by greed and need, creative work had become wage labor, the motives for which did not speak to the creative capacity that is essential to what it means to be human. For Marx, work had become inhuman in a literal sense – it contradicted human nature. Hence, the working classes were being both materially dispossessed and estranged from their own human nature as people. Marx suggested the image of the capitalist as a sort of vampire that literally drains away the productive life of the worker objectified in the goods that his labor has created.

Although this tendency was apparent throughout human history, it had become accelerated under industrial capitalism. Yet hope was not lost. Marx regarded capitalism as a system of *creative destruction*, as a force that provokes epochal social change. In the *Communist Manifesto* (excerpted here), Marx and Engels reveal how the forces of production unleashed by capitalism were sweeping away the old world while a new one was still in the making. Marx and Engels observed that in the modern world "Everything solid melts into air" including old ways of life, beliefs and social relations that dissolve under the pressure of material transformation. In view of the technological achievements and scientific spirit of the industrial revolution this was not altogether bad. Marx's analysis of capitalist production led him to conclude that the system was inherently unstable, destructive and exploitative. In time, it would become an obstacle to human progress. But the new industrial technology and productivity unleashed by capitalism offered a way out by freeing man from the shackles of subsistence and ignorance through universal enlightenment and prosperity. Revolution would achieve this by liberating workers and putting the ownership of the means of production in their own hands, thereby abolishing the exploiting class.

Capital was Marx's monumental effort to lay out a systematic theory of the capitalist economy, its genesis and its tendency towards terminal crisis. In the excerpts from this volume included in this section ("Commodities," "The General Formula for Capital," "Division of Labour and Manufacture," "The So-Called Primitive Accumulation," and "Classes") one can see the outline of Marx's sociology of capitalism and how his analysis led him to general propositions concerning the origins and probable fate of bourgeois society. Marx tried to show that the roots of all profit in the capitalist system could be traced to the extraction of surplus value from human labor. As capitalist competition increased, the owners of capital would be compelled by falling profit margins to attempt to increase the exploitation of workers. Capitalists would oversupply the market with commodities for which there were insufficient buyers. A cycle of boom and bust would result, and industrial depressions would become ever more frequent and destructive occurrences. At the same time, as the scale of production increased and workers were herded together into factories and industrial cities, they would begin to see themselves as members of the same social class with the same objective interests[In time, they would reject their increasing misery, band together as a political force and overturn the capitalist system.] In the place of private ownership of capital, social ownership of capital would be introduced. Gradually, the need for a coercive administration of economy and society would vanish as solidarity and cooperation replaced estrangement and competition. Marx suggested that the capitalist system of production was so riddled with contradictions and contending aims and the growing solidarity of the working classes so evidently apparent that the final crisis of capitalism and the great proletarian revolution was practically inevitable.

Marx envisioned the great social revolution as an opportunity to end humankind's self-alienation and make the Enlightenment dream of a "positive humanism" as a reality. In the new world of the future, human beings would become conscious producers and be free to engage in creative pursuits beyond the coercive dictates of the labor market. And once the estrangement of humankind from itself and from its product was eliminated, there was no longer a need for a state whose real purpose was the enforcement of this alienation. Marx's practical utopianism was thus not merely a scientific response to the irrationalities of the capitalist system, but also an ethical vision of human emancipation and self-realization.

Marx's Legacy

An advantge of Marx's thought is that it is grounded in material facts of human existence and inspired by the effort to apply scientific reason in the analysis of social life. In contrast to many social philosophies, Marx's theories yield testable propositions that allow rigorous evaluation and even falsification. Marx's influence can be clearly observed in a number of sociological traditions. Max Weber, in particular, was impressed by Marx's thought and much of his own work was inspired by it, even when he was critical of Marx's specific claims (see Part II of this volume).

Despite his contribution to empirical social science, it is only by considering the ethical appeal of Marx's thought that we can understand why it became the foundation not only of a school of sociological and historical analysis, but also of the modern socialist movement. Marx offered a way to understand society framed in a morally empowering language of critique that savaged the half-hearted and incremental reforms that were endorsed by many in Western societies and unflinchingly took the side of the oppressed.

In both its brilliance and menace Marx's thought represents a thorough indictment of capitalist modernity – the only theoretical system to offer such a complete repudiation of existing society and radical call to arms. The Critical Theory of the

Frankfurt School was directly inspired by this element of Marx's thought (see Part V). Over the century and half since Marx began his work, his radical rejection of the status quo and his indictment of exploitation have had enormous resonance, for good and for ill. Workers, women, colonized peoples and other marginalized and dispossessed groups have seen in Marx's theory a diagnosis of their oppression and a set of conceptual weapons in their struggles. However, for much of the twentieth century, Marx's thought was also used to promote dogmatism, intolerance and a dangerous strain of utopianism in which radical ends were thought to justify any ghastly means that might be used to achieve them. Marxism became a rigid and confining ideology that at worst justified the reign of tyrants and the exercise of mass murder against those deemed obstacles to the final triumph of the revolution.

In contemporary social science Marxian concepts are of continuing relevance, even if many of the specific propositions and predictions that Marx and his followers have made have been shown to be mistaken. Few today would argue that the capitalist system is so inherently flawed that it must collapse. Most would agree that profits are generated not only by extracting labor power, but also by investment in technology and human capital. In most Western nations working people are not worse off, as Marx predicted, but substantially better off than they were in the nineteenth century. Rather than the working class growing ever larger and more militant, in most developed nations the industrial "proletariat" is an ever-smaller fraction of the workforce as the service sector grows and new industries such as information technology and biological engineering expand. Moreover, as personal investment becomes common, even for people with modest incomes, the meaning of "ownership" of productive means is no longer so clear. And although Marx rejected the possibility of liberal reform, working-class movements did succeed in improving their living standards and political rights without overturning the system. At the same time, however, alienation is still felt. Even many well-paid workers would understand and agree with Marx's comment that in their work – which should be a satisfying and creative experience – they are often treated like expendable commodities. Moreover, contemporary processes such as economic globalization, commodity fetishism in a society of mass consumption, and the persistence of inequality and social conflict continue to provide fertile ground for Marxian analysis.

Select Bibliography

Aron, Raymond. 1968. *Main Currents in Sociological Thought*. Vol. 1. Garden City, NY: Anchor Books. (This volume contains a very long chapter on Marx that introduces the thinker's specifically sociological relevance.)

Avineri, Schlomo. 1968. *The Social and Political Thought of Karl Marx*. London: Cambridge University Press. (An excellent general introduction to the work of Marx.)

McClellan, David. 1973. *Karl Marx: His Life and Thought*. New York: Harper and Row, 1973. (An important intellectual biography of Marx.)

McClellan, David. 1974. *The Thought of Karl Marx: An Introduction*. New York: Harper & Row. (A basic introduction to Marx's work.)

Postone, Moishe. 1993. *Time, Labor and Social Domination*. London: Cambridge University Press. (A reevaluation of Marx's contribution to critical theory.)

Tucker, Robert C. (ed.) 1978. *The Marx–Engels Reader*. Second edition. New York: W. W. Norton & Company. (An indispensable volume that includes an excellent introduction and very good selection of key readings.)

A: ALIENATION AND HISTORICAL MATERIALSIM

1 Contribution to the Critique of Hegel's Philosophy of Law

Karl Marx

Introduction

For Germany the *criticism of religion* is in the main complete, and criticism of religion is the premise of all criticism.

The *profane* existence of error is discredited after its *heavenly oratio pro aris et focus*[a] has been disproved. Man, who looked for a superhuman being in the fantastic reality of heaven and found nothing there but the *reflection* of himself, will no longer be disposed to find but the *semblance* of himself, only an inhuman being, where he seeks and must seek his true reality.

The basis of irreligious criticism is: *Man makes religion*, religion does not make man. Religion is the self-consciousness and self-esteem of man who has either not yet found himself or has already lost himself again. But *man* is no abstract being encamped outside the world. Man is *the world of man*, the state, society. This state, this society, produce religion, an *inverted world-consciousness*, because they are an *inverted world*. Religion is the general theory of that world, its encyclopaedic compendium, its logic in a popular form, its spiritualistic *point d'honneur*, its enthusiasm, its moral sanction, its solemn complement, its universal source of consolation and justification. It is the *fantastic realisation* of the human essence because the *human essence* has no true reality. The struggle against religion is therefore indirectly a fight against *the world* of which religion is the spiritual *aroma*.

Religious distress is at the same time the *expression* of real distress and also the *protest* against real distress. Religion is the sigh of the oppressed creature, the heart of a heartless world, just as it is the spirit of spiritless conditions. It is the *opium* of the people.

To abolish religion as the *illusory* happiness of the people is to demand their *real* happiness. The demand to give up illusions about the existing state of affairs is the

Editorial footnotes in this and the following selections by Karl Marx and Friedrich Engels are reprinted as they appear in Marx and Engels, *Collected Works* (New York: International Publishers, 1975).

[a] Speech for the altars and hearths. – Ed.

demand to give up a state of affairs which needs illusions. The criticism of religion is therefore *in embryo the criticism of the vale of tears,* the *halo* of which is religion.

Criticism has torn up the imaginary flowers from the chain not so that man shall wear the unadorned, bleak chain but so that he will shake off the chain and pluck the living flower. The criticism of religion disillusions man to make him think and act and shape his reality like a man who has been disillusioned and has come to reason, so that he will revolve round himself and therefore round his true sun. Religion is only the illusory sun which revolves round man as long as he does not revolve round himself.

The *task of history,* therefore, once the *world beyond the truth* has disappeared, is to establish the *truth of this world.* The immediate *task of philosophy,* which is at the service of history, once the *holy form* of human self-estrangement has been unmasked, is to unmask self-estrangement in its *unholy forms.* Thus the criticism of heaven turns into the criticism of the earth, the *criticism of religion* into the *criticism of lay* and the *criticism of theology* into the *criticism of politics.*

The following exposition – a contribution to that task – deals immediately not with the original, but with a copy, the German *philosophy* of state and of law, for no other reason than that it deals with *Germany.*

If one wanted to proceed from the *status quo* itself in Germany, even in the only appropriate way, i.e., negatively, the result would still be an *anachronism.* Even the negation of our political present is a reality already covered with dust in the historical lumber-room of modern nations. If I negate powdered pigtails, I am still left with unpowdered pigtails. If I negate the German state of affairs in 1843, then, according to the French computation of time, I am hardly in the year 1789, and still less in the focus of the present.

Yes, German history flatters itself with a movement which no people in the firmament of history went through before it or will go through after it. For we shared the restorations of the modern nations although we had not shared their revolutions. We underwent a restoration, first because other nations dared to carry out a revolution and second because other nations suffered a counter-revolution, the first time because our rulers were afraid, and the second because our rulers were not afraid. We – and our shepherds first and foremost – never found ourselves in the company of freedom except once – on the *day of its burial.*

A school which legitimates the baseness of today by the baseness of yesterday, a school that declares rebellious every cry of the serf against the knout once that knout is a time-honoured, ancestral historical one, a school to which history only shows its *posterior* as the God of Israel did to his servant Moses[a] – the *historical school of law* – would hence have invented German history had it not been an invention of German history. For every pound of flesh cut from the heart of the people the historical school of law – Shylock, but Shylock the bondsman – swears on its bond, its historical bond, its Christian-Germanic bond.

Good-natured enthusiasts, Germanomaniacs by extraction and free-thinkers by reflection, on the contrary, seek our history of freedom beyond our history in the primeval Teutonic forests. But what difference is there between the history of our freedom and the history of the boar's freedom if it can be found only in the forests?

---

[a] The Holy Bible, Exodus 33:23 – Ed.

Besides, it is common knowledge that the forest echoes back what you shout into it. So let us leave the ancient Teutonic forests in peace!

War on the German conditions! By all means! They are *below the level of history, beneath any criticism*, but they are still an object of criticism like the criminal who is below the level of humanity but still an object for the *executioner*. In the struggle against those conditions criticism is no passion of the head, it is the head of passion. It is not a lancet, it is a weapon. Its object is its *enemy*, which it wants not to refute but to *exterminate*. For the spirit of those conditions is refuted. In themselves they are not objects *worthy of thought*, but *phenomena* which are as despicable as they are despised. Criticism does not need to make things clear to itself as regards this subject-matter, for it has already dealt with it. Criticism appears no longer as an *end in itself*, but only as a *means*. Its essential sentiment is *indignation*, its essential activity is *denunciation*.

It is a case of describing the dull reciprocal pressure of all social spheres on one another, a general inactive ill humour, a limitedness which recognises itself as much as it misjudges itself, within the frame of a government system which, living on the preservation of all wretchedness, is itself nothing but *wretchedness in office*.

What a sight! This infinitely proceeding division of society into the most manifold races opposed to one another by petty antipathies, uneasy consciences and brutal mediocrity, and which, precisely because of their reciprocal ambiguous and distrustful attitude, are all, without exception although with various formalities, treated by their *rulers as licensed existences*. And they must recognise and acknowledge as a *concession of heaven* the very fact that they are *mastered, ruled, possessed*! On the other side are the rulers themselves, whose greatness is in inverse proportion to their number!

Criticism dealing with this content is criticism in *hand-to-hand combat*, and in such a fight the point is not whether the opponent is a noble, equal, *interesting* opponent, the point is to *strike* him. The point is not to allow the Germans a minute for self-deception and resignation. The actual pressure must be made more pressing by adding to it consciousness of pressure, the shame must be made more shameful by publicising it. Every sphere of German society must be shown as the *partie honteuse*[a] of German society; these petrified relations must be forced to dance by singing their own tune to them! The people must be taught to be *terrified* at itself in order to give it *courage*. This will be fulfilling an imperative need of the German nation, and needs of the nations are in themselves the ultimate reason for their satisfaction.

This struggle against the limited content of the German *status quo* cannot be without interest even for the *modern* nations, for the German *status quo* is the *open completion of the ancien régime*, and the *ancien régime* is the *concealed deficiency of the modern state*. The struggle against the German political present is the struggle against the past of the modern nations, and they are still troubled by reminders of that past. It is instructive for them to see the *ancien régime*, which has been through its *tragedy* with them, playing its *comedy* as a German ghost. *Tragic* indeed was the history of the *ancien régime* so long as it was the pre-existing power of the world, and freedom, on the other hand, was a personal notion, i.e., as long

---

[a] Shameful part – Ed.

as this regime believed and had to believe in its own justification. As long as the *ancien régime*, as an existing world order, struggled against a world that was only coming into being, there was on its side a historical error, not a personal one. That is why its downfall was tragic.

On the other hand, the present German regime, an anachronism, a flagrant contradiction of generally recognised axioms, the nothingness of the *ancien régime* exhibited to the world, only imagines that it believes in itself and demands that the world should imagine the same thing. If it believed in its own *essence*, would it try to hide that essence under the *semblance* of an alien essence and seek refuge in hypocrisy and sophism? The modern *ancien régime* is only the *comedian* of a world order whose *true heroes* are dead. History is thorough and goes through many phases when carrying an old form to the grave. The last phase of a world-historical form is its *comedy*. The gods of Greece, already tragically wounded to death in Aeschylus' *Prometheus Bound*, had to re-die a comic death in Lucian's *Dialogues*. Why this course of history? So that humanity should part with its past *cheerfully*. This *cheerful* historical destiny is what we vindicate for the political authories of Germany.

However, once *modern* politico-social reality itself is subjected to criticism, once criticism rises to truly human problems, it finds itself outside the German *status quo* or else it would reach out for its object *below* its object. An example. The relation of industry, of the world of wealth generally, to the political world is one of the major problems of modern times. In what form is this problem beginning to engage the attention of the Germans? In the form of *protective duties*, of the *prohibitive system*, of *national economy*. Germanomania has passed out of man into matter, and thus one morning our cotton barons and iron champions saw themselves turned into patriots. People are therefore beginning in Germany to acknowledge the sovereignty of monopoly within the country by lending it *sovereignty abroad*. People are thus about to begin in Germany with what people in France and England are about to end. The old corrupt condition against which these countries are rebelling in theory and which they only bear as one bears chains is greeted in Germany as the dawn of a beautiful future which still hardly dares to pass from *cunning*[a] theory to the most ruthless practice. Whereas the problem in France and England is: *Political economy* or the *rule of society over wealth*, in Germany it is: *National economy* or the *mastery of private property over nationality*. In France and England, then, it is a case of abolishing monopoly that has proceeded to its last consequences; in Germany it is a case of proceeding to the last consequences of monopoly. There it is a case of solution, here as yet a case of collision. This is an adequate example of the *German* form of modern problems, an example of how our history, like a clumsy recruit, still has to do extra drill in matters that are old and hackneyed in history.

If therefore the *whole* German development did not exceed the German *political* development, a German could at the most participate in the problems of the present to the same extent as a *Russian* can. But, if the separate individual is not bound by the limitations of the nation, still less is the nation as a whole liberated by the

---

[a] In the German *listig*, probably an allusion to Friedrich List, who was an advocate of protectionism. – Ed.

liberation of one individual. The fact that Greece had a Scythian[a] among its philosophers did not help the Scythians to make a single step towards Greek culture.

Luckily we Germans are not Scythians.

As the ancient peoples went through their pre-history in imagination, in *mythology*, so we Germans have gone through our post-history in thought, in *philosophy*. We are *philosophical* contemporaries of the present without being its *historical* contemporaries. German philosophy is the *ideal prolongation* of German history. If therefore, instead of the *œuvres incomplètes* of our real history, we criticise the *œuvres posthumes* of our ideal history, *philosophy*, our criticism is among the questions of which the present says: *That is the question.*[b] What in advanced nations is a *practical* break with modern political conditions, is in Germany, where even those conditions do not yet exist, at first a *critical* break with the philosophical reflection of those conditions.

German philosophy of law and state is the only *German history* which is *al pari* with the *official* modern reality. The German nation must therefore take into account not only its present conditions but also its dream-history, and subject to criticism not only these existing conditions but at the same time their abstract continuation. Its future cannot be *limited* either to the immediate negation of its real conditions of state and law or to the immediate implementation of its ideal state and legal conditions, for it has the immediate negation of its real conditions in its ideal conditions, and it has almost *outlived* the immediate implementation of its ideal conditions in the contemplation of neighbouring nations. Hence it is with good reason that the *practical* political party in Germany demands the *negation of philosophy*. It is wrong, not in its demand, but in stopping at the demand, which it neither seriously implements nor can implement. It believes that it implements that negation by turning its back on philosophy and with averted face muttering a few trite and angry phrases about it. Owing to the limitation of its outlook it does not include philosophy in the circle of *German* reality or it even fancies it is *beneath* German practice and the theories that serve it. You demand that *real living germs* be made the starting point but you forget that the real living germ of the German nation has grown so far only inside its *cranium*. In a word – *you cannot supersede philosophy without making it a reality*.

The same mistake, but with the factors *reversed*, was made by the *theoretical* political party originating from philosophy.

In the present struggle it saw *only the critical struggle of philosophy against the German world*; it did not give a thought to the fact that the *hitherto prevailing philosophy* itself belongs to this world and is its *complement*, although an ideal one. Critical towards its adversary, it was uncritical towards itself when, proceeding from the *premises* of philosophy, it either stopped at the results given by philosophy or passed off demands and results from somewhere else as immediate demands and results of philosophy, although these, provided they are justified, can be obtained only by the *negation of hitherto existing philosophy*, of philosophy as such. We reserve ourselves the right to a more detailed description of this party. Its basic

---

[a] Anacharsis. – Ed.
[b] This sentence is in English in the original. – Ed.

deficiency may be reduced to the following: *It thought it could make philosophy a reality without superseding it.*

The criticism of the *German philosophy of state and law*, which attained its most consistent, richest and final formulation through *Hegel*, is both a critical analysis of the modern state and of the reality connected with it, and the resolute negation of the whole *German political and legal consciousness* as *practised* hitherto, the most distinguished, most universal expression of which, raised to the level of a *science*, is the *speculative philosophy of law* itself. If the speculative philosophy of law, that abstract extravagant *thinking* on the modern state, the reality of which remains a thing of the beyond, if only beyond the Rhine, was possible only in Germany, inversely the *German* thought-image of the modern state which disregards *real man* was possible only because and insofar as the modern state itself disregards *real man* or satisfies the *whole* of man only in imagination. In politics the Germans *thought* what other nations *did*. Germany was their *theoretical consciousness*. The abstraction and conceit of its thought always kept in step with the one-sidedness and stumpiness of its reality. If therefore the *status quo of German statehood* expresses the *perfection of the ancien régime*, the perfection of the thorn in the flesh of the modern state, the *status quo of German political theory* expresses the *imperfection of the modern state*, the defectiveness of its flesh itself.

Even as the resolute opponent of the previous form of *German* political consciousness the criticism of speculative philosophy of law turns, not towards itself, but towards *problems* which can only be solved by one means – *practice*.

It is not the *radical* revolution, not the *general human* emancipation which is a utopian dream for Germany, but rather the partial, the *merely* political revolution, the revolution which leaves the pillars of the house standing. On what is a partial, a merely political revolution based? On the fact that *part of civil society* emancipates itself and attains *general* domination; on the fact that a definite class, proceeding from its *particular situation*, undertakes the general emancipation of society. This class emancipates the whole of society but only provided the whole of society is in the same situation as this class, e.g., possesses money and education or can acquire them at will.

No class of civil society can play this role without arousing a moment of enthusiasm in itself and in the masses, a moment in which it fraternises and merges with society in general, becomes confused with it and is perceived and acknowledged as its *general representative*; a moment in which its demands and rights are truly the rights and demands of society itself; a moment in which it is truly the social head and the social heart. Only in the name of the general rights of society can a particular class lay claim to general domination. For the storming of this emancipatory position, and hence for the political exploitation of all spheres of society in the interests of its own sphere, revolutionary energy and intellectual self-confidence alone are not sufficient. For the *revolution of a nation* and the *emancipation of a particular class* of civil society to coincide, for *one* estate to be acknowledged as the estate of the whole society, all the defects of society must conversely be concentrated in another class, a particular estate must be the general stumbling-block, the incorporation of the general limitation, a particular social sphere must be looked upon as the *notorious crime* of the whole of society, so that liberation from that sphere appears as general self-liberation. For *one* estate to be *par excellence* the estate of liberation, another estate must conversely be the obvious estate of oppression. The negative general significance of the French nobility and the French clergy determined the positive general significance of the immediately adjacent and opposed class of the *bourgeoisie*.

But, no particular class in Germany has the consistency, the severity, the courage or the ruthlessness that could mark it out as the negative representative of society. No more has any estate the breadth of soul that identifies itself, even for a moment, with the soul of the nation, the genius that inspires material might be political violence, or that revolutionary audacity which flings at the adversary the defiant words: *I am nothing and I should be everything*. The main stem of German morals and honesty, of the classes as well as of individuals, is rather that *modest egoism* which asserts its limitedness and allows it to be asserted against itself. The relation of the various sections of German society is therefore not dramatic but epic. Each of them begins to be aware of itself and to settle down beside the others with all its particular claims not as soon as it is oppressed, but as soon as the circumstances of the time, without the section's own participation, create a social substratum on which it can in turn exert pressure. Even the *moral self-confidence of the German middle class* rests only on the consciousness that it is the general representative of the philistine mediocrity of all the other classes. It is therefore not only the German kings who accede to the throne *mal à propos*; every section of civil society goes through a defeat before it has celebrated victory, develops its own limitations before it has overcome the limitations facing it and asserts its narrow-hearted essence before it has been able to assert its magnanimous essence. Thus the very opportunity of a great role has on every occasion passed away before it is to hand, thus every class, once it begins the struggle against the class above it, is involved in the struggle against the class below it. Hence the princes are struggling against the monarchy, the bureaucrats against the nobility, and the bourgeois against them all, while the proletariat is already begging to struggle against the bourgeoisie. No sooner does the middle class dare to think of emancipation from its own standpoint than the development of the social conditions and the progress of political theory pronounce that standpoint antiquated or at least problematic.

In France it is enough for somebody to be something for him to want to be everything; in Germany one has to be nothing if one is not to forego everything. In France partial emancipation is the basis of universal emancipation; in Germany universal emancipation is the *conditio sine qua non* of any partial emancipation. In France it is the reality of gradual liberation, in Germany the impossibility of gradual liberation, that must give birth to complete freedom. In France every class is *politically idealistic* and becomes aware of itself at first not as a particular class but as the representative of social requirements generally. The role of *emancipator* therefore passes in dramatic motion to the various classes of the French nation one after the other until it finally comes to the class which implements social freedom no longer on the basis of certain conditions lying outside man and yet created by human society, but rather organises all conditions of human existence on the presupposition of social freedom. In Germany, on the contrary, where practical life is as spiritless as spiritual life is unpractical, no class in civil society has any need or capacity for general emancipation until it is forced by its *immediate* condition, by *material* necessity, by its *very chains*.

Where, then, is the *positive* possibility of a German emancipation?

Answer: In the formation of a class with *radical chains*, a class of civil society which is not a class of civil society, an estate which is the dissolution of all estates, a sphere which has a universal character by its universal suffering and claims no *particular right* because no *particular wrong* but *wrong generally* is perpetrated against it; which can no longer invoke a *historical* but only a *human* title; which does not stand in any one-sided antithesis to the consequences but in an all-round antithesis to the premises of the German state; a sphere, finally, which cannot emancipate itself without emancipating itself from all other spheres of society and thereby emancipating all other spheres of society, which, in a word, is the *complete loss* of man and hence can win itself only through the *complete rewinning of man*. This dissolution of society as a particular estate is the *proletariat*.

The proletariat is coming into being in Germany only as a result of the rising *industrial* development. For it is not the *naturally arising* poor but the *artificially impoverished*, not the human masses mechanically oppressed by the gravity of society but the masses resulting from the *drastic dissolution* of society, mainly of the middle estate, that form the proletariat, although it is obvious that gradually the naturally arising poor and the Christian-Germanic serfs also join its ranks.

By proclaiming the *dissolution of the hitherto existing world order* the proletariat merely states the *secret of its own existence*, for it *is in fact* the dissolution of that world order. By demanding the *negation of private property*, the proletariat merely raises to the rank of a *principle of society* what society has made the principle of the *proletariat*, what, without its own co-operation, is already incorporated in *it* as the negative result of society. In regard to the world which is coming into being the proletarian then finds himself possessing the same right as the *German king* in regard to the world which has come into being when he calls the people *his* people as he calls the horse *his* horse. By declaring the people his private property the king simply states that the property owner is king.

As philosophy finds its *material* weapons in the proletariat, so the proletariat finds its *spiritual* weapons in philosophy. And once the lightning of thought has squarely struck this ingenuous soil of the people the emancipation of the *Germans* into *human beings* will take place.

Let us sum up the result:

The only *practically* possible liberation of Germany is liberation that proceeds from the standpoint of *the* theory which proclaims man to be the highest being for man. In Germany emancipation from the *Middle Ages* is possible only as emancipation from the *partial* victories over the Middle Ages as well. In Germany *no* kind of bondage can be broken without breaking *every* kind of bondage. The *thorough* Germany cannot make a revolution without making a *thoroughgoing* revolution. The *emancipation of the German* is the *emancipation of the human being*. The *head* of this emancipation is *philosophy*, its *heart* is the *proletariat*. Philosophy cannot be made a reality without the abolition of the proletariat, the proletariat cannot be abolished without philosophy being made a reality.

When all inner requisites are fulfilled the *day of German resurrection* will be proclaimed by the *ringing call of the Gallic cock*.

2 Economic and Philosophic Manuscripts of 1844

Karl Marx

We have proceeded from the premises of political economy. We have accepted its language and its laws. We presupposed private property, the separation of labour, capital and land, and of wages, profit of capital and rent of land – likewise division of labour, competition, the concept of exchange-value, etc. On the basis of political economy itself, in its own words, we have shown that the worker sinks to the level of a commodity and becomes indeed the most wretched of commodities; that the wretchedness of the worker is in inverse proportion to the power and magnitude of his production; that the necessary result of competition is the accumulation of capital in a few hands, and thus the restoration of monopoly in a more terrible form; and that finally the distinction between capitalist and land rentier, like that between the tiller of the soil and the factory worker, disappears and that the whole of society must fall apart into the two classes – the *property owners* and the propertyless *workers*.

Political economy starts with the fact of private property; it does not explain it to us. It expresses in general, abstract formulas the *material* process through which private property actually passes, and these formulas it then takes for *laws*. It does not *comprehend* these laws, i.e., it does not demonstrate how they arise from the very nature of private property. Political economy throws no light on the cause of the division between labour and capital, and between capital and land. When, for example, it defines the relationship of wages to profit, it takes the interest of the capitalists to be the ultimate cause, i.e., it takes for granted what it is supposed to explain. Similarly, competition comes in everywhere. It is explained from external circumstances. As to how far these external and apparently accidental circumstances are but the expression of a necessary course of development, political economy teaches us nothing. We have seen how exchange itself appears to it as an accidental fact. The only wheels which political economy sets in motion are *greed* and the *war amongst the greedy – competition*.

Precisely because political economy does not grasp the way the movement is connected, it was possible to oppose, for instance, the doctrine of competition to the doctrine of monopoly, the doctrine of the freedom of the crafts to the doctrine of the guild, the doctrine of the division of landed property to the doctrine of the big estate – for competition, freedom of the crafts and the division of landed property were explained and comprehended only as accidental, premeditated and violent consequences of monopoly, of the guild system, and of feudal property, not as their necessary, inevitable and natural consequences.

Now, therefore, we have to grasp the intrinsic connection between private property, avarice, the separation of labour, capital and landed property; the connection of exchange and competition, of value and the devaluation of men, of monopoly and competition, etc. – we have to grasp this whole estrangement connected with the *money* system.

Do not let us go back to a fictitious primordial condition as the political economist does, when he tries to explain. Such a primordial condition explains nothing; it merely pushes the question away into a grey nebulous distance. The economist assumes in the form of a fact, of an event, what he is supposed to deduce – namely, the necessary relationship between two things – between, for example, division of labour and exchange. Thus the theologian explains the origin of evil by the fall of man; that is, he assumes as a fact, in historical form, what has to be explained.

We proceed from an *actual* economic fact.

The worker becomes all the poorer the more wealth he produces, the more his production increases in power and size. The worker becomes an ever cheaper commodity the more commodities he creates. The *devaluation* of the world of men is in direct proportion to the *increasing value* of the world of things. Labour produces not only commodities: it produces itself and the worker as a *commodity* – and this at the same rate at which it produces commodities in general.

This fact expresses merely that the object which labour produces – labour's product – confronts it as *something alien*, as a *power independent* of the producer. The product of labour is labour which has been embodied in an object, which has become material: it is the *objectification* of labour. Labour's realisation is its objectification. Under these economic conditions this realisation of labour appears as *loss of realisation* for the workers; objectification as *loss of the object and bondage to it*; appropriation as *estrangement, as alienation*.

So much does labour's realisation appear as loss of realisation that the worker loses realisation to the point of starving to death. So much does objectification appear as loss of the object that the worker is robbed of the objects most necessary not only for his life but for his work. Indeed, labour itself becomes an object which he can obtain only with the greatest effort and with the most irregular interruptions. So much does the appropriation of the object appear as estrangement that the more objects the worker produces the less he can possess and the more he falls under the sway of his product, capital.

All these consequences are implied in the statement that the worker is related to the *product of his labour* as to an *alien object*. For on this premise it is clear that the more the worker spends himself, the more powerful becomes the alien world of objects which he creates over and against himself, the poorer he himself – his inner world – becomes, the less belongs to him as his own. It is the same in religion. The more man puts into God, the less he retains in himself. The worker puts his life into the object; but now his life no longer belongs to him but to the object. Hence, the greater this activity, the more the worker lacks objects. Whatever the product of his labour is, he is not. Therefore the greater this product, the less is he himself. The *alienation* of the worker in his product means not only that his labour becomes an object, an *external* existence, but that it exists *outside him*, independently, as something alien to him, and that it becomes a power on its own confronting him. It means that the life which he has conferred on the object confronts him as something hostile and alien.

Let us now look more closely at the *objectification*, at the production of the worker; and in it at the *estrangement*, the *loss* of the object, of his product.

The worker can create nothing without *nature*, without the *sensuous external world*. It is the material on which his labour is realised, in which it is active, from which and by means of which it produces.

But just as nature provides labour with [the] *means of life* in the sense that labour cannot *live* without objects on which to operate, on the other hand, it also provides the *means of life* in the more restricted sense, i.e., the means for the physical subsistence of the *worker* himself.

Thus the more the worker by his labour *appropriates* the external world, sensuous nature, the more he deprives himself of *means of life* in two respects: first, in that the sensuous external world more and more ceases to be an object belonging to his labour – to be his labour's *means of life*; and secondly, in that it more and more ceases to be *means of life* in the immediate sense, means for the physical subsistence of the worker.

In both respects, therefore, the worker becomes a servant of his object, first, in that he receives an *object of labour*, i.e., in that he receives *work*; and secondly, in that he receives *means of subsistence*. This enables him to exist, first, as a *worker*, and, second, as a *physical subject*. The height of this servitude is that it is only as a *worker* that he can maintain himself as a *physical subject*, and that it is only as a *physical subject* that he is a worker.

(According to the economic laws the estrangement of the worker in his object is expressed thus: the more the worker produces, the less he has to consume; the more values he creates, the more valueless, the more unworthy he becomes; the better formed his product, the more deformed becomes the worker; the more civilised his object, the more barbarous becomes the worker; the more powerful labour becomes, the more powerless becomes the worker; the more ingenious labour becomes, the less ingenious becomes the worker and the more he becomes nature's servant.)

Political economy conceals the estrangement inherent in the nature of labour by not considering the **direct** *relationship between the* **worker** (labour) *and production.* It is true that labour produces wonderful things for the rich – but for the worker it produces privation. It produces palaces – but for the worker, hovels. It produces beauty – but for the worker, deformity. It replaces labour by machines, but it throws one section of the workers back to a barbarous type of labour, and it turns the other section into a machine. It produces intelligence – but for the worker, stupidity, cretinism.

The direct relationship of labour to its products is the relationship of the worker to the objects of his production. The relationship of the man of means to the objects of production and to production itself is only a *consequence* of this first relationship – and confirms it. We shall consider this other aspect later. When we ask, then, what is the essential relationship of labour we are asking about the relationship of the *worker* to production.

Till now we have been considering the estrangement; the alienation of the worker only in one of its aspects, i.e., the worker's *relationship to the products of his labour*. But the estrangement is manifested not only in the result but in the *act of production*, within the *producing activity* itself. How could the worker come to face the product of his activity as a stranger, were it not that in the very act of production he was estranging himself from himself? The product is after all but the summary of the activity, of production. If then the product of labour is alienation, production itself must be active alienation, the alienation of activity, the activity of alienation. In the estrangement of the object of labour is merely summarised the estrangement, the alienation, in the activity of labour itself.

What, then, constitutes the alienation of labour?

First, the fact that labour is *external* to the worker, i.e., it does not belong to his intrinsic nature; that in his work, therefore, he does not affirm himself but denies himself, does not feel content but unhappy, does not develop freely his physical and mental energy but mortifies his body and ruins his mind. The worker therefore only feels himself outside his work, and in his work feels outside himself. He feels at home when he is not working, and when he is working he does not feel at home. His labour is therefore not voluntary, but coerced; it is *forced labour*. It is therefore not the satisfaction of a need; it is merely a *means* to satisfy needs external to it. Its alien character emerges clearly in the fact that as soon as no physical or other compulsion exists, labour is shunned like the plague. External labour, labour in which man alienates himself, is a labour of self-sacrifice, of mortification. Lastly, the external character of labour for the worker appears in the fact that it is not his own, but someone else's, that it does not belong to him, that in it he belongs, not to himself, but to another. Just as in religion the spontaneous activity of the human imagination, of the human brain and the human heart, operates on the individual independently of him – that is, operates as an alien, divine or diabolical activity – so is the worker's activity not his spontaneous activity. It belongs to another; it is the loss of his self.

As a result, therefore, man (the worker) only feels himself freely active in his animal functions – eating, drinking, procreating, or at most in his dwelling and in dressing-up, etc.; and in his human functions he no longer feels himself to be anything but an animal. What is animal becomes human and what is human becomes animal.

Certainly eating, drinking, procreating, etc., are also genuinely human functions. But taken abstractly, separated from the sphere of all other human activity and turned into sole and ultimate ends, they are animal functions.

We have considered the act of estranging practical human activity, labour, in two of its aspects. (1) The relation of the worker to the *product of labour* as an alien object exercising power over him. This relation is at the same time the relation to the sensuous external world, to the objects of nature, as an alien world inimically opposed to him. (2) The relation of labour to the *act of production* within the *labour* process. This relation is the relation of the worker to his own activity as an alien activity not belonging to him; it is activity as suffering, strength as weakness, begetting as emasculating, the worker's *own* physical and mental energy, his personal life – for what is life but activity? – as an activity which is turned against him, independent of him and not belonging to him. Here we have *self-estrangement* as previously we had the estrangement of the *thing*.

We have still a third aspect of *estranged labour* to deduce from the two already considered.

Man is a species-being, not only because in practice and in theory he adopts the species (his own as well as those of other things) as his object, but – and this is only another way of expressing it – also because he treats himself as the actual, living species; because he treats himself as a *universal* and therefore a free being.

The life of the species, both in man and in animals, consists physically in the fact that man (like the animal) lives on inorganic nature; and the more universal man (or the animal) is, the more universal is the sphere of inorganic nature on which he lives. Just as plants, animals, stones, air, light, etc., constitute theoretically a part of human consciousness, partly as objects of natural science, partly as objects of art – his spiritual inorganic nature, spiritual nourishment which he must first prepare to make palatable and digestible – so also in the realm of practice they constitute a part of human life and human activity. Physically man lives only on these products of nature, whether they appear in the form of food, heating, clothes, a dwelling, etc. The universality of man appears in practice precisely in the universality which makes all nature his *inorganic* body – both inasmuch as nature is (1) his direct means of life, and (2) the material, the object, and the instrument of his life activity. Nature is man's *inorganic body* – nature, that is, insofar as it is not itself human body. Man *lives* on nature – means that nature is his *body*, with which he must remain in continuous interchange if he is not to die. That man's physical and spiritual life is linked to nature means simply that nature is linked to itself, for man is a part of nature.

In estranging from man (1) nature, and (2) himself, his own active functions, his life activity, estranged labour estranges the *species* from man. It changes for him the *life of the species* into a means of individual life. First it estranges the life of the species and individual life, and secondly it makes individual life in its abstract form the purpose of the life of the species, likewise in its abstract and estranged form.

For labour, *life activity, productive life* itself, appears to man in the first place merely as a *means* of satisfying a need – the need to maintain physical existence. Yet the productive life is the life of the species. It is life-engendering life. The whole character of a species – its species-character – is contained in the character of its life activity; and free, conscious activity is man's species-character. Life itself appears only as a *means to life*.

The animal is immediately one with its life activity. It does not distinguish itself from it. It is *its life activity*. Man makes his life activity itself the object of his will and of his consciousness. He has conscious life activity. It is not a determination with which he directly merges. Conscious life activity distinguishes man immediately from animal life activity. It is just because of this that he is a species-being. Or it is only because he is a species-being that he is a conscious being, i.e., that his own life is an object for him. Only because of that is his activity free activity. Estranged labour reverses this relationship, so that it is just because man is a conscious being that he makes his life activity, his *essential being*, a mere means to his *existence*.

In creating a *world of objects* by his practical activity, in his *work upon* inorganic nature, man proves himself a conscious species-being, i.e., as a being that treats the species as its own essential being, or that treats itself as a species-being. Admittedly animals also produce. They build themselves nests, dwellings, like the bees, beavers, ants, etc. But an animal only produces what it immediately needs for itself or its young. It produces one-sidedly, whilst man produces universally. It produces only under the dominion of immediate physical need, whilst man produces even when he is free from physical need and only truly produces in freedom therefrom. An animal produces only itself, whilst man reproduces the whole of nature. An animal's product belongs immediately to its physical body, whilst man freely confronts his product. An animal forms objects only in accordance with the standard and the need of the species to which it belongs, whilst man knows how to produce in accordance with the standard of every species, and knows how to apply everywhere the inherent standard to the object. Man therefore also forms objects in accordance with the laws of beauty.

It is just in his work upon the objective world, therefore, that man really proves himself to be a *species-being*. This production is his active species-life. Through this production, nature appears as *his* work and his reality. The object of labour is, therefore, the *objectification of man's species-life*; for he duplicates himself not only, as in consciousness, intellectually, but also actively, in reality, and therefore he sees himself in a world that he has created. In tearing away from man the object of his production, therefore, estranged labour tears from him his *species-life*, his real objectivity as a member of the species, and transforms his advantage over animals into the disadvantage that his inorganic body, nature, is taken away from him.

Similarly, in degrading spontaneous, free activity to a means, estranged labour makes man's species-life a means to his physical existence.

The consciousness which man has of his species is thus transformed by estrangement in such a way that species[-life] becomes for him a means.

Estranged labour turns thus:

(3) *Man's species-being*, both nature and his spiritual species-property, into a being *alien* to him, into a *means* for his *individual existence*. It estranges from man his own body, as well as external nature and his spiritual aspect, his *human* aspect.

(4) An immediate consequence of the fact that man is estranged from the product of his labour, from his life activity, from his species-being is the *estrangement of man* from *man*. When man confronts himself, he confronts the *other* man. What applies to a man's relation to his work, to the product of his labour and to himself, also holds of a man's relation to the other man, and to the other man's labour and object of labour.

In fact, the proposition that man's species-nature is estranged from him means that one man is estranged from the other, as each of them is from man's essential nature.

The estrangement of man, and in fact every relationship in which man [stands] to himself, is realised and expressed only in the relationship in which a man stands to other men.

Hence within the relationship of estranged labour each man views the other in accordance with the standard and the relationship in which he finds himself as a worker.

We took our departure from a fact of political economy – the estrangement of the worker and his product. We have formulated this fact in conceptual terms as *estranged, alienated* labour. We have analysed this concept – hence analysing merely a fact of political economy.

Let us now see, further, how the concept of estranged, alienated labour must express and present itself in real life.

If the product of labour is alien to me, if it confronts me as an alien power, to whom, then, does it belong?

If my own activity does not belong to me, if it is an alien, a coerced activity, to whom, then, does it belong?

To a being *other* than myself.

Who is this being?

The *gods*? To be sure, in the earliest times the principal production (for example, the building of temples, etc., in Egypt, India and Mexico) appears to be in the service of the gods, and the product belongs to the gods. However, the gods on their own were never the lords of labour. No more was *nature*. And what a contradiction it would be if, the more man subjugated nature by his labour and the more miracles of the gods were rendered superfluous by the miracles of industry, the more man were to renounce the joy of production and the enjoyment of the product to please these powers.

The *alien* being, to whom labour and the product of labour belongs, in whose service labour is done and for whose benefit the product of labour is provided, can only be *man* himself.

If the product of labour does not belong to the worker, if it confronts him as an alien power, then this can only be because it belongs to some *other man than the worker*. If the worker's activity is a torment to him, to another it must give *satisfaction* and pleasure. Not the gods, not nature, but only man himself can be this alien power over man.

We must bear in mind the previous proposition that man's relation to himself only becomes for him *objective* and *actual* through his relation to the other man. Thus, if the product of his labour, his labour objectified, is for him an *alien, hostile* powerful object independent of him, then his position towards it is such that someone else is master of this object, someone who is alien, hostile, powerful and independent of him. If he treats his own activity as an unfree activity, then he treats it as an activity performed in the service, under the dominion, the coercion, and the yoke of another man.

Every self-estrangement of man, from himself and from nature, appears in the relation in which he places himself and nature to men other than and differentiated from himself. For this reason religious self-estrangement necessarily appears in the relationship of the layman to the priest, or again to a mediator, etc., since we are here dealing with the intellectual world. In the real practical world self-estrangement can only become manifest through the real practical relationship to other men. The medium through which estrangement takes place is itself *practical*. Thus through estranged labour man not only creates his relationship to the object and to the act of production as to powers that are alien and hostile to him; he also creates the relationship in which other men stand to his production and to his product, and the relationship in which he stands to these other men. Just as he creates his own production as the loss of his reality, as his punishment; his own product as a loss, as a product not belonging to him; so he creates the domination of the person who does not produce over production and over the product. Just as he estranges his own activity from himself, so he confers upon the stranger an activity which is not his own.

We have until now considered this relationship only from the standpoint of the worker and later we shall be considering it also from the standpoint of the non-worker.

Through *estranged, alienated labour*, then, the worker produces the relationship to this labour of a man alien to labour and standing outside it. The relationship of the worker to labour creates the relation to it of the capitalist (or whatever one chooses to call the master of labour). *Private property* is thus the product, the result, the necessary consequence, of *alienated labour*, of the external relation of the worker to nature and to himself.

Private property thus results by analysis from the concept of *alienated labour*, i.e., of *alienated man*, of estranged labour, of estranged life, of *estranged* man.

True, it is as a result of the *movement of private property* that we have obtained the concept of *alienated labour* (*of alienated life*) in political economy. But analysis of this concept shows that though private property appears to be the reason, the cause of alienated labour, it is rather its consequence, just as the gods are *originally* not the cause but the effect of man's intellectual confusion. Later this relationship becomes reciprocal.

Only at the culmination of the development of private property does this, its secret, appear again, namely, that on the one hand it is the *product* of alienated labour, and that on the other it is the *means* by which labour alienates itself, the *realisation of this alienation*.

This exposition immediately sheds light on various hitherto unsolved conflicts.

(1) Political economy starts from labour as the real soul of production; yet to labour it gives nothing, and to private property everything. Confronting this contradiction, Proudhon has decided in favour of labour against private property. We understand, however, that this apparent contradiction is the contradiction of *estranged labour* with itself, and that political economy has merely formulated the laws of estranged labour.

We also understand, therefore, that *wages* and *private property* are identical. Indeed, where the product, as the object of labour, pays for labour itself, there the wage is but a necessary consequence of labour's estrangement. Likewise, in the wage of labour, labour does not appear as an end in itself but as the servant of the wage. We shall develop this point later, and meanwhile will only draw some conclusions.

An enforced *increase of wages* (disregarding all other difficulties, including the fact that it would only be by force, too, that such an increase, being an anomaly, could be maintained) would therefore be nothing but better *payment for the slave*, and would not win either for the worker or for labour their human status and dignity.

Indeed, even the *equality of wages*, as demanded by Proudhon, only transforms the relationship of the present-day worker to his labour into the relationship of all men to labour. Society is then conceived as an abstract capitalist.

Wages are a direct consequence of estranged labour, and estranged labour is the direct cause of private property. The downfall of the one must therefore involve the downfall of the other.

(2) From the relationship of estranged labour to private property it follows further that the emancipation of society from private property, etc., from servitude, is expressed in the *political* form of the *emancipation of the workers*; not that *their*

emancipation alone is at stake, but because the emancipation of the workers contains universal human emancipation – and it contains this, because the whole of human servitude is involved in the relation of the worker to production, and all relations of servitude are but modifications and consequences of this relation.

Just as we have derived the concept of *private property* from the concept of *estranged, alienated labour* by *analysis*, so we can develop every *category* of political economy with the help of these two factors; and we shall find again in each category, e.g., trade, competition, capital, money, only a *particular* and *developed expression* of these first elements.

Before considering this phenomenon, however, let us try to solve two other problems.

(1) To define the general *nature of private property*, as it has arisen as a result of estranged labour, in its relation to *truly human* and *social property*.

(2) We have accepted the *estrangement of labour*, its *alienation*, as a fact, and we have analysed this fact. How, we now ask, does *man* come to *alienate*, to estrange, his *labour*? How is this estrangement rooted in the nature of human development? We have already gone a long way to the solution of this problem by *transforming* the question of the *origin of private property* into the question of the relation of *alienated labour* to the course of humanity's development. For when one speaks of *private property*, one thinks of dealing with something external to man. When one speaks of labour, one is directly dealing with man himself. This new formulation of the question already contains its solution.

As to (1): The general nature of private property and its relation to truly human property.

Alienated labour has resolved itself for us into two components which depend on one another, or which are but different expressions of one and the same relationship. *Appropriation* appears as *estrangement*, as *alienation*; and *alienation* appears as *appropriation, estrangement* as truly *becoming a citizen*.

We have considered the one side – *alienated* labour in relation to the worker himself, i.e., the *relation of alienated labour to itself*. The product, the necessary outcome of this relationship, as we have seen, is the *property relation of the non-worker to the worker and to labour*. *Private property*, as the material, summary expression of alienated labour, embraces both relations – the *relation of the worker to labour and to the product of his labour and to the non-worker*, and the relation of the *non-worker to the worker and to the product of his labour*.

Having seen that in relation to the worker who *appropriates* nature by means of his labour, this appropriation appears as estrangement, his own spontaneous activity as activity for another and as activity of another, vitality as a sacrifice of life, production of the object as loss of the object to an alien power, to an *alien* person – we shall now consider the relation to the worker, to labour and its object of this person who is *alien* to labour and the worker.

First it has to be noted that everything which appears in the worker as an *activity of alienation, of estrangement*, appears in the non-worker as a *state of alienation, of estrangement*.

Secondly, that the worker's *real, practical attitude* in production and to the product (as a state of mind) appears in the non-worker confronting him as a *theoretical* attitude.

Thirdly, the non-worker does everything against the worker which the worker does against himself; but he does not do against himself what he does against the worker.

Let us look more closely at these three relations.[a]

---

[a] At this point the first manuscript breaks off unfinished. – Ed.

B: CAPITALISM AND COMMODITIES

3 Commodities

Karl Marx

The Two Factors of a Commodity: Use Value and Value (The substance of value and the magnitude of value)

The wealth of those societies in which the capitalist mode of production prevails, presents itself as "an immense accumulation of commodities", its unit being a single commodity. Our investigation must therefore begin with the analysis of a commodity.

A commodity is, in the first place, an object outside us, a thing that by its properties satisfies human wants of some sort or another. The nature of such wants, whether, for instance, they spring from the stomach or from fancy, makes no difference. Neither are we here concerned to know how the object satisfies these wants, whether directly as means of subsistence, or indirectly as means of production.

Every useful thing, as iron, paper, &c., may be looked at from the two points of view of quality and quantity. It is an assemblage of many properties, and may therefore be of use in various ways. To discover the various uses of things is the work of history. So also is the establishment of socially-recognised standards of measure for the quantities of these useful objects. The diversity of these measures has its origin partly in the diverse nature of the objects to be measured, partly in convention.

The utility of a thing makes it a use value. But this utility is not a thing of air. Being limited by the physical properties of the commodity, it has no existence apart from that commodity. A commodity, such as iron, corn, or a diamond, is therefore, so far as it is a material thing, a use value, something useful. This property of a commodity is independent of the amount of labour required to appropriate its useful qualities. When treating of use value, we always assume to be dealing with definite quantities, such as dozens of watches, yards of linen, or tons of iron. The use values of commodities furnish the material for a special study, that of the commercial knowledge of commodities.[1] Use values become a reality only by use or consumption: they also constitute the substance of all wealth, whatever may be the social form of that wealth. In the form of society we are about to consider, they are, in addition, the material depositories of exchange value.

Exchange value, at first sight, presents itself as a quantitative relation, as the proportion in which values in use of one sort are exchanged for those of another sort, a relation constantly changing with time and place. Hence exchange value appears to be something accidental and purely relative, and consequently an intrinsic value, i.e., an exchange value that is inseparably connected with, inherent in commodities, seems a contradiction in terms. Let us consider the matter a little more closely.

A given commodity, e.g., a quarter of wheat is exchanged for x blacking, y silk, or z gold, &c. – in short, for other commodities in the most different proportions. Instead of one exchange value, the wheat has, therefore, a great many. But since x blacking, y silk, or z gold, &c., each represents the exchange value of one quarter of wheat, x blacking, y silk, z gold, &c., must, as exchange values, be replaceable by each other, or equal to each other. Therefore, first: the valid exchange values of a given commodity express something equal; secondly, exchange value, generally, is only the mode of expression, the phenomenal form, of something contained in it, yet distinguishable from it.

Let us take two commodities, e.g., corn and iron. The proportions in which they are exchangeable, whatever those proportions may be, can always be represented by an equation in which a given quantity of corn is equated to some quantity of iron: e.g., 1 quarter corn = x cwt. iron. What does this equation tell us? It tells us that in two different things – in 1 quarter of corn and x cwt. of iron, there exists in equal quantities something common to both. The two things must therefore be equal to a third, which in itself is neither the one nor the other. Each of them, so far as it is exchange value, must therefore be reducible to this third.

A simple geometrical illustration will make this clear. In order to calculate and compare the areas of rectilinear figures, we decompose them into triangles. But the area of the triangle itself is expressed by something totally different from its visible figure, namely, by half the product of the base multiplied by the altitude. In the same way the exchange values of commodities must be capable of being expressed in terms of something common to them all, of which thing they represent a greater or less quantity.

This common "something" cannot be either a geometrical, a chemical, or any other natural property of commodities. Such properties claim our attention only in so far as they affect the utility of those commodities, make them use values. But the exchange of commodities is evidently an act characterised by a total abstraction from use value. Then one use value is just as good as another, provided only it be present in sufficient quantity. Or, as old Barbon says,

> "One sort of wares are as good as another, if the values be equal. There is no difference or distinction in things of equal value ... An hundred pounds' worth of lead or iron, is of as great a value as one hundred pounds' worth of silver or gold."

As use values, commodities are, above all, of different qualities, but as exchange values they are merely different quantities, and consequently do not contain an atom of use value.

If then we leave out of consideration the use value of commodities, they have only one common property left, that of being products of labour. But even the product of labour itself has undergone a change in our hands. If we make abstraction from its use value, we make abstraction at the same time from the material elements and shapes that make the product a use value; we see in it no longer a table, a house, yarn, or any other useful thing. Its existence as a material thing is put out of sight. Neither can it any longer be regarded as the product of the labour of the joiner, the mason, the spinner, or of any other definite kind of productive labour. Along with the useful qualities of the products themselves, we put out of sight both the useful character of the various kinds of labour embodied in them, and the concrete forms of that labour; there is nothing left but what is common to them all; all are reduced to one and the same sort of labour, human labour in the abstract.

Let us now consider the residue of each of these products; it consists of the same unsubstantial reality in each, a mere congelation of homogeneous human labour, of labour power expended without regard to the mode of its expenditure. All that these things now tell us is, that human labour power has been expended in their production, that human labour is embodied in them. When looked at as crystals of this social substance, common to them all, they are – Values.

We have seen that when commodities are exchanged, their exchange value manifests itself as something totally independent of their use value. But if we abstract from their use value, there remains their Value as defined above. Therefore, the common substance that manifests itself in the exchange value of commodities, whenever they are exchanged, is their value. The progress of our investigation will show that exchange value is the only form in which the value of commodities can manifest itself or be expressed. For the present, however, we have to consider the nature of value independently of this, its form.

A use value, or useful article, therefore, has value only because human labour in the abstract has been embodied or materialised in it. How, then, is the magnitude of this value to be measured? Plainly, by the quantity of the value-creating substance, the labour, contained in the article. The quantity of labour, however, is measured by its duration, and labour time in its turn finds its standard in weeks, days, and hours.

Some people might think that if the value of a commodity is determined by the quantity of labour spent on it, the more idle and unskilful the labourer, the more valuable would his commodity be, because more time would be required in its production. The labour, however, that forms the substance of value, is homogeneous human labour, expenditure of one uniform labour power. The total labour power of society, which is embodied in the sum total of the values of all commodities produced by that society, counts here as one homogeneous mass of human labour power, composed though it be of innumerable individual units. Each of these units is the same as any other, so far as it has the character of the average labour power of society, and takes effect as such; that is, so far as it requires for producing a commodity, no more time than is needed on an average, no more than is socially necessary. The labour time socially necessary is that required to produce an article under the normal conditions of production, and with the average degree of skill and intensity prevalent at the time. The introduction of power-looms into England probably reduced by one-half the labour required to weave a given quantity of yarn into cloth. The hand-loom weavers, as a matter of fact, continued to require the same time as before, but for all that, the product of one hour of their labour represented after the change only half an hour's social labour, and consequently fell to one-half its former value.

We see then that that which determines the magnitude of the value of any article is the amount of labour socially necessary, or the labour time socially necessary for its production.[2] Each individual commodity, in this connection, is to be considered as an average sample of its class.[3] Commodities, therefore, in which equal quantities of labour are embodied, or which can be produced in the same time, have the same value. The value of one commodity is to the value of any other, as the labour time necessary for the production of the one is to that necessary for the production of the other. "As values, all commodities are only definite masses of congealed labour time."

The value of a commodity would therefore remain constant, if the labour time required for its production also remained constant. But the latter changes with every variation in the productiveness of labour. This productiveness is determined by various circumstances, amongst others, by the average amount of skill of the workmen, the state of science, and the degree of its practical application, the social organisation of production, the extent and capabilities of the means of production, and by physical conditions. For example, the same amount of labour in favourable seasons is embodied in 8 bushels of corn, and in unfavourable, only in four. The same labour extracts from rich mines more metal than from poor mines. Diamonds are of very rare occurrence on the earth's surface, and hence their discovery costs, on an average, a great deal of labour time. Consequently much labour is represented in a small compass. Jacob doubts whether gold has ever been paid for at its full value. This applies still more to diamonds. According to Eschwege, the total produce of the Brazilian diamond mines for the eighty years, ending in 1823, had not realised the price of one-and-a-half years' average produce of the sugar and coffee plantations of the same country, although the diamonds cost much more labour, and therefore represented more value. With richer mines, the same quantity of labour would embody itself in more diamonds, and their value would fall. If we could succeed at a small expenditure of labour, in converting carbon into diamonds, their value might fall below that of bricks. In general, the greater the productiveness of labour, the less is the labour time required for the production of an article, the less is the amount of labour crystallised in that article, and the less is its value; and *vice versa*, the less the productiveness of labour, the greater is the labour time required for the production of an article, and the greater is its value. The value of a commodity, therefore, varies directly as the quantity, and inversely as the productiveness, of the labour incorporated in it.

A thing can be a use value, without having value. This is the case whenever its utility to man is not due to labour. Such are air, virgin soil, natural meadows, &c. A thing can be useful, and the product of human labour, without being a commodity. Whoever directly satisfies his wants with the produce of his own labour, creates, indeed, use values, but not commodities. In order to produce the latter, he must not only produce use values, but use values for others, social use values. //And not only for others, without more. The mediaeval peasant produced quit-rent-corn for his feudal lord and tithe-corn for his parson. But neither the quit-rent-corn nor the tithe-corn became commodities by reason of the fact that they had been produced for others. To become a commodity a product must be transferred to another, whom it will serve as a use value, by means of an exchange.//[a] Lastly nothing can have value, without being an object of utility. If the thing is useless, so is the labour contained in it; the labour does not count as labour, and therefore creates no value.

The Twofold Character of the Labour Embodied in Commodities

At first sight a commodity presented itself to us as a complex of two things – use value and exchange value. Later on, we saw also that labour, too, possesses the same twofold nature; for, so far as it finds expression in value, it does not possess the same characteristics that belong to it as a creator of use values. I was the first to point out and to examine critically this twofold nature of the labour contained in commodities. As this point is the pivot on which a clear comprehension of political economy turns, we must go more into detail.

Let us take two commodities such as a coat and 10 yards of linen, and let the former be double the value of the latter, so that, if 10 yards of linen = W, the coat = 2W

The coat is a use value that satisfies a particular want. Its existence is the result of a special sort of productive activity, the nature of which is determined by its aim, mode of operation, subject, means, and result. The labour, whose utility is thus represented by the value in use of its product, or which manifests itself by making its product a use value, we call useful labour. In this connection we consider only its useful effect.

As the coat and the linen are two qualitatively different use values, so also are the two forms of labour that produce them, tailoring and weaving. Were these two objects not qualitatively different, not produced respectively by labour of different quality, they could not stand to each other in the relation of commodities. Coats are not exchanged for coats, one use value is not exchanged for another of the same kind.

To all the different varieties of values in use there correspond as many different kinds of useful labour, classified according to the order, genus, species, and variety to which they belong in the social division of labour. This division of labour is a necessary condition for the production of commodities, but it does not follow, conversely, that the production of commodities is a necessary condition for the division of labour. In the primitive Indian community there is social division of labour, without production of commodities. Or, to take an example nearer home, in every factory the labour is divided according to a system, but this division is not brought about by the operatives mutually exchanging their individual products. Only such products can become commodities with regard to each other, as result from different kinds of labour, each kind being carried on independently and for the account of private individuals.

To resume, then: In the use value of each commodity there is contained useful

---

[a] //Note on the 4th German edition: I am inserting the parenthesis because its omission has often given rise to the misunderstanding that every product that is consumed by some one other than its producer is considered in Marx a commodity. – F. E.//

labour, i.e., productive activity of a definite kind and exercised with a definite aim. Use values cannot confront each other as commodities, unless the useful labour embodied in them is qualitatively different in each of them. In a community, the produce of which in general takes the form of commodities, i.e., in a community of commodity producers, this qualitative difference between the useful forms of labour that are carried on independently by individual producers, each on their own account, develops into a complex system, a social division of labour.

Anyhow, whether the coat be worn by the tailor or by his customer, in either case it operates as a use value. Nor is the relation between the coat and the labour that produced it altered by the circumstance that tailoring may have become a special trade, an independent branch of the social division of labour. Wherever the want of clothing forced them to it, the human race made clothes for thousands of years, without a single man becoming a tailor. But coats and linen, like every other element of material wealth that is not the spontaneous produce of Nature, must invariably owe their existence to a special productive activity, exercised with a definite aim, an activity that appropriates particular nature-given materials to particular human wants. So far therefore as labour is a creator of use value, is useful labour, it is a necessary condition, independent of all forms of society, for the existence of the human race; it is an eternal nature-imposed necessity, without which there can be no material exchanges between man and Nature, and therefore no life.

The use values, coat, linen, &c., i.e., the bodies of commodities, are combinations of two elements – matter and labour. If we take away the useful labour expended upon them, a material substratum is always left, which is furnished by Nature without the help of man. The latter can work only as Nature does, that is by changing the form of matter. Nay more, in this work of changing the form he is constantly helped by natural forces. We see, then, that labour is not the only source of material wealth, of use values produced by labour. As William Petty puts it, labour is its father and the earth its mother.

Let us now pass from the commodity considered as a use value to the value of commodities.

By our assumption, the coat is worth twice as much as the linen. But this is a mere quantitative difference, which for the present does not concern us. We bear in mind, however, that if the value of the coat is double that of 10 yds of linen, 20 yds of linen must have the same value as one coat. So far as they are values, the coat and the linen are things of a like substance, objective expressions of essentially identical labour. But tailoring and weaving are, qualitatively, different kinds of labour. There are, however, states of society in which one and the same man does tailoring and weaving alternately, in which case these two forms of labour are mere modifications of the labour of the same individual, and not special and fixed functions of different persons; just as the coat which our tailor makes one day, and the trousers which he makes another day, imply only a variation in the labour of one and the same individual. Moreover, we see at a glance that, in our capitalist society, a given portion of human labour is, in accordance with the varying demand, at one time supplied in the form of tailoring, at another in the form of weaving. This change may possibly not take place without friction, but take place it must.

Productive activity, if we leave out of sight its special form, viz., the useful character of the labour, is nothing but the expenditure of human labour power. Tailoring and weaving, though qualitatively different productive activities, are each a productive expenditure of human brains, nerves, and muscles, and in this sense are human labour. They are but two different modes of expending human labour power. Of course, this labour power, which means the same under all its modifications, must have attained a certain pitch of development before it can be expended in a multiplicity of modes. But the value of a commodity represents human labour in the abstract, the expenditure of human labour in general. And just as in society, a general or a banker plays a great part, but mere man, on the other hand, a very shabby part, so here with mere human labour. It is the expenditure of simple labour power, i.e., of the labour power which, on an average apart from any special development, exists in the organism of every ordinary individual. Simple average labour, it is true, varies in character in different countries and at different times, but in a particular society it is given. Skilled labour counts only as simple labour intensified, or rather, as multiplied simple labour, a given quantity of skilled being considered equal to a greater quantity of simple labour. Experience shows that this reduction is constantly being made. A commodity may be the product of the most skilled labour, but its value, by equating it to the product of simple unskilled labour, represents a definite quantity of the latter labour alone.[4] The different proportions in which different sorts of labour are reduced to unskilled labour as their standard, are established by a social process that goes on behind the backs of the producers, and, consequently, appear to be fixed by custom. For simplicity's sake we shall henceforth account every kind of labour to be unskilled, simple labour; by this we do no more than save ourselves the trouble of making the reduction.

Just as, therefore, in viewing the coat and linen as values, we abstract from their different use values, so it is with the labour represented by those values: we disregard the difference between its useful forms, weaving and tailoring. As the use values, coat and linen, are combinations of special productive activities with cloth and yarn, while the values, coat and linen, are, on the other hand, mere homogeneous congelations of undifferentiated labour, so the labour embodied in these latter values does not count by virtue of its productive relation to cloth and yarn, but only as being expenditure of human labour power. Tailoring and weaving are necessary factors in the creation of the use values, coat and linen, precisely because these two kinds of labour are of different qualities; but only in so far as abstraction is made from their special qualities, only in so far as both possess the same quality of being human labour, do tailoring and weaving form the substance of the values of the same articles.

Coats and linen, however, are not merely values, but values of definite magnitude, and according to our assumption, the coat is worth twice as much as the ten yards of linen. Whence this difference in their values? It is owing to the fact that the linen contains only half as much labour as the coat, and consequently, that in the production of the latter, labour power must have been expended during twice the time necessary for the production of the former.

While, therefore, with reference to use value, the labour contained in a commodity counts only qualitatively, with reference to value it counts only quantitatively, and must first be reduced to human labour pure and simple. In the former case, it is a question of How and What, in the latter of How much? How long a time? Since the magnitude of the value of a commodity represents only the quantity of labour embodied in it, it follows that all commodities, when taken in certain proportions, must be equal in value.

If the productive power of all the different sorts of useful labour required for the production of a coat remains unchanged, the sum of the values of the coats produced increases with their number. If one coat represents x days' labour, two coats represents 2x days' labour, and so on. But assume that the duration of the labour necessary for the production of a coat becomes doubled or halved. In the first case, one coat is worth as much as two coats were before; in the second case, two coats are only worth as much as one was before, although in both cases one coat renders the same service as before, and the useful labour embodied in it remains of the same quality. But the quantity of labour spent on its production has altered.

An increase in the quantity of use values is an increase of material wealth. With two coats two men can be clothed, with one coat only one man. Nevertheless, an increased quantity of material wealth may correspond to a simultaneous fall in the magnitude of its value. This antagonistic movement has its origin in the twofold character of labour. Productive power has reference, of course, only to labour of some useful concrete form, the efficacy of any special productive activity during a given time being dependent on its productiveness. Useful labour becomes, therefore, a more or less abundant source of products, in proportion to the rise or fall of its productiveness. On the other hand, no change in this productiveness affects the labour represented by value. Since productive power is an attribute of the concrete useful forms of labour, of course it can no longer have any bearing on that labour, so soon as we make abstraction from those concrete useful forms. However then productive power may vary, the same labour, exercised during equal period of time, always yields equal amounts of value. But it will yield, during equal periods of time, different quantities of values in use; more, if the productive power rise, fewer, if it fall. The same change in productive power, which increases the fruitfulness of labour, and, in consequence, the quantity of use values produced by that labour, will diminish the total value of this increased quantity of use values, provided such change shorten the total labour time necessary for their production; and *vice versa*.

On the one hand, all labour is, speaking physiologically, an expenditure of human labour power, and in its character of identical abstract human labour, it creates and forms the value of commodities. On the other hand, all labour is the expenditure of human labour power in a special form and with a definite aim, and in this, its character of concrete useful labour, it produces use values. . . .

The Fetishism of Commodities and the Secret Thereof

A commodity appears, at first sight, a very trivial thing, and easily understood. Its analysis shows that it is, in reality, a very queer thing, abounding in metaphysical subtleties and theological niceties. So far as it is a value in use, there is nothing mysterious about it, whether we consider it from the point of view that by its properties it is capable of satisfying human wants, or from the point that those properties are the product of human labour. It is as clear as noon-day, that man, by his industry, changes the forms of the materials furnished by Nature, in such a way as to make them useful to him. The form of wood, for instance, is altered, by making a table out of it. Yet, for all that, the table continues to be that common, every-day thing, wood. But, so soon as it steps forth as a commodity, it is changed into something transcendent. It not only stands with its feet on the ground, but, in relation to all other commodities, it stands on its head, and evolves out of its wooden brain grotesque ideas, far more wonderful than "table-turning" ever was.

The mystical character of commodities does not originate, therefore, in their use value. Just as little does it proceed from the nature of the determining factors of value. For, in the first place, however varied the useful kinds of labour, or productive activities, may be, it is a physiological fact, that they are functions of the human organism, and that each such function, whatever may be its nature or form, is essentially the expenditure of human brain, nerves, muscles, &c. Secondly, with regard to that which forms the ground-work for the quantitative determination of value, namely, the duration of that expenditure, or the quantity of labour, it is quite clear that there is a palpable difference between its quantity and quality. In all states of society, the labour time that it costs to produce the means of subsistence, must necessarily be an object of interest to mankind, though not of equal interest in different stages of development. And lastly, from the moment that men in any way work for one another, their labour assumes a social form.

Whence, then, arises the enigmatical character of the product of labour, so soon as it assumes the form of commodities? Clearly from this form itself. The equality of all sorts of human labour is expressed objectively by their products all being equally values; the measure of the expenditure of labour power by the duration of that expenditure, takes the form of the quantity of value of the products of labour; and finally, the mutual relations of the producers, within which the social character of their labour affirms itself, take the form of a social relation between the products.

A commodity is therefore a mysterious thing, simply because in it the social character of men's labour appears to them as an objective character stamped upon the product of that labour; because the relation of the producers to the sum total of their own labour is presented to them as a social relation, existing not between themselves, but between the products of their labour. This is the reason why the products of labour become commodities, social things whose qualities are at the same time perceptible and imperceptible by the senses. In the same way the light from an object is perceived by us not as the subjective excitation of our optic nerve, but as the objective form of something outside the eye itself. But, in the act of seeing, there is at all events, an actual passage of light from one thing to another, from the external object to the eye. There is a physical relation between physical things. But it is different with commodities. There, the existence of the things *qua* commodities, and the value relation between the products of labour which stamps them as commodities, have absolutely no connection with their physical properties and with the material relations arising therefrom. There it is a definite social relation between men, that assumes, in their eyes, the fantastic form of a relation between things. In order, therefore, to find an analogy, we must have recourse to the mist-enveloped regions of the religious world. In that world the productions of the human brain appear as independent beings endowed with life, and entering into relation both with one another and the human race. So it is in the world of commodities with the products of men's hands. This I call the Fetishism which attaches itself to the products of labour, so soon as they are produced as commodities, and which is therefore inseparable from the production of commodities.

This Fetishism of commodities has its origin, as the foregoing analysis has already shown, in the peculiar social character of the labour that produces them.

As a general rule, articles of utility become commodities, only because they are products of the labour of private individuals or groups of individuals who carry on their work independently of each other. The sum total of the labour of all these private individuals forms the aggregate labour of society. Since the producers do not come into social contact with each other until they exchange their products, the specific social character of each producer's labour does not show itself except in the act of exchange. In other words, the labour of the individual asserts itself as a part of the labour of society, only by means of the relations which the act of exchange establishes directly between the products, and indirectly, through them, between the producers. To the latter, therefore, the relations connectiong the labour of one individual with that of the rest appear, not as direct social relations between individuals at work, but as what they really are, material relations between persons and social relations between things. It is only by being exchanged that the products of labour acquire, as values, one uniform social status, distinct from their varied forms of existence as objects of utility. This division of a product into a useful thing and a value becomes practically important, only when exchange has acquired such an extension that useful articles are produced for the purpose of being exchanged, and their character as values has therefore to be taken into account, beforehand, during production. From this moment the labour of the individual producer acquires socially a twofold character. On the one hand, it must, as a definite useful kind of labour, satisfy a definite social want, and thus hold its place as part and parcel of the collective labour of all, as a branch of a social division of labour that has sprung up spontaneously. On the other hand, it can satisfy the manifold wants of the individual producer himself, only in so far as the mutual exchangeability of all kinds of useful private labour is an established social fact, and therefore the private useful labour of each producer ranks on an equality with that of all others. The equalisation of the most different kinds of labour can be the result only of an abstraction from their inequalities, or of reducing them to their common denominator, viz., expenditure of human labour power or human labour in the abstract. The twofold social character of the labour of the individual appears to him, when reflected in his brain, only under those forms which are impressed upon that labour in everyday practice by the exchange of products. In this way, the character that his own labour possesses of being socially useful takes the form of the condition, that the product must be not only useful, but useful for others, and the social character that his particular labour has of being the equal of all other particular kinds of labour, takes the form that all the physically different articles that are the products of labour, have one common quality, viz., that of having value.

Hence, when we bring the products of our labour into relation with each other as values, it is not because we see in these articles the material receptacles of homogeneous human labour. Quite the contrary: whenever, by an exchange, we equate as values our different products, by that very act, we also equate, as human labour, the different kinds of labour expended upon them. We are not aware of this, nevertheless we do it.[5] Value, therefore, does not stalk about with a label describing what it is. It is value, rather, that converts every product into a social hieroglyphic. Later on, we try to decipher the hieroglyphic, to get behind the secret of our own social products; for to stamp an object of utility as a value, is just as much a social product as language. The recent scientific discovery, that the products of labour, so far as they are values, are but material expressions of the human labour spent in their production, marks, indeed, an epoch in the history of the development of the human race, but, by no means, dissipates the mist through which the social character of labour appears to us to be an objective character of the products themselves. The fact, that in the particular form of production with which we are dealing, viz., the production of commodities, the specific social character of private labour carried on independently, consists in the equality of every kind of that labour, by virtue of its being human labour, which character, therefore, assumes in the product the form of value – this fact appears to the producers, notwithstanding the discovery above referred to, to be just as real and final, as the fact, that, after the discovery by science of the component gases of air, the atmosphere itself remained unaltered.

What, first of all, practically concerns producers when they make an exchange, is the question, how much of some other product they get for their own? in what proportions the products are exchangeable? When these proportions have, by custom, attained a certain stability, they appear to result from the nature of the products, so that, for instance, one ton of iron and two ounces of gold appear as naturally to be of equal value as a pound of gold and a pound of iron in spite of their different physical and chemical qualities appear to be of equal weight. The character of having value, when once impressed upon products, obtains fixity only by reason of their acting and reacting upon each other as quantities of value. These quantities vary continually, independently of the will, foresight and action of the producers. To them, their own social action takes the form of the action of objects, which rule the producers instead of being ruled by them. It requires a fully developed production of commodities before, from accumulated experience alone, the scientific conviction springs up, that all the different kinds of private labour, which are carried on independently of each other, and yet as spontaneously developed branches of the social division of labour, are continually being reduced to the quantitative proportions in which society requires them. And why? Because, in the midst of all the accidental and ever fluctuating exchange relations between the products, the labour time socially necessary for their production forcibly asserts itself like an overriding law of Nature. The law of gravity thus asserts itself when a house falls about our ears. The determination of the magnitude of value by labour time is therefore a secret, hidden under the apparent fluctuations in the relative values of commodities. Its discovery, while removing all appearance of mere accidentality from the determination of the magnitude of the values of products, yet in no way alters the mode in which that determination takes place.

Man's reflections on the forms of social life, and consequently, also, his scientific analysis of those forms, take a course directly opposite to that of their actual historical development. He begins, *post festum*,[a] with the results of the process of

---

[a] After the feast, i.e. after the events reflected on have taken place.

development ready to hand before him. The characters that stamp products as commodities, and whose establishment is a necessary preliminary to the circulation of commodities, have already acquired the stability of natural, self-understood forms of social life, before man seeks to decipher, not their historical character, for in his eyes they are immutable, but their meaning. Consequently it was the analysis of the prices of commodities that alone led to the determination of the magnitude of value, and it was the common expression of all commodities in money that alone led to the establishment of their characters as values. It is, however, just this ultimate money form of the world of commodities that actually conceals, instead of disclosing, the social character of private labour, and the social relations between the individual producers. When I state that coats or boots stand in a relation to linen, because it is the universal incarnation of abstract human labour, the absurdity of the statement is self-evident. Nevertheless, when the producers of coats and boots compare those articles with linen, or, what is the same thing, with gold or silver, as the universal equivalent, they express the relation between their own private labour and the collective labour of society in the same absurd form.

The categories of bourgeois economy consist of such like forms. They are forms of thought expressing with social validity the conditions and relations of a definite, historically determined mode of production, viz., the production of commodities. The whole mystery of commodities, all the magic and necromancy that surrounds the products of labour as long as they take the form of commodities, vanishes therefore, so soon as we come to other forms of production.

Since Robinson Crusoe's experiences are a favourite theme with political economists, let us take a look at him on his island. Moderate though he be, yet some few wants he has to satisfy, and must therefore do a little useful work of various sorts, such as making tools and furniture, taming goats, fishing and hunting. Of his prayers and the like we take no account, since they are a source of pleasure to him, and he looks upon them as so much recreation. In spite of the variety of his work, he knows that his labour, whatever its form, is but the activity of one and the same Robinson, and consequently, that it consists of nothing but different modes of human labour. Necessity itself compels him to apportion his time accurately between his different kinds of work. Whether one kind occupies a greater space in his general activity than another, depends on the difficulties, greater or less as the case may be, to be overcome in attaining the useful effect aimed at. This our friend Robinson soon learns by experience, and having rescued a watch, ledger, and pen and ink from the wreck, commences, like a true-born Briton, to keep a set of books. His stock-book contains a list of the objects of utility that belong to him, of the operations necessary for their production; and lastly, of the labour time that definite quantities of those objects have, on an average, cost him. All the relations between Robinson and the objects that form this wealth of his own creation, are here so simple and clear as to be intelligible without exertion, even to Mr Sedley Taylor. And yet those relations contain all that is essential to the determination of value.

Let us now transport ourselves from Robinson's island bathed in light to the European Middle Ages shrouded in darkness. Here, instead of the independent man, we find everyone dependent, serfs and lords, vassals and suzerains, laymen and clergy. Personal dependence here characterises the social relations of production just as much as it does the other spheres of life organised on the basis of that production. But for the very reason that personal dependence forms the ground-work of society, there is no necessity for labour and its products to assume a fantastic form different from their reality. They take the shape, in the transactions of society, of services in kind and payments in kind. Here the particular and natural form of labour, and not, as in a society based on production of commodities, its general abstract form is the immediate social form of labour. Compulsory labour is just as properly measured by time, as commodity-producing labour; but every serf knows that what he expends in the service of his lord, is a definite quantity of his own personal labour power. The tithe to be rendered to the priest is more matter of fact than his blessing. No matter, then, what we may think of the parts played by the different classes of people themselves in this society, the social relations between individuals in the performance of their labour, appear at all events as their own mutual personal relations, and are not disguised under the shape of social relations between the products of labour.

For an example of labour in common or directly associated labour, we have no occasion to go back to that spontaneously developed form which we find on the threshold of the history of all civilised races. We have one close at hand in the patriarchal industries of a peasant family, that produces corn, cattle, yarn, linen, and clothing for home use. These different articles are, as regards the family, so many products of its labour, but as between themselves, they are not commodities. The different kinds of labour, such as tillage, cattle tending, spinning, weaving and making clothes, which result in the various products, are in themselves, and such as they are, direct social functions, because functions of the family, which, just as much as a society based on the production of commodities, possesses a spontane-ously developed system of division of labour. The distribution of the work within the family, and the regulation of the labour time of the several members, depend as well upon differences of age and sex as upon natural conditions varying with the seasons. The labour power of each individual, by its very nature, operates in this case merely as a definite portion of the whole labour power of the family, and therefore, the measure of the expenditure of individual labour power by its duration, appears here by its very nature as a social character of their labour.

Let us now picture to ourselves, by way of change, a community of free individuals, carrying on their work with the means of production in common, in which the labour power of all the different individuals is consciously applied as the combined labour power of the community. All the characteristics of Robinson's labour are here repeated, but with this difference, that they are social, instead of individual. Everything produced by him was exclusively the result of his own personal labour, and therefore simply an object of use for himself. The total produce of our community is a social product. One portion serves as fresh means of production and remains social. But another portion is consumed by the members as means of subsistence. A distribution of this portion amongst them is consequently necessary. The mode of this distribution will vary with the productive organisation of the community, and the degree of historical development attained by the producers. We will assume, but merely for the sake of a parallel with the production of commodities, that the share of each individual producer in the means of subsistence is determined by his labour time. Labour time would, in that case, play a double part. Its apportionment in accordance with a definite social plan maintains the proper proportion between the different kinds of work to be done and the various wants of the community. On the other hand, it also serves as a measure of the portion of the common labour borne by each individual, and of his share in the part of the total product destined for individual consumption. The social relations of the individual producers, with regard both to their labour and to its products, are in this case perfectly simple and intelligible, and that with regard not only to production but also to distribution.

The religious world is but the reflex of the real world. And for a society based upon the production of commodities, in which the producers in general enter into social relations with one another by treating their products as commodities and values, whereby they reduce their individual private labour to the standard of homogeneous human labour – for such a society, Christianity with its *cultus* of abstract man, more especially in its bourgeois developments, Protestantism, Deism, &c., is the most fitting form of religion. In the ancient Asiatic and other ancient modes of production, we find that the conversion of products into commodities, and therefore the conversion of men into producers of commodities, holds a subordinate place, which, however, increases in importance as the primitive communities approach nearer and nearer to their dissolution. Trading nations, properly so called, exist in the ancient world only in its interstices, like the gods of Epicurus in the Intermundia, or like Jews in the pores of Polish society. Those ancient social organisms of production are, as compared with bourgeois society, extremely simple and transparent. But they are founded either on the immature development of man individually, who has not yet severed the umbilical cord that unites him with his fellowmen in a primitive tribal community, or upon direct relations of subjection. They can arise and exist only when the development of the productive power of labour has not risen beyond a low stage, and when, therefore, the social relations within the sphere of material life, between man and man, and between man and Nature, are correspondingly narrow. This narrowness is reflected in the ancient worship of Nature, and in the other elements of the popular religions. The religious reflex of the real world can, in any case, only then finally vanish, when the practical relations of every-day life offer to man none but perfectly intelligible and reasonable relations with regard to his fellowmen and to Nature.

The life-process of society, which is based on the process of material production, does not strip off its mystical veil until it is treated as production by freely associated men, and is consciously regulated by them in accordance with a settled plan. This, however, demands for society a certain material ground-work or set of conditions of existence which in their turn are the spontaneous product of a long and painful process of development.

Political economy has indeed analysed, however incompletely, value and its magnitude, and has discovered what lies beneath these forms. But it has never once asked the question why labour is represented by the value of its product and labour time by the magnitude of that value. These formulæ, which bear it stamped upon them in unmistakable letters that they belong to a state of society, in which the process of production has the mastery over man, instead of being controlled by him, such formulæ appear to the bourgeois intellect to be as much a self-evident necessity imposed by Nature as productive labour itself. Hence forms of social production that preceded the bourgeois form, are treated by the bourgeoisie in much the same way as the Fathers of the Church treated pre-Christian religions.

To what extent some economists are misled by the Fetishism inherent in commodities, or by the objective appearance of the social characteristics of labour, is shown, amongst other ways, by the dull and tedious quarrel over the part played by Nature in the formation of exchange value. Since exchange value is a definite social manner of expressing the amount of labour bestowed upon an object, Nature has no more to do with it, than it has in fixing the course of exchange.

The mode of production in which the product takes the form of a commodity, or is produced directly for exchange, is the most general and most embryonic form of bourgeois production. It therefore makes its appearance at an early date in history, though not in the same predominating and characteristic manner as now-a-days. Hence its Fetish character is comparatively easy to be seen through. But when we come to more concrete forms, even this appearance of simplicity vanishes. Whence arose the illusions of the monetary system? To it gold and silver, when serving as money, did not represent a social relation between producers, but were natural objects with strange social properties. And modern economy, which looks down with such disdain on the monetary system, does not its superstition come out as clear as noon-day, whenever it treats of capital? How long is it since economy discarded the physiocratic illusion, that rents grow out of the soil and not out of society?

But not to anticipate, we will content ourselves with yet another example relating to the commodity form. Could commodities themselves speak, they would say: Our use value may be a thing that interests men. It is no part of us as objects. What, however, does belong to us as objects, is our value. Our natural intercourse as commodities proves it. In the eyes of each other we are nothing but exchange values. Now listen how those commodities speak through the mouth of the economist.

"Value" – (i.e., exchange value) "is a property of things, riches" – (i.e., use value) "of man. Value, in this sense, necessarily implies exchanges, riches do not."

"Riches" (use value) "are the attribute of men, value is the attribute of commodities. A man or a community is rich, a pearl or a diamond is valuable . . ." A pearl or a diamond is valuable as a pearl or a diamond.

So far no chemist has ever discovered exchange value either in a pearl or a diamond. The economic discoverers of this chemical element, who by-the-bye lay special claim to critical acumen, find however that the use value of objects belongs to them independently of their material properties, while their value, on the other hand, forms a part of them as objects. What confirms them in this view, is the peculiar circumstance that the use value of objects is realised without exchange, by means of a direct relation between the objects and man, that is, by means of a social process. Who fails here to call to mind our good friend, Dogberry, who informs neighbour Seacoal, that, "To be a well-favoured man is the gift of fortune; but reading and writing comes by Nature."

Notes

1   In bourgeois societies the economic *fictio juris* prevails, that every one, as a buyer, possesses an encyclopaedic knowledge of commodities.

2   "The value of them" (the necessaries of life), "when they are exchanged the one for another, is regulated by the quantity of labour necessarily required, and commonly taken in producing them" (*Some Thoughts on the Interest of Money in General, and Particularly in the Publick Funds, &c.*, London, [p]p. 36 [,37]. This remarkable anonymous work, written in the last century, bears no date. It is clear, however, from internal evidence, that it appeared in the reign of George II about 1739 or 1740.

3   "Properly speaking, all products of the same kind form a single mass, and their price is determined in general and without regard to particular circumstances" (Le Trosne, l.c., p. 893).

4   The reader must note that we are not speaking here of the wages or value that the labourer gets for a given labour time, but of the value of the commodity in which that labour time is materialised. Wages is a category that, as yet, has no existence at the present stage of our investigation.

5   When, therefore, Galiani says: Value is a relation between persons – "La Richezza è una ragione tra due persone", – he ought to have added: a relation between persons expressed as a relation between things (Galiani, *Della Moneta*, p. 221, V. III of Custodi's collection of *Scrittori Classici Italiani di Economia Politica, Parte Moderna*, Milano, 1803).

4 The General Formula for Capital

Karl Marx

The circulation of commodities is the starting-point of capital. The production of commodities, their circulation, and that more developed form of their circulation called commerce, these form the historical ground-work from which it rises. The modern history of capital dates from the creation in the 16th century of a world-embracing commerce and a world-embracing market.

If we abstract from the material substance of the circulation of commodities, that is, from the exchange of the various use values, and consider only the economic forms produced by this process of circulation, we find its final result to be money: this final product of the circulation of commodities is the first form in which capital appears.

As a matter of history, capital, as opposed to landed property, invariably takes the form at first of money; it appears as moneyed wealth, as the capital of the merchant and of the usurer.[1] But we have no need to refer to the origin of capital in order to discover that the first form of appearance of capital is money. We can see it daily under our very eyes. All new capital, to commence with, comes on the stage, that is, on the market, whether of commodities, labour or money, even in our days, in the shape of money that by a definite process has to be transformed into capital.

The first distinction we notice between money that is money only, and money that is capital, is nothing more than a difference in their form of circulation.

The simplest form of the circulation of commodities is C—M—C, the transformation of commodities into money, and the change of the money back again into commodities; or selling in order to buy. But alongside of this form we find another specifically different form: M—C—M, the transformation of money into commodities, and the change of commodities back again into money; of buying in order to sell. Money that circulates in the latter manner is thereby transformed into, becomes capital, and is already potentially capital.

Now let us examine the circuit M—C—M a little closer. It consists, like the other, of two antithetical phases. In the first phase, M—C, or the purchase, the money is changed into a commodity. In the second phase, C—M, or the sale, the commodity is changed back again into money. The combination of these two phases constitutes the single movement whereby money is exchanged for a commodity, and the same commodity is again exchanged for money; whereby a commodity is bought in order to be sold, or neglecting the distinction in form between buying and selling, whereby a commodity is bought with money, and then money is bought with a commodity. The result, in which the phases of the process vanish, is the exchange of money for money, M—M. If I purhcase 2,000 lbs of cotton for £100, and resell the 2,000 lbs of cotton for £110, I have, in fact, exchanged £100 for £110, money for money.

Now it is evident that the circuit M−C−M would be absurd and without meaning if the intention were to exchange by this means two equal sums of money, £100 for £100. The miser's plan would be far simpler and surer; he sticks to his £100 instead of exposing it to the dangers of circulation. And yet, whether the merchant who has paid £100 for his cotton sells it for £110, or lets it go for £100, or even £50, his money has, at all events, gone through a characteristic and original movement, quite different in kind from that which it goes through in the hands of the peasant who sells corn, and with the money thus set free buys clothes. We have therefore to examine first the distinguishing characteristics of the forms of the circuits M−C−M and C−M−C, and in doing this the real difference that underlies the mere difference of form will reveal itself.

Let us see, in the first place, what the two forms have in common.

Both circuits are resolvable into the same two antithetical phases, C−M, a sale, and M C, a purchase. In each of these phases the same material elements – a commodity, and money, and the same economic *dramatis personæ*, a buyer and a seller – confront one another. Each circuit is the unity of the same two antithetical phases, and in each case this unity is brought about by the intervention of three contracting parties, of whom one only sells, another only buys, while the third both buys and sells.

What, however, first and foremost distinguishes the circuit C−M−C from the circuit M−C−M, is the inverted order of succession of the two phases. The simple circulation of commodities begins with a sale and ends with a purchase, while the circulation of money as capital begins with a purchase and ends with a sale. In the one case both the starting-point and the goal are commodities, in the other they are money. In the first form the movement is brought about by the intervention of money, in the second by that of a commodity.

In the circulation C−M−C, the money is in the end converted into a commodity, that serves as a use value; it is spent once for all. In the inverted form, M−C−M, on the contrary, the buyer lays out money in order that, as a seller, he may recover money. By the purchase of his commodity he throws money into circulation, in order to withdraw it again by the sale of the same commodity. He lets the money go, but only with the sly intention of getting it back again. The money, therefore, is not spent, it is merely advanced.[2]

In the circuit C−M−C, the same piece of money changes its place twice. The seller gets it from the buyer and pays it away to another seller. The complete circulation, which begins with the receipt, concludes with the payment, of money for commodities. It is the very contrary in the circuit M−C−M. Here it is not the piece of money that changes its place twice, but the commodity. The buyer takes it from the hands of the seller and passes it into the hands of another buyer. Just as in the simple circulation of commodities the double change of place of the same piece of money effects its passage from one hand into another, so here the double change of place of the same commodity brings about the reflux of the money to its point of departure.

Such reflux is not dependent on the commodity being sold for more than was paid for it. This circumstance influences only the amount of the money that comes back. The reflux itself takes place, so soon as the purchased commodity is resold, in other words, so soon as the circuit M—C—M is completed. We have here, therefore, a palpable difference between the circulation of money as capital, and its circulation as mere money.

The circuit C—M—C comes completely to an end, so soon as the money brought in by the sale of one commodity is abstracted again by the purchase of another.

If, nevertheless, there follows a reflux of money to its starting-point, this can only happen through a renewal or repetition of the operation. If I sell a quarter of corn for £3, and with this £3 buy clothes, the money, so far as I am concerned, is spent and done with. It belongs to the clothes merchant. If I now sell a second quarter of corn, money indeed flows back to me, not however as a sequel to the first transaction, but in consequence of its repetition. The money again leaves me, so soon as I complete this second transaction by a fresh purchase. Therefore, in the circuit C—M—C, the expenditure of money has nothing to do with its reflux. On the other hand, in M—C—M, the reflux of the money is conditioned by the very mode of its expenditure. Without this reflux, the operation fails, or the process is interrupted and incomplete, owing to the absence of its complementary and final phase, the sale.

The circuit C—M—C starts with one commodity, and finishes with another, which falls out of circulation and into consumption. Consumption, the satisfaction of wants, in one word, use value, is its end and aim. The circuit M—C—M, on the contrary, commences with money and ends with money. Its leading motive, and the goal that attracts it, is therefore mere exchange value.

In the simple circulation of commodities, the two extremes of the circuit have the same economic form. They are both commodities, and commodities of equal value. But they are also use values differing in their qualities, as, for example, corn and clothes. The exchange of products, of the different materials in which the labour of society is embodied, forms here the basis of the movement. It is otherwise in the circulation M—C—M, which at first sight appears purposeless, because tautological. Both extremes have the same economic form. They are both money, and therefore are not qualitatively different use values; for money is but the converted form of commodities, in which their particular use values vanish. To exchange £100 for cotton, and then this same cotton again for £100, is merely a roundabout way of exchanging money for money, the same for the same, and appears to be an operation just as purposeless as it is absurd. One sum of money is distinguishable from another only by its amount. The character and tendency of the process M—C—M, is therefore not due to any qualitative difference between its extremes, both being money, but solely to their quantitative difference. More money is withdrawn from circulation at the finish than was thrown into it at the start. The cotton that was bought for £100 is perhaps resold for £100 + £10 or £110. The exact form of this process is therefore M—C—M′, where M′ = M + $\triangle$M = the original sum advanced, plus an increment. This increment or excess over the original value I call "surplus value". The value originally advanced, therefore, not only remains intact while in circulation, but adds to itself a surplus value or expands itself. It is this movement that converts it into capital.

Of course, it is also possible, that in C—M—C, the two extremes C—C, say corn and clothes, may represent different quantities of value. The farmer may sell his corn above its value, or may buy the clothes at less than their value. He may, on the other hand, "be done" by the clothes merchant. Yet, in the form of circulation now under consideration, such differences in value are purely accidental. The fact that the corn and the clothes are equivalents, does not deprive the process of all meaning, as it does in M−C−M. The equivalence of their values is rather a necessary condition to its normal course.

The repetition or renewal of the act of selling in order to buy, is kept within bounds by the very object it aims at, namely, consumption or the satisfaction of definite wants, an aim that lies altogether outside the sphere of circulation. But when we buy in order to sell, we, on the contrary, begin and end with the same thing, money, exchange value; and thereby the movement becomes interminable. No doubt M becomes M + △M, £100 became £110. But when viewed in their qualitative aspect alone, £110 are the same as £100, namely money; and considered quantitatively, £110 is, like £100, a sum of definite and limited value. If now, the £110 be spent as money, they cease to play their part. They are no longer capital. Withdrawn from circulation, they become petrified into a hoard, and though they remained in that state till doomsday, not a single farthing would accrue to them. If, then, the expansion of value is once aimed at, there is just the same inducement to augment the value of the £110 as that of the £100; for both are but limited expressions for exchange value, and therefore both have the same vocation to approach, by quantitative increase, as near as possible to absolute wealth. Momentarily, indeed, the value originally advanced, the £100 is distinguishable from the surplus value of £10 that is annexed to it during circulation; but the distinction vanishes immediately. At the end of the process, we do not receive with one hand the original £100, and with the other, the surplus value of £10. We simply get a value of £110, which is in exactly the same condition and fitness for commencing the expanding process, as the original £100 was. Money ends the movement only to begin it again. Therefore, the final result of every separate circuit, in which a purchase and consequent sale are completed, forms of itself the starting-point of a new circuit. The simple circulation of commodities – selling in order to buy – is a means of carrying out a purpose unconnected with circulation, namely, the appropriation of use values, the satisfaction of wants. The circulation of money as capital is, on the contrary, an end in itself for the expansion of value takes place only within this constantly renewed movement. The circulation of capital has therefore no limits.

As the conscious representative of this movement, the possessor of money becomes a capitalist. His person, or rather his pocket, is the point from which the money starts and to which it returns. The expansion of value, which is the objective basis or mainspring of the circulation M−C−M, becomes his subjective aim, and it is only in so far as the appropriation of ever more and more wealth in the abstract becomes the sole motive of his operations, that he functions as a capitalist, that is, as capital personifed and endowed with consciousness and a will. Use values must therefore never be looked upon as the real aim of the capitalist; neither must the profit on any single transaction. The restless never-ending process of profit-making alone is what he aims at. This boundless greed after riches, this passionate chase after exchange value, is common to the capitalist and the miser; but while the miser is merely a capitalist gone mad, the capitalist is a rational miser. The never-ending augmentation of exchange value, which the miser strives after, by seeking to save his money from circulation, is attained by the more acute capitalist, by constantly throwing it afresh into circulation.

The independent form, i.e., the money form, which the value of commodities assumes in the case of simple circulation, serves only one purpose, namely, their exchange, and vanishes in the final result of the movement. On the other hand, in the circulation M—C—M, both the money and the commodity represent only different modes of existence of value itself, the money its general mode, and the commodity its particular, or, so to say, disguised mode. It is constantly changing from one form to the other without thereby becoming lost and thus assumes an automatically active character. If now we take in turn each of the two different forms which self-expanding value successively assumes in the course of its life, we then arrive at these two propositions: Capital is money: Capital is commodities.[3] In truth, however, value is here the active factor in a process, in which, while constantly assuming the form in turn of money and commodities, it at the same time changes in magnitude, differentiates itself by throwing off surplus value from itself; the original value, in other words, expands spontaneously. For the movement, in the course of which it adds surplus value, is its own movement, its expansion, therefore, is automatic expansion. Because it is value, it has acquired the occult quality of being able to add value to itself. It brings forth living offspring, or, at the least, lays golden eggs.

Value, therefore, being the active factor in such a process, and assuming at one time the form of money, at another that of commodities, but through all these changes preserving itself and expanding, it requires some independent form, by means of which its identity may at any time be established. And this form it possesses only in the shape of money. It is under the form of money that value begins and ends, and begins again, every act of its own spontaneous generation. It began by being £100, it is now £110, and so on. But the money itself is only one of the two forms of value. Unless it takes the form of some commodity, it does not become capital. There is here no antagonism, as in the case of hoarding, between the money and commodities. The capitalist knows that all commodities, however scurvy they may look, or however badly they may smell, are in faith and in truth money, inwardly circumcised Jews, and what is more, a wonderful means whereby out of money to make more money.

In simple circulation, C—M—C, the value of commodities attained at the most a form independent of their use values, i.e., the form of money; but that same value now in the circulation M—C—M, or the circulation of capital, suddenly presents itself as an independent substance, endowed with a motion of its own, passing through a life process of its own, in which money and commodities are mere forms which it assumes and casts off in turn. Nay, more: instead of simply representing the relations of commodities, it enters now, so to say, into private relations with itself. It differentiates itself as original value from itself as surplus value; as the father differentiates himself from himself *quâ* the son, yet both are one and of one age: for only by the surplus value of £10 does the £100 originally advanced become capital, and so soon as this takes place, so soon as the son, and by the son, the father, is begotten, so soon does their difference vanish, and they again become one, £110.

Value therefore now becomes value in process, money in process, and, as such, capital. It comes out of circulation, enters into it again, preserves and multiplies itself within its circuit, comes back out of it with expanded bulk, and begins the same round ever afresh. M—M', money which begets money, such is the description of Capital from the mouth of its first interpreters, the Mercantilists.

Buying in order to sell, or, more accurately, buying in order to sell dearer, M—C—M', appears certainly to be a form peculiar to one kind of capital alone, namely, merchants' capital. But industrial capital too is money, that is changed into commodities, and by the sale of these commodities, is re-converted into more money. The events that take place outside the sphere of circulation, in the interval between the buying and selling, do not affect the form of this movement. Lastly, in the case of interest-bearing capital, the circulation M—C—M' appears abridged. We have its result without the intermediate stage, in the form M—M', "*en style lapidaire*" so to say, money that is worth more money, value that is greater than itself.

M—C—M' is therefore in reality the general formula of capital as it appears *prima facie* within the sphere of circulation.

Notes

1 The contrast between the power, based on the personal relations of dominion and servitude, that is conferred by landed property, and the impersonal power that is given by money, is well expressed by the two French proverbs, "No land without its lord", and "Money has no master".

2 "When a thing is bought in order to be sold again, the sum employed is called money advanced; when it is bought not to be sold, it may be said to be expended." – James Steuart, *Works*, &c. Edited by Gen. Sir James Steuart, his son. London, 1805, Vol. I, p. 274).

3 "Currency (!) employed in producing articles . . . is capital" (Macleod, *The Theory and Practice of Banking*, London, 1855, v. 1, ch. i, p. 55). "Capital is commodities" (James Mill, *Elements of Pol. Econ.*, London, 1821, p. 74).

5 Division of Labour and Manufacture

Karl Marx

Twofold Origin of Manufacture

That co-operation which is based on division of labour, assumes its typical form in manufacture, and is the prevalent characteristic form of the capitalist process of production throughout the manufacturing period properly so called. That period, roughly speaking, extends from the middle of the 16th to the last third of the 18th century.

Manufacture takes its rise in two ways: –

(1) By the assemblage, in one workshop under the control of a single capitalist, of labourers belonging to various independent handicrafts, but through whose hands a given article must pass on its way to completion. A carriage, for example, was formerly the product of the labour of a great number of independent artificers, such as wheelwrights, harness-makers, tailors, locksmiths, upholsterers, turners, fringe-makers, glaziers, painters, polishers, gilders, &c. In the manufacture of carriages, however, all these different artificers are assembled in one building where they work into one another's hands. It is true that a carriage cannot be gilt before it has been made. But if a number of carriages are being made simultaneously, some may be in the hands of the gilders while others are going through an earlier process. So far, we are still in the domain of simple co-operation, which finds its materials ready to hand in the shape of men and things. But very soon an important change takes place. The tailor, the locksmith, and the other artificers, being now exclusively occupied in carriage-making, each gradually loses, through want of practice, the ability to carry on, to its full extent, his old handicraft. But, on the other hand, his activity now confined in one groove, assumes the form best adapted to the narrowed sphere of action. At first, carriage manufacture is a combination of various independent handicrafts. By degrees, it becomes the splitting up of carriage-making into its various detail processes, each of which crystallises into the exclusive function of a particular workman, the manufacture, as a whole, being carried on by the men in conjunction. In the same way, cloth manufacture, as also a whole series of other manufactures, arose by combining different handicrafts together under the control of a single capitalist.

(2) Manufacture also arises in a way exactly the reverse of this – namely, by one capitalist employing simultaneously in one workshop a number of artificers, who all do the same, or the same kind of work, such as making paper, type, or needles. This is co-operation in its most elementary form. Each of these artificers (with the help, perhaps, of one or two apprentices), makes the entire commodity, and he consequently performs in succession all the operations necessary for its production.

He still works in his old handicraft-like way. But very soon external circumstances cause a different use to be made of the concentration of the workmen on one spot, and of the simultaneousness of their work. An increased quantity of the article has perhaps to be delivered within a given time. The work is therefore re-distributed. Instead of each man being allowed to perform all the various operations in succession, these operations are changed into disconnected, isolated ones, carried on side by side; each is assigned to a different artificer, and the whole of them together are performed simultaneously by the co-operating workmen. This accidental repartition gets repeated, develops advantages of its own, and gradually ossifies into a systematic division of labour. The commodity, from being the individual product of an independent artificer, becomes the social product of a union of artificers, each of whom performs one, and only one, of the constituent partial operations. The same operations which, in the case of a papermaker belonging to a German Guild, merged one into the other as the successive acts of one artificer, became in the Dutch paper manufacture so many partial operations carred on side by side by numerous co-operating labourers. The needlemakers of the Nuremberg Guild was the cornerstone on which the English needle manufacture was raised. But while in Nuremberg that single artificer performed a series of perhaps 20 operations one after another, in England it was not long before there were 20 needlemakers side by side, each performing one alone of those 20 operations, and in consequence of further experience, each of those 20 operations was again split up, isolated, and made the exclusive function of a separate workman.

The mode in which manufacture arises, its growth out of handicrafts, is therefore twofold. On the one hand, it arises from the union of various independent handicrafts, which become stripped of their independence and specialised to such an extent as to be reduced to mere supplementary partial processes in the production of one particular commodity. On the other hand, it arises from the co-operation of artificers of one handicraft; it splits up that particular handicraft into its various detail operations, isolating, and making these operations independent of one another up to the point where each becomes the exclusive function of a particular labourer. On the one hand, therefore, manufacture either introduces division of labour into a process of production, or further develops that division; on the other hand, it unites together handicrafts that were formerly separate. But whatever may have been its particular starting-point, its final form is invariably the same – a productive mechanism whose parts are human beings.

For a proper understanding of the division of labour in manufacture, it is essential that the following points be firmly grasped. First, the decomposition of a process of production into its various successive steps coincides here, strictly with the resolution of a handicraft into its successive manual operations. Whether complex or simple, each operation has to be done by hand, retains the character of a handicraft, and is therefore dependent on the strength, skill, quickness, and sureness, of the individual workman in handling his tools. The handicraft continues to be the basis. This narrow technical basis excludes a really scientific analysis of any definite process of industrial production, since it is still a condition that each detail process gone through by the product must be capable of being done by hand and of forming, in its way, a separate handicraft. It is just because handicraft skill continues, in this way, to be the foundation of the process of production, that each workman becomes exclusively assigned to a partial function, and that for the rest of his life, his labour power is turned into the organ of this detail function.

Secondly, this division of labour is a particular sort of co-operation, and many of its disadvantages spring from the general character of co-operation, and not from this particular form of it. . . .

The Capitalistic Character of Manufacture

An increased number of labourers under the control of one capitalist is the natural starting-point, as well of co-operation generally, as of manufacture in particular. But the division of labour in manufacture makes this increase in the number of workmen a technical necessity. The minimum number that any given capitalist is bound to employ is here prescribed by the previously established division of labour. On the other hand, the advantages of further division are obtainable only by adding to the number of workmen, and this can be done only by adding multiples of the various detail groups. But an increase in the variable component of the capital employed necessitates an increase in its constant component, too, in the workshops, implements, &c., and, in particular, in the raw material, the call for which grows quicker than the number of workmen. The quantity of it consumed in a given time, by a given amount of labour, increases in the same ratio as does the productive power of that labour in consequence of its division. Hence, it is a law, based on the very nature of manufacture, that the minimum amount of capital, which is bound to be in the hands of each capitalist, must keep increasing; in other words, that the transformation into capital of the social means of production and subsistence must keep extending.[1]

In manufacture, as well as in simple co-operation, the collective working organism is a form of existence of capital. The mechanism that is made up of numerous individual detail labourers belongs to the capitalist. Hence, the productive power resulting from a combination of labours appears to be the productive power of capital. Manufacture proper not only subjects the previously independent workman to the discipline and command of capital, but, in addition, creates a hierarchic graduation of the workmen themselves. While simple co-operation leaves the mode of working by the individual for the most part unchanged, manufacture thoroughly revolutionises it, and seizes labour power by its very roots. It converts the labourer into a crippled monstrosity, by forcing his detail dexterity at the expense of a world of productive capabilities and instincts; just as in the States of La Plata they butcher a whole beast for the sake of his hide or his tallow. Not only is the detail work distributed to the different individuals, but the individual himself is made the automatic motor of a fractional operation, and the absurd fable of Menenius Agrippa, which makes man a mere fragment of his own body, becomes realised. If, at first, the workman sells his labour power to capital, because the material means of producing a commodity fail him, now his very labour power refuses its services unless it has been sold to capital. Its functions can be exercised only in an environment that exists in the workshop of the capitalist after the sale. By nature unfitted to make anything independently, the manufacturing labourer develops productive activity as a mere appendage of the capitalist's workshop. As the chosen people bore in their features the sign manual of Jehovah, so division of labour brands the manufacturing workman as the property of capital.

The knowledge, the judgment, and the will, which, though in ever so small a degree, are practised by the independent peasant or handicraftsman, in the same way as the savage makes the whole art of war consist in the exercise of his personal cunning – these faculties are now required only for the workshop as a whole. Intelligence in production expands in one direction, because it vanishes in many others. What is lost by the detail labourers, is concentrated in the capital that employs them. It is a result of the division of labour in manufactures, that the labourer is brought face to face with the intellectual potencies of the material process of production, as the property of another, and as a ruling power. This separation begins in simple cooperation, where the capitalist represents to the single workman, the oneness and the will of the associated labour. It is developed in manufacture which cuts down the labourer into a detail labourer. It is completed in modern industry, which makes science a productive force distinct from labour and presses it into the service of capital.

Notes

1   "It is not sufficient that the capital" (the writer should have said the necessary means of subsistence and of production) "required for the subdivision of handicrafts should be in readiness in the society: it must also be accumulated in the hands of the employers in sufficiently large quantities to enable them to conduct their operations on a large scale . . . (The more the division increases, the more does the constant employment of a given number of labourers require a greater outlay of capital in tools, raw material, &c." (Storch, *Cours d'Econ. Polit.* Paris Ed., t. I, pp. 250, 251).

6 The So-Called Primitive Accumulation

Karl Marx

The Secret of Primitive Accumulation

We have seen how money is changed into capital; how through capital surplus value is made, and from surplus value more capital. But the accumulation of capital presupposes surplus value; surplus value presupposes capitalistic production; capitalistic production presupposes the pre-existence of considerable masses of capital and of labour power in the hands of producers of commodities. The whole movement, therefore, seems to turn in a vicious circle, out of which we can only get by supposing a primitive accumulation (previous accumulation of Adam Smith) preceding capitalistic accumulation; an accumulation not the result of the capitalist mode of production, but its starting point.

This primitive accumulation plays in political economy about the same part as original sin in theology. Adam bit the apple, and thereupon sin fell on the human race. Its origin is supposed to be explained when it is told as an anecdote of the past. In times long gone by there were two sorts of people; one, the diligent, intelligent, and, above all, frugal élite; the other, lazy rascals, spending their substance, and more, in riotous living. The legend of theological original sin tells us certainly how man came to be condemned to eat his bread in the sweat of his brow; but the history of economic original sin reveals to us that there are people to whom this is by no means essential. Never mind! Thus it came to pass that the former sort accumulated wealth, and the latter sort had at last nothing to sell except their own skins. And from this original sin dates the poverty of the great majority that, despite all its labour, has up to now nothing to sell but itself, and the wealth of the few that increases constantly although they have long ceased to work. Such insipid childishness is every day preached to us in the defence of property. M. Thiers, e.g., had the assurance to repeat it with all the solemnity of a statesman, to the French people, once so *spirituel*. But as soon as the question of property crops up, it becomes a sacred duty to proclaim the intellectual food of the infant as the one thing fit for all ages and for all stages of development. In actual history it is notorious that conquest, enslavement, robbery, murder, briefly, force, play the great part. In the tender annals of political economy, the idyllic reigns from time immemorial. Right and "labour" were from all time the sole means of enrichment, the present year of course always excepted. As a matter of fact, the methods of primitive accumulation are anything but idyllic.

In themselves money and commodities are no more capital than are the means of production and of subsistence. They want transforming into capital. But this transformation itself can only take place under certain circumstances that centre in this, viz., that two very different kinds of commodity possessors must come face to face and into contact; on the one hand, the owners of money, means of production, means of subsistence, who are eager to increase the sum of values they possess, by buying other people's labour power; on the other hand, free labourers, the sellers of their own labour power, and therefore the sellers of labour. Free labourers, in the double sense that neither they themselves form part and parcel of the means of production, as in the case of slaves, bondsmen, &c., nor do the means of production belong to them, as in the case of peasant proprietors; they are, therefore, free from, unencumbered by, any means of production of their own. With this polarisation of the market for commodities, the fundamental conditions of capitalist production are given. The capitalist system presupposes the complete separation of the labourers from all property in the means by which they can realise their labour. As soon as capitalist production is once on its own legs, it not only maintains this separation, but reproduces it on a continually extending scale. The process, therefore, that clears the way for the capitalist system, can be none other than the process which takes away from the labourer the possession of his means of production; a process that transforms, on the one hand, the social means of subsistence and of production into capital, on the other, the immediate producers into wage labourers. The so-called primitive accumulation, therefore, is nothing else than the historical process of divorcing the producer from the means of production. It appears as primitive, because it forms the pre-historic stage of capital and of the mode of production corresponding with it.

The economic structure of capitalistic society has grown out of the economic structure of feudal society. The dissolution of the latter set free the elements of the former.

The immediate producer, the labourer, could only dispose of his own person after he had ceased to be attached to the soil and ceased to be the slave, serf, or bondman of another. To become a free seller of labour power, who carries his commodity wherever he finds a market, he must further have escaped from the regime of the guilds, their rules for apprentices and journeymen, and the impediments of their labour regulations. Hence, the historical movement which changes the producers into wage workers, appears, on the one hand, as their emancipation from serfdom and from the fetters of the guilds, and this side alone exists for our bourgeois historians. But, on the other hand, these new freedmen became sellers of themselves only after they had been robbed of all their own means of production, and of all the guarantees of existence afforded by the old feudal arrangements. And the history of this, their expropriation, is written in the annals of mankind in letters of blood and fire.

The industrial capitalists, these new potentates, had on their part not only to displace the guild masters of handicrafts, but also the feudal lords, the possessors of the sources of wealth. In this respect their conquest of social power appears as the fruit of a victorious struggle both against feudal lordship and its revolting prerogatives, and against the guilds and the fetters they laid on the free development of production and the free exploitation of man by man. The chevaliers d'industrie, however, only succeeded in supplanting the chevaliers of the sword by making use of events of which they themselves were wholly innocent. They have risen by means as vile as those by which the Roman freedman once on a time made himself the master of his *patronus*.

The starting point of the development that gave rise to the wage labourer as well as to the capitalist, was the servitude of the labourer. The advance consisted in a change of form of this servitude, in the transformation of feudal exploitation into capitalist exploitation. To understand its march, we need not go back very far. Although we come across the first begginings of capitalist production as early as the 14th or 15th century, sporadically, in certain towns of the Mediterranean, the capitalistic era dates from the 16th century. Wherever it appears, the abolition of serfdom has been long effected, and the highest development of the Middle Ages, the existence of sovereign towns, has been long on the wane.

In the history of primitive accumulation, all revolutions are epoch-making that act as levers for the capitalist class in our course of formation; but, above all, those moments when great masses of men are suddenly and forcibly torn from their means of subsistence, and hurled as free and "unattached" proletarians on the labour market. The expropriation of the agricultural producer, of the peasant, from the soil is the basis of the whole process. The history of this expropriation, in different countries, assumes different aspects, and runs through its various phases in different orders of succession, and at different periods. In England alone, which we take as our example, has it the classic form. . . .

Historical Tendency of Capitalist Accumulation

What does the primitive accumulation of capital, i.e., its historical genesis, resolve itself into? In so far as it is not immediate transformation of slaves and serfs into wage labourers, and therefore a mere change of form, it only means the expropriation of the immediate producers, i.e., the dissolution of private property based on the labour of its owner. Private property, as the antithesis to social, collective property, exists only where the means of labour and the external conditions of labour belong to private individuals. But according as these private individuals are labourers or not labourers, private property has a different character. The numberless shades, that it at first sight presents, correspond to the intermediate stages lying between these two extremes. The private property of the labourer in his means of production is the foundation of petty industry, whether agricultural, manufacturing, or both; petty industry, again, is an essential condition for the development of social production and of the free individuality of the labourer himself. Of course, this petty mode of production exists also under slavery, serfdom, and other states of dependence. But it flourishes, it lets loose its whole energy, it attains its adequate classical form, only where the labourer is the private owner of his own means of labour set in action by himself; the peasant of the land which he cultivates, the artisan of the tool which he handles as a virtuoso. This mode of production presupposes parcelling of the soil, and scattering of the other means of production. As it excludes the concentration of these means of production, so also it excludes co-operation, division of labour within each separate process of production, the control over, and the productive application of the forces of Nature by society, and the free development of the social productive powers. It is compatible only with a system of production, and a society, moving within narrow and more or less primitive bounds. To perpetuate it would be, as Pecqueur rightly says, "to decree universal mediocrity". At a certain stage of development it brings forth the material agencies for its own dissolution. From that moment new forces and new passions spring up in the bosom of society; but the old social organisation fetters them and keeps them down. It must be annihilated; it is annihilated. Its annihilation, the transformation of the individualised and scattered means of production into socially concentrated ones, of the pigmy property of the many into the huge property of the few, the expropriation of the great mass of the people from the soil, from the means of subsistence, and from the means of labour, this fearful and painful expropriation of the mass of the people forms the prelude to the history of capital. It comprises a series of forcible methods, of which we have passed in review only those that have been epoch-making as methods of the primitive accumulation of capital. The expropriation of the immediate producers was accomplished with merciless Vandalism, and under the stimulus of passions the most infamous, the most sordid, the pettiest, the most meanly odious. Self-earned private property, that is based, so to say, on the fusing together of the isolated, independent labouring individual with the conditions of his labour, is supplanted by capitalistic private property, which rests on exploitation of the nominally free labour of others, i.e., on wage labour.

As soon as this process of transformation has sufficiently decomposed the old society from top to bottom, as soon as the labourers are turned into proletarians, their means of labour into capital, as soon as the capitalist mode of production stands on its own feet, then the further socialisation of labour and further transformation of the land and other means of production into socially exploited and, therefore, common means of production, as well as the further expropriation of private proprietors, takes a new form. That which is now to be expropriated is no longer the labourer working for himself, but the capitalist exploiting many labourers. This expropriation is accomplished by the action of the immanent laws of capitalistic production itself, by the centralisation of capital. One capitalist always kills many. Hand in hand with this centralisation, or this expropriation of many capitalists by few, develop, on an ever-extending scale, the co-operative form of the labour process, the conscious technical application of science, the methodical cultivation of the soil, the transformation of the instruments of labour into instruments of labour only usable in common, the economising of all means of production by their use as the means of production combined, socialised labour, the entanglement of all peoples in the net of the world market, and with this, the international character of the capitalistic regime. Along with the constantly diminishing number of the magnates of capital, who usurp and monopolise all advantages of this process of transformation, grows the mass of misery, oppression, slavery, degradation, exploitation; but with this too grows the revolt of the working class, a class always increasing in numbers, and disciplined, united, organised by the very mechanism of the process of capitalist production itself. The monopoly of capital becomes a fetter upon the mode of production, which has sprung up and flourished along with, and under it. Centralisation of the means of production and socialisation of labour at last reach a point where they become incompatible with their capitalist integument. This integument is burst asunder. The knell of capitalist private property sounds. The expropriators are expropriated.

The capitalist mode of appropriation, the result of the capitalist mode of production, produces capitalist private property. This is the first negation of individual private property, as founded on the labour of the proprietor. But capitalist production begets, with the inexorability of a law of Nature, its own negation. It is the negation of negation. This does not re-establish private property for the producer, but gives him individual property based on the acquisitions of the capitalist era: i.e., on co-operation and the possession in common of the land and of the means of production.

The transformation of scattered private property, arising from individual labour, into capitalist private property is, naturally, a process, incomparably more protracted, violent, and difficult, than the transformation of capitalistic private property, already practically resting on socialised production, into socialised property. In the former case, we had the expropriation of the mass of the people by a few usurpers; in the latter, we have the expropriation of a few usurpers by the mass of the people.

7 Classes

Karl Marx

The owners merely of labour power, owners of capital, and land-owners, whose respective sources of income are wages, profit and ground rent, in other words, wage labourers, capitalists and landowners, constitute then three big classes of modern society based upon the capitalist mode of production.

In England, modern society is indisputably most highly and classically developed in economic structure. Nevertheless, even here the stratification of classes does not appear in its pure form. Middle and intermediate strata even here obliterate lines of demarcation everywhere (although incomparably less in rural districts than in the cities). However, this is immaterial for our analysis. We have seen that the continual tendency and law of development of the capitalist mode of production is more and more to divorce the means of production from labour, and more and more to concentrate the scattered means of production into large groups, thereby transforming labour into wage labour and the means of production into capital. And to this tendency, on the other hand, corresponds the independent separation of landed property from capital and labour, or the transformation of all landed property into the form of landed property corresponding to the capitalist mode of production.

The first question to be answered is this: What constitutes a class? – and the reply to this follows naturally from the reply to another question, namely: What makes wage labourers, capitalists and landlords constitute the three great social classes?

At first glance – the identity of revenues and sources of revenue. There are three great social groups whose members, the individuals forming them, live on wages, profit and ground rent respectively, on the realisation of their labour power, their capital, and their landed property.

However, from this standpoint, physicians and officials, e.g., would also constitute two classes, for they belong to two distinct social groups, the members of each of these groups receiving their revenue from one and the same source. The same would also be true of the infinite fragmentation of interest and rank into which the division of social labour splits labourers as well as capitalists and landlords – the latter, e.g., into owners of vineyards, farm owners, owners of forests, mine owners and owners of fisheries.

//Here the manuscript breaks off.//

C: HISTORY AND CLASS STRUGGLE

8 Manifesto of the Communist Party

Karl Marx and Friedrich Engels

A spectre is haunting Europe – the spectre of Communism. All the Powers of old Europe have entered into a holy alliance to exorcise this spectre: Pope and Czar, Metternich and Guizot, French Radicals and German police-spies.

Where is the party in opposition that has not been decried as Communistic by its opponents in power? Where the Opposition that has not hurled back the branding reproach of Communism, against the more advanced opposition parties, as well as against its reactionary adversaries?

Two things result from this fact:

I. Communism is already acknowledged by all European Powers to be itself a Power.

II. It is high time that Communists should openly, in the face of the whole world, publish their views, their aims, their tendencies, and meet this nursery tale of the Spectre of Communism with a Manifesto of the party itself.

To this end, Communists of various nationalities have assembled in London, and sketched the following Manifesto, to be published in the English, French, German, Italian, Flemish and Danish languages.

I
Bourgeois and Proletarians[1]

The history of all hitherto existing society is the history of class struggles.

Freeman and slave, patrician and plebeian, lord and serf, guild-master and journeyman, in a word, oppressor and oppressed, stood in constant opposition to one another, carried on an uninterrupted, now hidden, now open fight, a fight that

---

[1] By bourgeoisie is meant the class of modern Capitalists, owners of the means of social production and employers of wage-labour. By proletariat, the class of modern wage-labourers who, having no means of production of their own, are reduced to selling their labour-power in order to live. [*Note by Engels to the English edition of 1888.*]

each time ended, either in a revolutionary re-constitution of society at large, or in the common ruin of the contending classes.

In the earlier epochs of history, we find almost everywhere a complicated arrangement of society into various orders, a manifold gradation of social rank. In ancient Rome we have patricians, knights, plebeians, slaves; in the Middle Ages, feudal lords, vassals, guild-masters, journeymen, apprentices, serfs; in almost all of these classes, again, subordinate gradations.

The modern bourgeois society that has sprouted from the ruins of feudal society has not done away with class antagonisms. It has but established new classes, new conditions of oppression, new forms of struggle in place of the old ones.

Our epoch, the epoch of the bourgeoisie, possesses, however, this distinctive feature: it has simplified the class antagonisms. Society as a whole is more and more splitting up into two great hostile camps, into two great classes directly facing each other: Bourgeoisie and Proletariat.

From the serfs of the Middle Ages sprang the chartered burghers of the earliest towns. From these burgesses the first elements of the bourgeoisie were developed.

The discovery of America, the rounding of the Cape, opened up fresh ground for the rising bourgeoisie. The East-Indian and Chinese markets, the colonisation of America, trade with the colonies, the increase in the means of exchange and in commodities generally, gave to commerce, to navigation, to industry, an impulse never before known, and thereby, to the revolutionary element in the tottering feudal society, a rapid development.

The feudal system of industry, under which industrial production was monopolised by closed guilds, now no longer sufficed for the growing wants of the new markets. The manufacturing system took its place. The guild-masters were pushed on one side by the manufacturing middle class; division of labour between the different corporate guilds vanished in the face of division of labour in each single workshop.

Meantime the markets kept ever growing, the demand ever rising. Even manufacture no longer sufficed. Thereupon, steam and machinery revolutionised industrial production. The place of manufacture was taken by the giant, Modern Industry, the place of the industrial middle class, by industrial millionaires, the leaders of whole industrial armies, the modern bourgeois.

Modern industry has established the world market, for which the discovery of America paved the way. This market has given an immense development to commerce, to navigation, to communication by land. This development has, in its turn, reacted on the extension of industry; and in proportion as industry, commerce, navigation, railways extended, in the same proportion the bourgeoisie developed, increased its capital, and pushed into the background every class handed down from the Middle Ages.

We see, therefore, how the modern bourgeoisie is itself the product of a long course of development, of a series of revolutions in the modes of production and of exchange.

Each step in the development of the bourgeoisie was accompanied by a corresponding political advance of that class. An oppressed class under the sway of the feudal nobility, an armed and self-governing association in the medieval commune;[2] here independent urban republic (as in Italy and Germany), there taxable "third estate" of the monarchy (as in France), afterwards, in the period of manufacture proper, serving either the semi-feudal or the absolute monarchy as a counterpoise against the nobility, and, in fact, cornerstone of the great monarchies in general, the bourgeoisie has at last, since the establishment of Modern Industry and of the world market, conquered for itself, in the modern representative State, exclusive political sway. The executive of the modern State is but a committee for managing the common affairs of the whole bourgeoisie.

The bourgeoisie, historically, has played a most revolutionary part.

The bourgeoisie, wherever it has got the upper hand, has put an end to all feudal, patriarchal, idyllic relations. It has pitilessly torn asunder the motley feudal ties that bound man to his "natural superiors", and has left remaining no other nexus between man and man than naked self-interest, than callous "cash payment". It has drowned the most heavenly ecstasies of religious fervour, of chivalrous enthusiasm, of philistine sentimentalism, in the icy water of egotistical calculation. It has resolved personal worth into exchange value, and in place of the numberless indefeasible chartered freedoms, has set up that single, unconscionable freedom – Free Trade. In one word, for exploitation, veiled by religious and political illusions, it has substituted naked, shameless, direct, brutal exploitation.

The bourgeoisie has stripped of its halo every occupation hitherto honoured and looked up to with reverent awe. It has converted the physician, the lawyer, the priest, the poet, the man of science, into its paid wage-labourers.

The bourgeoisie has torn away from the family its sentimental veil, and has reduced the family relation to a mere money relation.

The bourgeoisie has disclosed how it came to pass that the brutal display of vigour in the Middle Ages, which Reactionists so much admire, found its fitting complement in the most slothful indolence. It has been the first to show what man's activity can bring about. It has accomplished wonders for surpassing Egyptian pyramids, Roman aqueducts, and Gothic cathedrals; it has conducted expeditions that put in the shade all former Exoduses of nations and crusades.

The bourgeoisie cannot exist without constantly revolutionising the instruments of production, and thereby the relations of production, and with them the whole relations of society. Conservation of the old modes of production in unaltered form, was, on the contrary, the first condition of existence for all earlier industrial classes. Constant revolutionising of production, uninterrupted disturbance of all social conditions, everlasting uncertainty and agitation distinguish the bourgeois epoch from all earlier ones. All fixed, fast-frozen relations, with their train of ancient and venerable prejudices and opinions, are swept away, all new-formed ones become antiquated before they can ossify. All that is solid melts into air, all that is holy is profaned, and man is at last compelled to face with sober senses, his real conditions of life, and his relations with his kind.

The need of a constantly expanding market for its products chases the bourgeoi-

---

[2] This was the name given their urban communities by the townsmen of Italy and France, after they had purchased or wrested their initial rights of self-government from their feudal lords. [*Note by Engels to the German edition of 1890.*]

sie over the whole surface of the globe. It must nestle everywhere, settle everywhere, establish connexions everywhere.

The bourgeoisie has through its exploitation of the world market given a cosmopolitan character to production and consumption in every country. To the great chagrin of Reactionists, it has drawn from under the feet of industry the national ground on which it stood. All old-established national industries have been destroyed or are daily being destroyed. They are dislodged by new industries, whose introduction becomes a life and death question for all civilised nations, by industries that no longer work up indigenous raw material, but raw material drawn from the remotest zones; industries whose products are consumed, not only at home, but in every quarter of the globe. In place of the old wants, satisfied by the productions of the country, we find new wants, requiring for their satisfaction the products of distant lands and climes. In place of the old local and national seclusion and self-sufficiency, we have intercourse in every direction, universal inter-dependence of nations. And as in material, so also in intellectual production. The intellectual creations of individual nations become common property. National one-sidedness and narrow-mindedness become more and more impossible, and from the numerous national and local literatures, there arises a world literature.

The bourgeoisie, by the rapid improvements of all instruments of production, by the immensely facilitated means of communication, draws all, even the most barbarian, nations into civilisation. The cheap prices of its commodities are the heavy artillery with which it batters down all Chinese walls, with which it forces the barbarians' intensely obstinate hatred of foreigners to capitulate. It compels all nations, on pain of extinction, to adopt the bourgeois mode of production; it compels them to introduce what it calls civilisation into their midst, i.e., to become bourgeois themselves. In one word, it creates a world after its own image.

The bourgeoisie has subjected the country to the rule of the towns. It has created enormous cities, has greatly increased the urban population as compared with the rural, and has thus rescued a considerable part of the population from the idiocy of rural life. Just as it has made the country dependent on the towns, so it has made barbarian and semi-barbarian countries dependent on the civilised ones, nations of peasants on nations of bourgeois, the East on the West.

The bourgeoisie keeps more and more doing away with the scattered state of the population, of the means of production, and of property. It has agglomerated population, centralised means of production, and has concentrated property in a few hands. The necessary consequence of this was political centralisation. Independent, or but loosely connected provinces with separate interests, laws, governments and systems of taxation, become lumped together into one nation, with one government, one code of laws, one national class-interest, one frontier and one customs-tariff.

The bourgeoisie, during its rule of scarce one hundred years, has created more massive and more colossal productive forces than have all preceding generations together. Subjection of Nature's forces to man, machinery, application of chemistry to industry and agriculture, steam-navigation, railways, electric telegraphs, clearing of whole continents for cultivation, canalisation of rivers, whole populations conjured out of the ground – what earlier century had even a presentiment that such productive forces slumbered in the lap of social labour?

We see then: the means of production and of exchange, on whose foundation the bourgeoisie built itself up, were generated in feudal society. At a certain stage in the development of these means of production and of exchange, the conditions under which feudal society produced and exchanged, the feudal organisation of agriculture and manufacturing industry, in one word, the feudal relations of property became no longer compatible with the already developed productive forces; they became so many fetters. They had to be burst asunder; they were burst asunder.

Into their place stepped free competition, accompanied by a social and political constitution adapted to it, and by the economical and political sway of the bourgeois class.

A similar movement is going on before our own eyes. Modern bourgeois society with its relations of production, of exchange and of property, a society that has conjured up such gigantic means of production and of exchange, is like the sorcerer, who is no longer able to control the powers of the nether world whom he has called up by his spells. For many a decade past the history of industry and commerce is but the history of the revolt of modern productive forces against modern conditions of production, against the property relations that are the conditions for the existence of the bourgeoisie and of its rule. It is enough to mention the commercial crises that by their periodical return put on its trial, each time more threateningly, the existence of the entire bourgeois society. In these crises a great part not only of the existing products, but also of the previously created productive forces, are periodically destroyed. In these crises there breaks out an epidemic that, in all earlier epochs, would have seemed an absurdity – the epidemic of over-production. Society suddenly finds itself put back into a state of momentary barbarism; it appears as if a famine, a universal war of devastation had cut off the supply of every means of subsistence; industry and commerce seem to be destroyed; and why? Because there is too much civilisation, too much means of subsistence, too much industry, too much commerce. The productive forces at the disposal of society no longer tend to further the development of the conditions of bourgeois property; on the contrary, they have become too powerful for these conditions, by which they are fettered, and so soon as they overcome these fetters, they bring disorder into the whole of bourgeois society, endanger the existence of bourgeois property. The conditions of bourgeois society are too narrow to comprise the wealth created by them. And how does the bourgeoisie get over these crises? On the one hand by enforced destruction of a mass of productive forces; on the other, by the conquest of new markets, and by the more thorough exploitation of the old ones. That is to say, by paving the way for more extensive and more destructive crises, and by diminishing the means whereby crises are prevented.

The weapons with which the bourgeoisie felled feudalism to the ground are now turned against the bourgeoisie itself.

But not only has the bourgeoisie forged the weapons that bring death to itself; it has also called into existence the men who are to wield those weapons – the modern working class – the proletarians.

In proportion as the bourgeoisie, *i.e.*, capital, is developed, in the same proportion is the proletariat, the modern working class, developed – a class of labourers, who live only so long as they find work, and who find work only so long as their labour increases capital. These labourers, who must sell themselves piecemeal, are a commodity, like every other article of commerce, and are consequently exposed to all the vicissitudes of competition, to all the fluctuations of the market.

Owing to the extensive use of machinery and to division of labour, the work of the proletarians has lost all individual character, and, consequently, all charm for the workman. He becomes an appendage of the machine, and it is only the most simple, most monotonous, and most easily acquired knack, that is required of him. Hence, the cost of production of a workman is restricted, almost entirely, to the means of subsistence that he requires for his maintenance, and for the propagation of his race. But the price of a commodity, and therefore also of labour, is equal to its cost of production. In proportion, therefore, as the repulsiveness of the work increases, the wage decreases. Nay more, in proportion as the use of machinery and division of labour increases, in the same proportion the burden of toil also increases, whether by prolongation of the working hours, by increase of the work exacted in a given time or by increased speed of the machinery, etc.

Modern industry has converted the little workshop of the patriarchal master into the great factory of the industrial capitalist. Masses of labourers, crowded into the factory, are organised like soldiers. As privates of the industrial army they are placed under the command of a perfect hierarchy of officers and sergeants. Not only are they slaves of the bourgeois class, and of the bourgeois State; they are daily and hourly enslaved by the machine, by the overlooker, and, above all, by the individual bourgeois manufacturer himself. The more openly this despotism proclaims gain to be its end and aim, the more petty, the more hateful and the more embittering it is.

The less the skill and exertion of strength implied in manual labour, in other words, the more modern industry becomes developed, the more is the labour of men superseded by that of women. Differences of age and sex have no longer any distinctive social validity for the working class. All are instruments of labour, more or less expensive to use, according to their age and sex.

No sooner is the exploitation of the labourer by the manufacturer, so far, at an end, and he receives his wages in cash, than he is set upon by the other portions of the bourgeoisie, the landlord, the shopkeeper, the pawnbroker, etc.

The lower strata of the middle class – the small tradespeople, shopkeepers, and retired tradesmen generally, the handicraftsmen and peasants – all these sink gradually into the proletariat, partly because their diminutive capital does not suffice for the scale on which Modern Industry is carried on, and is swamped in the competition with the large capitalists, partly because their specialised skill is rendered worthless by new methods of production. Thus the proletariat is recruited from all classes of the population.

The proletariat goes through various stages of development. With its birth begins its struggle with the bourgeoisie. At first the contest is carried on by individual labourers, then by the workpeople of a factory, then by the operatives of one trade, in one locality, against the individual bourgeois who directly exploits them. They direct their attacks not against the bourgeois conditions of production, but against the instruments of production themselves, they destroy imported wares that compete with their labour, they smash to pieces machinery, they set factories ablaze, they seek to restore by force the vanished status of the workman of the Middle Ages.

At this stage the labourers still form an incoherent mass scattered over the whole country, and broken up by their mutual competition. If anywhere they unite to form more compact bodies, this is not yet the consequence of their own active union, but of the union of the bourgeoisie, which class, in order to attain its own political ends, is compelled to set the whole proletariat in motion, and is moreover yet, for a time, able to do so. At this stage, therefore, the proletarians do not fight their enemies, but the enemies of their enemies, the remnants of absolute monarchy, the landowners, the non-industrial bourgeois, the petty bourgeoisie. Thus the whole historical movement is concentrated in the hands of the bourgeoisie; every victory so obtained is a victory for the bourgeoisie.

But with the development of industry the proletariat not only increases in number; it becomes concentrated in greater masses, its strength grows, and it feels that strength more. The various interests and conditions of life within the ranks of the proletariat are more and more equalised, in proportion as machinery obliterates all distinctions of labour, and nearly everywhere reduces wages to the same low level. The growing competition among the bourgeois, and the resulting commercial crises, make the wages of the workers ever more fluctuating. The unceasing improvement of machinery, ever more rapidly developing, makes their livelihood more and more precarious; the collisions between individual workmen and individual bourgeois take more and more the character of collisions between two classes. Thereupon the workers begin to form combinations (Trades' Unions) against the bourgeois; they club together in order to keep up the rate of wages; they found permanent associations in order to make provision beforehand for these occasional revolts. Here and there the contest breaks out into riots.

Now and then the workers are victorious, but only for a time. The real fruit of their battles lies, not in the immediate result, but in the ever-expanding union of the workers. This union is helped on by the improved means of communication that are created by modern industry and that place the workers of different localities in contact with one another. It was just this contact that was needed to centralise the numerous local struggles, all of the same character, into one national struggle between classes. But every class struggle is a political struggle. And that union, to attain which the burghers of the Middle Ages, with their miserable highways, required centuries, the modern proletarians, thanks to railways, achieve in a few years.

This organisation of the proletarians into a class, and consequently into a political party, is continually being upset again by the competition between the workers themselves. But it ever rises up again, stronger, firmer, mightier. It compels legislative recognition of particular interests of the workers, by taking advantage of the divisions among the bourgeoisie itself. Thus the ten-hours' bill in England was carried.

Altogether collisions between the classes of the old society further, in many ways, the course of development of the proletariat. The bourgeoisie finds itself involved in a constant battle. At first with the aristocracy; later on, with those portions of the bourgeoisie itself, whose interests have become antagonistic to the progress of industry; at all times, with the bourgeoisie of foreign countries. In all these battles it sees itself compelled to appeal to the proletariat, to ask for its help, and thus, to drag it into the political arena. The bourgeoisie itself, therefore, supplies the proletariat with its own elements of political and general education, in other words, it furnishes the proletariat with weapons for fighting the bourgeoisie.

Further, as we have already seen, entire sections of the ruling classes are, by the advance of industry, precipitated into the proletariat, or are at least threatened in their conditions of existence. These also supply the proletariat with fresh elements of enlightenment and progress.

Finally, in times when the class struggle nears the decisive hour, the process of dissolution going on within the ruling class, in fact within the whole range of old society, assumes such a violent, glaring character, that a small section of the ruling class cuts itself adrift, and joins the revolutionary class, the class that holds the future in its hands. Just as, therefore, at an earlier period, a section of the nobility went over to the bourgeoisie, so now a portion of the bourgeoisie goes over to the proletariat, and in particular, a portion of the bourgeois ideologists, who have raised themselves to the level of comprehending theoretically the historical movement as a whole.

Of all the classes that stand face to face with the bourgeoisie today, the proletariat alone is a really revolutionary class. The other classes decay and finally disappear in the face of Modern Industry; the proletariat is its special and essential product.

The lower middle class, the small manufacturer, the shopkeeper, the artisan, the peasant, all these fight against the bourgeoisie, to save from extinction their existence as fractions of the middle class. They are therefore not revolutionary, but conservative. Nay more, they are reactionary, for they try to roll back the wheel of history. If by chance they are revolutionary, they are so only in view of their impending transfer into the proletariat, they thus defend not their present, but their future interests, they desert their own standpoint to place themselves at that of the proletariat.

The "dangerous class", the social scum, that passively rotting mass thrown off by the lowest layers of old society may, here and there, be swept into the movement by a proletarian revolution; its conditions of life, however, prepare it far more for the part of a bribed tool of reactionary intrigue.

In the conditions of the proletariat, those of old society at large are already virtually swamped. The proletarian is without property; his relation to his wife and children has no longer anything in common with the bourgeois family relations; modern industrial labour, modern subjection to capital, the same in England as in France, in America as in Germany, has stripped him of every trace of national character. Law, morality, religion, are to him so many bourgeois prejudices, behind which lurk in ambush just as many bourgeois interests.

All the preceding classes that got the upper hand, sought to fortify their already acquired status by subjecting society at large to their conditions of appropriation. The proletarians cannot become masters of the productive forces of society, except by abolishing their own previous mode of appropriation, and thereby also every other previous mode of appropriation. They have nothing of their own to secure and to fortify; their mission is to destroy all previous securities for, and insurances of, individual property.

All previous historical movements were movements of minorities, or in the interest of minorities. The proletarian movement is the self-conscious, independent movement of the immense majority, in the interest of the immense majority. The proletariat, the lowest stratum of our present society, cannot stir, cannot raise itself up, without the whole superincumbent strata of official society being sprung into the air.

Though not in substance, yet in form, the struggle of the proletariat with the bourgeoisie is at first a national struggle. The proletariat of each country must, of course, first of all settle matters with its own bourgeoisie.

In depicting the most general phases of the development of the proletariat, we traced the more or less veiled civil war, raging within existing society, up to the point where that war breaks out into open revolution, and where the violent overthrow of the bourgeoisie lays the foundation for the sway of the proletariat.

Hitherto, every form of society has been based, as we have already seen, on the antagonism of oppressing and oppressed classes. But in order to oppress a class, certain conditions must be assured to it under which it can, at least, continue its slavish existence. The serf, in the period of serfdom, raised himself to membership in the commune, just as the petty bourgeois, under the yoke of feudal absolutism, managed to develop into a bourgeois. The modern labourer, on the contrary, instead of rising with the progress of industry, sinks deeper and deeper below the conditions of existence of his own class. He becomes a pauper, and pauperism develops more rapidly than population and wealth. And here it becomes evident, that the bourgeoisie is unfit any longer to be the ruling class in society, and to impose its conditions of existence upon society as an over-riding law. It is unfit to rule because it is incompetent to assure an existence to its slave within his slavery, because it cannot help letting him sink into such a state, that it has to feed him, instead of being fed by him. Society can no longer live under this bourgeoisie, in other words, its existence is no longer compatible with society.

The essential condition for the existence, and for the sway of the bourgeois class, is the formation and augmentation of capital; the condition for capital is wage-labour. Wage-labour rests exclusively on competition between the labourers. The advance of industry, whose involuntary promoter is the bourgeoisie, replaces the isolation of the labourers, due to competition, by their revolutionary combination, due to association. The development of Modern Industry, therefore, cuts from under its feet the very foundation on which the bourgeoisie produces and appropriates products. What the bourgeoisie, therefore, produces, above all, is its own grave-diggers. Its fall and the victory of the proletariat are equally inevitable.

II
Proletarians and Communists

In what relation do the Communists stand to the proletarians as a whole?

The Communists do not form a separate party opposed to other working-class parties.

They have no interests separate and apart from those of the proletariat as a whole.

They do not set up any sectarian principles of their own, by which to shape and mould the proletarian movement.

The Communists are distinguished from the other working-class parties by this only: 1. In the national struggles of the proletarians of the different countries, they point out and bring to the front the common interests of the entire proletariat, independently of all nationality. 2. In the various stages of development which the struggle of the working class against the bourgeoisie has to pass through, they always and everywhere represent the interests of the movement as a whole.

The Communists, therefore, are on the one hand, practically, the most advanced and resolute section of the working-class parties of every country, that section which pushes forward all others; on the other hand, theoretically, they have over the great mass of the proletariat the advantage of clearly understanding the line of march, the conditions, and the ultimate general results of the proletarian movement.

The immediate aim of the Communists is the same as that of all the other proletarian parties: formation of the proletariat into a class, overthrow of the bourgeois supremacy, conquest of political power by the proletariat.

The theoretical conclusions of the Communists are in no way based on ideas or principles that have been invented, or discovered by this or that would-be universal reformer.

They merely express, in general terms, actual relations springing from an existing class struggle, from a historical movement going on under our very eyes. The abolition of existing property relations is not at all a distinctive feature of Communism.

All property relations in the past have continually been subject to historical change consequent upon the change in historical conditions.

The French Revolution, for example, abolished feudal property in favour of bourgeois property.

The distinguishing feature of Communism is not the abolition of property generally, but the abolition of bourgeois property. But modern bourgeois private property is the final and most complete expression of the system of producing and appropriating products, that is based on class antagonisms, on the exploitation of the many by the few.

In this sense, the theory of the Communists may be summed up in the single sentence: Abolition of private property.

We Communists have been reproached with the desire of abolishing the right of personally acquiring property as the fruit of a man's own labour, which property is alleged to be the groundwork of all personal freedom, activity and independence.

Hard-won, self-acquired, self-earned property! Do you mean the property of the petty artisan and of the small peasant, a form of property that preceded the bourgeois form? There is no need to abolish that; the development of industry has to a great extent already destroyed it, and is still destroying it daily.

Or do you mean modern bourgeois private property?

But does wage-labour create any property for the labourer? Not a bit. It creates capital. i.e., that kind of property which exploits wage-labour, and which cannot increase except upon condition of begetting a new supply of wage-labour for fresh exploitation. Property, in its present form, is based on the antagonism of capital and wage-labour. Let us examine both sides of this antagonism.

To be a capitalist is to have not only a purely personal, but a social *status* in production. Capital is a collective product, and only by the united action of many members, nay, in the last resort, only by the united action of all members of society, can it be set in motion.

Capital is, therefore, not a personal, it is a social power.

When, therefore, capital is converted into common property, into the property of all members of society, personal property is not thereby transformed into social property. It is only the social character of the property that is changed. It loses its class character.

Let us now take wage-labour.

The average price of wage-labour is the minimum wage, i.e., that quantum of the means of subsistence, which is absolutely requisite to keep the labourer in bare existence as a labourer. What, therefore, the wage-labourer appropriates by means of his labour, merely suffices to prolong and reproduce a bare existence. We by no means intend to abolish this personal appropriation of the products of labour, an appropriation that is made for the maintenance and reproduction of human life, and that leaves no surplus wherewith to command the labour of others. All that we want to do away with is the miserable character of this appropriation, under which the labourer lives merely to increase capital, and is allowed to live only in so far as the interest of the ruling class requires it.

In bourgeois society, living labour is but a means to increase accumulated labour. In Communist society, accumulated labour is but a means to widen, to enrich, to promote the existence of the labourer.

In bourgeois society, therefore, the past dominates the present; in communist society, the present dominates the past. In bourgeois society capital is independent and has individuality, while the living person is dependent and has no individuality.

And the abolition of this state of things is called by the bourgeois, abolition of individuality and freedom! And rightly so. The abolition of bourgeois individuality, bourgeois independence, and bourgeois freedom is undoubtedly aimed at.

By freedom is meant, under the present bourgeois conditions of production, free trade, free selling and buying.

But if selling and buying disappears, free selling and buying disappears also. This talk about free selling and buying, and all the other "brave words" of our bourgeoisie about freedom in general, have a meaning, if any, only in contrast with restricted selling and buying, with the fettered traders of the Middle Ages, but have no meaning when opposed to the Communistic abolition of buying and selling, of the bourgeois conditions of production, and of the bourgeoisie itself.

You are horrified at our intending to do away with private property. But in your existing society, private property is already done away with for nine-tenths of the population; its existence for the few is solely due to its non-existence in the hands of those nine-tenths. You reproach us, therefore, with intending to do away with a form of property, the necessary condition for whose existence is the non-existence of any property for the immense majority of society.

In one word, you reproach us with intending to do away with your property. Precisely so; that is just what we intend.

From the moment when labour can no longer be converted into capital, money, or rent, into a social power capable of being monopolised, i.e., from the moment when individual property can no longer be transformed into bourgeois property, into capital, from that moment, you say, individuality vanishes.

You must, therefore, confess that by "individual" you mean no other person than the bourgeois, than the middle-class owner of property. This person must, indeed, be swept out of the way, and made impossible.

Communism deprives no man of the power to appropriate the products of society; all that it does is to deprive him of the power to subjugate the labour of others by means of such appropriation.

It has been objected that upon the abolition of private property all work will cease, and universal laziness will overtake us.

According to this, bourgeois society ought long ago to have gone to the dogs through sheer idleness; for those of its members who work, acquire nothing, and those who acquire anything, do not work. The whole of this objection is but another expression of the tautology: that there can no longer be any wage-labour when there is no longer any capital.

All objections urged against the Communistic mode of producing and appropriating material products, have, in the same way, been urged against the Communistic modes of producing and appropriating intellectual products. Just as, to the bourgeois, the disppearance of class property is the disappearance of production itself, so the disappearance of class culture is to him identical with the disappearance of all culture.

That culture, the loss of which he laments, is, for the enormous majority, a mere training to act as a machine.

But don't wrangle with us so long as you apply, to our intended abolition of bourgeois property, the standard of your bourgeois notions of freedom, culture, law, &c. Your very ideas are but the outgrowth of the conditions of your bourgeois production and bourgeois property, just as your jurisprudence is but the will of your class made into a law for all, a will, whose essential character and direction are determined by the economical conditions of existence of your class.

The selfish misconception that induces you to transform into eternal laws of nature and of reason, the social forms springing from your present mode of production and form of property – historical relations that rise and disappear in the progress of production – this misconception you share with every ruling class that has preceded you. What you see clearly in the case of ancient property, what you admit in the case of feudal property, you are of course forbidden to admit in the case of your own bourgeois form of property.

Abolition of the family! Even the most radical flare up at this infamous proposal of the Communists.

On what foundation is the present family, the bourgeois family, based? On capital, on private gain. In its completely developed form this family exists only among the bourgeoisie. But this state of things finds its complement in the practical absence of the family among the proletarians, and in public prostitution.

The bourgeois family will vanish as a matter of course when its complement vanishes, and both will vanish with the vanishing of captial.

Do you charge us with wanting to stop the exploitation of children by their parents? To this crime we plead guilty.

But, you will say, we destroy the most hallowed of relations, when we replace home education by social.

And your education! Is not that also social, and determined by the social conditions under which you educate, by the intervention, direct or indirect, of society, by means of schools, &c.? The Communists have not invented the intervention of society in education; they do but seek to alter the character of that intervention, and to rescue education from the influence of the ruling class.

The bourgeois clap-trap about the family and education, about the hallowed co-relation of parent and child, becomes all the more disgusting, the more, by the action of Modern Industry, all family ties among the proletarians are torn asunder, and their children transformed into simple articles of commerce and instruments of labour.

But you Communists would introduce community of women, screams the whole bourgeoisie in chorus.

The bourgeois sees in his wife a mere instrument of production. He hears that the instruments of production are to be exploited in common, and, naturally, can come to no other conclusion than that the lot of being common to all will likewise fall to the women.

He has not even a suspicion that the real point aimed at is to do away with the status of women as mere instruments of production.

For the rest, nothing is more ridiculous than the virtuous indignation of our bourgeois at the community of women which, they pretend, is to be openly and officially established by the Communists. The Communists have no need to introduce community of women; it has existed almost from time immemorial.

Our bourgeois, not content with having the wives and daughters of their proletarians at their disposal, not to speak of common prostitutes, take the greatest pleasure in seducing each other's wives.

Bourgeois marriage is in reality a system of wives in common and thus, at the most, what the Communists might possibly be reproached with, is that they desire to introduce, in substitution for a hypocritically concealed, an openly legalised community of women. For the rest, it is self-evident that the abolition of the present system of production must bring with it the abolition of the community of all women springing from that system, i.e., of prostitution both public and private.

The Communists are further reproached with desiring to abolish countries and nationality.

The working men have no country. We cannot take from them what they have not got. Since the proletariat must first of all acquire political supremacy, must rise to be the leading class of the nation, must constitute itself *the* nation, it is, so far, itself national, though not in the bourgeois sense of the word.

National differences and antagonism between peoples are daily more and more vanishing, owing to the development of the bourgeoisie, to freedom of commerce, to the world market, to uniformity in the mode of production and in the conditions of life corresponding thereto.

The supremacy of the proletariat will cause them to vanish still faster. United action, of the leading civilised countries at least, is one of the first conditions for the emancipation of the proletariat.

In proportion as the exploitation of one individual by another is put an end to, the exploitation of one nation by another will also be put an end to. In proportion as the antagonism between classes within the nation vanishes, the hostility of one nation to another will come to an end.

The charges against communism made from a religious, a philosophical, and, generally, from an idealogical standpoint, are not deserving of serious examination.

Does it require deep intuition to comprehend that man's ideas, views and conceptions, in one word, man's consciousness, changes with every change in the conditions of his material existence, in his social relations and in his social life?

What else does the history of ideas prove, than that intellectual production changes its character in proportion as material production is changed? The ruling ideas of each age have ever been the ideas of its ruling class.

When people speak of ideas that revolutionise society, they do but express the fact, that within the old society, the elements of a new one have been created, and that the dissolution of the old ideas keeps even pace with the dissolution of the old conditions of existence.

When the ancient world was in its last throes, the ancient religions were overcome by Christianity. When Christian ideas succumbed in the 18th century to rationalist ideas, feudal society fought its death battle with the then revolutionary bourgeoisie. The ideas of religious liberty and freedom of conscience merely gave expression to the sway of free competition within the domain of knowledge.

"Undoubtedly," it will be said, "religious, moral, philosophical and juridical ideas have been modified in the course of historical development. But religion, morality, philosophy, political science, and law, constantly survived this change.

"There are, besides, eternal truths, such as Freedom, Justice, etc., that are common to all states of society. But communism abolishes eternal truths, it abolishes all religion and all morality, instead of constituting them on a new basis; it therefore acts in contradiction to all past historical experience."

What does this accusation reduce itself to? The history of all past society has consisted in the development of class antagonisms, antagonisms that assumed different forms at different epochs.

But whatever form they may have taken, one fact is common to all past ages, *viz.*, the exploitation of one part of society by the other. No wonder, then, that the social consciousness of past ages, despite all the multiplicity and variety it displays, moves within certain common forms, or general ideas, which cannot completely vanish except with the total disappearance of class antagonisms.

The Communist revolution is the most radical rupture with traditional property relations; no wonder that its development involves the most radical rupture with traditional ideas.

But let us have done with the bourgeois objections to Communism.

We have seen above, that the first step in the revolution by the working class is to raise the proletariat to the position of ruling class, to win the battle of democracy.

The proletariat will use its political supremacy to wrest, by degrees, all capital from the bourgeoisie, to centralise all instruments of production in the hands of the State, i.e., of the proletariat organised as the ruling class; and to increase the total of productive forces as rapidly as possible.

Of course, in the beginning, this cannot be effected except by means of despotic inroads on the rights of property, and on the conditions of bourgeois production; by means of measures, therefore, which appear economically insufficient and untenable, but which, in the course of the movement, outstrip themselves, necessitate further inroads upon the old social order, and are unavoidable as a means of entirely revolutionising the mode of production.

These measures will of course be different in different countries.

Nevertheless in the most advanced countries, the following will be pretty generally applicable:

1   Abolition of property in land and application of all rents of land to public purposes.
2   A heavy progressive or graduated income tax.
3   Abolition of all right of inheritance.
4   Confiscation of the property of all emigrants and rebels.
5   Centralisation of credit in the hands of the State, by means of a national bank with State capital and an exclusive monopoly.
6   Centralisation of the means of communication and transport in the hands of the State.
7   Extension of factories and instruments of production owned by the State; the bringing into cultivation of waste-lands, and the improvement of the soil generally in accordance with a common plan.
8   Equal liability of all to labour. Establishment of industrial armies, especially for agriculture.
9   Combination of agriculture with manufacturing industries; gradual abolition of the distinction between town and country, by a more equable distribution of the population over the country.
10   Free education for all children in public schools. Abolition of children's factory labour in its present form. Combination of education with industrial production. &c., &c.

When, in the course of development, class distinctions have disappeared, and all production has been concentrated in the hands of a vast association of the whole nation, the public power will lose its political character. Political power, properly so called, is merely the organised power of one class for oppressing another. If the proletariat during its contest with the bourgeoisie is compelled, by the force of circumstances, to organise itself as a class, if, by means of a revolution, it makes itself the ruling class, and, as such, sweeps away by force the old conditions of production, then it will, along with these conditions, have swept away the conditions for the existence of class antagonisms and of classes generally, and will thereby have abolished its own supremacy as a class.

In place of the old bourgeois society, with its classes and class antagonisms, we shall have an association, in which the free development of each is the condition for the free development of all.

9 The Eighteenth Brumaire of Louis Bonaparte

Karl Marx

I

Hegel remarks somewhere that all facts and personages of great importance in world history occur, as it were, twice. He forgot to add: the first time as tragedy, the second as farce. Caussidière for Danton, Louis Blanc for Robespierre, the Montagne of 1848 to 1851 for the Montagne of 1793 to 1795, the Nephew for the Uncle. And the same caricature occurs in the circumstances attending the second edition of the eighteenth Brumaire!

Men make their own history, but they do not make it just as they please; they do not make it under circumstances chosen by themselves, but under circumstances directly encountered, given and transmitted from the past. The tradition of all the dead generations weighs like a nightmare on the brain of the living. And just when they seem engaged in revolutionising themselves and things, in creating something that has never yet existed, precisely in such periods of revolutionary crisis they anxiously conjure up the spirits of the past to their service and borrow from them names, battle-cries and costumes in order to present the new scene of world history in this time-honoured disguise and this borrowed language. Thus Luther donned the mask of the Apostle Paul, the revolution of 1789 to 1814 draped itself alternately as the Roman Republic and the Roman Empire, and the revolution of 1848 knew nothing better to do than to parody, now 1789, now the revolutionary tradition of 1793 to 1795. In like manner a beginner who has learnt a new language always translates it back into his mother tongue, but he has assimilated the spirit of the new language and can freely express himself in it only when he finds his way in it without recalling the old and forgets his native tongue in the use of the new.

Consideration of this world-historical necromancy reveals at once a salient difference. Camille Desmoulins, Danton, Robespierre, Saint-Just, Napoleon, the heroes as well as the parties and the masses of the old French Revolution, performed the task of their time in Roman costume and with Roman phrases, the task of unchaining and setting up modern *bourgeois* society. The first ones knocked the feudal basis to pieces and mowed off the feudal heads which had grown on it. The other created inside France the conditions under which free competition could first be developed, the parcelled landed property exploited and the unchained industrial productive forces of the nation employed; and beyond the French borders he everywhere swept the feudal institutions away, so far as was necessary to furnish bourgeois society in France with a suitable up-to-date environment on the European Continent. The new social formation once established, the antediluvian Colossi disappeared and with them resurrected Romanity – the Brutuses, Gracchi, Publicolas, the tribunes, the senators, and Caesar himself. Bourgeois society in its sober reality had begotten its true interpreters and mouthpieces in the Says, Cousins, Royer-Collards, Benjamin Constants and Guizots; its real commanders sat behind the counter, and the hogheaded Louis XVIII was its political chief. Wholly absorbed in the production of wealth and in peaceful competitive struggle, it no longer comprehended that ghosts from the days of Rome had watched over its cradle. But unheroic as bourgeois society is, it nevertheless took heroism, sacrifice, terror, civil war and battles of peoples to bring it into being. And in the classically austere traditions of the Roman Republic its gladiators found the ideals and the art forms, the self-deceptions that they needed in order to conceal from themselves the bourgeois limitations of the content of their struggles and to maintain their passion on the high plane of great historical tragedy. Similarly, at another stage of development, a century earlier, Cromwell and the English people had borrowed speech, passions and illusions from the Old Testament for their bourgeois revolution. When the real aim had been achieved, when the bourgeois transformation of English society had been accomplished, Locke supplanted Habakkuk.

Thus the resurrection of the dead in those revolutions served the purpose of glorifying the new struggles, not of parodying the old; of magnifying the given task in imagination, not of feeling from its solution in reality; of finding once more the spirit of revolution, not of making its ghost walk about again.

From 1848 to 1851 only the ghost of the old revolution walked about, from Marrast, the *républicain en gants jaunes*,[a] who disguised himself as the old Bailly, down to the adventurer who hides his commonplace repulsive features under the iron death mask of Napoleon. An entire people, which had imagined that by means of a revolution it had imparted to itself an accelerated power of motion, suddenly finds itself set back into a defunct epoch and, in order that no doubt as to the relapse may be possible, the old dates arise again, the old chronology, the old names, the old edicts, which had long become a subject of antiquarian erudition, and the old myrmidons of the law, who had seemed long decayed. The nation feels like that mad Englishman in Bedlam who fancies that he lives in the times of the ancient Pharoahs and daily bemoans the hard labour that he must perform in the Ethiopian mines as a gold digger, immured in this subterranean prison, a dimly burning lamp fastened to his head, the overseer of the slaves behind him with a long whip, and at the exits a confused welter of barbarian mercenaries, who understand neither the forced labourers in the mines nor one another, since they speak no common language. "And all this is expected of me," sighs the mad Englishman, "of me, a freeborn Briton, in order to make gold for the old Pharaohs." "In order to pay the debts of the Bonaparte family," sighs the French nation. The Englishman, so long as he was in his right mind, could not get rid of the fixed idea of making gold. The French, so long as they were engaged in revolution, could not get rid of the memory of Napoleon, as the election of December 10 proved. They hankered to return from the perils of revolution to the fleshpots of Egypt, and December 2, 1851 was the answer. They have not only a caricature of the old Napoleon, they have the old Napoleon himself, caricatured as he must appear in the middle of the nineteenth century.

---

[a] Republican in yellow gloves. – *Ed.*

The social revolution of the nineteenth century cannot draw its poetry from the past, but only from the future. It cannot begin with itself before it has stripped off all superstition about the past. Earlier revolutions required recollections of past world history in order to dull themselves to their own content. In order to arrive at its own content, the revolution of the nineteenth century must let the dead bury their dead.[a] There the words went beyond the content; here the content goes beyond the words.

The February revolution was a surprise attack, a *taking* of the old society *unawares*, and the people proclaimed this unexpected *coup de main* as a deed of historic importance, ushering in the new epoch. On December 2 the February revolution is conjured away by a cardsharper's trick, and what seems overthrown is no longer the monarchy but the liberal concessions that were wrung from it by centuries of struggle. Instead of *society* having conquered a new content for itself, it seems that the *state* only returned to its oldest form, to the shamelessly simple domination of the sabre and the cowl. This is the answer to the *coup de main* of February 1848, given by the *coup de tête*[b] of December 1851. Easy come, easy go. Meanwhile the intervening time has not passed by unused. During the years 1848 to 1851 French society made up, and that by an abbreviated because revolutionary method, for the studies and experiences which, in a regular, so to speak, textbook course of development, would have had to precede the February revolution, if it was to be more than a ruffling of the surface. Society now seems to have fallen back behind its point of departure; it has in truth first to create for itself the revolutionary point of departure, the situation, the relations, the conditions under which alone modern revolution becomes serious.

Bourgeois revolutions, like those of the eighteenth century, storm swiftly from success to success, their dramatic effects outdo each other, men and things seem set in sparkling brilliants, ecstasy is the everyday spirit, but they are short-lived, soon they have attained their zenith, and a long crapulent depression seizes society before it learns soberly to assimilate the results of its storm-and-stress period. On the other hand, proletarian revolutions, like those of the nineteenth century, criticise themselves constantly, interrupt themselves continually in their own course, come back to the apparently accomplished in order to begin it afresh, deride with unmerciful thoroughness the inadequacies, weaknesses and paltrinesses of their first attempts, seem to throw down their adversary only in order that he may draw new strength from the earth and rise again, more gigantic, before them, and recoil again and again from the indefinite prodigiousness of their own aims, until a situation has been created which makes all turning back impossible, and the conditions themselves cry out:

> Hic Rhodus, hic salta!
> Here is the rose, here dance!

For the rest, every fairly competent observer, even if he had not followed the course of French development step by step, must have had a presentiment that an unheard-of fiasco was in store for the revolution. It was enough to hear the self-

---

[a] Cf. Matthew 8:22. – *Ed.*
[b] Rash act. – *Ed.*

complacent howl of victory with which Messieurs the Democrats congratulated each other on the beneficial consequences of the second Sunday in May 1852. In their minds the second Sunday in May 1852 had become a fixed idea, a dogma, like the day on which Christ should reappear and the millennium begin, in the minds of the Chiliasts. As ever, weakness had taken refuge in a belief in miracles, fancied the enemy overcome when it had only conjured him away in imagination, and lost all understanding of the present in a passive glorification of the future in store for it and of the deeds it had *in petto*[a] but which it merely did not want as yet to make public. Those heroes who seek to disprove their proven incapacity by offering each other their sympathy and getting together in a crowd had tied up their bundles, collected their laurel wreaths in advance and were just then engaged in discounting on the exchange market the republics *in partibus*[b] for which they had already providently organised the government personnel with all the calm of their unassuming disposition. December 2 struck them like a thunderbolt from a clear sky, and the peoples that in periods of pusillanimous depression gladly let their inward apprehension be drowned out by the loudest bawlers will have perhaps convinced themselves that the times are past when the cackle of geese could save the Capitol.

The Constitution, the National Assembly, the dynastic parties, the blue and the red republicans, the heroes of Africa, the thunder from the platform, the sheet lightning of the daily press, the entire literature, the political names and the intellectual reputations, the civil law and the penal code, the *liberté, égalité, fraternité* and the second Sunday in May 1852 – all has vanished like a phantasmagoria before the spell of a man whom even his enemies do not make out to be a magician. Universal suffrage seems to have survived only for a moment, in order that with its own hand it may make its last will and testament before the eyes of all the world and declare in the name of the people itself: "All that comes to birth is fit for overthrow, as nothing worth."[c]

It is not enough to say, as the French do, that their nation was taken unawares. A nation and a woman are not forgiven the unguarded hour in which the first adventurer that came along could violate them. The riddle is not solved by such turns of speech, but merely formulated differently. It remains to be explained how a nation of thirty-six million can be surprised and delivered unresisting into captivity by three swindlers.

Let us recapitulate in general outline the phases that the French Revolution went through from February 24, 1848 to December 1851.

Three main periods are unmistakable: *the February period*; May 4, 1848 to May 28, 1849: *the period of the constitution of the republic* or *of the Constituent National Assembly*, May 28, 1849 to December 2, 1851: *the period of the constitutional republic* or *of the Legislative National Assembly*.

The *first period*, from February 24, or the overthrow of Louis Philippe, to May 4, 1848, the meeting of the Constituent Assembly, the *February period* proper, may

---

[a] In reserve. – *Ed.*

[b] *In partibus infidelium* – literally: in parts inhabited by infidels. The words are added to the title of Roman Catholic bishops holding purely nominal dioceses in non-Christian countries. In the figurative sense they mean: "not really existing". – *Ed.*

[c] Goethe, *Faust*, Erster Teil, "Studierzimmer". – *Ed.*

be described as the *prologue* to the revolution. Its character was officially expressed in the fact that the government improvised by it declared itself that it was *provisional* and, like the government, everything that was mooted, attempted or enunciated during this period proclaimed itself to be only *provisional*. Nothing and nobody ventured to lay claim to the right of existence and of real action. All the elements that had prepared or determined the revolution, the dynastic opposition, the republican bourgeoisie, the democratic–republican petty bourgeoisie and the Social-Democratic workers, provisionally found their place in the February *government*.

It could not be otherwise. The February days originally aimed at an electoral reform, by which the circle of the politically privileged among the possessing class itself was to be widened and the exclusive domination of the finance aristocracy overthrown. When it came to the actual conflict, however, when the people mounted the barricades, the National Guard maintained a passive attitude, the army offered no serious resistance and the monarchy ran away, the republic appeared to be a matter of course. Every party construed it in its own way. Having secured it arms in hand, the proletariat impressed its stamp upon it and proclaimed it to be a *social republic*. There was thus indicated the general content of the contradiction to everything that, with the material available, with the degree of education attained by the masses, under the given cirucmstances and relations, could be immediately realised in practice. On the other hand, the claims of all the remaining elements that had collaborated in the February revolution were recognised by the lion's share that they obtained in the government. In no period do we, therefore, find a more confused mixture of high-flown phrases and actual uncertainty and clumsiness, of more enthusiastic striving for innovation and more thorough domination of the old routine, of more apparent harmony of the whole of society and more profound estrangement of its elements. While the Paris proletariat still revelled in the vision of the wide prospects that had opened before it and indulged in earnest discussions on social problems, the old forces of society had grouped themselves, rallied, reflected and found unexpected support in the mass of the nation, the peasants and petty bourgeois, who all at once stormed on to the political stage, after the barriers of the July monarchy had fallen.

The *second period*, from May 4, 1848 to the end of May 1849, is the period of the *constitution*, the *foundation, of the bourgeois republic*. Directly after the February days not only had the dynastic opposition been surprised by the republicans and the republicans by the Socialists, but all France by Paris. The National Assembly, which met on May 4, 1848, had emerged from the national elections and represented the nation. It was a living protest against the aspirations of the February days and was to reduce the results of the revolution to the bourgeois scale. In vain the Paris proletariat, which immediately grasped the character of this National Assembly, attempted on May 15, a few days after it met, forcibly to negate its existence, to dissolve it, to disintegrate again into its constituent parts the organic form in which the proletariat was threatened by the reacting spirit of the nation. As is known, May 15 had no other result save that of removing Blanqui and his comrades, that is, the real leaders of the proletarian party, from the public stage for the entire duration of the cycle we are considering.

The *bourgeois monarchy* of Louis Philippe can be followed only by a *bourgeois republic*, that is to say, whereas a limited section of the bourgeoisie ruled in the name of the king, the whole of the bourgeoisie will now rule on behalf of the people. The demands of the Paris proletariat are utopian nonsense, to which an end must be put. To this declaration of the Constituent National Assembly the Paris proletariat replied with the *June insurrection*, the most colossal event in the history of European civil wars. The bourgeois republic triumphed. On its side stood the finance aristocracy, the industrial bourgeoisie, the middle class, the petty bourgeois, the army, the lumpenproletariat organised as the Mobile Guard, the intellectuals, the clergy and the rural population. On the side of the Paris proletariat stood none but itself. More than 3,000 insurgents were butchered after the victory, and 15,000 were deported without trial. With this defeat the proletariat recedes into the *background* of the revolutionary stage. It attempts to press forward again on every occasion, as soon as the movement appears to make a fresh start, but with ever decreased expenditure of strength and always slighter results. As soon as one of the social strata situated above it gets into revolutionary ferment, the proletariat enters into an alliance with it and so shares all the defeats that the different parties suffer, one after another. But these subsequent blows become the weaker, the greater the surface of society over which they are distributed. The more important leaders of the proletariat in the Assembly and in the press successively fall victim to the courts, and ever more equivocal figures come to head it. In part it throws itself into *doctrinaire experiments, exchange banks and workers' associations, hence into a movement in which it renounces the revolutionising of the old world by means of the latter's own great, combined resources, and seeks, rather, to achieve its salvation behind society's back, in private fashion, within its limited conditions of existence, and hence necessarily suffers shipwreck.* It seems to be unable either to rediscover revolutionary greatness in itself or to win new energy from the connections newly entered into, until *all classes* with which it contended in June themselves lie prostrate beside it. But at least it succumbs with the honours of the great, world-historic struggle; not only France, but all Europe trembles at the June earthquake, while the ensuing defeats of the upper classes are so cheaply bought that they require barefaced exaggeration by the victorious party to be able to pass for events at all, and become the more ignominious the further the defeated party is from the proletarian party.

The defeat of the June insurgents, to be sure, had indeed prepared and levelled the ground on which the bourgeois republic could be founded and built up, but it had shown at the same time that in Europe the questions at issue are other than that of "republic or monarchy". It had revealed that here *bourgeois republic* signifies the unlimited despotism of one class over other classes. It had proved that in countries with an old civilisation, with a developed formation of classes, with modern conditions of production and with an intellectual consciousness in which all traditional ideas have been dissolved by the work of centuries, *the republic* signifies *in general only the political form of the revolutionising of bourgeois society* and not its *conservative form of life*, as, for example, in the United States of North America, where, though classes already exist, they have not yet become fixed, but continually change and interchange their component elements in constant flux, where the modern means of production, instead of coinciding with a stagnant surplus population, rather compensate for the relative deficiency of heads and hands, and where, finally, the feverish, youthful movement of material production, which has to make a new world its own, has left neither time nor opportunity for abolishing the old spirit world.

During the June days all classes and parties had united in the *Party of Order* against the proletarian class as the *Party of Anarchy*, of socialism, of communism. They had "saved" society from "*the enemies of society*". They had given out the watch-words of the old society, "*property, family, religion, order*", to their army as passwords and had proclaimed to the counter-revolutionary crusaders: "By this sign thou shalt conquer!" From this moment, as soon as one of the numerous parties which had gathered under this sign against the June insurgents seeks to hold the revolutionary battlefield in its own class interest, it goes down before the cry: "property, family, religion, order." Society is saved just as often as the circle of its rulers contracts, as a more exclusive interest is maintained against a wider one. Every demand of the simplest bourgeois financial reform, of the most ordinary liberalism, of the most formal republicanism, of the most shallow democracy, is simultaneously castigated as an "attempt on society" and stigmatised as "social-ism". And, finally, the high priests of "religion and order" themselves are driven with kicks from their Pythian tripods, hauled out of their beds in the darkness of night, put in prison-vans, thrown into dungeons or sent into exile; their temple is razed to the ground, their mouths are sealed, their pens broken, their law torn to pieces in the name of religion, of property, of the family, of order. Bourgeois fanatics for order are shot down on their balconies by mobs of drunken soldiers, their domestic sanctuaries profaned, their houses bombarded for amusement – in the name of property, of the family, of religion and of order. Finally, the scum of bourgeois society forms the *holy phalanx of order* and the hero Krapülinski[a] installs himself in the Tuileries as the "*saviour of society*". . . .

As the executive authority which has made itself an independent power, Bona-parte feels it to be his mission to safeguard "bourgeois order". But the strength of this bourgeois order lies in the middle class. He looks on himself, therefore, as the representative of the middle class and issues decrees in this sense. Nevertheless, he is somebody solely due to the fact that he has broken the political power of this middle class and daily breaks it anew. Consequently, he looks on himself as the adversary of the political and literary power of the middle class. But by protecting its material power, he generates its political power anew. The cause must accord-ingly be kept alive; but the effect, where it manifests itself, must be done away with. But this cannot pass off without slight confusions of cause and effect, since in their interaction both lose their distinguishing features. New decrees that obliterate the border line. As against the bourgeoisie, Bonaparte looks on himself, at the same time, as the representative of the peasants and of the people in general, who wants to make the lower classes of the people happy within the framework of bourgeois society. New decrees that cheat the "true Socialists" of their statecraft in advance. But, above all, Bonaparte looks on himself as the chief of the Society of December 10, as the representative of the lumpenproletariat, to which he himself, his entourage, his government and his army belong, and whose price consideration is

---

[a] *Krapülinski* – one of the main characters in Heine's poem "Zwei Ritter" (*Romanzero*). Here Marx alludes to Louis Bonaparte. – *Ed.*

to benefit itself and draw California lottery prizes from the state treasury. And he vindicates his position as chief of the Society of December 10 with decrees, without decrees and despite decrees.

This contradictory task of the man explains the contradictions of his government, the confused, blind to-ing and fro-ing which seeks now to win, now to humiliate first one class and then another and arrays all of them uniformly against him, whose practical uncertainty forms a highly comical contrast to the imperious, categorical style of the government decrees, a style which is faithfully copied from the uncle.

Industry and trade, hence the business affairs of the middle class, are to prosper in hothouse fashion under the strong government. The grant of innumerable railway concessions. But the Bonapartist lumpenproletariat is to enrich itself. The initiated play *tripotage*[a] on the *bourse* with the railway concessions. But no capital is forthcoming for the railways. Obligation of the Bank to make advances on railway shares. But, at the same time, the Bank is to be exploited for personal ends and therefore must be cajoled. Release of the Bank from the obligation to publish its report weekly. Leonine agreement of the Bank with the government. The people are to be given employment. Initiation of public works. But the public works increase the obligations of the people in respect of taxes. Hence reduction of the taxes by an onslaught on the *rentiers*, by conversion of the five per cent bonds to four-and-a-half per cent. But, once more the middle class must receive a *douceur*.[b] Therefore doubling of the wine tax for the people, who buy it *en détail*,[c] and halving of the wine tax for the middle class, who drink it *en gros*.[d] Dissolution of the actual workers' associations, but promises of miracles of association in the future. The peasants are to be helped. Mortgage banks that expedite their getting into debt and accelerate the concentration of property. But these banks are to be used to make money out of the confiscated estates of the House of Orleans. No capitalist wants to agree to this condition, which is not in the decree, and the mortgage bank remains a mere decree, etc., etc.

Bonapart would like to appear as the patriarchal benefactor of all classes. But he cannot give to one class without taking from another. Just as at the time of the Fronde it was said of the Duke of Guise that he was the most *obligeant* man in France because he had turned all his estates into his partisans' obligations to him, so Bonaparte would fain be the most *obligeant* man in France and turn all the property, all the labour of France into a personal obligation to himself. He would like to steal the whole of France in order to be able to make a present of her to France or, rather, in order to be able to buy France anew with French money, for as the chief of the Society of December 10 he must needs buy what ought to belong to him. And all the state institutions, the Senate, the Council of State, the legislative body, the Legion of Honour, the soldiers' medals, the wash-houses, the public works, the railways, the *état-major*[e] of the National guard excluding privates, and the confiscated estates of the House of Orleans – all become parts of the institution

---

[a] Hanky-panky. – *Ed.*
[b] Sop. – *Ed.*
[c] Retail. – *Ed.*
[d] Wholesale. – *Ed.*
[e] General Staff. – *Ed.*

of purchase. Every place in the army and in the government machine becomes a means of purchase. But the most important feature of this process, whereby France is taken in order to be given back, is the percentages that find their way into the pockets of the head and the members of the Society of December 10 during the transaction. The witticism with which Countess L.,[a] the mistress of M. de Morny, characterised the confiscation of the Orleans estates: "*C'est le premier vol* de l'aigle*"[b] is applicable to every flight of this *eagle*, which is more like a *raven*. He himself and his adherents call out to one another daily like that Italian Carthusian admonishing the miser who, with boastful display, counted up the goods on which he could yet live for years to come: "*Tu fai conto sopra i beni, bisogna prima far il conto sopra gli anni.*"** Lest they make a mistake in the years, they count the minutes. A gang of shady characters push their way forward to the court, into the ministries, to the head of the administration and the army, a crowd of the best of whom it must be said that no one knows whence he comes, a noisy, disreputable, rapacious bohème that crawls into braided coats with the same grotesque dignity as the high dignitaries of Soulouque. One can visualise clearly this upper stratum of the Society of December 10, if one reflects that *Véron-Crevel**** is its preacher of morals and *Granier de Cassagnac* its thinker. When Guizot, at the time of his ministry, utilised this Granier on a hole-and-corner newspaper against the dynastic opposition, he used to boast of him with the quip: "*C'est le roi des drôles,*" "he is the king of buffoons."[c] One would do wrong to recall the Regency or Louis XV in connection with Louis Bonaparte's court and clique. For "often already, France has experienced a government of *hommes entretenus.*"****[d]

Driven by the contradictory demands of his situation and being at the same time, like a conjurer, under the necessity of keeping the public gaze fixed on himself, as Napoleon's substitute, by springing constant surprises, that is to say, under the necessity of executing a coup d'état *en miniature* every day, Bonaparte throws the entire bourgeois economy into confusion, violates everything that seemed inviolable to the revolution of 1848, makes some tolerant of revolution, others desirous of revolution, and produces actual anarchy in the name of order, while at the same time stripping its halo from the entire state machine, profanes it and makes it at once loathsome and ridiculous. The cult of the Holy Coat of Trier he duplicates in Paris with the cult of the Napoleonic imperial mantle. But when the imperial mantle finally falls on the shoulders of Louis Bonaparte, the bronze statue of Napoleon will crash from the top of the Vendôme Column.

---

* *Vol* means flight and theft.
** "Thou contest thy goods, thou shouldst first count thy years."
*** In this novel *Cousine Bette*, Blazac delineates the thoroughly dissolute Parisian philistine in Crevel, a character based on Dr Véron, owner of the *Constitutionnel*.
**** The words quoted are those of Madame Girardin.

---

[a] Lehon. – *Ed.*
[b] "It is the first flight (theft) of the eagle." – *Ed.*
[c] Quoted in the article by Dupont "Chronique de l'Interieur". *Voix du Proscrit*, No. 8. December 15, 1850. – *Ed.*
[d] *Hommes entretenus*: kept men. The 1852 edition further has: "and Cato, who took his life to be able to associate with heroes in the Elysian Fields! Poor Cato!" – *Ed.*

Part II

The Sociological Theory of Emile Durkheim

Introduction to Part II

Along with Karl Marx and Max Weber, Emile Durkheim (1858–1917) is one of the key classical theorists in sociology. Of the three, Durkheim was the only one to actually hold a chair in the discipline, and he was the author of some of the most programmatic statements about what sociology was and how it should be done. Durkheim's key theoretical contribution lies in his claim that social phenomena are *sui generis* realities that can only be explained by other social facts.

Durkheim's modern legacy is somewhat odd in the sense that his work is now considered central to sociologists of very different theoretical inclinations. Although Durkheim has recently come to be associated with positivism in sociology, his work also addresses important philosophical and cultural questions. Durkheim's theoretical writings have had wide-ranging influence on social anthropology, criminology, and studies of education, religion and social movements. To some degree, Durkheim's reputation suffered due to the reaction against functionalism (see Part VI in this volume), with which Durkheim's name has come to be associated in the English-speaking world. The recent renewal of "neo-functionalist" theory and analysis has brought interested readers again to Durkheim's work.

Durkheim's Life and Intellectual Context

Durkheim was born in Epinal, France in 1858 and grew up in a traditional Jewish family, which was part of the long-established Jewish community of Alsace-Lorraine. His father was the rabbi of the town and in fact, Durkheim's family had a long rabbinical tradition. In keeping with this tradition, Durkheim was expected to devote himself to religious studies. In general, Durkheim and his siblings were brought up in an austere atmosphere, with a strong sense of duty and moral discipline.

Durkheim's early education began at a rabbinical school. However, he soon decided against this course of study and switched to the local school. Durkheim was a serious student, and decided at an early age that he wanted to pursue higher education. After graduation, he moved to Paris in order to prepare for the entrance exam for the Ecole Normale Supérieure, the most distinguished college in France. After two failed attempts, he was admitted to the Ecole in 1879. He experienced intense anxiety about the academic competition there and he feared failure. At the same time, however, the Ecole provided a setting for exhilarating intellectual discussions, and Durkheim thrived on these. In the course of his studies at the Ecole, Durkheim became critical of its educational approach, which he found to be "too humanistic and literary, and too hostile to scientific attitudes" (Lukes, 1972: 52–3). Initially interested in psychology and philosophy, he soon turned his attention to the study of morality and society, and finally to sociology.

At the Ecole, Durkheim's intellectual development was shaped by the ideas of two neo-Kantian scholars, Renouvier and Boutroux. In particular, Durkheim was persuaded by Renouvier's commitment to rationalism, his central concern with the scientific study of morality, his anti-utilitarianism, and his advocacy of secular education. From Boutroux, Durkheim derived the principle that each science is irreducible to that of the preceding one, a principle that was to shape Durkheim's own conceptualization of the distinctive subject matter and methodology of sociology. Under Boutroux's guidance, he also engaged in a close reading of Auguste Comte, the inventor of the term "sociology." Methodologically, Durkheim was influenced by the historian Fustel de Coulanges, an advocate of the scientific method and a believer in the importance of religion in social life.

Following graduation, Durkheim taught philosophy at several provincial schools from 1882 to 1887. By this time, he had also settled on a topic for his doctoral thesis: the relation between individualism and socialism. He later recast the idea as the relation between the individual and society, and, finally, between individual personality and social solidarity. Although still quite abstract and philosophical, these ideas eventually spawned *The Division of Labor in Society*. By the time he completed the first draft of this work in 1886, Durkheim had committed himself to the establishment of the new science of sociology.

In this intellectual commitment, Durkheim was indebted to Comte's advocacy of scientific methods for the study of society. Although profound, this debt was not received uncritically by Durkheim. He believed that while Comte correctly identified "the social" as the object of sociology, Comte's work still amounted more to the philosophical contemplation of humanity in general rather than the study of any specific society. Although Comte coined the term "sociology" in 1822, the discipline itself was just being established in Durkheim's lifetime, and it was still struggling for recognition in the academic world. In his search for examples of sociology at work, Durkheim turned his attention to Germany. He spent the academic year 1885–6 visiting several German universities, where he became impressed with the German contribution to the emerging science of sociology.

In this respect, Durkheim found Herbert Spencer's earlier application of an organic analogy to societies a more satisfactory explanatory tool. The idea had become current in the work of many prominent German social thinkers. Organicism is based on the premise that the laws governing the functioning and evolution of animal organisms provide a model for a natural science of society. Durkheim was also impressed with the scientific study of morality that he encountered in Germany, for instance the work of social economists such as Wagner and Schmoller. However, it was the work of Wilhelm Wundt that Durkheim considered to be the greatest contribution to the sociological treatment of morality. Durkheim's articles on German social science and philosophy attracted public attention, and in 1887 he was appointed to teach the first university course in social science at the University of Bordeaux. At that time, the appointment of a social scientist to the predominantly humanist Faculty of Letters was in itself quite a significant event.

Durkheim's fifteen years at Bordeaux were extremely productive. In addition to numerous reviews and articles, he published *The Division of Labor* as well as *The Rules of Sociological Method* and *Suicide*. Durkheim's lectures on sociological subjects further staked the claim for sociology as a discipline. In addition, Durkheim founded the *L'Année Sociologique* (1898–1913), the first social science journal in France. These intellectual projects brought upon Durkheim charges of "sociological imperialism" (see Lukes, 1972: 103). While he was largely able to overcome opposition from his colleagues in Bordeaux, for a time these charges kept him from a professorship in Paris, something to which he had aspired.

While Durkheim held a strong antipathy for politics, he made two exceptions: the Dreyfus Affair and the First World War. It was Durkheim's involvement in the Dreyfus Affair that eventually brought Durkheim an appointment in Paris. In 1894, a Jewish staff officer named Captain Alfred Dreyfus was court-martialed for selling secrets to the German Embassy in Paris. When a later review of the case under a new chief of counter-intelligence found Dreyfus to be innocent, it became a public scandal. It was in the course of the public debate following this controversy that Durkheim published his only study addressing contemporary politics. The article, "Individualism and Intellectuals," published in 1898, responded to those who accused the intellectuals supporting Dreyfus's case of provoking individualism and anarchy. Durkheim argued in this article for a concept he called "moral individualism." Properly understood, he proposed, individualism was not the same thing as pure egotism.

Following the Dreyfus Affair, Durkheim's continued involvement in public debates led to his appointment in Paris. In 1902, Durkheim was appointed to a position in education at the Sorbonne. Although he became a full professor in 1906, it was not until 1913 that he was named Chair in "Education and Sociology." Durkheim's intellectual interests during his Paris years were the sociology of morality, knowledge, and religion. Following the outbreak of the First World War, Durkheim immersed himself in the war effort. By this time, his health had begun to decline, and he suffered a further blow with the death of his son in the war. Durkheim died in 1917 at the age of 59.

Durkheim's Work

Of the large body of work that Durkheim produced, the most influential are the four major books that were published during his lifetime: *The Division of Labor, The Rules of Sociological Method, Suicide,* and *The Elementary Forms of the Religious Life.* In these books, Durkheim developed some of his principal intellectual ideas. One project that he committed himself to was the establishment of sociology as a discipline. His goal was to provide a firm definition of the field and a scientific basis for its study. A second concern of Durkheim's was the issue of social integration in society. Durkheim wondered about the sources and nature of moral authority as an integrating force in society, as well as the rise of individualism. Finally, Durkheim held a strong interest in the practical implications of social scientific knowledge.

Durkheim intended *The Rules* as a programmatic statement about the cause of sociology as a discipline, which must have its own distinctive subject matter and methodology. Substantively, the domain of sociology must necessarily be "social facts" that are "external to individuals." Methodologically, sociologists must strive for objectivity by studying "social facts as things," that is, through empirical investigation. In demarcating the explanatory method of sociology from that of psychology, Durkheim proposed that sociology must focus on macro-level causal analysis, relating social causes to social effects. In addition to a causal analysis, he suggested that sociology must undertake a functional explanation of a social fact in terms of the needs of a social "organism."

Durkheim intended his book *Suicide* to be an example of his method. Durkheim took the suicide rate as an example of a social fact, and attempted to explain the variations in that rate scientifically. The suicide rate is an interesting example for several reasons. First, it is "external to individuals." Durkheim did not attempt to explain the inner feelings of someone contemplating suicide, nor even the causes of individual suicides. Instead, he examined variations in the suicide rate. What caused these variations? He argued that under different social conditions, different causes produced patterns of suicides. In modern societies, the most important cause was a disconnection of people from social bonds – resulting either from isolation or from disorienting changes in society at large.

In *The Division of Labor*, Durkheim confronted the basic question of what holds modern society together. Using an evolutionary approach, his central thesis in the book was that the increasing division of labor in modern societies was taking the place of the *conscience collective* – the moral consensus or the collective conscience – that marked traditional societies. Despite this, social cohesion still operated, but in a different way. Durkheim characterized the social integration that results from the division of labor in modern societies as "organic solidarity," a solidarity born out of mutual need. This was quickly replacing the "mechanical solidarity" typical of simpler societies. The term "organic" referred to the functional interconnectedness of elements in society, similar to the way that the parts of an organism are functionally connected. In modern societies, we may not feel morally or culturally connected to those around us, but as the division of labor increases we are more than ever functionally connected by our mutual needs.

The Elementary Forms of the Religious Life marked an explicitly cultural turn in Durkheim's work. It was ostensibly a study of Totemism, a "primitive and simple religion" of the aboriginal people of Australia. Durkheim picked this example because he believed that the simplest religions offered the purest examples of the essential elements of religious life. More broadly, Durkheim contributed in this work to a general theory of religion and the sociology of knowledge. *The Elementary Forms* can be seen as the study of collective representations, a concept that increasingly came to replace that of the *conscience collective* in Durkheim's work. In this direction, Durkheim traced the social origins and the social functions of religious beliefs. As the embodiment of collective ideals, religion is reinforced through ceremonials and rituals. Durkheim also advanced a sociological theory of knowledge that addresses old philosophical questions, such as the origin of categories of thought and action.

In doing so, he wanted to unite two philosophical claims that seemed to be opposed to one another. On the one hand, there was the claim that categories are constructed out of human experience. On the other hand, there was the claim that categories are logically prior to experience. Durkheim suggested that categories are collective representations; that is, categories are the product of society. To the extent that people collectively constitute society, our categories of knowledge can be said to be human creations. But because society is a *sui generis* phenomenon, they are prior to the experience of any particular person.

Durkheim's Legacy

By the turn of the century, Durkheim's hard work had paid off. Sociology had gained considerable popularity in Europe and the United States, and in France, Durkheim's vision of the discipline was well entrenched. Many of his students pursued his intellectual ideas in their own work. His nephew and collaborator Marcel Mauss studied reciprocity in the form of gift giving, and the notion of the person or "self;" Halbwachs did research on working-class consumption and collective memory; Bouglé studied caste.

Ironically, in recent decades Durkheim's methodology has been far more influential in America and Britain than in France. The British anthropologist Alfred Radcliffe-Brown first introduced Durkheim's ideas to the English-speaking world. Radcliffe-Brown also helped stimulate interest in Durkheim's writings in the United States. However, this interest became more widespread in the United States through the work of Talcott Parsons and Robert Merton.

Nevertheless, Durkheim's ideas influenced several major theoretical movements in the twentieth century. For instance, it was strongly present in the emergence of "structuralism" through the work of Jean Piaget and Claude Lévi-Strauss. Alexander (1988) points to the often-unacknowledged debt that the recent cultural revival in social theory owes to the ideas of Durkheim, for instance, in the work of Ferdinand de Saussure, Michel Foucault (see the sister volume to this reader, *Contemporary Sociological Theory*), and Clifford Geertz, as well as Peter Berger, Robert Bellah, and others.

Select Bibliography

Alexander, Jeffrey (ed.). 1988. *Durkheimian Sociology: Cultural Studies*. Cambridge: Cambridge University Press. (An excellent collection of essays on the contribution of Durkheim's work to cultural analysis and the study of religion.)

Bellah, Robert (ed.). 1973. *Emile Durkheim on Morality and Society, Selected Writings*. Chicago, IL: University of Chicago Press. (This volume includes a good introduction on morality and religion.)

Fenton, Steve with Robert Reiner and Ian Hamnett. 1984. *Durkheim and Modern Sociology*. Cambridge: Cambridge University Press. (A useful book for the general reader, organized around key sociological themes.)

Giddens, Anthony. 1978. *Emile Durkheim*. New York: Viking Press. (A short but useful introduction to Durkheim's work.)

Jones, Robert. 1986. *Emile Durkheim: An Introduction to Four Major Works*. Masters of Social Theory Vol. 2. Beverly Hills, CA: Sage Publications. (A good summary of Durkheim's major work.)

La Capra, Dominick. 1972. *Emile Durkheim: Sociologist and Philosopher*. Ithaca, NY: Cornell University Press. (A general introductory book with chapters devoted to Durkheim's important writings.)

Lukes, Steven. 1972. *Emile Durkheim: His Life and Work*. New York: Harper & Row. (One of the most detailed and authoritative interpretations of Durkheim's work.)

Lukes, Steven. 1982. "Introduction." *The Rules of Sociological Method.* New York: Free Press. (A good discussion of Durkheim's ideas on sociology as a science.)

Nisbet, Robert. 1974. *The Sociology of Emile Durkheim.* New York: Oxford University Press. (A good general introduction, but controversial for its treatment of Durkheim as a conservative.)

Pickering, W. S. F. 1984. *Durkheim's Sociology of Religion: Themes and Theories.* London: Routledge. (A valuable source for further reading on Durkheim's theory of religion.)

Thompson, Kenneth. 1982. *Emile Durkheim.* New York: Tavistock Publications. (A comprehensive summary and critique of Durkheim's work.)

Traugott, Mark (ed.). 1978. *Emile Durkheim on Institutional Analysis.* Chicago, IL: University of Chicago Press. (For those interested in a further reading of Durkheim's work, an interesting collection of his writings.)

Wallwork, Ernest. 1972. *Durkheim: Morality and Milieu.* Cambridge, MA: Harvard University Press. (A more specialized discussion of Durkheim's moral philosophy.)

Wolff, Kurt (ed.). 1960. *Emile Durkheim, 1858–1917.* Columbus, OH: Ohio State University Press. (An early collection of essays on various themes related to Durkheim's work.)

A: SOCIETY AND SOCIAL FACTS

10 The Rules of Sociological Method

Emile Durkheim

The proposition which states that social facts must be treated as things – the proposition which is at the very basis of our method – is among those which have stirred up the most opposition. It was deemed paradoxical and scandalous for us to assimilate to the realities of the external world those of the social world. This was singularly to misunderstand the meaning and effect of this assimilation, the object of which was not to reduce the higher forms of being to the level of lower ones but, on the contrary, to claim for the former a degree of reality at least equal to that which everyone accords to the latter. Indeed, we do not say that social facts are material things, but that they are things just as are material things, although in a different way.

What indeed is a thing? The thing stands in opposition to the idea, just as what is known from the outside stands in opposition to what is known from the inside. A thing is any object of knowledge which is not naturally penetrable by the understanding. It is all that which we cannot conceptualise adequately as an idea by the simple process of intellectual analysis. It is all that which the mind cannot understand without going outside itself, proceeding progressively by way of observation and experimentation from those features which are the most external and the most immediately accessible to those which are the least visible and the most profound. To treat facts of a certain order as things is therefore not to place them in this or that category of reality; it is to observe towards them a certain attitude of mind. It is to embark upon the study of them by adopting the principle that one is entirely ignorant of what they are, that their characteristic properties, like the unknown causes upon which they depend, cannot be discovered by even the most careful form of introspection.

The terms being so defined, our proposition, far from being a paradox, might almost pass for a truism if it were not too often still unrecognised in those sciences which deal with man, and above all in sociology. Indeed, in this sense it may be said that any object of knowledge is a thing, except perhaps for mathematical objects. Regarding the latter, since we construct them ourselves, from the most simple to the most complex, it is enough to look within ourselves and to analyse internally the mental process from which they arise, in order to know what they are. But as soon as we consider facts *per se*, when we undertake to make a science of them, they are of necessity unknowns for us, *things* of which we are ignorant, for the representations that we have been able to make of them in the course of our lives, since they have been made without method and uncritically, lack any scientific value and must be discarded. The facts of individual psychology themselves are of this nature and must be considered in this light. Indeed, although by definition they are internal to ourselves, the consciousness that we have of them reveals to us neither their inmost character nor their origin. Consciousness allows us to know them well up to a certain point, but only in the same way as our senses make us aware of heat or light, sound or electricity. It gives us muddled impressions of them, fleeting and subjective, but provides no clear, distinct notions or explanatory concepts. This is precisely why during this century an objective psychology has been founded whose fundamental rule is to study mental facts from the outside, namely as things. This should be even more the case for social facts, for consciousness cannot be more capable of knowing them than of knowing its own existence.[1] It will be objected that, since they have been wrought by us, we have only to become conscious of ourselves to know what we have put into them and how we shaped them. Firstly, however, most social institutions have been handed down to us already fashioned by previous generations; we have had no part in their shaping; consequently it is not by searching within ourselves that we can uncover the causes which have given rise to them. Furthermore, even if we have played a part in producing them, we can hardly glimpse, save in the most confused and often even the most imprecise way, the real reasons which have impelled us to act, or the nature of our action. Already, even regarding merely the steps we have taken personally, we know very inaccurately the relatively simple motives that govern us. We believe ourselves disinterested, whereas our actions are egoistic; we think that we are commanded by hatred whereas we are giving way to love, that we are obedient to reason whereas we are the slaves of irrational prejudices, etc. How therefore could we possess the ability to discern more clearly the causes, of a different order of complexity, which inspire the measures taken by the collectivity? For at the very least each individual shares in only an infinitesimally small part of them; we have a host of fellow-fashioners, and what is occurring in their different consciousnesses eludes us.

Thus our rule implies no metaphysical conception, no speculation about the innermost depth of being. What it demands is that the sociologist should assume the state of mind of physicists, chemists and physiologists when they venture into an as yet unexplored area of their scientific field. As the sociologist penetrates into the social world he should be conscious that he is penetrating into the unknown. He must feel himself in the presence of facts governed by laws as unsuspected as those of life before the science of biology was evolved. He must hold himself ready to make discoveries which will surprise and disconcert him. Yet sociology is far from having arrived at this degree of intellectual maturity. While the scientist who studies physical nature feels very keenly the resistances that it proffers, ones which he has great difficulty in overcoming, it really seems as if the sociologist operates among things immediately clear to the mind, so great is the ease with which he seems to resolve the most obscure questions. In the present state of the discipline, we do not really know the nature of the principal social institutions, such as the state or the family, property rights or contract, punishment and responsibility. We are virtually ignorant of the causes upon which they depend, the functions they fulfil, and their laws of evolution. It is as if, on certain points, we are only just beginning to perceive a few glimmers of light. Yet it suffices to glance through works of sociology to see how rare is any awareness of this ignorance and these difficulties. Not only is it deemed mandatory to dogmatise about every kind of problem at once, but it is believed that one is capable, in a few pages or sentences, of penetrating to the inmost essence of the most complex phenomena. This means that such theories express, not the facts, which could not be so swiftly fathomed, but the preconceptions of the author before he began his research. Doubtless the idea that we form of collective practices, of what they are, or what they should be, is a factor in their development. But this idea itself is a fact which, in order to be properly established, needs to be studied from the outside. For it is important to know not the way in which a particular thinker individually represents a particular institution, but the conception that the group has of it. This conception is ideed the only socially effective one. But it cannot be known through mere inner observation, since it is not wholly and entirely within any one of us; one must therefore find some external signs which make it apparent. Furthermore, it did not arise from nothing: it is itself the result of external causes which must be known in order to be able to appreciate its future role. Thus, no matter what one does, it is always to the same method that one must return. . . .

What is a Social Fact?

Before beginning the search for the method appropriate to the study of social facts it is important to know what are the facts termed 'social'.

The question is all the more necessary because the term is used without much precision. It is commonly used to designate almost all the phenomena that occur within society, however little social interest of some generality they present. Yet under this heading there is, so to speak, no human occurrence that cannot be called social. Every individual drinks, sleeps, eats, or employs his reason, and society has every interest in seeing that these functions are regularly exercised. If therefore these facts were social ones, sociology would possess no subject matter peculiarly its own, and its domain would be confused with that of biology and psychology.

However, in reality there is in every society a clearly determined group of phenomena separable, because of their distinct characteristics, from those that form the subject matter of other sciences of nature.

When I perform my duties as a brother, a husband or a citizen and carry out the commitments I have entered into, I fulfil obligations which are defined in law and custom and which are external to myself and my actions. Even when they conform to my own sentiments and when I feel their reality within me, that reality does not cease to be objective, for it is not I who have prescribed these duties; I have received them through education. Moreover, how often does it happen that we are ignorant of the details of the obligations that we must assume, and that, to know them, we must consult the legal code and its authorised interpreters! Similarly the believer has discovered from birth, ready fashioned, the beliefs and practices of his religious life; if they existed before he did, it follows that they exist outside him. The system of signs that I employ to express my thoughts, the monetary system I use to pay my debts, the credit instruments I utilise in my commercial relationships, the practices I follow in my profession, etc., all function independently of the use I make of them. Considering in turn each member of society, the foregoing remarks can be repeated for each single one of them. Thus there are ways of acting, thinking and feeling which possess the remarkable property of existing outside the consciousness of the individual.

Not only are these types of behaviour and thinking external to the individual, but they are endued with a compelling and coercive power by virtue of which, whether he wishes it or not, they impose themselves upon him. Undoubtedly when I conform to them of my own free will, this coercion is not felt or felt hardly at all, since it is unnecessary. None the less it is intrinsically a characteristic of these facts; the proof of this is that it asserts itself as soon as I try to resist. If I attempt to violate the rules of law they react against me so as to forestall my action, if there is still time. Alternatively, they annul it or make my action conform to the norm if it is already accomplished but capable of being reversed; or they cause me to pay the penalty for it if it is irreparable. If purely moral rules are at stake, the public conscience restricts any act which infringes them by the surveillance it exercises over the conduct of citizens and by the special punishments it has at its disposal. In other cases the constraint is less violent; nevertheless, it does not cease to exist. If I do not conform to ordinary conventions, if in my mode of dress I pay no heed to what is customary in my country and in my social class, the laughter I provoke, the social distance at which I am kept, produce, although in a more mitigated form, the same results as any real penalty. In other cases, although it may be indirect, constraint is no less effective. I am not forced to speak French with my compatriots, nor to use the legal currency, but it is impossible for me to do otherwise. If I tried to escape the necessity, my attempt would fail miserably. As an industrialist nothing prevents me from working with the processes and methods of the previous century, but if I do I will most certainly ruin myself. Even when in fact I can struggle free from these rules and successfully break them, it is never without being forced to fight against them. Even if in the end they are overcome, they make their constraining power sufficently felt in the resistance that they afford. There is no innovator, even a fortunate one, whose ventures do not encounter opposition of this kind.

Here, then, is a category of facts which present very special characteristics: they consist of manners of acting, thinking and feeling external to the individual, which are invested with a coercive power by virtue of which they exercise control over him. Consequently, since they consist of representations and actions, they cannot be confused with organic phenomena, nor with psychical phenomena, which have no existence save in and through the individual consciousness. Thus they constitute a new species and to them must be exclusively assigned the term *social*. It is appropriate, since it is clear that, not having the individual as their substratum, they can have none other than society, either political society in its entirety or one of the partial groups that it includes – religious denominations, political and literary schools, occupational corporations, etc. Moreover, it is for such as these alone that the term is fitting, for the word 'social' has the sole meaning of designating those phenomena which fall into none of the categories of facts already constituted and labelled. They are consequently the proper field of sociology. It is true that this word 'constraint', in terms of which we define them, is in danger of infuriating those who zealously uphold out-and-out individualism. Since they maintain that the individual is completely autonomous, it seems to them that he is diminished every time he is made aware that he is not dependent on himself alone. Yet since it is indisputable today that most of our ideas and tendencies are not developed by ourselves, but come to us from outside, they can only penetrate us by imposing themselves upon us. This is all that our definition implies. Moreover, we know that all social constraints do not necessarily exclude the individual personality.[2]

Yet since the examples just cited (legal and moral rules, religious dogmas, financial systems, etc.) consist wholly of beliefs and practices already well established, in view of what has been said it might be maintained that no social fact can exist except where there is a well defined social organisation. But there are other facts which do not present themselves in this already crystallised form but which also possess the same objectivity and ascendancy over the individual. These are what are called social 'currents'. Thus in a public gathering the great waves of ethusiasm, indignation and pity that are produced have their seat in no one individual consciousness. They come to each one of us from outside and can sweep us along in spite of ourselves. If perhaps I abandon myself to them I may not be conscious of the pressure that they are exerting upon me, but that pressure makes its presence felt immediately I attempt to struggle against them. If an individual tries to pit himself against one of these collective manifestations, the sentiments that he is rejecting will be turned against him. Now if this external coercive power asserts itself so acutely in cases of resistance, it must be because it exists in the other instances cited above without our being conscious of it. Hence we are the victims of an illusion which leads us to believe we have ourselves produced what has been imposed upon us externally. But if the willingness with which we let ourselves be carried along disguises the pressure we have undergone, it does not eradicate it. Thus air does not cease to have weight, although we no longer feel that weight. Even when we have individually and spontaneously shared in the common emotion, the impression we have experienced is utterly different from what we would have felt if we had been alone. Once the assembly has broken up and these social influences have ceased to act upon us, and we are once more on our own, the emotions we have felt seem an alien phenomenon, one in which we no longer recognise ourselves. It is then we perceive that we have undergone the emotions much more than generated them. These emotions may even perhaps fill us with horror, so much do they go against the grain. Thus individuals who are normally perfectly harmless may, when gathered together in a crowd, let themselves be drawn into acts of atrocity. And what we assert about these transitory outbreaks likewise applies to those more lasting movements of opinion which relate to religious, political, literary and artistic matters, etc., and which are constantly being produced around us, whether throughout society or in a more limited sphere.

Moreover, this definition of a social fact can be verified by examining an experience that is characteristic. It is sufficient to observe how children are brought up. If one views the facts as they are and indeed as they have always been, it is patently obvious that all education consists of a continual effort to impose upon the child ways of seeing, thinking and acting which he himself would not have arrived at spontaneously. From his earliest years we oblige him to eat, drink and sleep at regular hours, and to observe cleanliness, calm and obedience; later we force him to learn how to be mindful of others, to respect customs and conventions, and to work, etc. If this constraint in time ceases to be felt it is because it gradually gives rise to habits, to inner tendencies which render it superfluous; but they supplant the constraint only because they are derived from it. It is true that, in Spencer's view, a rational education should shun such means and allow the child complete freedom to do what he will. Yet as this educational theory has never been put into practice among any known people, it can only be the personal expression of a *desideratum* and not a fact which can be established in contradiction to the other facts given above. What renders these latter facts particularly illuminating is that education sets out precisely with the object of creating a social being. Thus there can be seen, as in an abbreviated form, how the social being has been fashioned historically. The pressure to which the child is subjected unremittingly is the same pressure of the social environment which seeks to shape him in its own image, and in which parents and teachers are only the representatives and intermediaries.

Thus it is not the fact that they are general which can serve to characterise sociological phenomena. Thoughts to be found in the consciousness of each individual and movements which are repeated by all individuals are not for this reason social facts. If some have been content with using this characteristic in order to define them it is because they have been confused, wrongly, with what might be termed their individual incarnations. What constitutes social facts are the beliefs, tendencies and practices of the group taken collectively. But the forms that these collective states may assume when they are 'refracted' through individuals are things of a different kind. What irrefutably demonstrates this duality of kind is that these two categories of facts frequently are manifested dissociated from each other. Indeed some of these ways of acting or thinking acquire, by dint of repetition, a sort of consistency which, so to speak, separates them out, isolating them from the particular events which reflect them. Thus they assume a shape, a tangible form peculiar to them and constitute a reality *sui generis* vastly distinct from the individual facts which manifest that reality. Collective custom does not exist only in a state of immanence in the successive actions which it determines, but, by a privilege without example in the biological kingdom, expresses itself once and for all in a formula repeated by word of mouth, transmitted by education and even enshrined in the written word. Such are the origins and nature of legal and moral rules, aphorisms and popular sayings, articles of faith in which religious or political sects epitomise their beliefs, and standards of taste drawn up by literary schools, etc. None of these modes of acting and thinking are to be found wholly in the application made of them by individuals, since they can even exist without being applied at the time.

Undoubtedly this state of dissociation does not always present itself with equal distinctiveness. It is sufficient for dissociation to exist unquestionably in the numerous important instances cited, for us to prove that the social fact exists separately from its individual effects. Moreover, even when the dissociation is not immediately observable, it can often be made so with the help of certain methodological devices. Indeed it is essential to embark on such procedures if one wishes to refine out the social fact from any amalgam and so observe it in its pure state. Thus certain currents of opinon, whose intensity varies according to the time and country in which they occur, impel us, for example, towards marriage or suicide, towards higher or lower birth-rates, etc. Such currents are plainly social facts. At first sight they seem inseparable from the forms they assume in individual cases. But statistics afford us a means of isolating them. They are indeed not inaccurately represented by rates of births, marriages and suicides, that is, by the result obtained after dividing the average annual total of marriages, births, and voluntary homicides by the number of persons of an age to marry, produce children, or commit suicide.[3] Since each one of these statistics includes without distinction all individual cases, the individual circumstances which may have played some part in producing the phenomenon cancel each other out and consequently do not contribute to determining the nature of the phenomenon. What it expresses is a certain state of the collective mind.

That is what social phenomena are when stripped of all extraneous elements. As regards their private manifestations, these do indeed having something social about them, since in part they reproduce the collective model. But to a large extent each one depends also upon the psychical and organic constitution of the individual, and on the particular circumstances in which he is placed. Therefore they are not phenomena which are in the strict sense sociological. They depend on both domains at the same time, and could be termed socio-psychical. They are of interest to the sociologist without constituting the immediate content of sociology. The same characteristic is to be found in the organisms of those mixed phenomena of nature studied in the combined sciences such as biochemistry.

It may be objected that a phenomenon can only be collective if it is common to all the members of society, or at the very least to a majority, and consequently, if it is general. This is doubtless the case, but if it is general it is because it is collective (that is, more or less obligatory); but it is very far from being collective because it is general. It is a condition of the group repeated in individuals because it imposes itself upon them. It is in each part because it is in the whole, but far from being in the whole because it is in the parts. This is supremely evident in those beliefs and practices which are handed down to us ready fashioned by previous generations. We accept and adopt them because, since they are the work of the collectivity and one that is centuries old, they are invested with a special authority that our education has taught us to recognise and respect. It is worthy of note that the vast majority of social phenomena come to us in this way. But even when the social fact is partly due to our direct co-operation, it is no different in nature. An outburst of collective emotion in a gathering does not merely express the sum total of what individual feelings share in common, but is something of a very different order, as we have demonstrated. It is a product of shared existence, of actions and reactions called into play between the consciousnesses of individuals. If it is echoed in each one of them it is precisely by virtue of the special energy derived from its collective origins. If all hearts beat in unison, this is not as a consequence of a spontaneous, pre-established harmony; it is because one and the same force is propelling them in the same direction. Each one is borne along by the rest.

We have therefore succeeded in delineating for ourselves the exact field of sociology. It embraces one single, well defined group of phenomena. A social fact is identifiable through the power of external coercion which it exerts or is capable of exerting upon individuals. The presence of this power is in turn recognisable because of the existence of some pre-determined sanction, or through the resistance that the fact opposes to any individual action that may threaten it. However, it can also be defined by ascertaining how widespread it is within the group, provided that, as noted above, one is careful to add a second essential characteristic; this is, that it exists independently of the particular forms that it may assume in the process of spreading itself within the group. In certain cases this latter criterion can even be more easily applied than the former one. The presence of constraint is easily ascertainable when it is manifested externally through some direct reaction of society, as in the case of law, morality, beliefs, customs and even fashions. But when constraint is merely indirect, as with that exerted by an economic organis-ation, it is not always so clearly discernible. Generality combined with objectivity may then be easier to establish. Moreover, this second definition is simply another formulation of the first one: if a mode of behaviour existing outside the conscious-nesses of individuals becomes general, it can only do so by exerting pressure upon them.[4]

However, one may well ask whether this definition is complete. Indeed the facts which have provided us with its basis are all *ways of functioning*: they are 'physiological' in nature. But there are also collective *ways of being*, namely, social facts of an 'anatomical' or morphological nature. Sociology cannot dissociate itself from what concerns the substratum of collective life. Yet the number and nature of the elementary parts which constitute society, the way in which they are articulated, the degree of coalescence they have attained, the distribution of population over the earth's surface, the extent and nature of the network of communications, the design of dwellings, etc., do not at first sight seem relatable to ways of acting, feeling or thinking.

Yet, first and foremost, these various phenomena present the same characteristic which has served us in defining the others. These ways of being impose themselves upon the individual just as do the ways of acting we have dealt with. In fact, when we wish to learn how a society is divided up politically, in what its divisions consist and the degree of solidarity that exists between them, it is not through physical inspection and geographical observation that we may come to find this out: such divisions are social, although they may have some physical basis. It is only through public law that we can study such political organisation, because this law is what determines its nature, just as it determines our domestic and civic relationships. The organisation is no less a form of compulsion. If the population clusters together in our cities instead of being scattered over the rural areas, it is because there exists a trend of opinion, a collective drive which imposes this concentration upon individ-uals. We can no more choose the design of our houses than the cut of our clothes – at least, the one is as much obligatory as the other. The communication network forcibly prescribes the direction of internal migrations or commercial exchanges, etc., and even their intensity. Consequently, at the most there are grounds for adding one further category to the list of phenomena already enumerated as bearing the distinctive stamp of a social fact. But as that enumeration was in no wise strictly exhaustive, this addition would not be indispensable.

Moreover, it does not even serve a purpose, for these ways of being are only ways of acting that have been consolidated. A society's political structure is only the way in which its various component segments have become accustomed to living with each other. If relationships between them are traditionally close, the segments tend to merge together; if the contrary, they tend to remain distinct. The type of dwelling imposed upon us is merely the way in which everyone around us and, in part, previous generations, have customarily built their houses. The communication network is only the channel which has been cut by the regular current of commerce and migrations, etc., flowing in the same direction. Doubtless if phenomena of a morphological kind were the only ones that displayed this rigidity, it might be thought that they constituted a separate species. But a legal rule is no less permanent an arrangement than an architectural style, and yet it is a 'physiological' fact. A simple moral maxim is certainly more malleable, yet it is cast in forms much more rigid than a mere professional custom or fashion. Thus there exists a whole range of gradations which, without any break in continuity, join the most clearly delineated structural facts to those free currents of social life which are not yet caught in any definite mould. This therefore signifies that the differences between them concern only the degree to which they have become consolidated. Both are forms of life at varying stages of crystallisation. It would undoubtedly be advantageous to reserve the term 'morphological' for those social facts which relate to the social substratum, but only on condition that one is aware that they are of the same nature as the others. Our definition will therefore subsume all that has to be defined if it states:

> A social fact is any way of acting, whether fixed or not, capable of exerting over the individual an external constraint;

or:

> which is general over the whole of a given society whilst having an existence of its own, independent of its individual manifestations.[5]

Rules for the Explanation of Social Facts

Most sociologists believe they have accounted for phenomena once they have demonstrated the purpose they serve and the role they play. They reason as if phenomena existed solely for this role and had no determining cause save a clear or vague sense of the services they are called upon to render. This is why it is thought that all that is needful has been said to make them intelligible when it has been established that these services are real and that the social need they satisfy has been demonstrated. Thus Comte relates all the drive for progress of the human species to this basic tendency, 'which directly impels man continually to improve his condition in all respects', whereas Spencer relates it to the need for greater happiness. It is by virtue of this principle that Spencer explains the formation of society as a function of the advantages which flow from co-operation, the institution of government by the utility which springs from regulating military co-operation, and the transformations which the family has undergone from the need for a more perfect reconciliation of the interests of parents, children and society.

But this method confuses two very different questions. To demonstrate the utility of a fact does not explain its origins, nor how it is what it is. The uses which it serves presume the specific properties characteristic of it, but do not create it. Our need for things cannot cause them to be of a particular nature; consequently, that need cannot produce them out of nothing, conferring in this way existence upon them. They spring from causes of another kind. The feeling we have regarding their utility can stimulate us to set these causes in motion and draw upon the effects they bring in their train, but it cannot conjure up these results out of nothing. This proposition is self-evident so long as only material or even psychological phenomena are being considered. It would also not be disputed in sociology if the social facts, because of their total lack of material substance, did not appear – wrongly, moreover – bereft of intrinsic reality. Since we view them as purely mental configurations, provided they are found to be useful, as soon as the idea of them occurs to us they seem to be self-generating. But since each fact is a force which prevails over the force of the individual and possesses its own nature, to bring a fact into existence it cannot suffice to have merely the desire or the will to engender it. Prior forces must exist, capable of producing this firmly established force, as well as natures capable of producing this special nature. Only under these conditions can facts be created. To revive the family spirit where it has grown weak, it is not enough for everybody to realise its advantages; we must set directly in operation those causes which alone can engender it. To endow a government with the authority it requires, it is not enough to feel the need for this. We must address ourselves to the sole sources from which all authority is derived: the establishment of traditions, a common spirit, etc. For this we must retrace our steps farther back along the chain of cause and effect until we find a point at which human action can effectively intervene.

What clearly demonstrates the duality of these two avenues of research is that a fact can exist without serving any purpose, either because it has never been used to further any vital goal or because, having once been of use, it has lost all utility but continues to exist merely through force of custom. There are even more instances of such survivals in society than in the human organism. There are even cases where a practice or a social institution changes its functions without for this reason changing its nature. The rule of *is pater est quem justae nuptiae declarant* has remained substantially the same in our legal code as it was in ancient Roman law. But while its purpose was to safeguard the property rights of the father over children born of his legitimate wife, it is much more the rights of the children that it protects today. The swearing of an oath began by being a kind of judicial ordeal before it became simply a solemn and impressive form of attestation. The religious dogmas of Christianity have not changed for centuries, but the role they play in our modern societies is no longer the same as in the Middle Ages. Thus words serve to express new ideas without their contexture changing. Moreover, it is a proposition true in sociology as in biology, that the organ is independent of its function, i.e. while staying the same it can serve different ends. Thus the causes which give rise to its existence are independent of the ends it serves.

Yet we do not mean that the tendencies, needs and desires of men never actively intervene in social evolution. On the contrary, it is certain that, according to the way they make an impact upon the conditions on which a fact depends, they can hasten or retard development. Yet, apart from the fact that they can never create something out of nothing, their intervention itself, regardless of its effects, can only occur by virtue of efficient causes. Indeed, a tendency cannot, even to this limited extent, contribute to the production of a new phenomenon unless it is itself new, whether constituted absolutely or arising from some transformation of a previous tendency. For unless we postulate a truly providential harmony established before-hand, we could not admit that from his origins man carried within him in potential all the tendencies whose opportuneness would be felt as evolution progressed, each one ready to be awakened when the circumstances called for it. Furthermore, a tendency is also a thing; thus it cannot arise or be modified for the sole reason that we deem it useful. It is a force possessing its own nature. For that nature to come into existence or be changed, it is not enough for us to find advantage in this occurring. To effect such changes causes must come into play which require them physically.

For example, we have explained the constant development of the social division of labour by showing that it is necessary in order for man to sustain himself in the new conditions of existence in which he is placed as he advances in history. We have therefore attributed to the tendency which is somewhat improperly termed the instinct of self-preservation an important role in our explanation. But in the first place the tendency alone could not account for even the most rudimentary form of specialisation. It can accomplish nothing if the conditions on which this phenom-enon depends are not already realised, that is, if individual differences have not sufficiently increased through the progressive state of indetermination of the com-mon consciousness and hereditary influences. The division of labour must even have begun already to occur for its utility to be perceived and its need to be felt. The mere development of individual differences, implying a greater diversity of tastes and abilities, had necessarily to bring about this first consequence. Moreover, the instinct of self-preservation did not come by itself and without cause to fertilise this first germ of specialisation. If it directed first itself and then us into this new path, it is because the course it followed and caused us to follow beforehand was as if blocked. This was because the greater intensity of the struggle for existence brought about by the greater concentration of societies rendered increasingly difficult the survival of those individuals who continued to devote themselves to more unspecialised tasks. Thus a change of direction was necessary. On the other hand if it turned itself, and for preference turned our activity, towards an ever increasing division of labour, it was also because it was the path of least resistance. The other possible solutions were emigration, suicide or crime. Now, on average, the ties that bind us to our country, to life and to feeling for our fellows are stronger and more resistant sentiments than the habits which can deter us from narrower specialisation. Thus these habits had inevitably to give ground as every advance occurred. Thus, since we are ready to allow for human needs in sociological explanations, we need not revert, even partially, to teleology. For these needs can have no influence over social evolution unless they themselves evolve, and the changes through which they pass can only be explained by causes which are in no way final.

What is even more convincing than the foregoing argument is the study of how social facts work out in practice. Where teleology rules, there rules also a fair margin of contingency, for there are no ends – and even fewer means – which necessarily influence all men, even supposing they are placed in the same circumstances. Given the same environment, each individual, according to his temperament, adapts himself to it in the way he pleases and which he prefers to all others. The one will seek to change it so that it better suits his needs; the other will prefer to change himself and to moderate his desires. Thus to arrive at the same goal, many different routes can be, and in reality are, followed. If then it were true that historical development occurred because of ends felt either clearly or obscurely, social facts would have to present an infinite diversity and all comparison would almost be impossible. But the opposite is true. Undoubtedly external events, the links between which constitute the superficial part of social life, vary from one people to another. Yet in this way each individual has his own history, although the bases of physical and social organisation remain the same for all. If, in fact, one comes even a little into contact with social phenomena, one is on the contrary surprised at the outstanding regularity with which they recur in similar circumstances. Even the most trivial and apparently most puerile practices are repeated with the most astonishing uniformity. A marriage ceremony, seemingly purely symbolic, such as the abduction of the bride-to-be, is found to be identical everywhere that a certain type of family exists, which itself is lined to a whole political organisation. The most bizarre customs, such as the 'couvade', the levirate, exogamy, etc. are to be observed in the most diverse peoples and are symptomatic of a certain social state. The right to make a will appears at a specific phase of history and, according to the severity of the restrictions which limit it, we can tell at what stage of social evolution we have arrived. It would be easy to multiply such examples. But the widespread character of collective forms would be inexplicable if final causes held in sociology the preponderance attributed to them.

Therefore when one undertakes to explain a social phenomenon the efficient cause which produces it and the function it fulfils must be investigated separately. We use the word 'function' in preference to 'end' or 'goal' precisely because social phenomena generally do not exist for the usefulness of the results they produce. We must determine whether there is a correspondence between the fact being considered and the general needs of the social organism, and in what this correspondence consists, without seeking to know whether it was intentional or not. All such questions of intention are, moreover, too subjective to be dealt with scientifically.

Not only must these two kinds of problems be dissociated from each other, but it is generally appropriate to deal with the first kind before the second. This order of precedence corresponds to that of the facts. It is natural to seek the cause of a phenomenon before attempting to determine its effects. This method is all the more logical because the first question, once resolved, will often help to answer the second. Indeed, the solid link which joins cause to effect is of a reciprocal character which has not been sufficiently recognised. Undoubtedly the effect cannot exist without its cause, but the latter, in turn, requires its effect. It is from the cause that the effect derives its energy, but on occasion it also restores energy to the cause and consequently cannot disappear without the cause being affected.[6] For example, the social reaction which constitutes punishment is due to the intensity of the collective sentiments that crime offends. On the other hand it serves the useful function of maintaining those sentiments at the same level of intensity, for they could not fail to weaken if the offences committed against them remained unpunished. Likewise, as the social environment becomes more complex and unstable, traditions and accepted beliefs arc shaken and take on a more indeterminate and flexible character, whilst faculties of reflection develop. These same faculties are indispensable for societies and individuals to adapt themselves to a more mobile and complex environment. As men are obliged to work more intensively, the products of their labour become more numerous and better in quality; but this increase in abundance and quality of the products is necessary to compensate for the effort that this more considerable labour entails. Thus, far from the cause of social phenomena consisting of a mental anticipation of the function they are called upon to fulfil, this function consists on the contrary, in a number of cases at least, in maintaining the pre-existent cause from which the phenomena derive. We will therefore discover more easily the function if the cause is already known.

If we must proceed only at a second stage to the determination of the function, it is none the less necessary for the complete explanation of the phenomenon. Indeed, if the utility of a fact is not what causes its existence, it must generally be useful to continue to survive. If it lacks utility, that very reason suffices to make it harmful, since in that case it requires effort but brings in no return. Thus if the general run of social phenomena had this parasitic character, the economy of the organism would be in deficit, and social life would be impossible. Consequently, to provide a satisfactory explanation of social life we need to show how the phenomena which are its substance come together to place society in harmony with itself and with the outside world. Undoubtedly the present formula which defines life as a correspondence between the internal and the external environments is only approximate. Yet in general it remains true; thus to explain a fact which is vital, it is not enough to show the cause on which it depends. We must also – at least in most cases – discover the part that it plays in the establishment of that general harmony.

Having distinguished between these two questions, we must determine the method whereby they must be resolved.

At the same time as being teleological, the method of explanation generally followed by sociologists is essentially psychological. The two tendencies are closely linked. Indeed, if society is only a system of means set up by men to achieve certain ends, these ends can only be individual, for before society existed there could only exist individuals. It is therefore from the individual that emanate the ideas and needs which have determined the formation of societies. If it is from him that everything comes, it is necessarily through him that everything must be explained. Moreover, in society there is nothing save individual consciousnesses, and it is consequently in these that is to be found the source of all social evolution. Thus sociological laws can only be a corollary of the more general laws of psychology. The ultimate explanation of collective life will consist in demonstrating how it derives from human nature in general, either by direct deduction from it without any preliminary observation, or by establishing links after having observed human nature. . . .

But such a method is not applicable to sociological phenomena unless one distorts their nature. For proof of this we need only refer to the definition we have given. Since their essential characteristic is the power they possess to exert outside pressure on individual consciousnesses, this shows that they do not derive from these consciousnesses and that consequently sociology is not a corollary of psychology. This constraining power attests to the fact that they express a nature different from our own, since they only penetrate into us by force or at the very least by bearing down more or less heavily upon us. If social life were no more than an extension of the individual, we would not see it return to its origin and invade the individual consciousness so precipitately. The authority to which the individual bows when he acts, thinks or feels socially dominates him to such a degree because it is a product of forces which transcend him and for which he consequently cannot account. It is not from within himself that can come the external pressure which he undergoes; it is therefore not what is happening within himself which can explain it. It is true that we are not incapable of placing constraints upon ourselves; we can restrain our tendencies, our habits, even our instincts, and halt their development by an act of inhibition. But inhibitive movements must not be confused with those which make up social constraint. The process of inhibitive movements is centrifugal; but the latter are centripetal. The former are worked out in the individual consciousness and then tend to manifest themselves externally; the latter are at first external to the individual, whom they tend afterwards to shape from the outside in their own image. Inhibition is, if one likes, the means by which social constraint produces its psychical effects, but is not itself that constraint.

Now, once the individual is ruled out, only society remains. It is therefore in the nature of society itself that we must seek the explanation of social life. We can conceive that, since it transcends infinitely the indivdual both in time and space, it is capable of imposing upon him the ways of acting and thinking that it has consecrated by its authority. This pressure, which is the distinctive sign of social facts, is that which all exert upon each individual.

But it will be argued that since the sole elements of which society is composed are individuals, the primary origin of sociological phenomena cannot be other than psychological. Reasoning in this way, we can just as easily establish that biological phenomena are explained analytically by inorganic phenomena. It is indeed certain that in the living cell there are only molecules of crude matter. But they are in association, and it is this association which is the cause of the new phenomena which characterise life, even the germ of which it is impossible to find in a single one of these associated elements. This is because the whole does not equal the sum of its parts; it is something different, whose properties differ from those displayed by the parts from which it is formed. Association is not, as has sometimes been believed, a phenomenon infertile in itself, which consists merely in juxtaposing externally facts already given and properties already constituted. On the contrary, is it not the source of all the successive innovations that have occurred in the course of the general evolution of things? What differences exist between the lower organisms and others, between the organised living creature and the mere protoplasm, between the latter and the inorganic molecules of which it is composed, if it is not differences in association? All these beings, in the last analysis, split up into elements of the same nature; but these elements are in one place juxtaposed, in another associated. Here they are associated in one way, there in another. We are even justified in wondering whether this law does not even extend to the mineral world, and whether the differences which separate inorganic bodies do not have the same origin.

By virtue of this principle, society is not the mere sum of individuals, but the system formed by their association represents a specific reality which has its own characteristics. Undoubtedly no collective entity can be produced if there are no individual consciousnesses: this is a necessary but not a sufficient condition. In addition, these consciousnesses must be associated and combined, but combined in a certain way. It is from this combination that social life arises and consequently it is this combination which explains it. By aggregating together, by interpenetrating, by fusing together, individuals give birth to a being, psychical if you will, but one which constitutes a psychical individuality of a new kind.[7] Thus it is in the nature of that individuality and not in that of its component elements that we must search for the proximate and determining causes of the facts produced in it. The group thinks, feels and acts entirely differently from the way its members would if they were isolated. If therefore we begin by studying these members separately, we will understand nothing about what is taking place in the group. In a word, there is between psychology and sociology the same break in continuity as there is between biology and the physical and chemical sciences. Consequently every time a social phenomenon is directly explained by a psychological phenomenon, we may rest assured that the explanation is false.

Some will perhaps argue that, although society, once formed, is the proximate cause of social phenomena, the causes which have determined its formation are of a psychological nature. They may concede that, when individuals are associated together, their association may give rise to a new life, but claim that this can only take place for individual reasons. But in reality, as far as one can go back in history, the fact of association is the most obligatory of all, because it is the origin of all other obligations. By reason of my birth, I am obligatorily attached to a given people. It may be said that later, once I am an adult, I acquiesce in this obligation by the mere fact that I continue to live in my own country. But what does that matter? Such acquiescence does not remove its imperative character. Pressure accepted and undergone with good grace does not cease to be pressure. Moreover, how far does such acceptance go? Firstly, it is forced, for in the immense majority of cases it is materially and morally impossible for us to shed our nationality; such a rejection is even generally declared to be apostasy. Next, the acceptance cannot relate to the past, when I was in no position to accept, but which nevertheless determines the present. I did not seek the education I received; yet this above all else roots me to my native soil. Lastly, the acceptance can have no moral value for the future, in so far as this is unknown. I do not even know all the duties which one day may be incumbent upon me in my capacity as a citizen. How then could I acquiesce in them in advance? Now, as we have shown, all that is obligatory has its origins outside the individual. Thus, provided one does not place oneself outside history, the fact of association is of the same character as the others and is consequently explicable in the same way. Furthermore, as all societies are born of other societies, with no break in continuity, we may be assured that in the whole course of social evolution there has not been a single time when individuals have really had to consult together to decide whether they would enter into collective life together, and into one sort of collective life rather than another. Such a question is only possible when we go back to the first origins of any society. But the solutions, always dubious, which can be brought to such problems could not in any case affect the method whereby the facts given in history must be treated. We have therefore no need to discuss them.

Yet our thought would be singularly misinterpreted if the conclusion was drawn from the previous remarks that sociology, in our view, should not even take into account man and his faculties. On the contrary, it is clear that the general characteristics of human nature play their part in the work of elaboration from which social life results. But it is not these which produce it or give it its special form: they only make it possible. Collective representations, emotions and tendencies have not as their causes certain states of consciousness in individuals, but the conditions under which the body social as a whole exists. Doubtless these can be realised only if individual natures are not opposed to them. But these are simply the indeterminate matter which the social factor fashions and transforms. Their contribution is made up exclusively of very general states, vague and thus malleable predispositions which of themselves could not assume the definite and complex forms which characterise social phenomena, if other agents did not intervene.

What a gulf, for example, between the feelings that man experiences when confronted with forces superior to his own and the institution of religion with its beliefs and practices, so multifarious and complicated, and its material and moral organisation! What an abyss between the psychical conditions of sympathy which two people of the same blood feel for each other, and that hotchpotch of legal and moral rules which determine the structure of the family, personal relationships, and the relationship of things to persons, etc.! We have seen that even when society is reduced to an unorganised crowd, the collective sentiments which arise within it can not only be totally unlike, but even opposed to, the average sentiments of the individuals in it. How much greater still must be the gap when the pressure exerted upon the individual comes from a normal society, where, to the influence exerted by his contemporaries, is added that of previous generations and of tradition! A purely psychological explanation of social facts cannot therefore fail to miss completely all that is specific, i.e. social, about them.

What has blinkered the vision of many sociologists to the insufficiency of this method is the fact that, taking the effect for the cause, they have very often highlighted as causal conditions for social phenomena certain psychical states, relatively well defined and specific, but which in reality are the consequence of the phenomena. Thus it has been held that a certain religiosity is innate in man, as is a certain minimum of sexual jealousy, filial piety or fatherly affection, etc., and it is in these that explanations have been sought for religion, marriage and the family. But history shows that these inclinations, far from being inherent in human nature, are either completely absent under certain social conditions or vary so much from one society to another that the residue left after eliminating all these differences, and which alone can be considered of psychological origin, is reduced to something vague and schematic, infinitely removed from the facts which have to be explained. Thus these sentiments result from the collective organisation and are far from being at the basis of it. It has not even been proved at all that the tendency to sociability was originally a congenital instinct of the human race. It is much more natural to see in it a product of social life which has slowly become organised in us, because it is an observable fact that animals are sociable or otherwise, depending on whether their environmental conditions force them to live in common or cause them to shun such a life. And even then we must add that a considerable gap remains between these well determined tendencies and social reality. . . .

Hence we arrive at the following rule: *The determining cause of a social fact must be sought among antecedent social facts and not among the states of the individual consciousness.* Moreover, we can easily conceive that all that has been stated above applies to the determination of the function as well as the cause of a social fact. Its function can only be social, which means that it consists in the production of socially useful effects. Undoubtedly it can and indeed does happen that it has repercussions which also serve the individual. But this happy result is not the immediate rationale for its existence. Thus we can complement the preceding proposition by stating: *The function of a social fact must always be sought in the relationship that it bears to some social end.*

It is because sociologists have often failed to acknowledge this rule and have considered sociological phenomena from too psychological a viewpoint that their theories appear to many minds too vague, too ethereal and too remote from the distinctive nature of the things which sociologists believe they are explaining. The historian, in particular, who has a close contact with social reality cannot fail to feel strongly how these too general interpretations are incapable of being linked to the facts. In part, this has undoubtedly produced the mistrust that history has often manifested towards sociology. Assuredly this does not mean that the study of psychological facts is not indispensable to the sociologist. If collective life does not derive from individual life, the two are none the less closely related. If the latter cannot explain the former, it can at least render its explanation easier. Firstly, as we have shown, it is undeniably true that social facts are produced by an elaboration *sui generis* of psychological facts. But in addition this action is itself not dissimilar to that which occurs in each individual consciousness and which progressively transforms the primary elements (sensations, reflexes, instincts) of which the consciousness was originally made up. Not unreasonably has the claim been made that the ego is itself a society, just as is the organism, although in a different way. For a long time psychologists have demonstrated the absolute importance of the factor of *association* in the explanation of mental activity. Thus a psychological education, even more than a biological one, constitutes a necessary preparation for the sociologist. But it can only be of service to him if, once he has acquired it, he frees himself from it, going beyond it by adding a specifically sociological education. He must give up making psychology in some way the focal point of his operations, the point of departure to which he must always return after his adventurous incursions into the social world. He must establish himself at the very heart of social facts in order to observe and confront them totally, without any mediating factor, while calling upon the science of the individual only for a general preparation and, if needs be, for useful suggestions.[8]

Notes

1   It can be seen that to concede this proposition it is unnecessary to maintain that social life is made up of anything save representations. It is sufficient to posit that representations, whether individual or collective, cannot be studied scientifically unless they are studied objectively.

2   Moreover, this is not to say that all constraint is normal.

3   Suicides do not occur at any age, nor do they occur at all ages of life with the same frequency.

4   It can be seen how far removed this definition of the social fact is from that which serves as the basis for the ingenious system of Tarde. We must first state that our research has nowhere led us to corroboration of the preponderant influence that Tarde attributes to imitation in the genesis of collective facts. Moreover, from this definition, which is not a theory but a mere résumé of the immediate data observed, it seems clearly to follow that imitation does not always express, indeed never expresses, what is essential and characteristic in the social fact. Doubtless every social fact is imitated and has, as we have just shown, a tendency to become generalised, but this is because it is social, i.e. obligatory. Its capacity for expansion is not the cause but the consequence of its sociological character. If social facts were unique in bringing about this effect, imitation might serve, if not to explain them, at least to define them. But an individual state which impacts on others none the less remains individual. Moreover, one may speculate whether the term 'imitation' is indeed appropriate to designate a proliferation which occurs through some coercive influence. In such a single term very different phenomena, which need to be distinguished, are confused.

5   This close affinity of life and structure, organ and function, can be readily established in sociology because there exists between these two extremes a whole series of intermediate stages, immediately observable, which reveal the link between them. Biology lacks this methodological resource. But one may believe legitimately that sociological inductions on this subject are applicable to biology and that, in organisms as in societies, between these two categories of facts only differences in degree exist.

6   We would not wish to raise questions of general philosophy which would be inappropriate here. However, we note that, if more closely studied, this reciprocity of cause and effect could provide a means of reconciling scientific mechanism with the teleology implied by the existence and, above all, the persistence of life.

7   In this sense and for these reasons we can and must speak of a collective consciousness distinct from individual consciousnesses. To justify this distinction there is no need to hypostatise the collective consciousness; it is something special and must be designated by a special term, simply because the states which constitute it differ specifically from those which make up individual consciousnesses. This specificity arises because they are not formed from the same elements. Individual consciousnesses result from the nature of the organic and psychical being taken in isolation, collective consciousnesses from a plurality of beings of this kind. The results cannot therefore fail to be different, since the component parts differ to this extent. Our definition of the social fact, moreover, did no more than highlight, in a different way, this demarcation line.

8   Psychical phenomena can only have social consequences when they are so closely linked to social phenomena that the actions of both are necessarily intermingled. This is the case for certain socio-psychical phenomena. Thus a public official is a social force, but at the same time he is an individual. The result is that he can employ the social force he commands in a way determined by his individual nature and thereby exert an influence

on the constitution of society. This is what occurs with statesmen and, more generally, with men of genius. The latter, although they do not fulfil a social role, draw from the collective sentiments of which they are the object an authority which is itself a social force, one which they can to a certain extent place at the service of their personal ideas. But it can be seen that such cases are due to individual chance and consequently cannot affect the characteristics which constitute the social species, which alone is the object of science. The limitation on the principle enunciated above is therefore not of great importance to the sociologist.

B: SOLIDARITY AND MODERN LIFE

11 The Division of Labor in Society

Emile Durkheim

The Problem

Although the division of labour is not of recent origin, it was only at the end of the last century that societies began to become aware of this law, to which up to then they had submitted almost unwittingly. Undoubtedly even from antiquity several thinkers had perceived its importance. Yet Adam Smith was the first to attempt to elaborate the theory of it. Moreover, it was he who first coined the term, which social science later lent to biology.

Nowadays the phenomenon has become so widespread that it catches everyone's attention. We can no longer be under any illusion about the trends in modern industry. It involves increasingly powerful mechanisms, large-scale groupings of power and capital, and consequently an extreme division of labour. Inside factories, not only are jobs demarcated, becoming extremely specialised, but each product is itself a speciality entailing the existence of others. Adam Smith and John Stuart Mill persisted in hoping that agriculture at least would prove an exception to the rule, seeing in it the last refuge of small-scale ownership. Although in such a matter we must guard against generalising unduly, nowadays it appears difficult to deny that the main branches of the agricultural industry are increasingly swept along in the general trend. Finally, commerce itself contrives ways to follow and reflect, in all their distinctive nuances, the boundless diversity of industrial undertakings. Although this evolution occurs spontaneously and unthinkingly, those economists who study its causes and evaluate its results, far from condemning such diversification or attacking it, proclaim its necessity. They perceive in it the higher law of human societies and the condition for progress.

Yet the division of labour is not peculiar to economic life. We can observe its increasing influence in the most diverse sectors of society. Functions, whether political, administrative or judicial, are becoming more and more specialised. The same is true in the arts and sciences. . . .

The Function of the Division of Labour

We have not merely to investigate whether, in these kinds of societies, there exists a social solidarity arising from the division of labour. This is a self-evident truth, since in them the division of labour is highly developed and it engenders solidarity. But above all we must determine the degree to which the solidarity it produces contributes generally to the integration of society. Only then shall we learn to what extent it is necessary, whether it is an essential factor in social cohesion, or whether, on the contrary, it is only an ancillary and secondary condition for it. To answer this question we must therefore compare this social bond to others, in order to measure what share in the total effect must be attributed to it. To do this it is indispensable to begin by classifying the different species of social solidarity.

However, social solidarity is a wholly moral phenomenon which by itself is not amenable to exact observation and especially not to measurement. To arrive at this classification, as well as this comparison, we must therefore substitute for this internal datum, which escapes us, an external one which symbolises it, and then study the former through the latter.

That visible symbol is the law. Indeed where social solidarity exists, in spite of its non-material nature, it does not remain in a state of pure potentiality, but shows its presence through perceptible effects. Where it is strong it attracts men strongly to one another, ensures frequent contacts between them, and multiplies the opportunities available to them to enter into mutual relationships. To state the position precisely, at the point we have now reached it is not easy to say whether it is social solidarity that produces these phenomena or, on the contrary, whether it is the result of them. Likewise it is a moot point whether men draw closer to one another because of the strong effects of social solidarity, or whether it is strong because men *have* come closer together. However, for the moment we need not concern ourselves with clarifying this question. It is enough to state that these two orders of facts are linked, varying with each other simultaneously and directly. The more closely knit the members of a society, the more they maintain various relationships either with one another or with the group collectively. For if they met together rarely, they would not be mutually dependent, except sporadically and somewhat weakly. Moreover, the number of these relationships is necessarily proportional to that of the legal rules that determine them. In fact, social life, wherever it becomes lasting, inevitably tends to assume a definite form and become organised. Law is nothing more than this very organisation in its most stable and precise form. Life in general within a society cannot enlarge in scope without legal activity simultaneously increasing in proportion. Thus we may be sure to find reflected in the law all the essential varieties of social solidarity.

It may certainly be objected that social relationships can be forged without necessarily taking on a legal form. Some do exist where the process of regulation does not attain such a level of consolidation and precision. This does not mean that they remain indeterminate; instead of being regulated by law they are merely regulated by custom. Thus law mirrors only a part of social life and consequently provides us with only incomplete data with which to resolve the problem. What is more, it is often the case that custom is out of step with the law. It is repeatedly stated that custom tempers the harshness of the law, corrects the excesses that arise from its formal nature, and is even occasionally inspired with a very different ethos. Might then custom display other kinds of social solidarity than those expressed in positive law?

But such an antithesis only occurs in wholly exceptional circumstances. For it to occur law must have ceased to correspond to the present state of society and yet, although lacking any reason to exist, is sustained through force of habit. In that event, the new relationships that are established in spite of it will become organised, for they cannot subsist without seeking to consolidate themselves. Yet, being at odds with the old law, which persists, and not succeeding in penetrating the legal domain proper, they do not rise beyond the level of custom. Thus opposition breaks out. But this can only happen in rare, pathological cases, and cannot even continue without becoming dangerous. Normally custom is not opposed to law; on the contrary, it forms the basis for it. It is true that sometimes nothing further is built upon this basis. There may exist social relationships governed only by that diffuse form of regulation arising from custom. But this is because they lack importance and continuity, excepting naturally those abnormal cases just mentioned. Thus if types of social solidarity chance to exist which custom alone renders apparent, these are assuredly of a very secondary order. On the other hand the law reproduces all those types that are essential, and it is about these alone that we need to know.

Should we go further and assert that social solidarity does not consist entirely in its visible manifestations; that these express it only partially and imperfectly; that beyond law and custom there exists an inner state from which solidarity derives; and that to know it in reality we must penetrate to its heart, without any intermediary? But in science we can know causes only through the effects that they produce. In order to determine the nature of these causes more precisely science selects only those results that are the most objective and that best lend themselves to quantification. Science studies heat through the variations in volume that changes in temperature cause in bodies, electricity through its physical and chemical effects, and force through movement. Why should social solidarity prove an exception?

Moreover, what remains of social solidarity once it is divested of its social forms? What imparts to it its specific characteristics is the nature of the group whose unity it ensures, and this is why it varies according to the types of society. It is not the same within the family as within political societies. We are not attached to our native land in the same way as the Roman was to his city or the German to his tribe. But since such differences spring from social causes, we can only grasp them through the differences that the social effects of solidarity present to us. Thus if we neglect the differences, all varieties become indistinguishable, and we can perceive no more than that which is common to all varieties, that is, the general tendency to sociability, a tendency that is always and everywhere the same and is not linked to any particular social type. But this residual element is only an abstraction, for sociability *per se* is met with nowhere. What exists and what is really alive are the special forms of solidarity – domestic, professional, national, that of the past and that of today, etc. Each has its own special nature. Hence generalities can in any case only furnish a very incomplete explanation of the phenomenon, since they necessarily allow to escape what is concrete and living about it.

Thus the study of solidarity lies within the domain of sociology. It is a social fact that can only be thoroughly known through its social effects. If so many moralists and psychologists have been able to deal with this question without following this method, it is because they have avoided the difficulty. They have divested the phenomenon of everything that is more specifically social about it, retaining only the psychological core from which it develops. It is certain that solidarity, whilst being pre-eminently a social fact, is dependent upon our individual organism. In order to be capable of existing it must fit our physical and psychological constitution. Thus, at the very least, we can content ourselves with studying it from this viewpoint. But in that case we shall perceive only that aspect of it which is the most indistinct and the least special. Strictly speaking, this is not even solidarity itself, but only what makes it possible.

Even so, such an abstract study cannot yield very fruitful results. For, so long as it remains in the state of a mere predisposition of our psychological nature, solidarity is something too indefinite to be easily understood. It remains an intangible virtuality too elusive to observe. To take on a form that we can grasp, social outcomes must provide an external interpretation of it. Moreover, even in such an indeterminate state, it depends on social conditions that explain it, and cannot consequently be detached from them. This is why some sociological perspectives are not infrequently to be found mixed up with these purely psychological analyses. For example, some mention is made of the influence of the *gregarious state* on the formation of social feeling in general; or the main social relationships on which sociability most obviously depends are rapidly sketched out. Undoubtedly such additional considerations, introduced unsystematically as examples and at random as they suggest themselves, cannot suffice to cast much light on the social nature of solidarity. Yet at least they demonstrate that the sociological viewpoint must weigh even with the psychologists.

Thus our method is clearly traced out for us. Since law reproduces the main forms of social solidarity, we have only to classify the different types of law in order to be able to investigate which types of social solidarity correspond to them. It is already likely that one species of law exists which symbolises the special solidarity engendered by the division of labour. Once we have made this investigation, in order to judge what part the division of labour plays it will be enough to compare the number of legal rules which give it expression with the total volume of law.

To undertake this study we cannot use the habitual distinctions made by jurisprudents. Conceived for the practice of law, from this viewpoint they can be very convenient, but science cannot be satisfied with such empirical classifications and approximations. The most widespread classification is that which divides law into public and private law. Public law is held to regulate the relationships of the individual with the state, private law those of individuals with one another. Yet when we attempt to define these terms closely, the dividing line, which appeared at first sight to be so clear-cut, disappears. All law is private, in the sense that always and everywhere individuals are concerned and are its actors. Above all, however, all law is public, in the sense that it is a social function, and all individuals are, although in different respects, functionaries of society. The functions of marriage and parenthood, etc. are not spelt out or organised any differently from those of ministers or legislators. Not without reason did Roman law term guardianship a *munus publicum*. Moreover, what is the state? Where does it begin, where does it end? The controversial nature of this question is well known. It is unscientific to base such a fundamental classification on such an obscure and inadequately analysed idea.

In order to proceed methodically, we have to discover some characteristic which, whilst essential to juridical phenomena, is capable of varying as they vary. Now, every legal precept may be defined as a rule of behaviour to which sanctions apply. Moreover, it is clear that the sanctions change according to the degree of seriousness attached to the precepts, the place they occupy in the public consciousness, and the role they play in society. Thus it is appropraite to classify legal rules according to the different sanctions that are attached to them.

These are of two kinds. The first consist essentially in some injury, or at least some disadvantage imposed upon the perpetrator of a crime. Their purpose is to do harm to him through his fortune, his honour, his life, his liberty, or to deprive him of some object whose possession he enjoys. These are said to be repressive sanctions, such as those laid down in the penal code. It is true that those that appertain to purely moral rules are of the same character. Yet such sanctions are administered in a diffuse way by everybody without distinction, whilst those of the penal code are applied only through the mediation of a definite body – they are organised. As for the other kind of sanctions, they do not necessarily imply any suffering on the part of the perpetrator, but merely consist in *restoring the previous state of affairs*, re-establishing relationships that have been disturbed from their normal form. This is done either by forcibly redressing the action impugned, restoring it to the type from which it has deviated, or by annulling it, that is depriving it of all social value. Thus legal rules must be divided into two main species, according to whether they relate to repressive, organised sanctions, or to ones that are purely restitutory. The first group covers all penal law; the second, civil law, commercial law, procedural law, administrative and constitutional law, when any penal rules which may be attached to them have been removed.

Let us now investigate what kind of social solidarity corresponds to each of these species. . . .

Mechanical Solidarity, or Solidarity by Similarities

The totality of beliefs and sentiments common to the average members of a society forms a determinate system with a life of its own. It can be termed the collective or common consciousness. Undoubtedly the substratum of this consciousness does not consist of a single organ. By definition it is diffused over society as a whole, but nonetheless possesses specific characteristics that make it a distinctive reality. In fact it is independent of the particular conditions in which individuals find themselves. Individuals pass on, but it abides. It is the same in north and south, in large towns and in small, and in different professions. Likewise it does not change with every generation but, on the contrary, links successive generations to one another. Thus it is something totally different from the consciousnesses of individuals, although it is only realised in individuals. It is the psychological type of society, one which has its properties, conditions for existence and mode of development, just as individual types do, but in a different fashion. For this reason it has the right to be designated by a special term. It is true that the one we have employed above is not without ambiguity. Since the terms 'collective' and 'social' are often taken as synonyms, one is inclined to believe that the collective consciousness is the entire social consciousness, that is, co-terminous with the psychological life of society, whereas, particularly in higher societies, it constitutes only a very limited part of it. Those functions that are judicial, governmental, scientific or industrial – in short, all the specific functions – appertain to the psychological order, since they consist of systems of representation and action. However, they clearly lie outside the common consciousness. To avoid a confusion[1] that has occurred it would perhaps be best to invent a technical expression which would specifically designate the sum total of social similarities. However, since the use of a new term, when it is not absolutely necessary, is not without its disadvantages, we shall retain the more generally used expression, 'collective (or common) consciousness', but always keeping in mind the restricted sense in which we are employing it.

Thus, we may state that an act is criminal when it offends the strong, well-defined states of the collective consciousness.[2]

This proposition, taken literally, is scarcely disputed, although usually we give it a meaning very different from the one it should have. It is taken as if it expressed, not the essential characteristics of the crime, but one of its repercussions. We well know that crime offends very general sentiments, but ones that are strongly held. But it is believed that their generality and strength spring from the criminal nature of the act, which consequently still remains wholly to be defined. It is not disputed that any criminal act excites universal disapproval, but it is taken for granted that this results from its criminal nature. Yet one is then hard put to it to state what is the nature of this criminality. Is it in a particularly serious form of immorality? I would concur, but this is to answer a question by posing another, by substituting one term for another. For what *is* immorality is precisely what we want to know – and particularly that special form of immorality which society represses by an organised system of punishments, and which constitutes criminality. Clearly it can only derive from one or several characteristics common to all varieties of crime. Now the only characteristic to satisfy that condition refers to the opposition that exists between crime of any kind and certain collective sentiments. It is thus the opposition which, far from deriving from the crime, constitutes the crime. In other words, we should not say that an act offends the common consciousness because it is criminal, but that it is criminal because it offends that consciousness. We do not condemn it because it is a crime, but it is a crime because we condemn it. As regards the intrinsic nature of these feelings, we cannot specify what that is. They have very diverse objects, so that they cannot be encompassed within a single formula. They cannot be said to relate to the vital interests of society or to a minimum of justice. All such definitions are inadequate. But by the mere fact that a sentiment, whatever may be its origin and purpose, is found in every consciousness and endowed with a certain degree of strength and precision, every act that disturbs it is a crime. Present-day psychology is increasingly turning back to Spinoza's idea that things are good because we like them, rather than that we like them because they are good. What is primary is the tendency and disposition: pleasure and pain are only facts derived from this. The same holds good for social life. An act is socially evil because it is rejected by society. But, it will be contended, are there no collective sentiments that arise from the pleasure or pain that society feels when it comes into contact with their objects? This is doubtless so, but all such sentiments do not originate in this way. Many, if not the majority, derive from utterly different causes. Anything that obliges our activity to take on a definite form can give rise to habits that result in dispositions which then have to be satisfied. Moreover, these dispositions alone are truly fundamental. The others are only special forms of them and are more determinate. Thus to find charm in a particular object, collective sensibility must already have been constituted in such a way as to be able to appreciate it. If the corresponding sentiments are abolished, an act most disastrous for society will not only be capable of being tolerated, but honoured and held up as an example. Pleasure cannot create a disposition out of nothing; it can only link to a particular end those dispositions that already exist, provided that end is in accordance with their original nature. . . .

Thus our analysis of punishment has substantiated our definition of crime. We began by establishing inductively that crime consisted essentially in an act contrary to strong, well-defined states of the common consciousness. We have just seen that in effect all the characteristics of punishment derive from the nature of crime. Thus the rules sanctioned by punishment are the expression of the most essential social similarities.

We can therefore see what kind of solidarity the penal law symbolises. In fact we all know that a social cohesion exists whose cause can be traced to a certain conformity of each individual consciousness to a common type, which is none other than the psychological type of society. Indeed under these conditions all members of the group are not only individually attracted to one another because they resemble one another, but they are also linked to what is the condition for the existence of this collective type, that is, to the society that they form by coming together. Not only do fellow-citizens like one another, seeking one another out in preference to foreigners, but they love their country. They wish for it what they would wish for themselves, they care that it should be lasting and prosperous, because without it a whole area of their psychological life would fail to function smoothly. Conversely, society insists upon its citizens displaying all these basic resemblances because it is a condition for its own cohesion. Two consciousnesses exist within us: the one comprises only states that are personal to each one of us, characteristic of us as individuals, whilst the other comprises states that are common to the whole of society.[3] The former represents only our individual personality, which it constitutes; the latter represents the collective type and consequently the society without which it would not exist. When it is an element of the latter determining our behaviour, we do not act with an eye to our own personal interest, but are pursuing collective ends. Now, although distinct, these two consciousnesses are linked to each other, since in the end they constitute only one entity, for both have one and the same organic basis. Thus they are solidly joined together. This gives rise to a solidarity *sui generis* which, deriving from resemblances, binds the individual directly to society. We propose to term this solidarity mechanical. It does not consist merely in a general, indeterminate attachment of the individual to the group, but is also one that concerts their detailed actions. Indeed, since such collective motives are the same everywhere, they produce everywhere the same effects. Consequently, whenever they are brought into play all wills spontaneously move as one in the same direction.

It is this solidarity that repressive law expresses, at least in regard to what is vital to it. Indeed the acts which such law forbids and stigmatises as crimes are of two kinds: either they manifest directly a too violent dissimilarity between the one who commits them and the collective type; or they offend the organ of the common consciousness. In both cases the force shocked by the crime and that rejects it is thus the same. It is a result of the most vital social similarities, and its effect is to maintain the social cohesion that arises from these similarities. It is that force which the penal law guards against being weakened in any way. At the same time it does this by insisting upon a minimum number of similarities from each one of us, without which the individual would be a threat to the unity of the body social, and by enforcing respect for the symbol which expresses and epitomises these resemblances, whilst simultaneously guaranteeing them.

By this is explained why some acts have so frequently been held to be criminal, and punished as such, without in themselves being harmful to society. Indeed, just like the individual type, the collective type has been fashioned under the influence of very diverse causes, and even of random events. A product of historical development, it bears the mark of those circumstances of every kind through which society has lived during its history. It would therefore be a miracle if everything to be found in it were geared to some useful end. Some elements, more or less numerous, cannot fail to have been introduced into it which are unrelated to social utility. Among the dispositions and tendencies the individual has received from his ancestors or has developed over time there are certainly many that serve no purpose, or that cost more than the benefits they bring. Undoubtedly most of these are not harmful, for if they were, in such conditions the individual could not live. But there are some that persist although lacking in all utility. Even those that do undisputedly render a service are frequently of an intensity disproportionate to their usefulness, because that intensity derives in part from other causes. The same holds good for collective emotions. Every act that disturbs them is not dangerous in itself, or at least is not so perilous as the condemnation it earns. However, the reprobation such acts incur is not without reason. For, whatever the origin of these sentiments, once they constitute a part of the collective type, and particularly if they are essential elements in it, everything that serves to undermine them at the same time undermines social cohesion and is prejudicial to society. In their origin they had no usefulness but, having survived it, it becomes necessary for them to continue despite their irrationality. This is generally why it is good that acts that offend these sentiments should not be tolerated. Doubtless, by reasoning in the abstract it can indeed be shown that there are no grounds for a society to prohibit the eating of a particular kind of meat, an action inoffensive in itself. But once an abhorrence of this food has become an integral part of the common consciousness it cannot disappear without social bonds becoming loosened, and of this the healthy individual consciousness is vaguely aware.[4]

The same is true of punishment. Although it proceeds from an entirely mechanical reaction and from an access of passionate emotion, for the most part unthinking, it continues to play a useful role. But that role is not the one commonly perceived. It does not serve, or serves only very incidentally, to correct the guilty person or to scare off any possible imitators. From this dual viewpoint its effectiveness may rightly be questioned; in any case it is mediocre. Its real function is to maintain inviolate the cohesion of society by sustaining the common consciousness in all its vigour. If that consciousness were thwarted so categorically, it would necessarily lose some of its power, were an emotional reaction from the community not forthcoming to make good that loss. Thus there would result a relaxation in the bonds of social solidarity. The consciousness must therefore be conspicuously reinforced the moment it meets with opposition. The sole means of doing so is to give voice to the unanimous aversion that the crime continues to evoke, and this by an official act, which can only mean suffering inflicted upon the wrongdoer. Thus, although a necessary outcome of the causes that give rise to it, this suffering is not a gratuitous act of cruelty. It is a sign indicating that the sentiments of the collectivity are still unchanged, that the communion of minds sharing the same beliefs remains absolute, and in this way the injury that the crime has inflicted upon society is made good. This is why it is right to maintain that the criminal should suffer in proportion to his crime, and why theories that deny to punishment any expiatory character appear, in the minds of many, to subvert the social order. In fact such theories could only be put into practice in a society from which almost every trace of the common consciousness has been expunged. Without this necessary act of satisfaction what is called the moral consciousness could not be preserved. Thus, without being paradoxical, we may state that punishment is above all intended to have its effect upon honest people. Since it serves to heal the wounds inflicted upon the collective sentiments, it can only fulfil this role where such sentiments exist, and in so far as they are active. Undoubtedly, by forestalling in minds already distressed any further weakening of the collective psyche, punishment can indeed prevent such attacks from multiplying. But such a result, useful though it is, is merely a particular side-effect. In short, to visualise an exact idea of punishment, the two opposing theories that have been advanced must be reconciled: the one sees in punishment an expiation, the other conceives it as a weapon for the defence of society. Certainly it does fulfil the function of protecting society, but this is because of its expiatory nature. Moreover, if it must be expiatory, this is not because suffering redeems error by virtue of some mystic strength or another, but because it cannot produce its socially useful effect save on this one condition.[5]. . .

Solidarity Arising From the Division of Labour, or Organic Solidarity

The very nature of the restitutory sanction is sufficient to show that the social solidarity to which that law corresponds is of a completely different kind.

The distinguishing mark of this sanction is that it is not expiatory, but comes down to a mere *restoration of the 'status quo ante'*. Suffering in proportion to the offence is not inflicted upon the one who has broken the law or failed to acknowledge it; he is merely condemned to submit to it. If certain acts have already been performed, the judge restores them to what they should be. He pronounces what the law is, but does not talk of punishment. Damages awarded have no penal character: they are simply a means of putting back the clock so as to restore the past, so far as possible, to its normal state. It is true that Tarde believed that he had discovered a kind of civil penal law in the awarding of costs, which are always borne by the losing party. Yet taken in this sense the term has no more than a metaphorical value. For there to be punishment there should at least be some proportionality between the punishment and the wrong, and for this one would have to establish exactly the degree of seriousness of the wrong. In fact the loser of the case pays its costs even when his intentions were innocent and he is guilty of nothing more than ignorance. The reasons for this rule therefore seem to be entirely different. Since justice is not administered free, it seems equitable that the costs should be borne by the one who has occasioned them. Moreover, although it is possible that the prospect of such costs may stop the overhasty litigant, this is not enough for them to be considered a punishment. The fear of ruin that is normally consequent upon idleness and neglect may cause the businessman to be energetic and diligent. Yet ruin, in the exact connotation of the term, is not the penal sanction for his shortcomings.

Failure to observe these rules is not even sanctioned by a diffused form of punishment. The plaintiff who has lost his case is not disgraced, nor is his honour impugned. We can even envisage these rules being different from what they are without any feeling of repugnance. The idea that murder can be tolerated sets us up in arms, but we very readily accept that the law of inheritance might be modified, and many even conceive that it could be abolished. At least it is a question that we are not unwilling to discuss. Likewise, we agree without difficulty that the laws regarding easements or usufruct might be framed differently, or that the mutual obligations of buyer and vendor might be determined in another way, and that administrative functions might be allocated according to different principles. Since these prescriptions do not correspond to any feeling within us, and as generally we do not know their scientific justification, since this science does not yet exist, they have no deep roots in most of us. Doubtless there are exceptions. We do not tolerate the idea that an undertaking entered into that is contrary to morals or obtained either by violence or fraud can bind the contracting parties. Thus when public opinion is faced with cases of this kind it shows itself less indifferent than we have just asserted, and it adds its disapprobation to the legal sanction, causing it to weigh more heavily. This is because there are no clear-cut partitions between the various domains of moral life. On the contrary, they form a continuum, and consequently adjacent areas exist where different characteristics may be found at one and the same time. Nevertheless the proposition we have enunciated remains true in the overwhelming majority of cases. It demonstrates that rules where sanctions are restitutory either constitute no part at all of the collective consciousness, or subsist in it in only a weak state. Repressive law corresponds to what is the heart and centre of the common consciousness. Purely moral rules are already a less central part of it. Lastly, restitutory law springs from the farthest zones of consciousness and extends well beyond them. The more it becomes truly itself, the more it takes its distance.

This characteristic is moreover evinced in the way that it functions. Whereas repressive law tends to stay diffused throughout society, restitutory law sets up for itself ever more specialized bodies: consular courts, and industrial and administrative tribunals of every kind. Even in its most general sector, that of civil law, it is brought into use only by special officials – magistrates, lawyers, etc., who have been equipped for their role by a very special kind of training.

But although these rules are more or less outside the collective consciousness, they do not merely concern private individuals. If this were the case, restitutory law would have nothing in common with social solidarity, for the relationships it regulates would join individuals to one another without their being linked to society. They would be mere events of private life, as are, for instance, relationships of friendship. Yet it is far from the case that society is absent from this sphere of legal activity. Generally it is true that it does not intervene by itself and of its own volition: it must be solicited to do so by the parties concerned. Yet although it has to be invoked, its intervention is none the less the essential cog in the mechanism, since it alone causes that mechanism to function. It is society that declares what the law is, through its body of representatives.

However, it has been maintained that this role is in no way an especially social one, but comes down to being that of a conciliator of private interests. Consequently it has been held that any private individual could fulfil it, and that if society adopted it, this was solely for reasons of convenience. Yet it is wholly inaccurate to make society a kind of third-party arbitrator between the other parties. When it is induced to intervene it is not to reconcile the interests of individuals. It does not investigate what may be the most advantageous solution for the protagonists, nor does it suggest a compromise. But it does apply to the particular case submitted to it the general and traditional rules of the law. Yet the law is pre-eminently a social matter, whose object is absolutely different from the interests of the litigants. The judge who examines a divorce petition is not concerned to know whether this form of separation is really desirable for the husband and wife, but whether the causes invoked for it fall into one of the categories stipulated by law.

Yet to assess accurately the importance of the intervention by society it must be observed not only at the moment when the sanction is applied, or when the relationship that has been upset is restored, but also when it is instituted.

Social action is in fact necessary either to lay a foundation for, or to modify, a number of legal relationships regulated by this form of law, and which the assent of the interested parties is not adequate enough either to institute or alter. Of this nature are those relationships in particular that concern personal status. Although marriage is a contract, the partners can neither draw it up nor rescind it at will. The same holds good for all other domestic relationships, and a fortiori for all those regulated by administrative law. It is true that obligations that are properly contractual can be entered into or abrogated by the mere will to agreement of the parties. Yet we must bear in mind that, if a contract has binding force, it is society which confers that force. Let us assume that it does not give its blessing to the obligations that have been contracted; these then become pure promises possessing only moral authority.[6] Every contract therefore assumes that behind the parties who bind each other, society is there, quite prepared to intervene and to enforce respect for any undertakings entered into. Thus it only bestows this obligatory force upon contracts that have a social value in themselves, that is, those that are in conformity with the rules of law. We shall even occasionally see that its intervention is still more positive. It is therefore present in every relationship determined by restitutory law, even in ones that appear the most completely private, and its presence, although not felt, at least under normal conditions, is no less essential.

Since the rules where sanctions are restitutory do not involve the common consciousness, the relationships that they determine are not of the sort that affect everyone indiscriminately. This means that they are instituted directly, not between the individual and society, but between limited and particular elements in society, which they link to one another. Yet on the other hand, since society is not absent it must necessarily indeed be concerned to some extent, and feel some repercussions. Then, depending upon the intensity with which it feels them, it intervenes at a greater or lesser distance, and more or less actively, through the mediation of special bodies whose task it is to represent it. These relationships are therefore very different from those regulated by repressive law, for the latter join directly, without any intermediary, the individual consciousness to that of society, that is, the individual himself to society. . . .

(1) The first kind links the individual directly to society without any intermediary. With the second kind he depends upon society because he depends upon the parts that go to constitute it.

(2) In the two cases, society is not viewed from the same perspective. In the first, the term is used to denote a more or less organised society composed of beliefs and sentiments common to all the members of the group: this is the collective type. On the contrary, in the second case the society to which we are solidly joined is a system of different and special functions united by definite relationships. Moreover, these two societies are really one. They are two facets of one and the same reality, but which none the less need to be distinguished from each other.

(3) From this second difference there arises another which will serve to allow us to characterise and delineate the features of these two kinds of solidarity.

The first kind can only be strong to the extent that the ideas and tendencies common to all members of the society exceed in number and intensity those that appertain personally to each one of those members. The greater this excess, the more active this kind of society is. Now what constitutes our personality is that which each one of us possesses that is peculiar and characteristic, what distinguishes it from others. This solidarity can therefore only increase in inverse relationship to the personality. As we have said, there is in the consciousness of each one of us two consciousnesses: one that we share in common with our group in its entirety, which is consequently not ourselves, but society living and acting within us; the other that, on the contrary, represents us alone in what is personal and distinctive about us, what makes us an individual.[7] The solidarity that derives from similarities is at its *maximum* when the collective consciousness completely envelops our total consciousness, coinciding with it at every point. At that moment our individuality is zero. That individuality cannot arise until the community fills us less completely. Here there are two opposing forces, the one centripetal, the other centrifugal, which cannot increase at the same time. We cannot ourselves develop simultaneously in two so opposing directions. If we have a strong inclination to think and act for ourselves we cannot be strongly inclined to think and act like other people. If the ideal is to create for ourselves a special, personal image, this cannot mean to be like everyone else. Moreover, at the very moment when this solidarity exerts its effect, our personality, it may be said by definition, disappears, for we are no longer ourselves, but a collective being.

The social molecules that can only cohere in this one manner cannot therefore move as a unit save in so far as they lack any movement of their own, as do the molecules of inorganic bodies. This is why we suggest that this kind of solidarity should be called mechanical. The word does not mean that the solidarity is produced by mechanical and artificial means. We only use this term for it by analogy with the cohesion that links together the elements of raw materials, in contrast to that which encompasses the unity of living organisms. What finally justifies the use of this term is the fact that the bond that thus unites the individual with society is completely analogous to that which links the thing to the person. The individual consciousness, considered from this viewpoint, is simply a dependency of the collective type, and follows all its motions, just as the object possessed follows those which its owner imposes upon it. In societies where this solidarity is highly developed the individual does not belong to himself; he is literally a thing at the disposal of society. Thus, in these same social types, personal rights are still not yet distinguished from 'real' rights.

The situation is entirely different in the case of solidarity that brings about the division of labour. Whereas the other solidarity implies that individuals resemble one another, the latter assumes that they are different from one another. The former type is only possible in so far as the individual personality is absorbed into the collective personality; the latter is only possible if each one of us has a sphere of action that is peculiarly our own, and consequently a personality. Thus the collective consciousness leaves uncovered a part of the individual consciousness, so that there may be established in it those special functions that it cannot regulate. The more extensive this free area is, the stronger the cohesion that arises from this solidarity. Indeed, on the one hand each one of us depends more intimately upon society the more labour is divided up, and on the other, the activity of each one of us is correspondingly more specialised, the more personal it is. Doubtless, however circumscribed that activity may be, it is never completely original. Even in the exercise of our profession we conform to usages and practices that are common to us all within our corporation. Yet even in this case, the burden that we bear is in a different way less heavy than when the whole of society bears down upon us, and this leaves much more room for the free play of our initiative. Here, then, the individuality of the whole grows at the same time as that of the parts. Society becomes more effective in moving in concert, at the same time as each of its elements has more movements that are peculiarly its own. This solidarity resembles that observed in the higher animals. In fact each organ has its own special characteristics and autonomy, yet the greater the unity of the organism, the more marked the individualisation of the parts. Using this analogy, we propose to call 'organic' the solidarity that is due to the division of labour. . . .

The Causes

Thus it is in certain variations of the social environment that we must seek the cause that explains the progress of the division of labour.

In fact we have seen that the organised structure, and consequently the division of labour, develops regularly as the segmentary structure vanishes. It is therefore this disappearance that is the cause of this development; alternatively, the latter may be the cause of the former. This last hypothesis is not acceptable, for we know that the segmentary arrangement is an insurmountable obstacle to the division of labour and that the arrangement must have disappeared, at least in part, for the division of labour to be able to appear. It can only do so when the arrangement no longer exists. Undoubtedly once the division of labour exists it can contribute to speeding up its disappearance, but it only becomes apparent after the segmentary arrangement has partly receded. The effect reacts upon the cause, but does not in consequence cease to be an effect. Thus the reaction that it exerts is a secondary one. The increase in the division of labour is therefore due to the fact that the social segments lose their individuality, that the partitions dividing them become more permeable. In short, there occurs between them a coalescence that renders the social substance free to enter upon new combinations.

But the disappearance of this type can only bring about this result for the following reason. It is because there occurs a drawing together of individuals who were separated from one another, or at least they draw more closely together than they had been. Hence movements take place between the parts of the social mass which up to then had no reciprocal effect upon one another. The more the alveolar system is developed, the more the relationships in which each one of us is involved become enclosed within the limits of the alveola to which we belong. There are, as it were, moral vacuums between the various segments. On the other hand these vacuums fill up as the system levels off. Social life, instead of concentrating itself in innumerable small foci that are distinct but alike, becomes general. Social relationships – more exactly we should say intra-social relationships – consequently become more numerous, since they push out beyond their original boundaries on all sides. Thus the division of labour progresses the more individuals there are who are sufficiently in contact with one another to be able mutually to act and react upon one another. If we agree to call dynamic or moral density this drawing together and the active exchanges that result from it, we can say that the progress of the division of labour is in direct proportion to the moral or dynamic density of society.

But this act of drawing together morally can only bear fruit if the real distance between individuals has itself diminished, in whatever manner. Moral density cannot therefore increase without physical density increasing at the same time, and the latter can serve to measure the extent of the former. Moreover, it is useless to investigate which of the two has influenced the other; it suffices to realise that they are inseparable.

The progressive increase in density of societies in the course of their historical development occurs in three main ways:

(1)   Whilst lower societies spread themselves over areas that are relatively vast in comparison with the number of individuals that constitute them, amongst more advanced peoples the population is continually becoming more concentrated. Spencer says: 'If we contrast the populousness of regions inhabited by wild tribes with the populousness of equal regions in Europe; or if we contrast the density of population in England under the Heptarchy with its present density; we see that besides the growth produced by union of groups there has gone an interstitial growth.

The changes wrought successively in the industrial life of nations demonstrate how general this transformation is. The activity of nomadic tribes, whether hunters or shepherds, entails in fact the absence of any kind of concentration and dispersion over as wide an area as possible. Agriculture, because it is of necessity a settled existence, already presumes a certain drawing together of the social tissues, but one still very incomplete, since between each family tracts of land are interposed. In the city, although the condensation process was greater, yet houses did not adjoin one another, for joined building was not known in Roman law. This was invented on our own soil and demonstrates that the social ties have become tighter.[8] Moreover, from their origins European societies have seen their density increase continuously in spite of a few cases of temporary regression.

(2)   The formation and development of towns are a further symptom, even more characteristic, of the same phenomenon. The increase in average density can be due solely to the physical increase in the birth rate and can consequently be reconciled with a very weak concentration of people, and the very marked maintenance of the segmentary type of society. But towns always result from the need that drives individuals to keep constantly in the closest possible contact with one another. They are like so many points where the social mass is contracting more strongly than elsewhere. They cannot therefore multiply and spread out unless the moral density increases. Moreover, we shall see that towns recruit their numbers through migration to them, which is only possible to the extent that the fusion of social segments is far advanced.

So long as the social organisation is essentially segmentary, towns do not exist. There are none in lower societies; they are not met with among the Iroquois, nor among the primitive German tribes. The same was true for the primitive populations of Italy. 'The peoples of Italy,' states Marquardt, 'originally used not to live in towns, but in family or village communities (*pagi*), over which farms (*vici, οἶχοῖ*) were scattered.' Yet after a fairly short period of time the town made its appearance. Athens and Rome were or became towns, and the same transformation was accomplished throughout Italy. In our Christian societies the town appears from the very beginning, for those that the Roman Empire had left behind did not disappear with it. Since then, they have not ceased to grow and multiply. The tendency of country dwellers to flow into the towns, so general in the civilised world, is only a consequence of this movement. But this phenomenon does not date from the present day: from the seventeenth century onwards it preoccupied statesmen.

Because societies generally start with an agricultural period we have occasionally been tempted to regard the development of urban centres as a sign of old age and decadence. But we must not lose sight of the fact that this agricultural phase is the shorter the more societies belong to a higher type. Whilst in Germany, among the American Indians and among all primitive peoples, it lasts as long as do these peoples themselves, in Rome or Athens it ceases fairly early on, and in France we may say that this agricultural state has never existed in a pure form. Conversely, urban life begins very early on, and consequently extends itself more. The regularly quicker acceleration of this development demonstrates that, far from constituting a kind of pathological phenomenon, it derives from the very nature of the higher social species. Even supposing therefore that today this movement has reached threatening proportions for our societies, which perhaps have no longer sufficient flexibility to adapt to it, it will not cease to continue, either through them, or after them, and the social types to be formed after our own will probably be distinguished by a more rapid and more complete regression of agricultural society.

(3)   Finally, there is the number and speed of the means of communication and transmission. By abolishing or lessening the vacuums separating social segments, these means increase the density of society. Moreover, there is no need to demonstrate that they are the more numerous and perfect the higher the type of society.

Since this visible and measurable symbol reflects the variations in what we have termed moral density,[9] we can substitute this symbol for the latter in the formula that we have put forward. We must, moreover, repeat here what we were saying earlier. If society, in concentrating itself, determines the development of the division of labour, the latter in its turn increases the concentration of society. But this is of no consequence, for the division of labour remains the derived action, and consequently the advances it makes are due to a parallel progress in social density, whatever may be the cause of this progress. This all we wished to establish.

But this factor is not the only one.

If the concentration of society produces this result, it is because it multiplies intra-social relationships. But these will be even more numerous if the total number of members in a society also becomes larger. If it includes more individuals, as well as their being in closer contact, the effect will necessarily be reinforced. Social volume has therefore the same influence over the division of labour as density.

In fact, societies are generally more voluminous the more advanced they are and consequently labour is more divided up in them. Spencer says that, 'Societies, like living bodies, begin as germs – originate from masses which are extremely minute in comparison with the masses some of them eventually reach. That out of small wandering hordes such as the lowest races now form, have arisen the largest societies, is a conclusion not to be contested.'

What we have said about the segmentary constitution makes this unquestionably true. We know in fact that societies are formed by a certain number of segments of unequal size that overlap with one another. These moulds are not artificial creations, particularly in the beginning. Even when they have become conventional they imitate and reproduce so far as possible the forms of natural arrangement that preceded them. Many ancient societies are maintained in this form. The largest among these subdivisions, those that include the others, correspond to the nearest lower social type. Likewise, among the segments of which they in turn are made up, the most extensive are the remains of the type that comes directly below the preceding one, and so on. Among the most advanced peoples we find traces of the most primitive social organisation. Thus the tribe is made up of an aggregate of hordes or clans; the nation (the Jewish nation, for example) and the city, of an aggregate of tribes; the city, in its turn, with the villages that are subordinate to it, is one element that enters into the most complex societies, etc. The social volume therefore cannot fail to grow, since each species is made up of a replication of societies of the immediately preceding species.

Yet there are exceptions. The Jewish nation, before the conquest, was probably more voluminous than the Roman city of the fourth century; yet it was of a lower species. China and Russia are much more populous than the most civilised nations in Europe. Consequently among these same peoples the division of labour did not develop in proportion to the social volume. This is because the growth in volume is not necessarily a mark of superiority if the density does not grow at the same time and in the same proportion. A society can reach very large dimensions because it contains a very large number of segments, whatever may be the nature of these. If therefore the largest of them only reproduces societies of a very inferior type, the segmentary structure will remain very pronounced, and in consequence the social organisation will be little advanced. An aggregate of clans, even if immense, ranks below the smallest society that is organised, since the latter has already gone through those stages of evolution below which the aggregate has remained. Likewise if the number of social units has some influence over the division of labour, it is not through itself and of necessity, but because the number of social relationships increases generally with the number of individuals. To obtain this result it is not enough for the society to comprise a large number of persons, but they must be in fairly intimate contact so as to act and react upon one another. If on the other hand they are separated by environments that are mutually impenetrable, only very rarely, and with difficulty, can they establish relationships, and everything occurs as if the number of people was small. An increase in social volume therefore does not always speed up the progress of the division of labour, but only when the mass condenses at the same time and to the same degree. Consequently it is, one may say, only an additional factor. Yet, when joined to the first factor, it extends the effects by an action peculiarly its own, and thus requires to be distinguished from it.

We can therefore formulate the following proposition:

> The division of labour varies in direct proportion to the volume and density of societies and if it progresses in a continuous manner over the course of social development it is because societies become regularly more dense and generally more voluminous.

At all times, it is true, it has been clearly understood that there was a relationship between these two orders of facts. This is because, for functions to specialise even more, there must be additional co-operating elements, which must be grouped close enough together to be able to co-operate. Yet in societies in this condition we usually see hardly more than the means by which the division of labour is developed, and not the cause of this development. The cause is made to depend upon individual aspirations towards wellbeing and happiness, which can be the better satisfied when societies are more extensive and more condensed. The law we have just established is completely different. We state, not that the growth and condensation of societies *permit* a greater division of labour, but that they *necessitate* it. It is not the instrument whereby that division is brought about; but it is its determining cause.[10] . . .

The Anomic Division of Labour

Although Auguste Comte recognised that the division of labour is a source of solidarity, he does not appear to have perceived that this solidarity is *sui generis* and is gradually substituted for that which social similarities engender. This is why, noticing that these similarities are very blurred where the functions are very specialised, he saw in this process of disappearance a morbid phenomenon, a threat to social cohesion, due to excessive specialisation. He explained in this way the fact of the lack of co-ordination which sometimes accompanies the development of the division of labour. Yet since we have established that the weakening of the collective consciousness is a normal phenomenon, we could not make it the cause of the abnormal phenomena we are at present studying. If in certain cases organic solidarity is not all that is needful, it is certainly not because mechanical solidarity has lost ground, but because all the conditions of existence for the former have not been realised.

Indeed we know that wherever it is to be observed, we meet at the same time a regulatory system sufficiently developed to determine the mutual relationships between functions. For organic solidarity to exist it is not enough for there to be a system of organs necessary to one another that feel their solidarity in a general way. The manner in which they should co-operate, if not on every kind of occasion when they meet, at least in the most common circumstances, must be predetermined. Otherwise, a fresh struggle would be required each time in order to bring them into a state of equilibrium with one another, for the conditions for this equilibrium can only be found by a process of trial and error, in the course of which each party treats the other as an opponent as much as an auxiliary. Such conflicts would therefore break out continually, and in consequence solidarity would be hardly more than virtual, and the mutual obligations would have to be negotiated anew in their entirety for each individual case. It will be objected that contracts exist. But firstly, not every social relationship is capable of assuming this legal form. Moreover, we know that a contract is not sufficient in itself, but supposes a regulatory system that extends and grows more complicated just as does contractual life itself. Moreover, the ties originating in this way are always of short duration. The contract is only a truce, and a fairly precarious one at that; it suspends hostilities only for a while. Doubtless, however precise the regulatory system may be, it will always leave room for much dispute. But it is neither necessary nor even possible for social life to be without struggle. The role of solidarity is not to abolish competition but to moderate it.

Moreover, in the normal state, these rules emerge automatically from the division of labour; they are, so to speak, its prolongation. Certainly if the division of labour only brought together individuals who unite for a brief space of time with a view to the exchange of personal services, it could not give rise to any regulatory process. But what it evokes are functions, that is, definite ways of acting that are repeated identically in given circumstances, since they relate to the general unchanging conditions of social life. The relationships entertained between these functions cannot therefore fail to arrive at the same level of stability and regularity. There are certain ways of reacting upon one another which, being more in accordance with the nature of things, are repeated more often and become habits. Then the habits, as they grow in strength, are transformed into rules of conduct. The past predetermines the future. In other words, there exists a certain allocation of rights and duties that is established by usage and that ends up by becoming obligatory. Thus the rule does not set up the state of mutual dependence in which the solidly linked organs are to be found, but only serves to express it in a perceptible, definite way, as a function of a given situation. Likewise the nervous system, far from dominating the evolution of the organism, as was once believed, is a result of it. The nerve tracts are probably only the paths along which have passed the wave-like movements and stimuli exchanged between the various organs. They are the channels that life has dug for itself by always flowing in the same direction, and the ganglions would only be the place where several of these paths intersect. It is because they have failed to recognise this aspect of the phenomenon that certain moralists have charged the division of labour with not producing real solidarity They have seen in it only individual exchanges, ephemeral combinations, without a past, just as they also have no tomorrow, in which the individual is abandoned to his own devices. They have not perceived that slow task of consolidation, that network of ties that gradually becomes woven of its own accord and that makes organic solidarity something that is permanent.

Now, in all the cases we have described above, this regulatory process either does not exist or is not related to the degree of development of the division of labour. Nowadays there are no longer any rules that fix the number of economic undertakings, and in each branch of industry production is not regulated in such a way that it remains exactly at the level of consumption. Moreover, we do not wish to draw from this fact any practical conclusion. We do not maintain that restrictive legislation is necessary. We have not to weigh here the advantages and disadvantages. What is certain is that this lack of regulation does not allow the functions to perform regularly and harmoniously. The economists show, it is true, that harmony is re-established by itself when necessary, thanks to the increase or decrease in prices, which, according to the need, stimulates or slows production. But in any case it is not re-established in this way until after breaks in equilibrium and more or less prolonged disturbances have occurred. Moreover, such disturbances are naturally all the more frequent the more specialised the functions, for the more complex an organisation is, the more the necessity for extensive regulation is felt.

The relationships between capital and labour have up to now remained in the same legal state of indeterminacy. The contract for the hiring of services occupies in our legal codes a very small place, particularly when we consider the diversity and complexity of the relationships it is called upon to regulate. Moreover, we need emphasise no further the deficiencies that all peoples feel at the present time and that they are attempting to remedy.

Methodological rules are to science what rules of law and morality are to conduct. They direct the thinking of the scientist just as the latter govern the actions of men. Yet if every science has its method, the order that is established is entirely an internal one. The method co-ordinates the procedures followed by scientists who are studying the same science, but not their relationships externally. There are hardly any disciplines that harmonise the efforts of the different sciences towards a common goal. This is especially true of the moral and social sciences, for the mathematical, physical, chemical and even biological sciences do not seem to such an extent foreign to one another. But the jurist, the psychologist, the anthropologist, the economist, the statistician, the linguist, the historian – all these go about their investigations as if the various orders of facts that they are studying formed so many independent worlds. Yet in reality these facts interlock with one another at every point. Consequently the same should occur for the corresponding sciences. This is how there has arisen the anarchy that has been pinpointed – moreover, not without some exaggeration – in science generally, but that is above all true for these special sciences. Indeed they afford the spectacle of an aggregate of disconnected parts that fail to co-operate with one another. If they therefore form a whole lacking in unity, it is not because there is no adequate view of their similarities, it is because they are not organised.

These various examples are therefore varieties of a same species. In all these cases, if the division of labour does not produce solidarity it is because the relationships between the organs are not regulated; it is because they are in a state of *anomie*.

But from where does this state spring?

Since a body of rules is the definite form taken over time by the relationships established spontaneously betwen the social functions, we may say *a priori* that a state of *anomie* is impossible wherever organs solidly linked to one another are in sufficient contact, and in sufficiently lengthy contact. Indeed, being adjacent to one another, they are easily alerted in every situation to the need for one another and consequently they experience a keen, continuous feeling of their mutual dependence. For the same reason, exchanges between them occur easily; being regular, they occur frequently; they regulate themselves and time gradually effects the task of consolidation. Finally, because the slightest reaction can be felt throughout, the rules formed in this way bear the mark of it, that is, they foresee and fix in some detail the conditions of equilibrium. Yet if, on the other hand, some blocking environment is interposed between them, only stimuli of a certain intensity can communicate from one organ to another. Contacts being rare, they are not repeated often enough to take on a determinate form. Each time the procedure is again one of trial and error. The paths along which pass the wave-like movements can no longer become definite channels because the waves themselves are too intermittent. If at least some rules are successfully constituted, these are general and vague, for in these conditions only the most general outlines of the phenomena can be fixed. The same is true of closeness of contact: whilst it is sufficient, it is too recent or has lasted too short a while.[11]

Very generally this condition of contiguity is realised by the nature of things. For a function cannot distribute itself between two or more parts of an organism unless these parts are more or less in contact. Moreover, once labour is divided up, as they have need of one another, they tend naturally to reduce the distance that separates them. This is why, as one rises in the animal scale, one sees organs growing closer together and, as Spencer puts it, insinuating themselves into one another's interstices. But a coincidence of exceptional circumstances can cause it to be otherwise.

This is what occurs in the cases with which we are dealing at present. So long as the segmentary type of society is strongly marked, there are roughly as many economic markets as there are different segments. In consequence, each one of them is very limited. The producers, being very close to the consumers, can easily estimate the extent of the needs that have to be satisfied. The equilibrium is therefore established without difficulty and production is regulated by itself. On the contrary, as the organised type of society develops, the fusion of the various segments entails the fusion of the markets into one single market, which embraces almost all of society. It even extends beyond and tends to become universal, for the barriers between peoples are lowered at the same time as those that separate the segments within each one of them. The result is that each industry produces for consumers who are dispersed over the length and breadth of the country, or even the whole world. The contact is therefore no longer sufficient. The producer can no longer keep the whole market within his purview, not even mentally. He can no longer figure out to himself its limits, since it is, so to speak, unlimited. Consequently production lacks any check or regulation. It can only proceed at random, and in the course of so doing it is inevitable that the yardstick is wrong, either in one way or the other. Hence the crises that periodically disturb economic functions. The increase in those local and limited crises represented by bankruptcies is likely to be an effect of the same cause.

As the market becomes more extensive, large-scale industry appears. The effect of it is to transform the relationship between employers and workers. The greater fatigue occasioned to the nervous system, linked to the contagious influence of large urban areas, causes the needs of the workers to increase. Machine work replaces that of the man, manufacturing that of the small workshop. The worker is regimented, removed for the whole day from his family. He lives ever more apart from the person who employs him, etc. These new conditions of industrial life naturally require a new organisation. Yet because these transformations have been accomplished with extreme rapidity the conflicting interests have not had time to strike an equilibrium.[12]

Notes

1   Such a confusion is not without its dangers. Thus it is occasionally asked whether the individual consciousness varies with the collective consciousness. Everything depends on the meaning assigned to the term. If it represents social similarities, the variation, as will be seen, is one of inverse relationship. If it designates the entire psychological life of society, the relationship is direct. Hence the need to draw a distinction.

2   We shall not go into the question as to whether the collective consciousness is like that of the individual. For us this term merely designates the sum total of social similarities, without prejudice to the category by which this system of phenomena must be defined.

3   In order to simplify our exposition we assume that the individual belongs to only one society. In fact we form a part of several groups and there exist in us several collective consciousnesses; but this complication does not in any way change the relationship we are establishing.

4   This does not mean that a penal rule should nonetheless be retained because at some given moment it corresponded to a particular collective feeling. The rule has no justification unless the feeling is still alive and active. If it has disappeared or grown weak nothing is so vain or even counter-productive as to attempt to preserve it artificially by force. It may even happen to become necessary to fight against a practice that was common once, but is no longer so, one that militates against the establishment of new and essential practices. But we need not enter into this problem of a casuistic nature.

5   In saying that punishment, as it is, has a reason for its existence we do not mean that it is perfect and cannot be improved upon. On the contrary, it is only too plain that, since it is produced by purely mechanical causes, it can only be very imperfectly attuned to its role. The justification can only be a rough and ready one.

6   Even that moral authority derives from custom, and hence from society.

7   Nevertheless these two consciousnesses are not regions of ourselves that are 'geographi-
     cally' distinct, for they interpenetrate each other at every point.

8   By reasoning in this way we do not mean that the increase in density is the result of
     economic changes. The two facts have a mutual conditioning effect upon each other,
     and this suffices for the presence of the one to attest to the presence of the other.

9   However, there are special cases of an exceptional kind, where material density and
     moral density are perhaps not entirely in proportion.

10   On this point we can again rely upon the authority of Comte. 'I need only,' he says,
     'point now to the progressive increase in density of our species as an ultimate general
     factor helping to regulate the effective rapidity of social movement. First, therefore, one
     may freely recognise that this influence contributes a great deal, above all at the
     beginning, in determining for human labour as a whole its increasingly specialised
     division, which is necessarily incompatible with a small number of people co-operating
     together. *Moreover, by a more intimate and less well-known property, although of even
     greater importance, such a densifying process directly and very powerfully stimulates
     the swifter development in social evolution*, either by stimulating individuals to put
     forth fresh efforts using refined methods, in order to ensure for themselves an existence
     which otherwise would become more difficult, or by obliging society also to react with
     greater energy and persistence, and in more concerted fashion, struggling against the
     increasedly powerful upsurge of particular divergences. On both counts we see that here
     it is not a question of the absolute increase in the number of individuals, but above all
     of the more intense competition between them in a given area' (*Cours de philosophie
     positive*, vol. IV, p. 455).

11   There is, however, one case where *anomie* can occur, although the contiguity is
     sufficient. This is when the necessary regulation can only be established at the expense
     of transformations that the social structure is no longer capable of carrying out, for the
     malleability of societies is not indefinite. When it has reached its limit, even necessary
     changes are impossible.

12   Let us nevertheless remember that this antagonism is not due wholly to the speed of
     these transformations, but to a considerable extent to the still too great inequality in the
     external conditions of the struggle. Over this factor time has no effect.

C: ORIGINS OF COLLECTIVE CONSCIENCE

12 The Elementary Forms of the Religious Life

Emile Durkheim

We cannot arrive at an understanding of the most recent religions except by following the manner in which they have been progressively composed in history. In fact, historical analysis is the only means of explanation which it is possible to apply to them. It alone enables us to resolve an institution into its constituent elements, for it shows them to us as they are born in time, one after another. On the other hand, by placing every one of them in the condition where it was born, it puts into our hands the only means we have of determining the causes which gave rise to it. Every time that we undertake to explain something human, taken at a given moment in history – be it a religious belief, a moral precept, a legal principle, an aesthetic style or an economic system – it is necessary to commence by going back to its most primitive and simple form, to try to account for the characteristics by which it was marked at that time, and then to show how it developed and became complicated little by little, and how it became that which it is at the moment in question. One readily understands the importance which the determination of the point of departure has for this series of progressive explanations, for all the others are attached to it. It was one of Descartes's principles that the first ring has a predominating place in the chain of scientific truths. But there is no question of placing at the foundation of the science of religions an idea elaborated after the cartesian manner, that is to say, a logical concept, a pure possibility, constructed simply by force of thought. What we must find is a concrete reality, and historical and ethnological observation alone can reveal that to us. But even if this cardinal conception is obtained by a different process than that of Descartes, it remains true that it is destined to have a considerable influence on the whole series of propositions which the science establishes. Biological evolution has been conceived quite differently ever since it has been known that monocellular beings do exist. In the same way, the arrangement of religious facts is explained quite differently, according as we put naturism, animism or some other religious form at the beginning of the evolution. Even the most specialized scholars, if they are unwilling to confine themselves to a task of pure erudition, and if they desire to interpret the facts which they analyse, are obliged to choose one of these hypotheses, and make it their starting-point. Whether they desire it or not, the questions which they raise necessarily take the following form: how has naturism or animism been led to take this particular form, here or there, or to enrich itself or impoverish itself in such and such a fashion? Since it is impossible to avoid taking sides on this initial problem, and since the solution given is destined to affect the whole science, it must be attacked at the outset: this is what we propose to do.

Besides this, outside of these indirect reactions, the study of primitive religions has of itself an immediate interest which is of primary importance.

If it is useful to know what a certain particular religion consists in, it is still more important to know what religion in general is. This is the problem which has aroused the interest of philosophers in all times; and not without reason, for it is of interest to all humanity. Unfortunately, the method which they generally employ is purely dialectic: they confine themselves to analysing the idea which they make for themselves of religion, except as they illustrate the results of this mental analysis by examples borrowed from the religions which best realize their ideal. But even if this method ought to be abandoned, the problem remains intact, and the great service of philosophy is to have prevented its being suppressed by the disdain of scholars. Now it is possible to attack it in a different way. Since all religions can be compared to each other, and since all are species of the same class, there are necessarily many elements which are common to all. We do not mean to speak simply of the outward and visible characteristics which they all have equally, and which make it possible to give them a provisional definition from the very outset of our researches; the discovery of these apparent signs is relatively easy, for the observation which it demands does not go beneath the surface of things. But these external resemblances suppose others which are profound. At the foundation of all systems of beliefs and of all cults there ought necessarily to be a certain number of fundamental representations or conceptions and of ritual attitudes which, in spite of the diversity of forms which they have taken, have the same objective significance and fulfil the same functions everywhere. These are the permanent elements which constitute that which is permanent and human in religion; they form all the objective contents of the idea which is expressed when one speaks of *religion* in general. How is it possible to pick them out?

Surely it is not by observing the complex religions which appear in the course of history. Every one of these is made up of such a variety of elements that it is very difficult to distinguish what is secondary from what is principal, the essential from the accessory. Suppose that the religion considered is like that of Egypt, India or the classical antiquity. It is a confused mass of many cults, varying according to the locality, the temples, the generations, the dynasties, the invasions, etc. Popular superstitions are there confused with the purest dogmas. Neither the thought nor the activity of the religion is evenly distributed among the believers; according to the men, the environment and the circumstances, the beliefs as well as the rites are thought of in different ways. Here they are priests, there they are monks, elsewhere they are laymen; there are mystics and rationalists, theologians and prophets, etc. In these conditions it is difficult to see what is common to all. In one or another of these systems it is quite possible to find the means of making a profitable study of some particular fact which is specially developed there, such as sacrifice or prophecy, monasticism or the mysteries; but how is it possible to find the common foundation of the religious life underneath the luxuriant vegetation which covers it? How is it possible to find, underneath the disputes of theology, the variations of ritual, the multiplicity of groups and the diversity of individuals, the fundamental states characteristic of religious mentality in general?

Things are quite different in the lower societies. The slighter development of individuality, the small extension of the group, the homogeneity of external circumstances, all contribute to reducing the differences and variations to a minimum. The group has an intellectual and moral conformity of which we find but rare examples in the more advanced societies. Everything is common to all. Movements are stereotyped; everybody performs the same ones in the same circumstances, and this conformity of conduct only translates the conformity of thought. Every mind being drawn into the same eddy, the individual type nearly confounds itself with that of the race. And while all is uniform, all is simple as well. Nothing is deformed like these myths, all composed of one and the same theme which is endlessly repeated, or like these rites made up of a small number of gestures repeated again and again. Neither the popular imagination nor that of the priests has had either the time or the means of refining and transforming the original substance of the religious ideas and practices; these are shown in all their nudity, and offer themselves to an examination, it requiring only the slightest effort to lay them open. That which is accessory or secondary, the development of luxury, has not yet come to hide the principal elements.[1] All is reduced to that which is indispensable, to that without which there could be no religion. But that which is indispensable is also that which is essential, that is to say, that which we must know before all else.

Primitive civilizations offer privileged cases, then, because they are simple cases. That is why, in all fields of human activity, the observations of ethnologists have frequently been veritable revelations, which have renewed the study of human institutions. For example, before the middle of the nineteenth century, everybody was convinced that the father was the essential element of the family; no one had dreamed that there could be a family organization of which the paternal authority was not the keystone. But the discovery of Bachofen came and upset this old conception. Up to very recent times it was regarded as evident that the moral and legal relations of kindred were only another aspect of the psychological relations which result from a common descent; Bachofen and his successors, MacLennan, Morgan and many others still laboured under this misunderstanding. But since we have become acquainted with the nature of the primitive clan, we know that, on the contrary, relationships cannot be explained by consanguinity. To return to religions, the study of only the most familiar ones had led men to believe for a long time that the idea of god was characteristic of everything that is religious. Now the religion which we are going to study presently is, in a large part, foreign to all idea of divinity; the forces to which the rites are there addressed are very different from those which occupy the leading place in our modern religions, yet they aid us in understanding these latter forces. So nothing is more unjust than the disdain with which too many historians still regard the work of ethnographers. Indeed, it is certain that ethnology has frequently brought about the most fruitful revolutions in the different branches of sociology. It is for this same reason that the discovery of unicellular beings, of which we just spoke, has transformed the current idea of life.

Since in these very simple beings, life is reduced to its essential traits, these are less easily misunderstood.

But primitive religions do not merely aid us in disengaging the constituent elements of religion; they also have the great advantage that they facilitate the explanation of it. Since the facts there are simpler, the relations between them are more apparent. The reasons with which men account for their acts have not yet been elaborated and denatured by studied reflection; they are nearer and more closely related to the motives which have really determined these acts. . . .

But our study is not of interest merely for the science of religion. In fact, every religion has one side by which it overlaps the circle of properly religious ideas, and there, the study of religious phenomena gives a means of renewing the problems which, up to the present, have only been discussed among philosophers.

For a long time it has been known that the first systems of representations with which men have pictured to themselves the world and themselves were of religious origin. There is no religion that is not a cosmology at the same time that it is a speculation upon divine things. If philosophy and the sciences were born of religion, it is because religion began by taking the place of the sciences and philosophy. But it has been less frequently noticed that religion has not confined itself to enriching the human intellect, formed beforehand, with a certain number of ideas; it has contributed to forming the intellect itself. Men owe to it not only a good part of the substance of their knowledge, but also the form in which this knowledge has been elaborated.

At the roots of all our judgments there are a certain number of essential ideas which dominate all our intellectual life, they are what philosophers since Aristotle have called the categories of the understanding: ideas of time, space,[2] class, number, cause, substance, personality, etc. They correspond to the most universal properties of things. They are like the solid frame which encloses all thought; this does not seem to be able to liberate itself from them without destroying itself, for it seems that we cannot think of objects that are not in time and space, which have no number, etc. Other ideas are contingent and unsteady; we can conceive of their being unknown to a man, a society or an epoch; but these others appear to be nearly inseparable from the normal working of the intellect. They are like the framework of the intelligence. Now when primitive religious beliefs are systematically analysed, the principal categories are naturally found. They are born in religion and of religion; they are a product of religious thought. . . .

The fundamental proposition of the apriorist theory is that knowledge is made up of two sorts of elements, which cannot be reduced into one another, and which are like two distinct layers superimposed one upon the other.[3] Our hypothesis keeps this principle intact. In fact, that knowledge which is called empirical, the only knowledge of which the theorists of empiricism have made use in constructing the reason, is that which is brought into our minds by the direct action of objects. It is composed of individual states which are completely explained[4] by the psychical nature of the individual. If, on the other hand, the categories are, as we believe they are, essentially collective representations, before all else, they should show the mental states of the group; they should depend upon the way in which this is founded and organized, upon its morphology, upon its religious, moral and economic institutions, etc. So between these two sorts of representations there is all the difference which exists between the individual and the social, and one can no more derive the second from the first than he can deduce society from the individual, the whole from the part, the complex from the simple.[5] Society is a reality *sui generis*; it has its own peculiar characteristics, which are not found elsewhere and which are not met with again in the same form in all the rest of the universe. The representations which express it have a wholly different contents from purely individual ones and we may rest assured in advance that the first add something to the second.

Even the manner in which the two are formed results in differentiating them. Collective representations are the result of an immense co-operation, which stretches out not only into space but into time as well; to make them, a multitude of minds have associated, united and combined their ideas and sentiments; for them, long generations have accumulated their experience and their knowledge. A special intellectual activity is therefore concentrated in them which is infinitely richer and complexer than that of the individual. From that one can understand how the reason has been able to go beyond the limits of empirical knowledge. It does not owe this to any vague mysterious virtue but simply to the fact that according to the well-known formula, man is double. There are two beings in him: an individual being which has its foundation in the organism and the circle of whose activities is therefore stricly limited, and a social being which represents the highest reality in the intellectual and moral order that we can know by observation – I mean society. This duality of our nature has as its consequence in the practical order, the irreducibility of a moral ideal to a utilitarian motive, and in the order of thought, the irreducibility of reason to individual experience. In so far as he belongs to society, the individual transcends himself, both when he thinks and when he acts.

This same social character leads to an understanding of the origin of the necessity of the categories. It is said that an idea is necessary when it imposes itself upon the mind by some sort of virtue of its own, without being accompanied by any proof. It contains within it something which constrains the intelligence and which leads to its acceptance without preliminary examination. The apriorist postulates this singular quality, but does not account for it; for saying that the categories are necessary because they are indispensable to the functioning of the intellect is simply repeating that they are necessary. But if they really have the origin which we attribute to them, their ascendancy no longer has anything suprising in it. They represent the most general relations which exist between things; surpassing all our other ideas in extension, they dominate all the details of our intellectual life. If men did not agree upon these essential ideas at every moment, if they did not have the same conception of time, space, cause, number, etc., all contact between their minds would be impossible, and with that, all life together. Thus society could not abandon the categories to the free choice of the individual without abandoning itself. If it is to live there is not merely need of a satisfactory moral conformity, but also there is a minimum of logical conformity beyond which it cannot safely go. For this reason it uses all its authority upon its members to forestall such dissidences. Does a mind ostensibly free itself from these forms of thought? It is no longer considered a human mind in the full sense of the word, and is treated accordingly. That is why we feel that we are no longer completely free and that something resists, both within and outside ourselves, when we attempt to rid ourselves of these fundamental notions, even in our own conscience. Outside of us there is public opinion which judges us; but more than that, since society is also represented inside of us, it sets itself against these revolutionary fancies, even inside of ourselves; we have the feeling that we cannot abandon them if our whole thought is not to cease being really human. This seems to be the origin of the exceptional authority which is inherent in the reason and which makes us accept its suggestions with confidence. It is the very authority of society,[6] transferring itself to a certain manner of thought which is the indispensable condition of all common action. The necessity with which the categories are imposed upon us is not the effect of simple habits whose yoke we could easily throw off with a little effort; nor is it a physical or metaphysical necessity, since the categories change in different places and times; it is a special sort of moral necessity which is to the intellectual life what moral obligation is to the will.[7]

But if the categories originally only translate social states, does it not follow that they can be applied to the rest of nature only as metaphors? If they were made merely to express social conditions, it seems as though they could not be extended to other realms except in this sense. Thus in so far as they aid us in thinking of the physical or biological world, they have only the value of artificial symbols, useful practically perhaps, but having no connection with reality. Thus we come back, by a different road, to nominalism and empiricism.

But when we interpret a sociological theory of knowledge in this way, we forget that even if society is a specific reality it is not an empire within an empire; it is a part of nature, and indeed its highest representation. The social realm is a natural realm which differs from the others only by a greater complexity. Now it is impossible that nature should differ radically from itself in the one case and the other in regard to that which is most essential. The fundamental relations that exist between things – just that which it is the function of the categories to express – cannot be essentially dissimilar in the different realms. If they are more clearly disengaged in the social world, it is nevertheless impossible that they should not be found elsewhere, though in less pronounced forms. Society makes them more manifest but it does not have a monopoly upon them. That is why ideas which have been elaborated on the model of social things can aid us in thinking of another department of nature. It is at least true that if these ideas play the rôle of symbols when they are thus turned aside from their original signification, they are well-founded symbols. If a sort of artificiality enters into them from the mere fact that they are constructed concepts, it is an artificiality which follows nature very closely and which is constantly approaching it still more closely.[8] From the fact that the ideas of time, space, class, cause or personality are constructed out of social elements, it is not necessary to conclude that they are devoid of all objective value. On the contrary, their social origin rather leads to the belief that they are not without foundation in the nature of things.[9]

Thus renovated, the theory of knowledge seems destined to unite the opposing advantages of the two rival theories, without incurring their inconveniences. It keeps all the essential principles of the apriorists; but at the same time it is inspired by that positive spirit which the empiricists have striven to satisfy. It leaves the reason its specific power, but it accounts for it and does so without leaving the world of observable phenomena. It affirms the duality of our intellectual life, but it explains it, and with natural causes. The categories are no longer considered as primary and unanalysable facts, yet they keep a complexity which falsifies any analysis as ready as that with which the empiricists content themselves. They no longer appear as very simple notions which the first comer can very easily arrange from his own personal observations and which the popular imagination has unluckily complicated, but rather they appear as priceless instruments of thought which the human groups have laboriously forged through the centuries and where they have accumulated the best of their intellectual capital.[10] A complete section of the history of humanity is resumed therein. This is equivalent to saying that to succeed in understanding them and judging them, it is necessary to resort to other means than those which have been in use up to the present. To know what these conceptions which we have not made ourselves are really made of, it does not suffice to interrogate our own consciousnesses; we must look outside of ourselves, it is history that we must observe, there is a whole science which must be formed, a complex science which can advance but slowly and by collective labour, and to which the present work brings some fragmentary contributions in the nature of an attempt. . . .

But, it is said, what society is it that has thus made the basis of religion? Is it the real society, such as it is and acts before our very eyes, with the legal and moral organization which it has laboriously fashioned during the course of history? This is full of defects and imperfections. In it, evil goes beside the good, injustice often reigns supreme, and the truth is often obscured by error. How could anything so crudely organized inspire the sentiments of love, the ardent enthusiasm and the spirit of abnegation which all religions claim of their followers? These perfect beings which are gods could not have taken their traits from so mediocre, and sometimes even so base a reality.

But, on the other hand, does someone think of a perfect society, where justice and truth would be sovereign, and from which evil in all its forms would be banished for ever? No one would deny that this is in close relations with the religious sentiment; for, they would say, it is towards the realization of this that all religions strive. But that society is not an empirical fact, definite and observable; it is a fancy, a dream with which men have lightened their sufferings, but in which they have never really lived. It is merely an idea which comes to express our more or less obscure aspirations towards the good, the beautiful and the ideal. Now these aspirations have their roots in us; they come from the very depths of our being; then there is nothing outside of us which can account for them. Moreover, they are already religious in themselves; thus it would seem that the ideal society presupposes religion, far from being able to explain it.

But, in the first place, things are arbitrarily simplified when religion is seen only on its idealistic side: in its way, it is realistic. There is no physical or moral ugliness, there are no vices or evils which do not have a special divinity. There are gods of theft and trickery, of lust and war, of sickness and of death. Christianity itself, howsoever high the idea which it has made of the divinity may be, has been obliged to give the spirit of evil a place in its mythology. Satan is an essential piece of the

Christian system; even if he is an impure being, he is not a profane one. The anti-god is a god, inferior and subordinated, it is true, but nevertheless endowed with extended powers; he is even the object of rites, at least of negative ones. Thus religion, far from ignoring the real society and making abstraction of it, is in its image; it reflects all its aspects, even the most vulgar and the most repulsive. All is to be found there, and if in the majority of cases we see the good victorious over evil, life over death, the powers of light over the powers of darkness, it is because reality is not otherwise. If the relation between these two contrary forces were reversed, life would be impossible; but, as a matter of fact, it maintains itself and even tends to develop.

But if, in the midst of these mythologies and theologies we see reality clearly appearing, it is none the less true that it is found there only in an enlarged, transformed and idealized form. In this respect, the most primitive religions do not differ from the most recent and the most refined. For example, we have seen how the Arunta place at the beginning of time a mythical society whose organization exactly reproduces that which still exists to-day; it includes the same clans and phratries, it is under the same matrimonial rules and it practises the same rites. But the personages who compose it are ideal beings, gifted with powers and virtues to which common mortals cannot pretend. Their nature is not only higher, but it is different, since it is at once animal and human. The evil powers there undergo a similar metamorphosis: evil itself is, as it were, made sublime and idealized. The question now raises itself of whence this idealization comes.

Some reply that men have a natural faculty for idealizing, that is to say, of substituting for the real world another different one, to which they transport themselves by thought. But that is merely changing the terms of the problem; it is not resolving it or even advancing it. This systematic idealization is an essential characteristic of religions. Explaining them by an innate power of idealization is simply replacing one word by another which is the equivalent of the first; it is as if they said that men have made religions because they have a religious nature. Animals know only one world, the one which they perceive by experience, internal as well as external. Men alone have the faculty of conceiving the ideal, of adding something to the real. Now where does this singular privilege come from? Before making it an initial fact or a mysterious virtue which escapes science, we must be sure that it does not depend upon empirically determinable conditions.

The explanation of religion which we have proposed has precisely this advantage, that it gives an answer to this question. For our definition of the sacred is that it is something added to and above the real: now the ideal answers to this same definition; we cannot explain one without explaining the other. In fact, we have seen that if collective life awakens religious thought on reaching a certain degree of intensity, it is because it brings about a state of effervescence which changes the conditions of psychic activity. Vital energies are over-excited, passions more active, sensations stronger; there are even some which are produced only at this moment. A man does not recognize himself; he feels himself transformed and consequently he transforms the environment which surrounds him. In order to account for the very particular impressions which he receives, he attributes to the things with which he is in most direct contact properties which they have not, exceptional powers and virtues which the objects of every-day experience do not possess. In a word, above the real world where his profane life passes he has placed another which, in one sense, does not exist except in thought, but to which he attributes a higher sort of dignity than to the first. Thus, from a double point of view it is an ideal world.

The formation of the ideal world is therefore not an irreducible fact which escapes science; it depends upon conditions which observation can touch; it is a natural product of social life. For a society to become conscious of itself and maintain at the necessary degree of intensity the sentiments which it thus attains, it must assemble and concentrate itself. Now this concentration brings about an exaltation of the mental life which takes form in a group of ideal conceptions where is portrayed the new life thus awakened; they correspond to this new set of psychical forces which is added to those which we have at our disposition for the daily tasks of existence. A society can neither create itself nor recreate itself without at the same time creating an ideal. This creation is not a sort of work of supererogation for it, by which it would complete itself, being already formed; it is the act by which it is periodically made and remade. Therefore when some oppose the ideal society to the real society, like two antagonists which would lead us in opposite directions, they materialize and oppose abstractions. The ideal society is not outside of the real society; it is a part of it. Far from being divided between them as between two poles which mutually repel each other, we cannot hold to one without holding to the other. For a society is not made up merely of the mass of individuals who compose it, the ground which they occupy, the things which they use and the movements which they perform, but above all is the idea which it forms of itself. It is undoubtedly true that it hesitates over the manner in which it ought to conceive itself; it feels itself drawn in divergent directions. But these conflicts which break forth are not between the ideal and reality, but between two different ideals, that of yesterday and that of to-day, that which has the authority of tradition and that which has the hope of the future. There is surely a place for investigating whence these ideals evolve; but whatever solution may be given to this problem it still remains that all passes in the world of the ideal.

Thus the collective ideal which religion expresses is far from being due to a vague innate power of the individual, but it is rather at the school of collective life that the individual has learned to idealize. It is in assimilating the ideals elaborated by society that he has become capable of conceiving the ideal. It is society which, by leading him within its sphere of action, had made him acquire the need of raising himself above the world of experience and has at the same time furnished him with the means of conceiving another. For society has constructed this new world in constructing itself, since it is society which this expresses. Thus both with the individual and in the group, the faculty of idealizing has nothing mysterious about it. It is not a sort of luxury which a man could get along without, but a condition of his very existence. He could not be a social being, that is to say, he could not be a man, if he had not acquired it. It is true that in incarnating themselves in individuals, collective ideals tend to individualize themselves. Each understands them after his own fashion and marks them with his own stamp; he suppresses certain elements and adds others. Thus the personal ideal disengages itself from the social ideal in proportion as the individual personality develops itself and becomes an autonomous source of action. But if we wish to understand this aptitude, so singular in appearance, of living outside of reality, it is enough to connect it with the social conditions upon which it depends.

Therefore it is necessary to avoid seeing in this theory of religion a simple restatement of historical materialism: that would be misunderstanding our thought to an extreme degree. In showing that religion is something essentially social, we do not mean to say that it confines itself to translating into another language the material forms of society and its immediate vital necessities. It is true that we take it as evident that social life depends upon its material foundation and bears its mark, just as the mental life of an individual depends upon his nervous system and in fact his whole organism. But collective consciousness is something more than a mere epiphenomenon of its morphological basis, just as individual consciousness is something more than a simple efflorescence of the nervous system. In order that the former may appear, a synthesis *sui generis* of particular consciousnesses is required. Now this synthesis has the effect of disengaging a whole world of sentiments, ideas and images which, once born, obey laws all their own. They attract each other, repel each other, unite, divide themselves, and multiply, though these combinations are not commanded and necessitated by the condition of the underlying reality. The life thus brought into being even enjoys so great an independence that it sometimes indulges in manifestations with no purpose or utility of any sort, for the mere pleasure of affirming itself. We have shown that this is often precisely the case with ritual activity and mythological thought. . . .

Thus there is something eternal in religion which is destined to survive all the particular symbols in which religious thought has successively enveloped itself. There can be no society which does not feel the need of upholding and reaffirming at regular intervals the collective sentiments and the collective ideas which make its unity and its personality. Now this moral remaking cannot be achieved except by the means of reunions, assemblies and meetings where the individuals, being closely united to one another, reaffirm in common their common sentiments; hence come ceremonies which do not differ from regular religious ceremonies, either in their object, the results which they produce, or the processes employed to attain these results. What essential difference is there between an assembly of Christians celebrating the principal dates of the life of Christ, or of Jews remembering the exodus from Egypt or the promulgation of the decalogue, and a reunion of citizens commemorating the promulgation of a new moral or legal system or some great event in the national life?

If we find a little difficulty to-day in imagining what these feasts and ceremonies of the future could consist in, it is because we are going through a stage of transition and moral mediocrity. The great things of the past which filled our fathers with enthusiasm do not excite the same ardour in us, either because they have come into common usage to such an extent that we are unconscious of them, or else because they no longer answer to our actual aspirations; but as yet there is nothing to replace them. We can no longer impassionate ourselves for the principles in the name of which Christianity recommended to masters that they treat their slaves humanely, and, on the other hand, the idea which it has formed of human equality and fraternity seems to us to-day to leave too large a place for unjust inequalities. Its pity for the outcast seems to us too Platonic; we desire another which would be more practicable; but as yet we cannot clearly see what it should be or how it could be realized in facts. In a word, the old gods are growing old or already dead, and others are not yet born. This is what rendered vain the attempt of Comte with the old historic souvenirs artificially revived: it is life itself, and not a dead past which can produce a living cult. But this state of incertitude and confused agitation cannot last for ever. A day will come when our societies will know again those hours of creative effervescence, in the course of which new ideas arise and new formulae are found which serve for a while as a guide to humanity; and when these hours shall have been passed through once, men will spontaneously feel the need of reliving them from time to time in thought, that is to say, of keeping alive their memory by means of celebrations which regularly reproduce their fruits.

Notes

1   But that is not equivalent to saying that all luxury is lacking to the primitive cults. On the contrary, we shall see that in every religion there are beliefs and practices which do not aim at strictly utilitarian ends. This luxury is indispensable to the religious life; it is at its very heart. But it is much more rudimentary in the inferior religions than in the others, so we are better able to determine its reason for existence here.

2   We say that time and space are categories because there is no difference between the rôle played by these ideas in the intellectual life and that which falls to the ideas of class or cause.

3   Perhaps some will be surprised that we do not define the apriorist theory by the hypothesis of innateness. But this conception really plays a secondary part in the doctrine. It is a simple way of stating the impossibility of reducing rational knowledge to empirical data. Saying that the former is innate is only a positive way of saying that it is not the product of experience, such as it is ordinarily conceived.

4   At least, in so far as there are any representations which are individual and hence wholly empirical. But there are in fact probably none where the two elements are not found closely united.

5   This irreducibility must not be taken in any absolute sense. We do not wish to say that there is nothing in the empirical representations which shows rational ones, nor that there is nothing in the individual which could be taken as a sign of social life. If experience were completely separated from all that is rational, reason could not operate upon it; in the same way, if the psychic nature of the individual were absolutely opposed to the social life, society would be impossible. A complete anlysis of the categories should seek these germs of rationality even in the individual consciousness. All that we wish to establish here is that between these indistinct germs of reason and the reason properly so called, there is a difference comparable to that which separates the properties of the mineral elements out of which a living being is composed from the characteristic attributes of life after this has once been constituted.

6   It has frequently been remarked that social disturbances result in multiplying mental disturbances. This is one more proof that logical discipline is a special aspect of social discipline. The first gives way as the second is weakened.

7   There is an analogy between this logical necessity and moral obligation, but there is not an actual identity. To-day society treats criminals in a different fashion than subjects whose intelligence only is abnormal; that is a proof that the authority attached to logical rules and that inherent in moral rules are not of the same nature, in spite of certain

similarities. They are two species of the same class. It would be interesting to make a study on the nature and origin of this difference, which is probably distinguished between the deranged and the delinquent. We confine ourselves to signalizing this question. By this example, one may see the number of problems which are raised by the analysis of these notions which generally pass as being elementary and simple, but which are really of an extreme complexity.

8   The rationalism which is imminent in the sociological theory of knowledge is thus midway between the classical empiricism and apriorism. For the first, the categories are purely artifical constructions; for the second, on the contrary, they are given by nature; for us, they are in a sense a work of art, but of an art which imitates nature with a perfection capable of increasing unlimitedly.

9   For example, that which is at the foundation of the category of time is the rhythm of social life; but if there is a rhythm in collective life, one may rest assured that there is another in the life of the individual, and more generally, in that of the universe. The first is merely more marked and apparent than the others. In the same way, we shall see that the notion of class is founded on that of the human group. But if men form natural groups, it can be assumed that among things there exist groups which are at once analogous and different. Classes and species are natural groups of things.

If it seems to many minds that a social origin cannot be attributed to the categories without depriving them of all speculative value, it is because society is still too frequently regarded as something that is not natural; hence it is concluded that the representations which express it express nothing in nature. But the conclusion is not worth more than the premise.

10   This is how it is legitimate to compare the categories to tools; for on its side, a tool is material accumulated capital. There is a close relationship between the three ideas of tool, category and institution.

Part III

The Sociological Theory of Max Weber

Introduction to Part III

This section is devoted to the work of Max Weber (1864–1920). Along with Marx and Durkheim, Weber stands as one of the central figures of sociological theory. Weber and Durkheim were both part of a generation of turn-of-the-century European academics who effectively founded sociology as a serious, and scientific, endeavor. Weber was only a few years younger than his French counterpart, but he was a very different theorist in both style and substance. Although Weber most likely read Durkheim's work, he made only a few general remarks about the "organic school" and he never mentioned Durkheim by name.

Compared with Marx and Durkheim, Weber's approach was more individualist in method and it was more cultural in orientation. Weber's individualism was particularly striking in his methodological essays. Weber insisted that the object of sociological analysis should be the action of individuals, insofar it is oriented towards others. Weber certainly did not ignore collective actors or institutions, but his analysis of these social formations was linked to the behaviour of the individuals that come under their influence. This set him apart particularly from Durkheim, who argued for the social collective as the unit of analysis. Weber was also profoundly interested in the cultural orientations of social actors. For Weber, ideas and value orientations – religious, political, economic and aesthetic – were important because they motivated action. Although ideas may be shaped by material conditions, Weber held that the reverse might also be true. This differentiated Weber most clearly from Karl Marx, especially in Marx's more programmatic statements on historical materialism.

Weber's Life and Work

Weber grew up in the suburbs of Berlin in a comfortably upper-middle class family, the son of Helene and Max, Sr., a city councilor and politician. Skinny and somewhat sickly as a child, Weber pursued his own intellectual interests rather than social or athletic ones. He studied history and philosophy in his free time and in class secretly read through a forty-volume edition of Goethe under his desk. At eighteen, Weber enrolled at the University of Heidelberg where he immersed himself in the social life of a bourgeois University student. After a year of military service, Weber resumed his studies at the University of Berlin in a more ascetic manner. He studied for a law degree while working as a junior barrister in the courts, and simultaneously completed his qualifications for an academic career. Though trained as a lawyer and a historian, Weber became drawn to the social sciences. He gained a professorship first in economics and later in political science.

Max Weber quickly became an influential scholar, but his work stopped suddenly three years after his first academic appointment. In 1897, Weber descended into a crippling depression that completely curtailed his research. When his capacity for work returned after several years, he channeled it in a different direction. Before his breakdown, Weber's studies were primarily in the fields of economic and legal history. His doctoral dissertation was a study of trading companies in the middle ages. This was followed quickly by a second thesis on the agrarian economics of the Roman Empire and by a massive survey of the conditions of agricultural workers in eastern Germany. After his depression however, Weber began to grapple with more fundamental theoretical issues of the social sciences. It was at this point that he laid out his own vision of the field of sociology. Virtually all of Weber's work that is read widely by sociologists today dates from after his breakdown.

Despite the fact that Weber never again felt well enough to take on full-time duties as a professor, he more than made up for lost time in his scholarship. In 1903, Weber began work on *The Protestant Ethic and the Spirit of Capitalism*. He also began to edit a journal, the *Archiv für Sozialwissenschaft und Sozialpolitik*, where he published many of his essays and lectures in the following years. He was completing the massive *Economy and Society* when he died. Weber also made up for lost time in his public life. With his wife Marianne, he remained part of an active social group of intellectuals that included Georg Simmel. He was also drawn to practical political action, although he was adamant that political beliefs should not cloud scholarship. Weber was a moderate nationalist, who criticized the parties of the extreme left and right for what he saw as their inability to accept political realities. Weber's public role expanded during the course of the First World War. He helped to found the German Democratic Party and had a hand in the construction of the Treaty of Versailles and the Weimar Constitution. Max Weber died in 1920, following a bout of pneumonia.

Social Theory and Social Science

Weber's approach to sociology was directly tied to the intellectual context of German philosophy and social science. Particularly important was the way that Weber's theory related to the *Methodenstreit* – the German debate about the proper method for the social sciences. On one side of the debate were those who felt that the social sciences should emulate the natural sciences by searching for general laws that govern all human behavior. On the other were those who argued that accounts of social action had to be rooted in particular historical contexts. These different goals were tied to different methods. The first group emphasized causal explanations of objective social conditions. The second group sought instead descriptive accounts of the subjective motivations of actors. Weber wanted to overcome this divide by insisting that social science should seek causal arguments that generalize past any particular case, even if it was not possible to build universal laws of human society. At the same time, Weber was very closely tied to the second position (known as the "historicist school") by training and by temperament. He stressed that the proper object of analysis was social action. Because the meaning of any particular action resides in the head of the actor, sociology must pay attention to the context in which an action happens, and it must involve "*verstehen*" – an interpretive understanding of subjective motivations.

Weber applied this method to his incredibly broad empirical interests which included religion, politics, organizations, the economy, stratification and law. There were two consistent themes that connected all of Weber's sociological work, however. One was an interest in the connection between forms of social action (especially relations of power) and patterns of social order. Bureaucracies, states and world religions were for Weber examples of social orders that supported certain forms of power relations among people. At the same time, Weber also argued that social action motivated by one kind of social order, such as religion, could lead to fundamental transformations in other domains, such as the economy. A second consistent theme in Weber's theory has to do with the gradual expansion of rationality in social life. Weber argued that the social action of individuals was becoming directed more and more by conscious cost/benefit calculation in all spheres of life. This had a profound advantage – we are no longer bound by traditional social guidelines – but it also entailed a loss of deeper meaning in our lives. The growth of rationality was marked by the reorganization of social institutions such as states and corporations around formal and explicit guidelines to increase efficiency, accountability and fairness. Both of these themes are apparent in the readings included in this section.

The readings in this section give an indication of the breadth of Weber's work, as well its unifying elements. The readings break roughly into three parts. The first exemplifies Weber's writing on methodology – how to do social science. The essay "'Objectivity' in the Social Sciences," falls into this category, as does "Basic Sociological Terms." The second, represented by "The Protestant Ethic and the Spirit of Capitalism," shows Weber's interest in rationality, and the ways that it relates to religion and the economy. The third inclues "Class, Status, Party," "Bureaucracy," and "The Types of Legitimate Domination" as examples of Weber's work on political and legal systems.

The methodological essays establish Weber's definition of sociology and how to do it. "'Objectivity' in Social Science," is a treatise on the use of "ideal type" constructs. Weber takes a position that is very different from Durkheim's social realism and from Marx's materialism. Weber claims the only way to escape from the subjectivity of the researcher is through the use of ideal types, which are concepts designed to capture the essential characteristics of a particular phenomenon. We can only define adequately the words we use to describe social realities when we admit that they are concepts, not historical realities, according to Weber. There is a more subtle argument about objectivity in this essay as well. Weber argues that the ideal types that social scientists use objectively should be concerned with the ideas that subjectively motivate action. Ideal types become Weber's way of connecting large-scale institutions and ideas to the social action of individuals.

The second methodological reading, "Basic Sociological Terms," provides Weber's views of sociology as a part of the social sciences. Weber here explicitly builds on the argument in "'Objectivity'" by defining sociology as the study of social action, a definition that stresses understanding (*verstehen*) of subjective motives rather than the building of law-like relationships. Still, Weber insists on the importance of generalization through the use of ideal-type concepts. Towards this end, Weber establishes a basic ideal-type scheme in outlining four types of social action. Since social action is the core of the field for Weber, the types of social action are a clear starting place. This outline, though basic, underlies much of the rest of his work. The two most important categories are instrumentally rational action (defined by the use of cost/benefit calculation) and traditional action (based on habit rather than calculation). In the readings that follow, Weber argues that instrumental rationality is gradually replacing traditional action in all spheres of life.

"The Protestant Ethic and the Spirit of Capitalism" is excerpted from Weber's celebrated book of the same name. Although the bulk of the text was completed in 1905, it was published only near the end of his life. The work develops Weber's interest in the link between religious ideas and economic institutions. Weber argues that a particular form of ascetic Protestantism fostered a "spirit" of modern capitalism, marked by a ceaseless obligation to earn money and to reinvest for profit. It is important to realize that Weber used both the terms "Protestant ethic" and "spirit of capitalism" as ideal-types and not as collective realities in Durkheim's sense. It is also important to recognize here Weber's critique of the materialist theories that Marx inspired. The emergence of Protestantism in Europe was partially related to economic factors, Weber argued, but this could not explain the relationship between ascetic Protestantism and capitalism in the "backwoods" of early America. "To speak here of a reflection of material conditions in the ideal superstructure would be patent nonsense," he said. In this case, a religious idea motivating the actions of individuals had a major world-historical effect on the economic structure.

The remaining essays, all from *Economy and Society*, focus in one way or another on the distribution of power and influence. "Class, Status, Party" provides a very different model of stratification from Marxist materialism. Most important is Weber's distinction between class (determined by market position) and status groups (based on social honor).

"Bureaucracy" and "The Types of Legitimate Domination" are both concerned with the role of rationality in political, economic and legal institutions. In "The Types of Legitimate Domination," Weber argues that people obey authority when they view it as legitimate. Claims to legitimacy may be based on rational grounds rooted in laws, traditional grounds, or charismatic grounds. Weber suggests a historical trend from traditional to rational types of authority. Movements based on the charismatic authority of political or religious reformers can bring about the end of traditional social orders, but they are also slippery. Because charismatic leadership is not easily passed on to a successor, such movements tend to revert to traditionalism or become more bureaucratic and hence provide a bridge to a rational social order.

Weber's Legacy in Sociology

The work of Max Weber stands second only to that of Marx in having become classic for historians, philosophers, and political scientists as well as for sociologists. Within the field of sociology, Weber's work has been influential substantively and methodologically. Substantively, the wide range of topics Weber covered has made his work required reading in political sociology, economic sociology, legal sociology, and stratification. Equally important, Weber's method and style allow his work to inform many of the problems currently debated hotly in sociology, including the agency/structure linkage, the nature of causality, and the tension between abstract, general theory and interpretive analysis of particular contexts (Kalberg, 1994).

Probably the best way to understand the enduring importance of Weber's work is to see how it relates to the more recent work in *Contemporary Sociological Theory*, the sister volume to this reader. Weber's focus on the growth of rationality and his studies of political, economic and legal structures clearly influenced much modern work on institutional analysis included in Part III. The influence is especially pronounced in Powell and Dimaggio's "The Iron Cage Revisited," the title of which refers to the famous phrase at the end of *The Protestant Ethic*. The muse of Weber is also clearly evident in the work of Anthony Giddens (Part V) and Pierre Bourdieu (Part VI). Both explicitly place the relationship between action and structure at the center of their theories. This renewed interest in action ("agency" in Giddens, "practice" in Bourdieu) as both reflecting and influencing existing structures has clear Weberian roots. In a more indirect way, Weber's work provided a model for at least some of the discussions of modernity and post-modernity (Part IX). Weber, of course, was among good company in grappling with the emergence of modernity. But Weber was the classical theorist who most clearly identified pervasive rationality as the ultimate condition of modernity. He also was the classical theorist to most clearly demonstrate the emergence of modernity as a process rather than a decisive break from traditionalism.

Select Bibliography

Bendix, Reinhard. 1977. *Max Weber: An Intellectual Portrait*. Berkeley: University of California Press. (A very thorough book on Weber's work. One of its most important features is that instead of treating broad themes, it covers the entire range of Weber's work in detail.)

Kalberg, Stephen. 1994. *Max Weber's Comparative-Historical Sociology*. Chicago: University of Chicago Press. (A discussion of the way Weber's work answers some of the recurring problems in historical and comparative sociology.)

Käsler, Dirk. 1988. *Max Weber: An Introduction to His Life and Work*. Philippa Hurd, translator. Chicago: University of Chicago Press. (An excellent advanced introduction to Weber and his work.)

Mitzman, Arthur. 1970. *The Iron Cage: An Historical Interpretation of Max Weber*. New York: Alfred A. Knopf. (Connects the developments of Weber's ideas to his biography. This book corrects some of the biases in Marianne Weber's biography.)

Mommsen, Wolfgang H. and Jürgen Osterhammel (eds.). 1987. *Weber and his Contemporaries*. Boston: Allen & Unwin. (Puts Weber into the context of his intellectual contemporaries in politics, social science and other fields.)

Turner, Bryan S. 1992. *Max Weber: From History to Modernity*. New York: Routledge. (A treatment of the theme of modernity in Weber's work and the way that Weber's work has itself contributed to current discussions of modernity.)

Turner, Stephen P. (ed.). 2000. *The Cambridge Companion to Max Weber*. New York: Cambridge University Press. (This volume presents an overview of Weber's thought, but also shows the legacy of Weber's work in the social sciences. It is especially useful as a guide to some of the intellectual debates about Weber's work.)

Weber, Marianne. 1988. *Max Weber: A Biography*. Harry Zohn, translator. Introduction by Guenther Roth. New Brunswick: Transaction Books. (The most thorough biography of Weber, written by his wife. It is an excellent source especially on the personal and political context of his work.)

A: METHOD OF SOCIAL SCIENCE

13   "Objectivity" in Social Science

Max Weber

We have in abstract economic theory an illustration of those synthetic constructs which have been designated as *"ideas"* of historical phenomena. It offers us an ideal picture of events on the commodity-market under conditions of a society organized on the principles of an exchange economy, free competition and rigorously rational conduct. This conceptual pattern brings together certain relationships and events of historical life into a complex, which is conceived as an internally consistent system. Substantively, this construct in itself is like a *utopia* which has been arrived at by the analytical accentuation of certain elements of reality. Its relationship to the empirical data consists solely in the fact that where market-conditioned relationships of the type referred to by the abstract construct are discovered or suspected to exist in reality to some extent, we can make the *characteristic* features of this relationship pragmatically *clear* and *understandable* by reference to an *ideal-type*. This procedure can be indispensable for heuristic as well as expository purposes. The ideal typical concept will help to develop our skill in imputation in *research*: it *is* no "hypothesis" but it offers guidance to the construction of hypotheses. It is not a *description* of reality but it aims to give unambiguous means of expression to such a description. It is thus the "idea" of the *historically* given modern society, based on an exchange economy, which is developed for us by quite the same logical principles as are used in constructing the idea of the medieval "city economy" as a "genetic" concept. When we do this, we construct the concept "city economy" not as an average of the economic structures actually existing in all the cities observed but as an *ideal-type*. An ideal type is formed by the one-sided *accentuation* of one or more points of view and by the synthesis of a great many diffuse, discrete, more or less present and occasionally absent *concrete individual* phenomena, which are arranged according to those one-sidedly emphasized viewpoints into a unified *analytical* construct (*Gedankenbild*). In its conceptual purity, this mental construct (*Gedankenbild*) cannot be found empirically anywhere in reality. It is a *utopia*. Historical research faces the task of determining in each individual case, the extent to which this ideal-construct approximates to or diverges from reality, to what extent for example, the economic structure of a certain city is to be classified as a "city-economy." When carefully applied, those concepts are particularly useful in research and exposition. In very much the same way one can work the "idea" of "handicraft" into a utopia by arranging certain traits, actually found in an unclear, confused state in the industrial enterprises of the most diverse epochs and countries, into a consistent ideal-construct by an accentuation of their essential tendencies. This ideal-type is then related to the idea (*Gedankenausdruck*) which one finds expressed there. One can further delineate a society in which all branches of economic and even intellectual activity are governed by maxims which appear to be applications of the same principle which characterizes the ideal-typical "handicraft" system. Furthermore, one can juxtapose alongside the ideal-typical "handicraft" system the antithesis of a correspondingly ideal-typical capitalistic productive system, which has been abstracted out of certain features of modern large scale industry. On the basis of this, one can delineate the utopia of a "capitalistic" culture, i.e., one in which the governing principle is the investment of private capital. This procecure would accentuate certain individual concretely diverse traits of modern material and intellectual culture in its unique aspects into an ideal construct which from our point of view would be completely self-consistent. This would then be the delineation of an *"idea" of capitalistic culture*. We must disregard for the moment whether and how this procedure could be carried out. It is possible, or rather, it must be accepted as certain that numerous, indeed a very great many, utopias of this sort can be worked out, of which *none* is like another, and *none* of which can be observed in empirical reality as an actually existing economic system, but *each* of which however claims that it is a representation of the "idea" of capitalistic culture. *Each* of these can claim to be a representation of the "idea" of capitalistic culture to the extent that it has really taken certain traits, meaningful in their essential features, from the empirical reality of our culture and brought them together into a unified ideal-construct. For those phenomena which interest us as cultural phenomena are interesting to us with respect to very different kinds of evaluative ideas to which we relate them. Inasmuch as the "points of view" from which they can become significant for us are very diverse, the most varied criteria can be applied to the selection of the traits which are to enter into the construction of an ideal-typical view of a particular culture.

What is the significance of such ideal-typical constructs for an *empirical* science, as we wish to constitute it? Before going any further, we should emphasize that the idea of an ethical *imperative*, of a "model" of what "ought" to exist is to be carefully distinguished from the analytical construct, which is "ideal" in the strictly logical sense of the term. It is a matter here of constructing relationships which our imagination accepts as plausibly motivated and hence as "objectively possible" and which appear as *adequate* from the nomological standpoint.

Whoever accepts the proposition that the knowledge of historical reality can or should be a "presuppositionless" copy of "objective" facts, will deny the value of the ideal-type. . . . Every conscientious examination of the conceptual elements of historical exposition shows however that the historian as soon as he attempts to go beyond the bare establishment of concrete relationships and to determine the *cultural* significance of even the simplest individual event in order to "characterize" it, *must* use concepts which are precisely and unambiguously definable only in the form of ideal types. Or are concepts such as "individualism," "imperialism," "feudalism," "mercantilism," "conventional," etc., and innumerable concepts of like character by means of which we seek analytically and empathically to understand reality constructed substantively by the "presuppositionless" *description* of some concrete phenomenon or through the abstract synthesis of those traits which are *common* to numerous concrete phenomena? Hundreds of words in the historian's vocabulary are ambiguous constructs created to meet the unconsciously felt need for adequate expression and the meaning of which is only concretely felt but not clearly thought out. In a great many cases, particularly in the field of descriptive political history, their ambiguity has not been prejudicial to the clarity of the presentation. It is sufficient that in each case the reader should *feel* what the historian had in mind; or, one can content one's self with the idea that the author used a *particular* meaning of the concept with special reference to the concrete case at hand. The greater the need however for a sharp appreciation of the significance of a cultural phenomenon, the more imperative is the need to operate with unambiguous concepts which are not only particularly but also systematically defined. . . .

In this function especially, the ideal-type is an attempt to analyze historically unique configurations or their individual components by means of genetic concepts. Let us take for instance the concepts "church" and "sect." They may be broken down purely classificatorily into complexes of characteristics whereby not only the distinction between them but also the content of the concept must constantly remain fluid. If however I wish to formulate the concept of "sect" genetically, e.g., with reference to certain important cultural significances which the "sectarian spirit" has had for modern culture, certain characteristics of both become *essential* because they stand in an adequate causal relationship to those influences. However, the concepts thereupon become ideal-typical in the sense that they appear in full conceptual *integrity* either not at all or only in individual instances. Here as elsewhere every concept which is not purely classificatory diverges from reality. But the discursive nature of our knowledge, i.e., the fact that we comprehend reality only through a chain of intellectual modifications postulates such a conceptual shorthand. Our imagination can often dispense with explicit conceptual formulations as a means of *investigation*. But as regards exposition, to the extent that it wishes to be unambiguous, the use of precise formulations in the sphere of cultural analysis is in many cases absolutely necessary. Whoever disregards it entirely must confine himself to the formal aspect of cultural phenomena, e.g., to legal history. The universe of legal norms is naturally clearly definable and is valid (in the *legal* sense!) for historical reality. But social science in our sense is concerned with practical *significance*. This significance however can very often be brought unambiguously to mind only by relating the empirical data to an ideal limiting case. If the historian (in the widest sense of the word) rejects an attempt to construct such ideal types as a "theoretical construction," i.e., as useless or dispensable for his concrete heuristic purposes, the inevitable consequence is either that he consciously or unconsciously uses other similar concepts without formulating them verbally and elaborating them logically or that he remains stuck in the realm of the vaguely "felt."

Nothing, however, is more dangerous than the *confusion* of theory and history stemming from naturalistic prejudices. This confusion expresses itself firstly in the belief that the "true" content and the essence of historical reality is portrayed in such theoretical constructs or secondly, in the use of these constructs as a procrustean bed into which history is to be forced or thirdly, in the hypostatization of such "ideas" as real "forces" and as a "true" reality which operates behind the passage of events and which works itself out in history.

This latter danger is especially great since we are also, indeed primarily, accustomed to understand by the "ideas" of an epoch the thoughts or ideals which dominated the mass or at least an historically decisive number of the persons living in that epoch itself, and who were therefore significant as components of its culture. Now there are two aspects to this: in the first place, there are certain relationships between the "idea" in the sense of a tendency of practical or theoretical thought and the "idea" in the sense of the ideal-*typical* portrayal of an epoch constructed as a heuristic device. An ideal type of certain situations, which can be abstracted from certain characteristic social phenomena of an epoch, might – and this is indeed quite often the case – have also been present in the minds of the persons living in that epoch as an ideal to be striven for in practical life or as a maxim for the regulation of certain social relationships. . . .

The relationship between the logical structure of the conceptual system in which we present such "ideas" and what is immediately given in empirical reality naturally varies considerably. It is relatively simple in cases in which one or a few easily formulated theoretical main principles as for instance Calvin's doctrine of predestination or clearly definable ethical postulates govern human conduct and produce historical effects, so that we can analyze the "idea" into a hierarchy of ideas which can be logically derived from those theses. It is of course easily overlooked that however important the significance even of the purely logically persuasive force of ideas – Marxism is an outstanding example of this type of force – nonetheless empirical-historical events occurring in men's minds must be understood as primarily *psychologically* and not logically conditioned. The ideal-typical character of such syntheses of historically effective ideas is revealed still more clearly when those fundamental main principles and postulates no longer survive in the minds of those individuals who are still dominated by ideas which were logically or associatively derived from them because the "idea" which was historically and originally fundamental has either died out or has in general achieved wide diffusion only for its broadest implications. The basic fact that the synthesis is an "idea" which *we* have created emerges even more markedly when those fundamental main principles have either only very imperfectly or not at all been raised to the level of explicit consciousness or at least have not taken the form of explicitly elaborated complexes of ideas. When we adopt this procedure, as it very often happens and must happen, we are concerned in these ideas, e.g., the "liberalism" of a certain period or "Methodism" or some intellectually unelaborated variety of "socialism," with a *pure* ideal type of much the same character as the synthetic "principles" of economic epochs in which we had our point of departure. The more inclusive the relationships to be presented, and the more many-sided their cultural *significance* has been, the *more* their comprehensive systematic exposition in a conceptual system approximates the character of an ideal type, and the less is it possible to operate with *one* such concept. In such situations the frequently repeated attempts to discover ever *new* aspects of significance by the construction of new ideal-typical concepts is all the more natural and unavoidable. All expositions for example of the "essence" of Christianity are ideal types enjoying only a necessarily very relative and problematic validity when they are intended to be regarded as the historical portrayal of empirically existing facts. On the other hand, such presentations are of great value for research and of high systematic value for expository purposes when they are used as conceptual instruments for *comparison* with and the *measurement* of reality. They are indispensable for this purpose.

There is still another even more complicated significance implicit in such ideal-typical presentations. They regularly seek to be, or are unconsciously, ideal-types not only in the *logical* sense but also in the *practical* sense, i.e., they are *model types* which – in our illustration – contain what, from the point of view of the expositor, *should* be and what *to him* is "essential" in Christianity *because it is enduringly valuable*. If this is consciously or – as it is more frequently – unconsciously the case, they contain ideals *to* which the expositor *evaluatively* relates Christianity. These ideals are tasks and ends towards which he orients his "idea" of Christianity and which naturally can and indeed doubtless always will differ greatly from the values which other persons, for instance, the early Christians, connected with Christianity. In this sense, however, the "ideas" are naturally no longer purely *logical* auxiliary devices, no longer concepts with which reality is compared, but ideals by which it is evaluatively *judged*. Here it is no longer a matter of the purely theoretical procedure of treating empirical rality with respect to values but of *value-judgments* which are integrated into the concept of "*Christianity.*" Because the ideal type claims empirical *validity* here, it penetrates into the realm of the evaluative *interpretation* of Christianity. The sphere of empirical science has been left behind and we are confronted with a profession of faith, not an ideal-typical construct. As fundamental as this distinction is in principle, the confusion of these two basically different meanings of the term "idea" appears with extraordinary frequency in historical writings. It is always close at hand whenever the descriptive historian begins to develop his "conception" of a personality or an epoch. . . . In contrast with this, the *elementary duty of scientific self-control* and the only way to avoid serious and foolish blunders requires a sharp, precise distinction between the logically *comparative* analysis of reality by ideal-*types* in the logical sense and the *value-judgment* of reality *on the basis of ideals*. An "ideal type" in our sense, to repeat once more, has no connection at all with *value-judgments*, and it has nothing to do with any type of perfection other than a purely *logical* one. There are ideal types of brothels as well as of religions; there are also ideal types of those kinds of brothels which are technically "expedient" from the point of view of police ethics as well as those of which the exact opposite is the case. . . .

We are now at the end of this discussion, the only purpose of which was to trace the course of the hair-line which separates science from faith and to make explicit the *meaning* of the quest for social and economic knowledge. The *objective* validity of all empirical knowledge rests exclusively upon the ordering of the given reality according to categories which are *subjective* in a specific sense, namely, in that they present the *presuppositions* of our knowledge and are based on the presupposition of the *value* of those *truths* which empirical knowledge alone is able to give us. The means available to our science offer nothing to those persons to whom this truth is of no value. It should be remembered that the belief in the value of scientific truth is the product of certain cultures and is not a product of man's original nature. Those for whom scientific truth is of no value will seek in vain for some other truth to take the place of science in just those respects in which it is unique, namely, in the provision of concepts and judgments which are neither empirical reality nor reproductions of it but which facilitate its analytical ordering in a valid manner. In the empirical social sciences, as we have seen, the possibility of meaningful knowledge of what is essential for us in the infinite richness of events is bound up with the unremitting application of viewpoints of a specifically particularized character, which, in the last analysis, are oriented on the basis of evaluative ideas. These evaluative ideas are for their part empirically discoverable and analyzable as elements of meaningful human conduct, but their validity can *not* be deduced from empirical data as such. The "objectivity" of the social sciences depends rather on the fact that the empirical data are always related to those evaluative ideas which alone make them worth knowing and the significance of the empirical data is derived from these evaluative ideas. But these data can never become the foundation for the empirically impossible proof of the validity of the evaluative ideas. The belief which we all have in some form or other, in the meta-empirical validity of ultimate and final values, in which the meaning of our existence is rooted, is not incompatible with the incessant changefulness of the concrete viewpoints, from which empirical reality gets its significance. Both these views are, on the contrary, in harmony with each other. Life with its irrational reality and its store of possible meanings is inexhaustible. The *concrete* form in which value-relevance occurs remains perpetually in flux, ever subject to change in the dimly seen future of human culture. The light which emanates from those highest evaluative ideas always falls on an ever changing finite segment of the vast chaotic stream of events, which flows away through time.

Now all this should not be misunderstood to mean that the proper task of the social sciences should be the continual chase for new viewpoints and new analytical constructs. *On the contrary*: nothing should be more sharply emphasized than the proposition that the knowledge of the *cultural significance* of *concrete historical events and patterns* is exclusively and solely the final end which, among other means, concept-construction and the criticism of constructs also seek to serve.

There are, to use the words of F. Th. Vischer, "subject matter specialists" and "interpretative specialists." The fact-greedy gullet of the former can be filled only with legal documents, statistical worksheets and questionnaires, but he is insensitive to the refinement of a new idea. The gourmandise of the latter dulls his taste for facts by ever new intellectual subtilities. That genuine artistry which, among the historians, Ranke possessed in such a grand measure, manifests itself through its ability to produce new knowledge by interpreting already *known* facts according to known viewpoints.

All research in the cultural sciences in an age of specialization, once it is oriented towards a given subject matter through particular settings of problems and has established its methodological principles, will consider the analysis of the data as an end in itself. It will discontinue assessing the value of the individual facts in terms of their relationships to ultimate value-ideas. Indeed, it will lose its awareness of its ultimate rootedness in the value-ideas in general. And it is well that should be so. But there comes a moment when the atmosphere changes. The significance of the unreflectively utilized viewpoints becomes uncertain and the road is lost in the twilight. The light of the great cultural problems moves on. Then science too prepares to change its standpoint and its analytical apparatus and to view the streams of events from the heights of thought. It follows those stars which alone are able to give meaning and direction to its labors:

> ". . . . . . . der neue Trieb erwacht,
> Ich eile fort, ihr ewiges Licht zu trinken,
> Vor mir den Tag und unter mir die Nacht,
> Den Himmel über mir und unter mir die Wellen."[1]

Note

1 *Faust*: Act I, Scene II. (Translated by Bayard-Taylor)
>   "The newborn impulse fires my mind,
>   I hasten on, his beams eternal drinking,
>   The Day before me and the Night behind,
>   Above me Heaven unfurled, the floor of waves beneath me."

14 Basic Sociological Terms

Max Weber

I. The Definition of Sociology and of Social Action

Sociology (in the sense in which this highly ambiguous word is used here) is a science concerning itself with the interpretive understanding of social action and thereby with a causal explanation of its course and consequences. We shall speak of "action" insofar as the acting individual attaches a subjective meaning to his behavior – be it overt or covert, omission or acquiescence. Action is "social" insofar as its subjective meaning takes account of the behavior of others and is thereby oriented in its course.

A. Methodological foundations

1   "Meaning" may be of two kinds. The term may refer first to the actual existing meaning in the given concrete case of a particular actor, or to the average or approximate meaning attributable to a given plurality of actors; or secondly to the theoretically conceived *pure type* of subjective meaning attributed to the hypothetical actor or actors in a given type of action. In no case does it refer to an objectively "correct" meaning or one which is "true" in some metaphysical sense. It is this which distinguishes the empirical sciences of action, such as sociology and history, from the dogmatic disciplines in that area, such as jurisprudence, logic, ethics, and esthetics, which seem to ascertain the "true" and "valid" meanings associated with the objects of their investigation.

2   The line between meaningful action and merely reactive behavior to which no subjective meaning is attached, cannot be sharply drawn empirically. A very considerable part of all sociologically relevant behavior, especially purely traditional behavior, is marginal between the two. In the case of some psychophysical processes, meaningful, i.e., subjectively understandable, action is not to be found at all; in others it is discernible only by the psychologist. Many mystical experiences which cannot be adequately communicated in words are, for a person who is not susceptible to such experiences, not fully understandable. At the same time the ability to perform a similar action is not a necessary prerequisite to understanding; "one need not have been Caeser in order to understand Caesar." "Recapturing an experience" is important for accurate understanding, but not an absolute precondition for its interpretation. Understandable and non-understandable components of a process are often intermingled and bound up together.

3   All interpretation of meaning, like all scientific observations, strives for clarity and verifiable accuracy of insight and comprehension (*Evidenz*). The basis for certainty in understanding can be either rational, which can be further subdivided into logical and mathematical, or it can be of an emotionally empathic or artistically

appreciative quality. Action is rationally evident chiefly when we attain a completely clear intellectual grasp of the action-elements in their intended context of meaning. Empathic or appreciative accuracy is attained when, through sympathetic participation, we can adequately grasp the emotional context in which the action took place. The highest degree of rational understanding is attained in cases involving the meanings of logically or mathematically related propositions; their meaning may be immediately and unambiguously intelligible. . . .

For the purposes of a typological scientific analysis it is convenient to treat all irrational, affectually determined elements of behavior as factors of deviation from a conceptually pure type of rational action. For example a panic on the stock exchange can be most conveniently analysed by attempting to determine first what the course of action would have been if it had not been influenced by irrational affects; it is then possible to introduce the irrational components as accounting for the observed deviations from this hypothetical course. Similarly, in analysing a political or military campaign it is convenient to determine in the first place what would have been a rational course, given the ends of the participants and adequate knowledge of all the circumstances. Only in this way is it possible to assess the causal significance of irrational factors as accounting for the deviations from this type. The construction of a purely rational course of action in such cases serves the sociologist as a type (ideal type) which has the merit of clear understandability and lack of ambiguity. By comparison with this it is possible to understand the ways in which actual action is influenced by irrational factors of all sorts, such as affects and errors, in that they account for the deviation from the line of conduct which would be expected on the hypothesis that the action were purely rational.

Only in this respect and for these reasons of methodological convenience is the method of sociology "rationalistic." It is naturally not legitimate to interpret this procedure as involving a rationalistic bias of sociology, but only as a methodological device. It certainly does not involve a belief in the actual predominance of rational elements in human life, for on the question of how far this predominance does or does not exist, nothing whatever has been said. That there is, however, a danger of rationalistic interpretations where they are out of place cannot be denied. All experience unfortunately confirms the existence of this danger.

4 In all the sciences of human action, account must be taken of processes and phenomena which are devoid of subjective meaning, in the role of stimuli, results, favoring or hindering circumstances. To be devoid of meaning is not identical with being lifeless or non-human; every artifact, such as for example a machine, can be understood only in terms of the meaning which its production and use have had or were intended to have; a meaning which may derive from a relation to exceedingly various purposes. Without reference to this meaning such an object remains wholly unintelligible. . . .

5 Understanding may be of two kinds: the first is the direct observational understanding of the subjective meaning of a given act as such, including verbal utterances. We thus understand by direct observation, in this case, the meaning of the proposition $2 \times 2 = 4$ when we hear or read it. This is a case of the direct rational understanding of ideas. We also understand an outbreak of anger as manifested by facial expression, exclamations or irrational movements. This is direct observational understanding of irrational emotional reactions. We can under-

stand in a similar observational way the action of a woodcutter or of somebody who reaches for the knob to shut a door or who aims a gun at an animal. This is rational observational understanding of actions.

Understanding may, however, be of another sort, namely explanatory understanding. Thus we understand in terms of *motive* the meaning an actor attaches to the proposition twice two equals four, when he states it or writes it down, in that we understand what makes him do this at precisely this moment and in these circumstances. Understanding in this sense is attained if we know that he is engaged in balancing a ledger or in making a scientific demonstration, or is engaged in some other task of which this particular act would be an appropriate part. This is rational understanding of motivation, which consists in placing the act in an intelligible and more inclusive context of meaning. Thus we understand the chopping of wood or aiming of a gun in terms of motive in addition to direct observation if we know that the woodchopper is working for a wage or is chopping a supply of firewood for his own use or possibly is doing it for recreation. But he might also be working off a fit of rage, an irrational case. Thus for a science which is concerned with the subjective meaning of action, explanation requires a grasp of the complex of meaning in which an actual course of understandable action thus interpreted belongs. In all such cases, even where the processes are largely affectual, the subjective meaning of the action, including that also of the relevant meaning complexes, will be called the intended meaning. (This involves a departure from ordinary usage, which speaks of intention in this sense only in the case of rationally purposive action.)

6   In all these cases understanding involves the interpretive grasp of the meaning present in one of the following contexts: (a) as in the historical approach, the actually intended meaning for concrete individual action; or (b) as in cases of sociological mass phenomena, the average of, or an approximation to, the actually intended meaning; or (c) the meaning appropriate to a scientifically formulated pure type (an ideal type) of a common phenomenon. . . .

Every interpretation attempts to attain clarity and certainty, but no matter how clear an interpretation as such appears to be from the point of view of meaning, it cannot on this account claim to be the causally valid interpretation. On this level it must remain only a peculiarly plausible hypothesis. . . .

More generally, verification of subjective interpretation by comparison with the concrete course of events is, as in the case of all hypotheses, indispensable. Unfortunately this type of verification is feasible with relative accuracy only in the few very special cases susceptible of psychological experimentation. In very different degrees of approximation, such verification is also feasible in the limited number of cases of mass phenomena which can be statistically described and unambiguously interpreted. For the rest there remains only the possibility of comparing the largest possible number of historical or contemporary processes which, while otherwise similar, differ in the one decisive point of their relation to the particular motive or factor the role of which is being investigated. This is a fundamental task of comparative sociology. Often, unfortunately, there is available only the uncertain procedure of the "imaginary experiment" which consists in thinking away certain elements of a chain of motivation and working out the course of action which would then probably ensue, thus arriving at a causal judgment. . . .

7   A motive is a complex of subjective meaning which seems to the actor himself or to the observer an adequate ground for the conduct in question. The interpretation of a coherent course of conduct is "subjectively adequate" (or "adequate on the level of meaning"), insofar as, according to our habitual modes of thought and feeling, its component parts taken in their mutual relation are recognized to constitute a "typical" complex of meaning. It is more common to say "correct." The interpretation of a sequence of events will on the other hand be called *causally* adequate insofar as, according to established generalizations from experience, there is a probability that it will always actually occur in the same way. . . .

Statistical uniformities constitute understandable types of action, and thus constitute sociological generalizations, only when they can be regarded as manifestations of the understandable subjective meaning of a course of social action. Conversely, formulations of a rational course of subjectively understandable action constitute sociological types of empirical process only when they can be empirically observed with a significant degree of approximation. By no means is the actual likelihood of the occurrence of a given course of overt action always directly proportional to the clarity of subjective interpretation. Only actual experience can prove whether this is so in a given case. There are statistics of processes devoid of subjective meaning, such as death rates, phenomena of fatigue, the production rate of machines, the amount of rainfall, in exactly the same sense as there are statistics of meaningful phenomena. But only when the phenomena are meaningful do we speak of sociological statistics. Examples are such cases as crime rates, occupational distributions, price statistics, and statistics of crop acreage. Naturally there are many cases where both components are involved, as in crop statistics.

8   Processes and uniformities which it has here seemed convenient not to designate as sociological phenomena or uniformities because they are not "understandable," are naturally not on that account any the less important. This is true even for sociology in our sense which is restricted to subjectively understandable phenomena – a usage which there is no intention of attempting to impose on anyone else. Such phenomena, however important, are simply treated by a different method from the others; they become conditions, stimuli, furthering or hindering circumstances of action.

9   Action in the sense of subjectively understandable orientation of behavior exists only as the behavior of one or more *individual* human beings. For other cognitive purposes it may be useful or necessary to consider the individual, for instance, as a collection of cells, as a complex of bio-chemical reactions, or to conceive his psychic life as made up of a variety of different elements, however these may be defined. Undoubtedly such procedures yield valuable knowledge of causal relationships. But the behavior of these elements, as expressed in such uniformities, is not subjectively understandable. . . .

For still other cognitive purposes – for instance, juristic ones – or for practical ends, it may on the other hand be convenient or even indispensable to treat social collectivities, such as states, associations, business corporations, foundations, as if they were individual persons. Thus they may be treated as the subjects of rights and duties or as the performers of legally significant actions. But for the subjective interpretation of action in sociological work these collectivities must be treated as *solely* the resultants and modes of organization of the particular acts of individual persons, since these alone can be treated as agents in a course of subjectively understandable action. Nevertheless, the sociologist cannot for his purposes afford to ignore these collective concepts derived from other disciplines. For the subjective interpretation of action has at least three important relations to these concepts. In the first place it is often necessary to employ very similar collective concepts, indeed often using the same terms, in order to obtain an intelligible terminology. Thus both in legal terminology and in everyday speech the term "state" is used both for the legal concept of the state and for the phenomena of social action to which its legal rules are relevant. . . .

Secondly, the subjective interpretation of action must take account of a fundamentally important fact. These concepts of collective entities which are found both in common sense and in juristic and other technical forms of thought, have a meaning in the minds of individual persons, partly as of something actually existing, partly as something with normative authority. This is true not only of judges and officials, but of ordinary private individuals as well. Actors thus in part orient their action to them, and in this role such ideas have a powerful, often a decisive, causal influence on the course of action of real individuals. . . .

Thirdly, it is the method of the so-called "organic" school of sociology – classical example: Schäffle's brilliant work, *Bau und Leben des sozialen Körpers* – to attempt to understand social interaction by using as a point of departure the "whole" within which the individual acts. His action and behavior are then interpreted somewhat in the way that a physiologist would treat the role of an organ of the body in the "economy" of the organism, that is from the point of view of the survival of the latter. (Compare the famous dictum of a well-known physiologist: "Sec. 10. The spleen. Of the spleen, gentlemen, we know nothing. So much for the spleen." Actually, of course, he knew a good deal about the spleen – its position, size, shape, etc.; but he could say nothing about its function, and it was his inability to do this that he called "ignorance.") How far in other disciplines this type of functional analysis of the relation of "parts" to a "whole" can be regarded as definitive, cannot be discussed here; but it is well known that the bio-chemical and bio-physical modes of analysis of the organism are on principle opposed to stopping there. For purposes of sociological analysis two things can be said. First this functional frame of reference is convenient for purposes of practical illustration and for provisional orientation. In these respects it is not only useful but indispensable. But at the same time if its cognitive value is overestimated and its concepts illegitimately "reified," it can be highly dangerous. Secondly, in certain circumstances this is the only available way of determining just what processes of social action it is important to understand in order to explain a given phenomenon. But this is only the beginning of sociological analysis as here understood. In the case of social collectivities, precisely as distinguished from organisms, we are in a position to go beyond merely demonstrating functional relationships and uniformities. We can accomplish something which is never attainable in the natural sciences, namely the subjective understanding of the action of the component individuals.

It is a tremendous misunderstanding to think that an "individualistic" *method* should involve what is in any conceivable sense an individualistic system of *values*. It is as important to avoid this error as the related one which confuses the unavoidable tendency of sociological concepts to assume a rationalistic character with a belief in the predominance of rational motives, or even a positive valuation of rationalism. Even a socialistic economy would have to be understood sociologically in exactly the same kind of "individualistic" terms; that is, in terms of the action of individuals, the types of officials found in it, as would be the case with a system of free exchange analysed in terms of the theory of marginal utility or a "better," but in this respect similar theory. The real empirical sociological investigation begins with the question: What motives determine and lead the individual members and participants in this socialistic community to behave in such a way that the community came into being in the first place and that it continues to exist? Any form of functional analysis which proceeds from the whole to the parts can accomplish only a preliminary preparation for this investigation – a preparation, the utility and indispensability of which, if properly carried out, is naturally beyond question.

10   It is customary to designate various sociological generalizations, as for example "Gresham's Law," as "laws." These are in fact typical probabilities confirmed by observation to the effect that under certain given conditions an expected course of social action will occur, which is understandable in terms of the typical motives and typical subjective intentions of the actors. These generalizations are both understandable and definite in the highest degree insofar as the typically observed course of action can be understood in terms of the purely rational pursuit of an end, or where for reasons of methodological convenience such a theoretical type can be heuristically employed. In such cases the relations of means and end will be clearly understandable on grounds of experience, particularly where the choice of means was "inevitable." In such cases it is legitimate to assert that insofar as the action was rigorously rational it could not have taken any other course because for technical reasons, given their clearly defined ends, no other means were available to the actors. This very case demonstrates how erroneous it is to regard any kind of psychology as the ultimate foundation of the sociological interpretation of action. . . .

11   We have taken for granted that sociology seeks to formulate type concepts and generalized uniformities of empirical process. This distinguishes it from history, which is oriented to the causal analysis and explanation of individual actions, structures, and personalities possessing cultural significance. The empirical material which underlies the concepts of sociology consists to a very large extent, though by no means exclusively, of the same concrete processes of action which are dealt with by historians. An important consideration in the formulation of sociological concepts and generalizations is the contribution that sociology can make toward the causal explanation of some historically and culturally important phenomenon. As in the case of every generalizing science the abstract character of the concepts of sociology is responsible for the fact that, compared with actual historical reality, they are relatively lacking in fullness of concrete content. To compensate for this disadvantage, sociological analysis can offer a greater precision of concepts. This precision is obtained by striving for the highest possible degree of adequacy on the level of meaning. It has already been repeatedly stressed that this aim can be realized in a particularly high degree in the case of concepts and generalizations which formulate rational processes. But sociological investigation attempts to include in its scope various irrational phenomena, such as prophetic, mystic, and affectual modes of action, formulated in terms of theoretical concepts which are

adequate on the level of meaning. In *all* cases, rational or irrational, sociological analysis both abstracts from reality and at the same time helps us to understand it, in that it shows with what degree of approximation a concrete historical phenomenon can be subsumed under one or more of these concepts. For example, the same historical phenomenon may be in one aspect feudal, in another patrimonial, in another bureaucratic, and in still another charismatic. In order to give a precise meaning to these terms, it is necessary for the sociologist to formulate pure ideal types of the corresponding forms of action which in each case involve the highest possible degree of logical integration by virtue of their complete adequacy on the level of meaning. But precisely because this is true, it is probably seldom if ever that a real phenomenon can be found which corresponds exactly to one of these ideally constructed pure types. . . .

The theoretical concepts of sociology are ideal types not only from the objective point of view, but also in their application to subjective processes. In the great majority of cases actual action goes on in a state of inarticulate half-consciousness or actual unconsciousness of its subjective meaning. The actor is more likely to "be aware" of it in a vague sense than he is to "know" what he is doing or be explicitly self-conscious about it. In most cases his action is governed by impulse or habit. Only occasionally and, in the uniform action of large numbers, often only in the case of a few individuals, is the subjective meaning of the action, whether rational or irrational, brought clearly into consciousness.

B. Social action

1   Social action, which includes both failure to act and passive acquiescence, may be oriented to the past, present, or expected future behavior of others. Thus it may be motivated by revenge for a past attack, defence against present, or measures of defence against future aggression. The "others" may be individual persons, and may be known to the actor as such, or may constitute an indefinite plurality and may be entirely unknown as individuals. (Thus, money is a means of exchange which the actor accepts in payment because he orients his action to the expectation that a large but unknown number of individuals he is personally unacquainted with will be ready to accept it in exchange on some future occasion.)

2   Not every kind of action, even of overt action, is "social" in the sense of the present discussion. Overt action is non-social if it is oriented solely to the behavior of inanimate objects. Subjective attitudes constitute social action only so far as they are oriented to the behavior of others. For example, religious behavior is not social if it is simply a matter of contemplation or of solitary prayer. The economic activity of an individual is social only if it takes account of the behavior of someone else. Thus very generally it becomes social insofar as the actor assumes that others will respect his actual control over economic goods. Concretely it is social, for instance, if in relation to the actor's own consumption the future wants of others are taken into account and this becomes one consideration affecting the actor's own saving. Or, in another connexion, production may be oriented to the future wants of other people.

3   Not every type of contact of human beings has a social character; this is rather confined to cases where the actor's behavior is meaningfully oriented to that

of others. For example, a mere collision of two cyclists may be compared to a natural event. On the other hand, their attempt to avoid hitting each other, or whatever insults, blows, or friendly discussion might follow the collision, would constitute "social action."

4 Social action is not identical either with the similar actions of many persons or with every action influenced by other persons. Thus, if at the beginning of a shower a number of people on the street put up their umbrellas at the same time, this would not ordinarily be a case of action mutually oriented to that of each other, but rather of all reacting in the same way to the like need of protection from the rain. It is well known that the actions of the individual are strongly influenced by the mere fact that he is a member of a crowd confined within a limited space. Thus, the subject matter of studies of "crowd psychology," such as those of Le Bon, will be called "action conditioned by crowds." It is also possible for large numbers, though dispersed, to be influenced simultaneously or successively by a source of influence operating similarly on all the individuals, as by means of the press. . . . But for this to happen there need not, at least in many cases, be any meaningful relation between the behavior of the individual and the fact that he is a member of a crowd. It is not proposed in the present sense to call action "social" when it is merely a result of the effect on the individual of the existence of a crowd as such and the action is not oriented to that fact on the level of meaning. At the same time the borderline is naturally highly indefinite. In such cases as that of the influence of the demagogue, there may be a wide variation in the extent to which his mass clientele is affected by a meaningful reaction to the fact of its large numbers; and whatever this relation may be, it is open to varying interpretations.

But furthermore, mere "imitation" of the action of others, such as that on which Tarde has rightly laid emphasis, will not be considered a case of specifically social action if it is purely reactive so that there is no meaningful orientation to the actor imitated. The borderline is, however, so indefinite that it is often hardly possible to discriminate. . . . On the other hand, if the action of others is imitated because it is fashionable or traditional or exemplary, or lends social distinction, or on similar grounds, it is meaningfully oriented either to the behavior of the source of imitation or of third persons or of both. . . .

2. Types of Social Action

Social action, like all action, may be oriented in four ways. It may be:

(1) *instrumentally rational* (*zweckrational*), that is, determined by expectations as to the behavior of objects in the environment and of other human beings; these expectations are used as "conditions" or "means" for the attainment of the actor's own rationally pursued and calculated ends;

(2) *value-rational* (*wertrational*), that is, determined by a conscious belief in the value for its own sake of some ethical, aesthetic, religious, or other form of behavior, independently of its prospects of success;

(3) *affectual* (especially emotional), that is, determined by the actor's specific affects and feeling states;

(4) *traditional*, that is, determined by ingrained habituation.

1   Strictly traditional behavior, like the reactive type of imitation discussed above, lies very close to the borderline of what can justifiably be called meaningfully oriented action, and indeed often on the other side. For it is very often a matter of almost automatic reaction to habitual stimuli which guide behavior in a course which has been repeatedly followed. The great bulk of all everyday action to which people have become habitually accustomed approaches this type. Hence, its place in a systematic classification is not merely that of a limiting case because, as will be shown later, attachment to habitual forms can be upheld with varying degrees of self-consciousness and in a variety of senses. In this case the type may shade over into value rationality (*Wertrationalität*).

2   Purely affectual behavior also stands on the borderline of what can be considered "meaningfully" oriented, and often it, too, goes over the line. It may, for instance, consist in an uncontrolled reaction to some exceptional stimulus. It is a case of sublimation when affectually determined action occurs in the form of conscious release of emotional tension. When this happens it is usually well on the road to rationalization in one or the other or both of the above senses.

3   The orientation of value-rational action is distinguished from the affectual type by its clearly self-conscious formulation of the ultimate values governing the action and the consistently planned orientation of its detailed course to these values. At the same time the two types have a common element, namely that the meaning of the action does not lie in the achievement of a result ulterior to it, but in carrying out the specific type of action for its own sake. Action is affectual if it satisfies a need for revenge, sensual gratification, devotion, contemplative bliss, or for working off emotional tensions (irrespective of the level of sublimation).

Examples of pure value-rational orientation would be the actions of persons who, regardless of possible cost to themselves, act to put into practice their convictions of what seems to them to be required by duty, honor, the pursuit of beauty, a religious call, personal loyalty, or the importance of some "cause" no matter in what it consists. In our terminology, value-rational action always involves "commands" or "demands" which, in the actor's opinion, are binding on him. . . .

4   Action is instrumentally rational (*zweckrational*) when the end, the means, and the secondary results are all rationally taken into account and weighed. This involves rational consideration of alternative means to the end, of the relations of the end to the secondary consequences, and finally of the relative importance of different possible ends. Determination of action either in affectual or in traditional terms is thus incompatible with this type. Choice between alternative and conflicting ends and results may well be determined in a value-rational manner. In that case, action is instrumentally rational only in respect to the choice of means. On the other hand, the actor may, instead of deciding between alternative and conflicting ends in terms of a rational orientation to a system of values, simply take them as given subjective wants and arrange them in a scale of consciously assessed relative urgency. He may then orient his action to this scale in such a way that they are satisfied as far as possible in order of urgency, as formulated in the principle of "marginal utility." Value-rational action may thus have various different relations to the instrumentally rational action. From the latter point of view, however, value-rationality is always irrational. . . .

5   It would be very unusual to find concrete cases of action, especially of social

action, which were oriented *only* in one or another of these ways. Furthermore, this classification of the modes of orientation of action is in no sense meant to exhaust the possibilities of the field, but only to formulate in conceptually pure form certain sociologically important types to which actual action is more or less closely approximated or, in much the more common case, which constitute its elements. The usefulness of the classification for the purposes of this investigation can only be judged in terms of its results.

B: RELIGION AND RATIONALITY

15 The Protestant Ethic and the Spirit of Capitalism

Max Weber

Religious Affiliation and Social Stratification

A glance at the occupational statistics of any country of mixed religious composition brings to light with remarkable frequency a situation which has several times provoked discussion in the Catholic press and literature, and in Catholic congresses in Germany, namely, the fact that business leaders and owners of capital, as well as the higher grades of skilled labour, and even more the higher technically and commercially trained personnel of modern enterprises, are overwhelmingly Protestant. This is true not only in cases where the difference in religion coincides with one of nationality, and thus of cultural development, as in Eastern Germany between Germans and Poles. The same thing is shown in the figures of religious affiliation almost wherever capitalism, at the time of its great expansion, has had a free hand to alter the social distribution of the population in accordance with its needs, and to determine its occupational structure. The more freedom it has had, the more clearly is the effect shown. It is true that the greater relative participation of Protestants in the ownership of capital, in management, and the upper ranks of labour in great modern industrial and commercial enterprises, may in part be explained in terms of historical circumstances which extend far back into the past, and in which religious affiliation is not a cause of the economic conditions, but to a certain extent appears to be a result of them. Participation in the above economic functions usually involves some previous ownership of capital, and generally an expensive education; often both. These are to-day largely dependent on the possession of inherited wealth, or at least on a certain degree of material well-being. A number of those sections of the old Empire which were most highly developed economically and most favoured by natural resources and situation, in particular a majority of the wealthy towns, went over to Protestantism in the sixteenth century. The results of that circumstance favour the Protestants even to-day in their struggle for economic existence. There arises thus the historical question: why were the districts of highest economic development at the same time particularly favourable to a revolution in the Church? The answer is by no means so simple as one might think.

The emancipation from economic traditionalism appears, no doubt, to be a factor which would greatly strengthen the tendency to doubt the sanctity of the religious tradition, as of all traditional authorities. But it is necessary to note, what has often been forgotten, that the Reformation meant not the elimination of the Church's control over everyday life, but rather the substitution of a new form of control for the previous one. It meant the repudiation of a control which was very lax, at that time scarcely perceptible in practice, and hardly more than formal, in favour of a regulation of the whole of conduct which, penetrating to all departments of private and public life, was infinitely burdensome and earnestly enforced. The rule of the Catholic Church, "punishing the heretic, but indulgent to the sinner", as it was in the past even more than to-day, is now tolerated by peoples of thoroughly modern economic character, and was borne by the richest and economically most advanced peoples on earth at about the turn of the fifteenth century. The rule of Calvinism, on the other hand, as it was enforced in the sixteenth century in Geneva and in Scotland, at the turn of the sixteenth and seventeenth centuries in large parts of the Netherlands, in the seventeenth in New England, and for a time in England itself, would be for us the most absolutely unbearable form of ecclesiastical control of the individual which could possibly exist. That was exactly what large numbers of the old commercial aristocracy of those times, in Geneva as well as in Holland and England, felt about it. And what the reformers complained of in those areas of high economic development was not too much supervision of life on the part of the Church, but too little. Now how does it happen that at that time those countries which were most advanced economically, and within them the rising bourgeois middle classes, not only failed to resist this unexampled tyranny of Puritanism, but even developed a heroism in its defence? For bourgeois classes as such have seldom before and never since displayed heroism. It was "the last of our heroisms", as Carlyle, not without reason, has said.

But further, and especially important: it may be, as has been claimed, that the greater participation of Protestants in the positions of ownership and management in modern economic life may to-day be understood, in part at least, simply as a result of the greater material wealth they have inherited. But there are certain other phenomena which cannot be explained in the same way. Thus, to mention only a few facts: there is a great difference discoverable in Baden, in Bavaria, in Hungary, in the type of higher education which Catholic parents, as opposed to Protestant, give their children. That the percentage of Catholics among the students and graduates of higher educational institutions in general lags behind their proportion of the total population, may, to be sure, be largely explicable in terms of inherited differences of wealth. But among the Catholic graduates themselves the percentage of those graduating from the institutions preparing, in particular, for technical studies and industrial and commercial occupations, but in general from those preparing for middle-class business life, lags still farther behind the percentage of Protestants. On the other hand, Catholics prefer the sort of training which the humanistic Gymnasium affords. That is a circumstance to which the above explanation does not apply, but which, on the contrary, is one reason why so few Catholics are engaged in capitalistic enterprise.

Even more striking is a fact which partly explains the smaller proportion of Catholics among the skilled labourers of modern industry. It is well known that the factory has taken its skilled labour to a large extent from young men in the handicrafts; but this is much more true of Protestant than of Catholic journeymen. Among journeymen, in other words, the Catholics show a stronger propensity to remain in their crafts, that is they more often become master craftsmen, whereas the Protestants are attracted to a larger extent into the factories in order to fill the upper ranks of skilled labour and administrative positions. The explanation of these cases is undoubtedly that the mental and spiritual peculiarities acquired from the environment, here the type of education favoured by the religious atmosphere of the home community and the parental home, have determined the choice of occupation, and through it the professional career.

The smaller participation of Catholics in the modern business life of Germany is all the more striking because it runs counter to a tendency which has been observed at all times including the present. National or religious minorities which are in a position of subordination to a group of rulers are likely, through their voluntary or involuntary exclusion from positions of political influence, to be driven with peculiar force into economic activity. Their ablest members seek to satisfy the desire for recognition of their abilities in this field since there is no opportunity in the service of the State. This has undoubtedly been true of the Poles in Russia and Eastern Prussia, who have without question been undergoing a more rapid economic advance than in Galicia, where they have been in the ascendant. It has in earlier times been true of the Huguenots in France under Louis XIV, the Nonconformists and Quakers in England, and, last but not least, the Jew for two thousand years. But the Catholics in Germany have shown no striking evidence of such a result of their position. In the past they have, unlike the Protestants, undergone no particularly prominent economic development in the times when they were persecuted or only tolerated, either in Holland or in England. On the other hand, it is a fact that the Protestants (especially certain branches of the movement to be fully discussed later) both as ruling classes and as ruled, both as majority and as minority, have shown a special tendency to develop economic rationalism which cannot be observed to the same extent among Catholics either in the one situation or in the other. Thus the principal explanation of this difference must be sought in the permanent intrinsic character of their religious beliefs, and not only in their temporary external historico-political situations.

It will be our task to investigate these religions with a view to finding out what peculiarities they have or have had which might have resulted in the behaviour we have described. . . .

The Spirit of Capitalism

In the title of this study is used the somewhat pretentious phrase, the *spirit* of capitalism. What is to be understood by it? The attempt to give anything like a definition of it brings out certain difficulties which are in the very nature of this type of investigation.

If any object can be found to which this term can be applied with any understandable meaning, it can only be an historical individual, i.e. a complex of elements associated in historical reality which we unite into a conceptual whole from the standpoint of their cultural significance.

Such an historical concept, however, since it refers in its content to a phenomenon significant for its unique individuality, cannot be defined according to the formula *genus proximum, differentia specifica*, but it must be gradually put together out of the individual parts which are taken from historical reality to make it up. Thus the final and definitive concept cannot stand at the beginning of the investigation, but must come at the end. We must, in other words, work out in the course of the discussion, as its most important result, the best conceptual formulation of what we here understand by the spirit of capitalism, that is the best from the point of view which interests us here. This point of view (the one of which we shall speak later) is, further, by no means the only possible one from which the historical phenomena we are investigating can be analysed. Other standpoints would, for this as for every historical phenomenon, yield other characteristics as the essential ones. The result is that it is by no means necessary to understand by the spirit of capitalism only what it will come to mean to *us* for the purposes of our analysis. This is a necessary result of the nature of historical concepts which attempt for their methodological purposes not to grasp historical reality in abstract general formulæ, but in concrete genetic sets of relations which are inevitably of a specifically unique and individual character.

Thus, if we try to determine the object, the analysis and historical explanation of which we are attempting, it cannot be in the form of a conceptual definition, but at least in the beginning only a provisional description of what is here meant by the spirit of capitalism. Such a description is, however, indispensable in order clearly to understand the object of the investigation. For this purpose we turn to a document of that spirit which contains what we are looking for in almost classical purity, and at the same time has the advantage of being free from all direct relationship to religion, being thus, for our purposes, free of preconceptions.

"Remember, that *time* is money. He that can earn ten shillings a day by his labour, and goes abroad, or sits idle, one half of that day, though he spends but sixpence during his diversion or idleness, ought not to reckon *that* the only expense; he has really spent, or rather thrown away, five shillings besides.

"Remember, that *credit* is money. If a man lets his money lie in my hands after it is due, he gives me the interest, or so much as I can make of it during that time. This amounts to a considerable sum where a man has good and large credit, and makes good use of it.

"Remember, that money is of the prolific, generating nature. Money can beget money, and its offspring can beget more, and so on. Five shillings turned is six, turned again it is seven and threepence, and so on, till it becomes a hundred pounds. The more there is of it, the more it produces every turning, so that the profits rise quicker and quicker. He that kills a breeding-sow, destroys all her offspring to the thousandth generation. He that murders a crown, destroys all that it might have produced, even scores of pounds."

"Remember this saying, *The good paymaster is lord of another man's purse*. He that is known to pay punctually and exactly to the time he promises, may at any time, and on any occasion, raise all the money his friends can spare. This is sometimes of great use. After industry and frugality, nothing contributes more to the raising of a young man in the world than punctuality and justice in all his dealings; therefore never keep borrowed money an hour beyond the time you promised, lest a disappointment shut up your friend's purse for ever.

"The most trifling actions that affect a man's credit are to be regarded. The sound of your hammer at five in the morning, or eight at night, heard by a creditor, makes him easy six months longer; but if he sees you at a billiard-table, or hears your voice at a tavern, when you should be at work, he sends for his money the next day; demands it, before he can receive it, in a lump.

"It shows, besides, that you are mindful of what you owe; it makes you appear a careful as well as an honest man, and that still increases your credit.

"Beware of thinking all your own that you possess, and of living accordingly. It is a mistake that many people who have credit fall into. To prevent this, keep an exact account for some time both of your expenses and your income. If you take the pains at first to mention particulars, it will have this good effect: you will discover how wonderfully small, trifling expenses mount up to large sums, and will discern what might have been, and may for the future be saved, without occasioning any great inconvenience."

"For six pounds a year you may have the use of one hundred pounds, provided you are a man of known prudence and honesty.

"He that spends a groat a day idly, spends idly above six pounds a year, which is the price for the use of one hundred pounds.

"He that wastes idly a groat's worth of his time per day, one day with another, wastes the privilege of using one hundred pounds each day.

"He that idly loses five shillings' worth of time, loses five shillings, and might as prudently throw five shillings into the sea.

"He that loses five shillings, not only loses that sum, but all the advantage that might be made by turning it in dealing, which by the time that a young man becomes old, will amount to a considerable sum of money."

It is Benjamin Franklin who preaches to us in these sentences, the same which Ferdinand Kürnberger satirizes in his clever and malicious *Picture of American Culture* as the supposed confession of faith of the Yankee. That it is the spirit of capitalism which here speaks in characteristic fashion, no one will doubt, however little we may wish to claim that everything which could be understood as pertaining to that spirit is contained in it. Let us pause a moment to consider this passage, the philosophy of which Kürnberger sums up in the words, "They make tallow out of cattle and money out of men". The peculiarity of this philosophy of avarice appears to be the ideal of the honest man of recognized credit, and above all the idea of a duty of the individual toward the increase of his capital, which is assumed as an end in itself. Truly what is here preached is not simply a means of making one's way in the world, but a peculiar ethic. The infraction of its rules is treated not as foolishness but as forgetfulness of duty. That is the essence of the matter. It is not mere business astuteness, that sort of thing is common enough, it is an ethos. *This* is the quality which interests us.

When Jacob Fugger, in speaking to a business associate who had retired and who wanted to persuade him to do the same, since he had made enough money and should let others have a chance, rejected that as pusillanimity and answered that "he (Fugger) though otherwise, he wanted to make money as long as he could", the spirit of his statement is evidently quite different from that of Franklin. What in the former case was an expression of commercial daring and a personal inclination morally neutral, in the latter takes on the character of an ethically coloured maxim for the conduct of life. The concept spirit of capitalism is here used in this specific sense, it is the spirit of modern capitalism. For that we are here dealing only with Western European and American capitalism is obvious from the way in which the problem was stated. Capitalism existed in China, India, Babylon, in the classic world, and in the Middle Ages. But in all these cases, as we shall see, this particular ethos was lacking.

Now, all Franklin's moral attitudes are coloured with utilitarianism. Honesty is useful, because it assures credit; so are punctuality, industry, frugality, and that is the reason they are virtues. A logical deduction from this would be that where, for instance, the appearance of honesty serves the same purpose, that would suffice, and an unnecessary surplus of this virtue would evidently appear to Franklin's eyes as unproductive waste. And as a matter of fact, the story in his autobiography of his conversion to those virtues, or the discussion of the value of a strict maintenance of the appearance of modesty, the assiduous belittlement of one's own deserts in order to gain general recognition later, confirms this impression. According to Franklin, those virtues, like all others, are only in so far virtues as they are actually useful to the individual, and the surrogate of mere appearance is always sufficient when it accomplishes the end in view. It is a conclusion which is inevitable for strict utilitarianism. The impression of many Germans that the virtues professed by Americanism are pure hypocrisy seems to have been confirmed by this striking case. But in fact the matter is not by any means so simple. Benjamin Franklin's own character, as it appears in the really unusual candidness of his autobiography, belies that suspicion. The circumstance that he ascribes his recognition of the utility of virtue to a divine revelation which was intended to lead him in the path of righteousness, shows that something more than mere garnishing for purely egocentric motives is involved.

In fact, the *summum bonum* of this ethic, the earning of more and more money, combined with the strict avoidance of all spontaneous enjoyment of life, is above all completely devoid of any eudæmonistic, not to say hedonistic, admixture. It is thought of so purely as an end in itself, that from the point of view of the happiness of, or utility to, the single individual, it appears entirely transcendental and absolutely irrational. Man is dominated by the making of money, by acquisition as the ultimate purpose of his life. Economic acquisition is no longer subordinated to man as the means for the satisfaction of his material needs. This reversal of what we should call the natural relationship, so irrational from a naïve point of view, is evidently as definitely a leading principle of capitalism as it is foreign to all peoples not under capitalistic influence. At the same time it expresses a type of feeling which is closely connected with certain religious ideas. If we thus ask, *why* should "money be made out of men", Benjamin Franklin himself, although he was a colourless deist, answers in his autobiography with a quotation from the Bible, which his strict Calvinistic father drummed into him again and again in his youth: "Seest thou a man diligent in his business? He shall stand before kings" (Prov. xxii.

29). The earning of money within the modern economic order is, so long as it is done legally, the result and the expression of virtue and proficiency in a calling; and this virtue and proficiency are, as it is now not difficult to see, the real Alpha and Omega of Franklin's ethic, as expressed in the passages we have quoted, as well as in all his works without exception.

And in truth this peculiar idea, so familiar to us to-day, but in reality so little a matter of course, of one's duty in a calling, is what is most characteristic of the social ethic of capitalistic culture, and is in a sense the fundamental basis of it. It is an obligation which the individual is supposed to feel and does feel towards the content of his professional activity, no matter in what it consists, in particular no matter whether it appears on the surface as a utilization of his personal powers, or only of his material possessions (as capital).

Of course, this conception has not appeared only under capitalistic conditions. On the contrary, we shall later trace its origins back to a time previous to the advent of capitalism. Still less, naturally, do we maintain that a conscious acceptance of these ethical maxims on the part of the individuals, entrepreneurs or labourers, in modern capitalistic enterprises, is a condition of the further existence of present-day capitalism. The capitalistic economy of the present day is an immense cosmos into which the individual is born, and which presents itself to him, at least as an individual, as an unalterable order of things in which he must live. It forces the individual, in so far as he is involved in the system of market relationships, to conform to capitalistic rules of action. The manufacturer who in the long run acts counter to these norms, will just as inevitably be eliminated from the economic scene as the worker who cannot or will not adapt himself to them will be thrown into the streets without a job.

Thus the capitalism of to-day, which has come to dominate economic life, educates and selects the economic subjects which it needs through a process of economic survival of the fittest. But here one can easily see the limits of the concept of selection as a means of historical explanation. In order that a manner of life so well adapted to the peculiarities of capitalism could be selected at all, i.e. should come to dominate others, it had to originate somewhere, and not in isolated individuals alone, but as a way of life common to whole groups of men. This origin is what really needs explanation. Concerning the doctrine of the more naïve historical materialism, that such ideas originate as a reflection or superstructure of economic situations, we shall speak more in detail below. At this point it will suffice for our purpose to call attention to the fact that without doubt, in the country of Benjamin Franklin's birth (Massachusetts), the spirit of capitalism (in the sense we have attached to it) was present before the capitalistic order. There were complaints of a peculiarly calculating sort of profit-seeking in New England, as distinguished from other parts of America, as early as 1632. It is further undoubted that capitalism remained far less developed in some of the neighbouring colonies, the later Southern States of the United States of America, in spite of the fact that these latter were founded by large capitalists for business motives, while the New England colonies were founded by preachers and seminary graduates with the help of small bourgeois, craftsmen and yeomen, for religious reasons. In this case the causal relation is certainly the reverse of that suggested by the materialistic standpoint.

But the origin and history of such ideas is much more complex than the theorists of the superstructure suppose. The spirit of capitalism, in the sense in which we are using the term, had to fight its way to supremacy against a whole world of hostile forces. A state of mind such as that expressed in the passages we have quoted from Franklin, and which called forth the applause of a whole people, would both in ancient times and in the Middle Ages have been proscribed as the lowest sort of avarice and as an attitude entirely lacking in self-respect. It is, in fact, still regularly thus looked upon by all those social groups which are least involved in or adapted to modern capitalistic conditions. This is not wholly because the instinct of acquisition was in those times unknown or underdeveloped, as has often been said. Nor because the *auri sacra fames*, the greed for gold, was then, or now, less powerful outside of bourgeois capitalism than within its peculiar sphere, as the illusions of modern romanticists are wont to believe. The difference between the capitalistic and pre-capitalistic spirits is not to be found at this point. The greed of the Chinese Mandarin, the old Roman aristocrat, or the modern peasant, can stand up to any comparison. And the *auri sacra fames* of a Neapolitan cab-driver or *barcaiuolo*, and certainly of Asiatic representatives of similar trades, as well as of the craftsmen of southern European or Asiatic countries, is, as anyone can find out for himself, very much more intense, and especially more unscrupulous than that of, say, an Englishman in similar circumstances.

The universal reign of absolute unscrupulousness in the pursuit of selfish interests by the making of money has been a specific characteristic of precisely those countries whose bourgeois-capitalistic development, measured according to Occidental standards, has remained backward. As every employer knows, the lack *of coscienziosità* of the labourers of such countries, for instance Italy as compared with Germany, has been, and to a certain extent still is, one of the principal obstacles to their capitalistic development. Capitalism cannot make use of the labour of those who practise the doctrine of undisciplined *liberum arbitrium*, any more than it can make use of the business man who seems absolutely unscrupulous in his dealings with others, as we can learn from Franklin. Hence the difference does not lie in the degree of development of any impulse to make money. The *auri sacra fames* is as old as the history of man. But we shall see that those who submitted to it without reserve as an uncontrolled impulse, such as the Dutch sea-captain who "would go through hell for gain, even though he scorched his sails", were by no means the representatives of that attitude of mind from which the specifically modern capitalistic spirit as a mass phenomenon is derived, and that is what matters. At all periods of history, wherever it was possible, there has been ruthless acquisition, bound to no ethical norms whatever. Like war and piracy, trade has often been unrestrained in its relations with foreigners and those outside the group. The double ethic has permitted here what was forbidden in dealings among brothers.

Capitalistic acquisition as an adventure has been at home in all types of economic society which have known trade with the use of money and which have offered it opportunities, through *commenda*, farming of taxes, State loans, financing of wars, ducal courts and officeholders. Likewise the inner attitude of the adventurer, which laughs at all ethical limitations, has been universal. Absolute and conscious ruthlessness in acquisition has often stood in the closest connection with the strictest conformity to tradition. Moreover, with the breakdown of tradition and the more or less complete extension of free economic enterprise, even to within the social group, the new thing has not generally been ethically justified and encouraged, but only tolerated as a fact. And this fact has been treated either as ethically indifferent or as reprehensible, but unfortunately unavoidable. This has not only been the normal attitude of all ethical teachings, but, what is more important, also that expressed in the practical action of the average man of pre-capitalistic times, pre-capitalistic in the sense that the rational utilization of capital in a permanent enterprise and the rational capitalistic organization of labour had not yet become dominant forces in the determination of economic activity. Now just this attitude was one of the strongest inner obstacles which the adaptation of men to the conditions of an ordered bourgeois-capitalistic economy has encountered everywhere.

The most important opponent with which the spirit of capitalism, in the sense of a definite standard of life claiming ethical sanction, has had to struggle, was that type of attitude and reaction to new situations which we may designate as traditionalism. In this case also every attempt at a final definition must be held in abeyance. On the other hand, we must try to make the provisional meaning clear by citing a few cases. We will begin from below, with the labourers. One of the technical means which the modern employer uses in order to secure the greatest possible amount of work from his men is the device of piece-rates. In agriculture, for instance, the gathering of the harvest is a case where the greatest possible intensity of labour is called for, since, the weather being uncertain, the difference between high profit and heavy loss may depend on the speed with which the harvesting can be done. Hence a system of piece-rates is almost universal in this case. And since the interest of the employer in a speeding up of harvesting increases with the increase of the results and the intensity of the work, the attempt has again and again been made, by increasing the piece-rates of the workmen, thereby giving them an opportunity to earn what is for them a very high wage, to interest them in increasing their own efficiency. But a peculiar difficulty has been met with surprising frequency: raising the piece-rates has often had the result that not more but less has been accomplished in the same time, because the worker reacted to the increase not by increasing but by decreasing the amount of his work. A man, for instance, who at the rate of 1 mark per acre mowed 2½ acres per day and earned 2½ marks, when the rate was raised to 1.25 marks per acre mowed, not 3 acres, as he might easily have done, thus earning 3.75 marks, but only 2 acres, so that he could still earn the 2½ marks to which he was accustomed. The opportunity of earning more was less attractive than that of working less. He did not ask: how much can I earn in a day if I do as much work as possible? but: how much must I work in order to earn the wage, 2½ marks, which I earned before and which takes care of my traditional needs? This is an example of what is here meant by traditionalism. A man does not "by nature" wish to earn more and more money, but simply to live as he is accustomed to live and to earn as much as is necessary for that purpose. Wherever modern capitalism has begun its work of increasing the productivity of human labour by increasing its intensity, it has encountered the immensely stubborn resistance of this leading trait of pre-capitalistic labour. And to-day it encounters it the more, the more backward (from a capitalistic point of view) the labouring forces are with which it has to deal.

Another obvious possibility, to return to our example, since the appeal to the acquisitive instinct through higher wage-rates failed, would have been to try the opposite policy, to force the worker by reduction of his wage-rates to work harder to earn the same amount than he did before. Low wages and high profits seem even to-day to a superficial observer to stand in correlation; everything which is paid out in wages seems to involve a corresponding reduction of profits. That road capitalism has taken again and again since its beginning. For centuries it was an article of faith, that low wages were productive, i.e. that they increased the material results of labour so that, as Pieter de la Cour, on this point, as we shall see, quite in the spirit of the old Calvinism, said long ago, the people only work because and so long as they are poor.

But the effectiveness of this apparently so efficient method has its limits. Of course the presence of a surplus population which it can hire cheaply in the labour market is a necessity for the development of capitalism. But though too large a reserve army may in certain cases favour its quantitative expansion, it checks its qualitative development, especially the transition to types of enterprise which make more intensive use of labour. Low wages are by no means identical with cheap labour. From a purely quantitative point of view the efficiency of labour decreases with a wage which is physiologically insufficient, which may in the long run even mean a survival of the unfit. The present-day average Silesian mows, when he exerts himself to the full, little more than two-thirds as much land as the better paid and nourished Pomeranian or Mecklenburger, and the Pole, the further East he comes from, accomplishes progressively less than the German. Low wages fail even from a purely business point of view wherever it is a question of producing goods which require any sort of skilled labour, or the use of expensive machinery which is easily damaged, or in general wherever any great amount of sharp attention or of initiative is required. Here low wages do not pay, and their effect is the opposite of what was intended. For not only is a developed sense of responsibility absolutely indispensable, but in general also an attitude which, at least during working hours, is freed from continual calculations of how the customary wage may be earned with a maximum of comfort and a minimum of exertion. Labour must, on the contrary, be performed as if it were an absolute end in itself, a calling. But such an attitude is by no means a product of nature. It cannot be evoked by low wages or high ones alone, but can only be the product of a long and arduous process of education. To-day, capitalism, once in the saddle, can recruit its labouring force in all industrial countries with comparative ease. In the past this was in every case an extremely difficult problem. And even to-day it could probably not get along without the support of a powerful ally along the way, which, as we shall see below, was at hand at the time of its development.

What is meant can again best be explained by means of an example. The type of backward traditional form of labour is to-day very often exemplified by women workers, especially unmarried ones. An almost universal complaint of employers of girls, for instance German girls, is that they are almost entirely unable and unwilling to give up methods of work inherited or once learned in favour of more efficient ones, to adapt themselves to new methods, to learn and to concentrate their intelligence, or even to use it at all. Explanations of the possibility of making work easier, above all more profitable to themselves, generally encounter a complete lack of understanding. Increases of piece-rates are without avail against the stone wall of habit. In general it is otherwise, and that is a point of no little importance from our view-point, only with girls having a specifically religious, especially a Pietistic, background. One often hears, and statistical investigation confirms it, that by far the best chances of economic education are found among this group. The ability of mental concentration, as well as the absolutely essential feeling of obligation to one's job, are here most often combined with a strict economy which calculates the possibility of high earnings, and a cool self-control and frugality which enormously increase performance. This provides the most favourable foundation for the conception of labour as an end in itself, as a calling which is necessary to capitalism: the chances of overcoming traditionalism are greatest on account of the religious upbringing. This observation of present-day capitalism in itself suggests that it is worth while to ask how this connection of adaptability to capitalism with religious factors may have come about in the days of the early development of capitalism. For that they were even then present in much the same form can be inferred from numerous facts. For instance, the dislike and the persecution which Methodist workmen in the eighteenth century met at the hands of their comrades were not solely nor even principally the result of their religious eccentricities, England had seen many of those and more striking ones. It rested rather, as the destruction of their tools, repeatedly mentioned in the reports, suggests, upon their specific willingness to work as we should say today.

However, let us again return to the present, and this time to the entrepreneur, in order to clarify the meaning of traditionalism in his case.

Sombart, in his discussions of the genesis of capitalism has distinguished between the satisfaction of needs and acquisition as the two great leading principles in economic history. In the former case the attainment of the goods necessary to meet personal needs, in the latter a struggle for profit free from the limits set by needs, have been the ends controlling the form and direction of economic activity. What he calls the economy of needs seems at first glance to be identical with what is here described as economic traditionalism. That may be the case if the concept of needs is limited to traditional needs. But if that is not done, a number of economic types which must be considered capitalistic according to the definition of capital which Sombart gives in another part of his work, would be excluded from the category of acquisitive economy and put into that of needs economy. Enterprises, namely, which are carried on by private entrepreneurs by utilizing capital (money or goods with a money value) to make a profit, purchasing the means of production and selling the product, i.e. undoubted capitalistic enterprises, may at the same time have a traditionalistic character. This has, in the course even of modern economic history, not been merely an occasional case, but rather the rule, with continual interruptions from repeated and increasingly powerful conquests of the capitalistic spirit. To be sure the capitalistic form of an enterprise and the spirit in which it is run generally stand in some sort of adequate relationship to each other, but not in one of necessary interdependence. Nevertheless, we provisionally use the expression spirit of (modern) capitalism to describe that attitude which seeks profit rationally and systematically in the manner which we have illustrated by the example of Benjamin Franklin. This, however, is justified by the historical fact that that attitude of mind has on the one hand found its most suitable expression in capitalistic enterprise, while on the other the enterprise has derived its most suitable motive force from the spirit of capitalism. . . .

Now, how could activity, which was at best ethically tolerated, turn into a calling in the sense of Benjamin Franklin? The fact to be explained historically is that in the most highly capitalistic centre of that time, in Florence of the fourteenth and fifteenth centuries, the money and capital market of all the great political Powers, this attitude was considered ethically unjustifiable, or at best to be tolerated. But in the backwoods small bourgeois circumstances of Pennsylvania in the eighteenth century, where business threatened for simple lack of money to fall back into barter, where there was hardly a sign of large enterprise, where only the earliest beginnings of banking were to be found, the same thing was considered the essence of moral conduct, even commanded in the name of duty. To speak here of a reflection of material conditions in the ideal superstructure would be patent nonsense. What was the background of ideas which could account for the sort of activity apparently directed toward profit alone as a calling toward which the individual feels himself to have an ethical obligation? For it was this idea which gave the way of life of the new entrepreneur its ethical foundation and justification.

The attempt has been made, particularly by Sombart, in what are often judicious and effective observations, to depict economic rationalism as the salient feature of modern economic life as a whole. Undoubtedly with justification, if by that is meant the extension of the productivity of labour which has, through the subordination of the process of production to scientific points of view, relieved it from its dependence upon the natural organic limitations of the human individual. Now this process of rationalization in the field of technique and economic organization undoubtedly determines an important part of the ideals of life of modern bourgeois society. Labour in the service of a rational organization for the provision of humanity with material goods has without doubt always appeared to representatives of the capitalist spirit as one of the most important purposes of their life-work. It is only necessary, for instance, to read Franklin's account of his efforts in the service of civic improvements in Philadelphia clearly to apprehend this obvious truth. And the joy and pride of having given employment to numerous people, of having had a part in the economic progress of his home town in the sense referring to figures of population and volume of trade which capitalism associated with the word, all these things obviously are part of the specific and undoubtedly idealistic satisfactions in life to modern men of business. Similarly it is one of the fundamental characteristics of an individualistic capitalistic economy that it is rationalized on the basis of rigorous calculation, directed with foresight and caution toward the economic success which is sought in sharp contrast to the hand-to-mouth existence of the peasant, and to the privileged traditionalism of the guild craftsman and of the adventurers' capitalism, oriented to the exploitation of political opportunities and irrational speculation.

It might thus seem that the development of the spirit of capitalism is best understood as part of the development of rationalism as a whole, and could be deduced from the fundamental position of rationalism on the basic problems of life. In the process Protestantism would only have to be considered in so far as it had formed a stage prior to the development of a purely rationalistic philosophy. But any serious attempt to carry this thesis through makes it evident that such a simple way of putting the question will not work, simply because of the fact that the history of rationalism shows a development which by no means follows parallel lines in the various departments of life. The rationalization of private law, for instance, if it is thought of as a logical simplification and rearrangement of the content of the law, was achieved in the highest hitherto known degree in the Roman law of late antiquity. But it remained most backward in some of the countries with the highest degree of economic rationalization, notably in England, where the Renaissance of Roman Law was overcome by the power of the great legal corporations, while it has always retained its supremacy in the Catholic countries of Southern Europe. The worldly rational philosophy of the eighteenth century did not find favour alone or even principally in the countries of highest capitalistic development. The doctrines of Voltaire are even to-day the common property of broad upper, and what is practically more important, middle-class groups in the Romance Catholic countries. Finally, if under practical rationalism is understood the type of attitude which sees and judges the world consciously in terms of the worldly interests of the individual ego, then this view of life was and is the special peculiarity of the peoples of the *liberum arbitrium*, such as the Italians and the French are in very flesh and blood. But we have already convinced ourselves that this is by no means the soil in which that relationship of a man to his calling as a task, which is necessary to capitalism, has preeminently grown. In fact, one may – this simple proposition, which is often forgotten, should be placed at the beginning of every study which essays to deal with rationalism – rationalize life from fundamentally different basic points of view and in very different directions. Rationalism is an historical concept which covers a whole world of different things. It will be our task to find out whose intellectual child the particular concrete form of rational thought was, from which the idea of a calling and the devotion to labour in the calling has grown, which is, as we have seen, so irrational from the standpoint of purely eudæmonistic self-interest, but which has been and still is one of the most characteristic elements of our capitalistic culture. We are here particularly interested in the origin of precisely the irrational element which lies in this, as in every conception of a calling. . . .

Asceticism and the Spirit of Capitalism

This worldly Protestant asceticism, as we may recapitulate up to this point, acted powerfully against the spontaneous enjoyment of possessions; it restricted consumption, especially of luxuries. On the other hand, it had the psychological effect of freeing the acquisition of goods from the inhibitions of traditionalistic ethics. It broke the bonds of the impulse of acquisition in that it not only legalized it, but (in the sense discussed) looked upon it as directly willed by God. The campaign against the temptations of the flesh, and the dependence on external things, was, as besides the Puritans the great Quaker apologist Barclay expressly says, not a struggle against the rational acquisition, but against the irrational use of wealth.

But this irrational use was exemplified in the outward forms of luxury which their code condemned as idolatry of the flesh, however natural they had appeared to the feudal mind. On the other hand, they approved the rational and utilitarian uses of wealth which were willed by God for the needs of the individual and the community. They did not wish to impose mortification on the man of wealth, but the use of his means for necessary and practical things. The idea of comfort characteristically limits the extent of ethically permissible expenditures. It is naturally no accident that the development of a manner of living consistent with that idea may be observed earliest and most clearly among the most consistent representatives of this whole attitude toward life. Over against the glitter and ostentation of feudal magnificence which, resting on an unsound economic basis, prefers a sordid elegance to a sober simplicity, they set the clean and solid comfort of the middle-class home as an ideal.

On the side of the production of private wealth, asceticism condemned both dishonesty and impulsive avarice. What was condemned as covetousness, Mammonism, etc., was the pursuit of riches for their own sake. For wealth in itself was a temptation. But here asceticism was the power "which ever seeks the good but ever creates evil", what was evil in its sense was possession and its temptations. For, in conformity with the Old Testament and in analogy to the ethical valuation of good works, asceticism looked upon the pursuit of wealth as an end in itself as highly reprehensible; but the attainment of it as a fruit of labour in a calling was a sign of God's blessing. And even more important: the religious valuation of restless, continuous, systematic work in a worldly calling, as the highest means to asceticism, and at the same time the surest and most evident proof of rebirth and genuine faith, must have been the most powerful conceivable lever for the expansion of that attitude toward life which we have here called the spirit of capitalism.

When the limitation of consumption is combined with this release of acquisitive activity, the inevitable practical result is obvious: accumulation of capital through ascetic compulsion to save. The restraints which were imposed upon the consumption of wealth naturally served to increase it by making possible the productive investment of capital. How strong this influence was is not, unfortunately, susceptible of exact statistical demonstration. In New England the connection is so evident that it did not escape the eye of so discerning a historian as Doyle. But also in Holland, which was really only dominated by strict Calvinism for seven years, the greater simplicity of life in the more seriously religious circles, in combination with great wealth, led to an excessive propensity to accumulations. . . .

As far as the influence of the Puritan outlook extended, under all circumstances – and this is, of course, much more important than the mere encouragement of capital accumulation – it favoured the development of a rational bourgeois economic life; it was the most important, and above all the only consistent influence in the development of that life. It stood at the cradle of the modern economic man.

To be sure, these Puritanical ideals tended to give way under excessive pressure from the temptations of wealth, as the Puritans themselves knew very well. With great regularity we find the most genuine adherents of Puritanism among the classes which were rising from a lowly status, the small bourgeois and farmers, while the *beati possidentes*, even among Quakers, are often found tending to repudiate the old ideals. It was the same fate which again and again befell the predecessor of this worldly asceticism, the monastic asceticism of the Middle Ages. In the latter case, when rational economic activity had worked out its full effects by strict regulation of conduct and limitation of consumption, the wealth accumulated either succumbed directly to the nobility, as in the time before the Reformation, or monastic discipline threatened to break down, and one of the numerous reformations became necessary.

In fact the whole history of monasticism is in a certain sense the history of a continual struggle with the problem of the secularizing influence of wealth. The same is true on a grand scale of the worldly asceticism of Puritanism. The great revival of Methodism, which preceded the expansion of English industry toward the end of the eighteenth century, may well be compared with such a monastic reform. We may hence quote here a passage from John Wesley himself which might well serve as a motto for everything which has been said above. For it shows that the leaders of these ascetic movements understood the seemingly paradoxical relationships which we have here analysed perfectly well, and in the same sense that we have given them. He wrote:

"I fear, wherever riches have increased, the essence of religion has decreased in the same proportion. Therefore I do not see how it is possible, in the nature of things, for any revival of true religion to continue long. For religion must necessarily produce both industry and frugality, and these cannot but produce riches. But as riches increase, so will pride, anger, and love of the world in all its branches. How then is it possible that Methodism, that is, a religion of the heart, though it flourishes now as a green bay tree, should continue in this state? For the Methodists in every place grow diligent and frugal; consequently they increase in goods. Hence they proportionately increase in pride, in anger, in the desire of the flesh, the desire of the eyes, and the pride of life. So, although the form of religion remains, the spirit is swiftly vanishing away. Is there no way to prevent this – this continual decay of pure religion? We ought not to prevent people from being diligent and frugal; *we must exhort all Christians to gain all they can, and to save all they can; that is, in effect, to grow rich.*"

There follows the advice that those who gain all they can and save all they can should also give all they can, so that they will grow in grace and lay up a treasure in heaven. It is clear that Wesley here expresses, even in detail, just what we have been trying to point out.

As Wesley here says, the full economic effect of those great religious movements, whose significance for economic development lay above all in their ascetic educative influence, generally came only after the peak of the purely religious enthusiasm was past. Then the intensity of the search for the Kingdom of God commenced gradually to pass over into sober economic virtue; the religious roots died out slowly, giving way to utilitarian worldliness. Then, as Dowden puts it, as in *Robinson Crusoe*, the isolated economic man who carries on missionary activities on the side takes the place of the lonely spiritual search for the Kingdom of Heaven of Bunyan's pilgrim, hurrying through the market-place of Vanity.

When later the principle "to make the most of both worlds" became dominant in the end, as Dowden has remarked, a good conscience simply became one of the means of enjoying a comfortable bourgeois life, as is well expressed in the German proverb about the soft pillow. What the great religious epoch of the seventeenth century bequeathed to its utilitarian successor was, however, above all an amazingly good, we may even say a pharisaically good, conscience in the acquisition of money, so long as it took place legally. Every trace of the *deplacere vix potest* has disappeared.

A specifically bourgeois economic ethic had grown up. With the consciousness of standing in the fullness of God's grace and being visibly blessed by Him, the bourgeois business man, as long as he remained within the bounds of formal correctness, as long as his moral conduct was spotless and the use to which he put his wealth was not objectionable, could follow his pecuniary interests as he would and feel that he was fulfilling a duty in doing so. The power of religious asceticism provided him in addition with sober, conscientious, and unusually industrious workmen, who clung to their work as to a life purpose willed by God.

Finally, it gave him the comforting assurance that the unequal distribution of the goods of this world was a special dispensation of Divine Providence, which in these differences, as in particular grace, pursued secret ends unknown to men. Calvin himself had made the much-quoted statement that only when the people, i.e. the mass of labourers and craftsmen, were poor did they remain obedient to God. In the Netherlands (Pieter de la Court and others), that had been secularized to the effect that the mass of men only labour when necessity forces them to do so. This formulation of a leading idea of capitalistic economy later entered into the current theories of the productivity of low wages. Here also, with the dying out of the religious root, the utilitarian interpretation crept in unnoticed, in the line of development which we have again and again observed. . . .

Now naturally the whole ascetic literature of almost all denominations is saturated with the idea that faithful labour, even at low wages, on the part of those whom life offers no other opportunities, is highly pleasing to God. In this respect Protestant Asceticism added in itself nothing new. But it not only deepened this idea most powerfully, it also created the force which was alone decisive for its effectiveness: the psychological sanction of it through the conception of this labour as a calling, as the best, often in the last analysis the only means of attaining certainty of grace. And on the other hand it legalized the exploitation of this specific willingness to work, in that it also interpreted the employer's business activity as a calling. It is obvious how powerfully the exclusive search for the Kingdom of God only through the fulfilment of duty in the calling, and the strict asceticism which Church discipline naturally imposed, especially on the propertyless classes, was bound to affect the productivity of labour in the capitalistic sense of the word. The treatment of labour as a calling became as characteristic of the modern worker as the corresponding attitude toward acquisition of the business man. It was a perception of this situation, new at his time, which caused so able an observer as Sir William Petty to attribute the economic power of Holland in the seventeenth century to the fact that the very numerous dissenters in that country (Calvinists and Baptists) "are for the most part thinking, sober men, and such as believe that Labour and Industry is their duty towards God".

Calvinism opposed organic social organization in the fiscal-monopolistic form which it assumed in Anglicanism under the Stuarts, especially in the conceptions of Laud, this alliance of Church and State with the monopolists on the basis of a Christian-social ethical foundation. Its leaders were universally among the most passionate opponents of this type of politically privileged commercial, putting-out, and colonial capitalism. Over against it they placed the individualistic motives of rational legal acquisition by virtue of one's own ability and initiative. And, while the politically privileged monopoly industries in England all disappeared in short order, this attitude played a large and decisive part in the development of the industries which grew up in spite of and against the authority of the State. The Puritans (Prynne, Parker) repudiated all connection with the large-scale capitalistic courtiers and projectors as an ethically suspicious class. On the other hand, they took pride in their own superior middle-class business morality, which formed the true reason for the persecutions to which they were subjected on the part of those circles. Defoe proposed to win the battle against dissent by boycotting bank credit and withdrawing deposits. The difference of the two types of capitalistic attitude went to a very large extent hand in hand with religious differences. The opponents of the Nonconformists, even in the eighteenth century, again and again ridiculed them for personifying the spirit of shopkeepers, and for having ruined the ideals of old England. Here also lay the difference of the Puritan economic ethic from the Jewish; and contemporaries (Prynne) knew well that the former and not the latter was the bourgeois capitalistic ethic.

One of the fundamental elements of the spirit of modern capitalism, and not only of that but of all modern culture: rational conduct on the basis of the idea of the calling, was born – that is what this discussion has sought to demonstrate – from the spirit of Christian asceticism. One has only to re-read the passage from Franklin, quoted at the beginning of this essay, in order to see that the essential elements of the attitude which was there called the spirit of capitalism are the same as what we have just shown to be the content of the Puritan worldly asceticism, only without the religious basis, which by Franklin's time had died away. The idea that modern labour has an ascetic character is of course not new. Limitation to specialized work, with a renunciation of the Faustian universality of man which it involves, is a condition of any valuable work in the modern world; hence deeds and renunciation inevitably condition each other to-day. This fundamentally ascetic trait of middle-class life, if it attempts to be a way of life at all, and not simply the absence of any, was what Goethe wanted to teach, at the height of his wisdom, in the *Wander-jahren*, and in the end which he gave to the life of his *Faust*. For him the realization meant a renunciation, a departure from an age of full and beautiful humanity, which can no more be repeated in the course of our cultural development than can the flower of the Athenian culture of antiquity.

The Puritan wanted to work in a calling; we are forced to do so. For when asceticism was carried out of monastic cells into everyday life, and began to dominate worldly morality, it did its part in building the tremendous cosmos of the modern economic order. This order is now bound to the technical and economic conditions of machine production which to-day determine the lives of all the individuals who are born into this mechanism, not only those directly concerned with economic acquisition, with irresistible force. Perhaps it will so determine them until the last ton of fossilized coal is burnt. In Baxter's view the care for external goods should only lie on the shoulders of the "saint like a light cloak, which can be thrown aside at any moment." But fate decreed that the cloak should become an iron cage.

Since asceticism undertook to remodel the world and to work out its ideals in the world, material goods have gained an increasing and finally an inexorable power over the lives of men as at no previous period in history. To-day the spirit of religious asceticism – whether finally, who knows? – has escaped from the cage. But victorious capitalism, since it rests on mechanical foundations, needs its support no longer. The rosy blush of its laughing heir, the Enlightenment, seems also to be irretrievably fading, and the idea of duty in one's calling prowls about in our lives like the ghost of dead religious beliefs. Where the fulfilment of the calling cannot directly be related to the highest spiritual and cultural values, or when, on the other hand, it need not be felt simply as economic compulsion, the individual generally abandons the attempt to justify it at all. In the field of its highest development, in the United States, the pursuit of wealth, stripped of its religious and ethical meaning, tends to become associated with purely mundane passions, which often actually give it the character of sport.

No one knows who will live in this cage in the future, or whether at the end of this tremendous development entirely new prophets will arise, or there will be a great rebirth of old ideas and ideals, or, if neither, mechanized petrification, embellished with a sort of convulsive self-importance. For of the last stage of this cultural development, it might well be truly said: "Specialists without spirit, sensualists without heart; this nullity imagines that it has attained a level of civilization never before achieved."

But this brings us to the world of judgments of value and of faith, with which this purely historical discussion need not be burdened. The next task would be rather to show the significance of ascetic rationalism, which has only been touched in the foregoing sketch, for the content of practical social ethics, thus for the types of organization and the functions of social groups from the conventicle to the State. Then its relations to humanistic rationalism, its ideals of life and cultural influence; further to the development of philosophical and scientific empiricism, to technical development and to spiritual ideals would have to be analysed. Then its historical development from the mediæval beginnings of worldly asceticism to its dissolution into pure utilitarianism would have to be traced out through all the areas of ascetic religion. Only then could the quantitative cultural significance of ascetic Protestantism in its relation to the other plastic elements of modern culture be estimated.

Here we have only attempted to trace the fact and the direction of its influence to their motives in one, though a very important point. But it would also further be necessary to investigate how Protestant Asceticism was in turn influenced in its development and its character by the totality of social conditions, especially economic. The modern man is in general, even with the best will, unable to give religious ideas a significance for culture and national character which they deserve. But it is, of course, not my aim to substitute for a one-sided materialistic an equally one-sided spiritualistic causal interpretation of culture and of history. Each is equally possible, but each, if it does not serve as the preparation, but as the conclusion of an investigation, accomplishes equally little in the interest of historical truth.

C: BUREAUCRACY AND POLITICS

16 The Distribution of Power Within the Political Community: Class, Status, Party

Max Weber

A. Economically Determined Power and the Status Order

The structure of every legal order directly influences the distribution of power, economic or otherwise, within its respective community. This is true of all legal orders and not only that of the state. In general, we understand by "power" the chance of a man or a number of men to realize their own will in a social action even against the resistance of others who are participating in the action.

"Economically conditioned" power is not, of course, identical with "power" as such. On the contrary, the emergence of economic power may be the consequence of power existing on other grounds. Man does not strive for power only in order to enrich himself economically. Power, including economic power, may be valued for its own sake. Very frequently the striving for power is also conditioned by the social honor it entails. Not all power, however, entails social honor: The typical American Boss, as well as the typical big speculator, deliberately relinquishes social honor. Quite generally, "mere economic" power, and especially "naked" money power, is by no means a recognized basis of social honor. Nor is power the only basis of social honor. Indeed, social honor, or prestige, may even be the basis of economic power, and very frequently has been. Power, as well as honor, may be guaranteed by the legal order, but, at least normally, it is not their primary source. The legal order is rather an additional factor that enhances the chance to hold power or honor; but it can not always secure them.

The way in which social honor is distributed in a community between typical groups participating in this distribution we call the "status order." The social order and the economic order are related in a similar manner to the legal order. However, the economic order merely defines the way in which economic goods and services are distributed and used. Of course, the status order is strongly influenced by it, and in turn reacts upon it.

Now: "classes," "status groups," and "parties" are phenomena of the distribution of power within a community.

B. Determination of Class Situation by Market Situation

In our terminology, "classes" are not communities; they merely represent possible, and frequent, bases for social action. We may speak of a "class" when (1) a number of people have in common a specific causal component of their life chances, insofar as (2) this component is represented exclusively by economic interests in the possession of goods and opportunities for income, and (3) is represented under the conditions of the commodity or labor markets. This is "class situation."

It is the most elemental economic fact that the way in which the disposition over material property is distributed among a plurality of people, meeting competitively in the market for the purpose of exchange, in itself creates specific life chances. The mode of distribution, in accord with the law of marginal utility, excludes the non-wealthy from competing for highly valued goods; it favors the owners and, in fact, gives to them a monopoly to acquire such goods. Other things being equal, the mode of distribution monopolizes the opportunities for profitable deals for all those who, provided with goods, do not necessarily have to exchange them. It increases, at least generally, their power in the price struggle with those who, being property-less, have nothing to offer but their labor or the resulting products, and who are compelled to get rid of these products in order to subsist at all. The mode of distribution gives to the propertied a monopoly on the possibility of transferring property from the sphere of use as "wealth" to the sphere of "capital," that is, it gives them the entrepreneurial function and all chances to share directly or indirectly in returns on capital. All this holds true within the area in which pure market conditions prevail. "Property" and "lack of property" are, therefore, the basic categories of all class situations. It does not matter whether these two categories become effective in the competitive struggles of the consumers or of the producers.

Within these categories, however, class situations are further differentiated: on the one hand, according to the kind of property that is usable for returns; and, on the other hand, according to the kind of services that can be offered in the market. Ownership of dwellings; workshops; warehouses; stores; agriculturally usable land in large or small holdings – a quantitative difference with possibly qualitative consequences; ownership of mines; cattle; men (slaves); disposition over mobile instruments of production, or capital goods of all sorts, especially money or objects that can easily be exchanged for money; disposition over products of one's own labor or of others' labor differing according to their various distances from consumability; disposition over transferable monopolies of any kind – all these distinctions differentiate the class situations of the propertied just as does the "meaning" which they can give to the use of property, especially to property which has money equivalence. Accordingly, the propertied, for instance, may belong to the class of rentiers or to the class of entrepreneurs.

Those who have no property but who offer services are differentiated just as much according to their kinds of services as according to the way in which they make use of these services, in a continuous or discontinuous relation to a recipient. But always this is the generic connotation of the concept of class: that kind of chance in the *market* is the decisive moment which presents a common condition for the individual's fate. Class situation is, in this sense, ultimately market situation. The effect of naked possession *per se*, which among cattle breeders gives the non-owning slave or serf into the power of the cattle owner, is only a fore-runner of real "class" formation. However, in the cattle loan and in the naked severity of the law of debts in such communities for the first time mere "possession" as such emerges as decisive for the fate of the individual; this is much in contrast to crop-raising communities, which are based on labor. The creditor–debtor relation becomes the basis of "class situations" first in the cities, where a "credit market," however primitive, with rates of interest increasing according to the extent of dearth and factual monopolization of lending in the hands of a plutocracy could develop. Therewith "class struggles" begin.

Those men whose fate is not determined by the chance of using goods or services for themselves on the market, e.g., slaves, are not, however, a class in the technical sense of the term. They are, rather, a status group.

C. Social Action Flowing from Class Interest.

According to our terminology, the factor that creates "class" is unambiguously economic interest, and indeed, only those interests involved in the existence of the market. Nevertheless, the concept of class-interest is an ambiguous one: even as an empirical concept it is ambiguous as soon as one understands it by something other than the factual direction of interests following with a certain probability from the class situation for a certain average of those people subjected to the class situation. The class situation and other circumstances remaining the same, the direction in which the individual worker, for instance, is likely to pursue his interests may vary widely, according to whether he is constitutionally qualified for the task at hand to a high, to an average, or to a low degree. In the same way, the direction of interests may vary according to whether or not social action of a larger of smaller portion of those commonly affected by the class situation, or even an association among them, e.g., a trade union, has grown out of the class situation, from which the individual may expect promising results for himself. The emergence of an association or even of mere social action from a common class situation is by no means a universal phenomenon.

The class situation may be restricted in its efforts to the generation of essentially *similar* reactions, that is to say, within our terminology, of "mass behavior." However, it may not even have this result. Furthermore, often merely amorphous social action emerges. For example, the "grumbling" of workers known in ancient Oriental ethics: The moral disapproval of the work-master's conduct, which in its practical significance was probably equivalent to an increasingly typical phenom-enon of precisely the latest industrial development, namely, the slowdown of laborers by virtue of tacit agreement. The degree in which "social action" and possibly associations emerge from the mass behavior of the members of a class is linked to general cultural conditions, especially to those of an intellectual sort. It is also linked to the extent of the contrasts that have already evolved, and is especially linked to the transparency of the connections between the causes and the consequences of the class situation. For however different life chances may be, this fact in itself, according to all experience, by no means gives birth to "class action" (social action by the members of a class). For that, the real conditions and the results of the class situation must be distinctly recognizable. For only then the contrast of life chances can be felt not as an absolutely given fact to be accepted, but as a resultant from either (1) the given distribution of property, or (2) the structure of the concrete economic order. It is only then that people may react against the class structure not only through acts of intermittent and irrational protest, but in the form of rational association. There have been "class situations" of the first category (1), of a specifically naked and transparent sort, in the urban centers of Antiquity and during the Middle Ages; especially then when great fortunes were accumulated by factually monopolized trading in local industrial products or in foodstuffs; furthermore, under certain conditions, in the rural economy of the most diverse periods, when agriculture was increasingly exploited in a profit-making manner. The most imporant historical example of the second category (2) is the class situation of the modern proletariat.

D. Types of Class Struggle

Thus every class may be the carrier of any one of the innumerable possible forms of class action, but this is not necessarily so. In any case, a class does not in itself constitute a group (*Gemeinschaft*). To treat "class" conceptually as being equivalent to "group" leads to distortion. That men in the same class situation regularly react in mass actions to such tangible situations as economic ones in the direction of those interests that are most adequate to their average number is an important and after all simple fact for the understanding of historical events. However, this fact must not lead to that kind of pseudo-scientific operation with the concepts of class and class interests which is so frequent these days and which has found its most classic expression in the statement of a talented author, that the individual may be in error concerning his interests but that the class is infallible about its interests.

If classes as such are not groups, nevertheless class situations emerge only on the basis of social action. However, social action that brings forth class situations is not basically action among members of the identical class; it is an action among members of different classes. Social actions that directly determine the class situation of the worker and the entrepreneur are: the labor market, the commodities market, and the capitalistic enterprise. But, in its turn, the existence of a capitalistic enterprise presupposes that a very specific kind of social action exists to protect the possession of goods *per se*, and especially the power of individuals to dispose, in principle freely, over the means of production: a certain kind of legal order. Each kind of class situation, and above all when it rests upon the power of property *per se*, will become most clearly efficacious when all other determinants of reciprocal relations are, as far as possible, eliminated in their significance. It is in this way that the use of the power of property in the market obtains its most sovereign importance.

Now status groups hinder the strict carrying through of the sheer market principle. In the present context they are of interest only from this one point of view. Before we briefly consider them, note that not much of a general nature can be said about the more specific kinds of antagonism between classes (in our meaning of the term). The great shift, which has been going on continuously in the past, and up to our times, may be summarized, although at a cost of some precision: the struggle in which class situations are effective has progressively shifted from consumption credit toward, first, competitive struggles in the commodity market and then toward wage disputes on the labor market. The class struggles of Antiquity – to the extent that they were genuine class struggles and not struggles between status groups – were initially carried on by peasants and perhaps also artisans threatened by debt bondage and struggling against urban creditors. . . .

E. Status Honor

In contrast to classes, *Stände* (*status groups*) are normally groups. They are, however, often of an amorphous kind. In contrast to the purely economically determined "class situation," we wish to designate as *status situation* every typical component of the life of men that is determined by a specific, positive or negative, social estimation of *honor*. This honor may be connected with any quality shared by a plurality, and, of course, it can be knit to a class situation: class distinctions are linked in the most varied ways with status distinctions. Property as such is not always recognized as a status qualification, but in the long run it is, and with extraordinary regularity. In the subsistence economy of neighborhood associations, it is often simply the richest who is the "chieftain." However, this often is only an honorific preference. For example, in the so-called pure modern democracy, that is, one devoid of any expressly ordered status privileges for individuals, it may be that only the families coming under approximately the same tax class dance with one another. This example is reported of certain smaller Swiss cities. But status honor need not necessarily be linked with a class situation. On the contrary, it normally stands in sharp opposition to the pretensions of sheer property.

Both propertied and propertyless people can belong to the same status group, and frequently they do with very tangible consequences. This equality of social esteem may, however, in the long run become quite precarious. The equality of status among American gentlemen, for instance, is expressed by the fact that outside the subordination determined by the different functions of business, it would be considered strictly repugnant – wherever the old tradition still prevails – if even the richest boss, while playing billiards or cards in his club would not treat his clerk as in every sense fully his equal in birthright, but would bestow upon him the condescending status-conscious "benevolence" which the German boss can never dissever from his attitude. This is one of the most important reasons why in America the German clubs have never been able to attain the attraction that the American clubs have.

In content, status honor is normally expressed by the fact that above all else a specific *style of life* is expected from all those who wish to belong to the circle. Linked with this expectation are restrictions on social intercourse (that is, intercourse which is not subservient to economic or any other purposes). These restrictions may confine normal marriages to within the status circle and may lead to complete endogamous closure. Whenever this is not a mere individual and socially irrelevant imitation of another style of life, but consensual action of this closing character, the status development is under way.

In its characteristic form, stratification by status groups on the basis of conventional styles of life evolves at the present time in the United States out of the traditional democracy. For example, only the resident of a certain street ("the Street") is considered as belonging to "society," is qualified for social intercourse, and is visited and invited. Above all, this differentiation evolves in such a way as to make for strict submission to the fashion that is dominant at a given time in society. This submission to fashion also exists among men in America to a degree unknown in Germany; it appears as an indication of the fact that a given man puts forward a *claim* to qualify as a gentleman. This submission decides, at least *prima facie*, that he will be treated as such. And this recognition becomes just as important for his employment chances in swank establishments, and above all, for social intercourse and marriage with "esteemed" families, as the qualification for dueling among Germans. As for the rest, status honor is usurped by certain families resident for a long time, and, of course, correspondingly wealthy (e.g. F.F.V., the First Families of Virginia), or by the actual or alleged descendants of the "Indian Princess" Pocahontas, of the Pilgrim fathers, or of the Knickerbockers, the members of almost inaccessible sects and all sorts of circles setting themselves apart by means of any other characteristics and badges. In this case stratification is purely conventional and rests largely on usurpation (as does almost all status honor in its beginning). But the road to legal privilege, positive or negative, is easily traveled as soon as a certain stratification of the social order has in fact been "lived in" and has achieved stability by virtue of a stable distribution of economic power.

F. Ethnic Segregation and Caste

Where the consequences have been realized to their full extent, the status group evolves into a closed caste. Status distinctions are then guaranteed not merely by conventions and laws, but also by religious sanctions. This occurs in such a way that every physical contact with a member of any caste that is considered to be lower by the members of a higher caste is considered as making for a ritualistic impurity and a stigma which must be expiated by a religious act. In addition, individual castes develop quite distinct cults and gods.

In general, however, the status structure reaches such extreme consequences only where there are underlying differences which are held to be "ethnic." The caste is, indeed, the normal form in which ethnic communities that believe in blood relationship and exclude exogamous marriage and social intercourse usually associate with one another. As mentioned before, such a caste situation is part of the phenomenon of pariah peoples and is found all over the world. These people form communities, acquire specific occupational traditions of handicrafts or of other arts, and cultivate a belief in their ethnic community. They live in a diaspora strictly segregated from all personal intercourse, except that of an unavoidable sort, and their situation is legally precarious. Yet, by virtue of their economic indispensability, they are tolerated, indeed frequently privileged, and they live interspersed in the political communities. The Jews are the most impressive historical example.

A status segregation grown into a caste differs in its structure from a mere ethnic segregation: the caste structure transforms the horizontal and unconnected coexistences of ethnically segregated groups into a vertical social system of super- and subordination. Correctly formulated: a comprehensive association integrates the ethnically divided communities into one political unit. They differ precisely in this way: ethnic coexistence, based on mutual repulsion and disdain, allows each ethnic community to consider its own honor as the highest one; the caste structure brings about a social subordination and an acknowledgement of "more honor" in favor of the privileged caste and status groups. This is due to the fact that in the caste structure ethnic distinctions as such have become "functional" distinctions within the political association (warriors, priests, artisans that are politically important for war and for building, and so on). But even pariah peoples who are most despised (for example, the Jews) are usually apt to continue cultivating the belief in their own specific "honor," a belief that is equally peculiar to ethnic and to status groups. . . .

G. Status Privileges

For all practical purposes, stratification by status goes hand in hand with a monopolization of ideal and material goods or opportunities, in a manner we have come to know as typical. Besides the specific status honor, which always rests upon distance and exclusiveness, honorific preferences may consist of the privilege of wearing special costumes, of eating special dishes taboo to others, of carrying arms – which is most obvious in its consequences – , the right to be a dilettante, for example, to play certain musical instruments. However, material monopolies provide the most effective motives for the exclusiveness of a status group; although, in themselves, they are rarely sufficient, almost always they come into play to some extent. Within a status circle there is the question of intermarriage: the interest of the families in the monopolization of potential bridegrooms is at least of equal importance and is parallel to the interest in the monopolization of daughters. The daughters of the members must be provided for. With an increased closure of the status group, the conventional preferential opportunities for special employment grow into a legal monopoly of special offices for the members. Certain goods become objects for monopolization by status groups, typically, entailed estates, and frequently also the possession of serfs or bondsmen and, finally, special trades. This monopolization occurs positively when the status group is exclusively entitled to own and to manage them; and negatively when, in order to maintain its specific way of life, the status group must *not* own and manage them. For the decisive role of a style of life in status honor means that status groups are the specific bearers of all conventions. In whatever way it may be manifest, all stylization of life either originates in status groups or is at least conserved by them. Even if the principles of status conventions differ greatly, they reveal certain typical traits, especially among the most privileged strata. Quite generally, among privileged status groups there is a status disqualification that operates against the performance of common physical labor. This disqualification is now "setting in" in America against the old tradition of esteem for labor. Very frequently every rational economic pursuit, and especially entrepreneurial activity, is looked upon as a disqualification of status. Artistic and literary activity is also considered degrading work as soon as it is exploited for income, or at least when it is connected with hard physical exertion. An example is the sculptor working like a mason in his dusty smock as over against the painter in his salon-like studio and those forms of musical practice that are acceptable to the status group.

H. Economic Conditions and Effects of Status Stratification

The frequent disqualification of the gainfully employed as such is a direct result of the principle of status stratification, and of course, of this principle's opposition to a distribution of power which is regulated exclusively through the market. These two factors operate along with various individual ones, which will be touched upon below.

We have seen above that the market and its processes knows no personal distinctions: "functional" interests dominate it. It knows nothing of honor. The status order means precisely the reverse: stratification in terms of honor and styles of life peculiar to status groups as such. The status order would be threatened at its very root if mere economic acquisition and naked economic power still bearing the stigma of its extra-status origin could bestow upon anyone who has won them the same or even greater honor as the vested interests claim for themselves. . . .

As to the general economic conditions making for the predominance of stratification by status, only the following can be said. When the bases of the acquisition and distribution of goods are relatively stable, stratification by status is favored. Every technological repercussion and economic transformation threatens stratification by status and pushes the class situation into the foreground. Epochs and countries in which the naked class situation is of predominant significance are regularly the periods of technical and economic transformations. And every slowing down of the change in economic stratification leads, in due course, to the growth of status structures and makes for a resuscitation of the important role of social honor.

I. Parties

Whereas the genuine place of classes is within the economic order, the place of status groups is within the social order, that is, within the sphere of the distribution of honor. From within these spheres, classes and status groups influence one another and the legal order and are in turn influenced by it. "*Parties*" reside in the sphere of power. Their action is oriented toward the acquisition of social power, that is to say, toward influencing social action no matter what its content may be.

In principle, parties may exist in a social club as well as in a state. As over against the actions of classes and status groups, for which this is not necessarily the case, party-oriented social action always involves association. For it is always directed toward a goal which is striven for in a planned manner. This goal may be a cause (the party may aim at realizing a program for ideal or material purposes), or the goal may be personal (sinecures, power, and from these, honor for the leader and the followers of the party). Usually the party aims at all these simultaneously. Parties are, therefore, only possible within groups that have an associational character, that is, some rational order and a staff of persons available who are ready to enforce it. For parties aim precisely at influencing this staff, and if possible, to recruit from it party members.

In any individual case, parties may represent interests determined through class situation or status situation, and they may recruit their following respectively from one or the other. But they need be neither purely class nor purely status parties; in fact, they are more likely to be mixed types, and sometimes they are neither. They may represent ephemeral or enduring structures. Their means of attaining power may be quite varied, ranging from naked violence of any sort to canvassing for votes with coarse or subtle means: money, social influence, the force of speech, suggestion, clumsy hoax, and so on to the rougher or more artful tactics of obstruction in parliamentary bodies.

The sociological structure of parties differs in a basic way according to the kind of social action which they struggle to influence; that means, they differ according to whether or not the community is stratified by status or by classes. Above all else, they vary according to the structure of domination. For their leaders normally deal with its conquest. In our general terminology, parties are not only products of modern forms of domination. We shall also designate as parties the ancient and medieval ones, despite the fact that they differ basically from modern parties. Since a party always struggles for political control (*Herrschaft*), its organization too is frequently strict and "authoritarian."

17 The Types of Legitimate Domination

Max Weber

The Basis of Legitimacy

Domination was defined as the probability that certain specific commands (or all commands) will be obeyed by a given group of persons. It thus does not include every mode of exercising "power" or "influence" over other persons. Domination ("authority") in this sense may be based on the most diverse motives of compliance: all the way from simple habituation to the most purely rational calculation of advantage. Hence every genuine form of domination implies a minimum of voluntary compliance, that is, an *interest* (based on ulterior motives or genuine acceptance) in obedience.

Not every case of domination makes use of economic means; still less does it always have economic objectives. However, normally the rule over a considerable number of persons requires a staff, that is, a *special* group which can normally be trusted to execute the general policy as well as the specific commands. The members of the administrative staff may be bound to obedience to their superior (or superiors) by custom, by affectual ties, by a purely material complex of interests, or by ideal (*wertrationale*) motives. The quality of these motives largely determines the type of domination. *Purely* material interests and calculations of advantages as the basis of solidarity between the chief and his administrative staff result, in this as in other connexions, in a relatively unstable situation. Normally other elements, affectual and ideal, supplement such interests. In certain exceptional cases the former alone may be decisive. In everyday life these relationships, like others, are governed by custom and material calculation of advantage. But custom, personal advantage, purely affectual or ideal motives of solidarity, do not form a sufficiently reliable basis for a given domination. In addition there is normally a further element, the belief in *legitimacy.*

Experience shows that in no instance does domination voluntarily limit itself to the appeal to material or affectual or ideal motives as a basis for its continuance. In addition every such system attempts to establish and to cultivate the belief in its legitimacy. But according to the kind of legitimacy which is claimed, the type of obedience, the kind of administrative staff developed to guarantee it, and the mode of exercising authority, will all differ fundamentally. Equally fundamental is the variation in effect. Hence, it is useful to classify the types of domination according to the kind of claim to legitimacy typically made by each. In doing this, it is best to start from modern and therefore more familiar examples. . . .

There are three pure types of legitimate domination. The validity of the claims to legitimacy may be based on:

(1)   Rational grounds – resting on a belief in the legality of enacted rules and the right of those elevated to authority under such rules to issue commands (legal authority).

(2)   Traditional grounds – resting on an established belief in the sanctity of immemorial traditions and the legitimacy of those exercising authority under them (traditional authority); or finally,

(3)   Charismatic grounds – resting on devotion to the exceptional sanctity, heroism or exemplary character of an individual person, and of the normative patterns or order revealed or ordained by him (charismatic authority).

In the case of legal authority, obedience is owed to the legally established impersonal order. It extends to the persons exercising the authority of office under it by virtue of the formal legality of their commands and only within the scope of authority of the office. In the case of traditional authority, obedience is owed to the *person* of the chief who occupies the traditionally sanctioned position of authority and who is (within its sphere) bound by tradition. But here the obligation of obedience is a matter of personal loyalty within the area of accustomed obligations. In the case of charismatic authority, it is the charismatically qualified leader as such who is obeyed by virtue of personal trust in his revelation, his heroism or his exemplary qualities so far as they fall within the scope of the individual's belief in his charisma. . . .

Legal Authority With a Bureaucratic Administrative Staff

Legal authority rests on the acceptance of the validity of the following mutually inter-dependent ideas.

1   That any given legal norm may be established by agreement or by imposition, on grounds of expediency or value-rationality or both, with a claim to obedience at least on the part of the members of the organization. This is, however, usually extended to include all persons within the sphere of power in question – which in the case of territorial bodies is the territorial area – who stand in certain social relationships or carry out forms of social action which in the order governing the organization have been declared to be relevant.

2   That every body of law consists essentially in a consistent system of abstract rules which have normally been intentionally established. Furthermore, administration of law is held to consist in the application of these rules to particular cases; the administrative process in the rational pursuit of the interests which are specified in the order governing the organization within the limits laid down by legal precepts and following principles which are capable of generalized formulation and are approved in the order governing the group, or at least not disapproved in it.

3   That thus the typical person in authority, the "superior," is himself subject to an impersonal order by orienting his actions to it in his own dispositions and commands. (This is true not only for persons exercising legal authority who are in the usual sense "officials," but, for instance, for the elected president of a state.)

4   That the person who obeys authority does so, as it is usually stated, only in his capacity as a "member" of the organization and what he obeys is only "the

law." (He may in this connection be the member of an association, of a community, of a church, or a citizen of a state.)

5   In conformity with point 3, it is held that the members of the organization, insofar as they obey a person in authority, do not owe this obedience to him as an individual, but to the impersonal order. Hence, it follows that there is an obligation to obedience only within the sphere of the rationally delimited jurisdiction which, in terms of the order, has been given to him. . . .

The purest type of exercise of legal authority is that which employs a bureaucratic administrative staff. Only the supreme chief of the organization occupies his position of dominance (*Herrenstellung*) by virtue of appropriation, of election, or of having been designated for the succession. But even *his* authority consists in a sphere of legal "competence." The whole administrative staff under the supreme authority then consists, in the purest type, of individual officials (constituting a "monocracy" as opposed to the "collegial" type, which will be discussed below) who are appointed and function according to the following criteria:

(1)   They are personally free and subject to authority only with respect to their impersonal official obligations.
(2)   They are organized in a clearly defined hierarchy of offices.
(3)   Each office has a clearly defined sphere of competence in the legal sense.
(4)   The office is filled by a free contractual relationship. Thus, in principle, there is free selection.
(5)   Candidates are selected on the basis of technical qualifications. In the most rational case, this is tested by examination or guaranteed by diplomas certifying technical training, or both. They are *appointed*, not elected.
(6)   They are remunerated by fixed salaries in money, for the most part with a right to pensions. Only under certain circumstances does the employing authority, especially in private organizations, have a right to terminate the appointment, but the official is always free to resign. The salary scale is graded according to rank in the hierarchy; but in addition to this criterion, the responsibility of the position and the requirements of the incumbent's social status may be taken into account.
(7)   The office is treated as the sole, or at least the primary, occupation of the incumbent.
(8)   It constitutes a career. There is a system of "promotion" according to seniority or to achievement, or both. Promotion is dependent on the judgment of superiors.
(9)   The official works entirely separated from ownership of the means of administration and without appropriation of his position.
(10)   He is subject to strict and systematic discipline and control in the conduct of the office.

This type of organization is in principle applicable with equal facility to a wide variety of different fields. It may be applied in profit-making business or in charitable organizations, or in any number of other types of private enterprises serving ideal or material ends. It is equally applicable to political and to hierocratic organizations. With the varying degrees of approximation to a pure type, its historical existence can be demonstrated in all these fields. . . .

Traditional Authority

Authority will be called traditional if legitimacy is claimed for it and believed in by virtue of the sanctity of age-old rules and powers. The masters are designated according to traditional rules and are obeyed because of their traditional status (*Eigenwürde*). This type of organized rule is, in the simplest case, primarily based on personal loyalty which results from common upbringing. The person exercising authority is not a "superior," but a personal master, his administrative staff does not consist mainly of officials but of personal retainers, and the ruled are not "members" of an association but are either his traditional "comrades" or his "subjects." Personal loyalty, not the official's impersonal duty, determines the relations of the administrative staff to the master.

Obedience is owed not to enacted rules but to the person who occupies a position of authority by tradition or who has been chosen for it by the traditional master. The commands of such a person are legitimized in one of two ways:

(a) partly in terms of traditions which themselves directly determine the content of the command and are believed to be valid within certain limits that cannot be overstepped without endangering the master's traditional status;

(b) partly in terms of the master's discretion in that sphere which tradition leaves open to him; this traditional prerogative rests primarily on the fact that the obligations of personal obedience tend to be essentially unlimited.

Thus there is a double sphere:

(a)   that of action which is bound to specific traditions;
(b)   that of action which is free of specific rules.

In the latter sphere, the master is free to do good turns on the basis of his personal pleasure and likes, particularly in return for gifts – the historical sources of dues (*Gebühren*). So far as his action follows principles at all, these are governed by considerations of ethical common sense, of equity or of utilitarian expediency. They are not formal principles, as in the case of legal authority. The exercise of power is oriented toward the consideration of how far master and staff can go in view of the subjects' traditional compliance without arousing their resistance. When resistance occurs, it is directed against the master or his servant personally, the accusation being that he failed to observe the traditional limits of his power. Opposition is not directed against the system as such – it is a case of "traditionalist revolution."

In the pure type of traditional authority it is impossible for law or administrative rule to be deliberately created by legislation. Rules which in fact are innovations can be legitimized only by the claim that they have been "valid of yore," but have only now been recognized by means of "Wisdom" [the *Weistum* of ancient Germanic law]. Legal decisions as "finding of the law" (*Rechtsfindung*) can refer only to documents of tradition, namely to precedents and earlier decisions. . . .

In the pure type of traditional rule, the following features of a bureaucratic administrative staff are absent:

(a) a clearly defined sphere of competence subject to impersonal rules,
(b) a rationally established hierarchy,
(c) a regular system of appointment on the basis of free contract, and orderly promotion,
(d) technical training as a regular requirement,
(e) (frequently) fixed salaries, in the type case paid in money. . . .

Charismatic Authority

The term "charisma" will be applied to a certain quality of an individual personality by virtue of which he is considered extraordinary and treated as endowed with supernatural, superhuman, or at least specifically exceptional powers or qualities. These are such as are not accessible to the ordinary person, but are regarded as of divine origin or as exemplary, and on the basis of them the individual concerned is treated as a "leader." In primitive circumstances this peculiar kind of quality is thought of as resting on magical powers, whether of prophets, persons with a reputation for therapeutic or legal wisdom, leaders in the hunt, or heroes in war. How the quality in question would be ultimately judged from any ethical, aesthetic, or other such point of view is naturally entirely indifferent for purposes of definition. What is alone important is how the individual is actually regarded by those subject to charismatic authority, by his "followers" or "disciples.". . .

I. It is recognition on the part of those subject to authority which is decisive for the validity of charisma. This recognition is freely given and guaranteed by what is held to be a proof, originally always a miracle, and consists in devotion to the corresponding revelation, hero worship, or absolute trust in the leader. But where charisma is genuine, it is not this which is the basis of the claim to legitimacy. This basis lies rather in the conception that it is the duty of those subject to charismatic authority to recognize its genuineness and to act accordingly. Psychologically this recognition is a matter of complete personal devotion to the possessor of the quality, arising out of enthusiasm, or of despair and hope. . . .

II. If proof and success elude the leader for long, if he appears deserted by his god or his magical or heroic powers, above all, if his leadership fails to benefit his followers, it is likely that his charismatic authority will disappear. This is the genuine meaning of the divine right of kings (*Gottesgnadentum*). . . .

III. An organized group subject to charismatic authority will be called a charismatic community (*Gemeinde*). It is based on an emotional form of communal relationship (*Vergemeinschaftung*). The administrative staff of a charismatic leader does not consist of "officials"; least of all are its members technically trained. It is not chosen on the basis of social privilege nor from the point of view of domestic or personal dependency. It is rather chosen in terms of the charismatic qualities of its members. The prophet has his disciples; the warlord his bodyguard; the leader, generally, his agents (*Vertrauensmänner*). There is no such thing as appointment or dismissal, no career, no promotion. There is only a call at the instance of the leader on the basis of the charismatic qualification of those he summons. There is no hierarchy; the leader merely intervenes in general or in individual cases when he considers the members of his staff lacking in charismatic qualification for a given task. There is no such thing as a bailiwick or definite sphere of competence, and no appropriation of official powers on the basis of social privileges. There may, however, be territorial or functional limits to charismatic powers and to the individual's mission. There is no such thing as a salary or a benefice. . . .

IV. Pure charisma is specifically foreign to economic considerations. Wherever it appears, it constitutes a "call" in the most emphatic sense of the word, a "mission" or a "spiritual duty." In the pure type, it disdains and repudiates economic exploitation of the gifts of grace as a source of income, though, to be sure, this often remains more an ideal than a fact. It is not that charisma always demands a renunciation of property or even of acquisition, as under certain circumstances prophets and their disciples do. The heroic warrior and his followers actively seek booty; the elective ruler or the charismatic party leader requires the material means of power. The former in addition requires a brilliant display of his authority to bolster his prestige. What is despised, so long as the genuinely charismatic type is adhered to, is traditional or rational everyday economizing, the attainment of a regular income by continuous economic activity devoted to this end. . . .

V. In traditionalist periods, charisma is *the* great revolutionary force. The likewise revolutionary force of "reason" works from *without*: by altering the situations of life and hence its problems, finally in this way changing men's attitudes toward them; or it intellectualizes the individual. Charisma, on the other hand, *may* effect a subjective or *internal* reorientation born out of suffering, conflicts, or enthusiasm. It may then result in a radical alteration of the central attitudes and directions of action with a completely new orientation of all attitudes toward the different problems of the "world." In prerationalistic periods, tradition and charisma between them have almost exhausted the whole of the orientation of action.

The Routinization of Charisma

In its pure form charismatic authority has a character specifically foreign to everyday routine structures. The social relationships directly involved are strictly personal, based on the validity and practice of charismatic personal qualities. If this is not to remain a purely transitory phenomenon, but to take on the character of a permanent relationship, a "community" of disciples or followers or a party organization or any sort of political or hierocratic organization, it is necessary for the character of charismatic authority to become radically changed. Indeed, in its pure form charismatic authority may be said to exist only *in statu nascendi*. It cannot remain stable, but becomes either traditionalized or rationalized, or a combination of both.

The following are the principal motives underlying this transformation: (a) The ideal and also the material interests of the followers in the continuation and the continual reactivation of the community, (b) the still stronger ideal and also stronger material interests of the members of the administrative staff, the disciples, the party workers, or others in continuing their relationship. Not only this, but they have an interest in continuing it in such a way that both from an ideal and a material point of view, their own position is put on a stable everyday basis. This means, above all, making it possible to participate in normal family relationships or at least to enjoy a secure social position in place of the kind of discipleship which is cut off from ordinary worldly connections, notably in the family and in economic relationships.

These interests generally become conspicuously evident with the disappearance of the personal charismatic leader and with the problem of *succession*. The way in which this problem is met – if it is met at all and the charismatic community continues to exist or now begins to emerge – is of crucial importance for the character of the subsequent social relationships. . . .

Concomitant with the routinization of charisma with a view to insuring adequate succession, go the interests in its routinization on the part of the administrative staff. It is only in the initial stages and so long as the charismatic leader acts in a way which is completely outside everyday social organization, that it is possible for his followers to live communistically in a community of faith and enthusiasm, on gifts, booty, or sporadic acquisition. Only the members of the small group of enthusiastic disciples and followers are prepared to devote their lives purely idealistically to their call. The great majority of disciples and followers will in the long run "make their living" out of their "calling" in a material sense as well. Indeed, this must be the case if the movement is not to disintegrate.

Hence, the routinization of charisma also takes the form of the appropriation of powers and of economic advantages by the followers or disciples, and of regulating recruitment. This process of traditionalization or of legalization, according to whether rational legislation is involved or not, may take any one of a number of typical forms. . . .

For charisma to be transformed into an everyday phenomenon, it is necessary that its anti-economic character should be altered. It must be adapted to some form of fiscal organization to provide for the needs of the group and hence to the economic conditions necessary for raising taxes and contributions. When a charismatic movement develops in the direction of prebendal provision, the "laity" becomes differentiated from the "clergy" – derived from κλῆρος, meaning a "share" – , that is, the participating members of the charismatic administrative staff which has now become routinized. These are the priests of the developing "church." Correspondingly, in a developing political body – the "state" in the rational case – vassals, benefice-holders, officials or appointed party officials (instead of voluntary party workers and functionaries) are differentiated from the "tax payers." . . .

It follows that, in the course of routinization, the charismatically ruled organization is largely transformed into one of the everyday authorities, the patrimonial form, especially in its estate-type or bureaucratic variant. Its original peculiarities are apt to be retained in the charismatic status honor acquired by heredity or office-holding. This applies to all who participate in the appropriation, the chief himself and the members of his staff. It is thus a matter of the type of prestige enjoyed by ruling groups. A hereditary monarch by "divine right" is not a simple patrimonial chief, patriarch, or sheik; a vassal is not a mere household retainer or official. Further details must be deferred to the analysis of status groups.

As a rule, routinization is not free of conflict. In the early stages personal claims on the charisma of the chief are not easily fogotten and the conflict between the charisma of the office or of hereditary status with personal charisma is a typical process in many historical situations.

18 Bureaucracy

Max Weber

Characteristics of Modern Bureaucracy

Modern officialdom functions in the following manner:

I. There is the principle of official *jurisdictional areas*, which are generally ordered by rules, that is, by laws or administrative regulations. This means:

(1) The regular activities required for the purposes of the bureaucratically governed structure are assigned as official duties.
(2) The authority to give the commands required for the discharge of these duties is distributed in a stable way and is strictly delimited by rules concerning the coercive means, physical, sacerdotal, or otherwise, which may be placed at the disposal of officials.
(3) Methodical provision is made for the regular and continuous fulfillment of these duties and for the exercise of the corresponding rights; only persons who qualify under general rules are employed.

In the sphere of the state these three elements constitute a bureaucratic *agency*, in the sphere of the private economy they constitute a bureaucratic *enterprise*. Bureaucracy, thus understood, is fully developed in political and ecclesiastical communities only in the modern state, and in the private economy only in the most advanced institutions of capitalism. Permanent agencies, with fixed jurisdiction, are not the historical rule but rather the exception. This is even true of large political structures such as those of the ancient Orient, the Germanic and Mongolian empires of conquest, and of many feudal states. In all these cases, the ruler executes the most important measures through personal trustees, table-companions, or court-servants. Their commissions and powers are not precisely delimited and are temporarily called into being for each case.

II. The principles of *office hierarchy* and of channels of appeal (*Instanzenzug*) stipulate a clearly established system of super- and subordination in which there is a supervision of the lower offices by the higher ones. Such a system offers the governed the possibility of appealing, in a precisely regulated manner, the decision of a lower office to the corresponding superior authority. With the full development of the bureaucratic type, the office hierarchy is *monocratically* organized. The principle of hierarchical office authority is found in all bureaucratic structures: in state and ecclesiastical structures as well as in large party organizations and private enterprises. It does not matter for the character of bureaucracy whether its authority is called "private" or "public."

When the principle of jurisdictional "competency" is fully carried through, hierarchical subordination – at least in public office – does not mean that the "higher" authority is authorized simply to take over the business of the "lower." Indeed, the opposite is the rule; once an office has been set up, a new incumbent will always be appointed if a vacancy occurs.

III. The management of the modern office is based upon written documents (the "files"), which are preserved in their original or draft form, and upon a staff of subaltern officials and scribes of all sorts. The body of officials working in an agency along with the respective apparatus of material implements and the files makes up a *bureau* (in private enterprises often called the "counting house," *Kontor*).

In principle, the modern organization of the civil service separates the bureau from the private domicile of the official and, in general, segregates official activity from the sphere of private life. Public monies and equipment are divorced from the private property of the official. This condition is everywhere the product of a long development. Nowadays, it is found in public as well as in private enterprises; in the latter, the principle extends even to the entrepreneur at the top. In principle, the *Kontor* (office) is separated from the household, business from private correspondence, and business assets from private wealth. The more consistently the modern type of business management has been carried through, the more are these separations the case. The beginnings of this process are to be found as early as the Middle Ages.

It is the peculiarity of the modern entrepreneur that he conducts himself as the "first official" of his enterprise, in the very same way in which the ruler of a specifically modern bureaucratic state [Frederick II of Prussia] spoke of himself as "the first servant" of the state. The idea that the bureau activities of the state are intrinsically different in character from the management of private offices is a continental European notion and, by way of contrast, is totally foreign to the American way.

IV. Office management, at least all specialized office management – and such management is distinctly modern – usually presupposes thorough training in a field of specialization. This, too, holds increasingly for the modern executive and employee of a private enterprise, just as it does for the state officials.

V. When the office is fully developed, official activity demands the *full working capacity* of the official, irrespective of the fact that the length of his obligatory working hours in the bureau may be limited. In the normal case, this too is only the product of a long development, in the public as well as in the private office. Formerly the normal state of affairs was the reverse: Official business was discharged as a secondary activity.

VI. The management of the office follows *general rules*, which are more or less stable, more or less exhaustive, and which can be learned. Knowledge of these rules represents a special technical expertise which the officials possess. It involves jurisprudence, administrative or business management.

The reduction of modern office management to rules is deeply embedded in its very nature. The theory of modern public administration, for instance, assumes that the authority to order certain matters by decree – which has been legally granted to an agency – does not entitle the agency to regulate the matter by individual commands given for each case, but only to regulate the matter abstractly. This stands in extreme contrast to the regulation of all relationships through individual privileges and bestowals of favor, which, as we shall see, is absolutely dominant in patrimonialism, at least in so far as such relationships are not fixed by sacred tradition.

The Position of the Official Within and Outside of Bureaucracy

All this results in the following for the internal and external position of the official:

I. Office holding as a vocation

That the office is a "vocation" (*Beruf*) finds expression, first, in the requirement of a prescribed course of training, which demands the entire working capacity for a long period of time, and in generally prescribed special examinations as prerequisites of employment. Furthermore, it finds expression in that the position of the official is in the nature of a "duty" (*Pflicht*). This determines the character of his relations in the folowing manner: Legally and actually, office holding is not considered ownership of a source of income, to be exploited for rents or emoluments in exchange for the rendering of certain services, as was normally the case during the Middle Ages and frequently up to the threshold of recent times, nor is office holding considered a common exchange of services, as in the case of free employment contracts. Rather, entrance into an office, including one in the private economy, is considered an acceptance of a specific duty of fealty to the purpose of the office (*Amtstreue*) in return for the grant of a secure existence. It is decisive for the modern loyalty to an office that, in the pure type, it does not establish a relationship to a *person*, like the vassal's or disciple's faith under feudal or patrimonial authority, but rather is devoted to *impersonal* and *functional* purposes. These purposes, of course, frequently gain an ideological halo from cultural values, such as state, church, community, party or enterprise, which appear as surrogates for a this-worldly or other-worldly personal master and which are embodied by a given group.

The political official – at least in the fully developed modern state – is not considered the personal servant of a ruler. Likewise, the bishop, the priest and the preacher are in fact no longer, as in early Christian times, carriers of a purely personal charisma, which offers other-worldly sacred values under the personal mandate of a master, and in principle responsible only to him, to everybody who appears worthy of them and asks for them. In spite of the partial survival of the old theory, they have become officials in the service of a functional purpose, a purpose which in the present-day "church" appears at once impersonalized and ideologically sanctified.

II. The social position of the official

A. SOCIAL ESTEEM AND STATUS CONVENTION. Whether he is in a private office or a public bureau, the modern official, too, always strives for and usually attains a distinctly elevated *social esteem* vis-à-vis the governed. His social position is protected by prescription about rank order and, for the political official, by special prohibitions of the criminal code against "insults to the office" and "contempt" of state and church authorities.

The social position of the official is normally highest where, as in old civilized countries, the following conditions prevail: a strong demand for administration by trained experts; a strong and stable social differentiation, where the official predominantly comes from socially and economically privileged strata because of the social distribution of power or the costliness of the required training and of status conventions. . . .

B. APPOINTMENT VERSUS ELECTION: CONSEQUENCES FOR EXPERTISE. Typically, the bureaucratic official is appointed by a superior authority. An official elected by the governed is no longer a purely bureaucratic figure. Of course, a formal election may hide an appointment – in politics especially by party bosses. This does not depend upon legal statutes, but upon the way in which the party mechanism functions. Once firmly organized, the parties can turn a formally free election into the mere acclamation of a candidate designated by the party chief, or at least into a contest, conducted according to certain rules, for the election of one of two designated candidates.

In all circumstances, the designation of officials by means of an election modifies the rigidity of hierarchical subordination. In principle, an official who is elected has an autonomous position vis-à-vis his superiors, for he does not derive his position "from above" but "from below," or at least not from a superior authority of the official hierarchy but from powerful party men ("bosses"), who also determine his further career. The career of the elected official is not primarily dependent upon his chief in the administration. The official who is not elected, but appointed by a master, normally functions, from a technical point of view, more accurately because it is more likely that purely functional points of consideration and qualities will determine his selection and career. As laymen, the governed can evaluate the expert qualifications of a candidate for office only in terms of experience, and hence only after his service. Moreover, if political parties are involved in any sort of selection of officials by election, they quite naturally tend to give decisive weight not to technical competence but to the services a follower renders to the party boss. This holds for the designation of otherwise freely elected officials by party bosses when they determine the slate of candidates as well as for the free appointment of officials by a chief who has himself been elected. The contrast, however, is relative: substantially similar conditions hold where legitimate monarchs and their subordinates appoint officials, except that partisan influences are then less controllable.

Where the demand for administration by trained experts is considerable, and the party faithful have to take into account an intellectually developed, educated, and free "public opinion," the use of unqualified officials redounds upon the party in power at the next election. Naturally, this is more likely to happen when the officials are appointed by the chief. The demand for a trained administration now exists in the United States, but wherever, as in the large cities, immigrant votes are "corralled," there is, of course, no effective public opinion. Therefore, popular election not only of the administrative chief but also of his subordinate officials usually endangers, at least in very large administrative bodies which are difficult to supervise, the expert qualification of the officials as well as the precise functioning of the bureaucratic mechanism, besides weakening the dependence of the officials upon the hierarchy. . . .

C. TENURE AND THE INVERSE RELATIONSHIP BETWEEN JUDICIAL INDEPENDENCE

AND SOCIAL PRESTIGE. Normally, the position of the official is held for life, at least in public bureaucracies, and this is increasingly the case for all similar structures. As a factual rule, *tenure for life* is presupposed even where notice can be given or periodic reappointment occurs. In a private enterprise, the fact of such tenure normally differentiates the official from the worker. Such legal or actual life-tenure, however, is not viewed as a proprietary right of the official to the possession of office as was the case in many structures of authority of the past. Wherever legal guarantees against discretionary dismissal or transfer are developed, as in Germany for all judicial and increasingly also for administrative officials, they merely serve the purpose of guaranteeing a strictly impersonal discharge of specific office duties. . . .

D. RANK AS THE BASIS OF REGULAR SALARY. The official as a rule receives a *monetary* compensation in the form of a *salary*, normally fixed, and the old age security provided by a pension. The salary is not measured like a wage in terms of work done, but according to "status," that is, according to the kind of function (the "rank") and, possibly, according to the length of service. The relatively great security of the official's income, as well as the rewards of social esteem, make the office a sought-after position, especially in countries which no longer provide opportunities for colonial profits. In such countries, this situation permits relatively low salaries for officials.

E. FIXED CAREER LINES AND STATUS RIGIDITY. The official is set for a "career" within the hierarchical order of the public service. He expects to move from the lower, less important and less well paid, to the higher positions. The average official naturally desires a mechanical fixing of the conditions of promotion: if not of the offices, at least of the salary levels. He wants these conditions fixed in terms of "seniority," or possibly according to grades achieved in a system of examinations. Here and there, such grades actually form a *character indelebilis* of the official and have lifelong effects on his career. To this is joined the desire to reinforce the right to office and to increase status group closure and economic security. All of this makes for a tendency to consider the offices as "prebends" of those qualified by educational certificates. The necessity of weighing general personal and intellectual qualifications without concern for the often subaltern character of such patents of specialized education, has brought it about that the highest political offices, especially the "ministerial" positions, are as a rule filled without reference to such certificates. . . .

The Technical Superiority of Bureaucratic Organization over Administration by Notables

The decisive reason for the advance of bureaucratic organization has always been its purely *technical* superiority over any other form of organization. The fully developed bureaucratic apparatus compares with other organizations exactly as does the machine with the non-mechanical modes of production. Precision, speed, unambiguity, knowledge of the files, continuity, discretion, unity, strict subordination, reduction of friction and of material and personal costs – these are raised to the optimum point in the strictly bureaucratic administration, and especially in its monocratic form. As compared with all collegiate, honorific, and avocational forms of administration, trained bureaucracy is superior on all these points. And as far as complicated tasks are concerned, paid bureaucratic work is not only more precise but, in the last analysis, it is often cheaper than even formally unremunerated honorific service. . . .

Today, it is primarily the capitalist market economy which demands that the official business of public administation be discharged precisely, unambiguously, continuously, and with as much speed as possible. Normally, the very large modern capitalist enterprises are themselves unequalled models of strict bureaucratic organization. Business management throughout rests on increasing precision, steadiness, and, above all, speed of operations. This, in turn, is determined by the peculiar nature of the modern means of communication, including, among other things, the news service of the press. The extraordinary increase in the speed by which public announcements, as well as economic and political facts, are transmitted exerts a steady and sharp pressure in the direction of speeding up the tempo of administrative reaction towards various situations. The optimum of such reaction time is normally attained only by a strictly bureaucratic organization. (The fact that the bureaucratic apparatus also can, and indeed does, create certain definite impediments for the discharge of business in a manner best adapted to the individuality of each case does not belong into the present context.)

Bureaucratization offers above all the optimum possibility for carrying through the principle of specializing administrative functions according to purely objective considerations. Individual performances are allocated to functionaries who have specialized training and who by constant practice increase their expertise. "Objective" discharge of business primarily means a discharge of business according to *calculable rules* and "without regard for persons."

"Without regard for persons," however, is also the watchword of the market and, in general, of all pursuits of naked economic interests. Consistent bureaucratic domination means the leveling of "status honor." Hence, if the principle of the free market is not at the same time restricted, it means the universal domination of the "class situation." That this consequence of bureaucratic domination has not set in everywhere proportional to the extent of bureaucratization is due to the differences between possible principles by which polities may supply their requirements. However, the second element mentioned, calculable rules, is the most important one for modern bureaucracy. The peculiarity of modern culture, and specifically of its technical and economic basis, demands this very "calculability" of results. When fully developed, bureaucracy also stands, in a specific sense, under the principle of *sine ira ac studio*. Bureaucracy develops the more perfectly, the more it is "dehumanized," the more completely it succeeds in eliminating from official business love, hatred, and all purely personal, irrational, and emotional elements which escape calculation. This is appraised as its special virtue by capitalism. . . .

The Leveling of Social Differences

In spite of its indubitable technical superiority, bureaucracy has everywhere been a relatively late development. A number of obstacles have contributed to this, and only under certain social and political conditions have they definitely receded into the background.

A. Administrative democratization

Bureaucratic organization has usually come into power on the basis of a leveling of economic and social differences. This leveling has been at least relative, and has concerned the significance of social and economic differences for the assumption of administrative functions.

Bureaucracy inevitably accompanies modern *mass democracy*, in contrast to the democratic self-government of small homogeneous units. This results from its characteristic principle: the abstract regularity of the exercise of authority, which is a result of the demand for "equality before the law" in the personal and functional sense – hence, of the horror of "privilege," and the principled rejection of doing business "from case to case." Such regularity also follows from the social precon-ditions of its origin. Any non-bureaucratic administration of a large social structure rests in some way upon the fact that existing social, material, or honorific preferences and ranks are connected with administrative functions and duties. This usually means that an economic or a social exploitation of position, which every sort of administrative activity provides to its bearers, is the compensation for the assumption of administrative functions.

Bureaucratization and democratization within the administration of the state therefore signify an increase of the cash expenditures of the public treasury, in spite of the fact that bureaucratic administration is usually more "economical" in character than other forms. Until recent times – at least from the point of view of the treasury – the cheapest way of satisfying the need for administration was to leave almost the entire local administration and lower judicature to the landlords of Eastern Prussia. The same is true of the administration by justices of the peace in England. Mass democracy which makes a clean sweep of the feudal, patrimonial, and – at least in intent – the plutocratic privileges in administration unavoidably has to put paid professional labor in place of the historically inherited "avoca-tional" administration by notables.

B. Mass parties and the bureaucratic consequences of democratization

This applies not only to the state. For it is no accident that in their own organizations the democratic mass parties have completely broken with traditional rule by notables based upon personal relationships and personal esteem. Such personal structures still persist among many old conservative as well as old liberal parties, but democratic mass parties are bureaucratically organized under the leadership of party officials, professional party and trade union secretaries, etc. In Germany, for instance, this has happened in the Social Democratic party and in the agrarian mass-movement; in England earliest in the caucus democracy of Gladstone and Chamberlain which spread from Birmingham in the 1870's. In the United States, both parties since Jackson's administration have developed bureaucratically. In France, however, attempts to organize disciplined political parties on the basis of an election system that would compel bureaucratic organization have repeatedly failed. The resistance of local circles of notables against the otherwise unavoidable bureaucratization of the parties, which would encompass the entire country and break their influence, could not be overcome. Every advance of simple election techniques based on numbers alone as, for instance, the system of proportional representation, means a strict and inter-local bureaucratic organization of the parties and therewith an increasing domination of party bureaucracy and discipline, as well as the elimination of the local circles of notables – at least this holds for large states.

The progress of bureaucratization within the state administration itself is a phenomenon paralleling the development of democracy, as is quite obvious in France, North America, and now in England. Of course, one must always remember that the term "democratization" can be misleading. The *demos* itself, in the sense of a shapeless mass, never "governs" larger associations, but rather is governed. What changes is only the way in which the executive leaders are selected and the measure of influence which the *demos*, or better, which social circles from its midst are able to exert upon the content and the direction of administrative activities by means of "public opinion." "Democratization," in the sense here intended, does not necessarily mean an increasingly active share of the subjects in government. This may be a result of democratization, but it is not necessarily the case.

We must expressly recall at this point that the political concept of democracy, deduced from the "equal rights" of the governed, includes these further postulates: (1) prevention of the development of a closed status group of officials in the interest of a universal accessibility of office, and (2) minimization of the authority of officialdom in the interest of expanding the sphere of influence of "public opinion" as far as practicable. Hence, wherever possible, political democracy strives to shorten the term of office through election and recall, and to be relieved from a limitation to candidates with special expert qualifications. Thereby democracy inevitably comes into conflict with the bureaucratic tendencies which have been produced by its very fight against the notables. The loose term "democratization" cannot be used here, in so far as it is understood to mean the minimization of the civil servants' power in favor of the greatest possible "direct" rule of the *demos*, which in practice means the respective party leaders of the *demos*. The decisive aspect here – indeed it is rather exclusively so – is the *leveling of the governed* in face of the governing and bureaucratically articulated group, which in its turn may occupy a quite autocratic position, both in fact and in form. . . .

The Objective and Subjective Bases of Bureaucratic Perpetuity

Once fully established, bureaucracy is among those social structures which are the hardest to destroy. Bureaucracy is *the* means of transforming social action into rationally organized action. Therefore, as an instrument of rationally organizing authority relations, bureaucracy was and is a power instrument of the first order for one who controls the bureaucratic apparatus. Under otherwise equal conditions, rationally organized and directed action (*Gesellschaftshandeln*) is superior to every kind of collective behavior (*Massenhandeln*) and also social action (*Gemeinschaftshandeln*) opposing it. Where administration has been completely bureaucratized, the resulting system of domination is practically indestructible.

The individual bureaucrat cannot squirm out of the apparatus into which he has been harnessed. In contrast to the "notable" performing administrative tasks as a honorific duty or as a subsidiary occupation (avocation), the professional bureaucrat is chained to his activity in his entire economic and ideological existence. In the great majority of cases he is only a small cog in a ceaselessly moving mechanism which prescribes to him an essentially fixed route of march. The official is entrusted with specialized tasks, and normally the mechanism cannot be put into motion or arrested by him, but only from the very top. The individual bureaucrat is, above all, forged to the common interest of all the functionaries in the perpetuation of the apparatus and the persistence of its rationally organized domination.

The ruled, for their part, cannot dispense with or replace the bureaucratic apparatus once it exists, for it rests upon expert training, a functional specialization of work, and an attitude set on habitual virtuosity in the mastery of single yet methodically integrated functions. If the apparatus stops working, or if its work is interrupted by force, chaos results, which it is difficult to master by improvised replacements from among the governed. This holds for public administration as well as for private economic management. Increasingly the material fate of the masses depends upon the continuous and correct functioning of the ever more bureaucratic organizations of private capitalism, and the idea of eliminating them becomes more and more utopian.

Increasingly, all order in public and private organizations is dependent on the system of files and the discipline of officialdom, that means, its habit of painstaking obedience within its wonted sphere of action. The latter is the more decisive element, however important in practice the files are. The naive idea of Bakuninism of destroying the basis of "acquired rights" together with "domination" by destroying the public documents overlooks that the settled orientation of *man* for observing the accustomed rules and regulations will survive independently of the documents. Every reorganization of defeated or scattered army units, as well as every restoration of an administrative order destroyed by revolts, panics, or other catastrophes, is effected by an appeal to this conditioned orientation, bred both in the officials and in the subjects, of obedient adjustment to such [social and political] orders. If the appeal is successful it brings, as it were, the disturbed mechanism to "snap into gear" again.

The objective indispensability of the once-existing apparatus, in connection with its peculiarly "impersonal" character, means that the mechanism – in contrast to the feudal order based upon personal loyalty – is easily made to work for anybody who knows how to gain control over it. A rationally ordered officialdom continues to function smoothly after the enemy has occupied the territory; he merely needs to change the top officials. It continues to operate because it is to the vital interest of everyone concerned, including above all the enemy. After Bismarck had, during the long course of his years in power, brought his ministerial colleagues into unconditional bureaucratic dependence by eliminating all independent statesmen, he saw to his surprise that upon his resignation they continued to administer their offices unconcernedly and undismayedly, as if it had not been the ingenious lord and very creator of these tools who had left, but merely some individual figure in the bureaucratic machine which had been exchanged for some other figure. In spite of all the changes of masters in France since the time of the First Empire, the power apparatus remained essentially the same.

Such an apparatus makes "revolution," in the sense of the forceful creation of entirely new formations of authority, more and more impossible – technically, because of its control over the modern means of communication (telegraph etc.), and also because of its increasingly rationalized inner structure. The place of "revolutions" is under this process taken by *coups d'état*, as again France demonstrates in the classical manner since all successful transformations there have been of this nature. . . .

Part IV

Self and Society in Sociological Theory

Introduction to Part IV

In this section, we have gathered work from four influential theorists active at the beginning of the century: Georg Simmel, Sigmund Freud, George Herbert Mead, and William Edward Burghardt (W. E. B.) Du Bois. Although there were significant differences among these theorists, there were also important similarities in their lives and their theories. In terms of biography, the four were born at around the same time, and were influenced by some of the same intellectual currents. In their work, each of these authors grappled with the same theoretical issue: the connection between an individual's sense of "self" and his or her social context. This concept of the self is the common theme connecting the authors in this section, even though that particular word is not used by all of them.

The concept of "self" makes the work in this section quite distinct from earlier social theory. These authors did not view society as the result of a contract among autonomous individuals, as did the early Enlightenment thinkers. Nor did they see social order composed largely of power relations, as did Marx and to some extent Weber as well. They can perhaps best be understood as claiming a middle ground between Weber's action-centered theory and Durkheim's understanding of society as a *sui generis* phenomenon. The authors began from the premise that humans are social animals by nature. Society is thus an innate part of human life. A human being could physically exist without any form of society, but that person would not be a "person" at all in the sense we normally mean. Such a person would have no social identity and no personality – in short, no sense of self.

A person's sense of self thus has a dual nature. On the one hand, it is the possession of the individual; it is in fact what makes a person unique from all other people. But at the same time, it is the reflection of the social group and the individual's places within it. Simmel for example claimed that a person's "individuality" is increased only when her social group is expanded. This dual nature is reflected in the terms that these authors use to talk about the self. Mead argued that a person's self is composed of a part that is completely unique and spontaneous (what he called the "I") and a part that comes from the internalized expectations of society (the "Me"). Freud made a similar claim with his famous distinction between "Id," "ego," and "superego."

The interest of these authors in the link between self and society had at least two important methodological ramifications. First, this interest led the authors to focus more specifically on the "micro" dimension of individuals as social beings without abandoning an interest in more "macro" social formations. Second, it led the authors to deal explicitly with the mental states of individuals.

Lives and Intellectual Contexts

Georg Simmel (1858–1918) and Sigmund Freud (1856–1939) were both German-speaking Europeans of the same intellectual generation as Max Weber. Both were

Jews who experienced the difficulties that their "otherness" entailed. Simmel was born in Berlin to middle-class parents and remained there nearly all his life. Despite his rejection of religious ties, anti-Jewish prejudice hampered his career. After earning his doctorate at the University of Berlin in 1881, Simmel became a popular teacher there from 1884 to 1914, but had no regular faculty appointment. He eventually attained a full professorship at the University of Strasbourg in 1914. During his academic career, Simmel worked out his own conception of sociology in a series of important articles and a few longer monographs. Throughout his work, emphasis on "sociability" as a central trait of humans is evident.

Freud grew up in Vienna. Like Simmel, Freud came from a Jewish family and experienced anti-Semitic prejudice despite his lack of religious faith. At the University of Vienna from 1873 to 1881, Freud studied medicine, philosophy, and science. In the 1880s, he studied in France and worked as a physician specializing in neurology. During the 1890s, Freud founded the psychoanalytic theory of the mind. He became an associate professor at the University of Vienna in 1902. He developed his psychoanalytic ideas through writing and teaching for the rest of his life. Freud's early work helped establish his psychoanalytic movement by the 1920s. His later works (especially *Civilization and its Discontents*, excerpted here) tie his perspective to more clearly sociological questions. He and his family fled to England in 1938 following the Nazi invasion of Austria. Freud died the following year.

By contrast, George Herbert Mead (1863–1931) and W. E. B. Du Bois (1868–1963) were Americans, and slightly younger than their European counterparts. Mead grew up in Oberlin, Ohio where his father, a Protestant clergyman, was a theology professor. After graduating from Oberlin College in 1883, Mead spent several years working as a teacher, a surveyor, and a laborer. He entered graduate studies at Harvard in 1887, studying philosophy and physiological psychology. Mead eventually abandoned his dissertation, married, and began to teach at the University of Michigan, and later at the University of Chicago. Through his popular course in social psychology, Mead influenced generations of Chicago sociology students. Mead published more than 60 articles during his academic career, but never published a longer programmatic discussion of his social thought. After his death, Mead's students published his four books, including *Mind, Self, and Society*, based on his lectures.

Du Bois, a Black American, grew up in a middle-class family in Massachusetts. He earned his undergraduate degree at Fisk University and completed his Ph.D. in history at Harvard, becoming the University's first Black graduate. After teaching briefly elsewhere, he became a professor of history and economics at Atlanta University until moving to head the National Association for the Advancement of Colored People (NAACP) in 1910. From then until 1934, Du Bois edited the NAACP's journal, *The Crisis*. He remained a prolific author of academic articles, speeches, poetry, fiction, and four autobiographies. Between 1896 and 1914, Du Bois published at least one book each year based on his research.

Both Mead and Du Bois became accomplished academics, but were also committed social activists. Mead worked with Jane Addams and others at Hull House, and was outspoken on issues of women's rights, penal reform, and education. Du Bois rose to national attention by opposing Booker T. Washington's ideas about social integration. Du Bois emphasized using political power to attain civil rights and encouraged the formation of a black elite that would work for the whole race's progress. He then remained politically active in Marxist and Pan-African movements until his death in 1963.

Self and Society

The work included in this section develops the relationship between the self and society in several different ways. The first is Mead's broad discussion of the development of the self and the importance of human communication in this process. While all humans carry the capacity to interpret the "significant symbols" used in communication, it is only by being involved in social life that we learn to do so, according to Mead. On the basis of this observation, Mead makes his distinction between "mind" (the ability to reflectively interpret symbols) and "self" (the experience of ourselves as unique individuals). Both, according to Mead, emerge through social interaction and thus must be distinguished from physical being. He further distinguishes the "I" and the "Me" as two moments of the self. The genius of Mead's writing lies in his ability to generate complex points about social life from simple examples. His discussion of children at play, for instance, shows how children learn to take on "the generalized other" and to see themselves and others in specific roles and thereby to enter into meaningful social interaction.

Simmel and Du Bois develop the theme of self and society in a different way. In contrast to Mead, both authors discuss the way aspects of the self are shaped under specific kinds of social circumstances. "Group Expansion and the Development of Individuality" demonstrates Simmel's "formal sociology" and its focus on the numerical characteristics of groups, differentiation within and between groups, and the resulting forms of individuation people experience within a group. Simmel argues that individuality increases as a person's social circle expands. Differentiation within groups also leads to social ties across group boundaries. The social context that an individual is in is thus extremely important for the way that she can define herself. This argument, like Durkheim's work on social solidarity that influenced it, suggests that differentiation can create its own form of social cohesion.

"The Stranger" is an example of Simmel's study of social types. Here, Simmel describes a social form in which physical and social distances are significant. Simmel suggests that all relationships have varying amounts of social distance. As a social being, the stranger is created by the individual's place in the social world – he or she is "both near and far" as Simmel describes it. Drawing on the historical example of Jewish traders in European society, Simmel shows how this combination of physical proximity and social distance leads to a certain freedom of interaction and objectivity in relationships. In a related passage in his 1905 article "How Is Society Possible?", which is not excerpted here, Simmel suggested that such distance creates a "veil" of inherent dissimilarity between people. Du Bois used the same metaphor of a veil to describe social distance between white and Black Americans. Black Americans, Du Bois argued, have a "double consciousness." The idea of double consciousness affected both social theory and political debates. He coined the term to describe the social selves of Black Americans, who have a self that contains competing goals – those appropriate to whites and Blacks. Like Simmel's "stranger," Du Bois shows that a Black American feels the distance of otherness, which can prevent the formation of a unified sense of self.

The theme of self and society is developed in a third way in the work of Freud. Like Simmel, Freud was concerned with the forces holding societies together. Freud, however, located these forces in individual and social drives rather than in the formal properties of groups. Freud's work also questioned earlier optimistic views of social progress because of its emphasis on conflicts between individuals and society and within individuals themselves. Freud's famous distinction between "Id," "ego" and "superego," for example, has a close parallel in Mead's distinction between the "I" and the "Me" as parts of the self. The reading included here, from *Civilization and its Discontents*, is Freud's most sociological work. The opening paragraphs of the excerpt set up Freud's argument. Society (or the process of "civilization," as Freud puts it) works to bind people together into social units (families, "races," nations, and so on). Ties of love and passion are an important element of cohesion at the collective level, which helps to check what Freud sees as the naturally aggressive instincts of humans. But such ties also lead to feelings of guilt and jealousy, which inevitably come with living in human society. This tension is then manifest as a constant struggle between "ego" and "superego." Although this view differs markedly from Simmel's claim that humans are inherently social beings, it nonetheless speaks to the broad claim made by all the authors that social life is deeply implicated in our experience of the self.

Legacies of the Self

The work of these four authors has had some important ramifications for later sociological work, much of which is evident in the second volume of this reader. Individually, each of these authors has left his own mark on the discipline. Du Bois' legacy is probably the most diffuse, in part because his very long public life had so many different facets. His work is now having a renaissance of sorts among theorists interested in questions of identity and difference. Simmel's influence is clearly seen in modern exchange theory and social networks. Peter Blau, once a central figure in exchange theory, has also brought aspects of Simmel's formal sociology to his more recent work on the properties of social structure. Freud's legacy has influenced social theorists who explore how unconscious desires shape individuals' lives and social patterns, including the critical social theorists of the Frankfurt School (see Part V of this volume). French poststructuralist theories and postmodern theories have also employed many of Freud's ideas about the contradictory forces of civilization and individuality. Mead is best known as the founding figure of the school of symbolic interactionism in sociology. Herbert Blumer, for example, developed symbolic interactionism by interpreting Mead's ideas. This work on the connection between the individual and society has had an extremely deep impact on modern social theory in a collective sense as well. The idea that the "self" – or whatever one wishes to call it – is both a personal property and a social structure is a distinctive claim of modern sociology. Although Marx, Weber and Durkheim all hinted at this idea, it was not until the second or third decade of the twentieth century that the claim became widely acknowledged.

Select Bibliography

Baldwin, John D. 1986. *George Herbert Mead: A Unifying Theory for Sociology*. Beverly Hills, CA: Sage Publications. (Baldwin summarizes Mead's model of the individual and society as a potentially unifying theory that includes all levels of society.)

Coser, Lewis, editor. 1965. *Georg Simmel*. Englewood Cliffs, NJ: Prentice-Hall. (This collection includes introductory and biographical information, and essays on Simmel's work by his contemporaries, including Durkheim, and discusses continuing uses of Simmel's ideas by other theorists.)

Deegan, Mary Jo. 1988. *Jane Addams and the Men of the Chicago School, 1892–1918*. New Brunswick, NJ: Transaction Books. (In a feminist engagement with Mead's ideas, Deegan analyzes how Mead's social activism with Jane Addams of Hull House influenced his theories and why this information is not widely known.)

Frisby, David. 1984. *Georg Simmel*. New York: Tavistock Publications. (Frisby offers a readable, yet comprehensive intellectual biography and overview of key issues in Simmel's work.)

Frisby, David. 1992. *Simmel and Since: Essays on Georg Simmel's Social Theory*. London: Routledge. (In this work focusing on modernity, Frisby outlines the historical and cultural context of Simmel's work, and examines his legacy to sociology including links with Weber.)

Gay, Peter. 1988. *Freud: A Life for Our Time*. New York: Norton. (Gay's critical intellectual biography traces Freud's development of ideas in the context of his life history. In a related series, *The Bourgeois Experience: Victoria to Freud*, Gay applies Freud's theory to interpret cultural history.)

Joas, Hans. 1985. *G. H. Mead: A Contemporary Re-examination of His Thought*. Translated by Raymond Meyer. Cambridge, MA: MIT Press. (Joas explores how Mead's ideas related to other pragmatists and how these ideas can be used.)

Jones, Ernest. 1961. *The Life and Work of Sigmund Freud*. Edited and abridged by Lionel Trilling and Steven Marcus. New York: Basic Books. (This is an abridged version of Jones' exhaustive, official biography that focuses on Freud's life and the context of his writings.)

Levine, Donald N. 1980. *Simmel and Parsons: Two Approaches to the Study of Society*. New York: Arno Press. (Levine explores Simmel and Parsons' structural-functionalist work as contrasting perspectives on sociology.)

Lewis, David Levering. 1994. *W. E. B. Du Bois: Biography of a Race, 1868–1919*. New York: Henry Holt. (Lewis's series traces Du Bois' life and thought discussing its contemporaneous and more recent effects.)

Zamir, Shamoon. 1995. *Dark Voices: W. E. B. Du Bois and American Thought, 1888–1903*. Chicago: University of Chicago Press. (Zamir's study is especially useful for those wishing a more sustained discussion of Du Bois' early work in its intellectual context.)

A: GEORGE HERBERT MEAD

19 The Self

George Herbert Mead

In our statement of the development of intelligence we have already suggested that the language process is essential for the development of the self. The self has a character which is different from that of the physiological organism proper. The self is something which has a development; it is not initially there, at birth, but arises in the process of social experience and activity, that is, develops in the given individual as a result of his relations to that process as a whole and to other individuals within that process. The intelligence of the lower forms of animal life, like a great deal of human intelligence, does not involve a self. In our habitual actions, for example, in our moving about in a world that is simply there and to which we are so adjusted that no thinking is involved, there is a certain amount of sensuous experience such as persons have when they are just waking up, a bare thereness of the world. Such characters about us may exist in experience without taking their place in relationship to the self. One must, of course, under those conditions, distinguish between the experience that immediately takes place and our own organization of it into the experience of the self. One says upon analysis that a certain item had its place in his experience, in the experience of his self. We do inevitably tend at a certain level of sophistication to organize all experience into that of a self. We do so intimately identify our experiences, especially our affective experiences, with the self that it takes a moment's abstraction to realize that pain and pleasure can be there without being the experience of the self. Similarly, we normally organize our memories upon the string of our self. If we date things we always date them from the point of view of our past experiences. We frequently have memories that we cannot date, that we cannot place. A picture comes before us suddenly and we are at a loss to explain when that experience originally took place. We remember perfectly distinctly the picture, but we do not have it definitely placed, and until we can place it in terms of our past experience we are not satisfied. Nevertheless, I think it is obvious when one comes to consider it that the self is not necessarily involved in the life of the organism, nor involved in what we term our sensuous experience, that is, experience in a world about us for which we have habitual reactions.

We can distinguish very definitely between the self and the body. The body can be there and can operate in a very intelligent fashion without there being a self involved in the experience. The self has the characteristic that it is an object to itself, and that characteristic distinguishes it from other objects and from the body.

It is perfectly true that the eye can see the foot, but it does not see the body as a whole. We cannot see our backs; we can feel certain portions of them, if we are agile, but we cannot get an experience of our whole body. There are, of course, experiences which are somewhat vague and difficult of location, but the bodily experiences are for us organized about a self. The foot and hand belong to the self. We can see our feet, especially if we look at them from the wrong end of an opera glass, as strange things which we have difficulty in recognizing as our own. The parts of the body are quite distinguishable from the self. We can lose parts of the body without any serious invasion of the self. The mere ability to experience different parts of the body is not different from the experience of a table. The table presents a different feel from what the hand does when one hand feels another, but it is an experience of something with which we come definitely into contact. The body does not experience itself as a whole, in the sense in which the self in some way enters into the experience of the self.

It is the characteristic of the self as an object to itself that I want to bring out. This characteristic is represented in the word "self," which is a reflexive, and indicates that which can be both subject and object. This type of object is essentially different from other objects, and in the past it has been distinguished as conscious, a term which indicates an experience with, an experience of, one's self. It was assumed that consciousness in some way carried this capacity of being an object to itself. In giving a behavioristic statement of consciousness we have to look for some sort of experience in which the physical organism can become an object to itself.[1]

When one is running to get away from someone who is chasing him, he is entirely occupied in this action, and his experience may be swallowed up in the objects about him, so that he has, at the time being, no consciousness of self at all. We must be, of course, very completely occupied to have that take place, but we can, I think, recognize that sort of a possible experience in which the self does not enter. We can, perhaps, get some light on that situation through those experiences in which in very intense action there appear in the experience of the individual, back of this intense action, memories and anticipations. Tolstoi as an officer in the war gives an account of having pictures of his past experience in the midst of his most intense action. There are also the pictures that flash into a person's mind when he is drowning. In such instances there is a contrast between an experience that is absolutely wound up in outside activity in which the self as an object does not enter, and an activity of memory and imagination in which the self is the principal object. The self is then entirely distinguishable from an organism that is surrounded by things and acts with reference to things, including parts of its own body. These latter may be objects like other objects, but they are just objects out there in the field, and they do not involve a self that is an object to the organism. This is, I think, frequently overlooked. It is that fact which makes our anthropomorphic reconstructions of animal life so fallacious. How can an individual get outside himself (experientially) in such a way as to become an object to himself? This is the essential psychological problem of selfhood or of self-consciousness; and its solution is to be found by referring to the process of social conduct or activity in which the given person or individual is implicated. The apparatus of reason would not be complete unless it swept itself into its own analysis of the field of experience; or unless the individual brought himself into the same experiential field as that of the other individual selves in relation to whom he acts in any given social situation. Reason cannot become impersonal unless it takes an objective, non-affective attitude toward itself; otherwise we have just consciousness, not *self*-consciousness. And it is necessary to rational conduct that the individual should thus take an objective, impersonal attitude toward himself, that he should become an object to himself. For the individual organism is obviously an essential and important fact or constituent element of the empirical situation in which it acts; and without taking objective account of itself as such, it cannot act intelligently, or rationally.

The individual experiences himself as such, not directly, but only indirectly, from the particular standpoints of other individual members of the same social group, or from the generalized standpoint of the social group as a whole to which he belongs. For he enters his own experience as a self or individual, not directly or immediately, not by becoming a subject to himself, but only in so far as he first becomes an object to himself just as other individuals are objects to him or in his experience; and he becomes an object to himself only by taking the attitudes of other individuals toward himself within a social environment or context of experience and behavior in which both he and they are involved.

The importance of what we term "communication" lies in the fact that it provides a form of behavior in which the organism or the individual may become an object to himself. It is that sort of communication which we have been discussing – not communication in the sense of the cluck of the hen to the chickens, or the bark of a wolf to the pack, or the lowing of a cow, but communication in the sense of significant symbols, communication which is directed not only to others but also to the individual himself. So far as that type of communication is a part of behavior it at least introduces a self. Of course, one may hear without listening; one may see things that he does not realize; do things that he is not really aware of. But it is where one does respond to that which he addresses to another and where that response of his own becomes a part of his conduct, where he not only hears himself but responds to himself, talks and replies to himself as truly as the other person replies to him, that we have behavior in which the individuals become objects to themselves.

Such a self is not, I would say, primarily the physiological organism. The physiological organism is essential to it, but we are at least able to think of a self without it. Persons who believe in immortality, or believe in ghosts, or in the possibility of the self leaving the body, assume a self which is quite distinguishable from the body. How successfully they can hold these conceptions is an open question, but we do, as a fact, separate the self and the organism. It is fair to say that the beginning of the self as an object, so far as we can see, is to be found in the experiences of people that lead to the conception of a "double." Primitive people assume that there is a double, located presumably in the diaphragm, that leaves the body temporarily in sleep and completely in death. It can be enticed out of the body of one's enemy and perhaps killed. It is represented in infancy by the imaginary playmates which children set up, and through which they come to control their experiences in their play.

The self, as that which can be an object to itself, is essentially a social structure, and it arises in social experience. After a self has arisen, it in a certain sense provides for itself its social experiences, and so we can conceive of an absolutely solitary self. But it is impossible to conceive of a self arising outside of social experience. When it has arisen we can think of a person in solitary confinement for the rest of his life, but who still has himself as a companion, and is able to think and to converse with himself as he had communicated with others. That process to which I have just referred, of responding to one's self as another responds to it, taking part in one's own conversation with others, being aware of what one is saying and using that awareness of what one is saying to determine what one is going to say thereafter – that is a process with which we are all familiar. We are continually following up our own address to other persons by an understanding of what we are saying, and using that understanding in the direction of our continued speech. We are finding out what we are going to say, what we are going to do, by saying and doing, and in the process we are continually controlling the process itself. In the conversation of gestures what we say calls out a certain response in another and that in turn changes our own action, so that we shift from what we started to do because of the reply the other makes. The conversation of gestures is the beginning of communication. The individual comes to carry on a conversation of gestures with himself. He says something, and that calls out a certain reply in himself which makes him change what he was going to say. One starts to say something, we will presume an unpleasant something, but when he starts to say it he realizes it is cruel. The effect on himself of what he is saying checks him; there is here a conversation of gestures between the individual and himself. We mean by significant speech that the action is one that affects the individual himself, and that the effect upon the individual himself is part of the intelligent carrying-out of the conversation with others. Now we, so to speak, amputate that social phase and dispense with it for the time being, so that one is talking to one's self as one would talk to another person.

This process of abstraction cannot be carried on indefinitely. One inevitably seeks an audience, has to pour himself out to somebody. In reflective intelligence one thinks to act, and to act solely so that this action remains a part of a social process. Thinking becomes preparatory to social action. The very process of thinking is, of course, simply an inner conversation that goes on, but it is a conversation of gestures which in its completion implies the expression of that which one thinks to an audience. One separates the significance of what he is saying to others from the actual speech and gets it ready before saying it. He thinks it out, and perhaps writes it in the form of a book; but it is still a part of social intercourse in which one is addressing other persons and at the same time addressing one's self, and in which one controls the address to other persons by the response made to one's own gesture. That the person should be responding to himself is necessary to the self, and it is this sort of social conduct which provides behavior within which that self appears. I know of no other form of behavior than the linguistic in which the individual is an object to himself, and, so far as I can see, the individual is not a self in the reflexive sense unless he is an object to himself. It is this fact that gives a critical importance to communication, since this is a type of behavior in which the individual does so respond to himself.

We realize in everyday conduct and experience that an individual does not mean a great deal of what he is doing and saying. We frequently say that such an individual is not himself. We come away from an interview with a realization that we have left out important things, that there are parts of the self that did not get into what was said. What determines the amount of the self that gets into communication is the social experience itself. Of course, a good deal of the self does not need to get expression. We carry on a whole series of different relationships to different people. We are one thing to one man and another thing to another. There are parts of the self which exist only for the self in relationship to itself. We divide ourselves up in all sorts of different selves with reference to our acquaintances. We discuss politics with one and religion with another. There are all sorts of different selves answering to all sorts of different social reactions. It is the social process itself that is responsible for the appearance of the self; it is not there as a self apart from this type of experience.

A multiple personality is in a certain sense normal, as I have just pointed out. There is usually an organization of the whole self with reference to the community to which we belong, and the situation in which we find ourselves. What the society is, whether we are living with people of the present, people of our own imaginations, people of the past, varies, of course, with different individuals. Normally, within the sort of community as a whole to which we belong, there is a unified self, but that may be broken up. To a person who is somewhat unstable nervously and in whom there is a line of cleavage, certain activities become impossible, and that set of activities may separate and evolve another self. Two separate "me's" and "I's," two different selves, result, and that is the condition under which there is a tendency to break up the personality. There is an account of a professor of education who disappeared, was lost to the community, and later turned up in a logging camp in the West. He freed himself of his occupation and turned to the woods where he felt, if you like, more at home. The pathological side of it was the forgetting, the leaving out of the rest of the self. This result involved getting rid of certain bodily memories which would identify the individual to himself. We often recognize the lines of cleavage that run through us. We would be glad to forget certain things, get rid of things the self is bound up with in past experiences. What we have here is a situation in which there can be different selves, and it is dependent upon the set of social reactions that is involved as to which self we are going to be. If we can forget everything involved in one set of activities, obviously we relinquish that part of the self. Take a person who is unstable, get him occupied by speech, and at the same time get his eye on something you are writing so that he is carrying on two separate lines of communication, and if you go about it in the right way you can get those two currents going so that they do not run into each other. You can get two entirely different sets of activities going on. You can bring about in that way the dissociation of a person's self. It is a process of setting up two sorts of communication which separate the behavior of the individual. For one individual it is this thing said and heard, and for the other individual there exists only that which he sees written. You must, of course, keep one experience out of the field of the other. Dissociations are apt to take place when an event leads to emotional upheavals. That which is separated goes on in its own way.

The unity and structure of the complete self reflects the unity and structure of the social process as a whole; and each of the elementary selves of which it is composed reflects the unity and structure of one of the various aspects of that process in which the individual is implicated. In other words, the various elementary selves which constitute, or are organized into, a complete self are the various aspects of the structure of that complete self answering to the various aspects of the structure of the social process as a whole; the structure of the complete self is thus a reflection of the complete social process. The organization and unification of a social group is identical with the organization and unification of any one of the selves arising within the social process in which that group is engaged, or which it is carrying on.[2]

The phenomenon of dissociation of personality is caused by a breaking up of the complete, unitary self into the component selves of which it is composed, and which respectively correspond to different aspects of the social process in which the person is involved, and within which his complete or unitary self has arisen; these aspects being the different social groups to which he belongs within that process. . . .

Another set of background factors in the genesis of the self is represented in the activities of play and the game.

Among primitive people, as I have said, the necessity of distinguishing the self and the organism was recognized in what we term the "double": the individual has a thing-like self that is affected by the individual as it affects other people and which is distinguished from the immediate organism in that it can leave the body and come back to it. This is the basis for the concept of the soul as a separate entity.

We find in children something that answers to this double, namely, the invisible, imaginary companions which a good many children produce in their own experience. They organize in this way the responses which they call out in other persons and call out also in themselves. Of course, this playing with an imaginary companion is only a peculiarly interesting phase of ordinary play. Play in this sense, especially the stage which precedes the organized games, is a play at something. A child plays at being a mother, at being a teacher, at being a policeman; that is, it is taking different rôles, as we say. We have something that suggests this in what we call the play of animals: a cat will play with her kittens, and dogs play with each other. Two dogs playing with each other will attack and defend, in a process which if carried through would amount to an actual fight. There is a combination of responses which checks the depth of the bite. But we do not have in such a situation the dogs taking a definite rôle in the sense that a child deliberately takes the rôle of another. This tendency on the part of the children is what we are working with in the kindergarten where the rôles which the children assume are made the basis for training. When a child does assume a rôle he has in himself the stimuli which call out that particular response or group of responses. He may, of course, run away when he is chased, as the dog does, or he may turn around and strike back just as the dog does in his play. But that is not the same as playing at something. Children get together to "play Indian." This means that the child has a certain set of stimuli which call out in itself the responses that they would call out in others, and which answer to an Indian. In the play period the child utilizes his own responses to these stimuli which he makes use of in building a self. The response which he has a tendency to make to these stimuli organizes them. He plays that he is, for instance, offering himself something, and he buys it; he gives a letter to himself and takes it away; he addresses himself as a parent, as a teacher; he arrests himself as a policeman. He has a set of stimuli which call out in himself the sort of responses they call out in others. He takes this group of responses and organizes them into a certain whole. Such is the simplest form of being another to one's self. It involves a temporal situation. The child says something in one character and responds in another character, and then his responding in another character is a stimulus to himself in the first character, and so the conversation goes on. A certain organized structure arises in him and in his other which replies to it, and these carry on the conversation of gestures between themselves.

If we contrast play with the situation in an organized game, we note the essential difference that the child who plays in a game must be ready to take the attitude of everyone else involved in that game, and that these different rôles must have a definite relationship to each other. Taking a very simple game such as hide-and-seek, everyone with the exception of the one who is hiding is a person who is hunting. A child does not require more than the person who is hunted and the one who is hunting. If a child is playing in the first sense he just goes on playing, but there is no basic organization gained. In that early stage he passes from one rôle to another just as a whim takes him. But in a game where a number of individuals are involved, then the child taking one rôle must be ready to take the rôle of everyone else. If he gets in a ball nine he must have the responses of each position involved in his own position. He must know what everyone else is going to do in order to carry out his own play. He has to take all of these rôles. They do not all have to be present in consciousness at the same time, but at some moments he has to have three or four individuals present in his own attitude, such as the one who is going to throw the ball, the one who is going to catch it, and so on. These responses must be, in some degree, present in his own make-up. In the game, then, there is a set of responses of such others so organized that the attitude of one calls out the appropriate attitudes of the other.

This organization is put in the form of the rules of the game. Children take a great interest in rules. They make rules on the spot in order to help themselves out of difficulties. Part of the enjoyment of the game is to get these rules. Now, the rules are the set of responses which a particular attitude calls out. You can demand a certain response in others if you take a certain attitude. These responses are all in yourself as well. There you get an organized set of such responses as that to which I have referred, which is something more elaborate than the rôles found in play. Here there is just a set of responses that follow on each other indefinitely. At such a stage we speak of a child as not yet having a fully developed self. The child responds in a fairly intelligent fashion to the immediate stimuli that comes to him, but they are not organized. He does not organize his life as we would like to have him do, namely, as a whole. There is just a set of responses of the type of play. The child reacts to a certain stimulus, and the reaction is in himself that is called out in others, but he is not a whole self. In his game he has to have an organization of these rôles; otherwise he cannot play the game. The game represents the passage in the life of the child from taking the rôle of others in play to the oranized part that is essential to self-consciousness in the full sense of the term.

We were speaking of the social conditions under which the self arises as an object. In addition to language we found two illustrations, one in play and the other in the game, and I wish to summarize and expand my account on these points. I have spoken of these from the point of view of children. We can, of course, refer also to the attitudes of more primitive people out of which our civilization has arisen. . . .

The fundamental difference between the game and play is that in the latter the child must have the attitude of all the others involved in that game. The attitudes of the other players which the participant assumes organize into a sort of unit, and it is that organization which controls the response of the individual. The illustration used was of a person playing baseball. Each one of his own acts is determined by his assumption of the action of the others who are playing the game. What he does is controlled by his being everyone else on that team, at least in so far as those attitudes affect his own particular response. We get then an "other" which is an organization of the attitudes of those involved in the same process.

The organized community or social group which gives to the individual his unity of self may be called "the generalized other." The attitude of the generalized other is the attitude of the whole community.[3] Thus, for example, in the case of such a social group as a ball team, the team is the generalized other in so far as it enters – as an organized process or social activity – into the experience of any one of the individual members of it.

If the given human individual is to develop a self in the fullest sense, it is not sufficient for him merely to take the attitudes of other human individuals toward himself and toward one another within the human social process, and to bring that social process as a whole into his individual experience merely in these terms: he must also, in the same way that he takes the attitudes of other individuals toward himself and toward one another, take their attitudes toward the various phases or aspects of the common social activity or set of social undertakings in which, as members of an organized society or social group, they are all engaged; and he must then, by generalizing these individual attitudes of that organized society or social group itself, as a whole, act toward different social projects which at any given time it is carrying out, or toward the various larger phases of the general social process which constitutes its life and of which these projects are specific manifestations. This getting of the broad activities of any given social whole or organized society as such within the experiential field of any one of the individuals involved or included in that whole is, in other words, the essential basis and prerequisite of the fullest development of that individual's self: only in so far as he takes the attitudes of the organized social group to which he belongs toward the organized, co-operative social activity or set of such activities in which that group as such is engaged, does he develop a complete self or possess the sort of complete self he has developed. And on the other hand, the complex co-operative processes and activities and institutional functionings of organized human society are also possible only in so far as every individual involved in them or belonging to that society can take the general attitudes of all other such individuals with reference to these processes and activities and institutional functionings, and to the organized social whole of experiential relations and interactions thereby constituted – and can direct his own behavior accordingly.

It is in the form of the generalized other that the social process influences the behavior of the individuals involved in it and carrying it on, i.e., that the community exercises control over the conduct of its individual members; for it is in this form that the social process or community enters as a determining factor into the individual's thinking. In abstract thought the individual takes the attitude of the generalized other toward himself, without reference to its expression in any particular other individuals; and in concrete thought he takes that attitude in so far as it is expressed in the attitudes toward his behavior of those other individuals with whom he is involved in the given social situation or act. But only by taking the attitude of the generalized other toward himself, in one or another of these ways, can he think at all; for only thus can thinking – or the internalized conversation of gestures which constitutes thinking – occur. And only through the taking by individuals of the attitude or attitudes of the generalized other toward themselves is the existence of a universe of discourse, as that system of common or social meanings which thinking presupposes at its context, rendered possible.

The self-conscious human individual, then, takes or assumes the organized social attitudes of the given social group or community (or of some one section thereof) to which he belongs, toward the social problems of various kinds which confront that group or community at any given time, and which arise in connection with the correspondingly different social projects or organized co-operative enterprises in which that group or community as such is engaged; and as an individual participant in these social projects or co-operative enterprises, he governs his own conduct accordingly. In politics, for example, the individual identifies himself with an entire political party and takes the organized attitudes of that entire party toward the rest of the given social community and toward the problems which confront the party within the given social situation; and he consequently reacts or responds in terms of the organized attitudes of the party as a whole. He thus enters into a special set of social relations with all the other individuals who belong to that political party; and in the same way he enters into various other special sets of social relations, with various other classes of individuals respectively, the individuals of each of these classes being the other members of some one of the particular organized subgroups (determined in socially functional terms) of which he himself is a member within the entire given society or social community. In the most highly developed, organized, and complicated human social communities – those evolved by civilized man – these various socially functional classes or subgroups of individuals to which any given individual belongs (and with the other individual members of which he thus enters into a special set of social relations) are of two kinds. Some of them are concrete social classes or subgroups, such as political parties, clubs, corporations, which are all actually functional social units, in terms of which their individual members are directly related to one another. The others are abstract social classes or subgroups, such as the class of debtors and the class of creditors, in terms of which their individual members are related to one another only more or less indirectly, and which only more or less indirectly function as social units, but which afford or represent unlimited possibilities for the widening and ramifying and enriching of the social relations among all the individual members of the given society as an organized and unified whole. The given individual's membership in several of these abstract social classes or subgroups makes posssible his entrance into definite social relations (however indirect) with an almost infinite number of other individuals who also belong to or are included within one or another of these abstract social classes or subgroups cutting across functional lines of demarcation which divide different human social communities from one another, and including individual members from several (in some cases from all) such communities. Of these abstract social classes or subgroups of human individuals the one which is most inclusive and extensive is, of course, the one defined by the logical universe of discourse (or system of universally significant symbols) determined by the participation and communicative interaction of individuals; for of all such classes or subgroups, it is the one which claims the largest number of individual members, and which enables the largest conceivable number of human individuals to enter into some sort of social relation, however indirect or abstract it may be, with one another – a relation arising from the universal functioning of gestures as significant symbols in the general human social process of communication.

I have pointed out, then, that there are two general stages in the full development of the self. At the first of these stages, the individual's self is constituted simply by an organization of the particular attitudes of other individuals toward himself and toward one another in the specific social acts in which he participates with them. But at the second stage in the full development of the individual's self that self is constituted not only by an organization of these particular individual attitudes, but also by an organization of the social attitudes of the generalized other or the social group as a whole to which he belongs. These social or group attitudes are brought within the individual's field of direct experience, and are included as elements in the structure or constitution of his self, in the same way that the attitudes of particular other individuals are; and the individual arrives at them, or succeeds in taking them, by means of further organizing, and then generalizing, the attitudes of particular other individuals in terms of their organized social bearings and implications. So the self reaches its full development by organizing these individual attitudes of others into the organized social or group attitudes, and by thus becoming an individual reflection of the general systematic pattern of social or group behavior in which it and the others are all involved – a pattern which enters as a whole into the individual's experience in terms of these organized group attitudes which, through the mechanism of his central nervous system, he takes toward himself, just as he takes the individual attitudes of others. . . .

I have so far emphasized what I have called the structures upon which the self is constructed, the framework of the self, as it were. Of course we are not only what is common to all: each one of the selves is different from everyone else; but there has to be such a common structure as I have sketched in order that we may be members of a community at all. We cannot be ourselves unless we are also members in whom there is a community of attitudes which control the attitudes of all. We cannot have rights unless we have common attitudes. That which we have acquired as self-conscious persons makes us such members of society and gives us selves. Selves can only exist in definite relationships to other selves. No hard-and-fast line can be drawn between our own selves and the selves of others, since our own selves exist and enter as such into our experience only in so far as the selves of others exist and enter as such into our experience also. The individual possesses a self only in relation to the selves of the other members of his social group; and the structure of his self expresses or reflects the general behavior pattern of this social group to which he belongs, just as does the structure of the self of every other individual belonging to this social group. . . .

The "I" and the "Me"

We have discussed at length the social foundations of the self, and hinted that the self does not consist simply in the bare organization of social attitudes. We may now explicitly raise the question as to the nature of the "I" which is aware of the social "me." I do not mean to raise the metaphysical question of how a person can be both "I" and "me," but to ask for the significance of this distinction from the point of view of conduct itself. Where in conduct does the "I" come in as over against the "me"? If one determines what his position is in society and feels himself as having a certain function and privilege, these are all defined with reference to an "I," but the "I" is not a "me" and cannot become a "me." We may have a better self and a worse self, but that again is not the "I" as over against the "me," because they are both selves. We approve of one and disapprove of the other, but when we bring up one or the other they are there for such approval as "me's." The "I" does not get into the limelight; we talk to ourselves, but do not see ourselves. The "I" reacts to the self which arises through the taking of the attitudes of others. Through taking those attitudes we have introduced the "me" and we react to it as an "I."

The simplest way of handling the problem would be in terms of memory. I talk to myself, and I remember what I said and perhaps the emotional content that went with it. The "I" of this moment is present in the "me"of the next moment. There again I cannot turn around quick enough to catch myself. I become a "me" in so far as I remember what I said. The "I" can be given, however, this functional relationship. It is because of the "I" that we say that we are never fully aware of what we are, that we surprise ourselves by our own action. It is as we act that we are aware of ourselves. It is in memory that the "I" is constantly present in experience. We can go back directly a few moments in our experience, and then we are dependent upon memory images for the rest. So that the "I" in the memory is there as the spokesman of the self of the second, or minute, or day ago. As given, it is a "me," but it is a "me" which was the "I" at the earlier time. If you ask, then, where directly in your own experience the "I" comes in, the answer is that it comes in as a historical figure. It is what you were a second ago that is the "I" of the "me." It is another "me" that has to take that rôle. You cannot get the immediate response of the "I" in the process. The "I" is in a certain sense that with which we do identify ourselves. The getting of it into experience constitutes one of the problems of most of our conscious experience; it is not directly given in experience.

The "I" is the repsonse of the organism to the attitudes of the others, the "me" is the organized set of attitudes of others which one himself assumes. The attitudes of the others constitute the organized "me," and then one reacts toward that as an "I." I now wish to examine these concepts in greater detail.

There is neither "I" nor "me" in the conversation of gestures; the whole act is not yet carried out, but the preparation takes place in this field of gesture. Now, in so far as the individual arouses in himself the attitudes of the others, there arises an organized group of responses. And it is due to the individual's ability to take the attitudes of these others in so far as they can be organized that he gets self-consciousness. The taking of all of those organized sets of attitudes gives him his "me"; that is the self he is aware of. He can throw the ball to some other member because of the demand made upon him from other members of the team. That is the self that immediately exists for him in his consciousness. He has their attitudes, knows what they want and what the consequence of any act of his will be, and he has assumed responsibility for the situation. Now, it is the presence of those organized sets of attitudes that constitutes that "me" to which he as an "I" is responding. But what that the response will be he does not know and nobody else knows. Perhaps he will make a brilliant play or an error. The response to that situation as it appears in his immediate experience is uncertain, and it is that which constitutes the "I."

The "I" is his action over against that social situation within his own conduct, and it gets into his experience only after he has carried out the act. Then he is aware of it. He had to do such a thing and he did it. He fulfils his duty and he may look with pride at the throw which he made. The "me" arises to do that duty – that is the way in which it arises in his experience. He had in him all the attitudes of others, calling for a certain response; that was the "me" of that situation, and his response is the "I."

I want to call attention particularly to the fact that this response of the "I" is something that is more or less uncertain. The attitudes of others which one assumes as affecting his own conduct constitute the "me," and that is something that is there, but the response to it is as yet not given. When one sits down to think anything out, he has certain data that are there. Suppose that it is a social situation which he has to straighten out. He sees himself from the point of view one individual or another in the group. These individuals, related all together, give him a certain self. Well, what is he going to do? He does not know and nobody else knows. He can get the situation into his experience because he can assume the attitudes of the various individuals involved in it. He knows how they feel about it by the assumption of their attitudes. He says, in effect, "I have done certain things that seem to commit me to a certain course of conduct." Perhaps if he does so act it will place him in a false position with another group. The "I" as a response to this situation, in contrast to the "me" which is involved in the attitudes which he takes, is uncertain. And when the response takes place, then it appears in the field of experience largely as a memory image. . . .

The "I" then, in this relation of the "I" and the "me," is something that is, so to speak, responding to a social situation which is within the experience of the individual. It is the answer which the individual makes to the attitude which others take toward him when he assumes an attitude toward them. Now, the attitudes he is taking toward them are present in his own experience, but his response to them will contain a novel element. The "I" gives the sense of freedom, of initiative. The situation is there for us to act in a self-conscious fashion. We are aware of ourselves, and of what the situation is, but exactly how we will act never gets into experience until after the action takes place.

Such is the basis for the fact that the "I" does not appear in the same sense in experience as does the "me." The "me" represents a definite organization of the community there in our own attitudes, and calling for a response, but the response that takes place is something that just happens. There is no certainty in regard to it. There is a moral necessity but no mechanical necessity for the act. When it does take place then we find what has been done. The above account gives us, I think, the relative position of the "I" and "me" in the situation, and the grounds for the separation of the two in behavior. The two are separated in the process but they belong together in the sense of being parts of a whole. They are separated and yet they belong together. The separation of the "I" and the "me" is not fictitious. They are not identical, for, as I have said, the "I" is something that is never entirely calculable. The "me" does call for certain sort of an "I" in so far as we meet the obligations that are given in conduct itself, but the "I" is always something different from what the situation itself calls for. So there is always that distinction, if you like, between the "I" and the "me." The "I" both calls out the "me" and responds to it. Taken together they constitute a personality as it appears in social experience. The self is essentially a social process going on with these two distinguishable phases. If it did not have these two phases there could not be conscious responsibility, and there would be nothing novel in experience.

Notes

1   Man's behavior is such in his social group that he is able to become an object to himself, a fact which constitutes him a more advanced product of evolutionary development than are the lower animals. Fundamentally it is this social fact – and not his alleged possession of a soul or mind with which he, as an individual, has been mysteriously and supernaturally endowed, and with which the lower animals have not been endowed – that differentiates him from them.
2   The unity of the mind is not identical with the unity of the self. The unity of the self is constituted by the unity of the entire relational pattern of social behavior and experience in which the individual is implicated, and which is reflected in the structure of the self; but many of the aspects or features of this entire pattern do not enter into consciousness, so that the unity of the mind is in a sense an abstraction from the more inclusive unity of the self.
3   It is possible for inanimate objects, no less than for other human organisms, to form parts of the generalized and organized – the completely socialized – other for any given human individual, in so far as he responds to such objects socially or in a social fashion (by means of the mechanism of thought, the internalized conversation of gestures).

B: GEORG SIMMEL

20 The Stranger

Georg Simmel

If wandering, considered as a state of detachment from every given point in space, is the conceptual opposite of attachment to any point, then the sociological form of "the stranger" presents the synthesis, as it were, of both of these properties. (This is another indication that spatial relations not only are determining conditions of relationships among men, but are also symbolic of those relationships.) The stranger will thus not be considered here in the usual sense of the term, as the wanderer who comes today and goes tomorrow, but rather as the man who comes today and stays tomorrow – the potential wanderer, so to speak, who, although he has gone no further, has not quite got over the freedom of coming and going. He is fixed within a certain spatial circle – or within a group whose boundaries are analogous to spatial boundaries – but his position within it is fundamentally affected by the fact that he does not belong in it initially and that he brings qualities into it that are not, and cannot be, indigenous to it.

In the case of the stranger, the union of closeness and remoteness involved in every human relationship is patterned in a way that may be succinctly formulated as follows: the distance within this relation indicates that one who is close by is remote, but his strangeness indicates that one who is remote is near. The state of being a stranger is of course a completely positive relation; it is a specific form of interaction. The inhabitants of Sirius are not exactly strangers to us, at least not in the sociological sense of the word as we are considering it. In that sense they do not exist for us at all; they are beyond being far and near. The stranger is an element of the group itself, not unlike the poor and sundry "inner enemies" – an element whose membership within the group involves both being outside it and confronting it.

The following statements about the stranger are intended to suggest how factors of repulsion and distance work to create a form of being together, a form of union based on interaction.

In the whole history of economic activity the stranger makes his appearance everywhere as a trader, and the trader makes his as a stranger. As long as production for one's own needs is the general rule, or products are exchanged within a relatively small circle, there is no need for a middleman within the group. A trader is required only for goods produced outside the group. Unless there are people who wander out into foreign lands to buy these necessities, in which case they are themselves "strange" merchants in this other region, the trader *must* be a stranger; there is no opportunity for anyone else to make a living at it.

This position of the stranger stands out more sharply if, instead of leaving the place of his activity, he settles down there. In innumerable cases even this is possible only if he can live by trade as a middleman. Any closed economic group where land and handicrafts have been apportioned in a way that satisfies local demands will still support a livelihood for the trader. For trade alone makes possible unlimited combinations, and through it intelligence is constantly extended and applied in new areas, something that is much harder for the primary producer with his more limited mobility and his dependence on a circle of customers that can be expanded only very slowly. Trade can always absorb more men than can primary production. It is therefore the most suitable activity for the stranger, who intrudes as a supernumerary, so to speak, into a group in which all the economic positions are already occupied. The classic example of this is the history of European Jews. The stranger is by his very nature no owner of land – land not only in the physical sense but also metaphorically as a vital substance which is fixed, if not in space, then at least in an ideal position within the social environment.

Although in the sphere of intimate personal relations the stranger may be attractive and meaningful in many ways, so long as he is regarded as a stranger he is no "landowner" in the eyes of the other. Restriction to intermediary trade and often (as though sublimated from it) to pure finance gives the stranger the specific character of *mobility*. The appearance of this mobility within a bounded group occasions that synthesis of nearness and remoteness which constitutes the formal position of the stranger. The purely mobile person comes incidentally into contact with *every* single element but is not bound up organically, through established ties of kinship, locality, or occupation, with any single one.

Another expression of this constellation is to be found in the objectivity of the stranger. Because he is not bound by roots to the particular constituents and partisan dispositions of the group, he confronts all of these with a distinctly "objective" attitude, an attitude that does not signify mere detachment and nonparticipation, but is a distinct structure composed of remoteness and nearness, indifference and involvement. I refer to my analysis of the dominating positions gained by aliens, in the discussion of superordination and subordination, typified by the practice in certain Italian cities of recruiting their judges from outside, because no native was free from entanglement in family interests and factionalism.

Connected with the characteristic of objectivity is a phenomenon that is found chiefly, though not exclusively, in the stranger who moves on. This is that he often receives the most surprising revelations and confidences, at times reminiscent of a confessional, about matters which are kept carefully hidden from everybody with whom one is close. Objectivity is by no means nonparticipation, a condition that is altogether outside the distinction between subjective and objective orientations. It is rather a positive and definite kind of participation, in the same way that the objectivity of a theoretical observation clearly does not mean that the mind is a passive tabula rasa on which things inscribe their qualities, but rather signifies the full activity of a mind working according to its own laws, under conditions that exclude accidental distortions and emphases whose individual and subjective differences would produce quite different pictures of the same object.

Objectivity can also be defined as freedom. The objective man is not bound by ties which could prejudice his perception, his understanding, and his assessment of data. This freedom, which permits the starnger to experience and treat even his close relationships as though from a bird's-eye view, contains many dangerous possibilities. From earliest times, in uprisings of all sorts the attacked party has claimed that there has been incitement from the outside, by foreign emissaries and agitators. Insofar as this has happened, it represents an exaggeration of the specific role of the stranger: he is the freer man, practically and theoretically; he examines conditions with less prejudice; he assesses them against standards that are more general and more objective; and his actions are not confined to custom, piety, or precedent.[1]

Finally, the proportion of nearness and remoteness which gives the stranger the character of objectivity also finds practical expression in the more *abstract* nature of the relation to him. That is, with the stranger one has only certain *more general* qualities in common, whereas the relation with organically connected persons is based on the similarity of just those specific traits which differentiate them from the merely universal. In fact, all personal relations whatsoever can be analyzed in terms of this scheme. They are not determined only by the existence of certain common characteristics which the individuals share in addition to their individual differences, which either influence the relationship or remain outside of it. Rather, the kind of effect which that commonality has on the relation essentially depends on whether it exists only among the participants themselves, and thus, although general within the relation, is specific and incomparable with respect to all those on the outside, or whether the participants feel that what they have in common is so only because it is common to a group, a type, or mankind in general. In the latter case, the effect of the common features becomes attenuated in proportion to the size of the group bearing the same characteristics. The commonality provides a basis for unifying the members, to be sure; but it does not specifically direct *these* particular persons to one another. A similarity so widely shared could just as easily unite each person with every possible other. This, too, is evidently a way in which a relationship includes both nearness and remoteness simultaneously. To the extent to which the similarities assume a universal nature, the warmth of the connection based on them will acquire an element of coolness, a sense of the contingent nature of precisely *this* relation – the connecting forces have lost their specific, centripetal character.

In relation to the stranger, it seems to me, this constellation assumes an extraordinary preponderance in principle over the individual elements peculiar to the relation in question. The stranger is close to us insofar as we feel between him and ourselves similarities of nationality or social position, of occupation or of general human nature. He is far from us insofar as these similarities extend beyond him and us, and connect us only because they connect a great many people.

A trace of strangeness in this sense easily enters even the most intimate relationships. In the stage of first passion, erotic relations strongly reject any thought of generalization. A love such as this has never existed before; there is nothing to compare either with the person one loves or with our feelings for that person. An estrangement is wont to set in (whether as cause or effect is hard to decide) at the moment when this feeling of uniqueness disappears from the relationship. A skepticism regarding the intrinsic value of the relationship and its value for us adheres to the very thought that in this relation, after all, one is only fulfilling a general human destiny, that one has had an experience that has occurred a thousand times before, and that, if one had not accidentally met this precise person, someone else would have acquired the same meaning for us.

Something of this feeling is probably not absent in any relation, be it ever so close, because that which is common to two is perhaps never common *only* to them but belongs to a general conception which includes much else besides, many *possibilities* of similarities. No matter how few of these possibilities are realized and how often we may forget about them, here and there, nevertheless, they crowd in like shadows between men, like a mist eluding every designation, which must congeal into solid corporeality for it to be called jealousy. Perhaps this is in many cases a more general, at least more insurmountable, strangeness than that due to differences and obscurities. It is strangeness caused by the fact that similarity, harmony, and closeness are accompanied by the feeling that they are actually not the exclusive property of this particular relation, but stem from a more general one – a relation that potentially includes us and an indeterminate number of others, and therefore prevents that relation which alone was experienced from having an inner and exclusive necessity.

On the other hand, there is a sort of "strangeness" in which this very connection on the basis of a general quality embracing the parties is precluded. The relation of the Greeks to the barbarians is a typical example; so are all the cases in which the general characteristics one takes as peculiarly and merely human are disallowed to the other. But here the expression "the stranger" no longer has any positive meaning. The relation with him is a non-relation; he is not what we have been discussing here: the stranger as a member of the group itself.

As such, the stranger is near and far *at the same time*, as in any relationship based on merely universal human similarities. Between these two factors of nearness and distance, however, a peculiar tension arises, since the consciousness of having only the absolutely general in common has exactly the effect of putting a special emphasis on that which is not common. For a stranger to the country, the city, the race, and so on, what is stressed is again nothing individual, but alien origin, a quality which he has, or could have, in common with many other strangers. For this reason strangers are not really perceived as individuals, but as strangers of a certain type. Their remoteness is no less general than their nearness.

This form appears, for example, in so special a case as the tax levied on Jews in Frankfurt and elsewhere during the Middle Ages. Whereas the tax paid by Christian citizens varied according to their wealth at any given time, for every single Jew the tax was fixed once and for all. This amount was fixed because the Jew had his social position as a *Jew*, not as the bearer of certain objective contents. With respect to taxes every other citizen was regarded as possessor of a certain amount of wealth, and his tax could follow the fluctuations of his fortune. But the Jew as taxpayer was first of all a Jew, and thus his fiscal position contained an invariable element. This appears most forcefully, of course, once the differing circumstances of individual Jews are no longer considered, limited though this consideration is by fixed assessments, and all strangers pay exactly the same head tax.

Despite his being inorganically appended to it, the stranger is still an organic member of the group. Its unified life includes the specific conditioning of this element. Only we do not know how to designate the characteristic unity of this position otherwise than by saying that it is put together of certain amounts of nearness and of remoteness. Although both these qualities are found to some extent in all relationships, a special proportion and reciprocal tension between them produce the specific form of the relation to the "stranger."

Note

1 Where the attacked parties make such an assertion falsely, they do so because those in higher positions tend to exculpate inferiors who previously have been in a close, solidary relationship with them. By introducing the fiction that the rebels were not really guilty, but only instigated, so they did not actually start the rebellion, they exonerate themselves by denying that there were any real grounds for the uprising.

21 Group Expansion and the Development of Individuality

Georg Simmel

Group Expansion and the Transformation of Social Bonds

Individuation of personality, on the one hand, and the influences, interests, and relationships that attach the personality to its social circle, on the other hand, show a pattern of interdependent development that appears in the most diverse historical and institutional setting as a typical form. *Individuality in being and action generally increases to the degree that the social circle encompassing the individual expands.*

Of the diverse modalities in which group expansion occurs and gives rise to the correlation just underscored, I will first mention the one that occurs when circles that are isolated from one another become approximately alike. Imagine that there are two social groups, M and N, that are sharply distinguished from one another both in characteristic attributes and in opposing systems of shared belief; and imagine further that each of these groups is composed of homogeneous and tightly cohesive elements. This being so, quantitative expansion will produce an increase in social differentation. What were once minimal differences in inner predilection, external resources, and actualizations of these will be accentuated by the necessity of competing for a livelihood with more and more people using more and more specialized means. Competition will develop the speciality of the individual in direct ratio to the number of participants.

Different as its points of origin in M and N may have been, this process will inevitably produce a gradually increasing likeness between the two groups. After all, the number of fundamental human formations upon which a group can build is relatively limited, and it can only slowly be increased. The more of these formations that are present in a group – that is, the greater the dissimilarity of constituent elements in M and N respectively – the greater is the likelihood that an ever increasing number of structures will develop in one group that have equivalents in the other. Deviation in all directions from what had thus far been the prevailing norm in each group complex must necessarily result in a likening – at first a qualitative or ideal equivalence – between parts of the two complexes.

This likening will come about if for no other reason than because even within very diverse groups, the forms of social differentiation are identical or approximately the same. What I have in mind here are such forms as the relational pattern of simple competition, the alliance of many who are weak against one who is strong, the pleonexy of lone individuals, the progression in which relationships among individuals, once initiated, become stabilized, the attraction or repulsion that arises between individuals by virtue of their qualitative differentiation, and so on.

This process, quite apart from all bonds based on shared substantive interests, will often lead to actual relations between the elements of any two – or of many – groups that have been made alike in this way. One observes this, for example, in the international sympathy that aristocrats hold for one another. To an astonishing degree, these feelings of solidarity are independent of the specific character of the individuals concerned, a matter that is otherwise decisive in determining personal attraction and repulsion. In the same way, by specialization within groups that were originally independent of one another, solidarities also develop at the other end of the social scale, as in the internationalism of social democrats and in the sentiments underlying the earlier journeymen's unions.

After the process of social differentiation has led to a separation between high and low, the mere formal fact of occupying a particular social position creates among the similarly characterized members of the most diverse groups a sense of solidarity and, frequently, actual relationships. Accompanying such a differentiation of social groups, there arise a need and an inclination to reach out beyond the original spatial, economic, and mental boundaries of the group and, in connection with the increase in individualization and concomitant mutual repulsion of group elements, to supplement the original centripetal forces of the lone group with a centrifugal tendency that forms bridges with other groups.

For example, the guilds were once ruled by the spirit of strict equality. On the one hand, the individual's production was limited to the level of quality and quantity that all other guild members attained; on the other hand, the guild's norms of sale and exchange sought to protect the individual from being outdone by other members. In the long run, it was impossible to maintain this condition of undifferentiation. The master who became rich under whatever circumstances was not inclined to submit further to regulations stipulating that he might sell only his own products, might maintain no more than one salesplace, might have no more than a very limited number of apprentices, and so forth.

Once the affluent masters had won the right – partly after intense struggle – to ignore these restrictions, a certain duality began to appear. The once homogeneous mass of guild members became differentiated with increasing decisiveness into rich and poor, capitalists and laborers. Once the principle of equality had been broken through to the extent that one member could have another labor for him and that he could select his sales market on the basis of his own personal capacity and energy, his knowledge of the market, and his assessment of its prospects, it was inevitable that just these personal attributes, once given the opportunity to unfold, would continue to develop, leading to an ever increasing specialization and individualization within the fellowship of the guild and, finally, to the dissolution of that fellowship. On the other hand, however, structural change made possible an extension far beyond the confines of previous sales regions. Formerly, producer and merchant had been united in *one* person; once they had been differentiated from one another, the merchant won an incomparable freedom of movement, and previously unattainable commercial relations were established.

Individual freedom and the expansion of commercial enterprise are interdependent. Thus, in the case of the coexistence of guild restrictions and large, factory-style workshops around the beginning of the nineteenth century in Germany, it always proved necessary to let the factories have freedoms of production and trade that could or would have been collectivistically restricted in the circles of smaller and more modest enterprises. In this manner, the development away from narrow, homogeneous guild circles prepared their dissolution along two lines: one led to individualizing differentiation, the other to expansion involving ties across great distances. For this reason, the differentiation of English guild members into merchants and actual workers was exhibited most strikingly by those, such as tanners and textile manufacturers, who produced articles of foreign demand.

A fissioning is inherent in this correlation with group expansion that involves not only the content of labor but also its sociological dimension. Even given a certain technical division of labor, as long as the small, primitive group is self-sufficient, a pervasive equality exists in that each member of the group works for the group itself; every achievement is sociologically centripetal. However, as soon as the boundaries of the group are ruptured and it enters into trade in special products with another group, internal differentiation develops between those who produce for export and those who produce for domestic consumption – two wholly opposed inner modes of being.

The history of the emancipation of the serfs, as for example in Prussia, demonstrates a process that is similar in this regard. As he existed in Prussia until about 1810, the enserfed peasant found himself in a peculiar intermediate position regarding both his lord and his land. The land belonged to the lord, to be sure, but not in such a way that the peasant himself could have no right at all to it. Likewise, the peasant was of course bound to work the lord's fields for him, but close by he also worked the land that had been allotted to him for his own benefit. With the abolition of serfdom, a certain part of the land that the peasant had formerly owned in a limited sense was converted into true, free property. The lord was left to seek wage laborers, whom he recruited for the most part from among the owners of smaller parcels that he had purchased. Thus, whereas the peasant had had within himself the partial attributes of owner and of laborer for another's benefit, a sharp differentiation of these attributes followed the abolition of serfdom: one part became pure owner, the other part pure laborer.

It is obvious how free movement of the person and his involvement in spatially more distant relations emerged from this situation. Not only the eradication of the external bond to the soil was involved, but also the very condition of the laborer as one who receives work first in one place, then in another. On the other hand, alienable property was involved, since it made possible sale and hence commercial relations, resettlement, and so on.

So it is that the observation made at the beginning of this section has its justification: differentiation and individualization loosen the bond of the individual with those who are most near in order to weave in its place a new one – both real and ideal – with those who are more distant. . . .

An Englishman who had lived for many years in India once told me that it was impossible for a European to get at all close to the natives where castes existed; but that where caste divisions did not prevail this was very easy. The insularity of the caste – maintained by an internal uniformity no less strict than its exclusion of outsiders – seems to inhibit the development of what one has to call a more universal humanity, which is what makes relationships between racial aliens possible.

Consistent with the above, the broad uneducated masses of one civilized people are more homogeneous internally, and they are separated from the masses of a second people by more distinct characteristics, than is the case either within or between the educated strata of these populations. This same pattern of synthesis and antithesis repeats itself intraculturally. The older German corporate system set out to unite guild *members* tightly in order to keep guild *memberships* strictly separated. The modern voluntary association, on the other hand, restricts its members and imposes uniformity upon them only so far as the strictly circumscribed organizational goal requires. In all other matters, it allows members complete freedom and tolerates every individuality and heterogeneity of their full personalities. But for all that, the modern association gravitates toward an all-embracing union of organizations by virtue of interpenetrating division of labor, leveling that results from equal justice and the cash economy, and solidarity of interests in the national economy.

These examples hint at a relation that will be found everywhere in the course of this inquiry. The nonindividuation of elements in the narrower circle and their differentiation in the wider one are phenomena that are found, synchronically, among coexistent groups and group elements, just as they appear, diachronically, in the sequence of stages through which a single group develops.

The Relation between Personal and Collective Individuality

This basic idea can be generalized to the proposition that in each person, other things being equal, there is, as it were, an unalterable ratio between individual and social factors that changes only its form. The narrower the circle to which we commit ourselves, the less freedom of individuality we possess; however, this narrower circle is itself something individual, and it cuts itself off sharply from all other circles precisely because it is small. Correspondingly, if the circle in which we are active and in which our interests hold sway enlarges, there is more room in it for the development of our individuality; but *as parts of this whole*, we have less uniqueness: the larger whole is less individual as a social group. Thus, the leveling of individual differences corresponds not only to the relative smallness and narrowness of the collectivity, but also – or above all – to its own individualistic coloring.

Expressed in a very terse schema, the elements of a distinctive social circle are undifferentiated, and the elements of a circle that is not distinctive are differentiated. Of course this is not a sociological "natural law," but rather what might be called a phenomenological formula that seeks to conceptualize the regular outcome of regularly coexisting sequences of events. It designates no cause of phenomena; instead, it designates a single phenomenon whose underlying, general structure is represented in each individual case as the effect of very diverse causes, but causes whose combined effect is always to release identical formative energies.

Illustrations of the Formula in Religious and Political Settings

The first aspect of this relationship – lack of differentiation among the members of a differentiated group – is exhibited by the social order of the Quakers, in a form that is based on the deepest motives of its members. As a whole, as a religious principle of the most extreme individualism and subjectivism, Quakerism binds members of the congregation to a style of life and a mode of being that are highly uniform and democratic, seeking to exclude, as far as possible, all individual differences. And in turn, Quakerism lacks all understanding for the higher political union and its goals so that the individuality of the smaller group not only precludes the individuality of the person, but also his commitment to the large group. The specific manifestation of this is as follows: in the affairs of the congregation, in the assemblies of worship, each person may act as preacher and may say whatever he likes whenever he likes. On the other hand, the congregation watches over personal affairs such as marriage, and these cannot occur without the permission of a committee that is appointed to investigate each case. Thus, the Quakers are individual only in collective matters, and in individual matters, they are socially regulated.

Both aspects of the formula are exemplified in the differences between the political structures in the Northern and Southern states in the United States, most clearly so during the period before the Civil War. The New England states in North America had a pronounced local orientation from the very beginning. They developed townships in which the individual was tightly bound by his obligations to the whole, and although this whole was relatively small, it was also self-sufficient. The Southern states, by contrast, were populated to a greater extent by lone adventurers who were not particularly predisposed to local self-government. The South very early developed extensive counties as units of administration. Indeed, for the Southerner, the state as a whole is the site of true political significance, whereas in New England, the state is more a combination of towns. The more abstract, less colorful general political structure corresponds to the more independent – to the point of anarchistic inclinations – Southern personalities that were included in it, whereas the more strictly regulated Northern personalities were inclined toward narrower municipal structures that each, as wholes, possessed strongly individual coloring and autonomous characters.

The Basic Relation as a Dualistic Drive

With all the above qualifications in mind, one could speak of a particular quantum of the tendency toward individualization and of the tendency toward nondifferentiation. This quantum is determined by personal, historical, and social circumstances; and it remains constant, whether it applies to purely psychological configurations or to the social community to which the personality belongs.

We lead, as it were, a doubled, or if one will, a halved existence. We live as an individual within a social circle, with tangible separation from its other members, but also as a member of this circle, with separation from everything that does not belong to it. If now there is a need within us both for individuation and for its opposite, then this need can be realized on either side of our existence. The differentiation drive receives satisfaction from the contrast of one's particular personality with one's fellow members, but this plus corresponds to a minus in the satisfaction that the same person, as a purely social being, derives from oneness with his fellows. That is to say: intensified individualization within the group is accompanied by decreased individualization of the group itself, and vice versa, whenever a certain portion of the drive is satiated.

A Frenchman has made the following observation about the mania for clubs in Germany: "It is this that accustoms the German, on the one hand, not to count solely on the state; on the other hand, not to count solely on himself. It keeps him from locking himself up in his particular interests, and from relying on the state in all matters of general interest." Thus, in this negative mode of expression it is argued that a tendency to the most individual and one to the most general are present, but that they cannot both be satisfied in radically separated special structures; rather, the club is said to constitute an intermediate structure that satiates the dualistic drive quantum in a certain fusion.

The Differentiation Drive as a Heuristic Principle

If one uses this notion as a heuristic principle (i.e., not as designating the actual causality of phenomena, but merely as maintaining that phenomena occur *as if* they were governed by such a dual drive whose manifestations on the two sides of our existence balance one another), then what we have here is a most universal norm that is particularly salient when differences in group size are involved, but one that also applies to other arrangements. For example, in certain circles, and perhaps even in certain peoples, where extravagance, nervous enthusiasm, and moody impulsiveness predominate, we notice nonetheless a decidedly slavish preoccupation with fashion. One person perpetrates some madness, and it is aped by all the others as though they were automatons. In contrast, there are other circles whose life style is of a more sober and soldierly cut, hardly as colorful as the former, but whose members have a far stronger individuality drive, and distinguish themselves much more sharply and concisely within their uniform and simple life style than do those others in their bright and transitory way. So in one case, the totality has a very individual character, but its parts are very much alike; in the other, the totality is less colorful and less modeled on an extreme, but its parts are strikingly differentiated from one another.

Fashion, in and of itself, as a form of social life, is a preeminent case of this correlation. The adornment and accentuation that it lends to the personality is accorded to it only as the member of a class that is collectively distinguishing itself from other classes by adopting the new fashion. (As soon as a fashion has diffused into the other classes, it is abandoned and replaced with another.) The adoption of a fashion represents an internal leveling of the class and its self-exaltation above all other classes.

For the moment, however, our principal concern is with the correlation that involves the *extent* of social circles, the one that generally relates the freedom of the group to the restriction of the individual. A good example of this is the coexistence of communal restrictions and political freedom as found in the Russian governmental system during the preczarist period. Especially in the period of the Mongol wars, Russia had a large number of territorial units, principalities, cities, and village communes that were not held together by any kind of unifying political bond; and thus on the whole they enjoyed great political freedom. For all that, however, the restriction of the individual in commune society was the narrowest imaginable, so much so that there was absolutely no private ownership of land, which only the commune possessed. This narrow confinement in the circle of the commune, which deprived the individual of personal property and often of freedom of movement as well, is the counterpart of the lack of all binding relations with a wider political circle.

Bismarck once said that there was a much more narrow-minded small-town provincialism in a French city of 200,000 than in a German city of 10,000, and he explained this by the fact that Germany was composed of a large number of smaller states. Apparently the very large state allows the local community to have a certain mental self-sufficiency and insularity; and if even a relatively small community views itself as a whole, it will exhibit that cherishing of minutiae which constitutes small-town provincialism. In a smaller state, the community can view itself more as a part of the whole; it is not so much thrown back upon itself. Because the community does not have so much individuality, it can dispense with that internal, coercive leveling of individuals which, because of our psychological sensitivity to differences, must produce a heightened awareness of the smallest and most petty events and interests.

In a narrow circle, one can preserve one's individuality, as a rule, in only two ways. Either one leads the circle (it is for this reason that strong personalities sometimes like to be "number one in the village"), or one exists in it only externally, being independent of it in all essential matters. The latter alternative is possible only through great stability of character or through eccentricity – both traits that are conspicuous most often in small towns.

Stages of Social Commitment

We are surrounded by concentric circles of special interests. The more narrowly they enclose us, the smaller they must be. However, a person is never merely a collective being, just as he is never merely an individual being. For that reason we are naturally speaking here only in terms of more or less, of single aspects and determinants of human existence in which we can see the development away from an excess of one and into an excess of the other.

This development can go through stages in which memberships in both the small and the larger social circle coincide in characteristic sequences. Thus, although commitment to a narrower circle is generally less conducive to the strength of individuality as such than it is in the most general realm possible, it is still psychologically significant that in a very large cultural community, belonging to a family promotes individuation. The lone individual cannot save himself from the totality: only by surrendering a part of his absolute ego to a few others, joining himself in with them, can he preserve his sense of individuality and still avoid excessive isolation, bitterness, and idiosyncrasy. And by extending his personality and his interests around those of a set of other persons, the individual opposes himself in the broader mass, as it were, to the remaining whole. To be sure, individuality in the sense of eccentricity and every kind of abnormality is given broader scope by life without a family in a wider social circle; but for the differentiation that also benefits the greatest whole, for the sort that derives from strength, not from succumbing to one-sided drives – for this, belonging to a narrower circle within the widest is often useful, frequently, to be sure, only as preparation or transition.

The family's significance is at first political and real; then with the growth of culture, it is more and more psychological and ideal. The family as a collective individual offers its members a preliminary differentiation that at least prepares them for differentiation in the sense of absolute individuality; on the other hand, the family offers members a shelter behind which that absolute individuality can develop until it has the strength to stand up against the greatest universality. Belonging to a family in a more advanced culture, where the rights of individuality and of the widest circle developed simultaneously, represents a mixture of the characteristic significance of the narrow and of the expanded circle.

The same observation has been made with respect to the animal kingdom. The tendencies to the creation of families and to the creation of large groups are inversely related. Monogamous and even polygamous relations have something so exclusive about them, and concern for the progeny demands so much from the parents, that a more extensive socialization suffers among such animals. Hence, organized groups are relatively rare among birds, whereas among wild dogs, to name an example in which complete sexual promiscuity and mutual indifference after the act are the rule, the animals live mostly in tightly cohesive packs.

Among the mammals that have both familial and social drives, we invariably notice that during those periods in which the former predominate, that is, during the period of pairing off and mating, the latter decline significantly. The union of parents and offspring is also tighter if the number of young is smaller. I will cite only one distinctive example: within the class of fishes, those whose offspring are left entirely on their own lay countless millions of eggs, whereas among the brooding and nesting fish, where the beginnings of a familial cohesion are found, few eggs are produced.

It is in this sense that it has been argued that social relations among the animals originated not in conjugal or filial ties, but rather in sibling ties alone, since the latter allow much greater freedom to the individual than do the former; hence, they make the individual more inclined to attach itself closely to the larger circle, which certainly first proffers itself in the individual's siblings. Being confined in an animal family has thus been viewed as the greatest hindrance to becoming involved in a larger animal society.

The Sociological Duality of the Family

The family has a peculiar sociological double role. On the one hand, it is an extension of one's own personality; it is a unit through which one feels one's own blood coursing, one which arises in being closed to all other social units and in enclosing us as a part of itself. On the other hand, the family also constitutes a complex within which the individual distinguishes himself from all others and in which, in opposition to other members, he develops a selfhood and an antithesis. This double role unavoidably results in the sociological ambiguity of the family: it appears sometimes as a unitary structure that acts as an individual, thereby assuming a characteristic position in larger and in the largest circles; and sometimes it appears as an intermediate circle that intervenes between the individual and the larger circle that encloses both family and individual.

The developmental history of the family, at least as it still seems to be recognizable from a series of points, recapitulates this schema. The family appears first as the embracing circle that entirely encloses the life horizons of the individual, while it is itself largely independent and exclusive. Then it contracts into a narrower structure and thereby becomes adapted to playing the role of an individual in a social circle that has expanded considerably beyond the boundaries of the previous one. After the matriarchal family had been displaced by the rise of masculine force, at first it was much less the fact of procreation by the father that established a family as *one* than it was the domination that he exercised over a particular number of people. Under his unitary authority, he held together not only his offspring, but also his followers, those whom he had bought, those whom he had married and their entire families, and so on. From this primal patriarchal family, the more recent family of mere blood relationship differentiated itself, a family in which parents and their children constitute an autonomous household. This one was naturally far smaller and more individual in character than the embracing patriarchal family had been. That older group had been self-sufficient in all matters, in gaining a livelihood as in carrying out warlike activity; but once it had individualized itself into small families, it became possible and necessary for these to be amalgamated into a newly expanded group, the superfamilial community of the state. The Platonic Ideal State merely extended this line of development by dissolving the family altogether, setting in place of this intermediate structure only individuals, on the one hand, and the state, on the other.

Methodological Implications

Incidentally, there is a typical epistemological difficulty in sociology that finds its clearest example in the double role of the family: when instead of having simply a larger and a smaller group standing opposed to one another so that the position of the individual in them can readily be compared, one has several continuously expanding, superimposed circles, this relation can seem to shift, since a circle can be the narrower one in relation to a second, but it can be the wider one in relation to a third. Short of the largest circle around us that is still effective, all circles included therein have a double meaning: on the one hand, they function as entities with an individual character, often directly as sociological individualities; while on the other hand, depending on their makeup, they function as higher-order complexes that may also include complexes of lower order in addition to their individual members.

It is always precisely the *intermediate* structure that exhibits the pattern in question – internal cohesion, external repulsion – when contrasted with a more general higher structure and a more individual lower structure. The latter is a *relative individual* in relation to the former, regardless of whether in relation to still others it is a collective structure. Thus, wherever one seeks, as we do here, the normal correlation between three levels that are distinguished by their magnitudes – between the primarily individual element, and the narrower and the wider circle – there one will find that under different circumstances one and the same complex can play all three roles, depending on the relationships into which it enters. This hardly diminishes the theoretical value of the statement of this correlation; on the contrary, it proves that the correlation has a formal character that is open to every determinate content.

The Individuation of Collectivities

There are naturally more than enough sociological constellations in which the value of individuality and the need for it focus exclusively on the individual person, where in comparison to him, every complex of several persons emerges under all circumstances as the essentially other level. But on the other hand, it has already been demonstrated that the meaning and the motive power of individuality do not always stop at the boundaries of individual personality, that this is something more general and more formal that can affect the group as a whole and the individual as its element as soon as something is present that is more inclusive, antithetical; over against this something, the (now relatively individual) collective structure can gain its conscious particularity, its character of uniqueness or indivisibility.

Given this formulation, we can explain phenomena that would seem to disconfirm the correlation at issue here, one of which is the following from the history of the United States. The Anti-Federalist party, which first called itself the Republicans, then the Whigs, then the Democrats, defended the autonomy and the sovereignty of the states at the expense of centralization and of national authority – but always with an appeal to the principle of individual freedom, of noninterference by the totality in the affairs of the individual. On no account does this contradict the relationship of individual freedom to just the relatively *large* circle, for here the sense of individuality has permeated the *narrower* circle enclosing many individual persons, and thus the narrower circle serves here the same sociological function as the discrete individual would otherwise. . . .

Freedom and Individuality

The meanings of freedom

The relatively most individual and the relatively most extensive configurations relate to one another over the head of the intermediate one, as it were. And at this point we have arrived at the basis of a fact that figures prominently in the foregoing discussion as well as in what now follows: the larger circle encourages individual freedom, the smaller one restricts it.

As it is used here, the concept of individual freedom covers various meanings that are differentiated according to the diversity of our provinces of interest. They range, say, from freedom in choosing a spouse to freedom in economic initiative. I will cite one example each for just these two.

During periods of strict group separation by clans, families, occupational and hereditary estates, castes, and so on, the circle within which a man or woman can marry tends to be a relatively narrow one – narrow, that is, relative to advanced or liberal conditions. But so far as we can survey this state of affairs, and so far as we can judge by certain contemporary analogies, selecting a partner from among the available individuals was not at all difficult. The lesser differentiation of persons and of marital relations had its counterpart in the fact that the individual male could take almost any girl from the appropriate circle, choosing on the basis of external attractiveness, since there were no highly specific internal impulses or aloof reservations to be considered by either side.

Culture as it has matured has now displaced this earlier condition in two directions. The circle of possible marriage partners has been vastly expanded by the mixing of status groups, the elimination of religious barriers, the decline of parental authority, free mobility in both the geographic and the social sense, and so forth. But for all that, individual selection is far more stern, a fact and a right of wholly personal inclination. The conviction that out of all mankind, two and only two people are "meant" for each other has now reached a stage of development that was still unheard of by the bourgeoisie of the eighteenth century.

A more profound meaning of freedom emerges here: individual freedom is freedom that is limited by individuality. Out of the uniqueness of the individual's being, there arises a corresponding uniqueness of that which can complement and free him, a specificity of needs whose correlate is the availability of the largest possible circle of possible selections, since as one's wishes and inner drives become more individual, it becomes that much less likely that they will find satisfaction in a narrowly bounded domain. In the earlier condition, conversely, there was far less restriction by the rigidity of personalities: *from the standpoint of his own concerns*, the individual was much more free in making a choice, since instead of a compelling differentiation of choice objects, there was an approximate equivalence of all those that might come under consideration. For this reason, there was no need for the circle of choice objects to be significantly more extensive. So the relatively undeveloped condition certainly imposed a social constraint on the individual; however, this was linked to the negative freedom of nondifferentiation, to the *liberum arbitrium* that was provided by the mere identical worth of objects. In the more advanced state, on the other hand, social possibilities are much enlarged, but now they are restricted by the positive meaning of freedom in which every choice is – or at least ideally should be – the unambiguously determined expression of an unalterable kind of personality.

Now in the general, societal meaning of freedom, I would say that feudalism generated nothing but narrow circles that bound individual to individual and restricted each by his obligation to the other. For this reason, within the feudal system there was room neither for national enthusiasm or public spirit, nor for the spirit of individual enterprise and private energy. The same restrictions that prevented the emergence of conceptions of a higher social union also prevented, at the lower level, the actualization of individual freedom. For just this reason, it is especially pertinent and profound that during the feudal period, the "freeman" is defined as a man who is subject to the law of the realm; bound and unfree is the man who is party to a feudal tie, that is, whose law derives from this narrower circle to the exclusion of the wider one.

If freedom swings to extremes; if the largest group, as I indicated above, affords greater play to extreme formations and malformations of individualism, to misanthropic detachment, to baroque and moody life styles, to crass egoism – then all this is merely the consequence of the wider group's requiring less of us, of its being less concerned with us, and thus of its lesser hindering of the full development even of perverse impulses. The size of the circle has a negative influence here, and it is more a matter, so to speak, of developments outside rather than inside the group, developments in which the larger circle gives its members more opportunity to get involved than does the smaller one.

The meanings of individuality

The meaning of individuality in general can be separated into two more specific meanings. One has been emphasized in the above, namely, individuality in the sense of the freedom and the responsibility for oneself that comes from a broad and fluid social environment, whereas the smaller group is "narrower" in a dual sense: not only with regard to its extent, but also with regard to the restraints it imposes upon the individual, the control it exercises over him, the trifling radius of the prospects and the kinds of impetus it allows him. The other meaning of individuality is qualitative: it means that the single human being distinguishes himself from all others; that his being and conduct – in form, content, or both – suit him alone; and that being different has a positive meaning and value for his life.

The elaborations that the principle or ideal of individualism has undergone in the modern era differ according to the accentuation given to the first or the second of these meanings. On the whole, the eighteenth century sought individuality in the form of freedom, the lack of every kind of restraint on personal powers, regardless whether this restraint came from the estates or from the church, whether it was political or economic. But at the same time, the assumption prevailed that once men had been freed from all sociohistorical fetters, they would show themselves to be essentially equal; that "man in general," along with all the goodness and perfection of his nature, was inherent in every personality, needing only to be emancipated from those distorting and diverting bonds. That once men had freedom, they would use it to differentiate themselves; to rule or to become enslaved; to be better or worse than others; in short, to unfold the full diversity of their individual powers – this fact escaped the kind of individualism for which "freedom and equality" were two peacefully coexisting – indeed, two mutually necessary – values.

It should be obvious how this kind of individualism was involved in blowing apart every narrow and narrowing accommodation; partly, this was its historical, real effect, and at least partly, it was involved as a yearning and a demand. In the French Revolution, even the workers were forbidden to join into unions for better working conditions: such a federation would limit the freedom of individual members! So it is that the correlate of this kind of individualism is a wholly "cosmopolitan" disposition; even national integration recedes behind the idea of "mankind." The particularistic rights of status groups and of circles are replaced in principle by the rights of the individual, and these, quite significantly, are called "human rights"; that is, they are the rights that derive from belonging to the widest conceivable circle.

It was the other meaning of individuality that was developed by the nineteenth century, and its contradiction of the meaning just described was not seen on the whole by the eighteenth. This other meaning found its preeminent theoretical expression in Romanticism and its practical expression in the ascendancy of the division of labor. Here individualism means that the person assumes and should assume a position that he and no one else can fill; that this position awaits him, as it were, in the organization of the whole, and that he should search until he finds it; that the personal and social, the psychological and metaphysical meaning of human existence is realized in this immutability of being, this intensified differentiation of performance. This ideal image of individualism seems to have nothing at all to do with the earlier notion of "the generally human," with the idea of a uniform human nature that is present in everyone and that only requires freedom for its emergence. Indeed, the second meaning fundamentally contradicts the first. In the first, the value emphasis is on what men have in common; in the second, it is on what separates them. But with regard to the correlation I am seeking to verify, they coincide.

The enlargement of the circle that is associated with the first conception of individuality also promotes the emergence of the second. Although the second conception does not look to the totality of mankind; although it makes individuals mutually complementary and dependent instead of atomizing society into uniform and absolutely "free" individuals; although historically it promotes nationalism and a certain illiberalism instead of free cosmopolitanism – nevertheless, it too requires a group of relatively considerable size for its origination and survival. One need only refer to the manner in which the mere expansion of the economic circle, the increase in population, or the geographic boundlessness of competition has directly compelled a specialization of performance.

It is no different for mental differentiation, especially since this usually originates in the meeting of latent mental abilities with objectively preexisting mental products. The unmediated interaction of subjectivities or the purely inner energy of a human being rarely elicits all the mental distinctiveness that one possesses; rather, this seems to be associated with the extent of what has been called "objective mind," that is, the traditions and the experiences of one's group, set down in thousands of forms; the art and learning that are present in tangible structures; all the cultural materials that the historical group possesses as something super-subjective and yet available to everyone. The peculiarity of this generally accessible Mind that crystallizes itself in objective structures is that it provides both the material and the impetus for the development of a distinct personal mental type. It is the essence of "being cultured" that our purely personal dispositions are sometimes realized as the *form* of what is given as a content of objective culture [*Geist*], sometimes as the *content* of what is given as a form in objective culture. Only in this synthesis does our mental life attain its full idiom and personality; only thereby do its unique and wholly individual attributes become tangibly incarnated.

This, then, is the connection that links mental differentiation to the size of the circle in which objective mind originates. The circle may be a social, real one, or it may be of a more abstract, literary, historical sort: as that circle enlarges, so too do the possibilities of developing our inner lives; as its cultural offerings increase, regardless of how objective or abstract they may be, so too do the chances of developing the distinctiveness, the uniqueness, the sufficiency of existence of our inner lives and their intellectual, aesthetic, and practical productivity.

The individualism of equality is not, from the very beginning, a *contradictio in adjecto* only if one takes it to mean the freedom and self-sufficiency that are not limited by narrower social bonds. The individualism of inequality is a consequence of that freedom, given the infinite variability of human capacities, and therefore it is incompatible with equality. In the fundamental antithesis of these two forms of individualism, there is one point at which they coincide: each of them has a potential for development to the degree that quantitative expansion of the circle that encloses the individual provides the necessary room, impetus, and material. . . .

Group Expansion and Consciousness of the Ego

Beyond the significance that expansion of the circle has for the differentiation of the determinants of will, one sees its significance for the emergence of the *sensation* of a personal ego. Surely no one can fail to recognize that the style of modern life – precisely because of its mass character, its rushing diversity, its unboundable equalization of countless previously conserved idiosyncrasies – has led to unprecedented levelings of the personality form of life. But neither should one fail to recognize the countertendencies, much as these may be diverted and paralyzed in the joint effect that ultimately appears.

Life in a wider circle and interaction with it develop, in and of themselves, more consciousness of personality than arises in a narrower circle; this is so above all because it is precisely through the *alternation* of sensations, thoughts, and activities that personality documents itself. The more uniformly and unwaveringly life progresses, and the less the extremes of sensate experience depart from an average level, the less strongly does the sensation of personality arise; but the farther apart they stretch, and the more energetically they erupt, the more intensely does a human being sense himself as a personality. Just as duration can be determined only in the presence of alternation, and just as it is only the alternation of nonessential properties that throws constancy of substance into bold relief, so too the ego is apparently perceived as the one constant in all the alternation of psychological contents, especially when these contents provide a particularly rich opportunity.

Personality is *not* a single immediate state, not a single quality or a single destiny, unique as this last may be; rather it is something that we sense beyond these singularities, something grown into consciousness out of their experienced reality. This is so even if this retroactively generated personality, as it were, is only the sign, the *ratio cognoscendi* of a more deeply unitary individuality that lies at the determinative root of the diverse singularities, an individuality that we cannot become aware of directly, but only as the gradual experience of these multiple contents and variations.

As long as psychic stimulations, especially the stimulations of sensation, occur only in small number, the ego is fused with them and stays latently embedded in them; it rises above them only to the degree that, precisely via a fullness of dissimilarity, it becomes clear to our awareness that the ego itself is common to all this variation. This is just the same as when a general concept cannot be abstracted out of single phenomena if we are familiar with only one or a few of their elaborations, but only if we know very many of them; and its abstractness and purity are all the greater as dissimilarity contrasts more distinctly with the generality. Now this alternation of the contents of the ego, which is what actually first poses the ego to consciousness as the stable pole in the play of psychic phenomena, is extraordinarily more lively within a large circle than it is for life in a narrower group. Stimulations of sensation, which are especially important for subjective ego consciousness, occur most where a highly differentiated individual stands amid other highly differentiated individuals, and where comparisons, frictions, and specialized relations release a profusion of reactions that remain latent in a narrower undifferentiated circle, but which in the larger circle, by virtue of their abundance and diversity, elicit the sensation of the ego as that which is absolutely "one's own."

C: SIGMUND FREUD

22 Civilization and its Discontents

Sigmund Freud

In all that follows I adopt the standpoint that the inclination to aggression is an original, self-subsisting instinctual disposition in man, and I return to my view that it constitutes the greatest impediment to civilization. At one point in the course of this enquiry I was led to the idea that civilization was a special process which mankind undergoes, and I am still under the influence of that idea. I may now add that civilization is a process in the service of Eros, whose purpose is to combine single human individuals, and after that families, then races, peoples and nations, into one great unity, the unity of mankind. Why this has to happen, we do not know; the work of Eros is precisely this. These collections of men are to be libidinally bound to one another. Necessity alone, the advantages of work in common, will not hold them together. But man's natural aggressive instinct, the hostility of each against all and of all against each, opposes this programme of civilization. This aggressive instinct is the derivative and the main representative of the death instinct which we have found alongside of Eros and which shares world-dominion with it. And now, I think, the meaning of the evolution of civilization is no longer obscure to us. It must present the struggle between Eros and Death, between the instinct of life and the instinct of destruction, as it works itself out in the human species. This struggle is what all life essentially consists of, and the evolution of civilization may therefore be simply described as the struggle for life of the human species. And it is this battle of the giants that our nurse-maids try to appease with their lullaby about Heaven.[1] . . .

Another question concerns us more nearly. What means does civilization employ in order to inhibit the aggressiveness which opposes it, to make it harmless, to get rid of it, perhaps? We have already become acquainted with a few of these methods, but not yet with the one that appears to be the most important. This we can study in the history of the development of the individual. What happens in him to render his desire for aggression innocuous? Something very remarkable, which we should never have guessed and which is nevertheless quite obvious. His aggressiveness is introjected, internalized; it is, in point of fact, sent back to where it came from – that is, it is directed towards his own ego. There it is taken over by a portion of the ego, which sets itself over against the rest of the ego as super-ego, and which now, in the form of 'conscience', is ready to put into action against the ego the same harsh aggressiveness that the ego would have liked to satisfy upon other, extraneous individuals. The tension between the harsh super-ego and the ego that is subjected to it, is called by us the sense of guilt; it expresses itself as a need for punishment. Civilization, therefore, obtains mastery over the individual's dangerous desire for aggression by weakening and disarming it and by setting up an agency within him to watch over it, like a garrison in a conquered city.

As to the origin of the sense of guilt, the analyst has different views from other psychologists; but even he does not find it easy to give an account of it. To begin with, if we ask how a person comes to have a sense of guilt, we arrive at an answer which cannot be disputed: a person feels guilty (devout people would say 'sinful') when he has done something which he knows to be 'bad'. But then we notice how little this answer tells us. Perhaps, after some hesitation, we shall add that even when a person has not actually *done* the bad thing but has only recognized in himself an *intention* to do it, he may regard himself as guilty; and the question then arises of why the intention is regarded as equal to the deed. Both cases, however, presuppose that one had already recognized that what is bad is reprehensible, is something that must not be carried out. How is this judgement arrived at? We may reject the existence of an original, as it were natural, capacity to distinguish good from bad. What is bad is often not at all what is injurious or dangerous to the ego; on the contrary, it may be something which is desirable and enjoyable to the ego. Here, therefore, there is an extraneous influence at work, and it is this that decides what is to be called good or bad. Since a person's own feelings would not have led him along this path, he must have had a motive for submitting to this extraneous influence. Such a motive is easily discovered in his helplessness and his dependence on other people, and it can best be designated as fear of loss of love. If he loses the love of another person upon whom he is dependent, he also ceases to be protected from a variety of dangers. Above all, he is exposed to the danger that this stronger person will show his superiority in the form of punishment. At the beginning, therefore, what is bad is whatever causes one to be threatened with loss of love. For fear of that loss, one must avoid it. This, too, is the reason why it makes little difference whether one has already done the bad thing or only intends to do it. In either case the danger only sets in if and when the authority discovers it, and in either case the authority would behave in the same way.

This state of mind is called a 'bad conscience'; but actually it does not deserve this name, for at this stage the sense of guilt is clearly only a fear of loss of love, 'social' anxiety. In small children it can never be anything else, but in many adults, too, it has only changed to the extent that the place of the father or the two parents is taken by the larger human community. Consequently, such people habitually allow themselves to do any bad thing which promises them enjoyment, so long as they are sure that the authority will not know anything about it or cannot blame them for it; they are afraid only of being found out. Present-day society has to reckon in general with this state of mind.

A great change takes place only when the authority is internalized through the establishment of a super-ego. The phenomena of conscience then reach a higher stage. Actually, it is not until now that we should speak of conscience or a sense of guilt. At this point, too, the fear of being found out comes to an end; the distinction, moreover, between doing something bad and wishing to do it disappears entirely, since nothing can be hidden from the super-ego, not even thoughts. It is true that the seriousness of the situation from a real point of view has passed away, for the new authority, the super-ego, has no motive that we know of for ill-treating the ego, with which it is intimately bound up; but genetic influence, which leads to the survival of what is past and has been surmounted, makes itself felt in the fact that fundamentally things remain as they were at the beginning. The super-ego torments the sinful ego with the same feeling of anxiety and is on the watch for opportunities of getting it punished by the external world. . . .

Thus we know of two origins of the sense of guilt: one arising from fear of an authority, and the other, later on, arising from fear of the super-ego. The first insists upon a renunciation of instinctual satisfactions; the second, as well as doing this, presses for punishment, since the continuance of the forbidden wishes cannot be concealed from the super-ego. We have also learned how the severity of the super-ego – the demands of conscience – is to be understood. It is simply a continuation of the severity of the external authority, to which it has succeeded and which it has in part replaced. We now see in what relationship the renunciation of instincts stands to the sense of guilt. Originally, renunciation of instinct was the result of fear of an external authority: one renounced one's satisfactions in order not to lose its love. If one has carried out this renunciation, one is, as it were, quits with the authority and no sense of guilt should remain. But with fear of the super-ego the case is different. Here, instinctual renunciation is not enough, for the wish persists and cannot be concealed from the super-ego. Thus, in spite of the renunciation that has been made, a sense of guilt comes about. This constitutes a great economic disadvantage in the erection of a super-ego, or, as we may put it, in the formation of a conscience. Instinctual renunciation now no longer has a completely liberating effect; virtuous continence is no longer rewarded with the assurance of love. A threatened external unhappiness – loss of love and punishment on the part of the external authority – has been exchanged for a permanent internal unhappiness, for the tension of the sense of guilt. . . .

Now, I think, we can at last grasp two things perfectly clearly: the part played by love in the origin of conscience and the fatal inevitability of the sense of guilt. Whether one has killed one's father or has abstained from doing so is not really the decisive thing. One is bound to feel guilty in either case, for the sense of guilt is an expression of the conflict due to ambivalence, of the external struggle between Eros and the instinct of destruction or death. This conflict is set going as soon as men are faced with the task of living together. So long as the community assumes no other form than that of the family, the conflict is bound to express itself in the Oedipus complex, to establish the conscience and to create the first sense of guilt. When an attempt is made to widen the community, the same conflict is continued in forms which are dependent on the past; and it is strengthened and results in a further intensification of the sense of guilt. Since civilization obeys an internal erotic impulse which causes human beings to unite in a closely-knit group, it can only achieve this aim through an ever-increasing reinforcement of the sense of guilt. What began in relation to the father is completed in relation to the group. If civilization is a necessary course of development from the family to humanity as a whole, then – as a result of the inborn conflict arising from ambivalence, of the eternal struggle between the trends of love and death – there is inextricably bound up with it an increase of the sense of guilt, which will perhaps reach heights that the individual finds hard to tolerate. . . .

When we look at the relation between the process of human civilization and the developmental or educative process of individual human beings, we shall conclude without much hesitation that the two are very similar in nature, if not the very same process applied to different kinds of object. The process of the civilization of the human species is, of course, an abstraction of a higher order than is the development of the individual and it is therefore harder to apprehend in concrete terms, nor should we pursue analogies to an obsessional extreme; but in view of the similarity between the aims of the two processes – in the one case the integration of a separate individual into a human group, and in the other case the creation of a unified group out of many individuals – we cannot be surprised at the similarity between the means employed and the resultant phenomena.

In view of its exceptional importance, we must not long postpone the mention of one feature which distinguishes between the two processes. In the developmental process of the individual, the programme of the pleasure principle, which consists in finding the satisfaction of happiness, is retained as the main aim. Integration in, or adaptation to, a human community appears as a scarcely avoidable condition which must be fulfilled before this aim of happiness can be achieved. If it could be done without that condition, it would perhaps be preferable. To put it in other words, the development of the individual seems to us to be a product of the interaction between two urges, the urge towards happiness, which we usually call 'egoistic', and the urge towards union with others in the community, which we call 'altruistic'. Neither of these descriptions goes much below the surface. In the process of individual development, as we have said, the main accent falls mostly on the egoistic urge (or the urge towards happiness); while the other urge, which may be described as a 'cultural' one, is usually content with the role of imposing restrictions. But in the process of civilization things are different. Here by far the most important thing is the aim of creating a unity out of the individual human beings. It is true that the aim of happiness is still there, but it is pushed into the background. It almost seems as if the creation of a great human community would be most successful if no attention had to be paid to the happiness of the individual. The developmental process of the individual can thus be expected to have special features of its own which are not reproduced in the process of human civilization. It is only in so far as the first of these processes has union with the community as its aim that it need coincide with the second process.

Just as a planet revolves around a central body as well as rotating on its own axis, so the human individual takes part in the course of development of mankind at the same time as he pursues his own path in life. But to our dull eyes the play of forces in the heavens seems fixed in a never-changing order; in the field of organic life we can still see how the forces contend with one another, and how the effects of the conflict are continually changing. So, also, the two urges, the one towards personal happiness and the other towards union with other human beings must struggle with each other in every individual; and so, also, the two processes of individual and of cultural development must stand in hostile opposition to each other and mutually dispute the ground. But this struggle between the individual and society is not a derivative of the contradiction – probably an irreconcilable one – between the primal instincts of Eros and death. It is a dispute within the economics of the libido, comparable to the contest concerning the distribution of libido between ego and objects; and it does admit of an eventual accommodation in the individual, as, it may be hoped, it will also do in the future of civilization, however much that civilization may oppress the life of the individual to-day.

The analogy between the process of civilization and the path of individual development may be extended in an important respect. It can be asserted that the community, too, evolves a super-ego under whose influence cultural development proceeds. It would be a tempting task for anyone who has a knowledge of human civilizations to follow out this analogy in detail. I will confine myself to bringing forward a few striking points. The super-ego of an epoch of civilization has an origin similar to that of an individual. It is based on the impression left behind by the personalities of great leaders – men of overwhelming force of mind or men in whom one of the human impulses has found its strongest and purest, and therefore often its most one-sided, expression. In many instances the analogy goes still further, in that during their lifetime these figures were – often enough, even if not always – mocked and maltreated by others and even despatched in a cruel fashion. In the same way, indeed, the primal father did not attain divinity until long after he had met his death by violence. The most arresting example of this fateful conjunction is to be seen in the figure of Jesus Christ – if, indeed, that figure is not a part of mythology, which called it into being from an obscure memory of that primal event. Another point of agreement between the cultural and the individual super-ego is that the former, just like the latter, sets up strict ideal demands, disobedience to which is visited with 'fear of conscience'. Here, indeed, we come across the remarkable circumstance that the mental processes concerned are actually more familiar to us and more accessible to consciousness as they are seen in the group than they can be in the individual man. In him, when tension arises, it is only the aggressiveness of the super-ego which, in the form of reproaches, makes itself noisily heard; its actual demands often remain unconscious in the background. If we bring them to conscious knowledge, we find that they coincide with the precepts of the prevailing cultural super-ego. At this point the two processes, that of the cultural development of the group and that of the cultural development of the individual, are, as it were, always interlocked. For that reason some of the manifestations and properties of the super-ego can be more easily detected in its behaviour in the cultural community than in the separate individual.

The cultural super-ego has developed its ideals and set up its demands. Among the latter, those which deal with the relations of human beings to one another are comprised under the heading of ethics. People have at all times set the greatest value on ethics, as though they expected that it in particular would produce especially important results. And it does in fact deal with a subject which can easily be recognized as the sorest spot in every civilization. Ethics is thus to be regarded as a therapeutic attempt – as an endeavour to achieve, by means of a command of the super-ego, something which has so far not been achieved by means of any other cultural activities. As we already know, the problem before us is how to get rid of the greatest hindrance to civilization – namely, the constitutional inclination of human beings to be aggressive towards one another; and for that very reason we are especially interested in what is probably the most recent of the cultural commands of the super-ego, the commandment to love one's neighbour as oneself. In our research into, and therapy of, a neurosis, we are led to make two reproaches against the super-ego of the individual. In the severity of its commands and prohibitions it troubles itself too little about the happiness of the ego, in that it takes insufficient account of the resistances against obeying them – of the instinctual strength of the id (in the first place), and of the difficulties presented by the real external environment (in the second). Consequently we are very often obliged, for therapeutic purposes, to oppose the super-ego, and we endeavour to lower its demands. Exactly the same objections can be made against the ethical demands of the cultural super-ego. It, too, does not trouble itself enough about the facts of the mental constitution of human beings. It issues a command and does not ask whether it is possible for people to obey it. On the contrary, it assumes that a man's ego is psychologically capable of anything that is required of it, that his ego has unlimited mastery over his id. This is a mistake; and even in what are known as normal people the id cannot be controlled beyond certain limits. If more is demanded of a man, a revolt will be produced in him or a neurosis, or he will be made unhappy. The commandment, 'Love thy neighbour as thyself', is the strongest defence against human aggressiveness and an excellent example of the unpsychological proceedings of the cultural super-ego. The commandment is impossible to fulfil; such an enormous inflation of love can only lower its value, not get rid of the difficulty. Civilization pays no attention to all this; it merely admonishes us that the harder it is to obey the precept the more meritorious it is to do so. But anyone who follows such a precept in present-day civilization only puts himself at a disadvantage *vis-à-vis* the person who disregards it. What a potent obstacle to civilization aggressiveness must be, if the defence against it can cause as much unhappiness as aggressiveness itself! 'Natural' ethics, as it is called, has nothing to offer here except the narcissistic satisfaction of being able to think oneself better than others. At this point the ethics based on religion introduces its promises of a better afterlife. But so long as virtue is not rewarded here on earth, ethics will, I fancy, preach in vain. I too think it quite certain that a real change in the relations of human beings to possessions would be of more help in this direction than any ethical commands; but the recognition of this fact among socialists has been obscured and made useless for practical purposes by a fresh idealistic misconception of human nature.

I believe the line of thought which seeks to trace in the phenomena of cultural development the part played by a super-ego promises still further discoveries. I hasten to come to a close. But there is one question which I can hardly evade. If the development of civilization has such a far-reaching similarity to the development of the individual and if it employs the same methods, may we not be justified in reaching the diagnosis that, under the influence of cultural urges, some civilizations, or some epochs of civilization – possibly the whole of mankind – have become 'neurotic'? An analytic dissection of such neuroses might lead to therapeutic recommendations which could lay claim to great practical interest. I would not say that an attempt of this kind to carry psycho-analysis over to the cultural community was absurd or doomed to be fruitless. But we should have to be very cautious and not forget that, after all, we are only dealing with analogies and that it is dangerous, not only with men but also with concepts, to tear them from the sphere in which they have originated and been evolved. Moreover, the diagnosis of communal neuroses is faced with a special difficulty. In an individual neurosis we take as our starting-point the contrast that distinguishes the patient from his environment, which is assumed to be 'normal'. For a group all of whose members are affected by one and the same disorder no such background could exist; it would have to be found elsewhere. And as regards the therapeutic application of our knowledge, what would be the use of the most correct analysis of social neuroses, since no one possesses authority to impose such a therapy upon the group? But in spite of all these difficulties, we may expect that one day someone will venture to embark upon a pathology of cultural communities.

For a wide variety of reasons, it is very far from my intention to express an opinion upon the value of human civilization. I have endeavoured to guard myself against the enthusiastic prejudice which holds that our civilization is the most precious thing that we possess or could acquire and that its path will necessarily lead to heights of unimagined perfection. I can at least listen without indignation to the critic who is of the opinion that when one surveys the aims of cultural endeavour and the means it employs, one is bound to come to the conclusion that the whole effort is not worth the trouble, and that the outcome of it can only be a state of affairs which the individual will be unable to tolerate. My impartiality is made all the easier to me by my knowing very little about all these things. One thing only do I know for certain and that is that man's judgements of value follow directly his wishes for happiness – that, accordingly, they are an attempt to support his illusions with arguments. I should find it very understandable if someone were to point out the obligatory nature of the course of human civilization and were to say, for instance, that the tendencies to a restriction of sexual life or to the institution of a humanitarian ideal at the expense of natural selection were developmental trends which cannot be averted or turned aside and to which it is best for us to yield as though they were necessities of nature. I know, too, the objection that can be made against this, to the effect that in the history of mankind, trends such as these, which were considered unsurmountable, have often been thrown aside and replaced by other trends. Thus I have not the courage to rise up before my fellow-men as a prophet, and I bow to their reproach that I can offer them no consolation: for at bottom that is what they are all demanding – the wildest revolutionaries no less passionately than the most virtuous believers.

The fateful question for the human species seems to me to be whether and to what extent their cultural development will succeed in mastering the disturbance of their communal life by the human instinct of aggression and self-destruction. It may be that in this respect precisely the present time deserves a special interest. Men have gained control over the forces of nature to such an extent that with their help they would have no difficulty in exterminating one another to the last man. They know this, and hence comes a large part of their current unrest, their unhappiness and their mood of anxiety. And now it is to be expected that the other of the two 'Heavenly Powers', eternal Eros, will make an effort to assert himself in the struggle with his equally immortal adversary. But who can foresee with what success and with what result?[2]

Notes

1 (*'Eiapopeia vom Himmel.'* A quotation from Heine's poem *Deutschland*, Caput 1.)
2 (The final sentence was added in 1931 – when the menace of Hitler was already beginning to be apparent.)

D: W. E. B. DU BOIS

23 The Souls of Black Folk

W. E. B. Du Bois

Of Our Spiritual Strivings

O water, voice of my heart, crying in the sand,
   All night long crying with a mournful cry,
As I lie and listen, and cannot understand
     The voice of my heart in my side or the voice of the sea,
   O water, crying for rest, is it I, is it I?
    All night long the water is crying to me.

Unresting water, there shall never be rest
   Till the last moon droop and the last tide fail,
And the fire of the end begin to burn in the west;
     And the heart shall be weary and wonder and cry like the sea,
   All life long crying without avail,
    As the water all night long is crying to me.

ARTHUR SYMONS

Between me and the other world there is ever an unasked question: unasked by some through feeling of delicacy; by others through the difficulty of rightly framing it. All, nevertheless, flutter round it. They approach me in a half-hesitant sort of way, eye me curiously or compassionately, and then, instead of saying directly, How does it feel to be a problem? they say, I know an excellent colored man in my town; or, I fought at Mechanicsville; or, Do not these Southern outrages make your blood boil? At these I smile, or am interested, or reduce the boiling to a simmer, as the occasion may require. To the real question, How does it feel to be a problem? I answer seldom a word.

And yet, being a problem is a strange experience, – peculiar even for one who has never been anything else, save perhaps in babyhood and in Europe. It is in the early days of rollicking boyhood that the revelation first bursts upon one, all in a day, as it were. I remember well when the shadow swept across me. I was a little thing, away up in the hills of New England, where the dark Housatonic winds between Hoosac and Taghkanic to the sea. In a wee wooden schoolhouse, something put it into the boys' and girls' heads to buy gorgeous visiting-cards – ten cents a package – and exchange. The exchange was merry, till one girl, a tall newcomer, refused my card, – refused it peremptorily, with a glance. Then it dawned upon me with a certain suddenness that I was different from the others; or like, mayhap, in heart and life and longing, but shut out from their world by a vast veil. I had thereafter no desire to tear down that veil, to creep through; I held all beyond it in common contempt, and lived above it in a region of blue sky and great wandering shadows. That sky was bluest when I could beat my mates at examination-time, or beat them at a foot-race, or even beat their stringy heads. Alas, with the years all this fine contempt began to fade; for the words I longed for, and all their dazzling opportunities, were theirs, not mine. But they should not keep these prizes, I said; some, all, I would wrest from them. Just how I would do it I could never decide: by reading law, by healing the sick, by telling the wonderful tales that swam in my head, – some way. With other black boys the strife was not so fiercely sunny: their youth shrunk into tasteless sycophancy, or into silent hatred of the pale world about them and mocking distrust of everything white; or wasted itself in a bitter cry, Why did God make me an outcast and a stranger in mine own house? The shades of the prison-house closed round about us all: walls strait and stubborn to the whitest, but relentlessly narrow, tall, and unscalable to sons of night who must plod darkly on in resignation, or beat unavailing palms against the stone, or steadily, half hopelessly, watch the streak of blue above.

After the Egyptian and Indian, the Greek and Roman, the Teuton and Mongolian, the Negro is a sort of seventh son, born with a veil, and gifted with second-sight in this American world, – a world which yields him no true self-consciousness, but only lets him see himself through the revelation of the other world. It is a peculiar sensation, this double-consciousness, this sense of always looking at one's self through the eyes of others, of measuring one's soul by the tape of a world that looks on in amused contempt and pity. One ever feels his twoness, – an American, a Negro; two souls, two thoughts, two unreconciled strivings; two warring ideals in one dark body, whose dogged strength alone keeps it from being torn asunder.

The history of the American Negro is the history of this strife, – this longing to attain self-conscious manhood, to merge his double self into a better and truer self. In this merging he wishes neither of the older selves to be lost. He would not Africanize America, for America has too much to teach the world and Africa. He would not bleach his Negro soul in a flood of white Americanism, for he knows that Negro blood has a message for the world. He simply wishes to make it possible for a man to be both a Negro and an American, without being cursed and spit upon by his fellows, without having the doors of Opportunity closed roughly in his face.

This, then, is the end of his striving: to be a co-worker in the kingdom of culture, to escape both death and isolation, to husband and use his best powers and his latent genius. These powers of body and mind have in the past been strangely wasted, dispersed, or forgotten. The shadow of a mighty Negro past flits through the tale of Ethiopia the Shadowy and of Egypt the Sphinx. Through history, the powers of single black men flash here and there like falling stars, and die sometimes before the world has rightly gauged their brightness. Here in America, in the few days since Emancipation, the black man's turning hither and thither in hesitant and doubtful striving has often made his very strength to lose effectiveness, to seem like absence of power, like weakness. And yet it is not weakness, – it is the contradiction of double aims. The double-aimed struggle of the black artisan – on the one hand to escape white contempt for a nation of mere hewers of wood and drawers of water, and on the other hand to plough and nail and dig for a poverty-stricken horde – could only result in making him a poor craftsman, for he had but half a heart in either cause. By the poverty and ignorance of his people, the Negro minister or doctor was tempted toward quackery and demagogy; and by the criticism of the other world, toward ideals that made him ashamed of his lowly tasks. The would-be black *savant* was confronted by the paradox that the knowledge his people needed was a twice-told tale to his white neighbors, while the knowledge which would teach the white world was Greek to his own flesh and blood. The innate love of harmony and beauty that set the ruder souls of his people a-dancing and a-singing raised but confusion and doubt in the soul of the black artist; for the beauty revealed to him was the soul-beauty of a race which his larger audience despised, and he could not articulate the message of another people. This waste of double aims, this seeking to satisfy two unreconciled ideals, has wrought sad havoc with the courage and faith and deeds of ten thousand thousand people, – has sent them often wooing false gods and invoking false means of salvation, and at times has even seemed about to make them ashamed of themselves.

Away back in the days of bondage they thought to see in one divine event the end of all doubt and disappointment; few men ever worshipped Freedom with half such unquestioning faith as did the American Negro for two centuries. To him, so far as he thought and dreamed, slavery was indeed the sum of all villainies, the cause of all sorrow, the root of all prejudice; Emancipation was the key to a promised land of sweeter beauty than ever stretched before the eyes of wearied Israelites. In song and exhortation swelled one refrain – Liberty; in his tears and curses the God he implored had Freedom in his right hand. At last it came, – suddenly, fearfully, like a dream. With one wild carnival of blood and passion came the message in his own plaintive cadences: –

> "Shout, O children!
> Shout, you're free!
> For God has bought your liberty!"

Years have passed away since then, – ten, twenty, forty; forty years of national life, forty years of renewal and development, and yet the swarthy spectre sits in its accustomed seat at the Nation's feast. In vain do we cry to this our vastest social problem: –

> "Take any shape but that, and my firm nerves
> Shall never tremble!"

The Nation has not yet found peace from its sins; the freedman has not yet found in freedom his promised land. Whatever of good may have come in these years of change, the shadow of a deep disappointment rests upon the Negro people, – a disappointment all the more bitter because the unattained ideal was unbounded save by the simple ignorance of a lowly people.

The first decade was merely a prolongation of the vain search for freedom, the boon that seemed ever barely to elude their grasp, – like a tantalizing will-o'-the-wisp, maddening and misleading the headless host. The holocaust of war, the terrors of the Ku-Klux Klan, the lies of carpet-baggers, the disorganization of industry, and the contradictory advice of friends and foes, left the bewildered serf with no new watchword beyond the old cry for freedom. As the time flew, however, he began to grasp a new idea. The ideal of liberty demanded for its attainment powerful means, and these the Fifteenth Amendment gave him. The ballot, which before he had looked upon as a visible sign of freedom, he now regarded as the chief means of gaining and perfecting the liberty with which war had partially endowed him. And why not? Had not votes made war and emancipated millions? Had not votes enfranchised the freedmen? Was anything impossible to a power that had done all this? A million black men started with renewed zeal to vote themselves into the kingdom. So the decade flew away, the revolution of 1876 came, and left the half-free serf weary, wondering, but still inspired. Slowly but steadily, in the following years, a new vision began gradually to replace the dream of political power, – a powerful movement, the rise of another ideal to guide the unguided, another pillar of fire by night after a clouded day. It was the ideal of "book-learning"; the curiosity, born of compulsory ignorance, to know and test the power of the cabalistic letters of the white man, the longing to know. Here at last seemed to have been discovered the mountain path to Canaan; longer than the highway of Emancipation and law, steep and rugged, but straight, leading to heights high enough to overlook life.

Up the new path the advance guard toiled, slowly, heavily, doggedly; only those who have watched and guided the faltering feet, the misty minds, the dull under-standings, of the dark pupils of these schools know how faithfully, how piteously, this people strove to learn. It was weary work. The cold statistician wrote down the inches of progress here and there, noted also where here and there a foot had slipped or some one had fallen. To the tired climbers, the horizon was ever dark, the mists were often cold, the Canaan was always dim and far away. If, however, the vistas disclosed as yet no goal, no resting-place, little but flattery and criticism, the journey at least gave leisure for reflection and self-examination; it changed the child of Emancipation to the youth with dawning self-consciousness, self-realiz-ation, self-respect. In those sombre forests of his striving his own soul rose before him, and he saw himself, – darkly as through a veil; and yet he saw in himself some faint revelation of his power, of his mission. He began to have a dim feeling that, to attain his place in the world, he must be himself, and not another. For the first time he sought to analyze the burden he bore upon his back, that dead-weight of social degradation partially masked behind a half-named Negro problem. He felt his poverty; without a cent, without a home, without land, tools, or savings, he had entered into competition with rich, landed, skilled neighbors. To be a poor man is hard, but to be a poor race in a land of dollars is the very bottom of hardships. He felt the weight of his ignorance, – not simply of letters, but of life, of business, of the humanities; the accumulated sloth and shirking and awkwardness of decades and centuries shackled his hands and feet. Nor was his burden all poverty and ignorance. The red stain of bastardy, which two centuries of systematic legal defilement of Negro women had stamped upon his race, meant not only the loss of ancient African chastity, but also the hereditary weight of a mass of corruption from white adulterers, threatening almost the obliteration of the Negro home.

A people thus handicapped ought not to be asked to race with the world, but rather allowed to give all its time and thought to its own social problems. But alas! while sociologists gleefully count his bastards and his prostitutes, the very soul of the toiling, sweating black man is darkened by the shadow of a vast despair. Men call the shadow prejudice, and learnedly explain it as the natural defence of culture against barbarism, learning against ignorance, purity against crime, the "higher" against the "lower" races. To which the Negro cries Amen! and swears that to so much of this strange prejudice as is founded on just homage to civilization, culture, righteousness, and progress, he humbly bows and meekly does obeisance. But before that nameless prejudice that leaps beyond all this he stands helpless, dismayed, and well-nigh speechless; before that personal disrespect and mockery, the ridicule and systematic humiliation, the distortion of fact and wanton license of fancy, the cynical ignoring of the better and the boisterous welcoming of the worse, the all-pervading desire to inculcate disdain for everything black, from Toussaint to the devil, – before this there rises a sickening despair that would disarm and discourage any nation save that black host to whom "discouragement" is an unwritten word.

But the facing of so vast a prejudice could not but bring the inevitable self-questioning, self-disparagement, and lowering of ideals which ever accompany repression and breed in an atmosphere of contempt and hate. Whisperings and portents came borne upon the four winds: Lo! we are diseased and dying, cried the dark hosts; we cannot write, our voting is vain; what need of education, since we must always cook and serve? And the Nation echoed and enforced this self-criticism, saying: Be content to be servants, and nothing more; what need of higher culture for halfmen? Away with the black man's ballot, by force or fraud, – and behold the suicide of a race! Nevertheless, out of the evil came something of good, – the more careful adjustment of education to real life, the clearer perception of the Negroes' social responsibilities, and the sobering realization of the meaning of progress.

So dawned the time of *Sturm und Drang*: storm and stress to-day rocks our little boat on the mad waters of the world-sea; there is within and without the sound of conflict, the burning of body and rending of soul; inspiration strives with doubt, and faith with vain questionings. The bright ideals of the past, – physical freedom, political power, the training of brains and the training of hands, – all these in turn have waxed and waned, until even the last grows dim and overcast. Are they all wrong, – all false? No, not that, but each alone was over-simple and incomplete, – the dreams of a credulous race-childhood, or the fond imaginings of the other world which does not know and does not want to know our power. To be really true, all these ideals must be melted and welded into one. The training of the schools we need to-day more than ever, – the training of deft hands, quick eyes and ears, and above all the broader, deeper, higher culture of gifted minds and pure hearts. The power of the ballot we need in sheer self-defence, – else what shall save us from a second slavery? Freedom, too, the long-sought, we still seek, – the freedom of life and limb, the freedom to work and think, the freedom to love and aspire. Work, culture, liberty, – all these we need, not singly but together, not successively but together, each growing and aiding each, and all striving toward that vaster ideal that swims before the Negro people, the ideal of human brotherhood, gained through the unifying ideal of Race; the ideal of fostering and developing the traits and talents of the Negro, not in opposition to or contempt for other races, but rather in large conformity to the greater ideals of the American Republic, in order that some day on American soil two world-races may give each to each those characteristics both so sadly lack. We the darker ones come even now not altogether empty-handed: there are to-day no truer exponents of the pure human spirit of the Declaration of Independence than the American Negroes; there is no true American music but the wild sweet melodies of the Negro slave; the American fairy tales and folklore are Indian and African; and, all in all, we black men seem the sole oasis of simple faith and reverence in a dusty desert of dollars and smartness. Will America be poorer if she replace her brutal dyspeptic blundering with light-hearted but determined Negro humility? or her coarse and cruel wit with loving jovial good-humor? or her vulgar music with the soul of the Sorrow Songs?

Merely a concrete test of the underlying principles of the great republic is the Negro Problem, and the spiritual striving of the freedmen's sons is the travail of souls whose burden is almost beyond the measure of their strength, but who bear it in the name of an historic race, in the name of this the land of their fathers' fathers, and in the name of human opportunity.

Part V

Knowledge and Critical Theory

Introduction to Part V

The sociology of knowledge and the related academic movement known as critical theory grew out of the fertile, if contentious, dialogue between German idealism, the radical critique of society and culture associated with Marxism (see Part I of this volume), and Freudian theory and the nascent science of psychoanalysis (see Part IV). It sought to understand the social foundation of ideas, the sociological conditions that shaped them, and the role of knowledge in the maintenance and reproduction of class-divided society. As Horkheimer announced in his programmatic essay "Traditional and Critical Theory" (excerpted below), critical theory would break with the conventions of both social philosophy and positivistic social science to offer a socioanalysis based on the negation of existing knowledge.

The chief figures in this movement were associated with the so-called Frankfurt School of critical theory established at the Institute for Social Research in Frankfurt. The Frankfurt School, founded in Germany but forced into exile in the United States in 1933 (to return again after German defeat), involved such prominent figures in German philosophy as Max Horkheimer, Theodor W. Adorno, Herbert Marcuse, and later Jürgen Habermas. Frankfurt School critical theory combined the thought of Marx, Weber, and Freud. Unlike traditional philosophers, the Frankfurt School theorists wished to engage the problems of the day by making critical interventions in the spheres of politics, social policy, and the arts. The Frankfurt School's project led to a sustained program of theoretically oriented sociological research that critically analyzed, among other things, the development of socialism, the eclipse of the labor movement, the rise of fascism, characteristics of authoritarian personality, and the emergence of mass consumer culture.

The Critical Theory of Society

This new sociology of knowledge was concerned particularly with the role of intellectuals in a society fraught with conflict. Could knowledge still be understood as the disinterested search for truth in accordance with Enlightenment ideals? Or was knowledge merely a serviceable good to be put to use in legitimating or opposing unequal social relations? In Karl Mannheim's *Ideology and Utopia*, which is excerpted in this section, the answer lay in moving beyond Marx's conception of the universal standpoint of knowledge based on the revolutionary proletariat. Mannheim argued that in the modern era, a "free-floating" class of autonomous intellectuals had emerged that was the only social force that could move beyond ideology to produce knowledge possessed of a progressive potential.

Confidence in this position was shaken by the mounting difficulties of the European democracies and the global economic disaster of the 1930s. In Germany, where the modern sociology of knowledge had developed, the triumph of the Nazis and with it the establishment of a totalitarian dictatorship enjoying broad popular support cemented a crisis in Western Marxism already divided by disappointment with the bureaucratic authoritarianism of the Bolshevik regime in the Soviet Union. For many, the rise of totalitarianism indicated both the eclipse of the European Enlightenment and the decline of the working class as a revolutionary subject. Confidence in the emancipatory potential of knowledge was replaced with a pessimistic appraisal of culture and society that drew upon Freudian theory. Theorists painted a picture of a pathological modernity in which the psychological need of the masses to be dominated promoted a masochistic desire for strong leaders and a taste for political violence. Fascism was portrayed as a reaction to the deep-seated alienation and frustrated desires of a modern world fractured by capitalism and aggression. In this, Weber's account of capitalist modernity as the progressive rationalization of society was also influential. For Weber, modernity was a process that inevitably entailed the decline of the religious worldview and the disenchantment of everyday life. For the Frankfurt School theorists, this aspect of modernity – the triumph of instrumental rationality at the expense of substantive values, authentic experience and the ethic of emancipation – became a chief concern, evident especially in Max Horkheimer and Theodor Adorno's *The Dialectic of Enlightenment* (1944).

The Frankfurt School theorists shared a deep sense of political disillusionment and profound pessimism concerning the question of critical consciousness and effective agency in an age of bureaucratic control and the mass media. In Marcuse's indictment of "One Dimensional Man," excerpted here, human capacities for autonomy and authentic self-expression had been smothered under the weight of techniques of domination – ranging from propaganda, advertisements and mass marketing to "scientific" management. If the Enlightenment ideal, expressed so clearly in Kant's political ethics, had been one of universal education and a liberated citizenship, it had been surrendered in the face of a "culture industry" that practiced mass deception and manipulation. In Adorno's "Cultural Criticism and Society," also excerpted here, the capacity for either artistic originality or aesthetic transcendence has been obliterated by the requirements of a professionalized culture industry. Its ringing indictment of the commercialization of culture and the unfulfilled promise of general enlightenment offered by communications technology have taken on new meaning in light of the proliferation of new media and postmodern enthusiasm for popular culture.

The radical critique of the drift toward totalitarianism in liberal capitalist society was clearly colored by its preoccupation with explaining the disaster of European fascism and the decline of European high culture. However, critical theory's fundamental insight into the overly rationalized, bureaucratic society that threatened to suffocate individual personality and self-expression – and its unmasking of the techniques of deception and manipulation that suffused a mass culture based on consumption – remain remarkably relevant today. In this regard a central, though often unacknowledged figure in the development of the sociology of knowledge and the Frankfurt School of Critical Theory was Max Weber. Weber's theories concerning the role of cultural change and the shift in values in the transition to modernity suggested how a revolution in consciousness might contribute to social revolutions. This contrasted with the common Marxian understanding of ideas as little more than after-the-fact justifications for material and social inequalities. For Marx and his followers, philosophy and learning reflected the material interests of rulers.

Knowledge became ideology that could only be dispelled through the proper scientific understanding of material conditions based on the concrete standpoint of a universal subject (i.e. the industrial proletariat). Weber's history of ideas, on the other hand, was hostile to the notion of a trans-historical subject and recognized a more independent role for culture and ideas in social development.

The Legacy of Critical Theory

Critical theory remains an important tradition in linking the contemporary sociology of knowledge to diverse strands of Marxism, feminism, and cultural studies (see *Contemporary Sociological Theory*, the sister volume to this reader). Its basic critique of social inequality and the corrosion of culture as well as its vigilant criticism of the forces that undermine a genuine democratic citizenship continue to inspire criticism and research. Concepts drawn from critical theory are essential to understanding the capacity of actors in society to communicate and act collectively on the basis of common understandings and interests. The problem of the standpoint of knowledge, explored by Mannheim and the Frankfurt School theorists in the sociology of knowledge, has become an important part of the theoretical arsenal of feminism and critical ethnic studies. By raising the issue of epistemological standpoint, the biases and theoretical lacunae of traditional social sciences can be revealed and false claims to universalism can be unseated. Perhaps most importantly, the legacy of Critical Theory has been to defend the liberating potential of knowledge in the face of new and continuing threats from ideology and inequality.

Select Bibliography

Adorno, Theodor W., et al. 1950. *The Authoritarian Personality*. New York: W. W. Norton & Company. (A major effort by a Frankfurt School intellectual to engage in a sustained empirical research project aimed at exploring the cultural and psychological conditions that support fascism. Famous for its development of an index to measure attitudinal and psychological attributes that make individuals susceptible to authoritarian control.)

Adorno, Theodor W. 1973. *Negative Dialectics*. New York: Seabury Press. (Adorno's most important philosophical writing that extends the dialectical tradition from its roots in Hegel and Marx.)

Adorno, Theodor W. 1967. *Prisms*. Translated by Samuel Weber and Shierry Weber. London: Spearman Press. (A set of wide-ranging essays on aesthetics and the sociology of culture that reflect the critical brilliance of Adorno's style.)

Horkheimer, Max and Theodor W. Adorno. 1972. *The Dialectic of Enlightenment*. John Cumming, translator. New York: Herder and Herder. (A devastating critique of modernity and of the triumph of instrumental reason over the ethical principles of the Enlightenment. Explores how mass culture and consumer capitalism is crippling the capacity for mankind's self-liberation from domination and unreason.)

Mannheim, Karl. 1936. *Ideology and Utopia*. New York: Harcourt, Brace & Company.

Mannheim, Karl. 1940. *Man and Society in an Age of Reconstruction*. London: K. Paul, Trench, Trubner & Company. (Mannheim was a founding figure in the sociology of knowledge. In these works he reveals the role intellectuals play in propagating ideology and the potential for the reconstruction of reason by ethically committed intellectuals.)

Marcuse, Herbert. 1964. *One Dimensional Man*. Boston: Beacon Press. (Marcuse's book helped to inspire the student radicals of the 1960s with its indictment of a society preoccupied with consumption and conformity and its call for a rebellion against apparent contentment and complacency.)

Jay, Martin. 1973. *The Dialectical Imagination*. Boston: Little, Brown. (This is the standard intellectual history of the Frankfurt School from its inception through the 1950s.)

Wiggershaus, Rolf. 1994. *The Frankfurt School: Its History, Theories, and Political Significance*. Cambridge, MA: MIT Press. (A brilliant history of the institution, personalities, and ideas of the Frankfurt School from its founding generation through present practitioners.)

A: KARL MANNHEIM

24 Ideology and Utopia

Karl Mannheim

In order to understand the present situation of thought, it is necessary to start with the problems of "ideology." For most people, the term "ideology" is closely bound up with Marxism, and their reactions to the term are largely determined by the association. It is therefore first necessary to state that although Marxism contributed a great deal to the original statement of the problem, both the word and its meaning go farther back in history than Marxism, and ever since its time new meanings of the word have emerged, which have taken shape independently of it.

There is no better introduction to the problem than the analysis of the meaning of the term "ideology": firstly we have to disentangle all the different shades of meaning which are blended here into a pseudo-unity, and a more precise statement of the variations in the meanings of the concept, as it is used to-day, will prepare the way for its sociological and historical analysis. Such an analysis will show that in general there are two distinct and separable meanings of the term "ideology" – the particular and the total.

The particular conception of ideology is implied when the term denotes that we are sceptical of the ideas and representations advanced by our opponent. They are regarded as more or less conscious disguises of the real nature of a situation, the true recognition of which would not be in accord with his interests. These distortions range all the way from conscious lies to half-conscious and unwitting disguises; from calculated attempts to dupe others to self-deception. This conception of ideology, which has only gradually become differentiated from the common-sense notion of the lie is particular in several senses. Its particularity becomes evident when it is contrasted with the more inclusive total conception of ideology. Here we refer to the ideology of an age or of a concrete historico-social group, e.g. of a class, when we are concerned with the characteristics and composition of the total structure of the mind of this epoch or of this group.

The common as well as the distinctive elements of the two concepts are readily evident. The common element in these two conceptions seems to consist in the fact that neither relies solely on what is actually said by the opponent in order to reach an understanding of his real meaning and intention. Both fall back on the subject, whether individual or group, proceeding to an understanding of what is said by the indirect method of analysing the social conditions of the individual or his group. The ideas expressed by the subject are thus regarded as functions of his existence. This means that opinions, statements, propositions, and systems of ideas are not taken at their face value but are interpreted in the light of the life-situation of the one who expresses them. It signifies further that the specific character and life-situation of the subject influence his opinions, perceptions, and interpretations.

Both these conceptions of ideology, accordingly, make these so-called "ideas" a function of him who holds them, and of his position in his social milieu. Although they have something in common, there are also significant differences between them. Of the latter we mention merely the most important: –

(a) Whereas the particular conception of ideology designates only a part of the opponent's assertions as ideologies – and this only with reference to their content, the total conception calls into question the opponent's total *Weltanschauung* (including his conceptual apparatus), and attempts to understand these concepts as an outgrowth of the collective life of which he partakes.

(b) The particular conception of "ideology" makes its analysis of ideas on a purely psychological level. If it is claimed for instance that an adversary is lying, or that he is concealing or distorting a given factual situation, it is still nevertheless assumed that both parties share common criteria of validity – it is still assumed that it is possible to refute lies and eradicate sources of error by referring to accepted criteria of objective validity common to both parties. The suspicion that one's opponent is the victim of an ideology does not go so far as to exclude him from discussion on the basis of a common theoretical frame of reference. The case is different with the total conception of ideology. When we attribute to one historical epoch one intellectual world and to ourselves another one, or if a certain historically determined social stratum thinks in categories other than our own, we refer not to the isolated cases of thought-content, but to fundamentally divergent thought-systems and to widely differing modes of experience and interpretation. We touch upon the theoretical or noological level whenever we consider not merely the content but also the form, and even the conceptual framework of a mode of thought as a function of the life-situation of a thinker. "The economic categories are only the theoretical expressions, the abstractions, of the social relations of production. . . . The same men who establish social relations conformably with their material productivity, produce also the principles, the ideas, the categories, conformably with their social relations" (Karl Marx, *The Poverty of Philosophy*). These are the two ways of analysing statements as functions of their social background; the first operates only on the psychological, the second on the noological level.

(c) Corresponding to this difference, the particular conception of ideology operates primarily with a psychology of interests, while the total conception uses a more formal functional analysis, without any reference to motivations, confining itself to an objective description of the structural differences in minds operating in different social settings. The former assumes that this or that interest is the cause of a given lie or deception. The latter presupposes simply that there is a correspondence between a given social situation and a given perspective, point of view, or apperception mass. In this case, while an analysis of constellations of interests may often be necessary it is not to establish causal connections but to characterize the total situation. Thus interest psychology tends to be displaced by an analysis of the correspondence between the situation to be known and the forms of knowledge.

Since the particular conception never actually departs from the psychological level, the point of reference in such analyses is always the individual. This is the case even when we are dealing with groups, since all psychic phenomena must finally be reduced to the minds of individuals. The term "group ideology" occurs frequently, to be sure, in popular speech. Group existence in this sense can only mean that a group of persons, either in their immediate reactions to the same situation or as a result of direct psychic interaction, react similarly. Accordingly, conditioned by the same social situation, they are subject to the same illusions. If we confine our observations to the mental processes which take place in the individual and regard him as the only possible bearer of ideologies, we shall never grasp in its totality the structure of the intellectual world belonging to a social group in a given historical situation. Although this mental world as a whole could never come into existence without the experiences and productive responses of the different individuals, its inner structure is not to be found in a mere integration of these individual experiences. The individual members of the working-class, for instance, do not experience *all* the elements of an outlook which could be called the proletarian *Weltanschauung*. Every individual participates only in certain fragments of this thought-system, the totality of which is not in the least a mere sum of these fragmentary individual experiences. As a totality the thought-system is integrated systematically, and is no mere casual jumble of fragmentary experiences of discrete members of the group. Thus it follows that the individual can only be considered as the bearer of an ideology as long as we deal with that conception of ideology which, by definition, is directed more to detached contents than to the whole structure of thought, uncovering false ways of thought and exposing lies. As soon as the total conception of ideology is used, we attempt to reconstruct the whole outlook of a social group, and neither the concrete individuals nor the abstract sum of them can legitimately be considered as bearers of this ideological thought-system as a whole. The aim of the analysis on this level is the reconstruction of the systematic theoretical basis underlying the single judgments of the individual. Analyses of ideologies in the particular sense, making the content of individual thought largely dependent on the interests of the subject, can never achieve this basic reconstruction of the whole outlook of a social group. They can at best reveal the collective psychological aspects of ideology, or lead to some development of mass psychology, dealing either with the different behaviour of the individual in the crowd, or with the results of the mass integration of the psychic experiences of many individuals. And although the collective-psychological aspect may very often approach the problems of the total ideological analysis, it does not answer its questions exactly. It is one thing to know how far my attitudes and judgments are influenced and altered by the co-existence of other human beings, but it is another thing to know what are the theoretical implications of my mode of thought which are identical with those of my fellow members of the group or social stratum. . . .

The Problem of False Consciousness

Through the dialectical process of history there inevitably proceeds the gradual transition from the non-evaluative, total, and general conception of ideology to the evaluative conception. The evaluation to which we now refer, however, is quite different from that previously known and described. We are no longer accepting the values of a given period as absolute, and the realization that norms and values are historically and socially determined can henceforth never escape us. The ontological emphasis is now transferred to another set of problems. Its purpose will be to distinguish the true from the untrue, the genuine from the spurious among the norms, modes of thought, and patterns of behaviour that exist alongside of one another in a given historical period. The danger of "false consciousness" nowadays is not that it cannot grasp an absolute unchanging reality, but rather that it obstructs comprehension of a reality which is the outcome of constant reorganization of the mental processes which make up our worlds. Hence it becomes intelligible why, compelled by the dialectical processes of thought, it is necessary to concentrate our attention with greater intensity upon the task of determining which of all the ideas current are really valid in a given situation. In the light of the problems we face in the present crisis of thought, the question of "false consciousness" is encountered in a new setting. The notion of "false consciousness" already appeared in one of its most modern forms when, having given up its concern with transcendental-religious factors, it transferred its search for the criterion of reality to the realm of practice and particularly political practice in a manner reminiscent of pragmatism. But contrasted with its modern formulation, it still lacked a sense of the historical. Thought and existence were still regarded as fixed and separate poles, bearing a static relationship to one another in an unchanging universe. It is only now that the new historical sense is beginning to penetrate and a dynamic concept of ideology and reality can be conceived of.

Accordingly, from our point of view, an ethical attitude is invalid if it is oriented with reference to norms, with which action in a given historical setting, even with the best of intentions, cannot comply. It is invalid then when the unethical action of the individual can no longer be conceived as due to his own personal transgression, but must be attributed rather to the compulsion of an erroneously founded set of moral axioms. The moral interpretation of one's own action is invalid, when, through the force of traditional modes of thought and conceptions of life, it does not allow for the accommodation of action and thought to a new and changed situation and in the end actually obscures and prevents this adjustment and transformation of man. A theory then is wrong if in a given practical situation it uses concepts and categories which, if taken seriously, would prevent man from adjusting himself at that historical stage. Antiquated and inapplicable norms, modes of thought, and theories are likely to degenerate into ideologies whose function it is to conceal the actual meaning of conduct rather than to reveal it. In the following paragraphs we cite a few characteristic examples of the most important types of the ideological thinking that has just been described.

The history of the taboo against taking interest on loans may serve as an example of the development of an antiquated ethical norm into an ideology. The rule that lending be carried out without interest could be put into practice only in a society which economically and socially was based upon intimate and neighbourly relations. In such a social world "lending without interest" is a usage that commands observance without difficulty, because it is a form of behaviour corresponding fundamentally to the social structure. Arising in a world of intimate and neighbourly relations this precept was assimilated and formalized by the Church in its ethical system. The more the real structure of society changed, the more this ethical precept took on an ideological character, and became virtually incapable of practical acceptance. Its arbitrariness and its unworldliness became even more evident in the period of rising capitalism when, having changed its function, it could be used as a weapon in the hands of the Church against the emergent economic force of capitalism. In the course of the complete emergence of capitalism, the ideological nature of this norm, which expressed itself in the fact that it could be only circumvented but not obeyed, became so patent that even the Church discarded it.

As examples of "false consciousness" taking the form of an incorrect interpretation of one's own self and one's role, we may cite those cases in which persons try to cover up their "real" relations to themselves and to the world, and falsify to themselves the elementary facts of human existence by deifying, romanticizing, or idealizing them, in short, by resorting to the device of escape from themselves and the world, and thereby conjuring up false interpretations of experience. We have a case of ideological distortion, therefore, when we try to resolve conflicts and anxieties by having recourse to absolutes, according to which it is no longer possible to live. This is the case when we create "myths," worship "greatness in itself," avow allegiance to "ideals," while in our actual conduct we are following other interests which we try to mask by simulating an unconscious righteousness, which is only too easily transparent.

Finally an example of the third type of ideological distortion may be seen when this ideology as a form of knowledge is no longer adequate for comprehending the actual world. This may be exemplified by a landed proprietor, whose estate has already become a capitalistic undertaking, but who still attempts to explain his relations to his labourers and his own function in the undertaking by means of categories reminiscent of the patriarchal order. If we take a total view of all these individual cases, we see the idea of "false consciousness" taking on a new meaning. Viewed from this standpoint, knowledge is distorted and ideological when it fails to take account of the new realities applying to a situation, and when it attempts to conceal them by thinking of them in categories which are inappropriate. . . .

Utopia, Ideology, and the Problem of Reality

A state of mind is utopian when it is incongruous with the state of reality within which it occurs.

This incongruence is always evident in the fact that such a state of mind in experience, in thought, and in practice, is oriented towards objects which do not exist in the actual situation. However, we should not regard as utopian every state of mind which is incongruous with and transcends the immediate situation (and in this sense, "departs from reality"). Only those orientations transcending reality will be referred to by us as utopian which, when they pass over into conduct, tend to shatter, either partially or wholly, the order of things prevailing at the time.

In limiting the meaning of the term "utopia" to that type of orientation which transcends reality and which at the same time breaks the bonds of the existing order, a distinction is set up between the utopian and the ideological states of mind. One can orient himself to objects that are alien to reality and which transcend actual existence – and nevertheless still be effective in the realization and the maintenance of the existing order of things. In the course of history, man has occupied himself more frequently with objects transcending his scope of existence than with those immanent in his existence and, despite this, actual and concrete forms of social life have been built upon the basis of such "ideological" states of mind which were incongruent with reality. Such an incongruent orientation became utopian only when in addition it tended to burst the bonds of the existing order. Consequently representatives of a given order have not in all cases taken a hostile attitude towards orientations transcending the existing order. Rather they have always aimed to control those situationally transcendent ideas and interests which are not realizable within the bounds of the present order, and thereby to render them socially impotent, so that such ideas would be confined to a world beyond history and society, where they could not affect the *status quo*.

Every period in history has contained ideas transcending the existing order, but these did not function as utopias; they were rather the appropriate ideologies of this stage of existence as long as they were "organically" and harmoniously integrated into the world-view characteristic of the period (i.e. did not offer revolutionary possibilities). As long as the clerically and feudally organized medieval order was able to locate its paradise outside of society, in some other-worldly sphere which transcended history and dulled its revolutionary edge, the idea of paradise was still an integral part of medieval society. Not until certain social groups embodied these wish-images into their actual conduct, and tried to realize them, did these ideologies become utopian. If for the moment we follow Landauer's terminology (G. Landauer, *Die Revolution*) and, in conscious opposition to the usual definition, call every actually existing and ongoing social order, a "topia" (from the word τόπος then these wish-images which take on a revolutionary function will become utopias.

It is clear that a definite conception of "existence" and a corresponding conception of the transcendence of existence underlies the above distinction. This assumption must be thoroughly investigated before proceeding farther. The nature of "reality" or "existence as such" is a problem which belongs to philosophy, and is of no concern here. However, what is to be regarded as "real" historically or sociologically at a given time is of importance to us and fortunately can be definitely ascertained. Inasmuch as man is a creature living primarily in history and society, the "existence" that surrounds him is never "existence as such," but is always a concrete historical form of social existence. For the sociologist, "existence" is that which is "concretely effective," i.e. a functioning social order, which does not exist only in the imagination of certain individuals but according to which people really act.

Every concretely "operating order of life" is to be conceived and characterized most clearly by means of the particular economical and political structure on which it is based. But it embraces also all those forms of human "living-together" (specific forms of love, sociability, conflict, etc.) which the structure makes possible or requires; and also all those modes and forms of experience and thought which are characteristic of this social system and are consequently congruous with it. (For the present statement of the problem this will be sufficiently precise. It is not to be denied that if the point of view from which the analysis is made were pressed further there would be much more to be explained. The extent to which a concept explains something can never be absolute; it always keeps step with the expansion and intensification of insight into the total structure.) But every "actually operating" order of life is at the same time enmeshed by conceptions which are to be designated as "transcendent" or "unreal" because their contents can never be realized in the societies in which they exist, and because one could not live and act according to them within the limits of the existing social order.

In a word, all those ideas which do not fit into the current order are "situationally transcendent" or unreal. Ideas which correspond to the concretely existing and *de facto* order are designated as "adequate" and situationally congruous. These are relatively rare and only a state of mind that has been sociologically fully clarified operates with situationally congruous ideas and motives. Contrasted with situationally congruous and adequate ideas are the two main categories of ideas which transcend the situation – ideologies and utopias.

Ideologies are the situationally transcendent ideas which never succeed *de facto* in the realization of their projected contents. Though they often become the good-intentioned motives for the subjective conduct of the individual, when they are actually embodied in practice their meanings are most frequently distorted. The idea of Christian brotherly love, for instance, in a society founded on serfdom remains an unrealizable and, in this sense, ideological idea, even when the intended meaning is, in good faith, a motive in the conduct of the individual. To live consistently, in the light of Christian brotherly love, in a society which is not organized on the same principle is impossible. The individual in his personal conduct is always compelled – in so far as he does not resort to breaking up the existing social structure – to fall short of his own nobler motives.

The fact that this ideologically determined conduct always falls short of its intended meaning may present itself in several forms – and corresponding to these forms there is a whole series of possible types of ideological mentality. As the first type in this series we may regard the case in which the conceiving and thinking subject is prevented from becoming aware of the incongruence of his ideas with reality by the whole body of axioms involved in his historically and socially determined thought. As a second type of ideological mentality we may present the "cant mentality," which is characterized by the fact that historically it has the possibility of uncovering the incongruence between its ideas and its conduct, but instead conceals these insights in response to certain vital-emotional interests. As a final type there is the ideological mentality based on conscious deception, where ideology is to be interpreted as a purposeful lie. In this case we are not dealing with self-delusion but rather with purposeful deception of another. There is an endless number of transitional stages ranging all the way from good-intentioned, situationally transcendent mentality through "cant mentality" to ideology in the sense of conscious lies. With these phenomena we need not occupy ourselves further at this point. It is necessary here to call attention to each of these types, however, in order to conceive more clearly in this connection the peculiarity of the utopian element.

Utopias too transcend the social situation, for they too orient conduct towards elements which the situation, in so far as it is realized at the time, does not contain. But they are not ideologies, i.e. they are not ideologies in the measure and in so far as they succeed through counteractivity in transforming the existing historical reality into one more in accord with their own conceptions. To an observer who has a relatively external view of them, this theoretical and completely formal distinction between utopias and ideologies seems to offer little difficulty. To determine concretely, however, what in a given case is ideological and what utopian is extremely difficult. We are confronted here with the application of a concept involving values and standards. To carry it out, one must necessarily participate in the feelings and motives of the parties struggling for dominance over historical reality.

What in a given case appears as utopian, and what as ideological, is dependent, essentially, on the stage and degree of reality to which one applies this standard. It is clear that those social strata which represent the prevailing social and intellectual order will experience as reality that structure of relationships of which they are the bearers, while the groups driven into opposition to the present order will be oriented towards the first stirrings of the social order for which they are striving and which is being realized through them. The representatives of a given order will label as utopian all conceptions of existence which *from their point of view* can in principle never be realized. According to this usage, the contemporary connotation of the term "utopian" is predominantly that of an idea which is in principle unrealizable. (We have consciously set apart this meaning of the term from the narrower definition.) Among ideas which transcend the situation there are, certainly, some which in principle can never be realized. Nevertheless, men whose thoughts and feelings are bound up with an order of existence in which they have a definite position will always evidence the tendency to designate as absolutely utopian all ideas which have been shown to be unrealizable only within the framework of the order in which they themselves live. In the following pages, whenever we speak of utopia we use the term merely in the relative sense, meaning thereby a utopia which seems to be unrealizable only from the point of view of a given social order which is already in existence.

The very attempt to determine the meaning of the concept "utopia" shows to what extent every definition in historical thinking depends necessarily upon one's perspective, i.e. it contains within itself the whole system of thought representing the position of the thinker in question and especially the political evaluations which lie behind this system of thought. The very way in which a concept is defined and the nuance in which it is employed already embody to a certain degree a prejudgment concerning the outcome of the chain of ideas built upon it. It is no accident that an observer who consciously or unconsciously has taken a stand in favour of the existing and prevailing social order should have such a broad and undifferentiated conception of the utopian; i.e. one which blurs the distinction between absolute and relative unrealizability. From this position, it is practically impossible to transcend the limits of the *status quo*. This reluctance to transcend the *status quo* tends towards the view of regarding something that is unrealizable merely in the given order as completely unrealizable in any order, so that by obscuring these distinctions one can suppress the validity of the claims of the relative utopia. By calling everything utopian that goes beyond the present existing order, one sets at rest the anxiety that might arise from the relative utopias that are realizable in another order.

At the other extreme is the anarchist, G. Landauer (*Die Revolution*), who regards the existing order as one undifferentiated whole, and who, by according esteem only to revolution and utopia, sees in every topia (the present existing order) evil itself. Just as the representatives of an existing order did not differentiate between the varieties of utopia (enabling us to speak of a utopia-blindness) so the anarchist may be accused of blindness to the existing order. We perceive in Landauer what is characteristic of all anarchists, namely the antithesis between the "authoritarian" and the "libertarian" – a contrast which simplifies everything and blurs all partial differences, which lumps together as authoritarian everything ranging from the police-state through the democratic-republican to the socialistic state, while only anarchism is regarded as libertarian. The same tendency towards simplification is also operative in the way history is pictured. This crude dichotomy obscures the undoubted qualitative differences in the individual forms of the state. Similarly, by laying the evaluative emphasis on utopia and revolution, the possibility of noting any kind of evolutionary trend in the realm of the historical and institutional is obscured. From this point of view every historical event is an ever-renewed deliverance from a topia (existing order) by a utopia, which arises out of it. Only in utopia and revolution is there true life, the institutional order is always only the evil residue which remains from ebbing utopias and revolutions. Hence, the road of history leads from one topia over a utopia to the next topia, etc.

The one-sidedness of this view of the world and conceptual structure is too obvious to require further elaboration. Its merit, however, is that in opposition to the "conservative" outlook which speaks for the established order, it prevents the existing order from becoming absolute, in that it envisages it as only one of the possible "topias" from which will emanate those utopian elements which in their turn will undermine the existing order. It is thus clear that in order to find the correct conception of utopia, or more modestly, the one most adequate for our present stage of thinking, the analysis based on the sociology of knowledge must be employed to set the one-sidedness of those individual positions over against one another and to eliminate them. This will make it clear precisely wherein the particularity of the previous conceptions consists. Not until this ground has been cleared is it possible on the basis of one's own judgment to arrive at a more inclusive solution, which overcomes the one-sidednesses that have become apparent. The conception of utopia which we have used above seems in this sense to be the most inclusive. It strives to take account of the dynamic character of reality, inasmuch as it assumes not a "reality as such" as its point of departure, but rather a concrete historically and socially determined reality which is in a constant process of change. It proposes further to arrive at a qualitatively, historically, and socially differentiated conception of utopia, and finally to keep distinct the "relatively" and "absolutely utopian."

All this happens in the last analysis because it is our intention not to establish purely abstractly and theoretically some sort of arbitrary relationship between existence and utopia, but rather if possible to do justice to the concrete fullness of the historical and social transformation of utopia in a given period. Furthermore, we do this because we not only seek to view contemplatively and to describe morphologically this transformation of form in the conception of utopia but also because we wish to single out the living principle which links the development of utopia with the development of an existing order. In this sense, the relationship between utopia and the existing order turns out to be a "dialectical" one. By this is meant that every age allows to arise (in differently located social groups) those ideas and values in which are contained in condensed form the unrealized and the unfulfilled tendencies which represent the needs of each age. These intellectual elements then become the explosive material for bursting the limits of the existing order. The existing order gives birth to utopias which in turn break the bonds of the existing order, leaving it free to develop in the direction of the next order of existence. This "dialectical relationship" was already well stated by the Hegelian Droysen, though in a formal and intellectualistic fashion. His definitions may serve for the preliminary clarifications of this dialectical aspect. He writes (J. G. Droysen, *Outline of the Principles of History*) as follows:

§ 77

"All movement in the historical world goes on in this way: Thought, which is the ideal counterpart of things as they really exist, develops itself as things ought to be. . . .

§ 78

"Thoughts constitute the criticism of that which is and yet is not as it should be. Inasmuch as they may bring conditions to their level, then broaden out and harden themselves into accord with custom, conservatism, and obstinacy, new criticism is demanded, and thus on and on.

§ 79

"That out of the already given conditions, new thoughts arise and out of the thoughts new conditions – this is the work of men."

This formulation of dialectical progression, of the situation, and of the contradictions to be found in the realm of thought should be regarded as nothing more than a formal outline. The real problem lies in tracing the concrete interplay of the differentiated forms of social existence with the corresponding differentiations in utopias. As a result, the problems raised become more systematic and more inclusive in so far as they reflect the richness and variety of history. The most immediate problem of research is to bring the conceptual system and empirical reality into closer contact with one another. . . .

Because the concrete determination of what is utopian proceeds always from a certain stage of existence, it is possible that the utopias of to-day may become the realities of to-morrow: "Utopias are often only premature truths" ("*Les utopies ne sont souvent que des verités prématurées*" – Lamartine). Whenever an idea is labelled utopian it is usually by a representative of an epoch that has already passed. On the other hand, the exposure of ideologies as illusory ideas, adapted to the present order, is the work generally of representatives of an order of existence which is still in process of emergence. It is always the dominant group which is in full accord with the existing order that determines what is to be regarded as utopian, while the ascendant group which is in conflict with things as they are is the one that determines what is regarded as ideological. Still another difficulty in defining precisely what, at a given period, is to be regarded as ideology, and what as utopia, results from the fact that the utopian and ideological elements do not occur separately in the historical process. The utopias of ascendant classes are often, to a large extent, permeated with ideological elements.

The utopia of the ascendant bourgeoisie was the idea of "freedom." It was in part a real utopia, i.e. it contained elements oriented towards the realization of a new social order which were instrumental in disintegrating the previously existing order and which, after their realization, did in part become translated into reality. Freedom in the sense of bursting asunder the bonds of the static, guild, and caste order, in the sense of freedom of thought and opinion, in the sense of political freedom and freedom of the unhampered development of the personality became to a large extent, or at least to a greater extent than in the preceding status-bound, feudal society, a realizable possibility. To-day we know just wherein these utopias became realities and to what extent the idea of freedom of that time contained not merely utopian but also ideological elements.

Wherever the idea of freedom had to make concessions to the concomitant idea of equality, it was setting up goals which were in contradiction to the social order which it demanded and which was later realized. The separation of the ideological elements in the dominant bourgeois mentality from those capable of subsequent realization, i.e. the truly utopian elements, could only be made by a social stratum that came later upon the scene to challenge the existing order.

All the hazards that we have pointed out as being involved in a specific definition of what is ideological and what utopian in the mentality of a given item, do indeed make the formulation of the problem more difficult, but do not preclude its investigation. It is only as long as we find ourselves in the very midst of mutually conflicting ideas that it is extremely difficult to determine what is to be regarded as truly utopian (i.e. realizable in the future) in the outlook of a rising class, and what is to be regarded as merely the ideology of dominant as well as ascendant classes. But, if we look into the past, it seems possible to find a fairly adequate criterion of what is to be regarded as ideological and what as utopian. This criterion is their realization. Ideas which later turned out to have been only distorted representations of a past or potential social order were ideological, while those which were adequately realized in the succeeding social order were relative utopias. The actualized realities of the past put an end to the conflict of mere opinions about what in earlier situationally transcendent ideas was relatively utopian bursting asunder the bonds of the existing order, and what was an ideology which merely served to conceal reality. The extent to which ideas are realized constitutes a supplementary and retroactive standard for making distinctions between facts which as long as they are contemporary are buried under the partisan conflict of opinion.

B: MAX HORKHEIMER

25 Traditional and Critical Theory

Max Horkheimer

What is "theory"? The question seems a rather easy one for contemporary science. Theory for most researchers is the sum-total of propositions about a subject, the propositions being so linked with each other that a few are basic and the rest derive from these. The smaller the number of primary principles in comparison with the derivations, the more perfect the theory. The real validity of the theory depends on the derived propositions being consonant with the actual facts. If experience and theory contradict each other, one of the two must be reexamined. Either the scientist has failed to observe correctly or something is wrong with the principles of the theory. . . .

The derivation as usually practiced in mathematics is to be applied to all science. The order in the world is captured by a deductive chain of thought.

> Those long chains of deductive reasoning, simple and easy as they are, of which geometricians make use in order to arrive at the most difficult demonstrations, had caused me to imagine that all those things which fall under the cognizance of men might very likely be mutually related in the same fashion; and that, provided only that we abstain from receiving anything as true which is not so, and always retain the order which is necessary in order to deduce the one conclusion from the other, there can be nothing so remote that we cannot reach to it, nor so recondite that we cannot discover it.[1]

Depending on the logician's own general philosophical outlook, the most universal propositions from which the deduction begins are themselves regarded as experiential judgments, as inductions (as with John Stuart Mill), as evident insights (as in rationalist and phenomenological schools), or as arbitrary postulates (as in the modern axiomatic approach). In the most advanced logic of the present time, as represented by Husserl's *Logische Untersuchungen*, theory is defined "as an enclosed system of propositions for a science as a whole."[2] Theory in the fullest sense is "a systematically linked set of propositions, taking the form of a systematically unified deduction."[3] Science is "a certain totality of propositions . . . , emerging in one or other manner from theoretical work, in the systematic order of which propositions a certain totality of objects acquires definition."[4] The basic requirement which any theoretical system must satisfy is that all the parts should intermesh thoroughly and without friction. Harmony, which includes lack of contradictions, and the absence of superfluous, purely dogmatic elements which have no influence on the observable phenomena, are necessary conditions, according to Weyl.[5]

In so far as this traditional conception of theory shows a tendency, it is towards a purely mathematical system of symbols. As elements of the theory, as components of the propositions and conclusions, there are ever fewer names of experiential objects and ever more numerous mathematical symbols. Even the logical operations themselves have already been so rationalized that, in large areas of natural science at least, theory formation has become a matter of mathematical construction.

The sciences of man and society have attempted to follow the lead of the natural sciences with their great successes. The difference between those schools of social science which are more oriented to the investigation of facts and those which concentrate more on principles has nothing directly to do with the concept of theory as such. The assiduous collecting of facts in all the disciplines dealing with social life, the gathering of great masses of detail in connection with problems, the empirical inquiries, through careful questionnaires and other means, which are a major part of scholarly activity, especially in the Anglo-Saxon universities since Spencer's time – all this adds up to a pattern which is, outwardly, much like the rest of life in a society dominated by industrial production techniques. . . .

There can be no doubt, in fact, that the various schools of sociology have an identical conception of theory and that it is the same as theory in the natural sciences. Empirically oriented sociologists have the same idea of what a fully elaborated theory should be as their theoretically oriented brethren. The former, indeed, are persuaded that in view of the complexity of social problems and the present state of science any concern with general principles must be regarded as indolent and idle. If theoretical work is to be done, it must be done with an eye unwaveringly on the facts; there can be no thought in the foreseeable future of comprehensive theoretical statements. These scholars are much enamored of the methods of exact formulation and, in particular, of mathematical procedures, which are especially congenial to the conception of theory described above. . . . There is always, on the one hand, the conceptually formulated knowledge and, on the other, the facts to be subsumed under it. Such a subsumption or establishing of a relation between the simple perception or verification of a fact and the conceptual structure of our knowing is called its theoretical explanation.

. . . For Weber, the historian's explanations, like those of the expert in criminal law, rest not on the fullest possible enumeration of all pertinent circumstances but on the establishment of a connection between those elements of an event which are significant for historical continuity, and particular, determinative happenings. This connection, for example the judgment that a war resulted from the policies of a statesman who knew what he was about, logically supposes that, had such a policy not existed, some other effect would have followed. If one maintains a particular causal nexus between historical events, one is necessarily implying that had the nexus not existed, then in accordance with the rules that govern our experience another effect would have followed in the given circumstances. The rules of experience here are nothing but the formulations of our knowledge concerning economic, social, and psychological interconnections. With the help of these we reconstruct the probable course of events, going beyond the event itself to what will serve as explanation.[6] We are thus working with conditional propositions as applied to a given situation. If circumstances a, b, c, and d are given, then event q must be expected; if d is lacking, event r; if g is added, event s, and so on. This kind of calculation is a logical tool of history as it is of science. It is in this fashion that theory in the traditional sense is actually elaborated.

What scientists in various fields regard as the essence of theory thus corresponds, in fact, to the immediate tasks they set for themselves. The manipulation of physical nature and of specific economic and social mechanisms demand alike the amassing of a body of knowledge such as is supplied in an ordered set of hypotheses. The technological advances of the bourgeois period are inseparably linked to this function of the pursuit of science. On the one hand, it made the facts fruitful for the kind of scientific knowledge that would have practical application in the circumstances, and, on the other, it made possible the application of knowledge already possessed. Beyond doubt, such work is a moment in the continuous transformation and development of the material foundations of that society. But the conception of theory was absolutized, as though it were grounded in the inner nature of knowledge as such or justified in some other ahistorical way, and thus it became a reified, ideological category.

As a matter of fact, the fruitfulness of newly discovered factual connections for the renewal of existent knowledge, and the application of such knowledge to the facts, do not derive from purely logical or methodological sources but can rather be understood only in the context of real social processes. When a discovery occasions the restructuring of current ideas, this is not due exclusively to logical considerations or, more particularly, to the contradiction between the discovery and particular elements in current views. If this were the only real issue, one could always think up further hypotheses by which one could avoid changing the theory as a whole. That new views in fact win out is due to concrete historical circumstances, even if the scientist himself may be determined to change his views only by immanent motives. Modern theoreticians of knowledge do not deny the importance of historical circumstance, even if among the most influential nonscientific factors they assign more importance to genius and accident than to social conditions. . . .

The traditional idea of theory is based on scientific activity as carried on within the division of labor at a particular stage in the latter's development. It corresponds to the activity of the scholar which takes place alongside all the other activities of a society but in no immediately clear connection with them. In this view of theory, therefore, the real social function of science is not made manifest; it speaks not of what theory means in human life, but only of what it means in the isolated sphere in which for historical reasons it comes into existence. Yet as a matter of fact the life of society is the result of all the work done in the various sectors of production. Even if therefore the division of labor in the capitalist system functions but poorly, its branches, including science, do not become for that reason self-sufficient and independent. They are particular instances of the way in which society comes to grips with nature and maintains its own inherited form. They are moments in the social process of production, even if they be almost or entirely unproductive in the narrower sense. Neither the structures of industrial and agrarian production nor the separation of the so-called guiding and executory functions, services, and works, or of intellectual and manual operations are eternal or natural states of affairs. They emerge rather from the mode of production practiced in particular forms of society. The seeming self-sufficiency enjoyed by work processes whose course is supposedly determined by the very nature of the object corresponds to the seeming freedom of the economic subject in bourgeois society. The latter believe they are acting according to personal determinations, whereas in fact even in their most complicated calculations they but exemplify the working of an incalculable social mechanism. . . .

The whole perceptible world as present to a member of bourgeois society and as interpreted within a traditional worldview which is in continuous interaction with that given world, is seen by the perceiver as a sum-total of facts; it is there and must be accepted. The classificatory thinking of each individual is one of those social reactions by which men try to adapt to reality in a way that best meets their needs. But there is at this point an essential difference between the individual and society. The world which is given to the individual and which he must accept and take into account is, in its present and continuing form, a product of the activity of society as a whole. The objects we perceive in our surroundings – cities, villages, fields, and woods – bear the mark of having been worked on by man. It is not only in clothing and appearance, in outward form and emotional make-up that men are the product of history. Even the way they see and hear is inseparable from the social life-process as it has evolved over the millennia. The facts which our senses present to us are socially preformed in two ways: through the historical character of the object perceived and through the historical character of the perceiving organ. Both are not simply natural; they are shaped by human activity, and yet the individual perceives himself as receptive and passive in the act of perception. The opposition of passivity and activity, which appears in knowledge theory as a dualism of sense-perception and understanding, does not hold for society, however, in the same measure as for the individual. The individual sees himself as passive and dependent, but society, though made up of individuals, is an active subject, even if a nonconscious one and, to that extent, a subject only in an improper sense. This difference in the existence of man and society is an expression of the cleavage which has up to now affected the historical forms of social life. The existence of society has either been founded directly on oppression or been the blind outcome of conflicting forces, but in any event not the result of conscious spontaneity on the part of free individuals. Therefore the meaning of "activity" and "passivity" changes according as these concepts are applied to society or to individual. In the bourgeois economic mode the activity of society is blind and concrete, that of individuals abstract and conscious.

Human production also always has an element of planning to it. To the extent then that the facts which the individual and his theory encounter are socially produced, there must be rationality in them, even if in a restricted sense. But social action always involves, in addition, available knowledge and its application. The perceived fact is therefore co-determined by human ideas and concepts, even before its conscious theoretical elaboration by the knowing individual. Nor are we to think here only of experiments in natural science. The so-called purity of objective event to be achieved by the experimental procedure is, of course, obviously connected with technological conditions, and the connection of these in turn with the material process of production is evident. But it is easy here to confuse two questions: the question of the mediation of the factual through the activity of society as a whole, and the question of the influence of the measuring instrument, that is, of a particular action, upon the object being observed. The latter problem, which continually plagues physics, is no more closely connected with the problem that concerns us here than is the problem of perception generally, including perception in everyday life. Man's physiological apparatus for sensation itself largely anticipates the order followed in physical experiment. As man reflectively records reality, he separates and rejoins pieces of it, and concentrates on some particulars while failing to notice others. This process is just as much a result of the modern mode of production, as the perception of a man in a tribe of primitive hunters and fishers is the result of the conditions of his existence (as well, of course, as of the object of perception). . . .

At least Kant understood that behind the discrepancy between fact and theory which the scholar experiences in his professional work, there lies a deeper unity, namely, the general subjectivity upon which individual knowledge depends. The activity of society thus appears to be a transcendental power, that is, the sum-total of spiritual factors. However, Kant's claim that its reality is sunk in obscurity, that is, that it is irrational despite all its rationality, is not without its kernel of truth. The bourgeois type of economy, despite all the ingenuity of the competing individuals within it, is not governed by any plan; it is not consciously directed to a general goal; the life of society as a whole proceeds from this economy only at the cost of excessive friction, in a stunted form, and almost, as it were, accidentally. The internal difficulties in the supreme concepts of Kantian philosophy, especially the ego of transcendental subjectivity, pure or original apperception, and conscious-ness-in-itself, show the depth and honesty of his thinking. The two-sidedness of these Kantian concepts, that is, their supreme unity and purposefulness, on the one hand, and their obscurity, unknownness, and impenetrability, on the other, reflects exactly the contradiction-filled form of human activity in the modern period. The collaboration of men in society is the mode of existence which reason urges upon them, and so they do apply their powers and thus confirm their own rationality. But at the same time their work and its results are alienated from them, and the whole process with all its waste of work-power and human life, and with its wars and all its senseless wretchedness, seems to be an unchangeable force of nature, a fate beyond man's control. . . .

We must go on now to add that there is a human activity which has society itself for its object.[7] The aim of this activity is not simply to eliminate one or other abuse, for it regards such abuses as necessarily connected with the way in which the social structure is organized. Although it itself emerges from the social structure, its purpose is not, either in its conscious intention or in its objective significance, the better functioning of any element in the structure. On the contrary, it is suspicious of the very categories of better, useful, appropriate, productive, and valuable, as these are understood in the present order, and refuses to take them as nonscientific presuppositions about which one can do nothing. The individual as a rule must simply accept the basic conditions of his existence as given and strive to fulfill them; he finds his satisfaction and praise in accomplishing as well as he can the tasks connected with his place in society and in courageously doing his duty despite all the sharp criticism he may choose to exercise in particular matters. But the critical attitude of which we are speaking is wholly distrustful of the rules of conduct with which society as presently constituted provides each of its members. The separation between individual and society in virtue of which the individual accepts as natural the limits prescribed for his activity is relativized in critical theory. The latter considers the overall framework which is conditioned by the blind interaction of individual activities (that is, the existent division of labor and the class distinctions) to be a function which originates in human action and therefore is a possible object of planful decision and rational determination of goals.

The two-sided character of the social totality in its present form becomes, for men who adopt the critical attitude, a conscious opposition. In recognizing the present form of economy and the whole culture which it generates to be the product of human work as well as the organization which mankind was capable of and has provided for itself in the present era, these men identify themselves with this totality and conceive it as will and reason. It is their own world. At the same time, however, they experience the fact that society is comparable to nonhuman natural processes, to pure mechanisms, because cultural forms which are supported by war and oppression are not the creations of a unified, self-conscious will. That world is not their own but the world of capital.

Previous history thus cannot really be understood; only the individuals and specific groups in it are intelligible, and even these not totally, since their internal dependence on an inhuman society means that even in their conscious action such individuals and groups are still in good measure mechanical functions. The identification, then, of men of critical mind with their society is marked by tension, and the tension characterizes all the concepts of the critical way of thinking. Thus, such thinkers interpret the economic categories of work, value, and productivity exactly as they are interpreted in the existing order, and they regard any other interpretation as pure idealism. But at the same time they consider it rank dishonesty simply to accept the interpretation; the critical acceptance of the categories which rule social life contains simultaneously their condemnation. This dialectical character of the self-interpretation of contemporary man is what, in the last analysis, also causes the obscurity of the Kantian critique of reason. Reason cannot become transparent to itself as long as men act as members of an organism which lacks reason. Organism as a naturally developing and declining unity cannot be a sort of model for society, but only a form of deadened existence from which society must emancipate itself. An attitude which aims at such an emancipation and at an alteration of society as a whole might well be of service in theoretical work carried on within reality as presently ordered. But it lacks the pragmatic character which attaches to traditional thought as a socially useful professional activity.

In traditional theoretical thinking, the genesis of particular objective facts, the practical application of the conceptual systems by which it grasps the facts, and the role of such systems in action, are all taken to be external to the theoretical thinking itself. This alienation, which finds expression in philosophical terminology as the separation of value and research, knowledge and action, and other polarities, protects the savant from the tensions we have indicated and provides an assured framework for his activity. Yet a kind of thinking which does not accept this framework seems to have the ground taken out from under it. . . .

. . . Its opposition to the traditional concept of theory springs in general from a difference not so much of objects as of subjects. For men of the critical mind, the facts, as they emerge from the work of society, are not extrinsic in the same degree as they are for the savant or for members of other professions who all think like little savants. The latter look towards a new kind of organization of work. But in so far as the objective realities given in perception are conceived as products which in principle should be under human control and, in the future at least, will in fact come under it, these realities lose the character of pure factuality.

The scholarly specialist "as" scientist regards social reality and its products as extrinsic to him, and "as" citizen exercises his interest in them through political articles, membership in political parties or social service organizations, and participation in elections. But he does not unify these two activities, and his other activities as well, except, at best, by psychological interpretation. Critical thinking, on the contrary, is motivated today by the effort really to transcend the tension and to abolish the opposition between the individual's purposefulness, spontaneity, and rationality, and those work-process relationships on which society is built. Critical thought has a concept of man as in conflict with himself until this opposition is removed. If activity governed by reason is proper to man, then existent social practice, which forms the individual's life down to its least details, is inhuman, and this inhumanity affects everything that goes on in the society. There will always be something that is extrinsic to man's intellectual and material activity, namely nature as the totality of as yet unmastered elements with which society must deal. But when situations which really depend on man alone, the relationships of men in their work, and the course of man's own history are also accounted part of "nature," the resultant extrinsicality is not only not a suprahistorical eternal category (even pure nature in the sense described is not that), but it is a sign of contemptible weakness. To surrender to such weakness is nonhuman and irrational. . . .

Critical thought and its theory are opposed to both the types of thinking just described. Critical thinking is the function neither of the isolated individual nor of a sum-total of individuals. Its subject is rather a definite individual in his real relation to other individuals and groups, in his conflict with a particular class, and, finally, in the resultant web of relationships with the social totality and with nature. . . .

How is critical thought related to experience? One might maintain that if such thought were not simply to classify but also to determine for itself the goals which classification serves, in other words its own fundamental direction, it would remain locked up within itself, as happened to idealist philosophy. If it did not take refuge in utopian fantasy, it would be reduced to the formalistic fighting of sham battles. The attempt legitimately to determine practical goals by thinking must always fail. If thought were not content with the role given to it in existent society, if it were not to engage in theory in the traditional sense of the word, it would necessarily have to return to illusions long since laid bare.

The fault in such reflections as these on the role of thought is that thinking is understood in a detachedly departmentalized and therefore spiritualist way, as it is today under existing conditions of the division of labor. . . . Now, inasmuch as every individual in modern times has been required to make his own the purposes of society as a whole and to recognize these in society, there is the possibility that men would become aware of and concentrate their attention upon the path which the social work process has taken without any definite theory behind it, as a result of disparate forces interacting, and with the despair of the masses acting as a decisive factor at major turning points. Thought does not spin such a possibility out of itself but rather becomes aware of its own proper function. In the course of history men have come to know their own activity and thus to recognize the contradiction that marks their existence. . . .

Yet, as far as the role of experience is concerned, there is a difference between traditional and critical theory. The viewpoints which the latter derives from historical analysis as the goals of human activity, especially the idea of a reasonable organization of society that will meet the needs of the whole community, are immanent in human work but are not correctly grasped by individuals or by the common mind. A certain concern is also required if these tendencies are to be perceived and expressed. According to Marx and Engels such a concern is necessarily generated in the proletariat. . . .

But it must be added that even the situation of the proletariat is, in this society, no guarantee of correct knowledge. The proletariat may indeed have experience of meaninglessness in the form of continuing and increasing wretchedness and injustice in its own life. Yet this awareness is prevented from becoming a social force by the differentiation of social structure which is still imposed on the proletariat from above and by the opposition between personal class interests which is transcended only at very special moments. Even to the proletariat the world superficially seems quite different than it really is. Even an outlook which could grasp that no opposition really exists between the proletariat's own true interests and those of society as a whole, and would therefore derive its principles of action from the thoughts and feelings of the masses, would fall into slavish dependence on the status quo. The intellectual is satisfied to proclaim with reverent admiration the creative strength of the proletariat and finds satisfaction in adapting himself to it and in canonizing it. He fails to see that such an evasion of theoretical effort (which the passivity of his own thinking spares him) and of temporary opposition to the masses (which active theoretical effort on his part might force upon him) only makes the masses blinder and weaker than they need be. His own thinking should in fact be a critical, promotive factor in the development of the masses. . . .

If critical theory consisted essentially in formulations of the feelings and ideas of one class at any given moment, it would not be structurally different from the special branches of science. It would be engaged in describing the psychological contents typical of certain social groups; it would be social psychology. The relation of being to consciousness is different in different classes of society. If we take seriously the ideas by which the bourgeoisie explains its own order – free exchange, free competition, harmony of interests, and so on – and if we follow them to their logical conclusion, they manifest their inner contradiction and therewith their real opposition to the bourgeois order. The simple description of bourgeois self-awareness thus does not give us the truth about this class of men. Similarly, a systematic presentation of the contents of proletarian consciousness cannot provide a true picture of proletarian existence and interests. . . .

If, however, the theoretician and his specific object are seen as forming a dynamic unity with the oppressed class, so that his presentation of societal contradictions is not merely an expression of the concrete historical situation but also a force within it to stimulate change, then his real function emerges. The course of the conflict between the advanced sectors of the class and the individuals who speak out the truth concerning it, as well as of the conflict between the most advanced sectors with their theoreticians and the rest of the class, is to be understood as a process of interactions in which awareness comes to flower along with its liberating but also its aggressive forces which incite while also requiring discipline. The sharpness of the conflict shows in the ever present possibility of tension between the theoretician and the class which his thinking is to serve. The unity of the social forces which promise liberation is at the same time their distinction (in Hegel's sense); it exists only as a conflict which continually threatens the subjects caught up in it. This truth becomes clearly evident in the person of the theoretician; he exercises an aggressive critique not only against the conscious defenders of the status quo but also against distracting, conformist, or utopian tendencies within his own household. . . .

One thing which this way of thinking has in common with fantasy is that an image of the future which springs indeed from a deep understanding of the present determines men's thoughts and actions even in periods when the course of events seems to be leading far away from such a future and seems to justify every reaction except belief in fulfillment. It is not the arbitrariness and supposed independence of fantasy that is the common bond here, but its obstinacy. Within the most advanced group it is the theoretician who must have this obstinacy. The theoretician of the ruling class, perhaps after difficult beginnings, may reach a relatively assured position, but, on the other hand, the theoretician is also at times an enemy and criminal, at times a solitary utopian; even after his death the question of what he really was is not decided. The historical significance of his work is not self-evident; it rather depends on men speaking and acting in such a way as to justify it. It is not a finished and fixed historical creation. . . .

Our consideration of the various functions of traditional and critical theory brings to light the difference in their logical structure. The primary propositions of traditional theory define universal concepts under which all facts in the field in question are to be subsumed; for example, the concept of a physical process in physics or an organic process in biology. . . .

The critical theory of society also begins with abstract determinations; in dealing with the present era it begins with the characterization of an economy based on exchange.[8] The concepts Marx uses, such as commodity, value, and money, can function as genera when, for example, concrete social relations are judged to be relations of exchange and when there is question of the commodity character of goods. But the theory is not satisfied to relate concepts of reality by way of hypotheses. The theory begins with an outline of the mechanism by which bourgeois society, after dismantling feudal regulations, the guild system, and vassalage, did not immediately fall apart under the pressure of its own anarchic principle but managed to survive. The regulatory effects of exchange are brought out on which bourgeois economy is founded. The conception of the interaction of society and nature, which is already exercising its influence here, as well as the idea of a unified period of society, of its self-preservation, and so on, spring from a radical analysis, guided by concern for the future, of the historical process. The relation of the primary conceptual interconnections to the world of facts is not essentially a relation of classes to instances. It is because of its inner dynamism that the exchange relationship, which the theory outlines, dominates social reality, as, for example, the assimilation of food largely dominates the organic life of plant and brute beast. . . .

Thus the critical theory of society begins with the idea of the simple exchange of commodities and defines the idea with the help of relatively universal concepts. It then moves further, using all knowledge available and taking suitable material from the research of others as well as from specialized research. Without denying its own principles as established by the special discipline of political economy, the theory shows how an exchange economy, given the condition of men (which, of course, changes under the very influence of such an economy), must necessarily lead to a heightening of those social tensions which in the present historical era lead in turn to wars and revolutions.

The necessity just mentioned, as well as the abstractness of the concepts, are both like and unlike the same phenomena in traditional theory. In both types of theory there is a strict deduction if the claim of validity for general definitions is shown to include a claim that certain factual relations will occur. For example, if you are dealing with electricity, such and such an event must occur because such and such characteristics belong to the very concept of electricity. To the extent that the critical theory of society deduces present conditions from the concept of simple exchange, it includes this kind of necessity, although it is relatively unimportant that the hypothetical form of statement be used. That is, the stress is not on the idea that wherever a society based on simple exchange prevails, capitalism must develop – although this is true. The stress is rather on the fact that the existent capitalist society, which has spread all over the world from Europe and for which the theory is declared valid, derives from the basic relation of exchange. Even the classificatory judgments of specialized science have a fundamentally hypothetical character, and existential judgments are allowed, if at all, only in certain areas, namely the descriptive and practical parts of the discipline.[9] But the critical theory of society is, in its totality, the unfolding of a single existential judgment. To put it in broad terms, the theory says that the basic form of the historically given commodity economy on which modern history rests contains in itself the internal and external tensions of the modern era; it generates these tensions over and over again in an increasingly heightened form; and after a period of progress, development of human powers, and emancipation for the individual, after an enormous extension of human control over nature, it finally hinders further development and drives humanity into a new barbarism. . . .

Even the critical theory, which stands in opposition to other theories, derives its statements about real relationships from basic universal concepts, as we have indicated, and therefore presents the relationships as necessary. Thus both kinds of theoretical structure are alike when it comes to logical necessity. But there is a difference as soon as we turn from logical to real necessity, the necessity involved in factual sequences. The biologist's statement that internal processes cause a plant to wither or that certain processes in the human organism lead to its destruction leaves untouched the question whether any influences can alter the character of these processes or change them totally. Even when an illness is said to be curable, the fact that the necessary curative measures are actually taken is regarded as purely extrinsic to the curability, a matter of technology and therefore nonessential as far as the theory as such is concerned. The necessity which rules society can be regarded as biological in the sense described, and the unique character of critical theory can therefore be called in question on the grounds that in biology as in other natural sciences particular sequences of events can be theoretically constructed just as they are in the critical theory of society. The development of society, in this view, would simply be a particular series of events, for the presentation of which conclusions from various other areas of research are used, just as a doctor in the course of an illness or a geologist dealing with the earth's prehistory has to apply various other disciplines. Society here would be the individual reality which is evaluated on the basis of theories in the special sciences.

However many valid analogies there may be between these different intellectual endeavors, there is nonetheless a decisive difference when it comes to the relation of subject and object and therefore to the necessity of the event being judged. The object with which the scientific specialist deals is not affected at all by his own theory. Subject and object are kept strictly apart. Even if it turns out that at a later point in time the objective event is influenced by human intervention, to science this is just another fact. The objective occurrence is independent of the theory, and this independence is part of its necessity: the observer as such can effect no change in the object. A consciously critical attitude, however, is part of the development of society: the construing of the course of history as the necessary product of an economic mechanism simultaneously contains both a protest against this order of things, a protest generated by the order itself, and the idea of self-determination for the human race, that is the idea of a state of affairs in which man's actions no longer flow from a mechanism but from his own decision. The judgment passed on the necessity inherent in the previous course of events implies here a struggle to change it from a blind to a meaningful necessity. If we think of the object of the theory in separation from the theory, we falsify it and fall into quietism or conformism. Every part of the theory presupposes the critique of the existing order and the struggle against it along lines determined by the theory itself.

The theoreticians of knowledge who started with physics had reason, even if they were not wholly right, to condemn the confusion of cause and operation of forces and to substitute the idea of condition or function for the idea of cause. For the kind of thinking which simply registers facts there are always only series of phenomena, never forces and counterforces; but this, of course, says something about this kind of thinking, not about nature. If such a method is applied to society, the result is statistics and descriptive sociology, and these can be important for many purposes, even for critical theory.

For traditional science either everything is necessary or nothing is necessary, according as necessity means the independence of event from observer or the possibility of absolutely certain prediction. But to the extent that the subject does not totally isolate himself, even as thinker, from the social struggles of which he is a part and to the extent that he does not think of knowledge and action as distinct concepts, necessity acquires another meaning for him. If he encounters necessity which is not mastered by man, it takes shape either as that realm of nature which despite the far-reaching conquests still to come will never wholly vanish, or as the weakness of the society of previous ages in carrying on the struggle with nature in a consciously and purposefully organized way. Here we do have forces and counterforces. Both elements in this concept of necessity – the power of nature and the weakness of society – are interconnected and are based on the experienced effort of man to emancipate himself from coercion by nature and from those forms of social life and of the juridical, political, and cultural orders which have become a straitjacket for him. The struggle on two fronts, against nature and against society's weakness, is part of the effective striving for a future condition of things in which whatever man wills is also necessary and in which the necessity of the object becomes the necessity of a rationally mastered event. . . .

Critical theory does not have one doctrinal substance today, another tomorrow. The changes in it do not mean a shift to a wholly new outlook, as long as the age itself does not radically change. The stability of the theory is due to the fact that amid all change in society the basic economic structure, the class relationship in its simplest form, and therefore the idea of the supercession of these two remain identical. The decisive substantive elements in the theory are conditioned by these unchanging factors and they themselves therefore cannot change until there has been a historical transformation of society. On the other hand, however, history does not stand still until such a point of transformation has been reached. The historical development of the conflicts in which the critical theory is involved leads to a reassignment of degrees of relative importance to individual elements of the theory, forces further concretizations, and determines which results of specialized science are to be significant for critical theory and practice at any given time.

In order to explain more fully what is meant, we shall use the concept of the social class which disposes of the means of production. In the liberalist period economic predominance was in great measure connected with legal ownership of the means of production. The large class of private property owners exercised leadership in the society, and the whole culture of the age bears the impress of this fact. Industry was still broken up into a large number of independent enterprises which were small by modern standards. The directors of factories, as was suitable for this stage of technological development, were either one or more of the owners or their direct appointees. Once, however, the development of technology in the last century had led to a rapidly increasing concentration and centralization of capital, the legal owners were largely excluded from the management of the huge combines which absorbed their small factories, and management became something quite distinct from ownership before the law. Industrial magnates, the leaders of the economy, came into being.

. . . Once the legal owners are cut off from the real productive process and lose their influence, their horizon narrows; they become increasingly unfitted for important social positions, and finally the share which they still have in industry due to ownership and which they have done nothing to augment comes to seem socially useless and morally dubious. These and other changes are accompanied by the rise of ideologies centering on the great personality and the distinction between productive and parasitic capitalists. The idea of a right with a fixed content and independent of society at large loses its importance. The very same sector of society which brutally maintains its private power to dispose of the means of production (and this power is at the heart of the prevailing social order) sponsors political doctrines which claim that unproductive property and parasitic incomes must disappear. The circle of really powerful men grows narrower, but the possibility increases of deliberately constructing ideologies, of establishing a double standard of truth (knowledge for insiders, a cooked-up story for the people), and of cynicism about truth and thought generally. The end result of the process is a society dominated no longer by independent owners but by cliques of industrial and political leaders.

Such changes do not leave the structure of the critical theory untouched. It does not indeed fall victim to the illusion that property and profit no longer play a key role, an illusion carefully fostered in the social sciences. On the one hand, even earlier it had regarded juridical relations not as the substance but as the surface of what was really going on in society. It knows that the disposition of men and things remains in the hands of a particular social group which is in competition with other economic power groups, less so at home but all the more fiercely at the international level. Profit continues to come from the same social sources and must in the last analysis be increased by the same means as before. On the other hand, in the judgment of the critical theorist the loss of all rights with a determined content, a loss conditioned by the concentration of economic power and given its fullest form in the authoritarian state, has brought with it the disappearance not only of an ideology but also of a cultural factor which has a positive value and not simply a negative one.

When the theory takes into account these changes in the inner structure of the entrepreneurial class, it is led to differentiate others of its concepts as well. The dependence of culture on social relationships must change as the latter change, even in details, if society indeed be a single whole. Even in the liberalist period political and moral interpretations of individuals could be derived from their economic situation. Admiration for nobility of character, fidelity to one's word, independence of judgment, and so forth, are traits of a society of relatively independent economic subjects who enter into contractual relationships with each other. But this cultural dependence was in good measure psychologically mediated, and morality itself acquired a kind of stability because of its function in the individual. (The truth that dependence on the economy thoroughly pervaded even this morality was brought home when in the recent threat to the economic position of the liberalist bourgeoisie the attitude of freedom and independence began to disintegrate.) Under the conditions of monopolistic capitalism, however, even such a relative individual independence is a thing of the past. The individual no longer has any ideas of his own. The content of mass belief, in which no one really believes, is an immediate product of the ruling economic and political bureaucracies, and its disciples secretly follow their own atomistic and therefore untrue interests; they act as mere functions of the economic machine.

The concept of the dependence of the cultural on the economic has thus changed. . . . This influence of social development on the structure of the theory is part of the theory's doctrinal content. Thus new contents are not just mechanically added to already existent parts. Since the theory is a unified whole which has its proper meaning only in relation to the contemporary situation, the theory as a whole is caught up in an evolution. The evolution does not change the theory's foundations, of course, any more than recent changes essentially alter the object which the theory reflects, namely contemporary society. Yet even the apparently more remote concepts of the theory are drawn into the evolution. The logical difficulties which understanding meets in every thought that attempts to reflect a living totality are due chiefly to this fact. . . .

There are no general criteria for judging the critical theory as a whole, for it is always based on the recurrence of events and thus on a self-reproducing totality. Nor is there a social class by whose acceptance of the theory one could be guided. It is possible for the consciousness of every social stratum today to be limited and corrupted by ideology, however much, for its circumstances, it may be bent on truth. For all its insight into the individual steps in social change and for all the agreement of its elements with the most advanced traditional theories, the critical theory has no specific influence on its side, except concern for the abolition of social injustice. This negative formulation, if we wish to express it abstractly, is the materialist content of the idealist concept of reason.

In a historical period like the present true theory is more critical than affirmative, just as the society that corresponds to it cannot be called "productive." The future of humanity depends on the existence today of the critical attitude, which of course contains within it elements from traditional theories and from our declining culture generally. Mankind has already been abandoned by a science which in its imaginary self-sufficiency thinks of the shaping of practice, which it serves and to which it belongs, simply as something lying outside its borders and is content with this separation of thought and action. Yet the characteristic mark of the thinker's activity is to determine for itself what it is to accomplish and serve, and this not in fragmentary fashion but totally. Its own nature, therefore, turns it towards a changing of history and the establishment of justice among men. Behind the loud calls for "social spirit" and "national community," the opposition between individual and society grows ever greater. The self-definition of science grows ever more abstract. But conformism in thought and the insistence that thinking is a fixed vocation, a self-enclosed realm within society as a whole, betrays the very essence of thought.

Notes

1 Descartes, *Discourse on Method*, in *The Philosophical Works of Descartes*, tr. by Elizabeth S. Haldane and G. R. T. Ross (Cambridge: Cambridge University Press, 1931), volume 1, p. 92.
2 Edmund Husserl, *Formale und transzendentale Logik* (Halle, 1929), p. 89.
3 Ibid., p. 79.
4 Ibid., p. 91.
5 Hermann Weyl, *Philosophie der Naturwissenschaft*, in *Handbuch der Philosophie*, Part 2 (Munich-Berlin, 1927), pp. 118ff.
6 Max Weber, "Critical Studies in the Logic of the Cultural Sciences I: A Critique of Eduard Meyer's Methodological Views," in *Max Weber on the Methodology of the Social Sciences*, ed. and tr. by Edward A. Shils and Henry A. Finch (Glencoe: Free Press, 1949), pp. 113–63.
7 In the following pages this activity is called "critical" activity. The term is used here less in the sense it has in the idealist critique of pure reason than in the sense it has in the dialectical critique of political economy. It points to an essential aspect of the dialectical theory of society.

8 On the logical structure of the critique of political economy, cf. the essay "Zum Problem der Wahrheit," in Horkheimer, *Kritische Theorie*, vol. 1 (Frankfurt, 1968), pp. 265ff.

9 There are connections between the forms of judgment and the historical periods. A brief indication will show what is meant. The classificatory judgment is typical of prebourgeois society: this is the way it is, and man can do nothing about it. The hypothetical and disjunctive forms belong especially to the bourgeois world: under certain circumstances this effect can take place; it is either thus or so. Critical theory maintains: it need not be so; man can change reality, and the necessary conditions for such change already exist.

C: THEODOR ADORNO

26 Cultural Criticism and Society

Theodor Adorno

To anyone in the habit of thinking with his ears, the words 'cultural criticism' (*Kulturkritik*) must have an offensive ring, not merely because, like 'automobile', they are pieced together from Latin and Greek. The words recall a flagrant contradiction. The cultural critic is not happy with civilization, to which alone he owes his discontent. He speaks as if he represented either unadulterated nature or a higher historical stage. Yet he is necessarily of the same essence as that to which he fancies himself superior. The insufficiency of the subject – criticized by Hegel in his apology for the *status quo* – which in its contingency and narrowness passes judgment on the might of the existent, becomes intolerable when the subject itself is mediated down to its innermost make-up by the notion to which it opposes itself as independent and sovereign. But what makes the content of cultural criticism inappropriate is not so much lack of respect for that which is critized as the dazzled and arrogant recognition which criticism surreptitiously confers on culture. The cultural critic can hardly avoid the imputation that he has the culture which culture lacks. His vanity aids that of culture: even in the accusing gesture, the critic clings to the notion of culture, isolated, unquestioned, dogmatic. He shifts the attack. Where there is despair and measureless misery, he sees only spiritual phenomena, the state of man's consciousness, the decline of norms. By insisting on this, criticism is tempted to forget the unutterable, instead of striving, however impotently, so that man may be spared.

The position of the cultural critic, by virtue of its difference from the prevailing disorder, enables him to go beyond it theoretically, although often enough he merely falls behind. But he incorporates this difference into the very culture industry which he seeks to leave behind and which itself needs the difference in order to fancy itself culture. Characteristic of culture's pretension to distinction, through which it exempts itself from evaluation against the material conditions of life, is that it is insatiable. The exaggerated claims of culture, which in turn inhere in the movement of the mind, remove it ever further from those conditions as the worth of sublimation becomes increasingly suspect when confronted both by a material fulfillment near enough to touch and by the threatening annihilation of uncounted human beings. The cultural critic makes such distinction his privilege and forfeits his legitimation by collaborating with culture as its salaried and honoured nuisance.

This, however, affects the substance of criticism. Even the implacable rigour with which criticism speaks the truth of an untrue consciousness remains imprisoned within the orbit of that against which it struggles, fixated on its surface manifestations. To flaunt one's superiority is, at the same time, to feel in on the job. Were one to study the profession of critic in bourgeois society as it progressed towards the rank of cultural critic, one would doubtless stumble on an element of usurpation in its origins, an element of which a writer like Balzac was still aware. Professional critics were first of all 'reporters': they oriented people in the market of intellectual products. In so doing, they occasionally gained insights into the matter at hand, yet remained continually traffic agents, in agreement with the sphere as such if not with its individual products. Of this they bear the mark even after they have discarded the role of agent. That they should have been entrusted with the roles of expert and then of judge was economically inevitable although accidental with respect to their objective qualifications. Their agility, which gained them privileged positions in the general competition – privileged, since the fate of those judged depends largely on their vote – invests their judgments with the semblance of competence. While they adroitly slipped into gaps and won influence with the expansion of the press, they attained that very authority which their profession already presupposed. Their arrogance derives from the fact that, in the forms of competitive society in which all being is merely there *for* something else, the critic himself is also measured only in terms of his marketable success – that is, in terms of his *being for* something else. Knowledge and understanding were not primary, but at most by-products, and the more they are lacking, the more they are replaced by Oneupmanship and conformity. When the critics in their playground – art – no longer understand what they judge and enthusiastically permit themselves to be degraded to propagandists or censors, it is the old dishonesty of trade fulfilling itself in their fate. The prerogatives of information and position permit them to express their opinion as if it were objectivity. But it is solely the objectivity of the ruling mind. They help to weave the veil.

The notion of the free expression of opinion, indeed, that of intellectual freedom itself in bourgeois society, upon which cultural criticism is founded, has its own dialectic. For while the mind extricated itself from a theological-feudal tutelage, it has fallen increasingly under the anonymous sway of the *status quo*. This regimentation, the result of the progressive societalization of all human relations, did not simply confront the mind from without; it immigrated into its immanent consistency. It imposes itself as relentlessly on the autonomous mind as heteronomous orders were formerly imposed on the mind which was bound. Not only does the mind mould itself for the sake of its marketability, and thus reproduce the socially prevalent categories. Rather, it grows to resemble ever more closely the *status quo* even where it subjectively refrains from making a commodity of itself. The network of the whole is drawn ever tighter, modelled after the act of exchange. It leaves the individual consciousness less and less room for evasion, preforms it more and more thoroughly, cuts it off *a priori* as it were from the possibility of differencing itself as all difference degenerates to a nuance in the monotony of supply. At the same time, the semblance of freedom makes reflection upon one's own unfreedom incomparably more difficult than formerly when such reflection stood in contradiction to manifest unfreedom, thus strengthening dependence. Such moments, in conjunction with the social selection of the 'spiritual and intellectual leaders', result in the regression of spirit and intellect. In accordance with the predominant social tendency, the integrity of the mind becomes a fiction. Of its freedom it develops only the negative moment, the heritage of the planless-monadological condition, irresponsibility. Otherwise, however, it clings ever more closely as a mere ornament to the material base which it claims to transcend. The strictures of Karl Kraus against freedom of the press are certainly not to be taken literally. To invoke seriously the censors against hack-writers would be to drive out the devil with Beelzebub. Nevertheless, the brutalization and deceit which flourish under the aegis of freedom of the press are not accidental to the historical march of the mind. Rather, they represent the stigma of that slavery within which the liberation of the mind – a false emancipation – has taken place. This is nowhere more striking than where the mind tears at its bonds: in criticism. When the German fascists defamed the word and replaced it with the inane notion of 'art appreciation', they were led to do so only by the rugged interests of the authoritarian state which still feared the passion of a Marquis Posa in the impertinence of the journalist. But the self-satisfied cultural barbarism which clamoured for the abolition of criticism, the incursion of the wild horde into the preserve of the mind, unawares repaid kind in kind. The bestial fury of the Brownshirt against 'carping critics' arises not merely from his envy of a culture which excludes him and against which he blindly rebels; nor is it merely his resentment of the person who can speak out the negative moment which he himself must repress. Decisive is that the critic's sovereign gesture suggests to his readers an autonomy which he does not have, and arrogates for itself a position of leadership which is incompatible with his own principle of intellectual freedom. This is innervated by his enemies. Their sadism was idiosyncratically attracted by the weakness, cleverly disguised as strength, of those who, in their dictatorial bearing, would have willingly excelled the less clever tyrants who were to succeed them. Except that the fascists succumbed to the same naivete as the critics, the faith in culture as such, which reduced it to pomp and approved spiritual giants. They regarded themselves as physicians of culture and removed the thorn of criticism from it. They thus not only degraded culture to the Official, but in addition, failed to recognize the extent to which culture and criticism, for better or for worse, are intertwined. Culture is only true when implicitly critical, and the mind which forgets this revenges itself in the critics it breeds. Criticism is an indispensable element of culture which is itself contradictory: in all its untruth still as true as culture is untrue. Criticism is not unjust when it dissects – this can be its greatest virtue – but rather when it parries by not parrying.

The complicity of cultural criticism with culture lies not in the mere mentality of the critic. Far more, it is dictated by his relation to that with which he deals. By making culture his object, he objectifies it once more. Its very meaning, however, is the suspension of objectification. Once culture itself has been debased to 'cultural goods', with its hideous philosophical rationalization, 'cultural values', it has already defamed its *raison d'être*. The distillation of such 'values' – the echo of commercial language is by no means accidental – places culture at the will of the market. Even the enthusiasm for foreign cultures includes the excitement over the rarity in which money may be invested. If cultural criticism, even at its best with Valéry, sides with conservativism, it is because of its unconscious adherence to a notion of culture which, during the era of late capitalism, aims at a form of property which is stable and independent of stock-market fluctuations. This idea of culture asserts its distance from the system in order, as it were, to offer universal security in the middle of a universal dynamic. The model of the cultural critic is no less the appraising collector than the art critic. In general, cultural criticism recalls the gesture of bargaining, of the expert questioning the authenticity of a painting or classifying it among the Master's lesser works. One devaluates in order to get more. The cultural critic evaluates and hence is inevitably involved in a sphere stained with 'cultural values', even when he rants against the mortgaging of culture. His contemplative stance towards culture necessarily entails scrutinizing, surveying, balancing, selecting: this piece suits him, that he rejects. Yet his very sovereignty, the claim to a more profound knowledge of the object, the separation of the idea from its object through the independence of the critical judgment threatens to succumb to the thinglike form of the object when cultural criticism appeals to a collection of ideas on display, as it were, and fetishizes isolated categories such as mind, life and the individual.

But the greatest fetish of cultural criticism is the notion of culture as such. For no authentic work of art and no true philosophy, according to their very meaning, has ever exhausted itself in itself alone, in its being-in-itself. They have always stood in relation to the actual life-process of society from which they distinguished themselves. Their very rejection of the guilt of a life which blindly and callously reproduces itself, their insistence on independence and autonomy, on separation from the prevailing realm of purposes, implies, at least as an unconscious element, the promise of a condition in which freedom were realized. This remains an equivocal promise of culture as long as its existence depends on a bewitched reality and, ultimately, on control over the work of others. That European culture in all its breadth – that which reached the consumer and which today is prescribed for whole populations by managers and psychotechnicians – degenerated to mere ideology resulted from a change in its function with regard to material *praxis*: its renunciation of interference. Far from being culture's 'sin', the change was forced upon culture by history. For it is only in the process of withdrawing into itself, only indirectly that is, that bourgeois culture conceives of a purity from the corrupting traces of a totalitarian disorder which embraces all areas of existence. Only in so far as it withdraws from a *praxis* which has degenerated into its opposite, from the ever-changing production of what is always the same, from the service of the customer who himself serves the manipulator – only in so far as it withdraws from Man, can culture be faithful to man. But such concentration on substance which is absolutely one's own, the greatest example of which is to be found in the poetry and theoretical writings of Paul Valéry, contributes at the same time to the impoverishment of that substance. Once the mind is no longer directed at reality, its meaning is changed despite the strictest preservation of meaning. Through its resignation before the facts of life and, even more, through its isolation as one 'field' among others, the mind aids the existing order and takes its place within it. The emasculation of culture has angered philosophers since the time of Rousseau and the 'ink-splattering age' of Schiller's *Robbers*, to Nietzsche and finally, to the preachers of commitment for its own sake. This is the result of culture's becoming self-consciously cultural, which in turn places culture in vigorous and consistent opposition to the growing barbarism of economic hegemony. What appears to be the decline of culture is its coming to pure self-consciousness. Only when neutralized and reified, does Culture allow itself to be idolized. Fetishism gravitates towards mythology. In general, cultural critics become intoxicated with idols drawn from antiquity to the dubious, long-evaporated warmth of the liberalist era, which recalled the origins of culture in its decline. Cultural criticism rejects the progressive integration of all aspects of consciousness within the apparatus of material production. But because it fails to see through the apparatus, it turns towards the past, lured by the promise of immediacy. This is necessitated by its own momentum and not merely by the influence of an order which sees itself obliged to drown out its progress in dehumanization with cries against dehumanization and progress. The isolation of the mind from material production heightens its esteem but also makes it a scapegoat in the general consciousness for that which is perpetrated in practice. Enlightenment as such – not as an instrument of actual domination – is held responsible. Hence, the irrationalism of cultural criticism. Once it has wrenched the mind out of its dialectic with the material conditions of life, it seizes it unequivocally and straightforwardly as the principle of fatality, thus undercutting the mind's own resistance. The cultural critic is barred from the insight that the reification of life results not from too much enlightenment but from too little, and that the mutilation of man which is the result of the present particularistic rationality is the stigma of the total irrationality. The abolition of this irrationality, which would coincide with the abolition of the divorce between mental and physical work, appears as chaos to the blindness of cultural criticism: whoever glorifies order and form as such, must see in the petrified divorce an archetype of the Eternal. That the fatal fragmentation of society might some day end is, for the cultural critic, a fatal destiny. He would rather that everything end than for mankind to put an end to reification. This tear harmonizes with the interests of those interested in the perpetuation of material denial. Whenever cultural criticism complains of 'materialism', it furthers the belief that the sin lies in man's desire for consumer goods, and not in the organization of the whole which withholds these goods from man: for the cultural critic, the sin is satiety, not hunger. Were mankind to possess the wealth of goods, it would shake off the chains of that civilized barbarism which cultural critics ascribe to the advanced state of the human spirit rather than to the retarded state of society. The 'eternal values' of which cultural criticism is so fond reflect the perennial catastrophe. The cultural critic thrives on the mythical obduracy of culture.

Because the existence of cultural criticism, no matter what its content, depends on the economic system, it is involved in the fate of the system. The more completely the life-process, including leisure, is dominated by modern social orders – those in the East, above all – the more all spiritual phenomena bear the mark of the order. Either, they may contribute directly to the perpetuation of the system as entertainment or edification, and are enjoyed as exponents of the system precisely because of their socially preformed character. Familiar, stamped and Approved by Good Housekeeping as it were, they insinuate themselves into a regressive consciousness, present themselves as 'natural', and permit identification with powers whose preponderance leaves no alternative but that of false love. Or, by being different, they become rarities and once again marketable. Throughout the liberalist era, culture fell within the sphere of circulation. Hence, the gradual withering away of this sphere strikes culture to the quick. With the elimination of trade and its irrational loopholes by the calculated distributive apparatus of industry, the commercialization of culture culminates in absurdity. Completely subdued, administered, thoroughly 'cultivated' in a sense, it dies out. Spengler's denunciation: that mind and money go together, proves correct. But because of his sympathy with direct rule, he advocated a structure of existence divested of all economic as well as spiritual mediations. He maliciously threw the mind together with an economic type which was in fact obsolete. What Spengler failed to understand was that no matter to what extent the mind is a product of that type, it implies at the same time the objective possibility of overcoming it. Just as culture sprang up in the marketplace, in the traffic of trade, in communication and negotiation, as something distinct from the immediate struggle for individual self-preservation, just as it was closely tied to trade in the era of mature capitalism, just as its representatives were counted among the class of 'third persons' who supported themselves in life as middlemen, so culture, considered 'socially necessary' according to classical rules, in the sense of reproducing itself economically, is in the end reduced to that as which it began, to mere communication. Its alienation from human affairs terminates in its absolute docility before a humanity which has been enchanted and transformed into clientele by the suppliers. In the name of the consumer, the manipulators suppress everything in culture which enables it to go beyond the total immanence in the existing society and allow only that to remain which serves society's unequivocal purpose. Hence, 'consumer culture' can boast of being not a luxury but rather the simple extension of production. Political slogans, designed for mass manipulation, unanimously stigmatize, as 'luxury', 'snobbism', and 'highbrow', everything cultural which displeases the commissars. Only when the established order has become the measure of all things does its mere reproduction in the realm of consciousness become truth. Cultural criticism points to this and rails against 'superficiality' and 'loss of substance'. But by limiting its attention to the entanglement of culture in commerce, such criticism itself becomes superficial. It follows the pattern of reactionary social critics who pit 'productive' against 'predatory' capital. In fact, all culture shares the guilt of society. It ekes out its existence only by virtue of injustice already perpetrated in the sphere of production, much as does commerce (cf. *Dialektik der Aufklärung*). Consequently, cultural criticism shifts the guilt: such criticism is ideology as long as it remains mere criticism of ideology. Totalitarian regimes of both kinds, seeking to protect the *status quo* from even the last traces of insubordination which they ascribe to culture even at its most servile, can conclusively convict culture and its introspection of servility. They suppress the mind, in itself already grown intolerable, and so feel themselves to be purifiers and revolutionaries. The ideological function of cultural criticism bridles its very truth which lies in its opposition to ideology. The struggle against deceit works to the advantage of naked terror. 'When I hear the word "culture", I reach for my gun,' said the spokesman of Hitler's Imperial Chamber of Culture.

Cultural criticism is, however, only able to reproach culture so penetratingly for prostituting itself, for violating in its decline the pure autonomy of the mind, because culture originates in the radical separation of mental and physical work. It is from this separation, the original sin as it were, that culture draws its strength. When culture simply denies the separation and feigns harmonious union, it falls back behind its own notion. Only the mind which, in the delusion of being absolute, removes itself entirely from the merely existent, truly defines the existent in its negativity. As long as even the least part of the mind remains engaged in the reproduction of life, it is its sworn bondsman. The anti-philistinism of Athens was both the most arrogant contempt of the man who need not soil his hands for the man from whose work he lives, and the preservation of an image of existence beyond the constraint which underlies all work. In projecting its own uneasy conscience on to its victims as their 'baseness', such an attitude also accuses that which they endure: the subjugation of men to the prevailing form in which their lives are reproduced. All 'pure culture' has always been a source of discomfort to the spokesmen of power. Plato and Aristotle knew why they would not permit the notion to arise. Instead, in questions concerning the evaluation of art, they advocated a pragmatism which contrasts curiously with the *pathos* of the two great metaphysicians. Modern bourgeois cultural criticism has, of course, been too prudent to follow them openly in this respect. But such criticism secretly finds a source of comfort in the divorce between 'high' and 'popular' culture, art and entertainment, knowledge and non-committal *Weltanschauung*. Its anti-philistinism exceeds that of the Athenian upper class to the extent that the proletariat is more dangerous than the slaves. The modern notion of a pure, autonomous culture indicates that the antagonism has become irreconcilable. This is the result both of an uncompromising oppositon to being-for-something else, and of an ideology which in its hybris enthrones itself as being-in-itself.

Cultural criticism shares the blindness of its object. It is incapable of allowing the recognition of its frailty to arise, a frailty set in the division of mental and physical work. No society which contradicts its very notion – that of mankind – can have full consciousness of itself. A display of subjective ideology is not required to obstruct this consciousness, although in times of historical upheaval it tends to contribute to the objective blindness. Rather, the fact that every form of repression, depending on the level of technology, has been necessary for the survival of society, and that society as it is, despite all absurdity, does indeed reproduce its life under the existing conditions, objectively produces the semblance of society's legitimation. As the epitome of the self-consciousness of an antagonistic society, culture can no more divest itself of this semblance than can cultural criticism, which measures culture against culture's own ideal. The semblance has become total in a phase in which irrationality and objective falsity hide behind rationality and objective necessity. Nevertheless, by virtue of their real force, the antagonisms reassert themselves in the realm of consciousness. Just because culture affirms the validity of the principle of harmony within an antagonistic society, albeit in order to glorify that society, it cannot avoid confronting society with its own notion of harmony and thereby stumbling on discord. The ideology which affirms life is forced into opposition to life by the immanent drive of the ideal. The mind which sees that reality does not resemble it in every respect but is instead subject to an unconscious and fatal dynamic, is impelled even against its will beyond apologetics. The fact that theory becomes real force when it moves men is founded in the objectivity of the mind itself which, through the fulfilment of its ideological function must lose faith in ideology. Prompted by the incompatibility of ideology and existence, the mind, in displaying its blindness also displays its effort to free itself of ideology. Disenchanted, the mind perceives naked existence in its nakedness and delivers it up to criticism. The mind either damns the material base, in accordance with the ever-questionable criterion of its 'pure principle', or it becomes aware of its own questionable position, by virtue of its incompatibility with the base. As a result of the social dynamic, culture becomes cultural criticism, which preserves the notion of culture while demolishing its present manifestations as mere commodities and means of brutalization. Such critical consciousness remains subservient to culture in so far as its concern with culture distracts from the true horrors. From this arises the ambivalent attitude of social theory towards cultural criticism. The procedure of cultural criticism is itself the object of permanent criticism, both in its general presuppositions – its immanence in the existing society – and in its concrete judgments. For the subservience of cultural criticism is revealed in its specific content, and only in this may it be grasped conclusively. At the same time, a dialectical theory which does not wish to succumb to 'Economism', the sentiment which holds that the transformation of the world is exhausted in the increase of production, must absorb cultural criticism, the truth of which consists in bringing untruth to consciousness of itself. A dialectical theory which is uninterested in culture as a mere epiphenomenon, aids pseudo-culture to run rampant and collaborates in the reproduction of the evil. Cultural traditionalism and the terror of the new Russian despots are in basic agreement. Both affirm culture as a whole, sight-unseen, while at the same time proscribing all forms of consciousness which are not made-to-order. They are thus no less ideological than is criticism when it calls a disembodied culture before its tribunal, or holds the alleged negativity of culture responsible for real catastrophes. To accept culture as a whole is to deprive it of the ferment which is its very truth – negation. The joyous appropriation of culture harmonizes with a climate of military music and paintings of battle-scenes. What distinguishes dialectical from cultural criticism is that it heightens cultural criticism until the notion of culture is itself negated, fulfilled and surmounted in one.

Immanent criticism of culture, it may be argued, overlooks what is decisive: the role of ideology in social conflicts. To suppose, if only methodologically, anything like an independent logic of culture is to collaborate in the hypostasis of culture, the ideological *proton pseudos*. The substance of culture, according to this argument, resides not in culture alone but in its relation to something external, to the material life-process. Culture, as Marx observed of juridical and political systems, cannot be fully 'understood either in terms of itself . . . or in terms of the so-called universal development of the mind'. To ignore this, the argument concludes, is to make ideology the basic matter and thus to establish it firmly. And in fact, having taken a dialectical turn, cultural criticism must not hypostasize the criteria of culture. Criticism retains its mobility in regard to culture by recognizing the latter's position within the whole. Without such freedom, without consciousness transcending the immanence of culture, immanent criticism itself would be inconceivable: the spontaneous movement of the object can be followed only by someone who is not entirely engulfed by it. But the traditional demand of the ideology-critique is itself subject to a historical dynamic. The critique was conceived against idealism, the philosophical form which reflects the fetishization of culture. Today, however, the definition of consciousness in terms of being has become a means of dispensing with all consciousness which does not conform to existence. The objectivity of truth, without which the dialectic is inconceivable, is tacitly replaced by vulgar positivism and pragmatism – ultimately, that is, by bourgeois subjectivism. During the bourgeois era, the prevailing theory was the ideology and the opposing *praxis* was in direct contradiction. Today, theory hardly exists any longer and the ideology drones, as it were, from the gears of an irresistible *praxis*. No notion dares to be conceived any more which does not cheerfully include, in all camps, explicit instructions as to who its beneficiaries are – exactly what the polemics once sought to expose. But the unideological thought is that which does not permit itself to be reduced to 'operational terms' and instead strives solely to help the things themselves to that articulation from which they are otherwise cut off by the prevailing language. Since the moment arrived when every advanced economic and political council agreed that what was important was to change the world and that to interpret it was *allotria*, it has become difficult simply to invoke the *Theses* against Feuerbach. Dialectics also includes the relation between action and contemplation. In an epoch in which bourgeois social science has, in Scheler's words, 'plundered' the Marxian notion of ideology and diluted it to universal relativism, the danger involved in overlooking the function of ideologies has become less than that of judging intellectual phenomena in a subsumptive, uninformed and administrative manner and assimilating them into the prevailing constellations of power which the intellect ought to expose. As with many other elements of dialectical materialism, the notion of ideology has changed from an instrument of knowledge into its strait-jacket. In the name of the dependence of superstructure on base, all use of ideology is controlled instead of criticized. No one is concerned with the objective substance of an ideology as long as it is expedient.

Yet the very function of ideologies becomes increasingly abstract. The suspicion held by earlier cultural critics is confirmed: in a world which denies the mass of human beings the authentic experience of intellectual phenomena by making genuine education a privilege and by shackling consciousness, the specific ideological content of these phenomena is less important than the fact that there should be anything at all to fill the vacuum of the expropriated consciousness and to distract from the open secret. Within the context of its social effect, the particular ideological doctrine which a film imparts to its audience is presumably far less important than the interest of the homeward bound movie-goer in the names and marital affairs of the stars. Vulgar notions such as 'amusement' and 'diversion' are more appropriate than pretentious explanations which designate one writer as a representative of the lower-middle class, another of the upper-middle. Culture has become ideological not only as the quintessence of subjectively devised manifestations of the objective mind, but even more as the sphere of private life. The illusory importance and autonomy of private life conceals the fact that private life drags on only as an appendage of the social process. Life transforms itself into the ideology of reification – a death mask. Hence, the task of criticism must be not so much to search for the particular interest-groups to which cultural phenomena are to be assigned, but rather to decipher the general social tendencies which are expressed in these phenomena and through which the most powerful interests realize themselves. Cultural criticism must become social physiognomy. The more the whole divests itself of all spontaneous elements, is socially mediated and filtered, is 'consciousness', the more it becomes 'culture'. In addition to being the means of subsistence, the material process of production finally unveils itself as that which it always was, from its origins in the exchange-relationship as the false consciousness which the two contracting parties have of each other: ideology. Inversely, however, consciousness becomes at the same time increasingly a mere transitional moment in the functioning of the whole. Today, ideology means society as appearance. Although mediated by the totality behind which stands the rule of partiality, ideology is not simply reducible to a partial interest. It is, as it were, equally near the centre in all its pieces.

The alternatives – either calling culture as a whole into question from outside under the general notion of ideology, or confronting it with the norms which it itself has crystallized – cannot be accepted by critical theory. To insist on the choice between immanence and transcendence is to revert to the traditional logic criticized in Hegel's polemic against Kant. As Hegel argued, every method which sets limits and restricts itself to the limits of its object thereby goes beyond them. The position transending culture is in a certain sense presupposed by dialectics as the conscious-ness which does succumb in advance to the fetishization of the intellectual sphere. Dialectics means intransigence towards all reification. The transcendent method, which aims at totality, seems more radical than the immanent method, which presupposes the questionable whole. The transcendent critic assumes an as it were Archimedean position above culture and the blindness of society, from which consciousness can bring the totality, no matter how massive, into flux. The attack on the whole draws strength from the fact that the semblance of unity and wholeness in the world grows with the advance of reification; that is, with division. But the summary dismissal of ideology which in the Soviet sphere has already become a pretext for cynical terror, taking the form of a ban on 'objectivism', pays that wholeness too high an honour. Such an attitude buys up culture *en bloc* from society, regardless of the use to which it is put. If ideology is defined as socially necessary appearance, then the ideology today is society itself in so far as its integral power and inevitability, its overwhelming existence-in-itself, surrogates the meaning which that existence has exterminated. The choice of a standpoint outside the sway of existing society is as fictitious as only the construction of abstract utopias can be. Hence, the transcendent criticism of culture, much like bourgeois cultural criticism, sees itself obliged to fall back upon the idea of 'naturalness', which itself forms a central element of bourgeois ideology. The transcendent attack on culture regularly speaks the language of false escape, that of the 'nature boy'. It despises the mind and its works, contending that they are, after all, only man-made and serve only to cover up 'natural' life. Because of this alleged worthlessness, the phenomena allow themselves to be manipulated and degraded for purposes of domination. This explains the inadequacy of most socialist contributions to cultural criticism: they lack the experience of that with which they deal. In wishing to wipe away the whole as if with a sponge, they develop an affinity to barbarism. Their sympathies are inevitably with the more primitive, more undifferentiated, no matter how much it may contradict the level of intellectual productive forces. The blanket rejection of culture becomes a pretext for promoting what is crudest, 'healthiest', even repressive; above all, the perennial conflict between individual and society, both drawn in like manner, which is obstinately resolved in favour of society according to the criteria of the administrators who have appropriated it. From there it is only a step to the official reinstatement of culture. Against this struggles the immanent procedure as the more essentially dialectical. It takes seriously the principle that it is not ideology in itself which is untrue but rather its pretension to correspond to reality. Immanent criticism of intellectual and artistic phenomena seeks to grasp, through the analysis of their form and meaning, the contradiction between their objective idea and that pretension. It names what the consistency or inconsistency of the work itself expresses of the structure of the existent. Such criticism does not stop at a general recognition of the servitude of the objective mind, but seeks rather to transform this knowledge into a heightened perception of the thing itself. Insight into the negativity of culture is binding only when it reveals the truth or untruth of a perception, the consequence or lameness of a thought, the coherence or incoherence of a structure, the substantiality or emptiness of a figure of speech. Where it finds inadequacies it does not ascribe them hastily to the individual and his psychology, which are merely the façade of the failure, but instead seeks to derive them from the irreconcilability of the object's moments. It pursues the logic of its aporias, the insolubility of the task itself. In such antinomies criticism perceives those of society. A successful work, according to immanent criticism, is not one which resolves objective contradictions in a spurious harmony, but one which expresses the idea of harmony negatively by embodying the contradictions, pure and uncompromised, in its innermost structure. Confronted with this kind of work, the verdict 'mere ideology' loses its meaning. At the same time, however, immanent criticism holds in evidence the fact that the mind has always been under a spell. On its own it is unable to resolve the contradictions under which it labours. Even the most radical reflection of the mind on its own failure is limited by the fact that it remains only reflection, without altering the existence to which its failure bears witness. Hence immanent criticism cannot take comfort in its own idea. It can neither be vain enough to believe that it can liberate the mind directly by immersing itself in it, nor naïve enough to believe that unflinching immersion in the object will inevitably lead to truth by virtue of the logic of things if only the subjective knowledge of the false whole is kept from intruding from the outside, as it were, in the determination of the object. The less the dialectical method can today presuppose the Hegelian identity of subject and object, the more it is obliged to be mindful of the duality of the moments. It must relate the knowledge of society as a totality and of the mind's involvement in it to the claim inherent in the specific content of the object that it be apprehended as such. Dialectics cannot, therefore, permit any insistence on logical neatness to encroach on its right to go from one *genus* to another, to shed light on an object in itself hermetic by casting a glance at society, to present society with the bill which the object does not redeem. Finally, the very opposition between knowledge which penetrates from without and that which bores from within becomes suspect to the dialectical method, which sees in it a symptom of precisely that reification which the dialectic is obliged to accuse. The abstract categorizing and, as it were, administrative thinking of the former corresponds in the latter to the fetishism of an object blind to its genesis, which has become the prerogative of the expert. But if stubbornly immanent comtemplation threatens to revert to idealism, to the illusion of the self-sufficient mind in command of both itself and of reality, transcendent contemplation threatens to forget the effort of conceptualization required and content itself instead with the prescribed label, the petrified invective, most often 'petty bourgeois', the ukase dispatched from above. Topological thinking, which knows the place of every phenomenon and the essence of none, is secretly related to the paranoic system of delusions which is cut off from experience of the object. With the aid of mechanically functioning categories, the world is divided into black and white and thus made ready for the very domination against which concepts were once conceived. No theory, not even that which is true, is safe from perversion into delusion once it has renounced a spontaneous relation to the object. Dialectics must guard against this no less than against enthrallment in the cultural object. It can subscribe neither to the cult of the mind nor to hatred of it. The dialectical critic of culture must both participate in culture and not participate. Only then does he do justice to his object and to himself.

The traditional transcendent critique of ideology is obsolete. In principle, the method succumbs to the very reification which is its critical theme. By transferring the notion of causality directly from the realm of physical nature to society, it falls back behind its own object. Nevertheless, the transcendent method can still appeal to the fact that it employs reified notions only in so far as society itself is reified. Through the crudity and severity, of the notion of causality, it claims to hold up a mirror to society's own crudity and severity, to its debasement of the mind. But the sinister, integrated society of today no longer tolerates even those relatively independent, distinct moments to which the theory of the causal dependence of superstructure on base once referred. In the open-air prison which the world is becoming, it is no longer so important to know what depends on what, such is the extent to which everything is one. All phenomena rigidify, become insignias of the absolute rule of that which is. There are no more ideologies in the authentic sense of false consciousness, only advertisements for the world through its duplication and the provocative lie which does not seek belief but commands silence. Hence, the question of the causal dependence of culture, a question which seems to embody the voice of that on which culture is thought only to depend, takes on a backwoods ring. Of course, even the immanent method is eventually overtaken by this. It is dragged into the abyss by its object. The materialistic transparency of culture has not made it more honest, only more vulgar. By relinquishing its own particularity, culture has also relinquished the salt of truth, which once consisted in its opposition to other particularities. To call it to account before a responsibility which it denies is only to confirm cultural pomposity. Neutralized and ready-made, traditional culture has become worthless today. Through an irrevocable process its heritage, hypocritically reclaimed by the Russians, has become expendable to the highest degree, superfluous, trash. And the hucksters of mass culture can point to it with a grin, for they treat it as such. The more total society becomes, the greater the reification of the mind and the more paradoxical its effort to escape reification on its own. Even the most extreme consciousness of doom threatens to degenerate into idle chatter. Cultural criticism finds itself faced with the final stage of the dialectic of culture and barbarism. To write poetry after Auschwitz is barbaric. And this corrodes even the knowledge of why it has become impossible to write poetry today. Absolute reification, which presupposed intellectual progress as one of its elements, is now preparing to absorb the mind entirely. Critical intelligence cannot be equal to this challenge as long as it confines itself to self-satisfied contemplation.

D: HERBERT MARCUSE

27 One Dimensional Man

Herbert Marcuse

A comfortable, smooth, reasonable, democratic unfreedom prevails in advanced industrial civilization, a token of technical progress. Indeed, what could be more rational than the suppression of individuality in the mechanization of socially necessary but painful performances; the concentration of individual enterprises in more effective, more productive corporations; the regulation of free competition among unequally equipped economic subjects; the curtailment of prerogatives and national sovereignties which impede the international organization of resources. That this technological order also involves a political and intellectual coordination may be a regrettable and yet promising development.

The rights and liberties which were such vital factors in the origins and earlier stages of industrial society yield to a higher stage of this society: they are losing their traditional rationale and content. Freedom of thought, speech, and conscience were – just as free enterprise, which they served to promote and protect – essentially *critical* ideas, designed to replace an obsolescent material and intellectual culture by a more productive and rational one. Once institutionalized, these rights and liberties shared the fate of the society of which they had become an integral part. The achievement cancels the premises. . . .

Contemporary industrial civilization demonstrates that it has reached the stage at which "the free society" can no longer be adequately defined in the traditional terms of economic, political, and intellectual liberties, not because these liberties have become insignificant, but because they are too significant to be confined within the traditional forms. New modes of realization are needed, corresponding to the new capabilities of society.

Such new modes can be indicated only in negative terms because they would amount to the negation of the prevailing modes. Thus economic freedom would mean freedom *from* the economy – from being controlled by economic forces and relationships; freedom from the daily struggle for existence, from earning a living. Political freedom would mean liberation of the individuals *from* politics over which they have no effective control. Similarly, intellectual freedom would mean the restoration of individual thought now absorbed by mass communication and indoctrination, abolition of "public opinion" together with its makers. The unrealistic sound of these propositions is indicative, not of their utopian character, but of the strength of the forces which prevent their realization. The most effective and enduring form of warfare against liberation is the implanting of material and intellectual needs that perpetuate obsolete forms of the struggle for existence.

The intensity, the satisfaction and even the character of human needs, beyond the biological level, have always been preconditioned. Whether or not the possibility of doing or leaving, enjoying or destroying, possessing or rejecting something is seized as a *need* depends on whether or not it can be seen as desirable and necessary for the prevailing societal institutions and interests. In this sense, human needs are historical needs and, to the extent to which the society demands the repressive development of the individual, his needs themselves and their claim for satisfaction are subject to overriding critical standards.

We may distinguish both true and false needs. "False" are those which are superimposed upon the individual by particular social interests in his repression: the needs which perpetuate toil, aggressiveness, misery, and injustice. Their satisfaction might be most gratifying to the individual, but this happiness is not a condition which has to be maintained and protected if it serves to arrest the development of the ability (his own and others) to recognize the disease of the whole and grasp the chances of curing the disease. The result then is euphoria in unhappiness. Most of the prevailing needs to relax, to have fun, to behave and consume in accordance with the advertisements, to love and hate what others love and hate, belong to this category of false needs.

Such needs have a societal content and function which are determined by external powers over which the individual has no control; the development and satisfaction of these needs is heteronomous. No matter how much such needs may have become the individual's own, reproduced and fortified by the conditions of his existence; no matter how much he identifies himself with them and finds himself in their satisfaction, they continue to be what they were from the beginning – products of a society whose dominant interest demands repression.

The prevalence of repressive needs is an accomplished fact, accepted in ignorance and defeat, but a fact that must be undone in the interest of the happy individual as well as all those whose misery is the price of his satisfaction. The only needs that have an unqualified claim for satisfaction are the vital ones – nourishment, clothing, lodging at the attainable level of culture. The satisfaction of these needs is the prerequisite for the realization of *all* needs, of the unsublimated as well as the sublimated ones. . . .

The distinguishing feature of advanced industrial society is its effective suffocation of those needs which demand liberation – liberation also from that which is tolerable and rewarding and comfortable – while it sustains and absolves the destructive power and repressive function of the affluent society. Here, the social controls exact the overwhelming need for the production and consumption of waste; the need for stupefying work where it is no longer a real necessity; the need for modes of relaxation which soothe and prolong this stupefication; the need for maintaining such deceptive liberties as free competition at administered prices, a free press which censors itself, free choice between brands and gadgets.

Under the rule of a repressive whole, liberty can be made into a powerful instrument of domination. The range of choice open to the individual is not the decisive factor in determining the degree of human freedom, but *what* can be chosen and what *is* chosen by the individual. The criterion for free choice can never be an absolute one, but neither is it entirely relative. Free election of masters does not abolish the masters or the slaves. Free choice among a wide variety of goods and services does not signify freedom if these goods and services sustain social controls over a life of toil and fear – that is, if they sustain alienation. And the spontaneous reproduction of superimposed needs by the individual does not establish autonomy; it only testifies to the efficacy of the controls. . . .

It is a rational universe which, by the mere weight and capabilities of its apparatus, blocks all escape. In its relation to the reality of daily life, the high culture of the past was many things – opposition and adornment, outcry and resignation. But it was also the appearance of the realm of freedom: the refusal to behave. Such refusal cannot be blocked without a compensation which seems more satisfying than the refusal. The conquest and unification of opposites, which finds its ideological glory in the transformation of higher into popular culture, takes place on a material ground of increased satisfaction. This is also the ground which allows a sweeping *desublimation*.

Artistic alienation is sublimation. It creates the images of conditions which are irreconcilable with the established Reality Principle but which, as cultural images, become tolerable, even edifying and useful. Now this imagery is invalidated. Its incorporation into the kitchen, the office, the shop; its commercial release for business and fun is, in a sense, desublimation – replacing mediated by immediate gratification. But it is desublimation practiced from a "position of strength" on the part of society, which can afford to grant more than before because its interests have become the innermost drives of its citizens, and because the joys which it grants promote social cohesion and contentment.

The Pleasure Principle absorbs the Reality Principle; sexuality is liberated (or rather liberalized) in socially constructive forms. This notion implies that there are repressive modes of desublimation,[1] compared with which the sublimated drives and objectives contain more deviation, more freedom, and more refusal to heed the social taboos. It appears that such repressive desublimation is indeed operative in the sexual sphere, and here, as in the desublimation of higher culture, it operates as the by-product of the social controls of technological reality, which extend liberty while intensifying domination. The link between desublimation and technological society can perhaps best be illuminated by discussing the change in the social use of instinctual energy.

In this society, not all the time spent on and with mechanisms is labor time (i.e., unpleasurable but necessary toil), and not all the energy saved by the machine is labor power. Mechanization has also "saved" libido, the energy of the Life Instincts – that is, has barred it from previous modes of realization. This is the kernel of truth in the romantic contrast between the modern traveler and the wandering poet or artisan, between assembly line and handicraft, town and city, factory-produced bread and the home-made loaf, the sailboat and the outboard motor, etc. True, this romantic pre-technical world was permeated with misery, toil, and filth, and these in turn were the background of all pleasure and joy. Still, there was a "landscape," a medium of libidinal experience which no longer exists.

With its disappearance (itself a historical prerequisite of progress), a whole dimension of human activity and passivity have been de-eroticized. The environment from which the individual could obtain pleasure – which he could cathect as gratifying almost as an extended zone of the body – has been rigidly reduced. Consequently, the "universe" of libidinous cathexis is likewise reduced. The effect is a localization and contraction of libido, the reduction of erotic to sexual experience and satisfaction.[2]

For example, compare love-making in a meadow and in an automobile, on a lovers' walk outside the town walls and on a Manhattan street. In the former cases, the environment partakes of and invites libidinal cathexis and tends to be eroticized. Libido transcends beyond the immediate erotogenic zones – a process of nonrepressive sublimation. In contrast, a mechanized environment seems to block such self-transcendence of libido. Impelled in the striving to extend the field of erotic gratification, libido becomes less "polymorphous," less capable of eroticism beyond localized sexuality, and the *latter* is intensified.

Thus diminishing erotic and intensifying sexual energy, the technological reality *limits the scope of sublimation*. It also reduces the *need* for sublimation. In the mental apparatus, the tension between that which is desired and that which is permitted seems considerably lowered, and the Reality Principle no longer seems to require a sweeping and painful transformation of instinctual needs. The individual must adapt himself to a world which does not seem to demand the denial of his innermost needs – a world which is not essentially hostile.

The organism is thus being preconditioned for the spontaneous acceptance of what is offered. Inasmuch as the greater liberty involves a contraction rather than extension and development of instinctual needs, it works *for* rather than *against* the status quo of general repression – one might speak of "institutionalized desublimation." The latter appears to be a vital factor in the making of the authoritarian personality of our time.

It has often been noted that advanced industrial civilization operates with a greater degree of sexual freedom – "operates" in the sense that the latter becomes a market value and a factor of social mores. Without ceasing to be an instrument of labor, the body is allowed to exhibit its sexual features in the everyday work world and in work relations. This is one of the unique achievements of industrial society – rendered possible by the reduction of dirty and heavy physical labor; by the availability of cheap, attractive clothing, beauty culture, and physical hygiene; by the requirements of the advertising industry, etc. The sexy office and sales girls, the handsome, virile junior executive and floor walker are highly marketable commodities, and the possession of suitable mistresses – once the prerogative of kings, princes, and lords – facilitates the career of even the less exalted ranks in the business community.

Functionalism, going artistic, promotes this trend. Shops and offices open themselves through huge glass windows and expose their personnel; inside, high counters and non-transparent partitions are coming down. The corrosion of privacy in massive apartment houses and suburban homes breaks the barrier which formerly separated the individual from the public existence and exposes more easily the attractive qualities of other wives and other husbands.

This socialization is not contradictory but complementary to the de-eroticization of the environment. Sex is integrated into work and public relations and is thus made more susceptible to (controlled) satisfaction. Technical progress and more comfortable living permit the systematic inclusion of libidinal components into the realm of commodity production and exchange. But no matter how controlled the mobilization of instinctual energy may be (it sometimes amounts to a scientific management of libido), no matter how much it may serve as a prop for the status quo – it is also gratifying to the managed individuals, just as racing the outboard motor, pushing the power lawn mower, and speeding the automobile are fun.

This mobilization and administration of libido may account for much of the voluntary compliance, the absence of terror, the pre-established harmony between individual needs and socially-required desires, goals, and aspirations. The technological and political conquest of the transcending factors in human existence, so characteristic of advanced industrial civilization, here asserts itself in the instinctual sphere: satisfaction in a way which generates submission and weakens the rationality of protest.

The range of socially permissible and desirable satisfaction is greatly enlarged, but through this satisfaction, the Pleasure Principle is reduced – deprived of the claims which are irreconcilable with the established society. Pleasure, thus adjusted, generates submission.

In contrast to the pleasures of adjusted desublimation, sublimation preserves the consciousness of the renunciations which the repressive society inflicts upon the individual, and thereby preserves the need for liberation. To be sure, all sublimation is enforced by the power of society, but the unhappy consciousness of this power already breaks through alienation. To be sure, all sublimation accepts the social barrier to instinctual gratification, but it also transgresses this barrier.

The Superego, in censoring the unconscious and in implanting conscience, also censors the censor because the developed conscience registers the forbidden evil act not only in the individual but also in his society. Conversely, loss of conscience due to the satisfactory liberties granted by an unfree society makes for a *happy consciousness* which facilitates acceptance of the misdeeds of this society. It is the token of declining autonomy and comprehension. Sublimation demands a high degree of autonomy and comprehension; it is mediation between the conscious and the unconscious, between the primary and secondary processes, between the intellect and instinct, renunciation and rebellion. In its most accomplished modes, such as in the artistic *oeuvre*, sublimation becomes the cognitive power which defeats suppression while bowing to it.

In the light of the cognitive function of this mode of sublimation, the desublimation rampant in advanced industrial society reveals its truly conformist function. This liberation of sexuality (and of aggressiveness) frees the instinctual drives from much of the unhappiness and discontent that elucidate the repressive power of the established universe of satisfaction. To be sure, there is pervasive unhappiness, and the happy consciousness is shaky enough – a thin surface over fear, frustration, and disgust. This unhappiness lends itself easily to political mobilization; without room for conscious development, it may become the instinctual reservoir for a new fascist way of life and death. But there are many ways in which the unhappiness beneath the happy consciousness may be turned into a source of strength and cohesion for the social order. The conflicts of the unhappy individual now seem far more amenable to cure than those which made for Freud's "discontent in civilization," and they seem more adequately defined in terms of the "neurotic personality of our time" than in terms of the eternal struggle between Eros and Thanatos.

The way in which controlled desublimation may weaken the instinctual revolt against the established Reality Principle may be illuminated by the contrast between the representation of sexuality in classical and romantic literature and in our contemporary literature. If one selects, from among the works which are, in their very substance and inner form, determined by the erotic commitment, such essentially different examples as Racine's *Phèdre*, Goethe's *Wahlverwandtschaften*, Baudelaire's *Les Fleurs du Mal*, Tolstoy's *Anna Karenina*, sexuality consistently appears in a highly sublimated, "mediated," reflective form – but in this form, it is absolute, uncompromising, unconditional. The dominion of Eros is, from the beginning, also that of Thanatos. Fulfillment is destruction, not in a moral or sociological but in an ontological sense. It is beyond good and evil, beyond social morality, and thus it remains beyond the reaches of the established Reality Principle, which this Eros refuses and explodes.

In contrast, desublimated sexuality is rampant in O'Neill's alcoholics and Faulkner's savages, in the *Streetcar Named Desire* and under the *Hot Tin Roof*, in *Lolita*, in all the stories of Hollywood and New York orgies, and the adventures of suburban housewives. This is infinitely more realistic, daring, uninhibited. It is part and parcel of the society in which it happens, but nowhere its negation. What happens is surely wild and obscene, virile and tasty, quite immoral – and, precisely because of that, perfectly harmless.

Freed from the sublimated form which was the very token of its irreconcilable dreams – a form which is the style, the language in which the story is told – sexuality turns into a vehicle for the bestsellers of oppression. It could not be said of any of the sexy women in contemporary literature what Balzac says of the whore Esther: that hers was the tenderness which blossoms only in infinity. This society turns everything it touches into a potential source of progress *and* of exploitation, of drudgery *and* satisfaction, of freedom *and* of oppression. Sexuality is no exception.

The concept of controlled desublimation would imply the possibility of a simultaneous release of repressed sexuality *and* aggressiveness, a possibility which seems incompatible with Freud's notion of the fixed quantum of instinctual energy available for distribution between the two primary drives. According to Freud, strengthening of sexuality (libido) would necessarily involve weakening of aggressiveness, and vice versa. However, if the socially permitted and encouraged release of libido would be that of partial and localized sexuality, it would be tantamount to an actual compression of erotic energy, and this desublimation would be compatible with the growth of unsublimated as well as sublimated forms of aggressiveness. The latter is rampant throughout contemporary industrial society.

Has it attained a degree of normalization where the individuals are getting used to the risk of their own dissolution and disintegration in the course of normal national preparedness? Or is this acquiescence entirely due to their impotence to do much about it? In any case, the risk of avoidable, man-made destruction has become normal equipment in the mental as well as material household of the people, so that it can no longer serve to indict or refute the established social system. Moreover, as part of their daily household, it may even tie them to this system. The economic and political connection between the absolute enemy and the high standard of living (and the desired level of employment!) is transparent enough, but also rational enough to be accepted.

Assuming that the Destruction Instinct (in the last analysis: the Death Instinct) is a large component of the energy which feeds the technical conquest of man and nature, it seems that society's growing capacity to manipulate technical progress also increases its *capacity to manipulate and control this instinct*, i.e., to satisfy it "productively." Then social cohesion would be strengthened at the deepest instinctual roots. The supreme risk, and even the fact of war would meet, not only with helpless acceptance, but also with instinctual approval on the part of the victims. Here too, we would have controlled desublimation.

Institutionalized desublimation thus appears to be an aspect of the "conquest of transcendence" achieved by the one-dimensional society. Just as this society tends to reduce, and even absorb opposition (the qualitative difference!) in the realm of politics and higher culture, so it does in the instinctual sphere. The result is the atrophy of the mental organs for grasping the contradictions and the alternatives and, in the one remaining dimension of technological rationality, the *Happy Consciousness* comes to prevail.

It reflects the belief that the real is rational, and that the established system, in spite of everything, delivers the goods. The people are led to find in the productive apparatus the effective agent of thought and action to which their personal thought and action can and must be surrendered. And in this transfer, the apparatus also assumes the role of a moral agent. Conscience is absolved by reification, by the general necessity of things.

In this general necessity, guilt has no place. One man can give the signal that liquidates hundreds and thousands of people, then declare himself free from all pangs of conscience, and live happily ever after. The antifascist powers who beat fascism on the battlefields reap the benefits of the Nazi scientists, generals, and engineers; they have the historical advantage of the late-comer. What begins as the horror of the concentration camps turns into the practice of training people for abnormal conditions – a subterranean human existence and the daily intake of radioactive nourishment. A Christian minister declares that it does not contradict Christian principles to prevent with all available means your neighbor from entering your bomb shelter. Another Christian minister contradicts his colleague and says it does. Who is right? Again, the neutrality of technological rationality shows forth over and above politics, and again it shows forth as spurious, for in both cases, it serves the politics of domination.

> "The world of the concentration camps ... was not an exceptionally monstrous society. What we saw there was the image, and in a sense the quintessence, of the infernal society into which we are plunged every day."[3]

It seems that even the most hideous transgressions can be repressed in such a manner that, for all practical purposes, they have ceased to be a danger for society. Or, if their eruption leads to functional disturbances in the individual (as in the case of one Hiroshima pilot), it does not disturb the functioning of society. A mental hospital manages the disturbance.

The Happy Consciousness has no limits – it arranges games with death and disfiguration in which fun, team work, and strategic importance mix in rewarding social harmony. . . .

Obviously, in the realm of the Happy Consciousness, guilt feeling has no place, and the calculus takes care of conscience. When the whole is at stake, there is no crime except that of rejecting the whole, or not defending it. Crime, guilt, and guilt feeling become a private affair. Freud revealed in the psyche of the individual the crimes of mankind, in the individual case history the history of the whole. This fatal link is successfully suppressed. Those who identify themselves with the whole, who are installed as the leaders and defenders of the whole can make mistakes, but they cannot do wrong – they are not guilty. They may become guilty again when this identification no longer holds, when they are gone.

Notes

1   See my book *Eros and Civilization* (Boston: Beacon Press, 1954), esp. Chapter X.
2   In accordance with the terminology used in the later works of Freud: sexuality as "specialized" partial drive; Eros as that of the entire organism.
3   E. Ionesco, in *Nouvelle Revue Française*, July 1956, as quoted in *London Times Literary Supplement*, March 4, 1960.

Part VI

Structural-Functional Analysis

Introduction to Part VI

Functionalism (sometimes called "structural-functionalism") refers to a body of theory first developed in the 1930s and 1940s that treats society as a set of interdependent systems. The theory rests on an organic analogy that likens a social system to a physical body, in which each subsystem is necessary to maintain the proper functioning of the entire organism. From a functionalist point of view, the key to understanding a social subsystem is to trace its function in the working of the whole.

According to such arguments, there are a number of functional "requisites" necessary to meet the basic needs of any society (see Aberle et al., 1950). Specific subsystems develop to meet those social needs. Functional theorists generally assumed that these subsystems would tend toward a stable equilibrium, with social change proceeding in a gradual evolutionary manner. For example, the social need for a common form of communication leads to a stable, slowly evolving language system. The need to control disruptive behavior leads to a relatively stable legal and political system. Perhaps most importantly, every society has some system for assigning people to different social positions and socializing them into the relevant roles, resulting in a relatively stable stratification system. To say that a system is "functional" is thus to say that it serves the needs of the society as a whole, not that it serves the interests of every individual.

The intellectual roots of functionalism stem largely from the organic perspectives of Auguste Comte, Herbert Spencer, and Émile Durkheim and the formal sociology of Georg Simmel. Spencer's work emphasized a social Darwinist position in which societies adapted to their environments through adaptation and natural selection, a position used to support laissez faire political perspectives in the late nineteenth century. Durkheim adopted this organic analogy, showing how social systems functioned to produce different forms of integration. Durkheim also influenced the later functionalists by noting that the cause of a given phenomenon and its function were separate.

This early work, and especially that of Durkheim, spawned two distinct legacies. In France, it influenced the work of structuralist anthropology, which in turn deeply influenced theorists such as Foucault and Bourdieu (see *Contemporary Sociological Theory*, the sister volume to this reader). In America, it fostered the functionalists. Functionalist ideas were rekindled by the theoretical efforts of Talcott Parsons and his students and colleagues, most notably Robert K. Merton. Substantive work in the functionalist tradition has focused on system-level properties, attempting to identify and understand how various elements of society fit together. Parsons claimed that the study of *social institutions* was the primary business of sociology, and a number of studies focused on how institutions develop and the functions they play.

Lives and Intellectual Contexts

Talcott Parsons and Robert Merton are the central figures in the American structural-functionalist tradition. As this introduction will detail below, Parsons and Merton differed in many ways; however, the two figures were immensely important in the development of functionalism as a central mode of inquiry in mid-twentieth-century American sociology. Structural-functionalism provided a coherent theoretical "center" for American sociologists – even though many bristled at its dominance.

Talcott Parsons (1902–79) was born in Colorado Springs, Colorado. He earned his undergraduate degree from Amherst College where he studied both biology and economics. After graduating, he spent a year at the London School of Economics. There, he was introduced to the field of sociology and took two classes with Bronislaw Malinowski, the famous structural anthropologist. After his year in London, Parsons accepted an exchange fellowship at Heidelberg. Max Weber had died several years before Parsons arrived at Heidelberg, but his thinking still held a strong influence there. Traces of Weber's thought are especially evident in Parsons' early work. His focus on social action as the proper subject for sociology is directly influenced by Weber's definition of the field. In fact, Parsons introduced Weber's work to much of the English-speaking academic world with his translation of the first part of *Economy and Society*. Weber's focus on social action became crucial to Parsons' early theoretical contributions.

Parsons' first academic position was as an instructor in the Harvard economics department. He moved to sociology when Pitirim Sorokin founded the department in 1930. Parsons published his first major work, *The Structure of Social Action*, in 1937. In 1939 he was given tenure at Harvard, and was appointed the chair of the Harvard sociology department in 1944. He went on to found the influential Program in Social Relations in 1946. The Program in Social Relations was Parsons' attempt to realize his vision of an integrated system of social sciences. He died in 1979 while returning to Heidelberg on the fiftieth anniversary of his Ph.D.

Robert K. Merton (1910–) was born in Philadelphia to a working-class Jewish immigrant family. After winning a scholarship to Temple University, where he became interested in sociology, he went on to do his graduate work at Harvard with Talcott Parsons and George Sarton. Merton, along with his colleague Paul Lazarsfeld, was largely responsible for making the sociology department at Columbia University famous by focusing attention away from grand theory and toward empirical research. He served as the associate director of Columbia's Bureau of Applied Social Research (1942–71) and is currently University Professor Emeritus at Columbia University.

American Structural-Functionalism

Of Parsons' many books and papers, *The Structure of Social Action* (1937) and *The Social System* (1951) are his most influential. In *The Structure of Social Action*, Parsons turned a critical eye on the work of four classical theorists (Alfred Marshall,

Vilfredo Pareto, Émile Durkheim and Max Weber), showing how each had responded to the inadaquacies of simple utilitarian perspectives in social thought. Through careful critique and comparison, Parsons showed that the four theorists converged on a single underlying vision of social order and action. This vision was neither individualistically rational (*utilitarian*) nor normatively determined (*idealistic*), but instead a synthesis that he termed "voluntaristic." Voluntaristic action implies that people make choices in a way that balances normative and self-interested pressures. For order to prevail in a system of such agents, Parsons suggests that some notion of value consensus was needed. Like Durkheim, Parsons did not suggest that a society would or should adopt any particular set of values. Rather, he argued that a society simply needs some common set of values as orienting principles.

Parsons and his colleagues extended the basic elements of voluntaristic action theory by introducing what they called *pattern variables*. The five pattern variables are value dimensions that characterize basic dilemmas facing actors, and are represented with labels that define extreme positions on each continuum. The first of the five pattern variables is gratification ↔ disicipline, relating to the extent of an actor's emotional involvement. The second is private ↔ collective, depending on whether action relates to the needs of the individual or the needs of a wider population. Universalism ↔ particularism refers to whether action relates to a particular person, such as one's child, or a wider class of generalized others. Fourth, interaction with others can be related to their achievements or their ascribed characteristics (achievement ↔ ascription). And finally, specificity ↔ diffuseness refers to the breadth of possible roles an actor can draw upon in any given interaction.

After his first book, Parsons broadened his focus on action to encompass the larger social context. Parsons argued that society was composed of three interdependent systems: a *cultural* system, consisting of shared symbols (i.e. language, arts, etc.) that serve as modes of expression among actors; a *personality* system, consisting of elements necessary for unique identity; and a *social* system, consisting of modes of interaction among actors. The cultural system connects to the personality system through a process of *internalization* in which actors incorporate cultural factors into their own identities. Understanding the connection between the personality system and the social system involves identifying social roles, which are defined through a process of *socialization*. Finally, Parsons argued that the cultural system and the social system are connected through *social institutions*, which systematize culture within social interaction and roles (see Münch, 1994, pp. 16–30).

Having identified the major systems of society and the relevant features of individual action, Parsons argued that the entire complex was governed by certain functional requirements. Parsons and his colleagues Robert F. Bales and Edward A. Shils described four spheres of activity that any society must accomplish to maintain itself. The four functions are usually referred to by their acronym, **AGIL**. The first element is **Adaptation**, which refers to how well the social system adapts to its material environment. The economic organization of any society is largely captured under this sphere. The second is **Goal attainment**, or the ability of the group to identify and pursue common goals, even though each member may have contrasting individual goals. Political organization is likely to fall under this sphere. Thirdly, Integration refers to dimensions of cohesion and solidarity that unite the group. Integration is complicated by the multiple roles that people play in diverse settings (work roles, family roles, etc.), but refers to norms that promote a sense of "we-ness" among the group (Alexander, 1987). Finally, Latent pattern maintenance refers to the sphere of general values. While largely subjective, these values tend to be institutionalized within any given society.

The excerpts below reflect Parsons' theoretical development over these periods. Starting with an excerpt from *The Structure of Social Action* (1937) we see Parsons' dissatisfaction with utilitarian thinking and his outline of a theory of voluntaristic action. In "The Position of Sociological Theory" (1948), Parsons presents an early statement of the central ideas that would be developed in *The Social System* (1951). We end with a selection from *Theories of Society* (1961) in which the later ideas developed with Bales and Shils are incorporated into the central points of Parsonian functionalism.

Merton's writings span multiple sub-fields in sociology. His most consistent empirical focus has been on the sociology of knowledge and science – early in his career he published *Science, Technology and Society in Seventeenth Century England* (1938) and he has continued to write in the field ever since. But he has also been influential in the areas of crime and deviance. His collection of work in *Social Theory and Social Structure* (1949/1957/1968) captures a great deal of this breadth, and provides a useful starting point for reading his work. Of the work not summarized here, "Social Structure and Anomie," "Contributions to the Theory of Reference Group Behavior," and "The Self-fulfilling Prophecy" are among the most widely read. Throughout his work, while maintaining a generally functionalist approach, his strong commitment to understanding phenomena of the "middle-range" – those phenomena cast at neither too abstract nor too particularistic a level – contrasts directly with the broad theoretical orientation of Parsons.

The three pieces abstracted below represent Merton's general statements on functionalism, the scope of scientific research and the interplay of empirical research and social theory. His distinction between manifest and latent functions provides an important answer to the teleological problem of functionalist theory – that is, the problem of conflating the cause of a given phenomenon with its functional ends. Merton argues that a given social action, such as a rain-dance, might be intended for a manifest function (producing rain). Nonetheless, it may also serve another end (building solidarity within the group). This distinction frees functionalists from needing to link actors' purposes with the functional needs of a society. In contrast to Parsons, Merton argues in "Theories of the Middle Range" that sociologists should develop theories that "lie between the minor but necessary working hypotheses" of research and the "all-inclusive systematic efforts to develop a unified theory" that would explain all social phenomena. Echoing this focus, Merton discusses the interplay of empirical research and middle-range theory in "The Bearing of Empirical Research on Sociological Theory," focusing on how unexpected findings lead to new theoretical development.

The Legacy of Functionalism

The decline of functionalism was swift, with few decidedly functional theoretical works appearing after the middle 1970s. Functionalism, especially Parsonian functionalism, was challenged on multiple fronts. Critics argued that there was an inherently conversative bias in the Parsonian focus on stability and function, which ignored important tensions within societies. With the rise of the Civil Rights movement and reactions to American action abroad, the harmonious self-balancing system seemed hard to square with direct observation. Aside from ideological implications, critics charged that Parsonian theory's inability to accommodate dramatic social change and conflict was itself problematic. Additionally, a general critique of functional theory is that it is *teleological*: that the ends of a given phenomenon are sufficient for *causing* the phenomenon. Since such theories reverse the causal order, the underlying logic appeared flawed (but it should be pointed out that Parsons saw this as a misreading of his work). Finally, contemporary theoretic work moved away from the macro level to the individual level with the simultaneous rise of social exchange theory and symbolic interactionism. While exchange theory largely rejected the normative aspects of Parsons in favor of a rational utilitarian perspective, symbolic internationalist approaches claimed a greater creative capacity for individuals than the pattern variable scheme would allow, resulting in both approaches being able to explain individual action without need for the overarching Parsonian frame.

Structural-functionalism thus fell deeply out of favor in American sociology by the 1970s. Interestingly, it was particularly Parsons' version, and not Merton's that was rejected. Merton's work remained relevant for particular sub-fields, such as the sociology of deviance, even while functionalism's dominance waned generally. In part this was also because Merton's middle-range theory seemed more suited to the increasingly individual-level empirical work in the discipline.

But just as this broad historical cycle took structural-functionalism out of favor, so it seems to be again on the upswing. In the mid-1980s, some aspects of functionalism reappeared, sparked largely through the work of Jeffrey C. Alexander. Alexander has argued that critics of Parsons were correct in many of their aspects, but that a desire to link individual action to wider social norms and a larger systemic view reflects many of the same goals as Parsons. As such, some of the basic systemic elements of a functional perspective provide useful theoretical tools for sociology today. A related body of work on social systems comes from the work of Niklas Luhmann (1995) and incorporates aspects of Parsons' work with that of General Systems Theory (Buckley, 1967).

Ironically, as rational choice theory becomes increasingly dominant in the social sciences, Parsons' emphasis on the contexts and limits of our choices – given by our personality systems, normative environment, and even our biological makeup – provides a necessary reminder of the boundedness of rational action.

Select Bibliography

Aberle, D. F., A. K. Cohen, A. K. Davis, M. J. Levy Jr., and F. X. Sutton. 1950. "The Functional Prerequisites of a Society." *Ethics* 60 (2): 100–11. (This piece provides a simple introduction to what the functionalists felt were the necessary elements for making a society work.)

Alexander, Jeffrey C. 1987. *Twenty Lectures: Sociological Theory Since World War II*. New York: Columbia University Press. (Alexander outlines the major currents of social thought during this time in a well-written and clear set of lectures. Most of the early lectures are devoted to Parsons' work.)

Buckley, Walter. 1967. *Sociology and Modern Systems Theory*. Englewood Cliffs, NJ: Prentice-Hall. (An early treatment of problems related to systems theory, cybernetics and communication-based social theory; provides an alternative systems reaction to Parsons' work.)

Luhmann, Niklas. 1995. *Social Systems*. Trans. John Bednarz, Jr. with Dirk Baecker. Stanford, CA: Stanford University Press. (The definitive statement of Luhmann's work on systems theory, covering his ideas about autopoietic communications systems and self-reference, as applied to the general problem of social order and action. Very difficult to read; described by Luhmann himself as a "labyrinth.")

Merton, Robert K. 1968. *Social Theory and Social Structure*. New York: The Free Press. (A collection of Merton's most central work, containing articles on a wide range of theoretical and empirical topics.)

Münch, Richard. 1994. *Sociological Theory: From the 1920s to the 1960s*. Chicago: Nelson-Hall Publishers. (This volume is dedicated almost entirely to Parsons and provides an excellent interpretation and introduction.

Parsons, Talcott. 1949 (1937). *The Structure of Social Action*. Glencoe, Illinois: The Free Press. (Parsons' major early work on the action frame of reference and its link to social structure.)

Parsons, Talcott. 1951. *The Social System*. New York: The Free Press. (The major work of Parsons' later multi-level theory of the social system.)

Parsons, Talcott. 1977. *The Evolution of Modern Societies*. Jackson Toby, editor. Englewood Cliffs, NJ: Prentice-Hall. (A synthetic presentation of a later version of Parsons' theory.)

Ritzer, George. 1992. *Sociological Theory*. New York: McGraw-Hill. (Provides a nice overview of functionalist theory, situating it well within the broader theoretical context of the time.)

Smelser, Neil J. 1963. *Theory of Collective Behavior*. New York: The Free Press. (Chapter 2 is a clear summary of Parsonian theory. Smelser uses this as a basis for his own more specialized theory.)

A: TALCOTT PARSONS

28 The Structure of Social Action

Talcott Parsons

The Unit of Action Systems

Attention was called to the fact that in the process of scientific conceptualization concrete phenomena come to be divided into units or parts. The first salient feature of the conceptual scheme to be dealt with lies in the character of the units which it employs in making this division. The basic unit may be called the "unit act." Just as the units of a mechanical system in the classical sense, particles, can be defined only in terms of their properties, mass, velocity, location in space, direction of motion, etc., so the units of action systems also have certain basic properties without which it is not possible to conceive of the unit as "existing." Thus, to continue the analogy, the conception of a unit of matter which has mass but which cannot be located in space is, in terms of the classical mechanics, non-sensical. It should be noted that the sense in which the unit act is here spoken of as an existent entity is not that of concrete spatiality or otherwise separate existence, but of conceivability as a unit in terms of a frame of reference. There must be a minimum number of descriptive terms applied to it, a minimum number of facts ascertainable about it, before it can be spoken of at all as a unit in a system.

In this sense then, an "act" involves logically the following: (1) It implies an agent, an "actor." (2) For purposes of definition the act must have an "end," a future state of affairs toward which the process of action is oriented.[1] (3) It must be initiated in a "situation" of which the trends of development differ in one or more important respects from the state of affairs to which the action is oriented, the end. This situation is in turn analyzable into two elements: those over which the actor has no control, that is which he cannot alter, or prevent from being altered, in conformity with his end, and those over which he has such control. The former may be termed the "conditions" of action, the latter the "means." Finally (4) there is inherent in the conception of this unit, in its analytical uses, a certain mode of relationship between these elements. That is, in the choice of alternative means to the end, in so far as the situation allows alternatives, there is a "normative orientation" of action. Within the area of control of the actor, the means employed cannot, in general, be conceived either as chosen at random or as dependent exclusively on the conditions of action, but must in some sense be subject to the influence of an independent, determinate selective factor, a knowledge of which is necessary to the understanding of the concrete course of action. What is essential to the concept of action is that there should be a normative orientation, not that this should be of any particular type. As will be seen, the discrimination of various possible modes of normative orientation is one of the most important questions with which this study will be confronted. . . .

The Utilitarian System

Thus far the discussion has been confined to the most general features of the action scheme of thought. Though the unit act is basic in all the theoretical structures encountered here, it is not surprising that the different possible permutations and combinations on this basis should not have been exhausted in the earlier stages of the process of development of the system as a whole. In fact, by the nineteenth century a subsystem (or, perhaps better, an interrelated group of several sub-subsystems) of the theory of action dominated Western European social thought. It was built essentially out of the kind of units described but put together in a peculiar way which distinguishes it sharply from the emerging system – the principal concern of the present discussion. Since the process of emergence of the later subsystem from the earlier must be traced, it is necessary to give a fairly extensive account of the starting point of the process, so that the nature and extent of the change may become clear.

The origin of the mode of thinking in terms of the action schema in general is so old and so obscure that it is fruitless to inquire into it here. It is sufficient to point out that, just like the schema of the classical physics, it is deeply rooted in the common-sense experience of everyday life, and it is of a range of such experience that it may be regarded as universal to all human beings. Proof of this claim can be found in the fact that the basic elements of the schema are imbedded in the structure of all languages, as in the universal existence of a verb corresponding to the English verb "to do." The peculiarity of the situation with which the analysis begins lies in the fact that for sophisticated thinkers this universal material of common-sense experience has become selectively ordered in a particular way so that a peculiar conceptual structure arises which, in spite of its many variants retains certain common features throughout. The peculiarities of this structure go back to a selective emphasis on certain problems and certain ways of looking at human action.

The first leading characteristic is a certain "atomism." It may be described as the strong tendency to consider mainly the properties of conceptually isolated unit acts and to infer the properties of systems of action only by a process of "direct" generalization from these. That is, only the simplest and most obvious modes of relationship of unit acts in systems – those indispensable to the idea of a system at all – are considered. They must be grouped according to whose acts they are, according to the actor as an aggregate unit. The potential acts of one may be relevant as means and conditions to the situation of action of another, and the like. It is not necessary to seek far for certain of the roots of this tendency. It is but natural that in the early stages of development of a theoretical system its adherents should work with the simplest conceptual scheme which seems adequate. It is only with the accumulation of factual knowledge and the more refined and subtle working out of logical implications and difficulties that the more complex possibilities are brought into consideration. At the stage of development closest to the common-sense level there is generally found an atomistic tendency in scientific theories. . . .

The general effect of the individualistic elements of the European cultural tradition so far as they concern the present discussion has been to emphasize the discreteness of the different individuals who make up a society, particularly with regard to their ends. The result has been to inhibit the elaboration of certain of the most important possibilities of the theory of action, those having to do with the integration of ends in systems, especially those involving a plurality of actors. The tendency has been rather to concentrate for analytical purposes on the unit act itself and to leave the relations between the ends of different acts in a system entirely out of consideration or, when they were considered, to lay emphasis on their diversity and lack of integration.

The other principal element of the subsystem of action which is of special interest here may now be approached – the character of the normative element of the means–end relationship in the unit act. There has been, in the thought with which this discussion is concerned, an overwhelming stress upon one particular type, which may be called the "rational norm of efficiency." Hence the second predominant feature of the developing system here outlined, "atomism" being the first, is the problem of "rationality" action. It would not be correct to speak of the "rationalism" of the wider body of thought since a large section of it has been marked by the minimization of the role of rational norms. But in spite of this disagreement over the concrete role of rationality there has been, on the whole, a common standard of rationality and, equally important, the absence of any other *positive* conception of a normative element governing the means–end relationship. Departures from the rational norm have been described in such negative terms as "irrational" and "non-rational." With a more sophisticated development of systematic thinking these have, as will be shown later, taken on quite specific meanings, but for the present the important thing is the fact that attention has been concentrated on this particular type of norm. . . .

The simplest and most widespread concept is that which defines a particular type of norm for the means–end relationship, accepting the end as given without inquiry as to its rationality or "reasonableness." It may be stated as follows:

Action is rational in so far as it pursues ends possible within the conditions of the situation, and by the means which, among those available to the actor, are intrinsically best adapted to the end for reasons understandable and verifiable by positive empirical science.

Since science is the rational achievement par excellence, the mode of approach here outlined is in terms of the analogy between the scientific investigator and the actor in ordinary practical activities. The starting point is that of conceiving the actor as coming to know the facts of the situation in which he acts and thus the conditions necessary and means available for the realization of his ends. As applied to the means–end relationship this is essentially a matter of the accurate prediction of the probable effects of various possible ways of altering the situation (employment of alternative means) and the resultant choice among them. Apart from questions relating to the choice of ends and from those relating to "effort" – the ways in which action is more than an automatic result of knowledge – there is, where the standard is applicable at all, little difficulty in conceiving the actor as thus analogous to the scientist whose knowledge is the principal determinant of his action so far as his actual course conforms with the expectations of an observer who has, as Pareto says, "a more extended knowledge of the circumstances."

Thus far there have been laid down, with some indication of their origins, two of the main features of the system of theory on the action basis on which initial interest will be centered. It is a theory which is predominantly atomistic in the above sense, employing the "rational unit act" as the unit of the systems of action which it considers. It is unnecessary to go further in considering other features of the unit itself; it is now time to turn to the way the units are built up into systems and consider certain characteristics of the general systems thus arrived at.

The rational unit act which has been described – ficitious or not is immaterial – is a concrete unit of concrete systems of action. It is a unit which is, within the framework of the general action schema, arrived at by maximizing one important property of unit acts – rationality. By assuming that a concrete system as a whole is made up only of units of this character we get the picture of a complete concrete system of rational action. This is the simplest and most obvious mode of employment of this conceptual scheme – the assumption, often naïvely made without full realization of what it implies, that the concrete action systems being studied are simply aggregates of such rational unit acts. Even on this basis certain complications can arise, but for the present the discussion must be confined to the more general issues involved in the question of the relation of such a conceptual scheme to concrete reality.

The naïve empiricist view just stated has certain very important implications. If the concrete system be considered as analyzable exclusively into rational unit acts it follows that though the conception of action as consisting in the pursuit of ends is fundamental, there is nothing in the theory dealing with the relations of the ends to each other, but only with the character of the means–end relationship. If the conceptual scheme is not consciously "abstract" but is held to be literally descriptive of concrete reality, at least so far as the latter is "important," this gap is of great significance. For the failure to state anything positive about the relations of ends to each other can then have only one meaning – that there are no significant relations, that is, that ends are random in the statistical sense. It is by this indirect path of implication rather than by that of any positive theorem that the last defining feature of the system is arrived at – the randomness of the ends, at least the ultimate ends, of action. Though seldom brought out into the open, it will be found to be continually lurking in the background as one of the implicit logical assumptions upon which the whole structure rests.

The theoretical action system characterized by these four features, atomism, rationality, empiricsm and randomness of ends will be called in the present study the utilitarian system of social theory. The term, like most of its kind, is partly in conformity, partly at variance with general usage. Unfortunately usage is not consistent and some choice must be made. What has been outlined is, however, the logical center of the historical body of thought usually called utilitarianism, though various other doctrines, partly consistent with the above, partly not, have been historically associated with it. But above all the choice is justified by the fact that it is in connection with the modern economic doctrine of utility that the logic of the situation just developed has been clearly worked out. Subject to the corrections necessitated by placing these elements in a wider system of thought which takes account of others as well, the utility elements of human action are in fact, as will be seen, those to which utilitarian theory in the above sense came relatively near doing justice.

The Positivistic Theory of Action

It has been stated that developing modern science constituted one of the principal influences in establishing a main feature of the utilitarian system of thought, its emphasis on the problem of rationality. The same influence may be followed out on a still deeper level, involving still wider issues, in relation to the question last brought under consideration – that concerning the properties of systems of action taken as wholes.

It has been stated that when combined with an empiricist view of the relation of the theory to concrete reality, the utilitarian failure to consider the relations of ends to each other amounts to the implicit theorem that they have no such relations that are important to the logical structure of the theory. That is, that relative to the considerations affecting the rational choice of means, the center of gravity of theoretical interest, they may be held to vary at random. Focusing theoretical interest on the relation of science to rational action and failure to consider other elements explicitly result in still further implications which define a wider closed system of thought of which the utilitarian must be regarded as a subsystem. This is most easily seen in connection with the subjective point of view which is throughout the decisive one for purposes of the action schema. Starting with the utilitarian case we can see that the actor is conceived as possessing a certain amount of rational scientific knowledge of the situation of his action. But at the same time it is freely granted that this knowledge is so limited as to be inadequate for the complete determination of action. Specifically, in utilitarian terms, it is irrelevant to the choice of ends. But the fact that there is *no alternative selective standard*, in the choice either of ends or of means, throws the system, with its tendency to become logically closed, into the negative concept of randomness. Then, from the point of view of the actor, scientifically verifiable knowledge of the situation in which he acts becomes the only *significant orienting medium* in the action system. It is that alone which makes of his action an intelligible order rather than a response to the "meaningless" forces impinging upon him. It should be remembered that the actor is here being considered as if he were a scientific investigator. This throws the emphasis on the *cognitive elements* in the subjective aspect of action. The peculiarity of the point of view under consideration now is that it involves explicitly or implicitly (more often the latter) the view that positive science constitutes man's sole possible significant cognitive relation to external (nonego) reality, man as actor, that is. In so far as this inference is drawn, or as the reasoning dealt with implies it as a premise, the system of social theory in question may be called "positivistic." From this point of view utilitarianism as it has been herein defined is a true positivistic system but by no means the only possible one. On the contrary, deviations from it are possible in a number of different ways, all f which remain within the positivistic framework. . . .

The utilitarian version of positivism is not only on the whole historically prior but forms a convenient starting point for analysis of the logical alternatives which are open within the framework of the wider system. If the atomism of rational unit acts be accepted as its most distinguishing feature, it is clear that there are two fundamental respects in which a departure from the utilitarian basis can be made: in the status of the ends of action, on the one hand; in that of the property of rationality, on the other. In both respects the positivistic framework imposes certain limitations on what kinds of departures from the utilitarian position are logically acceptable. In both respects, also, these positivistically acceptable alternatives to utilitarianism fail to exhaust the logical possibilities of the more general action schema. In fact the transition from a positivistic position consists precisely in opening up those possibilities which are perfectly consistent with the general scheme of action, but which involve abandonment of the positivistic version of it. For the present, however, only those alternatives will be outlined which make it possible to retain the positivistic position.

First, then, the status of ends in the utilitarian scheme. Here the distinction between ends of action in the analytical sense and the elements of action belonging to the situation is vital and essential. In conformity with the voluntarism of the Christian background the reality of the agency of the actor was never doubted. The positivistic element consisted only in the implication that ends must be taken as given, not only in a heuristic sense for certain analytical purposes, but on the empiricist basis, with the assumption that they varied at random relative to the means-end relationship and its central component, the actor's knowledge of his situation. Only thus could their analytical independence be preserved in terms of the utilitarian scheme. But what happens when this assumption is questioned without abandoning the positivistic basis? And it was sure to be questioned, for such an assumption could hardly be considered scientifically satisfying in the long run. It is, indeed, the statement of an ultimate limit to scientific investigation, and science has always been reluctant to accept such limitations, especially when they are arbitrarily imposed a priori.

On positivistic ground there was only one possible way of escaping this unsatisfactory limitation. If ends were not random, it was because it must be possible for the actor to base his choice of ends on scientific knowledge of some empirical reality. But this tenet had the inevitable logical consequences of assimilating ends to the situation of action and destroying their analytical independence, so essential to the utilitarian position. For the only possible basis of empirical knowledge of a future state of affairs is prediction on the basis of knowledge of present and past states. Then action becomes determined entirely by its conditions, for without the independence of ends the distinction between conditions and means becomes meaningless. Action becomes a process of rational adaptation to these conditions. The active role of the actor is reduced to one of the understanding of his situation and forecasting of its future course of development. Indeed, it becomes somewhat mysterious what the function is of this rational process, how it is possible for the actor ever to err, if there is no other determinant of his action than knowledge and the conditions through this knowledge.

Thus with respect to the status of ends, positivistic thought is caught in the "utilitarian dilemma." That is, either the active agency of the actor in the choice of ends is an independent factor in action, and the end element must be random;[2] or the objectionable implication of the randomness of ends is denied, but then their independence disappears and they are assimilated to the conditions of the situation, that is to elements analyzable in terms of nonsubjective categories, principally heredity and environment, in the analytical sense of biological theory. . . .

The second problem involves the status of the norm of rationality. Here, as has already been pointed out, the utilitarian position represents the polar type of case where rationality is maximized. It is the case where the actor's knowledge of the situation is, if not complete in any ultimate sense, fully adequate to the realization of his ends. Departures from the rational norm must be associated with falling short in some respect of this adequacy of knowledge. Now the significant thing in this connection is that on a utilitarian or, more generally, a positivistic basis, there is no other, alternative type of norm in relation to which such departures from rationality may be measured. Their characterization must be purely negative. There are two current terms which quite satisfactorily describe this – "ignorance" and "error." Any failure to live up to the rational norm must be imputed to one or both of these two elements. Either the actor simply did not know certain facts relevant to his action and would have acted differently had he known them, or he based his action on considerations which a more extensive knowledge would have proved to be erroneous. He thought he knew, but in fact he did not.

The terms ignorance and error may, on a common-sense basis, be taken to mean merely the absence of adequate knowledge. But in positivistic terms they must have a more specific connotation. Since scientific knowledge is held to be man's only significant cognitive relation to external reality, then there are open only two alternatives in explaining why the actor in question was the victim of ignorance or error or both. Either this subjective fact may be the reflection of elements in the situation which are intrinsically incapable of being understood in scientific terms in their relations to action – then they are random elements and must be taken as ultimate data without further inquiry into whys and wherefores – or, on the other hand, they can be explained. The explanation must be that they are due to intrinsically understandable factors which the actor has either failed to understand or positively misunderstood. Then the only possible course for the scientific investigator is to "get behind" the actor's subjective experience, that is to abandon the subjective categories of the schema of action in favor of objective processes which may be thought of as influencing action by acting upon the actor without his knowledge or awareness of what is "really" happening.

But one point must be kept clearly in mind. It follows directly from these considerations that, if and in so far as the actor comes to know these elements in his action, and is able to act rationally relative to them, it must be in the form of acquiring scentifically valid knowledge of them, of eliminating the ignorance and error. Being rational consists in these terms precisely in becoming a scientist relative to one's own action. Short of the ultimate boundaries of science, irrationality, then, is only possible so long as actors are not in possession of the logically possible complement of knowledge affecting human affairs.

It follows further: If the explanation of irrationality on a positivistic basis must lie in factors not in fact known, but intrinsically capable of being known scientifically to the actor, then these factors must be found, on analytical generalization, to lie in categories capable of nonsubjective formulation, that is in the *conditions* of action. Thus, remarkable as it may seem, departure from the utilitarian position, so long as it remains within the positivistic framework leads in both the major problems, that of the status of ends and that of the norm of rationality, to the same analytical result: explanation of action in terms of the ultimate nonsubjective conditions, conveniently designated as heredity and environment. The difference lies merely in the account of the process by which their influence on action is exerted. In the one case it is through the medium of a rational scientific appreciation on the part of the actor of his situation; in the other, this medium is dispensed with and it is by means of an "automatic" process which, if it is subjectively manifest to the actor at all, is so only in terms which render effective adaptation and control impossible, positively only as error. This position may be called radical anti-intellectualistic positivism. Thus the utilitarian dilemma is broadened into a more inclusive form. It may, in this form, be stated in the following proposition: In so far as the utilitarian position is abandoned in either of its two major tenets, the only alternative on a positivistic basis in the explanation of action lies in the conditions of the situation of action objectively rather than subjectively considered, which for most practical purposes may be taken to mean in the factors of heredity and environment in the analytical sense of biological theory.

The principal reason for the common failure to see this implication seems to lie in the fact that thinkers have been principally concerned with what has been called the concrete use of the action schema and have failed to carry their reasoning through systematically to a general analytical plane. In the latter terms it is inescapable.

This striking result raises a fundamental methodological problem. At the outset of this chapter attention was called to the fact that the subjective point of view is central to the structure of the conceptual scheme under consideration – the theory of action. But at the radically positivistic pole of thought, whether in the rationalistic or the anti-intellectualistic form, the analytical necessity for it disappears. It is true that the facts relevant to the explanation of action are always *capable of statement* in terms at least of the concrete action schema, actually in the rationalistic case, potentially in the anti-intellectualistic, on the assumption of the actor coming to know the extent of his ignorance and the sources of his error. But the analytical categories of heredity and environment are, in the sense here used, characterized by the fact that for purposes of adequate scientific explanation they are able to dispense with subjective categories. Then in so far as they or other nonsubjective categories prove adequate to the task of understanding the concrete facts of human action, the scientific status of the action schema itself must be called into question. It may be a convenient heuristic tool, a scaffolding to use in building up a theory, but no more. It can be torn down and dispensed with at the end to the general benefit of the scientific virtues of simplicity and elegance.

This is, of course, true only at the "radically positivistic" pole of positivistic thought, and ceases to be so in so far as the utilitarian position is adhered to. But, as will be seen in the next chapter, where reasons will be entered into, there is as an adequate general explanation of human action an inherent instability in the utilitarian system. If this is so, there has been raised in radical form the question whether the preoccupation of so many generations of acute thinkers with the theory of action has not been based on delusion, or has at best been a stage of scientific development which is now happily past. This is one solution of the dilemma, and one which certainly enjoys wide acceptance at the present time. But this study will present as one of its main theses an alternative, namely to accept the incompatibility of the two principal elements here considered, the action schema and positivism, but to maintain that the evidence indicates that by freeing the former from its involvement with the latter its most valuable services to social science can best be taken advantage of. It will be the task . . . to present this thesis, backed by a careful analytical study of the empirical consequences of taking one or the other of these two alternatives. For scientific theory is one thing to which the pragmatic formula applies; it is justified only by its usefulness in understanding the facts of empirical experience. . . .

Verified Conclusions

1   That in the works of the four principal writers here treated there has appeared the outline of what *in all essentials*, is the *same* system of generalized social theory, the structural aspect of what has been called the voluntaristic theory of action. Theoretically important differences between these writers can be reduced to three circumstances: (*a*) Differences of terminology, different names for the same thing (for instance Pareto calls "logical" what Weber calls "rational"). (*b*) Differences in the point to which the structural analysis has been carried in order to arrive at the explicit distinction of all the major elements. In this respect Marshall represents hardly more than a beginning of the advance beyond the utilitarian position. But it is a beginning at such a strategic point as to be of great interest here. (*c*) Differences in mode of statement due to the different empirical centers of attention and theoretical approaches of the different writers. Thus the moral element appeared for Pareto first as ultimate ends, one element of the residues; for Durkheim as institutional norms.

2   That this generalized system of theoretical categories common to the writers here treated is, taken as a total system, a *new* development of theory and is not simply taken over from the traditions on which they built. It is not, of course, a creation *ex nihilo* but was arrived at by a gradual process of critical re-examination of certain aspects and elements of the older systems, a process standing in closest relation to empirical observation and verification. Indeed, given the diversity of starting points, the fact alone that it is essentially the same system precludes its being simply taken over from the older systems. Above all, it does not contain only elements common to all the previous traditions. Though every one of its major groups of elements had some place in at least one of the other traditions as something more than part of a residual category, this is not true of the system as a whole looked at as a specific total structure of conceptual elements. The

completed structure is at some vital point incompatible with each of these older systems.

3 That the development of this theoretical system has in each case stood in the closest relation to the principal empirical generalizations which the writer in question formulated. First, negatively, the closeness of Marshall's empirical views to those dominant in the utilitarian tradition is possible only by virtue of the relatively slight extent of his departure from their theoretical system. To take only one crucial instance, if from his insight into the role of one common value system he had come to see the possibilities of different value systems, he could not have upheld linear evolutionism in the sense he did. In the cases of Pareto and Durkheim their departures from all the major positivistic empirical theories, such as linear evolutionism, *laissez faire*, Social Darwinism, religion and magic conceived as pre-science, are most intimately related to the voluntaristic theory of action. In part, their development of this theory is due to the criticism of positivistic theories which has followed from their new empirical discoveries and insights; in part, their new theoretical ideas have led them to new factual insights. The same is true of Weber, with the exception that he was fighting on two fronts – on the one side against idealistic, emanationist views and the empirical theories associated with them; on the other against the positivistic tendencies of Marxian historical materialism.

Above all, the important empirical interpretations of none of the three thinkers could be adequately developed or stated in terms of either a positivistic or an idealistic conceptual scheme. It is to be remembered that their "theories" in this sense are not merely such bald propositions as "Social change follows in certain respects a cyclical pattern" or "There are social factors in suicide" or "The Protestant ethic had an important effect on Western economic development." All these propositions could be fitted into other schemes. The "empirical interpretations" here spoken of are rather their specific accounts of the modes, processes and relations of elements of the phenomena concerned, which underlie these most general propositions. The more deeply one goes into the detail of their explanations of these things the more central do the categories of the voluntaristic theory of action become.

4 That one major factor in the emergence of the voluntaristic theory of action lies in correct observation of the empirical facts of social life, especially corrections of and additions to the observations made by proponents of the theories against which these writers stood in polemical opposition. It has naturally been impossible, within the scope of this study, to present all the empirical evidence which each writer studied brought forward himself or which could be introduced. Hence the possibilities of empirical proof of this proposition have not been exhausted. The evidence that has been presented is, however, adequate. In the first place a considerable amount of this evidence has been cited and on the whole found to be sound. Secondly, various criticisms brought against these empirical theories have been considered and found to be lacking in conclusiveness. Finally, there is the very impressive fact of convergence, that the work of these men who started from markedly different points of view converges upon a single theory.

It is, of course, conceivable that the convergence does not exist at all, but that its appearance in this study is the result of an accumulation of errors of interpretation by the present author. It is also conceivable, though very improbable, that it is the result of an accumulation of random errors on the part of the various theorists themselves. If either of these possibilities is to be considered, it might be instructive to calculate the probabilities that this might occur, considering the number of different elements and their combinations to be taken into account.

That it is due to a congruence of purely personal sentiments seems highly improbable in view of the great diversity of the four men in these respects. . . . For instance, the anticlerical, radical humanitarianism that was at the basis of Durkheim's personal values was the commonest target for Pareto's biting irony. Finally, the diversities of individualistic positivism, sociologistic positivism and the idealistic social theories as conceptual schemes are so great as to eliminate as an adequate explanation the immanent development of previous theoretical systems without reference to the facts. Each of these theoretical systems could have developed in any one of several different ways – there was no general predetermination in favor of a voluntaristic theory of action. Above all, the utilitarian position could have developed, and did develop, into radical positivism, especially the theory of natural selection and psychological anti-intellectualism. Equally a critique of Marxian historical materialism in favor of the role of "ideas" could perfectly well have developed into a radically idealistic emanationist theory, and, with Sombart, did so develop.

In the matter of convergence, then, there remain two other possible explanations. One is the determination of the convergence by the adequacy of the theories to the facts. The other is that it is due to certain features of the total movement of European thought, independent of the facts observed by scientists, but common to all the intellectual traditions considered here out of which the voluntaristic theory of action has emerged. It is by no means argued that the latter element cannot be involved at all – it certainly is involved – but only that, taken by itself, it cannot serve as the exclusive or an adequate explanation.[3] In addition to the evidence already presented the following may be noted: Eliminating observation of the facts as an important element in the development of the theory of action really amounts to eliminating action itself, unless there be a purely fortuitous harmony between the outline of the theory and the facts to which it refers. For action itself in the relevant sense is not conceivable without some degree of correctness in observation of facts. This would place the whole problem of the nature of science itself, to say nothing of this particular set of scientific ideas, on so radically different a footing from the position taken here that the whole study would fall to the ground.

This is, then, the basic thesis of the study. On it the whole structure must stand or fall. There is no possible explanation of this convergence into a single theoretical system which does not include the proposition that correct observation and interpretation of the facts themselves constitutes a major element.

This conclusion is particularly important for the following reason: If this be true, and it is reasonable to think that it has been demonstrated, then the concepts of the voluntaristic theory of action must be sound theoretical concepts. It is not, of course, asserted that they are in the present formulation final and will never develop further. But they have been through the test and proved to constitute a conceptual scheme usable in empirical research. Hence they furnish a feasible starting point for further theoretical work, since science always develops further from a given theoretical point of departure. To advocate the use of this scheme, then, is not to lay down a Utopian program of what the social sciences should do but never have done. It is, on the contrary, to take the position that what has proved useful in the past and has greatly contributed to the attainment of important empirical results is likely to continue to do so in the course of its future use and development.

5   That the four above conclusions, taken together, constitute the hoped-for empirical verification, for this particular case, of the theory of the development of scentific theory stated at the outset. It is, indeed, impossible to understand the processes of scientific change which have been demonstrated on any other basis. In particular it has been shown that this change cannot be understood adequately (*a*) as the resultant of a process of accumulation of new knowledge of empirical fact arrived at independently of the statement of problems and the direction of interest inherent in the structure of the initial theoretical systems; (*b*) as resulting from processes of the purely "immanent" development of the initial theoretical systems without reference to the facts; (*c*) as only the result of elements external to science altogether such as the personal sentiments of the authors, their class position, nationality, etc. That leaves the mutual interdependence of the structure of the theoretical systems with observation and verification of fact in a position of great, though by no means exclusive, importance.

It is worth while pointing out that if the last conclusion be accepted, especially in combination with the other four, this study has a legitimate claim to be considered, not only as a contribution to the understanding of certain social theories and their processes of development, but also as a contribution to social dynamics. For in view of its exceedingly close relations to rational action, which have constituted a main theme of the study as a whole, the development of empirical knowledge must be considered a factor of major importance in social change; the rationalistic positivists erred only in making it of exclusively dominating importance. This is as true of knowledge of human action as it is of that of nature. Hence an understanding of the kind of processes by which such knowledge, particularly in the form of science, develops is an indispensable preliminary to any accurate comprehension of its social role. Of course this study has not solved these problems, but it may lay claim to have contributed to their solution.

Notes

1   In this sense and this only, the schema of action is inherently teleological.
2   This is really an impossible position for there can be no choice between random ends.
3   It is presumably the common source of the similarity of *Wertbeziehung* which is essential to such a theoretical agreement.

29 The Position of Sociological Theory

Talcott Parsons

A Few Basic Postulates

It seems possible to lay down a few fundamental propositions which can serve as general guiding lines for the more technical task of building a systematic treatment of sociological theory. I shall try to state these in sufficiently general form to leave room for a variety of different approaches in working out their implications in considerable detail. The following five seem to me the most essential of these basic postulates:

A. Systematic theory itself is of fundamental importance to any science. There is, of course, no intention to deny that work which can be quite legitimately called scientific can develop without systematic theory. Morphologies, classifications and empirical generalizations of various sorts have played very important parts in the development of a variety of sciences. The highest levels of scientific development, however, are not reached without conceptualization on the level of what is ordinarily called that of the theoretical system. The closer social science approaches to realizing this possibility, the more mature will it be considered as a science and the greater the predictive power which it will command.

B. The theoretical system which is basic to sociology must be broader than that of the science of sociology itself. It must be a theory of social systems. There has historically been an important so-called "encyclopedic" view which considered sociology the synthesis of all our knowledge of human social behavior. This has the consequence of making economics, political science, etc., branches of sociology, which is not in accord either with current academic reality or with good analytical procedure. We must somehow work out a theoretical scheme which articulates our own field with others which are equally part of the same broader fundamental system.

C. The systematic theory which is most fruitful for our field must conform with the "structural-functional" type, which is current in biological theory, notably physiology. Intrinsically the type of theoretical system best exemplified by analytical mechanics is more desirable, but is not now attainable in our field either as a theoretical system as such or as a useful tool of empirical analysis over a wide range. The most notable attempt to develop such a system was that of Pareto, which with all its merits has not proved very fruitful as a tool in empirical research. The most essential point about a structural-functional theory is that by the use of structural categories it simplifies dynamic problems to the point where a significant proportion of them became empirically manageable with the observational and analytical resources we can hope to command in the near future.

D. The theory must be formulated within what may be called the "action" frame of reference. It cannot, that is, be completely behavioristic in the sense of excluding all reference to the point of view of the actor himself and to what is imputed as belonging to his internal or subjective mental processes. This postulate is essential in order to make it possible to achieve a high degree of articulation with the motivational categories of contemporary psychology which deal with such things as attitudes, sentiments, goals, complexes, and the like.

E. The theoretical system must so far as possible be framed in terms of genuinely operational concepts. The ideal is to have theoretical categories of such a character that the empirical values of the variables concerned are the immediate products of our observational procedures. In relatively few fields of social science is any close approach to this yet possible, but with further development both on the theoretical side and in the invention of new observational and experimental procedures great progress in this direction is to be expected.

Some Methodological Prerequisites of the Formulation of a System

A. *Analysis of the action frame of reference.* In order to be clear about the implications of postulate D above, it is essential to work out some of the major features and implication of the action schema. There are a variety of ways of doing this, but it has seemed on the whole most fruitful in the first instance to distinguish the orientation of the actor on the one hand, and the structure of the situation on the other. Though the situation includes both the physical environment and other persons, the point of view from which it must be analyzed for this purpose is not that of the physical or biological sciences as such, but the various types of significance of situational facts *to the actor.* This means that the analysis of the situation must be fully integrated with the analysis of action itself. Action, in turn, it seems convenient to analyze in terms of three fundamental modes of orientation, which may be called cognitive, goal directed, and affective, respectively. We can, that is, have an adequate analysis of the action of the individual only so far as we understand his action and his situation in terms of his attempts to know it cognitively, in terms of the goals he is striving to achieve, and in terms of his affective attitudes toward these components and toward the situation. This is a very broad and noncommital schema which is, in fundamental respects, in general current use.

B. *The functional prerequisites of the social system.* Somewhat analogous to the spelling out of the action frame of reference is an analysis of the functional prerequisites of the social system; that is, of a system of social action involving a plurality of interacting individuals. If the social system is to be the major unit of reference of the total theoretical schema as a whole, it must be treated in functional terms. It is assumed as a matter of empirical fact that it has either certain given characteristics as a system which differentiate it from other systems and from the non-social situation, or there is a relatively definite empirically observed pattern of change in these characteristics analogous to the pattern of maturation of the young organism. Functional requirements of the maintenance of any such pattern system or pattern line of change can be generalized to a certain degree. In the first place, of course, a social system must somehow provide for the minimum biological and psychological needs of a sufficient proportion of its component members. On a more strictly social level, there seem to be two primary fundamental foci of its functional prerequisites. One lies in the problem of order, in the problem of the coordination of the activities of the various members in such a way that they are prevented from mutually blocking each other's action or destroying one another by actual physical destruction of the organisms, and, on the other hand, they are sufficiently geared in with each other so that they do mutually contribute to the functioning of the system as a whole. The second focus is on adequacy of motivation. The system can only function if a sufficient proportion of its members perform the essential social roles with an adequate degree of effectiveness. If they are not adequately motivated to this minimum level of contribution to the system, the system itself, of course, can not operate. A variety of further elaborations of the problem of functional prerequisites can be worked out from these starting points.

C. *The bases of structure in social systems.* A third fundamental methodological focus is in the nature of the structuring of the social system and the points of reference which must be considered in order to analyze that structuring. A structural category in its significance for a structural-functional system must be treated as a relatively stable patterning of the relationships of the parts, which in this connection may be treated either as component actors or as the roles in terms of which they participate in social relationships. One aspect of the structuring of the system must be what is conveniently called "institutionalization";[1] that is, the organization of action around sufficiently stable patterns so that it may be treated as structured from the point of view of the system. This theoretical function is to enable their assumption as constants for the treatment of limited dynamic problems. There are varying degrees of institutionalization of action in different parts of the total social system.

The second major aspect of the structuring of social systems is differentiation and the patterns according to which differentiation must be studied. This is a very complicated problem, and in general, treatment of it must be conceded to be in a rather unsatisfactory state. It is above all essential, however, that modes of differentiation be treated in terms of a system of catgories which make different social structures comparable with each other on the structural level. Without this, any high level of dynamic generalization will prove to be impossible. The most promising lead to solving this problem seems to lie in the demonstration of the existence of certain invariant points of reference about which differentiated structures focus. Some of these may lie in the external non-social situation or action; for instance, it is possible to systematize the comparison of kinship structures by using the fundamental biological facts of relatedness through biological descent as a set of invariant points of reference. Seen in this light, social systems of kinship become as it were variations on the biological theme. In a somewhat comparable way, it is possible to treat certain elements of the structure of action in terms of the pursuit of specific goals and the social relationship complexes which grow out of that pursuit, as another set of invariant points of reference which makes structures in such areas as technology, exchange, property, organization, and the like, fundamentally comparable with each other. This is one aspect of the field which is in need of the most intensive analytical development.

The Main Conceptual Components of the Social System

In the terms most immediately relevant to the sociological level of theoretical analysis, it seems convenient to classify the major conceptual components under the following four categories:

A. The structure of the situation.
B. The cultural tradition.
C. Institutional structure.
D. Motivational forces and mechanisms.

A. The role of the structure of the situation has already been commented on above. Here it is necessary only to say that it is essential to keep continually in mind a distinction of two major levels. The first is the structure of the situation from the point of view of any given individual actor; the second, from the point of view of the functioning of the social system under consideration as a whole. Failure to distinguish these two levels was, for instance, the primary source of the dilemma into which Durkheim fell which was responsible for most of the controversy over the group mind problem. For the most part, the categorization of this area is relatively familiar. It should only be stated that there will be refinements and shifts of emphasis as a result of further development of the more distinctively sociological elements of the total theoretical system.

B. The cultural tradition. In general the usual anthropological definition of culture is applicable in this context.[2] Culture in this sense consists in those patterns relative to behavior and the products of human action which may be transmitted, that is, passed on from generation to generation independently of the biological genes. It is an exceedingly varied and complex entity, and one of the most imperative theoretical tasks is to work out careful and analytical distinctions of the different elements which make it up and of their different relations to the levels of social structure and action. The difference from the usual anthropological usage of the concept culture lies in our interest in the particularly strategic role which is played by those elements in the cultural tradition which define ideal patterns governing the action of individuals. Their strategic significance derives from the fact that these are the patterns of culture which are susceptible of institutionalization, thereby forming components of the main structure of the social system itself. It clarifies discussion of this field, it seems to me, to make clear that there is not a substantive distinction between cultural and institutional patterns, but rather it should be held that all institutional patterns are cultural. However, only some cultural patterns become institutionalized and therefore have the special significance for the social system which institutions have. The distinction is one of functional relationship to the social system.

C. Institutional structure. This is that aspect of the conceptual analysis of the social system which is of closest relevance to the sociologist. Its most generalized role in the social system has been adequately described under C in the preceding section, and will be further elaborated below.

D. Motivational forces and mechanisms. It is here that the psychological theory which is essential to the theory of social systems finds its place. It should be made quite clear that many elements of psychological theory are of only secondary relevance to the theory of social systems. This is true of a great deal of physiological psychology and also of the more idiosyncratic elements of the theory of personality. Fundamentally the basic concern of the theory of social systems is with those elements of motivation which deal with the motivation of typical or expected behavior in social roles, and those tendencies which motivate socially significant deviance. It is important to make clear that the very common statement that psychology provides certain premises or underlying assumptions for the theory of social systems is not correct. This psychological component does not constitute a set of assumptions which lie outside the system, but an indispensable component *of the system itself*. It seems to me that the relation between the psychological theory of motivation of social action and the sociological aspect of the theory of social systems is closely analogous to that between biochemistry and physiology. They are both inextricably interlocked in the same body of analytical thinking in such a way that they are only analytically distinguishable.

Institutions as the Theoretical Focus of Sociological Science

It has been stated above that sociology should not claim to be the encyclopedic science of all human social behavior, but should find a place *among* the various social sciences. In terms of this point of view, institutions constitute the logical focus of sociology. When, for instance, some of the difficulties associated with group mind problems are stripped away, I think this is what is left of Durkheim's emphasis on the study of society as a phenomenon *sui generis*. This point of view should not, however, be interpreted to mean that sociology should be confined to the formal classificatory treatment of the structure of institutions. I should prefer the formula that institutions are the *focus* of its interest and that almost any component of the social system which bears on the functional and dynamic problems of institutions should be defined as sociological. From this point of view, sociological theory would, it seems to me, fall principally into the five following divisions.

A. The systematization of the study of the structural differentiation and integration of institutional patterns on a comparative basis. This includes not simply formal morphology but the theoretical analysis of the relations of structure and structural variation to the functional needs of social systems. However, relatively speaking, this could be called "pure" or "formal" sociology. Its difference from the program of Simmel or von Wiese lies in its relations to the other branches of sociological theory rather than in a difference in specific content. As has been remarked above, it is a grossly undeveloped part of sociological theory, and is much in need of attention. Promising beginnings, however, are to be found.

B. The theory of the dynamic interrelationships of institutions and culture. This is the major point of articulation between sociology and those aspects of anthropology which may be regarded as theoretically distinctive. What may be called the sociology of nonliterate societies cannot be regarded as distinctive of anthropology as a *theoretical* science. It would deal with the selected processes and patterns of the institutionalization of different elements of culture which are not functionally appropriate for institutionalization, such as traditions of science or speculative philosophy or magic. It is within this field that primarily the sociology of knowledge and, for example, the sociology of religion should be placed.

C. The theory of the motivation of institutional behavior. In my opinion, this theory should center about the concept of role, which is the primary name for the focus of the integration of motivation of the individual within the social system. It also would include the sociologically relevant theory of the process of socialization and of what is sometimes called basic personality or character structure. Another important aspect is the theoretical analysis of the structural generalization of goals in institutional behavior. This whole field is, of course, one of the major points of articulation between the theory of social systems and psychology. One may perhaps speak of this and the next category as in a very broad sense constituting either "psychological sociology" or an essential part of social psychology.

D. The theory of the motivation of deviant behavior and the problem of social control. This branch of sociological theory within the general framework of a theory of motivation and institutional behavior would be particularly concerned with the dynamics of the balance between conforming and deviant behavior. It would analyze the sources of the motivation to deviant behavior in terms of their relations to the social status and role of the individuals concerned, and the strains placed upon them in those situations. Conversely, it would analyze the mechanisms of social control by which deviance is kept at a relatively low level. It assumes both knowledge of institutional structure and of the basic motivation of institutional behavior as a starting point.

E. The final branch of sociological theory according to this conception is the dynamic theory of institutional change. It is most important to realize that this from a theoretical point of view would involve a synthesis of all the other branches of the total theoretical system. It is impossible to understand the dynamics of change without a knowledge of the structural base from which any given process of change starts. It is also impossible to understand it without some knowledge of the possibilities of new definitions of the situation which are available in the cultural tradition. Finally, the motivation of any such change requires explicit analysis of the relevant motivational problems. This is above all true of the starting points of the process of change in terms of what, from the point of view of the initial starting point of a process of change, must be defined as deviant behavior. It must include an analysis of the ways in which deviant behavior becomes socially structured and linked with legitimizing cultural patterns. It is unquestionably the culminating synthetic aspect of the theoretical structure of our science, and high levels of achievement in this aspect must depend on the development of the tools in the other branches with which the theorist of dynamic change must work.

Notes

1   To avoid misunderstanding it should be clearly stated what concept of institutions and correspondingly of institutionalization is being employed in this paper. A pattern governing action in a social system will be called "institutionalized" in so far as it defines the main modes of the *legitimately expected* behavior of the persons acting in the relevant

social roles, and in so far as comformity with these expectations is of strategic structural significance to the social system. An institutional pattern is thus a culture pattern (see below) to which a certain structured complex of motivations and social sanctions have become attached. It is an *ideal* pattern, but since conformity is legitimately expected it is not a "utopian" pattern. An institution is a complex of such institutional patterns which it is convenient to treat as a structural unit in the social system.

2   There is, of course, no single standardized definition of culture accepted by all anthropologists. The theme of "social heredity" may, however, be considered the dominant one.

30 An Outline of the Social System

Talcott Parsons

Let us now turn to a more detailed discussion of our conception of a social system. First, the concept of interpenetration implies that, however important *logical* closure may be as a theoretical ideal, *empirically* social systems are conceived as *open* systems, engaged in complicated processes of interchange with environing systems. The environing systems include, in this case, cultural and personality systems, the behavioral and other subsystems of the organism, and, through the organism, the physical environment. The same logic applies internally to social systems, conceived as differentiated and segmented into a plurality of subsystems, each of which must be treated analytically as an open system interchanging with environing subsystems of the larger system.

The concept of an open system interchanging with environing systems also implies *boundaries* and their maintenance. When a set of interdependent phenomena shows sufficiently definite patterning and stability over time, then we can say that it has a "structure" and that it is fruitful to treat it as a "system." A boundary means simply that a theoretically and empirically significant difference between structures and processes internal to the system and those external to it exists and tends to be maintained. In so far as boundaries in this sense do not exist, it is not possible to identify a set of interdependent phenomena as a system; it is merged in some other, more extensive system. It is thus important to distinguish a set of phenomena not meant to constitute a system in the theoretically relevant sense – e.g., a certain type of statistical sample of a population – from a true system.

Structural and Functional Modes of Analysis. Besides identifying a system in terms of its patterns and boundaries, a social system can and should be analyzed in terms of three logically independent – i.e., cross-cutting – but also interdependent, bases or axes of variability, or as they may be called, bases of selective abstraction.

The first of these is best defined in relation to the distinction between "structural" and "functional" references for analysis. However relative these two concepts may be, the distinction between them is highly important. The concept of structure focuses on those elements of the patterning of the system which may be regarded as indepenent of the lower-amplitude and shorter time-range fluctuations in the relation of the system to its external situation. It thus designates the features of the system which can, in certain strategic respects, be treated as constants over certain ranges of variation in the behavior of other significant elements of the theoretical problem.

Thus, in a broad sense, the American Constitution has remained a stable reference point over a period of more than a century and a half. During this time, of course, the structure of American society has changed very greatly in certain respects; there have been changes in legal terms, through legislation, through legal interpretations, and through more informal processes. But the federal state, the division between legislative and executive branches of government, the independent judiciary, the separation of church and state, the basic rights of personal liberty, of assembly, and of property, and a variety of other features have for most purposes remained constant.

The functional reference, on the other hand, diverges from the structural in the "dynamic" direction. Its primary theoretical significance is integrative; functional considerations relate to the problem of *mediation* between two fundamental sets of exigencies: those imposed by the relative constancy or "givenness" of a structure, and those imposed by the givenness of the environing situation external to the system. Since only in a theoretically limiting case can these two be assumed to stand in a constant relation to each other, there will necessarily exist a system of dynamic processes and mechanisms.

Concepts like "structure" and "function" can be considered as either concrete or analytical. Our present concern is with their analytical meaning; we wish to state in a preliminary way a fundamental proposition about the structure of social systems that will be enlarged upon later – namely, that their structure as treated within the frame of reference of action *consists* in institutionalized patterns of normative culture. It consists in components of the organisms or personalities of the participating individuals only so far as these "interpenetrate" with the social and cultural systems, i.e., are "internalized" in the personality and organism of the individual. I shall presently discuss the problem of classifying the elements of normative culture that enter into the structure of social systems.

The functional categories of social systems concern, then, those features in terms of which systematically ordered modes of adjustment operate in the changing relations between a given set of patterns of institutionally established structure in the system and a given set of properties of the relevant environing systems. Historically, the most common model on which this relationship has been based is that of the behaving organism, as used in psychological thinking. From this point of view, the functional problem is that of analyzing the mechanisms which make orderly response to environmental conditions possible. When using this model in analyzing social systems, however, we treat not only the environment but the structure of the system as problematical and subject to change, in a sense which goes farther than the traditional behavior psychologist has been accustomed to go.

In interpreting this position, one should remember that the immediately environing systems of a social system are not those of the physical environment. They are, rather, the other primary subsystems of the general system of action – i.e., the personalities of its individual members, the behaviorally organized aspects of the organisms underlying those personalities, and the relevant cultural systems in so far as they are not fully institutionalized in the social system but involve components other than "normative patterns of culture" that are institutionalized.

"Dynamic" Modes of Analysis. The importance of the second basis or axis of empirical variability, and hence of theoretical problem formulation, follows directly. A fundamental distinction must be made between two orders of "dynamic" problems relative to a given system. The first of these concerns the processes which go on under the assumption that the structural patterns of institutionalized culture

are given, i.e., are assumed to remain constant. This is the area of problems of *equilibrium* as that concept has been used by Pareto, Henderson, and others, and of homeostasis as used by Cannon. The significance of such problems is directly connected with both the concept of system and the ways in which we have defined the relation between structure and function.

The concept of equilibrium is a fundamental reference point for analyzing the processes by which a system either comes to terms with the exigencies imposed by a *changing* environment, without essential change in its own structure, or fails to come to terms and undergoes other processes, such as structural change, dissolution as a boundary-maintaining system (analogous to biological death for the organism), or the consolidation of some impairment leading to the establishment of secondary structures of a "pathological" character. Theoretically, the concept of equilibrium has a normative reference in only one sense. Since the structure of social systems consists in institutionalized normative culture, the "maintenance" of these normative patterns is a basic reference point for analyzing the equilibrium of the system. However, whether this maintenance actually occurs or not, and in what measure, is entirely an empirical question. Furthermore, "disequilibrium" may lead to structural change which, from a higher-order normative point of view, is desirable.

The second set of dynamic problems concerns processes involving change in the structure of the system itself. This involves, above all, problems of interchange with the cultural system, however much these may in turn depend upon the internal state of the social system and its relations to other environing systems. Leaving distinctions within the category of internal adjustive processes aside for the moment, one can say that, with respect to its external interchanges, problems of equilibrium for the social system involve primarily its relations to its individual members as personalities and organisms, and, through these, to the physical environment. Problems of structural change, on the other hand, primarily involve its relations to the cultural systems affecting its patterns of institutionalized normative culture.

However fundamental the distinction between dynamic problems which do and do not involve structural change may be, the great importance of an intermediate or mixed case should be emphasized. This is the problem of change involving the structure of subsystems of the social system, but not the over-all structural pattern. The most important case in this category is that of processes of structural differentiation. Structural differentiation involves genuine *reorganization* of the system and, therefore, fundamental structural change of various subsystems and their relations to each other. Its analysis therefore presents problems of structural change for the relevant subsystems, but not in the same sense for the system as a whole. The problems involved concern the organization of the structural components of social systems, particularly the hierarchical order in which they are placed. Further discussion will have to await clarification of these problems.

The Hierarchy of Relations of Control. The third of the three essential axes of theoretical analysis may be defined as concerning a hierarchy of relations of control. The development of theory in the past generation in both the biological and the behavioral sciences has revealed the primary source of the difficulty underlying the prominent reductionism of so much earlier thought. This was the reductionist tendency to ignore the importance of the ways in which the organization of living systems involved structures and mechanisms that operated as agencies of control –

in the cybernetic sense of control – of their metabolic and behavioral processes. The concept of the "behavioral organism" put forward above is that of a cybernetic system located mainly in the central nervous system, which operates through several intermediary mechanisms to control the metabolic processes of the organism and the behavioral use of its physical facilities, such as the motions of limbs.

The basic subsystems of the general system of action constitute a hierarchical series of such agencies of control of the behavior of individuals or organisms. The behavioral organism is the point of articulation of the system of action with the anatomical–physiological features of the physical organism and is its point of contact with the physical environment. The personality system is, in turn, a system of control over the behavioral organism; the social system, over the personalities of its participating members; and the cultural system, a system of control relative to social systems.

It may help if we illustrate the nature of this type of hierarchical relationship by discussing the sense in which the social system "controls" the personality. There are two main empirical points at which this control operates, though the principles involved are the same in both cases. First, the situation in which any given individual acts is, far more than any other set of factors, composed of *other* individuals, not discretely but in ordered sets of relationship to the individual in point. Hence, as the source of his principal facilities of action and of his principal rewards and deprivations, the concrete social system exercises a powerful control over the action of any concrete, adult individual. However, the *patterning* of the motivational system in terms of which he faces this situation also depends upon the social system, because his own personality *structure* has been shaped through the internalization of systems of social objects and of the patterns of institutionalized culture. This point, it should be made clear, is independent of the sense in which individuals are concretely autonomous or creative rather than "passive" or "conforming," for individuality and creativity are, to a considerable extent, phenomena of the institutionalization of expectations. The social system which controls the personality is here conceived analytically, not concretely.

Control Relations within the Social System. The same basic principle of cybernetic hierarchy that applies to the relations between general subsystems of action applies again *within* each of them, notably to social systems, which is of primary concern here. The principle of the order of cybernetic priority, combined with primacy of relevance to the different boundary-interchange exigencies of the system, will be used as the fundamental basis for classifying the components of social systems. The relevance of this hierarchy applies, of course, to all the components distinguished according to the first of our three ranges of variation, to structures, functions, mechanisms, and categories of input and output.

The most strategic starting point for explaining this basic set of classifications is the category of functions, the link between the structural and the dynamic aspects of the system. I have suggested that it is possible to reduce the essential functional imperatives of any system of action, and hence of any social system, to four, which I have called pattern-maintenance, integration, goal-attainment, and adaptation. These are listed in order of significance from the point of view of cybernetic control of action processes in the system type under consideration.

The Function of Pattern-Maintenance. The function of pattern-maintenance refers to the imperative of maintaining the stability of the patterns of institutional-ized culture defining the structure of the system. There are two distinct aspects of this functional imperative. The first concerns the character of the normative pattern itself; the second concerns its state of "institutionalization." From the point of view of the individual participant in a social system, this may be called his motivational *commitment* to act in accordance with certain normative patterns; this, as we shall see, involves their "internalization" in the structure of his personality.

Accordingly, the focus of pattern-maintenance lies in the structural category of *values,* which will be discussed presently. In this connection, the essential function is maintenance, at the cultural level, of the stability of institutionalized values through the processes which articulate values with the belief system, namely, religious beliefs, ideology, and the like. Values, of course, are subject to change, but whether the empirical tendency be toward stability or not, the potentialities of disruption from this source are very great, and it is essential to look for mechanisms that tend to protect such order – even if it is orderliness in the process of change.

The second aspect of this control function concerns the motivational commit-ment of the individual – elsewhere called "tension-management." A very central problem is that of the mechanisms of socialization of the individual, i.e., of the processes by which the values of the society are internalized in his personality. But even when values have become internalized, the commitments involved are subject to different kinds of strain. Much insight has recently been gained about the ways in which such mechanisms as ritual, various types of expressive symbolism, the arts, and indeed recreation, operate in this connection. Durkheim's analysis of the functions of religious ritual may be said to constitute the main point of departure here.

Pattern-maintenance in this sense plays a part in the theory of social systems, as of other systems of action, comparable to that of the concept of inertia in mechanics. It serves as the most fundamental reference point to which the analysis of other, more variable factors can be related. Properly conceived and used, it does not imply the empirical predominance of stability over change. However, when we say that, because of this set of functional exigencies, social systems show a *tendency* to maintain their structural patterns, we say essentially two things. First, we provide a reference point for the orderly analysis of a whole range of problems of variation which can be treated as arising from sources *other* than processes of structural change in the system, including, in the latter concept, its dissolution. Second, we make it clear that when we do analyze structural change we are dealing with a different kind of theoretical problem than that involved in equilibration. Hence, there is a direct relation between the function of pattern-maintenance – as distin-guished from the other three funcational imperatives – and the distinction between problems of equilibrium analysis, on the one hand, and the analysis of structural change on the other. The distinction between these two types of problems comes to focus at this point in the paradigm.

The Function of Goal-Attainment. For purposes of exposition it seems best to abandon the order of control set forth above and to concentrate next upon the function of goal-attainment and its relation to adaptation. In contrast to the constancy of institutionalized cultural patterns, we have emphasized the variability of a system's relation to its situation. The functions of goal-attainment and adaptation concern the structures, mechanisms, and processes involved in this relation.

We have compared pattern-maintenance with inertia as used in the theory of mechanics. Goal-attainment then becomes a "problem" in so far as there arises some discrepancy between the inertial tendencies of the system and its "needs" resulting from interchange with the situation. Such needs necessarily arise because the internal system and the environing ones cannot be expected to follow immediately the changing patterns of process.[1] A goal is therefore defined in terms of equilibrium. It is a directional change that tends to reduce the discrepancy between the needs of the system, with respect to input-output interchange, and the conditions in the environing systems that bear upon the "fulfilment" of such needs. Goal-attainment or goal-orientation is thus, by contrast with pattern-maintenance, essentially tied to a specific situation.

A social system with only one goal, defined in relation to a generically crucial situational problem, is conceivable. Most often, however, the situation is complex, with many goals and problems. In such a case two further considerations must be taken into account. First, to protect the integrity of the system, the several goals must be arranged in some scale of relative urgency, a scale sufficiently flexible to allow for variations in the situation. For any complex system, therefore, it is necessary to speak of a system of goals rather than of a single unitary goal, a system, however, which must have some balance between integration as a system and flexible adjustment to changing pressures.

For the social system as such, the focus of its goal-orientation lies in its relation as a system to the personalities of the participating individuals. It concerns, therefore, not commitment to the values of the society, but motivation to contribute what is necessary for the functioning of the system; these "contributions" vary according to particular exigencies. For example, considering American society, one may suggest that, given the main system of values, there has been in the cold-war period a major problem of motivating large sectors of the population to the level of national effort required to sustain a position of world leadership in a very unstable and rapidly changing situation. I would interpret much of the sense of frustration expressed in isolationism and McCarthyism as manifestations of the strains resulting from this problem.[2]

The Function of Adaptation. The second consequence of plurality of goals, however, concerns the difference between the functions of goal-attainment and adaptation. When there is only one goal, the problem of evaluating the usefulness of facilities is narrowed down to their relevance to attaining this particular goal. With a plurality of goals, however, the problem of "cost" arises. That is, the same scarce facilities will have *alternative* uses within the system of goals, and hence their use for one purpose means sacrificing the gains that would have been derived from their use for another. It is on this basis that an analytical distinction must be made between the function of effective goal-attainment and that of providing disposable facilities independent of their relevance to any particular goal. The adaptive function is defined as the provision of such facilities.

Just as there is a pluralism of lower-order, more concrete goals, there is also a pluralism of relatively concrete facilities. Hence there is a parallel problem of the organization of such facilities in a system. The primary criterion is the provision of flexibility, so far as this is compatible with effectiveness, for the system, this means a maximum of generalized disposability in the processes of allocation between alternative uses. Within the complex type of social system, this disposability of facilities crystallizes about the institutionalization of money and markets. More generally, at the macroscopic social-system level, the function of goal-attainment is the focus of the political organization of societies, while that of adaptation is the focus of economic organization.[3]

The most important kinds of facilities involve control of physical objects, access to the services of human agents and certain cultural elements. For their mechanisms of control to be at all highly generalized, particular units of such resources must be "alienable," i.e., not bound to specific uses through ascription. The market system is thus a primary focus of the society's organization for adaptation. Comparable features operate in less differentiated societies, and in more differentiated subsystems where markets do not penetrate, such as the family.

Within a given system, goal-attainment is a more important control than adaptation. Facilities subserve the attainment of goals, not vice versa – though of course the provision or "production" of facilities may itself be a goal, with a place within the more general system of goals. There are, however, complications in the implications of this statement.

The Function of Integration. The last of the four functional imperatives of a system of action – in our case, a social system – is that of integration. In the control hierarchy, this stands between the functions of pattern-maintenance and goal-attainment. Our recognition of the significance of integration implies that all systems, except for a limiting case, are differentiated and segmented into relatively independent units, i.e., must be treated as boundary-maintaining systems within an environment of other systems, which in this case are other subsystems of the same, more inclusive system. The functional problem of integration concerns the mutual adjustment of these "units" or subsystems from the point of view of their "contributions" to the effective functioning of the system as a whole. This, in turn, concerns their relation to the pattern-maintenance problem, as well as to the external situation through processes of goal-attainment and adaptation.

In a highly differentiated society, the primary focus of the integrative function is found in its system of legal norms and the agencies associated with its management, notably the courts and the legal profession. Legal norms at this level, rather than that of a supreme constitution, govern the *allocation* of rights and obligations, of facilities and rewards, between different units of the complex system; such norms facilitate internal adjustments compatible with the stability of the value system or its orderly change, as well as with adaptation to the shifting demands of the external situation. The institutionalization of money and power are primarily integrative phenomena, like other mechanisms of social control in the narrower sense. These problems will be further discussed in later sections of this essay.

For any given type of system – here, the social – the integrative function is the focus of its most distinctive properties and processes. We contend, therefore, that the problems focusing about the integrative functions of social systems constitute the central core of the concerns of sociological theory. . . .

Categories of Social Structure

Historically, the theoretical preoccupations of sociological theory have emerged from two main points of reference. One concerns the relations of social systems and culture and focuses on the problem of values and norms in the social system. The second concerns the individual as organism and personality and focuses on the individuals' participation in social interaction. Generally, neither of these reference points may be considered more important than the other. However, since the foregoing discussion of functional imperatives has started with pattern-maintenance, which chiefly concerns the institutionalization of normative culture, it may help to balance the picture if we begin our detailed discussion of structure at the other end, with the problem of the interaction of individuals.

Social interaction and roles

For sociology, the essential concept here is that of *role*. I should like to treat this concept as the "bottom" term of a series of structural categories, of which the other terms, in ascending order, are *collectivity, norm,* and *value*. (It is interesting, and I think significant, that systematic introduction of the concept of role has been, perhaps, the most distinctively American contribution to the structural aspects of sociological theory.)

The essential starting point is the conception of two (or more) individuals interacting in such a way as to constitute an interdependent system. As personalities, each individual may be considered a system with its own values, goals, etc., facing the others as part of an "environment" that provides certain opportunities for goal-attainment as well as certain limitations and sources of frustration. Though interdependence can be taken into account at this level, this is not equivalent to treating the process of interaction as a social system. True, the action of Alter is an essential part of the conditions bearing on the attainment of Ego's goals, but the vital sociological question concerns the nature and degree of the integration of the *system* of interaction as a social system. Here the question arises of the conditions under which the interaction process can be treated as stable – in the sense, at least, that it does not prove to be so mutually frustrating that dissolution of the system (i.e., for the individual, "leaving the field") seems more likely than its continuation.

The problem of stability introduces considerations of temporal continuity, which immediately brings us to the relevance of normative orientation. It can be shown that, within the action frame of reference, stable interaction implies that acts acquire "meanings" which are interpreted with reference to a common set of normative conceptions. The particularity of specific acts is transcended in terms of the generalization of the normative common culture as well as in the normative component of the expectations that get built into the guiding mechanisms of the process. This means that the response to Alter to an act of Ego may be interpreted as a sanction expressing an evaluation of the past act and serving as a guide to desirable future behavior.

The essentials of the interaction situation can be illustrated by any two-player game, such as chess. Each player is presumed to have some motivation to participate in the game, including a "desire to win." Hence, he has a goal, and, relative to this, some conception of effective "strategies." He may plan an opening gambit but he cannot carry advance planning too far, because the situation is not stable: it is contingent on the moves made both by himself and by his opponent as the game proceeds. The basic facilities at his command consist of his knowledge of the opportunities implicit in the changing situation; his command of these opportunities means performance of the adaptive function. Hence, at the goal-attainment and adaptive levels, goals are defined and facilities are provided, but *specific acts are not prescribed*. The facilities are generalized, and their allocation between the players depends upon each player's capacities to take advantage of opportunities.

In turn, the meaningfulness of the goals and the stability of the generalized pattern of facilities depend on the existence of a well defined set of rules, which forms the center of the integration of the system. The roles, in this case, are not differentiated on a permanent basis; rather, the rules define the consequences of any given move by one player for the situation in which the other must make his next choice. Without such rules the interactive process could not be stable, and the system of adaptive facilities would break down; neither player would know what was expected of him or what the consequences of a given set of moves would be. Finally, the differentiated and contingent rules must be grounded in a set of values which define the nature of a "good game" of this sort, including the value of equality of opportunity for both contestants and the meaningfulness of the goal of "winning."

A stable system of interaction, therefore, orients its participants in terms of mutual expectations which have the dual significance of expressing normative evaluations and stating contingent predictions of overt behavior. This mutuality of expectations implies that the *evaluative* meanings of acts are shared by the interacting units in two ways: what a member does can be categorized in terms meaningful to both; also, they share criteria of behavior, so that there are common standards of evaluation for particular acts.

We can say that even such an elementary two-member system of social interaction has most of the structural essentials of a social system. The essential property is mutuality of orientation, defined in terms of shared patterns of normative culture. Such normative patterns are *values*; the normatively regulated complex of behavior of one of the participants is a *role*; and the system composed by the interaction of the two participants, so far as it shares a common normative culture and is distinguishable from others by the participation of these two and not others, is a *collectivity*.

One further condition, not present in our chess game example, is necessary in order to complete the roster of structural components, namely, differentiation between the roles of the participants. This is to say that, in most social systems, participants do not *do* the same things; their performances may be conceived as *complementary* contributions to the "functioning" of the interaction system. When there are two or more structurally distinct units which perform essentially *the same* function in the system (e.g., nuclear families in a community) we will speak of segmentation as distinguished from differentiation. When differentiation of roles is present, it becomes necessary to distinguish between two components of the normative culture of the system: that of values, which are shared by the members over and above their particular roles, and that of role-expectations, which are differentiated by role and therefore define rights and obligations applicable to one role but not to the other. I propose to use the term *values* for the shared normative component, and the term (differentiated) *norm* for the component that is specific to a given role or, in more complex systems, to other empirical units of the system, i.e., various collectivities such as families, churches, business firms, governmental agencies, universities.

Where roles are differentiated, the sharing of values becomes an essential condition of integration of the system. Only on this assumption can the reactions of Alter to Ego's performances have the character of sanctions regulating Ego's action in the interests of the system. However, it should be clear that for Alter to be in a position to evaluate Ego's acts, the acts need not be such that Alter is, by virtue of his role, expected to perform. Thus, in marriage, one of the most important diadic relationships in all societies, the roles of the partners are differentiated by sex. The mutual evaluation of performance is an essential regulatory mechanism, but to be in a position to evaluate the partner's performance is not to assume his role.

The Concepts of Role and Collectivity. A role may now be defined as the structured, i.e., normatively regulated, participation of a person in a concrete process of social interaction with specified, concrete role-partners. The system of such interaction of a plurality of role-performers is, so far as it is normatively regulated in terms of common values and of norms sanctioned by these common values, a collectivity. Performing a role within a collectivity defines the category of *membership*, i.e., the assumption of obligations of performance in that concrete interaction system. Obligations correlatively imply rights.

Since the normal individual participates in many collectivities, it is a commonplace, though a crucial one, that only in a limiting case does a single role constitute the entire interactive behavior of a concrete individual. The role is rather a *sector* in his behavioral system, and hence of his personality. For most purposes, therefore, it is not the individual, or the person as such, that is a unit of social systems, but rather his role-participation at the boundary directly affecting his personality. It is largely when interpreted as this particular boundary-concept that the concept of role has an important theoretical significance for sociology.

So long as we restrict our illustrations to the diadic interaction system it may seem that the distinction of four analytical structural components – role, collectivity, norm, and value – is overelaborate. At this level it is still possible to identify values and the collectivity, norms and the role. In more complex social systems, however, there is not just one collectivity but many; and a differentiated norm does not define expectations for just one role but for a class of roles (and also for classes of collectivities). The social systems with which the sociologist normally deals are complex networks of many different types or categories of roles and collectivities on many different levels of organization. It therefore becomes essential to conceptualize values and norms independently of any particular collectivity or role. . . .

The structure of complex systems

Having outlined these essential structural components of a social system and their rank in the general hierarchy of control, we can now outline their main pattern of organization so as to constitute a relatively complex system. What is here presented is necessarily a schematic "ideal type," one that pretends merely to define and distinguish rather broad structural categories; we cannot take into account the immense richness of various concrete social structures.

The main guiding line of the analysis is the concept that a complex social system consists of a network of interdependent and interpenetrating subsystems, each of which, seen at the appropriate level of reference, is a social system in its own right, subject to all the functional exigencies of any such system relative to *its* institutionalized culture and situation and possessing all the essential structural components, organized on the appropriate levels of differentiation and specification.

The Concept of a Society. The starting point must be the concept of a *society*, defined as a collectivity, i.e., a system of concrete interacting human individuals, which is the primary bearer of a distinctive institutionalized culture and which cannot be said to be a differentiated subsystem of a higher-order collectivity oriented to most of the functional exigencies of a social system. It will be noted that this conception is stated in terms that leave the question of the "openness" of a society in various directions to be treated empirically. At the social-system level, however, rather than the cultural,[4] the main criterion is *relative* self-sufficiency.

To approach the structural analysis of the subsystem organization of a society, we must refer to the appropriate functional exigencies of both the societal system itself and its various subsystems. The primary, over-all principle is that of differentiation in relation to functional exigency; this is the master concept for the analysis of social structure. By itself, however, it is not adequate; it must be supplemented by the two principles of specification and segmentation. The first refers primarily to the institutionalized culture components of the structure, the second to the exigencies confronting the concrete behaving units, i.e., to collectivities and roles. It seems preferable to discuss the latter first.

We have noted that, in *one* (but only one) of its aspects, a society is a *single* collectivity with a specifiable, though naturally changing, membership of individuals. This fact is related to three fundamental imperatives. First, there must be, to some degree and on some level, a unitary system of institutionalized values, in this aspect a common culture. In so far as maintenance of a common value system requires the kinds of functions collectivities must perform, the society will have to constitute a single collectivity – what Durkheim called a "moral community." Second, however, since the system is differentiated, the implementation of these values for different units requires a relatively *consistent* system of norms that receive a unitary formulation and interpretation. In highly differentiated societies this system of norms takes the form of an integrated legal system administered by courts. The need for co-ordinated dealing with the external situation is also relevant, as will be brought out presently.

The Segmentation of Social Units. But if, for one set of reasons, a society must be a single collectivity, other reasons prevent its being only that. These reasons can be summed up in the generalized principles economists refer to as determining the "economies of scale." Beyond certain points, that is to say, "costs" increase as the size of the unit of organization increases, though what the points are varies greatly according to the specific factors involved. Thus, under modern industrial conditions the manufacture of such commodities as automobiles takes place in very large units indeed, whereas there seem to be important reasons which inhibit entrusting the early socialization of children primarily to units with membership much larger than the nuclear family.

Perhaps the most fundamental determinant underlying the segmentation of social systems is the indispensability of the human individual as an agency of performance. But there are essential limits, not only to what a given individual can do, but to the effectiveness with which individuals can co-operate. The problems of communication and other aspects of integration may thus multiply as a result of an increasing scale of organization; in certain respects, therefore, subcollectivities may acquire a distinctive organization, including a special integration or solidarity relative to the larger systems of which they are parts.

By the concept *segmentation* I refer, in discussing the formation of collectivities, to the development of subcollectivities, within a larger collectivity system, in which some of the members of the larger system participate more intimately than in others. In this sense, segmentation is a factor independent of the differentiation of function between the subcollectivities. Thus a large-scale society may comprise millions of nuclear families, all of which perform essentially similar functions in the socialization of children; here the structure is highly segmented but not highly differentiated.

The necessity of segmentation derives largely from the problems of integration resulting from the other exigencies to which units of the system are subject. At the same time, however, it gives rise to new problems of integration: the more units there are, the less likely they will be just "naturally" to co-ordinate their activities in ways compatible with the smooth functioning of the system as a whole. This tends, in more complex systems, to give rise to special mechanisms of integration, which will have to be discussed in due course.

The Specification of Normative Culture. As already noted, there is an important relation between the hierarchy of control and the levels of generality of the components of normative culture. Thus, values were defined as standing at the highest level of generality of "conceptions of the desirable," i.e., without specification of function or situation. In comparison to values, therefore, norms are differentiated on the basis of specification of function of the units or subunits to which they apply. Subcollectivities, in turn, involve further specification on the basis of situation. This is to say that, given its function(s), a collectivity is identified in terms of specified memberships of concrete individuals acting in concrete situations. When the collectivity is treated as a differentiated system, there must be further specifications applicable to the roles of the participating members.

There is, therefore, a hierarchy of generality of the patterns of normative culture institutionalized in a social system, one that corresponds to the general hierarchical relations of its structural components. Each subunit of the society, as collectivity, will have its own institutionalized values, which should be conceived as specifications, at the appropriate level, of the more general values of the society. To cope with its own internal differentiation of function, then, each subunit will have a set of differentiated norms, which should be regarded as specifications both of the subcollectivity values and of the more general norms applicable both to it and to other types of subcollectivity. The principle of specification restricts the generality of the pattern of culture by introducing qualifications arising from specialization of function, on the one hand, and from specificity of situation, on the other.

The last of the three principles of organization of complex systems, functional differentiation, has already been discussed in general terms. In accord with this principle, structured units acquire specialized significance in the functioning of the system. The general scheme of functional categories that we have presented is very simple, being limited to four categories. In using it, however, one must do justice to the empirical complexity of the situation by taking account of the many steps in segmentation and specification, and hence of the compounding of the patterns of differentiation by their repetition for subsystems at each level of segmentation.

Since our general approach has been in terms of the hierarchy of control observed in descending order, a brief account should now be given of the "anchorage" of social systems at the base. This anchorage is in the personalities and behavioral organisms of the individual members and, *through* these, in the lower-order subsystems of the organism and in the physical environment. Concretely, all social interaction is bound to the physical task performance of individuals in a physical environment; it is bound to spatial location in the physical sense. Following the usage of ecologically oriented theory, I have elsewhere referred to this spatial location as the "community" aspect of social structure.[5] It can be broken down most conveniently into four complexes: (1) residential location and the crystalliza- tion of social structure around that focus; (2) functional task-performance through occupation, and the attendant locational problems; (3) jurisdictional application of normative order through the specification of categories of persons, and the relevance of this to the spatial locations of their interests and activities; and (4) the physical exigencies of communication and of the movements of persons and commodities. More generally, the category of technology – not only what is usually called "physical production," but all task-performance involving the physical organism in relation to its physical environment – belongs in this area of borderline problems. Technology relates to physical exigencies, but it is also based on *cultural* resources in their significance as facilities for social action. Empirical knowledge of the physical world is an instance of such a cultural resource.

The Integration of Societies as Collectivities. Let us now approach the problem of outlining the structure of a complex society as a social system. As we have said, three different exigencies underlie the fact that a society can always be regarded as a single collectivity, namely, the maintenance of its patterns of institutionalized culture at the value level, the integration of its system of differentiated norms, and the co-ordinated handling of external situations.

The prevalence of fundamental patterns of value and the general commitment of units to common values are so crucial that the problem of the relation of the over- all collectivity to values is a universal one. At the other end, however, the problems of jurisdiction and enforcement with reference to normative order are equally crucial; the over-all collectivity structure cannot be divorced from political organiz- ation, oriented to maintaining commitments to this order and to the jurisdictional functions associated with it, in relation both to its own population and to other societies. This means that the boundaries of a society tend to coincide with the territorial jurisdiction of the highest-order units of political organization.

The primary area in which the problems of value-commitment are played out is that of religion; for most societies, the paramount over-all collectivity has been at the same time a religious collectivity and a political collectivity, both a "church" and a "state." Law, we may say, has tended to stand in the middle, to be legitimized by religion and enforced by political authority; often the function of interpreting it has been a serious bone of contention.

However, the formula of religio-political-legal unity is not, by itself, adequate as a universal generalization. In the first place, within the over-all collectivity these functions have tended to be differentiated with respect to personnel and subcollectivities. But, in a more radical sense, in the Western world since the Christian era there has been a process of fundamental differentiation of church and state. In interpreting the sociological implications of this, one must consider this process in terms of the relation between social and cultural systems. Even before its Protestant phase, Western Christianity was characterized by a special type of religious "individualism." In the present context, this means that, except on the most general level of over-all societal membership, the individual's religious and social status did not necessarily coincide. The church was an organization of the religious interests and orientations of the population conceived as independent of (but not unrelated to) their secular or temporal orientations, especially at the level of societal value-commitment. It was a "Christian society," but one in which the function of religion was more specialized than in other pre- and non-Christian types.

This I interpret to mean that, in societal as distinguished from cultural terms, the "moral community" aspect shifted from religious organization as such to the area of interpenetration between the religious and the secular. The paramount societal collectivity became the "state," administered by laymen – or when administered, in fact, by priests, not in their special clerical capacity. This differentiation was never fully carried out in medieval Europe – for instance, it was impossible to divest bishops of secular functions that went beyond the administration of ecclesiastical affairs – but it was, nevertheless, the main pattern.

Since the Reformation, this process has gone farther, particularly where the principle of the separation, as distinguished from the differentiation, of church and state has prevailed. As in the United States today, the values are still clearly anchored in theistic religion ("In God We Trust"), but on the level of collectivity organization the "moral community" is clearly the "politically organized community." What has happened, essentially, is that any agency whose orientation is primarily cultural rather than societal has been deprived of legitimate authority to prescribe values and enforce norms for the society; in this sense the society has become "secularized." The religious anchorage of the values is still there, but religion is pluralistically and "privately" organized. Formally, the values are embodied in the Constitution and in the official interpretations of it, above all by judicial and legislative agencies.

The universal association of the over-all collectivity structure with political organization is based on another set of imperatives, involving the special significance of physical force as a sanction. The central point here is that, while there are many limitations on the efficacy of this sanction, control of sufficiently superior socially organized force is almost always a completely effective preventive of any undesired action. Therefore, without the control that includes "neutralization" of organized force, which is inherently territorial in its reference, the guarantee of the binding power of a normative order is not possible.

I conceive of political organization as functionally organized about the attainment of *collective* goals, i.e., the attainment or maintenance of states of interaction between the system and its environing situation that are relatively desirable from the point of view of the system. The maintenance of security against the adverse use of force is a crucial collective goal for every society. Considerations such as these underlie the general tendency of the over-all collectivity to develop an effective monopoly of the internal organization of force through police and military agencies. Such statements are not meant to imply that the control of force is the paramount function of political organization. Force is not the only function that is primarily negative, i.e., "protective" in significance, and, in general, government is a central agency of positive societal goal-attainment. But force is so strategically significant that its control is an indispensable function, a necessary, but not sufficient, condition of social order. Accordingly, in a well-integrated society, most sub-collectivities except those specifically concerned with force are almost totally deprived of it.

Because of the problems involved in the use and control of force, the political organization must always be integrated with the legal system, which is concerned with administering the highest order of norms regulating the behavior of units within the society. No society can afford to permit any other normative order to take precedence over that sanctioned by "politically organized society." Indeed, the promulgation of any such alternative order is a revolutionary act, and the agencies responsible for it must assume the responsibility of political organization.

In this context it is of great significance that in a few societies, notably in the modern West, the organization of the legal system has attained a significant degree of independence in the judicial and, to some extent, in the legislative departments. There are two main aspects of this independent collectivity structure: the judiciary, with certain types of insulation from the pressures of "politics"; second, very notable, the development of a legal profession whose members occupy an interstitial status, partly through membership in the bar, functioning as "officers of the court," and partly by dealing privately with clients – indeed, protected from even governmental intervention by such institutions as privileged communication.

Summing up, we may say that the highest over-all collectivity in even a modern society is, to an important degree, necessarily "multifunctional," or functionally "diffuse." At the same time, under certain circumstances the diffuseness characteristic of the more "monolithic" religio-political structures – even of such high development as classical China or late Republican Rome – has tended to differentiate further. The most notable of these differentiations have been the "secularization" of political organization, which has gone through many stages and modes, and the institutionalization of a relatively independent legal function.[6]

The problem of the kind and degree of differentiation likely to occur at this highest level of societal collectivity organization may be described as a function of four primary sets of factors, all variable over considerable ranges. These are: (1) the *type* of societal values which are more or less fully institutionalized in the society (classified in terms of modes of categorizations of the society, at the highest level of generality, as an evaluated object – the appropriate categories seem to be pattern variables); (2) the degree and mode of their institutionalization, including its "security" relative particularly to the religious and cultural foundations of value-commitments in the society (long-range institutionalization of new values implies a relatively low level of such security); (3) the kind and level of structural differentiation of the society, with special reference to the severity and kinds of integrative problems they impose on the society; and (4) the kinds of situational exigencies to which the system is exposed. . . .

The Problem of Structural Change

According to the program laid out above, the last major problem area is the analysis of processes of structural change in social systems. The process of structural change may be considered the obverse of equilibrating process; the distinction is made in terms of boundary-maintenance. Boundary implies both that there is a difference of state between phenomena internal and external to the system; and that the type of process tending to maintain that difference of state is different from the type tending to break it down. In applying this concept to social systems, one must remember that their essential boundaries are those vis-à-vis personalities, organisms, and cultural systems, and not those directly vis-à-vis the physical environment.

A boundary is thus conceived as a kind of watershed. The control resources of the system are adequate for its maintenance up to a well-defined set of points in one direction: beyond that set of points, there is a tendency for a *cumulative* process of change to begin, producing states progressively farther from the institutionalized patterns. The metaphor of the watershed, however, fails to demonstrate the complexity of the series of control levels and, hence, of the boundaries of subsystems within larger systems. The mechanisms discussed earlier are involved in the dynamic aspects of such a hierarchical series of subboundaries; if a subboundary is broken, resources within the larger system counteract the implicit tendency to structural change. This is most dramatically shown in the capacity of social control mechanisms, in a narrow sense, to reverse cumulative processes of deviance. The conception of the nature of the difference between processes of equilibration and processes of structural change seems inherent in the conception of a social system as a cybernetic system of control over behavior.

As observed, structural change in subsystems is an inevitable part of equilibrating process in larger systems. The individual's life-span is so short that concrete role-units in any social system of societal scope must, through socialization, continually undergo structural change. Closely bound to this is a low-order collectivity like the nuclear family. Though the institutional norms defining "the family" in a society or a social sector may remain stable over long periods, *the family* is never a collectivity; and real families are continually being established by marriages, passing through the "family cycle," and, eventually, disappearing, with the parents' death and the children's dispersion. Similar considerations apply to other types of societal subsystems.

Within this frame of reference, the problem of structural change can be considered under three headings, as follows: (1) the sources of tendencies toward change; (2) the impact of these tendencies on the affected structural components, and the possible consequences; and (3) possible generalizations about trends and patterns of change.

The sources of structural change

The potential sources of structural change are exogenous and endogenous – usually in combination. The foregoing discussion has stressed the instability of the relations between any system of action and its situation, because this is important for defining the concepts of goal and the political function. We were emphasizing *relation*, and a relation's internal sources of instability may derive from external tendencies to change.

Exogenous Sources of Change. The exogenous sources of social structural change consist in endogenous tendencies to change in the organisms, personalities, and cultural systems articulated with the social systems in question. Among such sources are those operating through genetic changes in the constituent human organisms and changes in the distribution of genetic components within populations, which have an impact on behavior as it affects social role-performance, including the social system's capacities for socialization. Changes in the physical environment are mediated most directly either through the organism – e.g., through perception – or through appropriate aspects of the cultural system – e.g., technological knowledge.

One particularly important source of exogenous change is a change originating in other social systems. For the politically organized society, the most important are other politically organized societies. To consider change in this context, it is essential to treat the society of reference as a unit in a more inclusive social system. Even when the system's level of integration is relatively low and chronic conflicts between its subunits continually threaten to break into war, *some* element of more or less institutionalized order always governs their interrelations – otherwise, a concept like "diplomacy" would be meaningless. Of course, exogenous cultural borrowing and diffusion are mediated through interrelations among societies.

Endogenous Sources: "Strains." The most general, commonly used term for an endogenous tendency to change is "strain." *Strain* here refers to a condition in the *relation* between two or more structured units (i.e., subsystems of the system) that constitutes a tendency or pressure toward changing that relation to one incompatible with the equilibrium of the relevant part of the system. If the strain becomes great enough, the mechanisms of control will not be able to maintain that conformity to relevant normative expectations necessary to avoid the breakdown of the structure. A strain is a tendency to disequilibrium in the input-output balance between two or more units of the system.

Strains can be relieved in various ways. For the system's stability, the ideal way is resolution – i.e., restoring full conformity with normative expectations, as in complete recovery from motivated illness. A second relieving mechanism is arrestation or isolation – full conformity is not restored, but some accommodation is made by which less than normal performance by the deficient units is accepted, and other units carry the resulting burden. However, it may be extremely difficult to detect a unit's failure to attain full potentiality, as in the case of handicap contrasted with illness. Completely eliminating the unit from social function is the limiting case here.

Strain may also be relieved by change in the structure itself. Since we have emphasized strain in the *relations* of units (instability internal to the unit itself would be analyzed at the next lower level of system reference), structural change must be defined as alteration in the normative culture defining the expectations governing that relation – thus, at the systemic level, comprising all units standing in strained relations. The total empirical process may also involve change in the structure of typical units; but the essential reference is to *relational pattern*. For example, chronic instability in a typical kind of market might lead to a change in the norms governing that market; but if bargaining units change their tactics in the direction of conforming with the old norms, this would not constitute *structural* change of *this* system. In line with the general concepts of inertia and of the hierarchy of controls, we may say that endogenous change occurs only when the lower-order mechanisms of control fail to contain the factors of strain.

Factors in Change. In introducing our discussion of the factors in structural change, we must establish the essential point that the conception of a system of interdependent variables, on the one hand, and of units or parts, on the other, by its nature implies that there is no necessary order of teleological significance in the sources of change. This applies particularly to such old controversies as economic or interest explanations *versus* explanations in terms of ideas or values. This problem is logically parallel to the problem of the relations between heredity and environment. Of a set of "factors," *any or all may be sources of change*, whose nature will depend on the ways an initial impetus is propagated through the system by the types of dynamic process analyzed above.

To avoid implying a formless eclecticism we must add two other points. First, careful theoretical identifications must be made of the nature of the factors to which an impetus to structural change is imputed. Many factors prominent in the history of social thought are, according to the theory of social systems, exogenous – including factors of geographical environment and biological heredity, and outstanding personalities, as "great men," who are never conceived of simply as products of their societies. This category of exogenous factors also includes cultural explanations, as those in terms of religious ideas. Furthermore, these different exogenous sources are not alike in the nature of their impact on the social system.

Among these exogenous sources of change is the size of the population of any social system. Perhaps the most important relevant discussion of this was Durkheim's, in the *Division of Labor*, where he speaks of the relations between "material" and "dynamic" density. Populations are partially resultants of the processes of social systems, but their size is in turn a determinant.

The second, related point concerns the implications of the hierarchy of control in social systems. It may be difficult to define magnitude of impact; however, given approximate equality of magnitude, the probability of producing structural change is greater in proportion to the position in the order of control at which the impact of its principal disturbing influence occurs. This principle is based on the assumption that stable systems have mechanisms which can absorb considerable internal strains, and thus endogenous or exogenous variabilities impinging at lower levels in the hierarchy of control may be neutralized before extending structural changes to higher levels. It follows that the crucial focus of the problem of change lies in the stability of the value system.

The analytical problems in this area are by no means simple. Difficulties arise because of the complex ways in which societies are composed of interpenetrating subsystems, and because of the ways in which the exogenous factors impinge somehow on every role, collectivity norm, and subvalue. Thus the collectivity component of social structure has been placed, in general analytical terms, only third in the general control hierarchy. Yet every society must be organized as a whole on the collectivity level, integrating goal-attainment, integrative, and pattern-maintenance functions. Hence an important change in the leadership composition of the over-all societal collectivity *may* have a far greater impact on the norms and values of the society generally than would a value change in lower-order subsystems. Hence a naïve use of the formula, the higher in the control hierarchy the greater the impact, is not recommended.

Notes

1   When we speak of the *pattern* of the system tending to remain constant, we mean this in an analytical sense. The outputs to environing systems need not remain constant in the same sense, and their variations may disturb the relationship to the environing system. Thus scientific investigation may be stably institutionalized in a structural sense but result in a continuing output of new knowledge, which is a dynamic factor in the system's interchanges with its situation.

2   Cf. the paper, Parsons, "McCarthyism and American Social Tension," *Yale Review*, Winter, 1955. Reprinted as Chap. 7, *Structure and Process in Modern Societies*.

3   It should be noted that the above formulation of the function of adaptation carefully avoids any implication that "passive" adjustment is the keynote of adaptation. Adaptation is relative to the values and goals of the system. "Good adaptation" may consist either in passive acceptance of conditions with a minimization of risk or in active mastery of conditions. The inclusion of active mastery in the concept of adaptation is one of the most important tendencies of recent developments in biological theory. An important relation between the two functional categories of goal-attainment and adaptation and the old categories of ends and means should be noted. The basic discrimination of ends and means may be said to be the special case, for the personality system, of the more general discrimination of the functions of goal-attainment and adaptation. In attempting to squeeze analysis of social behavior into this framework, utilitarian theory was guilty both of narrowing it to the personality case (above all, denying the independent analytical significance of social systems) and of overlooking the independent significance of the functions of pattern-maintenance and of integration of social systems themselves.

4   By this criterion a system such as the Catholic Church is not a society. It clearly transcends and interpenetrates with a number of different societies in which its values are more or less fully institutionalized and its subunits are constituent collectivities. But the Church, primarily a *culturally* oriented social system, is not itself capable of meeting very many of the functional exigencies of a society, especially the political and economic needs. Similarly, even a "world government," should anything approaching that conception come into being, need not itself constitute a "world-society," though its effectiveness would imply a level of normative integration which would make the degree of separateness we have traditionally attributed to "national societies" problematical.

5   Cf. Parsons, "The Principal Structures of Community" in C. J. Friedrich, ed., *Community*, Nomos, Vol. II, Liberal Arts Press, 1959, and in Parsons, *Structure and Process in Modern Societies*, Free Press, 1959, Chap. 8.

6   It may be noted that allowing the institutionalized values to be determined through agencies not fully controlled by the paramount political collectivity involves a certain risk to it. The relatively full institutionalization of anything like the separation of church and state is therefore probably an index of the completeness of institutionalization of values. Modern totalitarian regimes are partly understandable in terms of the insecurity of this institutionalization. Therefore totalitarian parties are functionally equivalent to "churches," though they may put their value focus at a nontranscendental level, which is, e.g., allegedly "economic," which attempts to establish the kind of relation to government typical of a less differentiated state of the paramount collectivity than has existed in the modern West.

B: ROBERT K. MERTON

31 On Sociological Theories of the Middle Range

Robert K. Merton

Like so many words that are bandied about, the word theory threatens to become meaningless. Because its referents are so diverse – including everything from minor working hypotheses, through comprehensive but vague and unordered speculations, to axiomatic systems of thought – use of the word often obscures rather than creates understanding.

The term *sociological theory* refers to logically interconnected sets of propositions from which empirical uniformities can be derived. Throughout we focus on what I have called *theories of the middle range*: theories that lie between the minor but necessary working hypotheses that evolve in abundance during day-to-day research and the all-inclusive systematic efforts to develop a unified theory that will explain all the observed uniformities of social behavior, social organization and social change.

Middle-range theory is principally used in sociology to guide empirical inquiry. It is intermediate to general theories of social systems which are too remote from particular classes of social behavior, organization and change to account for what is observed and to those detailed orderly descriptions of particulars that are not generalized at all. Middle-range theory involves abstractions, of course, but they are close enough to observed data to be incorporated in propositions that permit empirical testing. Middle-range theories deal with delimited aspects of social phenomena, as is indicated by their labels. One speaks of a theory of reference groups, of social mobility, or role-conflict and of the formation of social norms just as one speaks of a theory of prices, a germ theory of disease, or a kinetic theory of gases.

The seminal ideas in such theories are characteristically simple: consider Gilbert on magnetism, Boyle on atmospheric pressure, or Darwin on the formation of coral atolls. Gilbert *begins* with the relatively simple idea that the earth may be conceived as a magnet; Boyle, with the simple idea that the atmosphere may be conceived as a 'sea of air'; Darwin, with the idea that one can conceive of the atolls as upward and outward growths of coral over islands that had long since subsided into the sea. Each of these theories provides an image that gives rise to inferences. To take but one case: if the atmosphere is thought of as a sea of air, then, as Pascal inferred, there should be less air pressure on a mountain top than at its base. The initial idea thus suggests specific hypotheses which are tested by seeing whether the inferences from them are empirically confirmed. The idea itself is tested for its fruitfulness by noting the range of theoretical problems and hypotheses that allow one to identify new characteristics of atmospheric pressure.

In much the same fashion, the theory of reference groups and relative deprivation starts with the simple idea, initiated by James, Baldwin, and Mead and developed by Hyman and Stouffer, that people take the standards of significant others as a basis for self-appraisal and evaluation. Some of the inferences drawn from this idea are at odds with common-sense expectations based upon an unexamined set of 'self-evident' assumptions. Common sense, for example, would suggest that the greater the actual loss experienced by a family in a mass disaster, the more acutely it will feel deprived. This belief is based on the unexamined assumption that the magnitude of objective loss is related linearly to the subjective appraisal of the loss and that this appraisal is confined to one's own experience. But the theory of relative deprivation leads to quite a different hypothesis – that self-appraisals depend upon people's comparisons of their own situation with that of other people perceived as being comparable to themselves. This theory therefore suggests that, under specifiable conditions, families suffering serious losses will feel *less* deprived than those suffering smaller losses if they are in situations leading them to compare themselves to people suffering even more severe losses. For example, it is people in the area of greatest impact of a disaster who, though substantially deprived themselves, are most apt to see others around them who are even more severely deprived. Empirical inquiry supports the theory of relative deprivation rather than the common-sense assumptions: "the feeling of being relatively *better off* than others *increases with objective loss* up to the category of highest loss" and only then declines. This pattern is reinforced by the tendency of public communications to focus on "the *most extreme sufferers* [which] tends to fix them as a reference group against which even other sufferers can compare themselves favorably." As the inquiry develops, it is found that these patterns of self-appraisal in turn affect the distribution of morale in the community of survivors and their motivation to help others.[1] Within a particular *class* of behavior, therefore, the theory of relative deprivation directs us to a set of hypotheses that can be empirically tested. The confirmed conclusion can then be put simply enough: when few are hurt to much the same extent, the pain and loss of each seems great; where many are hurt in greatly varying degree, even fairly large losses seem small as they are compared with far larger ones. The probability that comparisons will be made is affected by the differing visibility of losses of greater and less extent.

The specificity of this example should not obscure the more general character of middle-range theory. Obviously, behavior of people confronted with a mass disaster is only one of an indefinitely large array of particular situations to which the theory of reference groups can be instructively applied, just as is the case with the theory of change in social stratification, the theory of authority, the theory of institutional interdependence, or the theory of anomie. But it is equally clear that such middle-range theories have not been logically *derived* from a single all-embracing theory of social systems, though once developed they may be consistent with one. Furthermore, each theory is more than a mere empirical generalization – an isolated proposition summarizing observed uniformities of relationships between two or more variables. A theory comprises a set of assumptions from which empirical generalizations have themselves been derived.

Another case of middle-range theory in sociology may help us to identify its character and uses. The theory of role-sets[2] begins with an image of how social status is organized in the social structure. This image is as simple as Boyle's image of the atmosphere as a sea of air or Gilbert's image of the earth as a magnet. As with all middle-range theories, however, the proof is in the using not in the immediate response to the originating ideas as obvious or odd, as derived from more general theory or conceived of to deal with a particular class of problems.

Despite the very diverse meanings attached to the concept of *social status*, one sociological tradition consistently uses it to refer to a position in a social system, with its distinctive array of designated rights and obligations. In this tradition, as exemplified by Ralph Linton, the related concept of *social role* refers to the behavior of status-occupants that is oriented toward the patterned expectations of others (who accord the rights and exact the obligations). Linton, like others in this tradition, went on to state the long recognized and basic observation that each person in society inevitably occupies multiple statuses and that each of these statuses has its associated role.

It is at this point that the imagery of the role-set theory departs from this long-established tradition. The difference is initially a small one – some might say so small as to be insignificant – but the shift in the angle of vision leads to successively more fundamental theoretical differences. Role-set theory begins with the concept that each social status involves not a single associated role, but an array of roles. This feature of social structure gives rise to the concept of role-set: that complement of social relationships in which persons are involved simply because they occupy a particular social status. Thus, a person in the status of medical student plays not only the role of student *vis-à-vis* the correlative status of his teachers, but also an array of other roles relating him diversely to others in the system: other students, physicians, nurses, social workers, medical technicians, and the like. Again, the status of school teacher has its distinctive role-set which relates the teacher not only to the correlative status, pupil, but also to colleagues, the school principal and superintendent, the Board of Education, professional associations and, in the United States, local patriotic organizations.

Notice that the role-set differs from what sociologists have long described as 'multiple roles.' The latter term has traditionally referred not to the complex of roles associated with a single social status but to the various social statuses (often, in different institutional spheres) in which people find themselves – for example, one person might have the diverse statuses of physician, husband, father, professor, church elder, Conservative Party member and army captain. . . .

Up to this point, the concept of role-set is *merely* an image for thinking about a component of the social structure. But this image is a beginning, not an end, for it leads directly to certain analytical problems. The notion of the role-set at once leads to the inference that social structures confront men with the task of articulating the components of countless role-sets – that is, the functional task of managing somehow to organize these so that an appreciable degree of social regularity obtains, sufficient to enable most people most of the time to go about their business without becoming paralyzed by extreme conflicts in their role-sets.

If this relatively simple idea of role-set has theoretical worth, it should generate distinctive problems for sociological inquiry. The concept of role-set does this. It raises the general but definite problem of identifying the social mechanisms – that is, the social processes having designated consequences for designated parts of the social structure – which articulate the expectations of those in the role-set sufficiently to reduce conflicts for the occupant of a status. It generates the further problem of discovering how these mechanisms come into being, so that we can also explain why the mechanisms do not operate effectively or fail to emerge at all in some social systems. Finally, like the theory of atmospheric pressure, the theory of role-set points directly to relevant empirical research. Monographs on the workings of diverse types of formal organization have developed empirically-based theoretical extensions of how role-sets operate in practice.

The theory of role-sets illustrates another aspect of sociological theories of the middle range. They are frequently consistent with a variety of so-called systems of sociological theory. So far as one can tell, the theory of role-sets is not inconsistent with such broad theoretical orientations as Marxist theory, functional analysis, social behaviorism, Sorokin's integral sociology, or Parsons' theory of action. This may be a horrendous observation for those of us who have been trained to believe that systems of sociological thought are logically close-knit and mutually exclusive sets of doctrine. But in fact, as we shall note later in this introduction, comprehensive sociological theories are sufficiently loose-knit, internally diversified, and mutually overlapping that a *given theory of the middle range*, which has a measure of empirical confirmation, can often be subsumed under comprehensive theories which are themselves discrepant in certain respects.

This reasonably unorthodox opinion can be illustrated by reexamining the theory of role-sets as a middle-range theory. We depart from the traditional concept by assuming that a single status in society involves, not a single role, but an array of associated roles, relating the status-occupant to diverse others. Second, we note that this concept of the role-set gives rise to distinctive theoretical problems, hypotheses, and so to empirical inquiry. One basic problem is that of identifying the social mechanisms which articulate the role-set and reduce conflicts among roles. Third, the concept of the role-set directs our attention to the structural problem of identifying the social arrangements which integrate as well as oppose the expectations of various members of the role-set. The concept of multiple roles, on the other hand, confines our attention to a different and no doubt important issue: how do *individual* occupants of statuses happen to deal with the many and sometimes conflicting demands made of them? Fourth, the concept of the role-set directs us to the further question of how these social mechanisms come into being; the answer to this question enables us to account for the many concrete instances in which the role-set operates ineffectively. (This no more assumes that all social mechanisms are functional than the theory of biological evolution involves the comparable assumption that no dysfunctional developments occur.) Finally, the logic of analysis exhibited in this sociological theory of the middle range is developed wholly in terms of the elements of social structure rather than in terms of providing concrete *historical descriptions* of particular social systems. Thus, middle-range theory enables us to transcend the mock problem of a theoretical conflict between the nomothetic and the idiothetic, between the general and the altogether particular, between generalizing sociological theory and historicism.

From all this, it is evident that according to role-set theory there is always a *potential* for differing expectations among those in the role-set as to what is appropriate conduct for a status-occupant. The basic source of this potential for conflict – and it is important to note once again that on this point we are at one with such disparate general theorists as Marx and Spencer, Simmel, Sorokin and Parsons – is found in the structural fact that the other members of a role-set are apt to hold various social positions differing from those of the status-occupant in question. To the extent that members of a role-set are diversely located in the social structure, they are apt to have interests and sentiments, values and moral expectations, differing from those of the status-occupant himself. This, after all, is one of the principal assumptions of Marxist theory as it is of much other sociological theory: social differentiation generates distinct interests among those variously located in the structure of the society. For example, the members of a school board are often in social and economic strata that differ significantly from the stratum of the school teacher. The interests, values, and expectations of board members are consequently apt to differ from those of the teacher who may thus be subject to conflicting expectations from these and other members of his role-set: professional colleagues, influential members of the school board and, say, the Americanism Committee of the American Legion. An educational essential for one is apt to be judged as an educational frill by another, or as downright subversion, by the third. What holds conspicuously for this one status holds, in identifiable degree, for occupants of other statuses who are structurally related through their role-set to others who themselves occupy differing positions in society.

As a theory of the middle range, then, the theory of role-sets begins with a concept and its associated imagery and generates an array of theoretical problems. Thus, the assumed structural basis for potential disturbance of a role-set gives rise to a double question (which, the record shows, has not been raised in the absence of the theory): which social mechanisms, if any, operate to counteract the theoretically assumed instability of role-sets and, correlatively, under which circumstances do these social mechanisms fail to operate, with resulting inefficiency, confusion, and conflict? Like other questions that have historically stemmed from the general orientation of functional analysis, these do not assume that role-sets invariably operate with substantial efficiency. For this middle-range theory is not concerned with the historical generalization that a degree of social order or conflict prevails in society but with the analytical problem of identifying the social mechanisms which produce a greater degree of order or less conflict than would obtain if these mechanisms were not called into play.

Total Systems of Sociological Theory

The quest for theories of the middle range exacts a distinctly different commitment from the sociologist than does the quest for an all-embracing, unified theory. The pages that follow assume that this search for a total system of sociological theory, in which observations about every aspect of social behavior, organization, and change promptly find their preordained place, has the same exhilarating challenge and the same small promise as those many all-encompassing philosophical systems which have fallen into deserved disuse. The issue must be fairly joined. Some sociologists still write as though they expect, here and now, formulation of *the* general sociological theory broad enough to encompass the vast ranges of precisely observed details of social behavior, organization, and change and fruitful enough to direct the attention of research workers to a flow of problems for empirical research. This I take to be a premature and apocalyptic belief. We are not ready. Not enough preparatory work has been done.

An historical sense of the changing intellectual contexts of sociology should be sufficiently humbling to liberate these optimists from this extravagant hope. For one thing, certain aspects of our historical past are still too much with us. We must remember that early sociology grew up in an intellectual atmosphere in which vastly comprehensive systems of philosophy were being introduced on all sides. Any philosopher of the eighteenth and early nineteenth centuries worth his salt had to develop his own philosophical system – of these, Kant, Fichte, Schelling, Hegel were only the best known. Each system was a personal bid for the definitive overview of the universe of matter, nature and man.

These attempts of philosophers to create total systems became a model for the early sociologists, and so the nineteenth century was a century of sociological systems. Some of the founding fathers, like Comte and Spencer, were imbued with the *esprit de système*, which was expressed in their sociologies as in the rest of their wider-ranging philosophies. Others, such as Gumplowicz, Ward, and Giddings, later tried to provide intellectual legitimacy for this still "new science of a very ancient subject." This required that a general and definitive framework of sociological thought be built rather than developing special theories designed to guide the investigation of specific sociological problems within an evolving and provisional framework.

Within this context, almost all the pioneers in sociology tried to fashion his own system. The multiplicity of sytems, each claiming to be the genuine sociology, led naturally enough to the formation of schools, each with its cluster of masters, disciples and epigoni. Sociology not only became differentiated with other disciples, but it became internally differentiated. This differentiation, however, was not in terms of specialization, as in the sciences, but rather, as in philosophy, in terms of total systems, typically held to be mutually exclusive and largely at odds. As Bertrand Russell noted about philosophy, this total sociology did not seize "the advantage, as compared with the [sociologies] of the system-builders, of being able to tackle its problems one at a time, instead of having to invent at one stroke a block theory of the whole [sociological] universe."[3]

Another route has been followed by sociologists in their quest to establish the intellectual legitimacy of their discipline: they have taken as their prototype systems of scientific theory rather than systems of philosophy. This path too has sometimes led to the attempt to create total systems of sociology – a goal that is often based on one or more of three basic misconceptions about the sciences.

The first misinterpretation assumes that systems of thought can be effectively developed before a great mass of basic observations has been accumulated.

According to this view, Einstein might follow hard on the heels of Kepler, without the intervening centuries of investigation and systematic thought about the results of investigation that were needed to prepare the terrain. The systems of sociology that stem from this tacit assumption are much like those introduced by the system-makers in medicine over a span of 150 years: the systems of Stahl, Boissier de Sauvages, Broussais, John Brown and Benjamin Rush. Until well into the nineteenth century eminent personages in medicine thought it necessary to develop a theoretical system of disease long before the antecedent empirical inquiry had been adequately developed. These garden-paths have since been closed off in medicine but this sort of effort still turns up in sociology. It is this tendency that led the biochemist and avocational sociologist, L. J. Henderson, to observe:

> A difference between most system-building in the social sciences and systems of thought and classification in the natural sciences is to be seen in their evolution. In the natural sciences both theories and descriptive systems grow by adaptation to the increasing knowledge and experience of the scientists. *In the social sciences, systems often issue fully formed from the mind of one man.* Then they may be much discussed if they attract attention, but *progressive adaptive modification as a result of the concerted efforts of great numbers of men is rare.*[4]

The second misconception about the physical sciences rests on a mistaken assumption of historical contemporaneity – *that all cultural products existing at the same moment of history have the same degree of maturity.* In fact, to perceive differences here would be to achieve a sense of proportion. The fact that the discipline of physics and the discipline of sociology are both identifiable in the mid-twentieth century does not mean that the achievements of the one should be the measure of the other. True, social scientists today live at a time when physics has achieved comparatively great scope and precision of theory and experiment, a great aggregate of tools of investigation, and an abundance of technological by-products. Looking about them, many sociologists take the achievements of physics as the standard for self-appraisal. They want to compare biceps with their bigger brothers. They, too, want to *count.* And when it becomes evident that they neither have the rugged physique nor pack the murderous wallop of their big brothers, some sociologists despair. They begin to ask: is a science of society really possible unless we institute a total system of sociology? But this perspective ignores the fact that between twentieth-century physics and twentieth-century sociology stand billions of man-hours of sustained, disciplined, and cumulative research. Perhaps sociology is not yet ready for its Einstein because it has not yet found its Kepler – to say nothing of its Newton, Laplace, Gibbs, Maxwell or Planck.

Third, sociologists sometimes misread the actual state of theory in the physical sciences. This error is ironic, for physicists agree that they have not achieved an all-encompassing system of theory, and most see little prospect of it in the near future. What characterizes physics is an array of special theories of greater or less scope, coupled with the historically-grounded hope that these will continue to be brought together into families of theory. As one observer puts it: "though most of us hope, it is true, for an all embracive future theory which will unify the various postulates of physics, we do not wait for it before proceeding with the important business of science."[5] More recently, the theoretical physicist, Richard Feynman, reported without dismay that "today our theories of physics, the laws of physics, are a multitude of different parts and pieces that do not fit together very well."[6] But perhaps most telling is the observation by that most comprehensive of theoreticians who devoted the last years of his life to the unrelenting and unsuccessful search "for a unifying theoretical basis for all these single disciplines, consisting of a minimum of concepts and fundamental relationships, from which all the concepts and relationships of the single disciplines might be derived by logical process." Despite his own profound and lonely commitment to this quest, Einstein observed:

> The greater part of physical research is devoted to the development of the various branches in physics, in each of which the object is the theoretical understanding of more or less restricted fields of experience, and in each of which the laws and concepts remain as closely as possible related to experience.[7]

These observations might be pondered by those sociologists who expect a sound general system of sociological theory in our time – or soon after. If the science of physics, with its centuries of enlarged theoretical generalizations, has not managed to develop an all-encompassing theoretical system, then *a fortiori* the science of sociology, which has only begun to accumulate empirically grounded theoretical generalizations of modest scope, would seem well advised to moderate its aspirations for such a system.

Utilitarian Pressures for Total Systems of Sociology

The conviction among some sociologists that we must, here and now, achieve a grand theoretical system not only results from a misplaced comparison with the physical sciences, it is also a response to the ambiguous position of sociology in contemporary society. The very uncertainty about whether the accumulated knowledge of sociology is adequate to meet the large demands now being made of it – by policy-makers, reformers and reactionaries, by business-men and government-men, by college presidents and college sophomores – provokes an overly-zealous and defensive conviction on the part of some sociologists that they must somehow be equal to these demands, however premature and extravagant they may be.

This conviction erroneously assumes that a science must be adequate to meet *all* demands, intelligent or stupid, made of it. This conviction is implicitly based on the sacrilegious and masochistic assumption that one must be omniscient and omnicompetent – to admit to less than total knowledge is to admit to total ignorance. So it often happens that the exponents of a fledgling discipline make extravagant claims to total systems of theory, adequate to the entire range of problems encompassed by the discipline. It is this sort of attitude that Whitehead referred to in the epigraph to this book: "It is characteristic of a science in its earlier stages . . . to be both ambitiously profound in its aims and trivial in its handling of details."

Like the sociologists who thoughtlessly compared themselves with contemporary physical scientists because they both are alive at the same instant of history, the general public and its strategic decision-makers often err in making a definitive appraisal of social science on the basis of its ability to solve the urgent problems of society today. The misplaced masochism of the social scientist and the inadvertent sadism of the public both result from the failure to remember that social science, like all science, is continually developing and that there is no providential dispensation providing that at any given moment it will be adequate to the entire array of problems confronting men. In historical perspective this expectation would be equivalent to having forever prejudged the status and promise of medicine in the seventeenth century according to its ability to produce, then and there, a cure or even a preventative for cardiac diseases. If the problem had been widely acknowledged – look at the growing rate of death from coronary thrombosis – its very importance would have obscured the *entirely independent question* of how adequate the medical knowledge of 1650 (or 1850 or 1950) was for solving a wide array of other health problems. Yet it is precisely this illogic that lies behind so many of the practical demands made on the social sciences. Because war and exploitation and poverty and racial discrimination and psychological insecurity plague modern societies, social science must justify itself by providing solutions for all of these problems. Yet social scientists may be no better equipped to solve these urgent problems today than were physicians, such as Harvey or Sydenham, to identify, study, and cure coronary thrombosis in 1655. Yet, as history testifies, the inadequacy of medicine to cope with this particular problem scarcely meant that it lacked powers of development. If everyone backs only the sure thing, who will support the colt yet to come into its own?

My emphasis upon the gap between the practical problems assigned to the sociologist and the state of his accumulated knowledge and skills does not mean of course, that the sociologist should not seek to develop increasingly comprehensive theory or should not work on research directly relevant to urgent practical problems. Most of all, it does not mean that sociologists should deliberately seek out the pragmatically trivial problem. Different sectors in the spectrum of basic research and theory have different probabilities of being germane to particular practical problems; they have differing potentials of relevance.[8] But it is important to re-establish an historical sense of proportion. The urgency or immensity of a practical social problem does not ensure its immediate solution.[9] At any given moment, men of science are close to the solutions of some problems and remote from others. It must be remembered that necessity is only the mother of invention; socially accumulated knowledge is its father. Unless the two are brought together, necessity remains infertile. She may of course conceive at some future time when she is properly mated. But the mate requires time (and sustenance) if he is to attain the size and vigor needed to meet the demands that will be made upon him.

This book's orientation toward the relationship of current sociology and practical problems of society is much the same as its orientation toward the relationship of sociology and general sociological theory. It is a developmental orientation, rather than one that relies on the sudden mutations of one sociologist that suddenly bring solutions to major social problems or to a single encompassing theory. Though this orientation makes no marvellously dramatic claims, it offers a reasonably realistic assessment of the current condition of sociology and the ways in which it actually develops.

Total Systems of Theory and Theories of the Middle Range

From all this it would seem reasonable to suppose that sociology will advance insofar as its major (but not exclusive) concern is with developing theories of the middle range, and it will be retarded if its primary attention is focussed on developing total sociological systems. So it is that in his inaugural address at the London School of Economics, T. H. Marshall put in a plea for sociological "stepping-stones in the middle distance."[10] Our major task today is to develop special theories applicable to limited conceptual ranges – theories, for example, of deviant behavior, the unanticipated consequences of purposive action, social perception, reference groups, social control, the interdependence of social institutions – rather than to seek immediately the total conceptual structure that is adequate to derive these and other theories of the middle range.

Sociological theory, if it is to advance significantly, must proceed on these interconnected planes: (1) by developing special theories from which to derive hypotheses that can be empirically investigated and (2) by evolving, not suddenly revealing, a progressively more general conceptual scheme that is adequate to consolidate groups of special theories.

To concentrate entirely on special theories is to risk emerging with specific hypotheses that account for limited aspects of social behavior, organization and change but that remain mutually inconsistent.

To concentrate entirely on a master conceptual scheme for deriving all subsidiary theories is to risk producing twentieth-century sociological equivalents of the large philosophical systems of the past, with all their varied suggestiveness, their architectonic splendor, and their scientific sterility. The sociological theorist who is *exclusively* committed to the exploration of a total system with its utmost abstractions runs the risk that, as with modern décor, the furniture of his mind will be bare and uncomfortable.

The road to effective general schemes in sociology will only become clogged if, as in the early days of sociology, each charismatic sociologist tries to develop his own general system of theory. The persistence of this practice can only make for the balkanization of sociology, with each principality governed by its own theoretical system. Though this process has periodically marked the development of other sciences – conspicuously, chemistry, geology and medicine – it need not be reproduced in sociology if we learn from the history of science. We sociologists can look instead toward progressively comprehensive sociological theory which, instead of proceeding from the head of one man, gradually consolidates theories of the middle range, so that these become special cases of more general formulations.

Developments in sociological theory suggest that emphasis on this orientation is needed. Note how few, how scattered, and how unimpressive are the specific sociological hypotheses which are *derived* from a master conceptual scheme. The proposals for an all-embracing theory run so far ahead of confirmed special theories as to remain unrealized programs rather than *consolidations* of theories that at first seemed discrete. Of course, as Talcott Parsons and Pitirim Sorokin (in his *Sociological Theories of Today*) have indicated, significant progress has recently been made. The gradual convergence of streams of theory in sociology, social psychology and anthropology records large theoretical gains and promises even more. Nonetheless, a large part of what is now described as sociological theory consists of *general orientations toward data, suggesting types of variables which theories must somehow take into account, rather than clearly formulated, verifiable statements of relationships between specified variables.* We have many concepts but fewer confirmed theories; many points of view, but few theorems; many "approaches" but few arrivals. Perhaps some further changes in emphasis would be all to the good.

Consciously or unconsciously, men allocate their scant resources as much in the production of sociological theory as they do in the production of plumbing supplies, and their allocations reflect their underlying assumptions. Our discussion of middle-range theory in sociology is intended to make explicit a policy decision faced by all sociological theorists. Which shall have the greater share of our collective energies and resources: the search for confirmed theories of the middle range or the search for an all-inclusive conceptual scheme? I believe – and beliefs are of course notoriously subject to error – that theories of the middle range hold the largest promise, *provided that* the search for them is coupled with a pervasive concern with consolidating special theories into more general sets of concepts and mutually consistent propositions. Even so, we must adopt the provisional outlook of our big brothers and of Tennyson:

> Our little systems have their day;
> They have their day and cease to be.

Notes

1   Allen Barton, 1963, *Social Organization Under Stress: A Sociological Review of Disaster Studies*, Washington, DC: National Academy of Sciences – National Research Council.
2   Robert K. Merton, 1957, "The Role Set: Problems in Sociological Theory," *The British Journal of Sociology* 8: 106—20.
3   Bertrand Russell, *A History of Western Philosophy* (New York: Simon and Schuster, 1945), 834.
4   Lawrence J. Henderson, *The Study of Man* (Philadelphia: University of Pennsylvania Press, 1941), 19—20, italics supplied; for that matter, the entire book can be read with profit by most of us sociologists.
5   Henry Margenau, "The basis of theory in physics," unpublished ms., 1949, 5—6.
6   Richard Feynman, *The Character of Physical Law* (London: Cox & Wyman Ltd., 1965), 30.
7   Albert Einstein, "The fundamentals of theoretical physics," in L. Hamalian and E. L. Volpe, eds., *Great Essays by Nobel Prize Winners* (New York: Noonday Press, 1960), 219—30 at 220.
8   This conception is developed in R. K. Merton, "Basic research and potentials of relevance," *American Behavioral Scientist*, May 1963, VI, 86–90 on the basis of my earlier discussion, "The role of applied social science in the formation of policy," *Philosophy of Science*, 1949, 16, 161—81.
9   As can be seen in detail in such works as the following: Paul F. Lazarsfeld, William Sewell and Harold Wilensky, eds., *The Uses of Sociology* (New York: Basic Books, in press); Alvin W. Gouldner and S. M. Miller, *Applied Sociology: Opportunities and Problems* (New York: The Free Press, 1965); Bernard Rosenberg, Israel Gerver and F.

William Howton, *Mass Society in Crisis: Social Problems and Social Pathology* (New York: The Macmillan Company, 1964); Barbara Wootton, *Social Science and Social Pathology* (New York: The Macmillan Company, 1959).

10   The inaugural lecture was delivered 21 February 1946. It is printed in T. H. Marshall, *Sociology at the Crossroads* (London: Heinemann, 1963), 3—24.

32 Manifest and Latent Functions

Robert K. Merton

The distinction between manifest and latent functions was devised to preclude the inadvertent confusion, often found in the sociological literature, between conscious *motivations* for social behavior and its *objective consequences*. Our scrutiny of current vocabularies of functional analysis has shown how easily, and how unfortunately, the sociologist may identify *motives* with *functions*. It was further indicated that the motive and the function vary independently and that the failure to register this fact in an established terminology has contributed to the unwitting tendency among sociologists to confuse the subjective categories of motivation with the objective categories of function. This, then, is the central purpose of our succumbing to the not-always-commendable practice of introducing new terms into the rapidly growing technical vocabulary of sociology, a practice regarded by many laymen as an affront to their intelligence and an offense against common intelligibility.

As will be readily recognized, I have adapted the terms "manifest" and "latent" from their use in another context by Freud (although Francis Bacon had long ago spoken of "latent process" and "latent configuration" in connection with processes which are below the threshold of superficial observation). . . .

Since the occasion for making the distinction arises with great frequency, and since the purpose of a conceptual scheme is to direct observations toward salient elements of a situation and to prevent the inadvertent oversight of these elements, it would seem justifiable to designate this distinction by an appropriate set of terms. This is the rationale for the distinction between manifest functions and latent functions; the first referring to those objective consequences for a specified unit (person, subgroup, social or cultural system) which contribute to its adjustment or adaptation and were so intended; the second referring to unintended and unrecognized consequences of the same order.

There are some indications that the christening of this distinction may serve a heuristic purpose by becoming incorporated into an explicit conceptual apparatus, thus aiding both systematic observation and later analysis. In recent years, for example, the distinction between manifest and latent functions has been utilized in analyses of racial intermarriage,[1] social stratification,[2] affective frustration,[3] Veblen's sociological theories,[4] prevailing American orientations toward Russia,[5] propaganda as a means of social control,[6] Malinowski's anthropological theory,[7] Navajo witchcraft,[8] problems in the sociology of knowledge,[9] fashion,[10] the dynamics of personality,[11] national security measures,[12] the internal social dynamics of bureaucracy,[13] and a great variety of other sociological problems.

The very diversity of these subject-matters suggests that the theoretic distinction between manifest and latent functions is not bound up with a limited and particular range of human behavior. But there still remains the large task of ferreting out the specific uses to which this distinction can be put, and it is to this large task that we devote the remaining pages of this chapter.

Heuristic Purposes of the Distinction

Clarifies the analysis of seemingly irrational social patterns. In the first place, the distinction aids the sociological interpretation of many social practices which persist even though their manifest purpose is clearly not achieved. The time-worn procedure in such instances has been for diverse, particularly lay, observers to refer to these practices as "superstitions," irrationalities," "mere inertia of tradition," *etc.* In other words, when group behavior does not - and, indeed, often cannot – attain its ostensible purpose there is an inclination to attribute its occurrence to lack of intelligence, sheer ignorance, survivals, or so-called inertia. Thus, the Hopi ceremonials designed to produce abundant rainfall may be labelled a superstitious practice of primitive folk and that is assumed to conclude the matter. It should be noted that this in no sense accounts for the group behavior. It is simply a case of name-calling; it substitutes the epithet "superstition" for an analysis of the actual role of this behavior in the life of the group. Given the concept of latent function, however, we are reminded that this behavior *may* perform a function for the group, although this function may be quite remote from the avowed purpose of the behavior.

The concept of latent function extends the observer's attention beyond the question of whether or not the behavior attains its avowed purpose. Temporarily ignoring these explicit purposes, it directs attention *toward* another range of consequences: those bearing, for example, upon the individual personalities of Hopi involved in the ceremony and upon the persistence and continuity of the larger group. Were one to confine himself to the problem of whether a manifest (purposed) function occurs, it becomes a problem, not for the sociologist, but for the meteorologist. And to be sure, our meteorologists agree that the rain ceremonial does not produce rain; but this is hardly to the point. It is merely to say that the ceremony does not have this technological use; that this purpose of the ceremony and its actual consequences do not coincide. But with the concept of latent function, we continue our inquiry, examining the consequences of the ceremony not for the rain gods or for meteorological phenomena, but for the groups which conduct the ceremony. And here it may be found, as many observers indicate, that the ceremonial does indeed have functions – but functions which are non-purposed or latent.

Ceremonials may fulfill the latent function of reinforcing the group identity by providing a periodic occasion on which the scattered members of a group assemble to engage in a common activity. As Durkheim among others long since indicated, such ceremonials are a means by which collective expression is afforded the sentiments which, in a further analysis, are found to be a basic source of group unity. Through the systematic application of the concept of latent function, therefore, *apparently* irrational behavior may *at times* be found to be positively functional for the group. Operating with the concept of latent function we are not too quick to conclude that if an activity of a group does not achieve its nominal purpose, then its persistence can be described only as an instance of "inertia," "survival," or "manipulation by powerful subgroups in the society."

In point of fact, some conception like that of latent function has very often, almost invariably, been employed by social scientists observing *a standardized practice designed to achieve an objective which one knows from accredited physical science cannot be thus achieved.* This would plainly be the case, for example, with Pueblo rituals dealing with rain or fertility. *But with behavior which is not directed toward a clearly unattainable objective, sociological observers are less likely to examine the collateral or latent functions of the behavior.*

Directs attention to theoretically fruitful fields of inquiry. The distinction between manifest and latent functions serves further to direct the attention of the sociologist to precisely those realms of behavior, attitude and belief where he can most fruitfully apply his special skills. For what is his task if he confines himself to the study of manifest functions? He is then concerned very largely with determining whether a practice instituted for a particular purpose does, in fact, achieve this purpose. He will then inquire, for example, whether a new system of wage-payment achieves its avowed purpose of reducing labor turnover or of increasing output. He will ask whether a propaganda campaign has indeed gained its objective of increasing "willingness to fight" or "willingness to buy war bonds," or "tolerance toward other ethnic groups." Now, these are important, and complex, types of inquiry. But, so long as sociologists *confine* themselves to the study of manifest functions, their inquiry is set for them by practical men of affairs (whether a captain of industry, a trade union leader, or, conceivably, a Navaho chieftain, is for the moment immaterial), rather than by the theoretic problems which are at the core of the discipline. By dealing primarily with the realm of manifest functions, with the key problem of whether deliberately instituted practices or organizations succeed in achieving their objectives, the sociologist becomes converted into an industrious and skilled recorder of the altogether familiar pattern of behavior. *The terms of appraisal are fixed and limited by the question put to him by the non-theoretic men of affairs*, e.g., has the new wage-payment program achieved such-and-such purposes?

But armed with the concept of latent function, the sociologist extends his inquiry in those very directions which promise most for the theoretic development of the discipline. He examines the familiar (or planned) social practice to ascertain the latent, and hence generally unrecognized, functions (as well, of course, as the manifest functions). He considers, for example, the consequences of the new wage plan for, say, the trade union in which the workers are organized or the consequences of a propaganda program, not only for increasing its avowed purpose of stirring up patriotic fervor, but also for making larger numbers of people reluctant to speak their minds when they differ with official policies, *etc.* In short, it is suggested that the *distinctive* intellectual contributions of the sociologist are found primarily in the study of unintended consequences (among which are latent functions) of social practices, as well as in the study of anticipated consequences (among which are manifest functions).

There is some evidence that it is precisely at the point where the research attention of sociologists has shifted from the plane of manifest to the plane of latent functions that they have made their *distinctive* and major contributions. This can be extensively documented but a few passing illustrations must suffice.

THE HAWTHORNE WESTERN ELECTRIC STUDIES:[14] As is well known, the early stages of this inquiry were concerned with the problem of the relations of "illumination of efficiency" of industrial workers. For some two and a half years, attention was focused on problems such as this: do variations in the intensity of lighting affect production? The initial results showed that within wide limits there was no uniform relation between illumination and output. Production output increased *both* in the experimental group where illumination was increased (or *decreased*) *and* in the control group where no changes in illumination were introduced. In short, the investigators confined themselves wholly to a search for the manifest functions. Lacking a concept of latent social function, no attention whatever was initially paid to the social consequences *of the experiment* for relations among members of the test and control groups or for relations between workers and the test room authorities. In other words, the investigators lacked a sociological frame of reference and operated merely as "engineers" (just as a group of meteorologists might have explored the "effects" upon rainfall of the Hopi ceremonial).

Only after continued investigation, did it occur to the research group to explore the consequences of the new "experimental situation" for the self-images and self-conceptions of the workers taking part in the experiment, for the interpersonal relations among members of the group, for the coherence and unity of the group. As Elton Mayo reports it, "the illumination fiasco had made them alert to the need that very careful records should be kept of everything that happened in the room in addition to the obvious engineering and industrial devices. Their observations therefore included not only records of industrial and engineering changes but also records of physiological or medical changes, and, *in a sense*, of social and anthropological. This last took the form of a 'log' that gave as full an account as possible of the actual events of every day. . . ."[15] In short, it was only after a long series of experiments which wholly neglected the latent social functions of the experiment (as a contrived social situation) that this distinctly sociological framework was introduced. "With this realization," the authors write, "the inquiry changed its character. No longer were the investigators interested in testing for the effects of single variables. In the place of a controlled experiment they substituted the notion of a social situation which needed to be described and understood as a system of interdependent elements." Thereafter, as is now widely known, inquiry was directed very largely toward ferreting out the latent functions of standardized practices among the workers, of informal organization developing among workers, of workers' games instituted by "wise administrators," of large programs of worker counselling and interviewing, etc. The new conceptual scheme entirely altered the range and types of data gathered in the ensuing research.

One has only to turn to Thomas and Znaniecki in their classical work of some thirty years ago[16], to recognize the correctness of Shils' remark:

> . . . indeed the history of the study of primary groups in American sociology is a supreme instance of the *discontinuities of the development of this discipline*: a problem is stressed by one who is an acknowledged founder of the discipline, the problem is

left unstudied, then, some years later, it is taken up with enthusiasm as if no one had ever thought of it before.[17]

For Thomas and Znaniecki had repeatedly emphasized the sociological view that, whatever its major purpose, "the association as a concrete group of human personalities unofficially involves many other interests; the social contacts between its members are not limited to their common pursuit. . . ." In effect, then, it had taken years of experimentation to turn the attention of the Western Electric research team to the latent social functions of primary groups emerging in industrial organizations. It should be made clear that this case is not cited here as an instance of defective experimental design; that is not our immediate concern. It is considered only as an illustration of the pertinence for *sociological* inquiry of the concept of latent function, and the associated concepts of functional analysis. It illustrates how the inclusion of this concept (whether the term is used or not is inconsequential) can sensitize sociological investigators to a range of significant social variables which are otherwise easily overlooked. The explicit ticketing of the concept may perhaps lessen the frequency of such occasions of discontinuity in future sociological research.

The discovery of latent functions represents significant increments in sociological knowledge. There is another respect in which inquiry into latent functions represents a distinctive contribution of the social scientist. It is precisely the latent functions of a practice or belief which are *not* common knowledge, for these are unintended and generally unrecognized social and psychological consequences. As a result, findings concerning latent functions represent a greater increment in knowledge than findings concerning manifest functions. They represent, also, greater departures from "common-sense" knowledge about social life. Inasmuch as the latent functions depart, more or less, from the avowed manifest functions, the research which uncovers latent functions very often produces "paradoxical" results. The seeming paradox arises from the sharp modification of a familiar popular preconception which regards a standardized practice or belief *only* in terms of its manifest functions by indicating some of its subsidiary or collateral latent functions. The introduction of the concept of latent function in social research leads to conclusions which show that "social life is not as simple as it first seems." For as long as people confine themselves to *certain* consequences (*e.g.* manifest consequences), it is comparatively simple for them to pass moral judgments upon the practice or belief in question. Moral evaluations, generally based on these manifest consequences, tend to be polarized in terms of black or white. But the perception of further (latent) consequences often complicates the picture. Problems of moral evaluation (which are not our immediate concern) and problems of social engineering (which are our concern) both take on the additional complexities usually involved in responsible social decisions. . . .

Precludes the substitution of naive moral judgments for sociological analysis. Since moral evaluations in a society tend to be largely in terms of the manifest consequences of a practice or code, we should be prepared to find that analysis in terms of latent functions at times runs counter to prevailing moral evaluations. For it does not follow that the latent functions will operate in the same fashion as the manifest consequences which are ordinarily the basis of these judgments. Thus, in large sectors of the American population, the political machine or the "political racket" are judged as unequivocally "bad" and "undesirable." The grounds for such moral judgment vary somewhat, but they consist substantially in pointing out that political machines violate moral codes: political patronage violates the code of selecting personnel on the basis of impersonal qualifications rather than on grounds of party loyalty or contributions to the party war-chest; bossism violates the code that votes should be based on individual appraisal of the qualifications of candidates and of political issues, and not on abiding loyalty to a feudal leader; bribery, and "honest graft" obviously offend the proprieties of property; "protection" for crime clearly violates the law and the mores; and so on.

In view of the manifold respects in which political machines, in varying degrees, run counter to the mores and at times to the law, it becomes pertinent to inquire how they manage to continue in operation. The familiar "explanations" for the continuance of the political machine are not here in point. To be sure, it may well be that if "respectable citizenry" would live up to their political obligations, if the electorate were to be alert and enlightened; if the number of elective officers were substantially reduced from the dozens, even hundreds, which the average voter is now expected to appraise in the course of town, county, state and national elections; if the electorate were activated by the "wealthy and educated classes without whose participation," as the not-always democratically oriented Bryce put it, "the best-framed government must speedily degenerate"; – if these and a plethora of similar changes in political structure were introduced, perhaps the "evils" of the political machine would indeed be exorcized. But it should be noted that these changes are often not introduced, that political machines have had the phoenix-like quality of arising strong and unspoiled from their ashes, that, in short, this structure has exhibited a notable vitality in many areas of American political life.

Proceeding from the functional view, therefore, that we should *ordinarily* (not invariably) expect persistent social patterns and social structures to perform positive functions *which are at the time not adequately fulfilled by other existing patterns and structures*, the thought occurs that perhaps this publicly maligned organization is, *under present conditions*, satisfying basic latent functions. . . .

Notes

1   Robert K. Merton, "Intermarriage and the Social Structure," *Psychiatry*, 1941, 4:361–74.
2   Kingsley Davis, "A conceptual analysis of stratification," *American Sociological Review*, 1942, 7, 309–21.
3   Isidor Thorner, "Sociological Aspects of Affectional Frustration," *Psychiatry*, 1943, 6:157–73, esp. at 165.
4   A. K. Davis, *Thorstein Veblen's Social Theory*, Harvard Ph.D. dissertation, 1941 and "Veblen on the decline of the Protestant Ethic," *Social Forces*, 1944, 22, 282–86; Louis Schneider, *The Freudian Psychology and Veblen's Social Theory* (New York: King's Crown Press, 1948), esp. Chapter 2.
5   A. K. Davis, "Some sources of American hostility to Russia," *American Journal of Sociology*, 1947, 53, 174–83.
6   Talcott Parsons, "Propaganda and social control," in his *Essays in Sociological Theory*.

7   Clyde Kluckhohn, "Bronislaw Malinowski, 1884–1942," *Journal of American Folklore*, 1943, 56, 208–19.

8   Clyde Kluckhohn, *Navaho Witchcraft*, Papers of the Peabody Museum of American Archaeology and Ethnology, Harvard University, XXII, No. 2, 1944, 47a, esp. at 46–7 and ff.

9   Robert K. Merton, "The Sociology of Knowledge," in R. K. Merton, *Social Theory and Social Structure*, 1968, 510–42.

10 Bernard Barber and L. S. Lobel, " 'Fashion' in women's clothes and the American social system," *Social Forces*, 1952, 31, 124–31.

11 O. H. Mowrer and C. Kluckhohn, "Dynamic theory of personality," in J. M. Hunt, ed., *Personality and the Behavior Disorders* (New York: Ronald Press, 1944), 1, 69–135, esp. at 72.

12 Marie Jahoda and S. W. Cook, "Security measures and freedom of thought: an exploratory study of the impact of loyalty and security programs," *Yale Law Journal* 1952, 61, 296–333.

13 Philip Selznick, *TVA and the Grass Roots* (University of California Press, 1949); A. W. Gouldner, *Patterns of Industrial Bureaucracy* (Glencoe, Illinois: The Free Press, 1954); P. M. Blau, *The Dynamics of Bureaucracy* (University of Chicago Press, 1955); A. K. Davis, "Bureaucratic patterns in Navy officer corps," *Social forces*, 1948, 27, 142–53.

14 This is cited as a case study of how *an elaborate research was wholly changed in theoretic orientation and in the character of its research findings by the introduction of a concept approximating the concept of latent function.* Selection of the case for this purpose does not, of course, imply full acceptance of the *interpretations* which the authors give their findings. Among the several volumes reporting the Western Electric research, see particularly F. J. Roethlisberger and W. J. Dickson, *Management and the Worker* (Harvard University Press, 1939).

15 Elton Mayo, *The Social Problems of an Industrial Civilization* (Harvard University Press, 1945), 70.

16 W. I. Thomas and F. Znaniecki, *The Polish Peasant in Europe and America* (New York: Knopf, 1927).

17 Edward Shils, *The Present State of American Sociology* (Glencoe, Illinois: The Free Press, 1948), 42 [italics supplied].

33 The Bearing of Empirical Research on Sociological Theory

Robert K. Merton

The Theoretic Functions of Research

With a few conspicuous exceptions, recent sociological discussions have assigned but one major function to empirical research: the testing or verification of hypotheses. The model for the proper way of performing this function is as familiar as it is clear. The investigator begins with a hunch or hypothesis, from this he draws various inferences and these, in turn, are subjected to empirical test which confirms or refutes the hypothesis. But this is a logical model, and so fails, of course, to describe much of what actually occurs in fruitful investigation. It presents a set of logical norms, not a description of the research experience. And, as logicians are well aware, in purifying the experience, the logical model may also distort it. Like other models, it abstracts from the temporal sequence of events. It exaggerates the creative role of explicit theory just as it minimizes the creative role of observation. For research is not merely logic tempered with observation. It has its psychological as well as its logical dimensions, although one would scarcely suspect this from the logically rigorous sequence in which research is usually reported. It is both the psychological and logical pressures of research upon social theory which we seek to trace.

It is my central thesis that empirical research goes far beyond the passive role of verifying and testing theory: it does more than confirm or refute hypotheses. Research plays an active role: it performs at least four major functions which help shape the development of theory. It *initiates*, it *reformulates*, it *deflects* and it *clarifies* theory.[1]

1. The serendipity pattern
   (THE UNANTICIPATED, ANOMALOUS AND STRATEGIC DATUM EXERTS PRESSURE FOR INITIATING THEORY)

Under certain conditions, a research finding gives rise to social theory. In a previous paper, this was all too briefly expressed as follows: "Fruitful empirical research not only tests theoretically derived hypotheses; it also originates new hypotheses. This might be termed the 'serendipity' component of research, i.e., the discovery, by change or sagacity, of valid results which were not sought for."[2]

The serendipity pattern refers to the fairly common experience of observing an *unanticipated, anomalous and strategic* datum which becomes the occasion for developing a new theory or for extending an existing theory. Each of these elements of the pattern can be readily described. The datum is, first of all, unanticipated. A research directed toward the test of one hypothesis yields a fortuitous by-product, an unexpected observation which bears upon theories not in question when the research was begun.

Second, the observation is anomalous, surprising, either because it seems inconsistent with prevailing theory or with other established facts. In either case, the seeming inconsistency provokes curiosity; it stimulates the investigator to "make sense of the datum," to fit it into a broader frame of knowledge. He explores further. He makes fresh observations. He draws inferences from the observations, inferences depending largely, of course, upon his general theoretic orientation. The more he is steeped in the data, the greater the likelihood that he will hit upon a fruitful direction of inquiry. In the fortunate circumstances that his new hunch proves justified, the anomalous datum leads ultimately to a new or extended theory. The curiosity stimulated by the anomalous datum is temporarily appeased.

And thirdly, in noting that the unexpected fact must be strategic, *i.e.*, that it must permit of implications which bear upon generalized theory, we are, of course, referring rather to what the observer brings to the datum than to the datum itself. For it obviously requires a theoretically sensitized observer to detect the universal in the particular. After all, men had for centuries noticed such "trivial" occurrences as slips of the tongue, slips of the pen, typographical errors, and lapses of memory, but it required the theoretic sensitivity of a Freud to see these as strategic data through which he could extend his theory of repression and symptomatic acts.

The serendipity pattern, then, involves the unanticipated, anomalous and strategic datum which exerts pressure upon the investigator for a new direction of inquiry which extends theory. Instances of serendipity have occurred in many disciplines, but I should like to draw upon a recent sociological research for illustration. In the course of our research into the social organization of Craftown,[3] a suburban housing community of some 700 families, largely of working class status, we observed that a large proportion of residents were affiliated with more civic, political and other voluntary organizations than had been the case in their previous places of residence. Quite incidentally, we noted further that this increase in group participation had occurred also among the parents of infants and young children. This finding was rather inconsistent with common-sense knowledge. For it is well known that, particularly on the lower economic levels, youngsters usually tie parents down and preclude their taking active part in organized group life outside the home. But Craftown parents themselves readily explained their behavior. "Oh, there's no real problem about getting out in the evenings," said one mother who belonged to several organizations. "It's easy to find teen-agers around here to take care of the kids. There are so many more teen-agers around here than where I used to live."

The explanation appears adequate enough and would have quieted the investigator's curiosity, had it not been for one disturbing datum: like most new housing communities, Craftown actually has a very small proportion of adolescents – only 3.7 per cent for example, in the 15–19 year age group. What is more, the majority of the adults, 63 per cent, are under 34 years of age, so that their children include an exceptionally large proportion of infants and youngsters. Thus, far from there being many adolescents to look after the younger children in Craftown, quite the contrary is true: the ratio of adolescents to children under ten years of age is 1:10, whereas in the communities of origin, the ratio hovers about 1:1.5. . . .

The clue was inadvertently provided by further interviews with residents. In the words of an active participant in Craftown affairs, herself the mother of two children under six years of age:

> My husband and I get out together much more. You see, there are more people around to mind the children. *You feel more confident about having some thirteen-or-fourteen-year-old in here when you know most of the people. If you're in a big city, you don't feel so easy about having someone who's almost a stranger come in.*

This clearly suggests that the sociological roots of the "illusion" are to be found in the structure of community relations in which Craftown residents are enmeshed. The belief is an unwitting reflection, not of the statistical reality, but of the community cohesion. It is not that there are objectively more adolescents in Craftown, but more who are *intimately known* and who, therefore, *exist socially* for parents seeking aid in child supervision. Most Craftown residents having lately come from an urban setting now find themselves in a community in which proximity has developed into reciprocal intimacies. The illusion expresses the perspective of people for whom adolescents as potential child-care aides "exist" only if they are well-known and therefore merit confidence. In short, perception was a function of confidence and confidence, in turn, was a function of social cohesion. . . .

2. The recasting of theory
(NEW DATA EXERT PRESSURE FOR THE ELABORATION OF A CONCEPTUAL SCHEME)

But it is not only through the anomalous fact that empirical research invites the extension of theory. It does so also through the repeated observation of hitherto neglected facts. When an existing conceptual scheme commonly applied to a subject-matter does not adequately take these facts into account, research presses insistently for its reformulation. It leads to the introduction of variables which have not been systematically included in the scheme of analysis. Here, be it noted, it is not that the data are anomalous or unexpected or incompatible with existing theory; it is merely that they had not been considered pertinent. Whereas the serendipity pattern centers in an apparent inconsistency which presses for resolution, the reformulation pattern centers in the hitherto neglected but relevant fact which presses for an extension of the conceptual scheme.

Examples of this in the history of social science are far from limited. Thus it was a series of fresh empirical facts which led Malinowski to incorporate new elements into a theory of magic. It was his Trobrianders, of course, who gave him the clue to the distinctive feature of his theory. When these islanders fished in the inner lagoon by the reliable method of poisoning, an abundant catch was assured and danger was absent. Neither uncertainty nor uncontrollable hazards were involved. And here, Malinowski noted, magic was not practiced. But in the open-sea fishing, with the uncertain yield and its often grave dangers, the rituals of magic flourished. Stemming from these pregnant observations was his theory that magical belief arises to bridge the uncertainties in man's practical pursuits, to fortify confidence, to reduce anxieties, to open up avenues of escape from the seeming impasse. Magic was construed as a supplementary technique for reaching practical objectives. It was these empirical facts which suggested the incorporation of new dimensions into earlier theories of magic – particularly the relations of magic to the fortuitous, the dangerous and the uncontrollable. It was not that these facts were *inconsistent* with previous theories; it was simply that these conceptual schemes had not taken them adequately into account. Nor was Malinowski testing a preconceived hypothesis – he was developing an enlarged and improved theory on the basis of suggestive empirical data. . . .

3. The re-focusing of theoretic interest
(NEW METHODS OF EMPIRICAL RESEARCH EXERT PRESSURE FOR NEW FOCI OF THEORETIC INTEREST)

To this point we have considered the impact of research upon the development of particular theories. But empirical research also affects more general trends in the development of theory. This occurs chiefly through the invention of research procedures which tend to shift the foci of theoretic interest to the growing points of research.

The reasons for this are on the whole evident. After all, sound theory thrives only on a rich diet of pertinent facts and newly invented procedures help provide the ingredients of this diet. The new, and often previously unavailable, data stimulate fresh hypotheses. Moreover, theorists find that their hypotheses can be put to immediate test in those spheres where appropriate research techniques have been designed. It is no longer necessary for them to wait upon data as they happen to turn up – researches directed to the verification of hypotheses can be instituted at once. The flow of relevant data thus increases the tempo of advance in certain spheres of theory whereas in others, theory stagnates for want of adequate observations. Attention shifts accordingly.

In noting that new centers of theoretic interest have followed upon the invention of research procedures, we do not imply that these alone played a decisive role.[4] The growing interest in the theory of propaganda as an instrument of social control, for example, is in large part a response to the changing historical situation, with its conflict of major ideological systems, new technologies of mass communication which have opened up new avenues for propaganda and the rich research treasuries provided by business and government interested in this new weapon of war, both declared and undeclared. But this shift is also a byproduct of accumulated facts made available through such newly developed, and confessedly crude, procedures as content-analysis, the panel technique and the focused interview.

Examples of this impact in the recent history of social theory are numerous but we have time to mention only a few. Thus, the increasing concern with the theory of character and personality formation in relation to social structure became marked after the introduction of new projective methods; the Rorschach test, the thematic apperception test, play techniques and story completions being among the most familiar. So, too, the sociometric techniques of Moreno and others, and fresh advances in the technique of the "passive interview" have revived interest in the theory of interpersonal relations. Stemming from such techniques as well is the trend toward what might be called the "rediscovery of the primary group," particularly in the shape of theoretic concern with informal social structures as mediating between the individual and large formal organizations. This interest has found expression in an entire literature on the role and structure of the informal group, for example, in factory social systems, bureaucracy and political organizations. Similarly, we may anticipate that the recent introduction of the panel technique – the repeated interviewing of the same group of informants – will in due course more sharply focus the attention of social psychologists upon the theory of attitude formation, decisions among alternative choices, factors in political participation and determinants of behavior in cases of conflicting role demands, to mention a few types of problems to which this technique is especially adapted. . . .

What we have said does not mean that the piling up of statistics in itself advances theory; it does mean that theoretic interest tends to shift to those areas in which there is an abundance of *pertinent* statistical data. Moreover, we are merely calling attention to this shift of focus, not evaluating it. It may very well be that it sometimes deflects attention to problems which, in a theoretic or humanistic sense, are "unimportant"; it may divert attention from problems with larger implications onto those for which there is the promise of immediate solutions. Failing a detailed study, it is difficult to come to any overall assessment of this point. But the pattern itself seems clear enough in sociology as in other disciplines; as new and previously unobtainable data become available through the use of new techniques, theorists turn their analytical eye upon the implications of these data and bring about new directions of inquiry.

4. The clarification of concepts
(EMPIRICAL RESEARCH EXERTS PRESSURE FOR CLEAR CONCEPTS)

A good part of the work called "theorizing" is taken up with the clarification of concepts – and rightly so. It is in this matter of clearly defined concepts that social science research is not infrequently defective. Research activated by a major interest in methodology may be centered on the *design* of establishing causal relations without due regard for analyzing the variables involved in the inquiry. This methodological empiricism, as the design of inquiry without correlative concern with the clarification of substantive variables may be called, characterizes a large part of current research. Thus, in a series of effectively designed experiments Chapin finds that "the rehousing of slum families in a public housing project results in improvement of the living conditions and the social life of these families."[5] Or through controlled experiments, psychologists search out the effects of foster home placement upon children's performances in intelligence tests.[6] Or, again through experimental inquiry, researchers seek to determine whether a propaganda film has achieved its purpose of improving attitudes toward the British. These several cases, and they are representative of a large amount of research which has advanced social science method, have in common the fact that the empirical variables are not analyzed in terms of their conceptual elements. As Rebecca West, with her characteristic lucidity, put this general problem of methodological empiricism, one might "know that A and B and C were linked by certain causal connexions, but he would never apprehend with any exactitude the nature of A or B or C." In consequence, these researches advance the procedures of inquiry, but their findings do not enter into the repository of cumulative social science theory.

But in general, the clarification of concepts, commonly considered a province peculiar to the theorist, is a frequent result of empirical research. Research sensitive to its own needs cannot easily escape this pressure for conceptual clarification. *For a basic requirement of research is that the concepts, the variables, be defined with sufficient clarity to enable the research to proceed*, a requirement easily and unwittingly not met in the kind of discursive exposition which is often miscalled sociological theory.

The clarification of concepts ordinarily enters into empirical research in the shape of establishing *indices* of the variables under consideration. In non-research speculations, it is possible to talk loosely about "morale" or "social cohesion" without any clear conceptions of what is entailed by these terms, but they *must* be clarified if the researcher is to go about his business of systematically observing instances of low and high morale, of social cohesion or social cleavage. If he is not to be blocked at the outset, he must devise indices which are observable, fairly precise and meticulously clear. The entire movement of thought which was christened "operationalism" is only one conspicuous case of the researcher demanding that concepts be defined clearly enough for him to go to work.

This has been typically recognized by those sociologists who combine a theoretic orientation with systematic empirical research. Durkheim, for example, despite the fact that his terminology and indices now appear crude and debatable, clearly perceived the need for devising indices of his concepts. Repeatedly, he asserted that "it is necessary . . . to substitute for the internal fact which escapes us an external fact that symbolizes it and to study the former through the latter."[7] The index, or sign of the conceptualized item, stands ideally in a one-to-one correlation with what it signifies (and the difficulty of establishing this relation is of course one of the critical problems of research). Since the index and its object are so related, one may ask for the grounds on which one is taken as the index and the other as the indexed variable. As Durkheim implied and as Suzanne Langer has indicated anew, the index is that one of the correlated pair which is perceptible and the other, harder or impossible to perceive, is theoretically relevant.[8] Thus, attitude scales make available indices of otherwise not discriminable attitudes, just as ecological statistics represent indices of diverse social structures in diffferent areas.

What often appears as a tendency in research for quantification (through the development of scales) can thus be seen as a special case of attempting to clarify concepts sufficiently to permit the conduct of empirical investigation. The development of valid and observable indices becomes central to the use of concepts in the prosecution of research. A final illustration will indicate how research presses for the clarification of ancient sociological concepts which, on the plane of discursive exposition, have remained ill-defined and unclarified.

A conception basic to sociology holds that individuals have multiple social roles and tend to organize their behavior in terms of the structurally defined expectations assigned to each role. Further, it is said, the less integrated the society, the more often will individuals be subject to the strain of incompatible social roles. Type-cases are numerous and familiar: the Catholic Communist subjected to conflicting pressures from party and church, the marginal man suffering the pulls of conflicting societies, the professional woman torn between the demands of family and career. Every sociological textbook abounds with illustrations of incompatible demands made of the multiselved person.

Perhaps because it has been largely confined to discursive interpretations and has seldom been made the focus of systematic research, this central problem of conflicting roles has yet to be materially clarified and advanced beyond the point reached decades ago. Thomas and Znaniecki long since indicated that conflicts between social roles *can* be reduced by conventionalization and by role-segmentation (by assigning each set of role-demands to different situations).[9] And others have noted that frequent conflict between roles is dysfunctional for the society as well as for the individual. But all this leaves many salient problems untouched: on which grounds does one predict the behavior of persons subject to conflicting roles? And when a decision must be made, which role (or which group solidarity) takes precedence? Under which conditions does one or another prove controlling? On the plane of discursive thought, it has been suggested that the role with which the individual identifies most fully will prove dominant, thus banishing the problem through a tautological pseudo-solution. Or, the problem of seeking to predict behavior consequent to incompatibility of roles a research problem requiring operational clarification of the concepts of solidarity, conflict, role-demands and situation, has been evaded by observing that conflicts of roles, typically ensue in frustration.

More recently, empirical research has pressed for clarification of the key concepts involved in this problem. Indices of conflicting group pressures have been devised and the resultant behavior observed in specified situations. Thus, as a beginning in this direction, it has been shown that in a concrete decision-situation, such as voting, individuals subject to these cross-pressures respond by delaying their vote-decision. And, under conditions yet to be determined, they seek to reduce the conflict by escaping from the field of confict: they lose interest in the political campaign. Finally, there is the intimation in these data that in cases of cross-pressures upon the voter, it is socio-economic position which is typically controlling.[10]

Notes

1   The fourth function, clarification, has been elaborated in publications by Paul F. Lazarsfeld.
2   R. K. Merton, "Sociological Theory," *American Journal of Sociology*, 1945, 50, 469n.
3   Drawn from studies in the Sociology and Social Psychology of Housing, under a grant from the Lavanburg Foundation.
4   It is perhaps needless to add that these procedures, instruments and apparatus are in turn dependent upon prior theory. But this does not alter their stimulating effect upon the further development of theory.
5   F. S. Chapin, "The effects of slum clearance and rehousing on family and community relationships in Minneapolis," *American Journal of Sociology*, 1938, 43, 744–63.
6   R. R. Sears, "Child Psychology," in Wayne Dennis, ed., *Current Trends in Psychology* (University of Pittsburgh Press, 1947), 55–6.
7   Emile Durkheim, *Division of Labor in Society* (New York: Macmillan, 1933), 66; also

his *Les règles de la méthode sociologique* (Paris, 1895), 55–8; *Le Suicide* (Paris, 1930), 356 and *passim*.

8   Suzanne K. Langer, *Philosophy in a New Key* (New York: Penguin Books, 1948), 46–7.

9   W. I. Thomas and F. Znaniecki, *The Polish Peasant* (New York: Knopf, 1927), 1866–70, 1888, 1899 ff.

10   Lazarsfeld, Berelson and Gaudet, *The People's Choice*, Chapter VI and the subsequent study by B. Berelson, P. F. Lazarsfeld and W. N. McPhee, *Voting* (University of Chicago Press, 1954).

Index